1 MONTH OF
FREE
READING

at

www.ForgottenBooks.com

By purchasing this book you are
eligible for one month membership to
ForgottenBooks.com, giving you
unlimited access to our entire
collection of over 1,000,000 titles via
our web site and mobile apps.

To claim your free month visit:
www.forgottenbooks.com/free930673

ISBN 978-0-260-14660-1
PIBN 10930673

Reports of Causes Determined

in the

ted States District Court

for the

District of Hawaii

APRIL 1, 1911 - JANUARY 15, 1917

VOLUME IV.

HONOLULU, T. H.
Printed at The New Freedom Press, 13-19 Pauahi St.
1918

/

ERRATA

Page	Line	Read	For
179	1	Unaccustomed	Accustomed
301	15	Award	Reward
321	30	42	12
322	5	$365,000	$465,000
342	15	Nobu	Nobe
418	18	Kishi	Kihi
476	8	sources	source
480	36	here	hereto
481	14	effected	affected
535	14	27	12
545	17	usual	unusual
573	4	dual marriages	marriages
699	16	1	2
786	1	Georgia	George
789	19	to	of

OFFICERS

OF THE

United States District Court

FOR THE TERRITORY OF HAWAII

Judges

SANFORD B. DOLE, November 18, 1903—December 16, 1915.

CHARLES F. CLEMONS, March 9, 1911—January 15, 1917 (resigned December 7, 1916).

HORACE W. VAUGHAN, May 15, 1916—

United States District Attorneys

ROBERT W. BRECKONS. February 26, 1902—December 15, 1913 (resigned March 4, 1913).

JEFF McCARN, December 15, 1913—December 22, 1915.

HORACE W. VAUGHAN, December 22, 1915—May 15, 1916.

SEBA C. HUBER, May 15, 1916—

Assistant United States Attorneys

WILLIAM T. RAWLINS, December 16, 1907—November 9, 1911.

CHARLES CARROLL BITTING, November 9, 1911—March 17, 1914.

J. WESLEY THOMPSON, March 27, 1914—October 1, 1915.

HORACE W. VAUGHAN, October 1, 1915—December 22, 1915.

SAMUEL B. KEMP, February 23, 1916—March 19, 1917.

United States Marshals

EUGENE R. HENDRY, September 17, 1901—April 23, 1904 (deceased).

HARRY H. HOLT, April 24, 1914—October 3, 1914 (marshal pro tem. under appointment of court).

JEROME J. SMIDDY, October 3, 1914—

Clerks of Court

AUGUSTUS E. MURPHY, November 16, 1908—October 25, 1915 (deceased).

FOSTER L. DAVIS, November 17, 1915—March 14, 1916.

GEORGE R. CLARK, March 15, 1916—February 20, 1917.

TABLE OF CASES REPORTED.

PAGE

TABLE OF CASES CITED.

TABLE OF CASES CITED.

TABLE OF CASES CITED.

TABLE OF STATUTES CITED.

UNITED STATES.

CONSTITUTION.

STATUTES AT LARGE.

TABLE OF STATUTES CITED.

REVISED STATUTES.

HAWAII.

CAUSES DETERMINED

IN THE

United States District Court

FOR THE

District of Hawaii

UNITED STATES OF AMERICA

v.

LORRIN A. THURSTON *et al.*

April 17, 1911.

1. *Judge—Disqualification—Acting as counsel, or other participation, in cause:* Under Rev. Stat. sec. 601, the fact of having been counsel of record as member of a firm of attorneys who had been retained in a suit, disqualifies a judge from sitting in that suit even though he had never taken any part in the cause and has no further pecuniary, or other, interest in it.

2. *Same—Same; exception in case of necessity: Quare,* whether a judge, though disqualified by having been of counsel, may not sit in case of absolute necessity, in order to prevent failure of justice.

3. *Same—Same; exception in merely formal matters:* A judge though disqualified, may act in merely formal matters.

Eminent Domain: Suggestion of disqualification of judge.

R. W. Breckons, U. S. District Attorney, for the plaintiff.
Holmes, Stanley & Olson; Kinney, Ballou, Prosser & Anderson; Thompson & Wilder; Smith, Warren & Hemenway; and *Lorrin Andrews* for the defendants.

CLEMONS, J. In this case counsel for the defendants have declared in open court their intention to suggest my disqualification to pass upon the pending demurrers, as well as to preside at the trial, on the ground of my having been of counsel for one of the defendants previous to becoming a judge of this court; and the plaintiff having meantime moved to set the demurrers for hearing, several of the defendants have now joined in filing such suggestion. Aside from this action of the parties, I also had been considering the question with the view of declining, on my own motion, to sit in the case if I should find myself disqualified. See *Moses v. Julian*, 45 N. H. 52, 53; 84 Am. Dec., 114, 116.

It is a fact that previous to my accession to the bench of this court, I had been a member of a firm of attorneys representing one of the defendants, and counsel of record herein, but I never had any part in the case whatsoever, never discussed it with the clients or with my associates in this firm, and know nothing of the facts or pleadings, though, of course, I have knowledge in a general way of the nature of the suit; also, I have no further pecuniary interest in the matter by way of compensation as attorney, and have no other interest in the outcome of the suit, except such interest as any judge could not help but have in desiring the reasonably prompt determination of a condemnation proceeding, preliminary, as this particular proceeding is, to his court's having quarters of its own.

[1] The Organic Act creating a government for Hawaii, 31 Stat. 141, sec. 5, makes effective in this Territory all laws of the United States, which are not locally inapplicable, saving only certain specified statutes. These special exceptions strengthen the general application of this statutory rule. See 23 Ops. Atty. Gen., 177; Id., 169; 19 Id., 678.

The Federal law relating to disqualification of judges of District Courts, Rev. Stat., sec. 601, provides that:

"Whenever it appears that the judge of any District

Court is in any way concerned in interest in any suit pending therein, or has been of counsel for either party, or is so related to or connected with either party as to render it improper, in his opinion, for him to sit on the trial, it shall be his duty, on application by either party, to cause the fact to be entered on the records of the court."

This section, having defined disqualification, then provides a method of procedure whereby a disqualified judge shall certify to another court such cases as are within the definition.

Insofar as this section expresses what Congress regards as disqualifying a judge, it is applicable to any District Court; Congress could not be presumed to have intended anything else, in view of the principle of equality fundamental in our institutions.

The procedure provided by section 601 cannot, however, apply here, because of the limiting effect of the word "adjoining" used by Congress about a century ago in its short view of territorial expansion. See *Lewis v. Johnson*, 90 Fed., 673. And the procedure clause of this section has given me the only difficulty in reaching an immediate conclusion, the question arising whether the inapplicability, or rather "unworkability" of the provision as to procedure would render the whole section inapplicable. But I feel that, Congress having declared itself against a judge's sitting in a case in which he had been of counsel, I must regard that expression of the legislative will, even though the procedure provision of the statute was not made broad enough to cover non-contiguous territory; Congress, undoubtedly, intended this procedure to apply everywhere, as it also undoubtedly intended its definition of disqualification to apply without limitation, and we can only regret that our legislators of the early days, though "wise in their own generation", did not foresee conditions in generations to follow, but we cannot disregard their will so plainly spoken as to the matter of disqualification. The reasons for my not sitting in this case, "the reason and spirit of the law", which moved Congress to prescribe these disqualifications, exist none the less, even though the procedure provided for assignment to another court or judge, is here inadequate.

Does the fact of my having been only nominally of counsel, or of having had no active part in the case, make any difference? The courts have held that it does not. *State v. Hocker*, 34 Fla. 43; 15 So. 581, 583; 25 L. R. A. 114; *Keeffe v. Third Nat'l. Bank*, 177 N. Y. 305: 69 N. E. 593, 595; *East Rome Town Co. v. Cothran*, 81 Ga. 359; 8 S. E. 737, 740-741. And with this view I heartily agree, for if we leave to a judge the determination of border-line cases, or cases of different degrees, of disqualification, we offend the very principle under consideration, expressed by the ancient maxim, *nemo debet esse judex in propria sua causa.* Broom, Maxims, 7th Eng. ed., 92. "It is of the last importance," said Lord Campbell, "that the maxim that 'no man is to be judge in his own case' should be held sacred." Id., 93. See, also, Id., 96.

It is suggested that my disqualification would result, at all events, under the provision of section 84 of the Organic Act, 31 Stat., 157, relating to disqualification of judges of the Hawaiian Territorial courts, as amended by the Act of May 27, 1910, 36 Stat. 447, sec. 6; on the ground that this section is made operative by section 914 of the Revised Statutes, enforcing in the District Courts, as near as may be, the practice of the State courts within the same District. But, while this latter section applies to Hawaii, as well as to the States: *United States v. Honolulu Plantation Co.,* 122 Fed., 581, 586; *Work v. Northern Pacific R. Co.,* 11 Mont. 513, 519, 29 Pac. 280; I must hold that it does not make section 84 of the Organic Act applicable in this case. where a Federal statute already exists expressly defining disqualification of District Judges. *United States v. Indian Grave Drainage Dist.,* 85 Fed. 928; 3 Gould & Tucker, Notes on Rev. Stat., 95. Nevertheless I regard section 84 of the Organic Act, as amended, as of strong force as an argument for my conclusion, it being a very recent declaration by Congress of its view of disqualification, and made in the face of local practice in the Territorial courts as determined in *Notley v. Brown*, 17 Haw. 393, which held that even active participation in a case was not a disqualification in the absence of statute.

The ruling is, therefore, that I am disqualified to sit in this case.

[2] There is reserved, however, for future determina-. tion, if required, the question whether some judge of this court may not sit in case of absolute necessity in order to prevent failure of justice, in this particular cause under consideration, as well as in any other cause. *Ten Eick v. Simpson*, 11 Paige, 177, 179; *Notley v. Brown*, 17 Haw. 393, 414 (Frear, C.J., dissenting); and see *In re Sime*, 22 Fed. Cas. 145, 147, No. 12,861. It may be noted, that the Judiciary Act of March 3, 1911, recently approved, 36 Stat. 1087, in effect next January, would in any event soon relieve the case of any possible embarrassment for want of some judge to dispose of it. Id., secs. 14, 15, 20, 116, 301.

[3] The senior judge of this court, to whose charge this suit will now fall, will, of course, determine his own qualifications. Meanwhile, I shall be ready at all times to act herein in merely formal matters. *McFarlane v. Clark*, 44 Mich. 44, 46. See 25 L. R. A., 116, note d.

The clerk will cause the fact of my disqualification to be entered on the records of the court.

UNITED STATES OF AMERICA

v.

LORRIN A. THURSTON *et al.*

March 8, 1912.

1. *Evidence—Expert testimony—Appraisement of real estate on information:* In proceedings requiring proof of the value of real estate and improvements attached thereto, expert testimony based upon information alone, as to rentals, sales of neighborhood property, and areas, some of which is correct and some incorrect is inadmissible before a jury.

2. *Same—Same—Appraisement on experience and examination:* In such proceedings, when it appears that the testimony of an expert witness is based upon his own experience as a real estate broker and on his examination of the property, independently of his opinion based upon his estimate of the values of neighboring properties arrived at from information as to their rentals and sales, some of which is incorrect, it should be allowed to stand.

Eminent Domain: Motion to strike out certain testimony.

R. W. Breckons, U. S. District Attorney, for the motion. *Holmes, Stanley & Olson,* contra.

Dole, J. The case of *Delaware, L. & W. R. Co. v. Roqlefs,* 70 Fed. 21, was one to recover compensation for injuries received in an accident. A doctor, who had been called in a year after the accident, testified as to the plaintiff's condition from information obtained from his declarations at the time respecting his symptoms past and present, and also based on his own personal observations. The court ruled that such of his information as rested on the declarations of the patient as to past conditions and symptoms could not be received and that the opinion of the doctor was indivisible and must be accepted or rejected as a whole, there being nothing to show how much of it rested on declarations of the patient and how much on personal observation, and stated that the jury should not have been allowed to guess what it would have been in the absence of the declarations, and to try to estimate the damages upon such a guess.

[1] This ruling applies to the present case insofar as the evidence of Mr. Reidford states that among his reasons for arriving at his appraisement of the Cummins block were statements, later shown to be inaccurate, of the net rentals of the McIntyre building and statements of the area of the Jordan block, also shown to be inaccurate, and a consideration of a sale of the Chambers drug store property, which took place after the date of the summons in this case.

[2] On the other hand, the claimants have submitted the case of *People v. Benham,* 160 N. Y. 402, 445, this, also, being a case of medical expert testimony, in which it appears that the medical witnesses based their conclusion on a number of grounds, some of which were found to be unproved or disproved. The court was requested to instruct the jury that the testimony of such physicians must be considered valueless and disregarded if one of the symptoms enumerated should be disproved. The court said, "We think there is no authority for this; the disproof of one symptom may, to some extent, weaken the conclusion of these witnesses, but may not totally destroy it, so that their testimony should be wholly disregarded by the jury."

Is there any difference in the nature of expert testimony in appraising the value of property based on that of neighboring property shown by sales and rentals, and the case of medical testimony as to the cause of death? There is this difference—that the investigation of values is on a sliding scale, the issue being whether it is worth so much or less or more; whereas the investigation of the cause of a death contains no such field, but is limited as to question of fact as to whether deceased died a natural death or whether he came to his death through some violent or poisonous agent.

The opinion in the New York case seems reasonable because the physician, leaving out some of the facts upon which he based his conclusion, still had other facts and the court in that case deemed it safe to leave it to the jury to consider those facts in weighing the testimony of the expert. In the case of valuation of property, the question to be answered being answerable by a hundred possible estimates, is not the case much more difficult for a jury to consider as to the amount of influence the incompetent evidence had on the mind of the expert witness in reaching his conclusion, and how much his opinion can be discounted by the fact that certain of such evidence was incompetent; or, can the jury size up the case and say that his testimony should be discounted so much or so much? In the New York case the jury could say, well, there is still testimony upon which the decision as to the presence of poison could be sustained; and, although to my mind the case was not free from doubt, yet I feel that the allowance of such an opinion was on a somewhat different basis than exists in the present case. It will be seen that this point is raised in view of the difficulty a jury would have in fixing the influence the incompetent and disproved testimony had had upon the mind of the expert witness in reaching his conclusion, where such a conclusion is based both upon correct and incorrect and competent and incompetent information. Where such expert testimony might be based upon information which has gone to the jury, it would be for the jury to weigh the evidence of such information and to deal accordingly with the expert opinion under the instructions of the court, which might be to disregard the opinion if they found the information on which the expert testified to be in whole or in part unfounded. The district attorney argued that if there was any inaccuracy, even to a cent, that the opinion should not be given to the jury. I think he is wrong there. The estimation of damages in cases like this is a reaching out for an approximate figure;

no figure can be obtained which may be considered as absolutely correct. Therefore, where the difference is slight and not sufficient to materially influence the mind of the expert I should ignore it. In this case, however, we find that the information relied on by Mr. Reidford in regard to the McIntyre building was inaccurate as to the net rentals of the block, to the extent of about a thousand dollars a year, and that his information in regard to the area of the Jordan block was inaccurate to the extent of over 201 square feet, and as to the rentals of the same in the neighborhood of five hundred dollars a year; that he took into consideration the sale of the Chambers drug store block which occurred subsequent to the date of the summons in this case. Such incompetent evidence, and evidence involving such considerable mistakes of fact, are too great to pass over. It also appears that a considerable portion of the information relied on by Mr. Reidford was hearsay testimony which may be found to be, and probably was, correct; but it has not been proven before this court to be so. I do not find in the testimony, any record showing that Mr. Reidford made any independent appraisement of the Cummins property based on his own experience as a real estate man, and on his examination of the building clear of and free from his examination of the valuations of neighboring property based on sales and rentals. If there is any such I think it may stand; otherwise the motion to strike is allowed.

UNITED STATES OF AMERICA
v.
LORRIN A. THURSTON *et al.*

March 14, 1912.

1. *Eminent Domain—Just compensation for property taken for public use:* Just compensation for property taken for public use includes not only "a full and perfect equivalent for the property taken," but also for the necessary and direct loss produced by the taking.

2. *Movable fixtures:* There is a distinction between "movable fixtures" and loose furniture like chairs and tables. They are not "fixtures" strictly; although fixed, they may be moved without injury to the building, making a distinction between them and fixtures that cannot be moved without such injury.

3. *Same—Damages for their removal:* Movable fixtures made to fit certain rooms or vaults sometimes cannot be moved without injury, and usually without expense in fitting them to a different building. Lessee entitled to damage for such injury and expense or compensation for their value, if he elects to leave them.

Eminent Domain: On objection to question in evidence.

R. W. Breckons, U. S. District Attorney, for the motion. *Holmes, Stanley & Olson,* contra.

DOLE, J. The points reserved are substantially covered by the question it was desired to ask the witness as to the cost of the removal of the furniture from the Cummins block and installing it in another building; also as to depreciation of furniture and fittings to be removed if they were sold.

[1] It is an established rule of policy in the Federal courts that the constitutional provision for the security of persons and property, which applies to this case, should be liberally construed in favor of property owners. The constitutional provision in this case is that private property shall not be taken for public use without "just compensation." The Supreme Court, in the case of *Monogahela Navi-*

gation Co. v. United States, 148 U. S. 312, 326, defines "just compensation" as "a full and perfect equivalent for the property taken." There is a tendency in some of the courts to interpret this to mean that compensation is limited to the intrinsic value of the property at the time of the taking. This does not appear to me to fill the demand of the constitution, because the compensation mentioned in the fifth amendment is enlarged by the word "just", and compensation, in order to be just, must be, not only "a full and perfect equivalent for the property taken", but also for the necessary loss produced by the taking.

I do not wish to tie up the court as to the future consideration of consequential damages. I wish to leave my mind free on that point, but the obvious loss, the necessary and immediate loss, I think must be compensated in order to carry out the constitutional provision. Compensation means ·making amends. There are other constructions, but they all—or nearly all—come down to these words, making amends.

[2] [3] Now, the kind of furniture under consideration in this motion is the kind which has been sometimes described as "movable fixtures", making a distinction between such furniture and loose office furniture like chairs and tables. They are not fixtures strictly; that is, although fixed, they may be removed without injury to the building, making a distinction between them and fixtures which cannot be removed without such injury. These movable fixtures were made for the building and fitted to it; the vault furniture was made for the vault and will not fit any other, unless one is made for it or it is changed to fit some other vault. The counters cannot be removed without cutting them up somewhat because of the iron pillars that run through them. Their removal will cause no damage to the building, but considerable damage to them; and would require further cutting up to fit them to another building. The same is true of the semi-partitions. The

lessee should not be compelled to remove these for use in another building, or put them on the market in order to reimburse itself for their value, without compensation to make up to it the loss and expense which would accrue in such an operation.

The lessee may elect to remove such fixtures or to leave them in the building. If it elects to remove them it should be allowed the cost of such removal and the damages consequent thereon. If it elects to leave them it must be compensated for their value at the date of the summons.

The objection to the question is overruled.

UNITED STATES OF AMERICA

v.

LORRIN A. THURSTON *et al.*

June 6, 1912.

1. *Eminent Domain—"Just compensation":* The rule established by the precedents of the Supreme Court of the United States in regard to compensation to be made for the taking of private property for public uses under the law of eminent domain is, that the "just compensation" required by the Constitution is limited to an equivalent for the property taken.

2. *Same—Same—Movable Fixtures:* Such rule taken to include damages resulting from the necessary removal of movable fixtures from the property taken, but not the expense of such removal.

Eminent Domain: On objection to testimony.

R. W. Breckons, U. S. District Attorney, and *C. C. Bitting,* Assistant U. S. Attorney, for the objection.

M. F. Prosser for the testimony.

Dole, J. A question arose as to the introduction of testimony on the following points: To show damages for depreciation of fixtures by removal; damages for cost of removal of property on the premises; and damages for loss of business and profits in consequence of removal from the premises.

[1] The most pronounced opinion in the decisions of the Supreme Court of the United States, in regard to damages or compensation for anything outside of the market value of the property taken, is in the *Monongahela Case*, 148 U. S. 312, 326. The decision in this case is based on its construction of the Fifth Amendment, referring to the clause relating to the taking of private property for public purposes. It says: "And this just compensation, it will be noticed, is for the property, and not to the owner. Every other clause in this Fifth Amendment is personal. 'No person shall be held to answer for a capital or otherwise infamous crime,' etc. Instead of continuing that form of statement, and saying that no person shall be deprived of his property without just compensation, the personal element is left out, and the 'just compensation' is to be a full equivalent for the property taken."

The case of *Shoemaker v. United States*, 147 U. S. 282, 321, lays down the rule that an owner who has suffered inconveniences by delay in connection with the proceedings under eminent domain, is presumed to compensated therefor by the jury in fixing the amount of the award. This conclusion does not appear to be consistent with the rule referred to in the *Monongahela* case, the reasoning in which is that because previous sentences used the word "persons", the following sentence relating to the taking of property for public use must be considered as having no reference to persons but merely to the property taken, because the word "persons" does not appear. If persons are not meant, what becomes of the "just compensation" referred to in the sentence? It seems to me that the language does not require such a construction, and that the statement of principles in the *Monongahela* case would require a more liberal interpretation, if that is practicable. One of such statements in the early part of the decision, quoted from *Boyd v. United States*, 116 U. S. 616, 635, is as follows: "Constitutional provisions for the security of persons and property shall be liberally construed. A close and literal construction deprives them of half their efficacy, and leads to the gradual depreciation of the right."

Some of the decisions under provisions of state constitutions, which correspond to the Fifth Amendment of the United States Constitution, throw some light upon this discussion. The following is from *M'Intire v. State*, 5 Blackf. (Ind.) 384: "The clause in the constitution which provides that a just compensation shall be made for private property taken for public use, means, not that the property thus taken shall be valued and its price paid in money, but that the owner shall be recompensed for the actual injury he may have sustained—all circumstances considered—by the measure of which he complains."

The case of *Phillips v. Town of Scales Mound*, 63 N. E. (Ill.) 183, says: "Just compensation means the payment of such sum of money as will make the defender whole, so that, on receipt by the defendant of the compensation and damages awarded, he will not be poorer by reason of his property being taken or damaged."

The constitution of Michigan contains the following, article 18, section 2: "When private property is taken for the use or benefit of the public, the necessity for using such property, and the just compensation to be made therefor * * * shall be ascertained by a jury." Section 14 of article 18 says, "The property of no person shall be taken for public use without just compensation therefor."

These are quoted to show how exactly they correspond

to the enactment of the United States Constitution. Under this provision, the case of *G. R. & I. R. R. Co. v. Weiden*, 70 Mich. 390, 395, has the following:

"Both of the appellants were using their property in lucrative business, in which the locality and its surroundings had some bearing on its value. Apart from the money value of the property itself, they were entitled to be compensated so as to lose nothing by the interruption of their business and its damage by the change. A business stand is of some value to the owner of the business, whether he owns the fee of the land or not, and a diminution of business facilities may lead to serious results. There may be cases where a loss of a particular location may destroy business altogether, for want of access to any other that is suitable for it. Whatever damage is suffered must be compensated. Appellants are not legally bound to suffer for petitioner's benefit. Petitioner can only be authorized to oust them from their possessions by making up to them the whole of their losses."

In *Commissioners of Parks v. Moesta*, 91 Mich. 149, 155· is the following: "In the present case appellants should have been permitted to recover for such loss occasioned by the interruption of their business as they were able to show, with reasonable certainty, will occur during the time it will necessarily be interrupted."

Counsel for the government have referred the court to a number of cases which appear to take the view of the Supreme Court of the United States in the *Monongahela* case, but I feel that the construction which tends to place the person whose property is taken by the United States in, as near as possible, the same financial condition as he was before the taking, is the view that is best supported by those considerations of justice and fair dealing which all governments should insist upon, not only as to their own interests but in relation to the interests of all with whom they deal, and is not inconsistent with the language of the Amendment. This court, however, recognizes the fact that the weight of authority is against this construction and that it is controlled in its application of the law ,by the precedents of the Supreme Court of the United States. Under that authority, therefore, the third point, i. e., damages for loss of business and profits caused by removal to another locality, cannot be allowed.

[2] The taking will cause damage to the removable fixtures of the lessees in their detachment from the building and removal to another locality. Evidence may be received to show such damage.

I have doubts as to allowing the expense of removing movable fixtures under precedents which refuse such expenses on the ground that at the expiration of the lease they would have to be removed in any case, unless such lease was extended· and will therefore rule against the admission of testimony showing the cost of removal.

UNITED STATES OF AMERICA

v.

LORRIN A. THURSTON et al.

June 24, 1912.

1, 2. *Eminent Domain:* Statement of the case.

3. *Same:* Private property may not be taken for public use without "just compensation."

3, 5. *Same—Just compensation:* Just compensation includes a full equivalent for the property taken and for any injury to other property of the owner, caused by the taking. It is the fair market value of the property at the time of the taking, which is what it would bring at a sale without pressure, together with the damage caused by the taking to other property of the owner.

4a. *Same—Appraisement of value:* Ordinarily the lessor's interests, together with the interests of the lessees and sub-lessees, represent about the value of the property unincumbered.

4b. *Same—Market value of a lease:* Ordinarily obtained by ascertaining how much the unexpired term is worth, considering the expense of maintaining it. If such expense is greater than the money that can be realized from it by sub-leasing or otherwise, it is worth nothing. If the rental is less than the yearly value, compensation should be allowed the lessee for the difference.   Same is the case with sub-leases.

4c. *Same—Lessor's interests:* Surplus of the rent over his expense in keeping the property in rentable condition, and present worth of permanent improvements placed on the leasehold by lessee to go to lessor at end of lease.

6. *Same—Permanent improvements made by lessee:* As such improvements increase the value of the leased premises they consequently increase the value of the lease, which to the lessee is a diminishing value from year to year.

7. *Same—Method of assessment:* Ascertain whole value, then apportion the amount between parties in interest—owners, lessees and sub-lessees.   Rule not applicable in case of radical depreciation of property.

8. *Same—Expert Witnesses:* Valuations by expert witnesses based upon previous sales and rentals of similar adjacent property, or upon their general experience, is evidence to be considered by the jury in fixing the value of the property in question.

9. *Same—Elements of value:* Conditions and surroundings of the property; its availability for valuable purposes in view of its situation; the business demands of the locality and as they may be reasonably expected to develop in the near future, and its adaptability for other uses so far as they might enhance its market value, all belong to the owners of the several interests ,as elements of the money's worth of the property, and may be considered so far as supported by the evidence.

10. *Same—Testimony of possible improvements:* Testimony concerning improvements that might profitably be added to the property in the future, cannot be considered as evidence of damage by the taking, but may be considered as showing the uses to which the property is adapted for the purpose of ascertaining its present value.

11, 12. *Same:* Instruction as to interest rates and rates of discount.

13, 16a. *Same—Tax returns; insufficient return:* Tax returns are competent evidence as admissions against interest. Fact of insufficient tax return not to prejudice party making it, in these proceedings.

14, 15. *Same—Hawaiian rule:* Instruction as to Hawaiian rule of eight years' rental as a basis of value for taxation purposes.

16a. *Same—Same:* Evidence of aggregate eight years' rental not binding but to be considered with all the evidence.

16b. *Same—Interest:* Duty of jury to determine value of property at the initiation of these proceedings without any question of interest.

17, 18. *Same:* Instruction as to weighing the testimony including the knowledge gained by the jury in its "actual view" of the premises.

19, 20. *Same:* Instructions as to expert testimony, expert witnesses being usually paid for their services and work of preparation by the parties calling them.

21. *Same—Preponderance of evidence:* Instructions.

22. *Same—Movable fixtures:* Award to include damage to "movable fixtures" caused by their detachment from buildings and removal to another locality.

23. *Same—Decree of condemnation—Leases, lessees and tenants:* Leases are cancelled and subsequent rent dues otherwise to accrue, are extinguished by a decree of condemnation.

24. *Same—Burden of proof:* Instructions.

25. *Same—Vigilance of counsel; inferences:* Instructions.

26. *Same:* General instructions to jury.

27. *Same:* Suggestions as to form of verdict.

Eminent Domain: Instructions to jury.

R. W. Breckons. U. S. District Attorney, and *C. C. Bitting,* Assistant U. S. Attorney, for plaintiff.

C. H. Olson (*Holmes, Stanley & Olson* with him) for defendants H. Cushman Carter, Herbert Austin and Walter Austin.

L. J. Warren (*Smith, Warren & Hemenway* with him) for defendants Bank of Hawaii, Limited, and Charles M. Cooke, Limited.

M. F. Prosser (*Frear, Prosser, Anderson & Marx* with him) for defendant Hawaiian Trust Company, Limited.

DOLE, J. Charging the jury:

[1]. Under proceedings by the United States of America to condemn certain lands in Honolulu of the Territory

of Hawaii, for the enlargement of the existing site for government offices of the United States under an act of the Congress of the United States approved June 25, 1910, a separate trial was allowed to the parties interested in that portion of the premises sought to be condemned, held by the Hawaiian Trust Company, Limited, a corporation, the Bank of Hawaii, Limited, a corporation, and Charles M. Cooke, Limited, a corporation, to wit: the heirs at law of James W. Austin, deceased, and the trustees under his will, H. Cushman Carter, Trustee of John H. Cummins and others, his relations and connections, as owners in fee simple of such portion of the said premises; and the Bank of Hawaii, Limited, the Hawaiian Trust Company, Limited, and Charles M. Cooke, Limited, as lessees of such portion of the said premises;—all respondents herein.

[2] It is admitted that the said heirs at law of the said James W. Austin, deceased, and the trustees under his will, and the said H. Cushman Carter, trustee aforesaid, are the owners in fee simple of such portion of the land sought to be condemned according to their respective divisions thereof as shown by the evidence, to wit: 2832 square feet to the Austin Estate, and 664 square feet to the Cummins Estate, and of the improvements respectively situated thereon, subject only to the leases which have been admitted in evidence as follows: The ownership of the Austin Estate is subject to a lease to E. A. Jones (Exhibit F), dated October 1, 1893, and assigned to the Bank of Hawaii, Limited, December 27, 1897, expiring October 1, 1918; to a sublease of E. A. Jones to Charles M. Cooke (Exhibit 36), dated September 1, 1894 and expiring September 1, 1918—admitted to have been assigned to Charles M. Cooke, Limited, and by it subleased to the Hawaiian Trust Company, Limited, by a sublease (Exhibit J), which subleases the floor space of the building erected upon the area leased by Exhibit 36 and the area leased by lease (Exhibit C) to the Hawaiian Trust Company, Lim-

ited, dated August 19, 1905, expiring September 1, 1918; to a sublease of the Bank of Hawaii, Limited, to the Hawaiian Trust Company, Limited (Exhibit H), dated August 19, 1905, expiring October 1, 1918; to a lease to the Hawaiian Trust Company, Limited (Exhibit E), dated April 14, 1910, expiring April 1, 1918; to a lease from the Bank of Hawaii, Limited, to Charles M. Cooke, Limited (Exhibit I), dated January 15, 1909, expiring October 1, 1918; and to a lease from Charles M. Cooke, Limited, to the Hawaiian Trust Company, Limited (Exhibit J), dated August 19, 1905, expiring September 1, 1918. The ownership of H. Cushman Carter, Trustee, is subject to a lease to Charles M. Cooke (Exhibit C), dated September 1, 1894, expiring September 1, 1918—admitted to have been assigned to Charles M. Cooke, Limited, sub-leased to the Hawaiian Trust Company, Limited (Exhibit J), and to a lease to the Hawaiian Trust Company, Limited (Exhibit D), dated August 19, 1905, expiring September 1, 1918.

[3] The Constitution of the United States provides that private property shall not be taken for public use without just compensation. It is your duty to see that the compensation is just, not merely to those whose property is taken but to the public which is to pay for it; you are to treat both sides fairly and impartially. The values are not to be diminished or depreciated because the owners are compelled to part with their titles to the United States, nor increased or exaggerated because the government desires to acquire the premises. The compensation, in order to be just, must be not only a full equivalent for the property taken but also for any injury to other property of the respondents caused by the taking. Such compensation must be estimated as the fair market value of the property at the time of the taking, which, in this case, is December 23, 1910, together with the damage caused by the taking to other property of the respondents. This market value is not to be ascertained by what the property would bring

at a forced sale, but by what it would fairly bring for any purpose if the owners themselves, without pressure, should offer it for sale.

[4a] In assessing the value of property like this, where there are fee simple interests subject to leases and subleases, the aggregate value of all the interests will ordinarily equal the value of the property, as if it stood without incumbrance of any kind; that is, if the leases and subleases have been consummated in good faith under ordinary business conditions, and if the property has experienced no violent or unusual injury whereby its value has been radically diminished, the lessors' interests together with the interests of the lessees and sublessees represent about the value of the property unincumbered. This is evident when we consider that each lease and sublease made under ordinary conditions, is, at the time it is made, evidence of the approximate value of the property leased. The reason for this is that in the open market business men will hold a property for lease at a figure which will net them so much per cent upon its market value, according to the business conditions of the locality.

[4b] The market value of a lease to the lessee is of course what it will sell for in the open market. This is ordinarily estimated by ascertaining how much the unexpired term is worth, taking into consideration the rents, taxes and other charges which the lessee must pay to maintain it. Some leases are worth nothing in the market because the rent and fixed charges absorb the whole rental value of the property, and there is nothing left of value to tempt a purchaser. If the rental is less than the yearly value, compensation should be allowed the lessee in accordance with the difference.

[4c] The lessor's interest in a leasehold is determined by the net rental over and above the expenses he is required to assume in keeping the property in a rentable condition. This rule applies to sublessors, the value of their interests

being ascertained by the rent they receive discounted by
the rent they have to pay as well as by the other expenses
they must assume, and should include the present worth of
such permanent improvements as are placed on the premises by the lessee, to become the property of the lessor at
the termination of the lease. The accumulation of such net
rentals for the balance of the lease, discounted according to
the table in evidence at such rate of discount as you may
adopt, will give the present value as of December 23, 1910.

[5]   Counsel representing lessees in this case have made
the point that a lease may have a value independent of the
value of the land; that it is valuable as a contract for the
payment of money, even though the property should have
ceased to be worth what it was. This is true, but hardly has
a practical application to this case, inasmuch as the evidence tends to show that the property upon which the
leases are based has been rising in value for several years
previous to the time these proceedings were begun. In any
case the holder of a lease is entitled to such amount as it
could be sold for if freely offered for sale by the owner. It
is admitted in this case that there is no reason to doubt
the continuing ability of the Hawaiian Trust Company,
Limited, to meet its rents under the leases held by it.

[6]   It is urged by counsel for the Hawaiian Trust Company, Limited, that it has made permanent improvements
upon the premises held by it under lease, and therefore it
should be awarded the value to it for the use of such improvements during the balance of the term of its leases in
addition to such award as you may make in its favor for
the value of its leasehold interests. You are, however, instructed on this point, that permanent improvements
placed on the leased premises in question by the lessees,
which will revert to the owner of the land at the end of
the term, are to be considered only as enhancing the value
of the property leased and consequently the value of the
leases. The amount they have cost is, of course, one of the

elements which enters into this question. How much such improvements have increased the value of the leasehold is for you to say. They represent a value to the lessees that would gradually decrease as the use thereof continues through the diminishing term of the lease. In this regard I further instruct you that it is admitted that the Hawaiian Trust Company, Limited, pays an annual rental for the improvements referred to of $620 per year and that such rental has been paid in advance for the entire term of the respective leases; in considering the value of the leasehold interest of the Hawaiian Trust Company, Limited, this should be considered.

[7] In assessing the value of property under eminent domain proceedings, the usual rule is to ascertain first the value as it would stand without incumbrance of any kind, and then to apportion the amount arrived at between the parties in interest—the owners of the property· and, as in this case, the lessees and sublessees. Although there are some circumstances which would render this rule unsuitable, as for instance, the radical depreciation in value of the property subsequent to the execution of leases thereof, no such condition exists in this case. You are therefore instructed to follow the rule above set forth,—the aggregate interests of the lessors and lessees making up the value of the whole property. In so doing the statement of the witness Reidford, giving the present worth of one dollar under different contingencies and rates of interest and discount, and the application thereof, may be taken into the jury room by you to assist in your calculations.

As there are two owners of the real estate in this trial, to-wit: the Austin Estate and the Cummins Estate, I suggest to you that you first reach a conclusion as to the unincumbered value of the whole property and then apportion such value between the said owners of the fee, and thereafter make the apportionment of such valuations be-

tween the leasehold interests of lessors and lessees and sub-
lssees of each title respectively.

[8]   In arriving at a valuation of the property involved
in this trial, the expert witnesses had the right to take into
consideration sales and rentals of similar adjacent property
occurring before December 23, 1910, and their valuations
based upon evidence of such sales and rentals, or based upon
their general experience, may be considered by you in establishing the rental value of the property in question.

[9]   In estimating the value of the leasehold interests
in the premises as well as the present value of the whole
property, you are to take into consideration under the evidence the conditions and surroundings of the property, and
its availability for valuable purposes, having regard to its
situation and the business wants of the locality, or such
as may reasonably be expected in the near future, as far as
the same appears by the evidence. The adaptability of the
property to uses other than those to which it is applied, so
far as such other uses may enhance the market value of the
same, may be considered. This includes every element of
usefulness and advantage in the property. If it possesses
advantage of location, either generally or for any particular
kind or kinds of business, including the kind of business
actually carried on on the premises; if it be available for
any other beneficial purpose for which you can see from
the evidence it might reasonably be suited and which would
affect the amount of compensation;—all these elements of
value belong to the owners of the several interests and are
to be considered in estimating its value. It matters not that
the property might be used even for the least valuable of all
the ends to which it is adapted. or might be put to no profitable use at all.   All of its capabilities are theirs, and
must be taken into the estimate. It does not necessarily
follow, from the fact that a piece of land may be unim-
proved or unused, that it has no rental or market value.

[10]   I charge you that while you cannot properly con-

sider testimony respecting improvements that might in the future be added to the property, as evidence of damage by showing that such improvements would be a profitable investment, you are nevertheless entitled to regard such testimony as illustrative of the uses to which the property may be adapted, for the purpose of ascertaining its present value.

[11] If, in arriving at your conclusions in this case, you should consider in any way the rental value of the property and the amount of interest which money should yield in the Territory of Hawaii, you have the right to take into consideration, together with all the other facts in the case, the laws of the Territory of Hawaii relative to interest rates. In this connection I charge you that under the laws of the Territory of Hawaii, when there is no express contract in writing fixing a different rate, interest shall be allowed on contracts at the rate of eight per cent. per annum, and that in condemnation cases the judgment finally entered shall, if payment be delayed for more than thirty days after the entry of the judgment, bear interest at the rate of seven per cent. per annum; and that interest at the rate of six per cent. per annum shall be allowed on any judgment before any court in any civil suit. These rates are not binding on you in your consideration of the question of value as based on rents, but may be considered by you together with all of the facts in the case.

[12] It is further provided by the laws of the Territory of Hawaii that the rate of discount to be assessed in computing the present value of future interests and contingencies liable under the inheritance tax shall be five per cent. per annum. This rate also is not binding on you.

[13] In this case evidence has been introduced by the government tending to show certain valuations of this property, sworn to by the agents of the owners before the commencement of these proceedings, to-wit, certain tax returns filed with the assessor, pursuant to the laws of the Territory of Hawaii. Such sworn returns, made by the

agents of the owners of the property to the assessor, are admissions against interest, and are competent evidence tending to show what such agents then believed the value of the property to be. You may therefore consider such returns along with other evidence in the case, upon the valuation of this property, and give them such weight as you may deem just.

[14] In considering, under the instructions of the court, the weight or effect to be given to the returns for the purpose of taxation admitted during the trial of this case, you are instructed that the term "full cash value" as used in the returns, and as used in the laws of the Territory of Hawaii, means market value. You are further instructed that the provision of the laws of the Territory of Hawaii fixing as a basis for the purpose of taxation of real property under lease, a figure equal to the sum of eight years' rental thereof, applies only in cases where such amount is not "manifestly unfair." It is a rule of law established for the determination of values in cases where it cannot be said that the rate is unfair. It is not a rule which arbitrarily permits the taxpayer to return his property for taxation on that basis, or permits the government to fix the value of the property for the purpose of taxation on that basis arbitrarily. A return of property by a taxpayer on this basis amounts to a declaration by him, under oath, that the value so fixed is not in his estimation "manifestly unfair."

[15] This rule of valuation based on the sum of eight years' rental of leased property to be followed unless the result is "manifestly unfair," is somewhat misleading and confusing to the taxpayer, who is required to swear that his return is the full cash value of the property. "Manifestly" is a strong word, and the conscientious taxpayer feels that under its protection, he is safe in adopting the assessment of the previous year or otherwise of making a conservative return somewhere near the sum of eight years' rental, unless some strong and positive reason for making a radical change

is forced on his consciousness; and this is more easily the
case, as any return is merely tentative, and as such is submitted to the assessor for his approval and revision.

[16a]   If you find that any of the tax returns admitted
in evidence are lower than they should have been, in that
case you should nevertheless award the full value of the
property sought to be condemned as supported by the consideration of all of the evidence in the case.   It is not
within your province to punish in this suit any person for
making a lower return for taxes than the law requires; the
sole question you should consider is the actual value of the
property being condemned.

[16b]   In determining any damages or compensation,
you are not to award interest, or to make any allowance for
interest, but your duty is to determine the value of the
property at the date of the commencement of these proceedings, December 23, 1910, without interest.

[17]   In ascertaining the market value of the property
as a whole and of the leaseholds, you are to consider and
weigh the testimony of the witnesses and all the facts
proven in the case, and apply also your own knowledge of
the premises, their nature, character and surroundings, as
ascertained by the actual view which you had there on the
ground.   And in determining what weight the testimony of
the witnesses shall have, you are to take into consideration
the testimony both for the government and for the claimants, the witnesses' opportunities of knowledge of the subject on which they have spoken, whether they are conversant with all the elements that go to make up or assist
in determining the value of this particular piece of property; and, taking into consideration the facts, you may
look to the reasons which the witnesses both for the government and the claimants have given, and decide whether the
conclusions which they have arrived at and to which they
have testified are supported by the reasons which they
have assigned as leading to or supporting such conclusions.

[18]   In determining values you are to consider and weigh the testimony of the witnesses, and all the facts proven in the case, in the light of your own knowledge of these premises, and their nature, character and surroundings, as ascertained by the actual view which you had there on the ground, but not your special knowledge, if any, of the premises, gained otherwise than from the view itself and from the evidence in the case.

[19]   The question of the credibility of witnesses is one for your sole consideration. In passing on this question you have the right to take into consideration the fact, if it has been established in the case, that any of the witnesses have been employed by any one of the parties for the purpose of preparing estimates for use as testimony in this case, giving to this fact, if it has been established, such consideration as you think it may be entitled to, under all of the facts in the case. And in considering this point, if you come to the consideration of it, you may take it as the common practice to pay expert witnesses for their work and time in preparing and giving such testimony.

[20]   Testimony as to value may be received from the mouths of witnesses who are duly qualified to testify in relation to the subject of inquiry, although the jury, even if such testimony be uncontradicted, may exercise their independent judgment. You are not bound by the opinions which these witnesses have given as to the value of the premises. They are proper to be considered by you as part of the proof on the question of value, as the testimony of men experienced in such matters, and whose judgment may aid yours, but it is your duty to settle and determine this question of value from all the testimony in the case, and to award to the owners of the land such amount as you believe to be just compensation as defined in these instructions.

[21]   I further instruct you that you are to reach a final conclusion in this case by a preponderance of the evi-

dence, by which is not meant the evidence given by the greater number of witnesses, but the superior strength of certain evidence, and the greater weight which that evidence may in your judgment be entitled to. In weighing the testimony you should take into consideration the opportunities of the witnesses for seeing or knowing the things about which they testify, and especially so when testifying as experts as to the value, and also their interest or lack of interest in the result of the action, their competency from a standpoint of general knowledge and experience, the probability or improbability of the truth of their several statements and the reasonableness of their opinions when testifying as experts, and from all the circumstances, you are to determine where the weight or preponderance of the evidence rests.

[22] In addition to the amount which you will award to the Hawaiian Trust Company, Limited, for the taking of its leasehold interests in the land and permanent improvements, you must separately assess and award to it the damage to its movable fixtures caused by their detachment from the buildings where they are placed and their removal to another locality.

[23] As a matter of law, a decree of condemnation of real estate operates to cancel all leases of the property, and to extinguish the obligations of lessees and tenants thereafter to pay their rents which would otherwise subsequently accrue.

[24] The government has established its right to take the property of the respondents and the necessity for the taking, and it has become incumbent upon them to establish the fair market value thereof as defined in these instructions. The burden of proof is upon them, therefore, to establish such value by a preponderance of evidence.

[25] The fact that counsel on all sides have shown earnestness and vigilance in the conduct of the case, does not justify you in a conclusion that the United States is

trying to acquire the land in question for a consideration which would be less than a just compensation to the owners and lessees, or, on the other hand that the owners and lessees are trying to get at your hands a consideration for the property which would be more than a just compensation therefor. Such vigilance on both sides—the one inevitably taking a conservative view and the other an optimistic one as to the value, is desirable for the exhaustive investigation of the question at issue, inasmuch as the real responsibility is with you, a disinterested body which only cares to reach a right and fair judgment between the parties.

[26] The work of jurors in trying a case like this is one of public importance and one requiring unusual patience, attention and study, and when it is taken up, as from my observation I feel that you have taken it up, cheerfully and faithfully, it is evidence of a high degree of public spirit. The inconvenience attending the trial lasting for many weeks must have been very serious to you all. I feel that you have given that careful attention to the great mass of detail which is necessary in order that you may be able to approach the case with a clear understanding of all its various aspects, and decide it not only from an impartial standpoint, but also from the standpoint of good judgment. This case is one of such complication as will severely tax your powers of analysis and comparison, and will call for your best study in order to reach a point of view that will enable you to clearly and logically see your way to a just conclusion upon the rights of all the parties as set forth in the evidence.

[27] Finally, I instruct you that you are not bound to use any particular form of verdict, but you are at liberty to use the following: and although you are free to take any other form, the third part must be given in any case:

VERDICT.

We, the jury in the above entitled cause, upon the issues framed therein between the plaintiff the *United States of America*, and the respondents *Herbert Austin, Walter Austin* and *Edith Austin, H. Cushman Carter, Trustee, The Bank of Hawaii, Limited, Charles M. Cooke, Limited*, and *The Hawaiian Trust Company, Limited*, find the following verdict:

FIRST.

That the fair market value on December 23, 1910, of the land and permanent improvements thereon upon the southeast side of Fort Street between King and Merchant Streets in Honolulu, the area whereof is 3496 square feet as shown upon the map in evidence as Exhibit A, was the sum of ———————— dollars (————————) which sum we hereby apportion between and award to the several parties in interest on this trial as follows:

Award No. 1.

To *Herbert Austin, Walter Austin* and *Edith Austin*, individually and as Trustees under the will of James W. Austin, deceased, the sum of ———————— dollars ($————————) as compensation for their interest in the said land and improvements and rentals accruing to them under the outstanding leases.

Award No. 2.

To *H. Cushman Carter*, Trustee for the Cummins Estate, the sum of ———————— dollars ($————————) as full compensation for his interest in the said land and improvements and rentals accruing to him under the outstanding leases.

Award No. 3.

To *The Bank of Hawaii, Limited*, the sum of ———————— dollars ($————————) as compensation for its interest as lessee under the lease made by James W. Austin to E. A. Jones, October 1, 1893, and assigned by Jones to The Bank of Hawaii, Limited, December 27, 1897.

Award No. 4.

To *Charles M. Cooke, Limited, the* sum of ——————
dollars ($——————) as compensation for its leasehold in-
terests held under the lease made to it by The Bank of
Hawaii, Limited, January 15, 1909, and the lease made by
E. A. Jones to C. M. Cooke, September 1, 1894, assigned by
C. M. Cooke to Charles M. Cooke, Limited, and the lease
made by the Cummins Estate to Charles M. Cooke, September 1, 1894, assigned by C. M. Cooke to Charles M.
Cooke, Limited.

Award No. 5.

To *The Hawaiian Trust Company, Limited,* the sum of
—————— dollars ($——————) as compensation for its
leasehold interests under the lease made to it by The Bank
of Hawaii, Limited, August 19, 1905, and the lease made to
it by Charles M. Cooke, Limited, August 19, 1905, and the
lease made to it by the Austin Estate, April 14, 1910, and
the lease made to it by the Cummins Estate, dated August
19, 1905.

SECOND.

We further award to *The Hawaiian Trust Company, Limited,* as the amount of damage that will be sustained by it
by reason of the taking under these proceedings, being the
damage to movable fixtures by way of detachment and
removal, the sum of —————— dollars ($——————).

THIRD.

We find that all of the interest of *John A. Cummins, Kapeka M. Cummins, Charles Mahoe* and *Hattie Mahoe,* in
the property is held and owned by the defendant *H. Cushman Carter* as *Trustee,* and that the award herein made to
H. Cushman Carter, Trustee, covers all of the interest held
by the said *John A. Cummins, Kapeka M. Cummins,
Charles Mahoe* and *Hattie Mahoe* in and to said property.

UNITED STATES OF AMERICA

v.

LORRIN A. THURSTON *et al.*

March 6, 1913.

1. *Eminent domain—Interest—Just compensation:* The jury was instructed not to make any allowance for interest in determining the compensation, but simply to determine the value of the lessors' ownership as it stood at the beginning of the proceedings. *Held*, that the lessors would not, under such instruction, receive "just compensation", inasmuch as the rental under the lease—an old one, with still a long time to run, is far below what the premises would now bring, if unincumbered; and the time elapsed since proceedings began, has by diminishing the term of the lease, increased the value of the lessors' interest.

2. *Same—Constitutional rule for just compensation, opposing statutes:* Even if the silence of the Federal and local statutes as to interest upon such awards, can be construed as prohibiting it, they must give way to the constitutional provision for "just compensation," whenever the owners would be deprived of it without the payment of interest.

3. *Same—Interest—Net profits:* A reasonable remedy for this state of things is to allow interest on the award, for the time elapsed before payment, to be discounted by the net profits that have accrued to the lessors during that time.

4. *Same—Rate of interest:* Legal rates of interest in the Territory are eight per cent. ordinarily and six per cent. on judgments of a court in a civil suit. *Held*, that interest be six per cent. on the award, as fixed by a verdict of a jury and to be formulated into a decree.

5. *Same—Interest on award when payment delayed:* Though having as above allowed interest at six per cent per annum on the award from date of instituting proceedings, in order to secure "just compensation", yet the court following the rule of the Hawaiian statute, Rev. L. 1905, sec. 505, holds that, if the judgment is not satisfied within thirty days, interest should run on the amount so fixed, at the rate of seven per cent per annum from the expiration of such thirty days.

Eminent Domain: Motion for allowance of interest

Holmes, Stanley & Olson for the motion.
R. W. Breckons, U. S. District Attorney, contra.

Dole, J. After verdict had been rendered in the two trials in the case of United States v. L. A. Thurston, et al., to-wit, the one in which the Austin Estate and the Hawaiian Office Supply Company were respondents, and the one in which the Austin Estate was respondent, counsel for the Austin Estate, represented by Herbert Austin, Walter Austin and Edith Austin, moved that the court in making up its decree should allow and decree interest on the awards in favor of the Austins in such trials from the date of the beginning of the proceedings in this case, to-wit, December 23, 1910. Counsel for the government opposed such motion and referred the court to the following cases in support of his contention:

In *Bauman v. Ross,* 167 U. S. 548, 598, the act under which suit was brought, 27 Stat. 532, c. 197 (1893), is silent as to interest pending the proceedings. Such silence is no obstacle to the rule of the Constitution for "just compensation" if that rule requires payment of such interest. The case of *Shoemaker v. United States,* 147 U. S. 282, 320-321, is not applicable here, inasmuch as the court in ruling against the claim of interest pending proceedings, said, "The inconveniences to which he [the owner] was subjected by the delay are presumed to be considered and allowed for in fixing the amount of compensation;" whereas in the present case the jury were instructed as follows: "In determining damages or compensation, you are not to award interest or to make any allowance for interest, but your duty is to determine the value of the lessors' interest at the date of the commencement of these procedings." It is therefore clear that the respondents did not have the benefit of the presumption recognized in the *Shoemaker* case. The case of *Town of Hingham v. United States*, 161 Fed. 295, 299-300, cites the *Bauman* case with some misgiving and, referring to the Massachusetts law in conformity with which the case was brought, as allowing interest where loss of use of land or trouble or expense is shown, refused interest as no basis for it was produced. This case does not offer much assistance to the solution of the question in the present case. The case of *Kerr v. South Park Commissioners*, 117 U. S. 379, 382-383, has nothing to say about interest except upon accounts paid in and upon the balance remaining to be paid to the claimant. The case of *United States v. Town of Nahant*, 153 Fed. 520, is indecisive on this question. In the case of *United States v. Sargent*, 162 Fed. 81, 84, the United States proceeded under the provisions of the local law of Minnesota for the condemnation of a site for post office. This law allowed interest on such awards from same date not made clear by the decision; the court did not not base its decision on such law, but conformed to it as a "fair and reasonable method" of reaching the amount of "just compensation" due the owner.

The district attorney argues that the Hawaiian statute on eminent domain, which is silent as to the payment of interest on the award from the time with reference to which the award is made to the time of payment, forbids the allowance of interest for such period, but that the only interest that the respondents are entitled to is that which is provided in such local statute, i. e., that if payment shall be delayed more than thirty days after final judgment then interest shall be allowed at the rate of seven per cent. per annum.

The act of August 1, 1888, 25 Stat. 357, c. 728, provides that "the practice, pleadings, forms and modes of proceeding in causes arising under the provisions of this act shall conform, as near as may be, to the practice, pleadings, forms and proceedings existing at the time in like causes in the courts of record of the State within which such circuit or

district courts are held, any rule of the court to the contrary
notwithstanding." This is section 2 of the statute, the title
of which is "An act to authorize condemnation of land for
sites of public buildings, and for other purposes." Whether
such reference to the practice, pleadings, forms and proceedings of local courts in such cases includes the matter of
interest, is a question which the court in the case of *United
States v. Sargent,* supra, at page 84, declined to decide, but
acted in harmony therewith as a fair and reasonable method
of reaching the "just compensation" required by the Constitution.

[2]   Even if a court should consider that the act of 1888
meant to include the requirement in the local statute for
payment of interest, as covered by the words practice, pleadings, forms and proceedings, yet if, following our local statute and refusing to pay interest should deprive land owners
in proceedings under condemnation, of a part of the "just
compensation" which the Constituion assures them, then
the statutes must give way. As both the Hawaiian law and
the United States law are silent on the subject of interest
upon an award from the time with reference to which the
property is appraised to the time of payment, there seems
to be no obstacle to carrying out the requirements of the
Constitution as to "just compensation" if interest on such
award is called for. *Nudd v. Burrows,* 91 U. S. 426, 441-442.

"Where damages are assessed for property to be afterwards taken, the award or verdict should include interest
from the time with reference to which the damages are estimated, to be reduced by the value of the use of the property
to the owner while he continues to have such use   *   *   *
This is just to the owner. But he should not have more
than is just, and justice to the party condemning requires
that the value of the possession to the owner should be
deducted from the interest." 2 Lewis on Eminent Domain,
3d ed., sec. 742, pp. 1320-1321.

"While the assessed value, if paid at the date taken for
the assessment, might be just compensation, it certainly
would not be, if payment be delayed, as might happen in

many cases, and as did happen in this case, till several years after that time. This difference is the same as between a sale for cash and a sale on time." *Warren v. R. R. Co.*, 21 Minn. 424, 427.

[1] The circumstances in this case are peculiar. The larger and more valuable part of the premises is held under an old lease at a rental which the evidence taken in the case would clearly show to be proximately about between one-tenth and one-twelfth of the rents that the property would receive at the present time if unincumbered. This lease had eight years and four months to run from the date when proceedings were begun, December 23, 1910. Over two years have elapsed from then to the time of the verdict of the jury. It is obvious that the value of this property to the lessors was improving with every year's diminution of the term of the lease; for instance if there had been no lease on the place the lessors would have been able to acquire the total value of the premises, being the aggregate of what has been awarded to them and to the lessees; but if the lessors are awarded only the value of the place as it was in December 1910 with eight years and four months of the lease unexpired, and without interest, it would be a loss to them as compared with an award which might be made as to the value of their interest at the present time with over two years of such balance of the term removed. This prejudicial loss to them is clear and undoubted. To hold them to the valuation of the place as it was two years ago would be to fail to award them "just compensation" as called for by the Constitution.

[3] The reasonable and obvious way of remedying this loss is to allow them interest for the time elapsed, to be discounted by the net profits which have accrued to them during that period.

[4] Counsel for the lessors has asked that eight per cent. be allowed upon the award, which is the legal rate where no special rate is provided. The law provides that interest

at the rate of six per cent. per annum shall be allowed on any judgment in any court in any civil suit. The interest asked for is upon an award established by the verdict of the jury to be formulated into a decree by the court. It appears to me that the provision as to fixing the rate of six per cent. for judgments in civil suits is the rule here, this being interest on a judgment, and I so rule.

March 29, 1913.

[5] In the opinion rendered March 6, 1913, as to interest on the awards in this case, relating to the proceedings for estimating the compensation due the Austin Estate, in which the Office Supply Company, Limited, and E. O. Hall & Son, Limited, were respondents, the ruling was made that, inasmuch as the court had instructed the juries in those proceedings not to allow any interest on their valuation of the interests of the Austin Estate as of December 23, 1910, the date of the filing of the proceedings, interest should be allowed at the rate of six per cent. to the date of decree, upon such valuation less the net profits of the Austins from the premises during such period. Now the question arises whether, in case payment should not be made within thirty days after the date of the decree, interest at seven per cent. on the amount of the decree, under the Hawaiian statute, should be allowed upon the award as fixed by the verdict of the jury, or should such interest run on the amount fixed by the decree, which includes interest on the amount found by such verdict, as part compensation.

In this case, although compensation due to the Austin Estate includes such jury award with interest from the initiation of proceedings, yet such interest is in the nature of damages for the taking, and makes up the full compensation. The charging of interest is simply a method of arriving at the just compensation required by the Constitution. There would seem, therefore, to be no reason why the matter should be treated differently from what would have been the rule had the jury found the full compensation under instructions of the court covering the point.

Following the Hawaiian statute, then, interest should run upon the amount fixed by the decree, if unpaid within thirty days thereafter, from he expiration of such thirty days until paid, at the rate of seven per cent. per annum.

GEORGE R. MAYNE v. THE STEAMSHIP MAKURA.

June 5, 1911.

1. *Admiralty—Process—Issuance—Necessity of order for:* To set in motion the service of a libel in admiralty and of a simple monition to appear and answer (without attachment), process may issue as a matter of course without special order of court.

2. *Same—Same—Service upon foreign corporation:* Service of process upon a foreign corporation in the manner prescribed by the laws of the Territory of Hawaii, is valid, in the absence of any special governing provision of Federal statute or practice.

3. *Same—Same—Same—Motion to quash:* Where a motion to quash, together with its supporting affidavit, leaves uncertain facts upon which the motion is based, relief is refused, but with leave to amend.

4. *Foreign corporations—Failure to comply with local laws—Jurisdiction of Federal court:* Failure of a foreign corporation, respondent in an admiralty suit, to comply with local laws requiring such corporations to provide persons upon whom service of process may be made, does not deprive the United States District Court of jurisdiction of that respondent when duly served through its agent. *Spreckels v. The Nevadan,* 1 U. S. Dist. Ct. Haw. 354, followed.

In Admiralty: Motions to quash and set aside service.

Holmes, Stanley & Olson for the motions.
Lorrin Andrews and *George A. Davis,* contra.

CLEMONS, J. This is a libel against the steamship Ma-

kura and her owner and the Canadian-Australian Royal
Mail Steamship Line, wherein the owner and the Canadian-
Australian Line, by separate motions, move to quash and to
set aside service of summons.

The first ground, common to both motions, is that no
order was made or authority given by this court or by any
judge thereof for the issue of any process *in personam* directed to or against the movants.

[1] The libel contains the usual prayer for process
against the ship and for citation to the libellees and all persons in interest to appear and answer. Whereupon an order
was made that process issue against the ship as prayed for,
and, also, upon a proper showing it was ordered that the
clerk "file suit and issue process" and the marshal serve
process without payment of fees or costs.

The court does not agree with the inevitable conclusion
of this ground of the motions. While the order may be
necessary as to the attachment, *Manro v. Almeida*, 10
Wheat. 473, 496, and as to the remission of costs, we are
not ready to hold that for setting in motion the service of
a libel and of a simple monition to appear and answer, anything more is necessary than the mere filing of the complaint and payment of costs, or obtaining of an order for
their remission. As regards the simple citation to parties in
interest, process is commonly issued by the clerk as a matter of course. Benedict, Adm., 4th ed., sec. 342; 1 Enc. Pl.
& Pr., 261. See 1 Street, Fed. Eq. Pr., sec. 588. And the
rules of this court so contemplate. See rules of May 5,
1902, rule 45, p. 20, and note the *exceptions* to the common
practice.

The objection may be disposed of, also, by the fact that
the conclusion of the order, providing for the filing of suit
and issuance of process, fairly intends the issuance of
process as prayed for in the broad prayer of the libel.

[2] The second ground, common to both motions, is
that neither the original nor the amended return of process

shows any valid service upon the movants. The original return shows personal service on Mr. T. Clive Davies by handing to and leaving with him certified copies of libel and citation and shows his refusal to accept service on the ground that the firm of Theo. H. Davies & Company, Limited, has no authority to act for or represent either the ship's owner the Union Steamship Company of New Zealand, Limited, or the Canadian-Australian Royal Mail Steamship Line. There was no showing, however, of Mr. Davies' connection with the Davies company. The marshal, with the court's approval, amended his returns to show service upon Mr. Davies, a person in charge of the business and office of the libellees, and a director of the Davies company, their agent.

This manner of service accords with the provisions of the local laws applicable to foreign corporations. Session Laws, Hawaii, 1909, Act 43, sec. 1, p. 53. But it is contended, that the local practice is excluded by Rev. Stat. sec. 914, under which "the practice * * * in civil causes, *other than equity and admiralty causes* * * * shall conform, as near as may be, to the practice" of the local courts of record; and, especially, taken in connection with Rev. Stat. sec. 917, by which the Supreme Court is empowered to prescribe the practice in admiralty suits.

The latter court having prescribed no practice as to service on foreign corporations, this court is free to adopt, even in admiralty, the local practice in civil cases generally. Section 914 in making the local practice the rule in certain cases, cannot be held to have excluded the local practice in other cases for which no special provisions have been made. And in the absence of such special provisions, we approve of the local practice. *Insurance Co. v. Leyland*, 139 Fed. 67, 68; *Doe v. Springfield Boiler & Mfg. Co.*, 104 Fed. 684, 686; *Christie v. Davis Coal & Coke Co.*, 92 Fed. 3; *In re Louisville Underwriters*, 134 U. S. 488, 493. See *Laweliilii v. Hind, Rolph & Co.*, 3 U. S. Dist. Ct. Haw. 184; *Steam*

chants' Mfg. Co. v. Grand Trunk Ry. Co., 13 Fed. 358, 359-360.

[4] The contention made in argument, that there was no showing in the return, of compliance of these respondents with the local law, Revised Laws, Hawaii, 1905, sec. 2623, requiring foreign corporations to provide persons upon whom service of process may be made, is disposed of by the ruling in *Spreckels v. The Nevadan*, 1 U. S. Dist. Ct. Haw. 354.

[3] The motion of the Canadian-Australian Line has the further ground, "that this movant is a foreign corporation and has not now and has not at any time since the institution of the above-entitled cause had any agent whatever within the Territory of Hawaii, and no service of process herein has been made upon movant in any way whatever." In support of this the affidavit of Mr. Davies shows that the Davies company is the agent of the Union Steamship Company and that the latter company operates a line of steamships calling at the port of Honolulu and known as the Canadian-Australian Royal Mail Steamship Line to distinguish it from other lines operated by the Union Steamship Company, and that the advertisements and declarations made or published by the Davies company stating it to be agent of the Canadian-Australian Line refer only to the said line of steamships and not to any company or corporation having the name of "The Canadian-Australian Royal Mail Steamship Line. It being admitted that the Canadian-Australian Line is a corporation (ground 3 of its motion), and from the whole record it not appearing to the satisfaction of the court that this movant is not doing business here, with the person served "in charge" of the business or office, the motion will not now be sustained on this ground, but the Canadian-Australian Line is given leave to file within five days an amended motion and affidavit, in order to remove, if it can, the uncertainty on this point.

GEORGE R. MAYNE·*v*. THE STEAMSHIP MAKURA.

August 3, 1912.

1.. *Admiralty—Jurisdiction in rem—Breach* of *contract* of *carriage:* A suit *in* rem is not maintainable for breach of an executory contract to carry a passenger on a particular vessel, where the vessel has never entered upon the performance thereof, even though there has been full prepayment of fare..

2. *Same—Lien:* A lien in admiralty cannot, as a general rule at least, attach to a vessel other than the one involved in the breach of contract or other wrongful act which is the basis of the claim.

3. *Principal and agent—Pleading—Joinder* of *principal and agent as defendants:* One who contracts with a disclosed principal through the latter's agent, has no right of action against the agent for breach of the agreement, and it is improper to join the agent as a party defendant in an action against the principal on such agreement.

4. *Pleading—Damages—Breach* of *contract—Expected profits:* An objection to an alleged claim of damages as "largely composed of loss of expected profits," overruled.

5. *Same—Argumentative or inferential allegations:* Allegations of ownership of the *res* in a libel *in rem* should be direct and not by way of inference.

6. *Same—Amendment—Joinder* of *actions in rem and in personam:* The libelant having brought his action substantially *in rem* and *in personam*, the action *in rem* having been held to be unfounded, and the respondents having withdrawn an exception to such joinder, the court allows the libelant by amendment to proceed *in personam*.

In Admiralty: Exceptions to libel.

Lorrin Andrews and *George A. Davis*, for libelant.
Holmes, Stanley & Olson for libellees.

CLEMONS, J. To this libel in a cause of contract, civil and maritime, against the steamship Makura and her appurtenances, and the Union Steamship Company of New Zealand, Limited, her owner, and the Canadian-Australian

Royal Mail Steamship Line, there have been interposed in behalf of the libellees, the Union Steamship Company and the Canadian-Australian Royal Mail Steamship line, and the master of the steamship Makura, as claimant the exceptions hereinafter set forth.

The libel alleges the following facts: The libelant, on February 1, 1911, had entered into a contract with three actors to perform at such places as the libelant should designate, for which they were to receive fifteen hundred dollars per month, costs of transportation and reasonable expenses, the contract to continue for two years from that date. The Union Steamship Company was then and at the time of filing the libel agent for the Canadian-Australian Line and owned and operated a line of steamships plying between New Zealand and Australia on the one hand and Vancouver and San Francisco on the other, and calling at Fiji and elsewhere. The Union Steamship Company was a common carrier of passengers and as such carrier and, in the language of the libel, "acting for the Canadian-Australian Line", and upon applicantion of the libelant, entered into a contract for hire to carry and convey these three actors from Suva, Fiji, to Honolulu, Hawaii, at which port the steamships of the Union Steamship Company and the Canadian-Australian Line touched and to which these ships conveyed passengers; and pursuant to said contract the libelant paid to the Canadian-Australian Line three hundred dollars as passage money for the transportation of these actors from Suva to Honolulu, which money was received and is held by the Union Steamship Company under and by virtue of said agreement, and the Union Steamship Company, by this contract, agreed to carry these actors from Suva to Honolulu on one of its steamships, the Moana, which was scheduled to sail and did sail from Suva to Honolulu, on or about February 14, 1911. This steamship had ample accomodation and room for the transportation and conveyance of the said actors, when she arrived at Suva at that time and on her departure thereafter. But the Union Steamship Company in violation of its contract and of its duty as a common carrier of passengers for hire, and without just cause or excuse, refused to receive these actors on board of the steamship Moana and to carry them to Honolulu, although they presented themselves for conveyance as passengers aforesaid and in a fit and proper state and at a reasonable time before the departure of the vessel, had complied with every reasonable rule and regulation in that behalf, and were fit and proper persons to be carried as such passengers, and although the libelant was ready and willing on said February 1, 1911, to pay to the agents of the Union Steamship Company any further sums of money or reasonable charges which the Union Steamship Company or its agents might require for the carriage of these passengers. By reason of the breaches of contract, the libelant was deprived of the services of the actors, was unable to fulfill his engagements and contracts which he had entered into with divers persons to give public performances in Honolulu after the arrival of the steamship Moana sailing from Suva as aforesaid, and "lost large sums of money which he would have obtained from the sale of tickets for such performances and otherwise," and also "became liable for the salaries" of the said actors at the rate of fifteen hundred dollars per month, and was forced and required to expend a large sum of money for expenses, telegrams, and other charges; for which he claims damages of fifteen thousand dollars.

It is then alleged that the steamship Makura, theretofore described by inference and not directly as owned by the Union Steamship Company, was, at the date of the libel, lying in the port of Honolulu and would on that day proceed to sea and out of the jurisdiction of this court, and that the said company "has no property or assets" within this jurisdiction "other than the said steamship Makura."

The Union Steamship Company is described throughout

as a corporation, but no suggestion is made anywhere in the libel as to the status of the Canadian-Australian Line.

The libel concludes with a prayer for process against the steamship Moana, with citation of the libellee companies and all claiming interest in the said vessel, to appear and answer, and for return of the passage money and payment of the said damages, and for condemnation and sale of the said steamship to satisfy the libelant's demands. By the court's order, process issued as prayed. The vessel was seized by the marshal and by stipulation of the proctors for the libelant released under bond, and the respondents Union Steamship Company and Canadian-Australian Line were, as this court has heretofore held, duly served (*Mayne* v. *The Makura*, ante, p. 39) through their agents in charge of their business and office at Honolulu.

The objection common to both exceptions, "That two causes of action are improperly joined in said libel, to-wit: a claim *in personam* and a claim *in rem*," was withdrawn at the time of the oral argument. The other exceptions of the libellee companies are the same as those of the claimant master, save that the latter includes an exception, "that the allegations * * * do not disclose any admiralty claim or lien upon the said steamship Makura," and that the former urge: "that there is a misjoinder of party libellees," and "that the said libel is ambiguous, unintelligible and uncertain in that it does not appear therefrom that these libellees, or either of them, are under any liability to the libelant."

[1] As to the exception of the master, claimant, founded on the non-disclosure of an admiralty or maritime lien upon the ship Makura: The contention in this behalf is, that this is a proceeding *in rem* and as such must fail because the esential, basic, lien is wanting. In reply, the libellant cites the ruling in *The Stanley Dollar*, 2 U. S. Dist. Ct. Haw., 337, 342 (see, also, 160 Fed. 914), supported by Benedict on Admiralty, 3rd ed., sec. 286, holding a ship to

be liable *in rem* "if the ship, her masters and owners, do
not faithfully and fully perform their contracts to carry
goods or passengers." But, the libellees argue, the ruling
in the case of *The Stanley Dollar* does not apply to the
present case, for the reason that the contract here remained
executory on the part of the carrier, as in the case of *The
Eugene*, 83 Fed. 222, in which it was held that even prepayment of the passenger fare made no difference in favor
of a lien, when the vessel herself had not entered upon performance, or, in other words, that the lien does not attach
until the passenger has placed himself within the care and
under the control of the master. This particular ruling was
affirmed on appeal, *The Eugene*, 87 Fed. 1001, 1003, and
adhered to by the lower court in the later case of *The Bella*,
91 Fed. 540, 542. To the decisions reviewed in *The Eugene*,
83 Fed. 222, there may be added *The Missouri*, 30 Fed. 384.

The considerable study which I have given to the point
raised in the case of *The Eugene* has convinced me that
the decision in that case is well founded. The only question
suggested which caused hesitation in accepting that decision
as final, was this: If, in the carriage of goods, the remedy
against the ship is the reciprocal of the ship's right of re-
course against the goods (*The Schooner Freeman v. Buck-
ingham*, 18 How. 182, 188; *Vandewater v. Mills*, 19 How.
82, 89-90; *The Rebecca*, 1 Ware, 187, 20 Fed. Cas. 373, 374-
375, No. 11,619), and if in a contract of carriage of passengers, the passage money is the equivalent of freight (The
Aberfoyle, 1 Blatch. 360, 1 Fed. Cas. 35, No. 17, s. c. Abb.
Adm. 242, 1 Fed. Cas. 30, No. 16; *The Moses Taylor*, 4
Wall. 411, 427. And see *The Pacific*, 1 Blatch. 569, 18 Fed.
Cas. 935, 942, No. 10,643), why should not the remedy *in
rem* be allowed against the ship when the carrier has, instead of mere security for her compensation, the actual payment of that compensation in advance? But the question
must be answered in the negative, for others have interests just as worthy of consideration as the interests of the

man who has parted with his money in the prepayment of freight or of passenger-fare:

"The maritime 'privilege' or lien is adopted from the civil law, and imports a tacit hypothecation of the subject of it. It is a '*jus in re*,' without actual possession or any right of possession. It accompanies the property into the hands of a bona fide purchaser. It can be executed and divested only by a proceeding *in rem*. This sort of proceeding against personal property is unknown to the common law, and is peculiar to the process of courts of admiralty. The foreign and other attachments of property in the State courts, though by analogy loosely termed proceedings *in rem*, are evidently not within the category. But this privilege or lien, though adhering to the vessel, is a secret one; it may operate to the prejudice of general creditors and purchasers without notice; it is therefore '*stricti juris*,' and cannot be extended by construction, analogy, or inference. 'Analogy,' says Pardessus, (Droit Civ., vol. 3, 597) 'cannot afford a decisive argument, because privileges are of *strict right*. They are an exception to the rule by which all creditors have equal rights in the property of their debtor, and an exception should be declared and described in express words; we cannot arrive at it by reasoning from one case to another.'" *Vandewater v. Mills* (*The Yankee Blade*), 19 How. 82, 89. See, also, *The Larch*, 2 Curtis, 427; 14 Fed. Cas. 1139, 1141, No. 8,085.

To create a lien for mere money-loss would be to create a lien in very nearly every case. Such an extraordinary remedy should not be weakened by being made universal, but should best be reserved for extraordinary contingencies.

The authorities offer no suggestion that any protection against mere money-loss was in view in giving a lien to the shipper of goods or to the passenger, for any loss of money paid in advance for carriage must always be small in comparison with the value of the object to be carried; indeed, in the case of a passenger, there is no comparison between the fare and the value of a human life. It is, rather, the safe-carriage, the general safety, of the object itself, while more or less at the mercy of the carrier, whether that object be a person or a thing, which seems to be the concern of the law in giving the lien against the ship. Wherefore, it is held to be of so great importance that the object of carriage must come within the care and custody of the carrier before this extraordinary lien attaches.

[2]   The exception is well taken. But, in any event, it may be upheld, also, by the fact that the case presents a claim against a ship other than that to which the contract of carriage applied—a ship other than the one on which passage was engaged. It is fundamental that no maritime lien can attach to any object except the offending thing, or the thing in default, itself: at least such seems to be the general rule, and nothing has been suggested or discovered to make the present case an exception. See *The Pacific*, 1 Blatch. 569, 18 Fed. Cas. 935, 942, No. 10,643; Holmes, Com. Law, 25-29. In the early days of the Hawaiian judiciary, the learned Chief Justice Lee had occasion to say on this very point, in the course of a decision in admiralty. "Now, clearly the plaintiff had no lien on the 'Nile' for supplies furnished to the 'Walter Claxton' ": *Spencer v. Bailey*, 1 Haw. 187 (*108); and also, "The 'Nile' is not attached for any 'maritime lien or liability' attaching to that *particular vessel*, but is seized like any other property of the defendants, under a process *in personam*." Id. I93 (*112). See, also, Id., 192 (*111).

[3a]   The exception of misjoinder of party libellees is well taken. This proceeding makes parties respondent both the principal, Canadian-Australian Line, and the agent, Union Steamship Company, which is also owner of the steamship Makura. The only instance known to the court in which, under any authority, both principal and agent may be sued together for breach of contract, is where the agent acted ostensibly as principal but really as agent for a principal undisclosed. See 31 Cyc. 1624 and cases cited. Even the soundness of such authority may be questionable (see *Tuthill v. Wilson*, 90 N. Y. 423), but it is beyond ques-

tion, that one who contracts with a known principal through an authorized agent, has no right of action against the agent, and no right of action against any one but the principal or his privies. The exception is well taken, as is also the allied exception of want of showing of any liability of the respondent Union Steamship Company: for it was a disclosed agent contracting only for and in the name of a disclosed principal. But the exception of want of showing of any liability of the respondent principal, is untenable.

The exception of ambiguity, unintelligibility and uncertainty, in that it does not appear who were the parties to the alleged contract of February 1, 1911, is not without excuse, for the allegations of the libel are wanting in simplicity and clearness. But they are capable of being understood, and can be understood only as stating a contract between the libelant and the Canadian-Australian Line (presumably a corporation, though this is not alleged) through its agent the Union Steamship Company.

[5] The exception, that it does not appear that the steamship Makura was the property of any person or persons legally liable under the alleged contract, is well taken: for the sake of good pleading. There is nowhere a distinct allegation of ownership. The nearest approach to it is mere inference, suggestion of ownership. The libelant leaves ownership to be discovered only from the introductory paragraph of the libel naming the parties respondent as "the steamship Makura * ' * and the Union Steamship Company * * * owner of the said steamship," from a mere descriptive phrase in the body of the libel, "The Union Steamship Company * * * owner of the said steamship." and from the indirect allegation that the Union Steamship Company "has no other property or assets within the jurisdiction * * * other than the said steamship." In view of the adverse ruling on the question of lien, the question of ownership is ·not vital, but the court takes occasion to

emphasize its disapproval of argumentative pleading, or pleading by inference.

[4] The objection to the claim of damages as "largely composed of loss of expected profits" which are not "recoverable in this proceeding", is directed to an allegation that the libelant by reason of the breach of contract was "deprived of large sums of money which he would have obtained from the sale of tickets for such performances" of these three actors, also possibly directed to the allegation of liability for salaries of the actors and expenses, including telegrams and other items, incurred by reason of the failure of the carrier to transport these "intending passengers". The line between lost profits which may be shown in evidence as a basis of damages and those which may not be shown, is so difficult to draw, that the court is not inclined to narrow the libelant's line of proof of damages in advance of the trial, though it might require more particularity of allegations of special damages if the objection had been made on that ground. The not dissimilar case of *Foster v. Cleveland &c. Ry. Co.*, 56 Fed. 434, is suggestive of the proper limits of proof as to engagements of actors, interfered with by fault of a common carrier. See, also, 3 Sutherland, Damages, 3rd ed., sec. 947; 13 Cyc. 179.

[3b] The exception, that the libel "does not set forth any good cause of action against either of these libellees, or any matter or thing whereon any decree against either of these libellees can be made or granted," must be sustained as to the agent libellee but overruled as to the libellee principal, the Canadian-Australian Line, for reasons which are disclosed in the discussion of principles of agency.

[6] Let the libel be dismissed as against the steamship Makura and her appurtenances, and the bond given upon her release be canceled. The ruling on the point of agency justifies the immediate dismissal of the libel as against the Union Steamship Company, but on counsel's confession, in the course of oral argument, of a possible confusion of prin-

cipal and agent in the allegations of the libel, the court will not now order such dismissal, but grants the libelant five days within which to amend to cover any error in that regard; unless such amendment, verified, and approved by the court, is filed within that time, the libel will be dismissed as against the Union Steamship Company. The objection having been waived, as to joinder of an action *in rem* with one *in personam*, and there appearing from the libel a clear right of recovery against the person, the libelant may proceed *in personam* upon amending his libel in accordance with this opinion. See *The Monte A*, 12 Fed. 331, 337, 338; Betts, Adm. Pr. 99, as quoted in 12 Fed. 337.

IN THE MATTER OF THE APPLICATION OF SUEKICHI TSUJI, FOR A WRIT OF HABEAS CORPUS.

July 29, 1911.

1. *Aliens—Immigration laws—Right of domiciled alien criminal to re-enter:* Domiciled aliens returning from a temporary absence abroad, are not excluded from admission to the United States by the Immigration Act (Act of Feb. 20, 1907, 34 Stat. 898, amended by Act of March 26, 1910, 36 Stat. 263), evven though of the criminal class (Act, section 2).

2. *Courts—Rules of decision—Decision of appellate court:* This court is bound, as a rule, to follow the decision of its superior court, the Circuit Court of Appeals for the Ninth Circuit, in a similar case. *United States v. Nakashima*, 160 Fed. 842, followed.

3. *Same—Decision of associate judge:* The ruling of one member of this court should be followed by his associate unless extraordinary reasons require its reconsideration.

4. *Statutes—Construction:* As a rule, the intent of a statute is to be ascertained solely from the language used.

Habeas Corpus: On traverse to return to writ.

J. Lightfoot for petitioner.
R. W. Breckons, U. S. District Attorney, for respondent.

CLEMONS, J. A writ of habeas corpus issued herein directed to the United States Immigration Inspector at the port of Honolulu as respondent, based upon the claim of the petitioner, Suekichi Tsuji, that he was illegally held in custody by the inspector. From the petition, the respondent's return and supplemental return, and the petitioner's traverse to the returns, the following facts appear: The petitioner, a subject of the Emperor of Japan, came to Honolulu, in July, 1906, and a month later was followed by his wife. Ever since arrival they have both had their residence and domicil in Honolulu, except that the petitioner was absent temporarily on a visit to Japan from September, 1910, to June, 1911, when he returned to Hawaii. In April, 1909, he was in this court indicted for the crime of harboring an alien woman, his own wife, for the purpose of prostitution, and in November, 1909, on a plea of guilty, was sentenced to three months' imprisonment, which sentence was duly executed. On his return to Honolulu he was examined by a board of special inquiry which, after due hearing, determined that he had no right to land in the United States, and ordered him deported as a person convicted of a crime involving moral turpitude.

The contentions of the petitioner are: (1) That the above indictment and all proceedings thereon including the plea of guilty, are null and void as founded on an unconstitutional statute; (2) That he is a nonimmigrant alien and not subject to the immigration laws.

The question suggested in argument, of this court's jurisdiction, or of the finality of the decision of the board of special inquiry, is not raised by the pleadings, and was by counsel practically conceded to have been settled for this

court by its previous decisions and the affirmance of the
Circuit Court of Appeals. *In re Chop Tin*, 2 U. S. Dist. Ct.
Haw. 153; *In re Nakashima*, 3 U. S. Dist. Ct. Haw. 168;
United States v. Nakashima, 160 Fed. 842, 846, 847.

The question of the constitutionality of the statute under
which the petitioner was indicted has, also, been settled
here. *In re Shigematsu Umeno*, 3 U. S. Dist. Ct. Haw. 481,
now pending on appeal to the Supreme Court [appeal dismissed, pursuant to tenth rule. *Shigematsu v. Hackfeld*, 227
U.S. 684]. See *United States v. Weis*, 181 Fed. 860.

It remains to be determined, whether the petitioner is
within the provisions of the immigration laws,—whether
these laws apply to nonimmigrant aliens.

The contention in the respondent's behalf is that the immigration laws now in force (Act of February 20, 1907, 34
Stat. 898, as amended by Act of March 26, 1910, 36 Stat.
263), and those superseded by the Act of 1907 (Act of
March 3, 1903, 32 Stat. 1213) do not purport to amend previous laws, but to remodel and reconstruct the entire immigration system; that Congress had in view not only undesirable immigrants, in the narrower sense of the word, i. e.,
aliens coming to our country for the first time to seek residence here, but also all aliens of the undesirable classes
specified in section 2 of the act, whether coming for the
first time, or returning after an abandonment of their domicil here, or returning after a temporary absence. And it is
attempted to distinguish the decision in the *Nakashima*
case, 160 Fed. 843, by the fact of that decisions' being based
on laws enacted prior to 1907 and not so broad as the
statute of that year (34 Stat. 898). It is also argued in
favor of a broad interpretation of the act as against persons convicted, or admitting the commission, of a crime of
the particular character of which the petitioner had been
convicted, that Congress in its deliberations over the new
act of 1907, had before it especially the matters of preventing the importation of alien women for the purpose of

prostitution, and of suppressing the traffic of pimps and procurers, and that diplomatic negotiations were then pending which, about the time of the passage of the act, culminated in a treaty directed against these evils; that this contemporaneous history shows Congress to have intended to prevent the coming in of all aliens of the petitioner's class.

Beyond question, the petitioner would, if a newcomer, be proscribed by section 2 of the act as amended, 36 Stat. 263. Does this section apply only to new-comers? Or, does it apply to all aliens whether coming here for the first time or returning from a temporary absence?

[1]   As to the respondent's reliance upon the adoption, in the act of 1903 and subsequent acts, of the broader term "alien" instead of the narrower term "immigrant" used in earlier acts, the question has been settled for this jurisdiction adversely to his contention. *United States v. Nakashima*, 160 Fed. 842

[2]   Though the Supreme Court in overruling the decision in *Taylor v. United States*, 152 Fed. 1, in which the same question is raised, leaves the question open, 207 U. S. 120, 126, we are bound, by the general rule at least, to follow the decision of our superior court of the Ninth Circuit in the *Nakashima* case. *Roche v. Jordan*, 175 Fed. 234, 235; *Continental Securities Co. v. Interborough R. Co.*, 165 Fed. 945, 959-960; *In re Baird*, 154 Fed. 215; *Edison Electric Light Co. v. Bloomingdale*, 65 Fed. 212, 214; *Norton v. Wheaton*, 57 Fed. 927-928; *Dent v. United States*, 8 Ariz. 413, 76 Pac. 455.

[3]   Also, the present judge would, unless for very good reasons not existing here, follow the decision of his senior associate in the *Nakashima* case, 3 U. S. Dist. Ct. Haw. 168. See *United States v. Hoshi*, 3 Id. 439; *United States v. Ichitaro Ishibashyi*, 3 Id. 517.

And, at all event, in spite of some rulings to the contrary, e. g., *Taylor v. United States*, 152 Fed. 1, *United States v.*

Villet, 173 Fed. 500, *Ex parte Hoffman,* 179 Fed. 839,
United States v. Williams, 186 Fed. 354, we believe the decisions in the *Nakashima case,* 3 Haw. Fed. 168, and 160
Fed. 842, 844-845, and the reasoning of Circuit Judge Wallace, dissenting, in the *Taylor* case, 152 Fed. 1, 7-8, to be
sound. The contra decisions seem not to give due, if any
attention to the parol evidence rule as applied to the interpretation of statutes. See 4 Wigmore, Ev., sec. 2478; 2
Lewis' Sutherland on Statutory Construction, 882-883, sec.
470; *United States v. Freight Ass'n,* 166 U. S. 290, 318-319;
United States v. Union Pacific R. Co., 91 U. S. 72, 79;
United States v. Oregon & C. R. Co., 57 Fed. 426, 429; *Keyport Steamboat Co. v. Farmers' Transportation Co.,* 18 N. J.
Eq., 13, 24.

[4] Further, it is no violent supposition that the law-
makers had in mind what everyone is presumed to know, the
law as declared by the courts. And, in the face of contemporaneous decisions such as those of *Rodgers v. United
States,* 152 Fed. 346; s. c. (*In re Buchsbaum*) 141 Fed. 221;
United States v. Aultman, 143 Fed. 922, and even of the
contra decision in *Taylor v. United States,* 152 Fed. 1,
wherein doubt was raised by a strong dissent, it would seem
that Congress, if intending so radical a change, would, and
should, have placed beyond any question the expression of
its intent. *In re Nakashima,* 3 U. S. Dist. Ct. Haw. 168;
United States v. Aultman, 143 Fed. 922, 928. And legis-
latures should not be encouraged in putting the people, who
are presumed to know the law, to the necessity of looking
for the intent of a statute beyond its face 18 N. J. Eq., 13,
24, above cited.

The petitioner is discharged subject to the taking of an
appeal, in which case he may be released upon giving a recognizance with surety in an amount to be fixed by the
court to answer the judgment of the appellate court.

Affirmed: United States v. Tsuji Suekichi, 199 Fed. 750,

which has since been overruled by *Lapina v. Williams*, 232 U. S. 78, as to the holding that the Immigration Act does not apply to domiciled aliens.

UNITED STATES OF AMERICA *v.* GEORGE LOW.

September 13, 1911.

1. *Indictment—Designation of defendant—Omission of middle initial of name:* The failure of an indictment in designating the defendant, to give the middle initial of his name, is not fatal.

2. *Same—Same—Spelling of defendant's surname—Idem sonans:* In an indictment the spelling of the defendant's surname "Low" instead of "Lowe," is no misnomer.

Indictment: Plea in abatement.

C. C. Bitting for the plea.
W. T. Rawlins, Assistant U. S. Attorney, contra.

CLEMONS, J. The defendant, named in the indictment as "George Low," pleads in abatement misnomer, in that his true name is "George K. Lowe."

[1] The absence of the middle initial "K" is no misnomer. *Edmundson v. State,* 17 Ala. 179: 52 Am. Dec. 169; 29 Cyc. 265, and cases cited; 14 Enc. Pl. & Pr. 275-276; 21 A. & E. Enc. L. 2d. ed., 307; Clark Crim. Proc., 145-146. See *Keene v. Meade.* 3 Pet. (U. S.) 1, 7; *Games v. Dunn,* 14 Pet. (U. S.) 322, 326; *Dunn v. Games,* 8 Fed. Cas. 98 (No. 4,176): 1 McLean, 321; *Choen v. State,* 52 Ind. 347: 21 Am. Rep. 179, 181, note. The reason of the rule is often given as the fact that "the law knows of but one Christian name," and such is the reasoning of the United States Supreme

Court, *Keene v. Meade,* supra; *Games v. Dunn,* supra; but a better ground would seem to be that the omission, in a case like this, cannot in any reasonable view prejudice the defendant. See *State v. White,* 34 So. Car. 59: 27 Am. St. Rep. 783, 784.

[2] As to the spelling of the surname, the indictment must stand, under the modern application of the rule of *idem sonans,* that the defect is not fatal "where the name, as written in the indictment, may be pronounced (although such may not be the strictly correct pronunciation) in the same way as the name given." *State v. White,* 34 So. Car. 59: 27 Am. St. Rep. 783-785; *Faust v. United States,* 163 U. S. 452, 454; *United States v. Hinman,* 26 Fed. Cas. 324 (No. 15,370), Bald. 292; *Territory v. Johnson,* 16 Haw. 743, 748; Clark, Crim. Proc., 145-149; 29 Cyc. 275-276; 21 A. & E. Enc. L., 2d. ed., 313

These well-settled rules dispose of the plea, without considering whether the defects, if any, are matters of form, immaterial under the curative provisions of Rev. Stat. sec. 1025; Rose's Code, sec. 1579; 2 Fed. Stat. Ann., 340. See *People v. Ferris,* 56 Cal. 442, 444; *Burroughs v. State,* 17 Fla. 643, 655-656.

The rule of the California Federal Court of the Northern District, abolishing pleas in abatement for misnomer, might well be adopted here. See 3 Rose's Code, 2295-2296, rule 98, providing that "when the defendant is arraigned, he shall be informed that if the name by which he is indicted is not his true name, he must then declare his true name or be proceeded against by the name in the indictment."

The plea is overruled.

IN THE MATTER OF THE APPLICATION OF WONG ON FOR A WRIT OF HABEAS CORPUS.

October 3 1911.

Habeas Corpus—Practice—Order to show cause—Chinese exclusion law: Where a petition for a writ of habeas corpus for relief of one ordered deported under the Chinese exclusion law, discloses the same facts as those of a case previously determined here (*In re Su Yen Hoon*, 3 U. S. Dist. Ct. Haw. 606), the court instead of granting the writ in the first instance, orders the respondent to show cause why the writ should not issue, and upon the hearing on the return to the order denies the writ, following the decision in the previous case.

Habeas Corpus: Petition for writ; order to show cause.

Thompson, Wilder, Watson & Lymer for petitioner.
R. W. Breckons, U. S. District Attorney, for respondent.

CLEMONS, J. It appearing that the grounds of the petition herein were identical with those presented in behalf of the petition in *In re Su Yen Hoon,* 3 U. S. Dist. Ct. Haw. 606, and Judge Robertson in that similar case having rendered a decision adverse to the petitioner, I deemed it the best practice not to issue the writ, and, instead, ordered the respondent to show cause why the writ should not issue. See 9 Enc. Pl. & Pr. 1024-1025, and notes; Church, Hab. Corp., 2nd ed., sec. 101; also, *Soga v. Jarrett,* 3 U. S. Dist. Ct. Haw. 502, 517.

At the hearing on the return to the order to show cause, the respondent's counsel urged that, admitting the facts alleged in the petition, the writ must be denied, in view of the decision of this court in the case of *Su Yen Hoon,* supra.

As that decision appears to be sound in its disposition of the questions raised, it should be followed. See *United States v. Hoshi,* 3 U. S. Dist. Ct. Haw. 439; *United States v. Ishibashyi,* 3 U. S. Dist. Ct. Haw. 517.

The rule to show cause is discharged, and the writ denied.

IN THE MATTER OF THE PETITION OF ERNST BISCHOF FOR NATURALIZATION.

October 28, 1911.

Naturalization—Residence—Member of marine corps, honorably discharged: Under 28 Stat. 124, an alien who has been honorably discharged from service in the marine corps after having served for the term of one enlistment, may be admitted to citizenship without other proof of residence, such service being taken in lieu thereof.

Naturalization: Application under act of July 26, 1894, 28 Stat. 124.

W. T. Rawlins, Assistant U. S. Attorney, for the United States.

CLEMONS, J. The petitioner, having served one enlistment in the United States marine corps and having been honorably discharged from service, applied for naturalization, and his vouching witnesses made affidavit to his residence for a term of three years within the Territory of Hawaii. Upon the hearing of the petition, the assistant United States attorney raised the query whether the full five years' residence required in ordinary cases by subdivision "fourth" of section 4 of the naturalization act, 34 Stat. 596, as amended, must not be shown by the affidavit.

Under the practice, as I understand it to have been observed heretofore in similar cases, the statute applying to the navy and marine corps, 28 Stat. 124, has uniformly been interpreted as entitling those who have received an honorable discharge after having served the specified length of time, to admission to citizenship without other proof of residence. See Van Dyne, Naturalization, 110. The statutes enacted for the benefit of those in the service of the army, navy and marine corps were not repealed by the general naturalization act of June 29, 1906, 34 Stat. 596. *Bessho v.*

United States, 178 Fed. 245, 247; *United States v. Rodiek,* 162 Fed. 469, 471-472. Although they are in the nature of exceptions to the general naturalization laws, they were intended as a special inducement to those in the army and navy service and should be construed to fully effect the intention. The statute relating to merchant seamen is another provision of the same class. In all of these statutes the intention appears to be to make service the substitute for residence; except that in case of soldiers one year's residence is required instead of the usual five year's residence. Rev. Stat. sec. 2166; Van Dyne, Naturalization, 109-111. The statute in question, 28 Stat. 124, appears, in the final clause thereof, to contemplate all that is required in the way of proof, when it says:

"Any alien of the age of twenty-one years and upward who has enlisted or may enlist in the United States Navy or Marine Corps, and has served or may hereafter serve five consecutive years in the United States Navy or one enlistment in the United States Marine Corps, and has been or may hereafter be honorably discharged, shall be admitted to become a citizen of the United States upon his petition, without any previous declaration of his intention to become such; and the court admitting such alien shall, in addition to proof of good moral character, be satisfied by competent proof of such person's service in and honorable discharge from the United States Navy or Marine Corps."

This is exactly the same as the provision of Rev. Stat. sec. 2166, relating to soldiers, except that it omits any reference to proof of residence. It is thus significant that the statute in question does not say "the court admitting such alien, shall in addition to proof of good moral character, *and residence,* be satisfied by competent proof of such person's service and honorable discharge from the United States Navy or Marine Corps."

So far as the reference to previous declaration of intention is concerned, it seems that this is added merely to remove any doubt of the necessity of such declaration, and the reference is not the main object of the statute,—which is, to declare what may be taken as a substitute for the usual term of residence.

The prayer of the petition is granted.

UNITED STATES OF AMERICA v. KAUCHI MOTO-HARA.

UNITED STATES OF AMERICA *v.* MATSUNAGA.

November 20, 1911.

1. *Evidence—Judicial notice—Executive orders:* The court takes judicial notice of executive orders of the President of the United States reserving lands within its jurisdiction for military purposes.

2. *United States courts—Jurisdiction—Military reservations:* The United States District Court for the District of Hawaii has jurisdiction of an assault committed upon a military reservation in the Territory of Hawaii. The words "exclusive jurisdiction of the United States" (Penal Code, sec. 272, subdiv. third) construed.

Criminal Law: Indictment under Penal Code, section 276.

R. W. Breckons, U. S. District Attorney, for the United States.

A. K. Ozawa for defendant Kauchi Motohara.

A. L. C. Atkinson for defendant Matsunaga.

CLEMONS, J.   In the case of Motohara, the indictment charges the defendant with an assault with a deadly weapon (Penal Code, sec. 276), committed "within and upon certain lands reserved and acquired" and "held and owned by the

United States of America for the exclusive use of the United
·States of America and under the exclusive jurisdiction
thereof, to-wit, certain lands reserved and acquired by the
said United States and then and there held and owned by
it for military purposes on the island of Oahu, within the
Territory and District of Hawaii, and within the jurisdiction of this court."

[1]   The prosecution adduced evidence showing the alleged act to have been committed on a military reservation
known as "Schofield Barracks," situate on the island of
Oahu, Territory of Hawaii, this land having been, as was
also shown, and as the court takes judicial notice, set aside
by executive order dated July 20, 1899, and amended November 15, 1909.   At the close of the government's case,
the defendant moved for his discharge by reason of the
court's want of jurisdiction.

[2]   The statute upon which this indictment is based, so
far as jurisdiction is concerned, is section 272 of the penal
code, providing punishment for certain offenses, including
assault, committed in the following places; among others:

"When committed within or on any lands reserved or acquired for the exclusive use of the United States, and under
the exclusive jurisdiction thereof, or any place purchased or
otherwise acquired by the United States by consent of the
legislature of the State in which the same shall be, for the
erection of a fort, magazine, arsenal, dock-yard, or other
needful building."

The latter clause of the section would seem to apply not
to Territories, but to places "purchased or otherwise acquired" within the limits of States, and evidently was in-
serted to provide for those places, within State limits, contemplated by section 8 of Article 1 of the Constitution.
Territory v. Carter, 19 Haw. 198, 199; *Reynolds v. People,*
1 Colo. 179, 181; *Franklin v. United States,* Id. 35, 38-39.
The indictment must, therefore, be justified, if at all, by the
first clause of the section, relating to "lands reserved or ac-

quired for the exclusive use of the United States, and under
the exclusive jurisdiction thereof."

It is admitted that the place of the assault was land reserved and acquired for the exclusive use of the United
States," but the contention is that this is not a place "under
the exclusive jurisdiction thereof" within the meaning of
the statute.

The Organic Act, sec. 6, 31 Stat. 142, gives jurisdiction to
the Territorial courts of Hawaii, in ordinary cases, and in
Territory v. Carter, 19 Haw. 198, it has been held that the
Territorial courts have jurisdiction of an assault committed
on a naval reservation.

Would the fact that the Territory might have jurisdiction (without, however, intimating an opinion), negative
the exercise of jurisdiction by the Federal government? It
would if the words "exclusive jurisdiction" were used in the
narrow sense of, "*so long as,* or *while,* the Federal courts as
distinguished from the Territorial courts, are exercising jurisdiction without Congress' having conferred it wholly or
partially upon the Territorial courts or without Congress'
having permitted its exercise by the Territorial courts."
But it would not, if the words "exclusive jurisdiction" mean
merely to indicate lands which the United States has acquired for its exclusive use in places which are within its
exclusive control, whether it be exercising that control directly by legislation of Congress, or indirectly by legislation
which it permits the Territory to enact and the Territorial
courts to enforce, or indirectly by continuing in operation
local laws which Congress can repeal at any time. A use of
the word jurisdiction in the latter sense seems to have been
in the mind of the court in several instances.

Mr. Justice Field says, in *Fort Leavenworth R. R. Co. v.
Lowe,* 114 U. S. 525, at 526:

"The land constituting the reservation was part of the
territory acquired in 1803 by cession from France, and, until
the formation of the State of Kansas, and her admission

into the Union, the United States possessed the rights of a
proprietor, and had political dominion and sovereignty over
it. For many years before that admission it had been reserved from sale by the proper authorities of the United
States for military purposes, and occupied by them as a
military post. *The jurisdiction of the United States over it
during this time was necessarily paramount."*

Also, at 538, Mr. Justice Field quotes from a New York
decision:

"If the United States had the right of exclusive legislation over the Fortress of Niagara [as the United States has
over Schofield Barracks], they would have also exclusive
jurisdiction."

The same language is quoted in *Baker v. State*, 47 Tex.
Cr. 482, at 485.

See, also, *Reynolds v. People*, 1 Colo. 179, at 182,

Mr. Justice Story in *United States v. Cornell*, 25 Fed. Cas.
648, says that "exclusive jurisdiction is the attendant upon
exclusive legislation," and also says, by implication, that exclusive jurisdiction and exclusive legislation "import the
same thing." Attorney General Knox, in 24 Ops. Atty. Gen.
617, 619, regards the words "exclusive jurisdiction" and "exclusive legislation" as synonymous. See, also, 26 Ops. Atty.
Gen. 94, as to the "paramount authority" of Congress.

A use of the word "jurisdiction" in the sense of "political
jurisdiction" is made in the *Lowe* case, 114 U. S. at 531, and
in a Missouri decision it is said that "jurisdicton . . .
signifies the *authority* to declare, and the power to enforce
the law, as well as the territory within which such power
and authority may be exercised. . . . The jurisdiction
of a State is coextensive with its *sovereignty." Sanders v.
St. L. & N. O. Anchor Line*, 3 L. R. A. 390, 391, 97 Mo. 26,
10 S. W. 595, 597. Jurisdiction is, thus, coextensive with
authority and sovereignty.

In *Gon-Shay-Ee, Petitioner*, 130 U. S. 343, 352, it is said:

"This phrase, 'within the exclusive jurisdiction of the
United States,' is well understood as applying to the crimes

which are committed within the premises, grounds, forts, arsenals, navy-yards, and other places within the boundaries of a State, or even within a Territory, over which the federal government has by cession, by agreement, or by reservation exclusive jurisdiction. Those cases are tried by circuit or district courts of the United States, administering the laws of the United States, and not by the courts of the State or those of the Territory."

This view is also suggested by the language of the court in *Burgess v. Territory*, 8 Mont. at 66-67, 19 Pac. at 560-561, where, however, the court upholds the jurisdiction of the Territorial courts. A reference to the case of *Grafton v. United State*, 206 U. S. 333, 354-355, is pertinent, and to the case of *United States v. Perez*, 3 U. S. Dist. Ct. Haw. 295, 298, in which the words "jurisdiction of the United States" are used in this broad sense.

Of course, in the broad sense of the words, the whole Territory of Hawaii is within the jurisdiction of the United States, but, in answer to a possible adverse argument it may be said that that fact would not give the United States courts jurisdiction everywhere throughout the Territory under section 272 of the Penal Code; for, to come within its provisions, the lands must also be those reserved or acquired, as they were in the case at bar, "for the exclusive use of the United States." But when once exclusive use and exclusive jurisdiction of the United States concur, then the courts of the United States may try offenses committed in such places.

It may be noted, also, in support of the suggested broad signification of the words in question, that the statute does not, as defendant's contention would imply, limit them to "exclusive jurisdiction" of the United States *courts*, but applies them unqualifiedly to "exclusive jurisdiction" of the United States government.

Madison, in the Federalist, letter No. XLIII, pointed out the necessity of *Federal* control over certain places including the seat of government, forts, etc. Though he referred to the provision of Article I, section 8, of the Constitution, which applies to States, the same necessity would apply to military reservations in Territories, and Congress may fairly be presumed to have so intended in enacting section 272 of the Penal Code, which not only gives jurisdiction in case of forts within the limits of States where the State has consented to the acquirement of the land, but also gives jurisdiction in case of places described in language general enough to include forts or military reservations in places other than States.

It would seem that the words "under the exclusive jurisdiction" are used to exclude States and to contemplate especially the District of Columbia (see Rev. Stat. sec. 2145) and other territory of the United States, as distinguished from places within States used for forts and other purposes and provided for by the latter part of clause third of section 272.

Some support is lent to the foregoing view by the fact that statutes in existence from the earliest times, which the present law was intended to codify, apparently regarded places of this kind, to-wit, "forts, arsenals, dock-yards, magazines," as being places "under the sole and exclusive jurisdiction of the United States." Act of April 30, 1790, 1 Stat. 113, et seq. See *Franklin v. United States*, 1 Colo. 35, 36, 37-38, 42-43. Rev. Stat. sec. 5339. For, in the earlier statutes, the use of the word "other" in the expression "other places under the exclusive jurisdiction," or similar expressions, would seem to give color to the preceding places enumerated in the context and bring them also within the same "exclusive jurisdiction." The principle of *noscitur a sociis* would support this construction. Indeed, it is difficult to see what places can be intended by the portion of the statute in question, if not places of the kind here shown, —military reservations.

Having thus indicated my view of the question, some

authorities cited in support of an opposite conclusion should be considered.

The opinion of Attorney General Cushing holds that under a statute covering offenses committed within a fort or other building or place, the site whereof is "ceded to, and is under the jurisdiction of the United States," the Federal courts would not have jurisdiction in an organized Territory, but his opinion is influenced by the fact that "the apparent sense of the act" is to apply to cessions made by States. 7 Ops. Atty. Gen. 564. Mr. Cushing, in a later opinion, says, "I will not undertake, until the question arises, to determine whether in a military or other reservation within a Territory, the legislative jurisdiction of Congress be complete and exclusive or not." Id. 574.

The case of *Burgess v. Territory*, 8 Mont. 57, 19 Pac. 558, is authority only for the jurisdiction of Territorial courts, though its reasoning would seem to exclude Federal jurisdiction. It relies mainly on Mr. Cushing's opinion discussed above.

The case of *Reynolds v. People*, 1 Colo. 179, also supports Territorial jurisdiction but indicates a view of Federal jurisdiction in the broad sense, Id. 182, and, affirms *Franklin v. United States*, Id. 35, which clearly indicates that the United States would have jurisdiction. Id. 37, 38, 42-43.

The opinion of Solicitor-General Hoyt, 26 Ops. Atty. Gen. 91, only supports local jurisdiction in case of a military reservation in the Philippines, where there is no Federal court, but suggests nothing as to jurisdiction where Federal courts are provided.

The case of *Territory v. Carter*, 19 Haw. 198, supports local jurisdiction, but goes no further.

These authorities, upon analysis, lend little, if any support to jurisdiction of Territorial courts to the exclusion of that of Federal courts.

The only case found which passes directly and squarely

upon the point here involved, *Scott v. Wyoming*, 1 Wyo. 40, rules in support of Federal jurisdiction, though it is weakened by want of discussion or statement of its reasons.

While realizing that if we construe the words "exclusive jurisdiction" as not giving the United States jurisdiction where it has parted with any of its jurisdiction to a subordinate Territory, the motion might be granted, nevertheless these words in an unqualified sense mean the power and authority of the United States, whether partly exercised through its subordinate, or not, and I find nothing to justify my qualifying them in any way.

In accordance with the foregoing views, the motion to dismiss is denied.

The foregoing opinion disposes of the case of Matsunaga, in which the defendant interposed a demurrer on the ground of want of jurisdiction,—the offense charged being larceny (Penal Code, sec. 287), committed in a place identical in description with that described in the indictment in the Motohara case.

The demurrer is, accordingly, overruled.

UNITED STATES OF AMERICA

v.

FONG HING.

December 22, 1911.

1. *Indictment—Offenses charged in general language of statute—Bill of particulars:* The allegations of an indictment for violation of the statute against the importation and use of opium, 35 Stat. 614, being in the general language of the statute, the court on motion orders

a bill of particulars as to time and place of importation (under one count), time and place of other alleged acts (under another count), and names of persons whom the defendant is charged with having assisted in importation (under another count). A bill of particulars as to certain other items refused.

2. *Same—Election between counts:* When two or more distinct offenses are properly charged in separate counts of an indictment, the government will not be required to elect before the trial upon which one of such counts it will proceed against the defendant, unless it appears that the defendant would be prejudiced or embarrassed without such election. *United States v. Leau Hung,* 3 U. S. Dist. Ct. Haw. 552, followed.

Indictment: Motion for bill of particulars and to compel election between counts.

Thompson, Wilder, Watson & Lymer for the motion.
W. T. Rawlins, Assistant U. S. Attorney, contra.

CLEMONS, J. The defendant is here charged, in an indictment of three counts, with the unlawful importation of smoking opium (first count), the unlawful assisting in such importation (second count), and the unlawful receiving, buying, selling and concealing of smoking opium, and facilitating in such receipt, purchase, sale, and concealment (third count), the allegations in each count being in the general language of the statute as in the indictments under consideration in the cases of *United States v. Ah Foo,* 3 U. S. Dist. Ct. Haw. 487, and the *United States v. Leau Hung,* Id. 553. He moves for a bill of particulars of many items, the nature of which will hereinafter appear, the motion being supported by defendant's affidavit, in which he deposes that by reason of the generality of the indictment and the lack of information contained therein, he is unable to duly prepare for trial, or to prepare such preliminary motions as counsel may advise.

[1] The decision in the case of *United States v. Ah Foo*, supra, at p. 490, suggests that under an indictment of this kind, "circumstances might require a bill of particulars." No clear rule is laid down by the authorities as to what these circumstances are, but a guide is suggested by some expressions of the Supreme Court of the United States, as to the defendant's being entitled to know matters "essential in the preparation of his defense," *Kirby v. United States*, 174 U. S. 47, 64, and as to the defendant's being protected against "surprise by evidence for which he is unprepared." *Dunlop v. United States*, 165 U. S. 486, 491. Perhaps, the best statement of the matter is contained in the language of a New York court, to the effect that the defendant is entitled to such particulars as will "identify the transaction." *Wray v. Penn. R. Co.*, 4 N. Y. Supp. 354, 355. Courts never refuse a bill of particulars where there is any reason "to believe such particulars necessary to inform the defendant of the particular transactions, or instances," charged, *People v. McKnight*, 10 Mich. 54, 92; and especially, should they be liberal in protecting defendants against what are aptly termed "drag-net" proceedings. See *Gary v. Circuit Judge*, 132 Mich. 205; 92 N. W. 774; *Chipman v. People*, 39 Mich. 357, 362; *Williams v. Commonwealth*, 91 Pa. 493, 502.

On the other hand, the court should be somewhat guarded in the exercise of its discretion, as the bill of particulars necessarily limits the prosecution in its proof, and at all events the prosecution should not be required to disclose its evidence, or to do anything more than state ultimate facts which it is to prove. See *Com. v. Buccieri*, 153 Pa. St. 535, 547; *Higenbotham v. Green*, 25 Hun, 214, 216.

The case falls within the class "where the charges of a valid indictment are, nevertheless, so general in their nature that they do not fully advise the accused of the specific acts with which he is charged, so that he may properly prepare his defense." 22 Cyc. 371. It seems that at least the following items should be furnished, to fairly enable the defendants to identify the transactions alleged. The motion is accordingly granted as to these items, insofar as the prosecution is able to furnish the desired information:

First count: The time, as near as possible, of the said importation (see *People v. Davis*, 52 Mich. 569, 571); the port or place or such importation (*United States v. Miyamura*, 2 U. S. Dist. Ct. Haw. 1, 3).

Second count: The time and port or place, all aforesaid; also, a description by name or otherwise, of the person or persons whom the defendant is alleged to have assisted in such importation (*Kirby v. United States*, 174 U. S. 47, 64. See *Wray v. Penn. R. Co.*, 4 N. Y. Supp. 354, 355; *Kee v. McSweeney*, 15 Abb. N. C. 229).

Third count: The time (as near as possible) and place of the act or series of acts alleged; the port or place of delivery of the opium.

[2] Insofar as the motion requires an election as to which of the series of acts alleged in the third count the prosecution will rely upon, the motion is denied. *United States v. Leau Hung*, 3 U. S. Dist. Ct. Haw. 552. See also *Burt v. State*, 48 So. 851, par. 5 (Ala.).

As to all other items requested, including the following, the motion is denied:

First count: The means employed in effecting the alleged importation; the exact date of the arrival of the ship or carrier; the port or place of arrival of the ship or carrier; the port or place within the United States at which the contraband opium is alleged to have been received and discharged; the exact amount of opium imported, and description and number of the containers.

Second count: The nature of the assistance rendered by defendant to other persons in importing opium; the means employed; the exact amount of opium imported, and description and number of the containers.

Third count: The exact act or series of acts upon which

the prosecution relies to establish the charge; whether the same constituted the receiving, buying, selling, or concealing of opium, or consisted in facilitating the purchase, sale, receipt and/or concealment of opium; the date or dates of importation; the exact amount of opium imported, and description and number of the containers.

The prosecution may have three weeks within which to furnish the bill of particulars ordered.

UNITED STATES OF AMERICA

v.

FONG HING.

December 6, 1913.

1. *Constitutional law—Search and seizure—Self-incrimination:* The incidental seizure of an incriminating account book in the execution of a search warrant for contraband opium, is not an unreasonable search or seizure or an infringement of the guaranty against self-incrimination.

2. *Search warrant—Federal statutes:* Statutory authority for search warrants in case of contraband opium, discussed.

Indictment: Motion for return of seized property, evidence of crime.

E. M. Watson (*Thompson, Wilder, Watson & Lymer* with him) for the motion.

R. W. Breckons, U. S. District Attorney, contra.

CLEMONS, J. The defendant, here indicted for unlawfully importing opium, petitions for an order directing the district attorney and the collector of customs for the port of Honolulu to return to him an account book alleged to have been wrongfully seized by the collector. The seizure was made by the collector in the execution of a search warrant issued by a United States commissioner, authorizing search for opium unlawfully brought into the United States and concealed in and upon the defendant's premises.

The defendant had been arrested with six tins of opium in his possession. On the following morning the police who had him in custody turned over to the district attorney a bunch of keys and a book containing the combination of a safe, which were found by the police on search of his person at the time of his arrest. With the aid of the keys and combination, the collector, in executing the search warrant, on the same day entered the defendant's place of business and opened his safe. The collector there found the book in question which he turned over to the district attorney.

In the petition it is alleged under oath of the defendant that the account book contains a record and his only record of moneys owing to him without which it is "impossible to accurately and adequately collect said debts;" that he is informed and believes that the district attorney is about to use certain entries therein as evidence against him in this action; that he is advised by counsel and believes that these entries will tend to incriminate him upon his trial under the above indictment; that the use of these entries would be a violation of his right of freedom from compulsion to give testimony against himself (Constitution, Amendment V); and that the acts of the collector violated his right to be protected against unreasonable searches and seizures (Constitution, Amendment IV).

Perhaps the defendant might justly be precluded from the peremptory remedy which he seeks, by reason of his long delay in moving for it. But as the extended delays in this case have been due largely to the indulgence given, with the acquiescence of the district attorney, because of the protracted illness of that one of the defendant's counsel who has had the defense especially in charge, I shall dispose of the petition on other and more vital grounds.

[1] It is the law of the Supreme Court of the United States and of this court, " 'that though papers and other subjects of evidence may have been illegally taken from the possession of the party against whom they are offered or otherwise unlawfully obtained, this is no valid objection to their admissibility if they are pertinent to the issue. The court will not take notice how they were obtained, whether lawfully or unlawfully, nor will it form an issue to determine that question.' " *Adams v. New York*, 192 U. S. 585, 594-595, 597, 598; *United States v. Miyamura*, 2 U. S. Dist. Ct. Haw. 3, 7; *Lum Yan v. United States*, 193 Fed. 970, affirming a judgment of this court. See also *Territory v. Sing Kee*, 14 Haw. 586, 588. I can see no reason why the same considerations which have led these controlling authorities to give no heed to a defendant's complaint that he has been deprived of his constitutional right of immunity from unreasonable searches and seizures and from self-incrimination, when this complaint is made on the offering in evidence of papers obtained on an illegal search and seizure, do not lead to a similar conclusion, when the complaint is made before trial. In other words, in such cases the papers are to be used for the purposes of the prosecution, notwithstanding any trespass or other wrong to the defendant in their obtention, and the defendant is left to whatever direct remedies the law may afford. See 4 Wig. Ev., secs. 2183, 2264. The fact that they are to be used as evidence by the prosecution, or that the prosecuting attorney declares such purpose, is enough in ordinary cases at least to stay the court from making any peremptory order disposing of the papers on an issue collateral to the real issue in the case. See *Com. v. Dana*, 2 Metc. (Mass.) 329, 337. The fact of their prospective use as evidence would make a case different from that of *Ex parte Craig*, 4 Wash. (C. C.) 710, 6 Fed. Cas. 710, No. 3321, in which Justice Washington ordered re-

turned to a defendant in a criminal case money taken from his person upon his arrest; for the Justice adverted to the fact that the "notes in question are admitted to be true and genuine [the offense charged being forgery], and no case of any kind is made aginst the prisoner in relation to them, *nor can they be used as evidence against the prisoner,* upon his trial for having counterfeited other notes."

As regards expressions in the books to the effect that the constitutional prohibitions against seizures are "limitations upon the power of the State   .   .   .   and have no reference to unauthorized acts of individuals," 35 Cyc. 1274 and cases cited, the restriction is held by authority which has the approval of Mr. Wigmore, as intended to act upon legislative bodies, or upon executives in attempts to enforce inhibited legislation, or upon the judiciary in respect to such legislation, but not upon private persons or upon officials who, exceeding or abusing their authority, are deemed to act as individuals and not as agents of the State. 4 Wig. Ev., sec. 2183, quoting *Williams v. State,* 100 Ga. 511, 28 S. E. 624, 627-628.   The general principle above quoted from the encyclopaedia is, I take it, what is referred to in the dictum of this court in the *Miyamura* case, supra, at page 7, in the first part of the following sentence (the last part only being the court's conclusion on the facts involved): "Seizures of papers and other property, *by process of the court,* to be used as evidence against the party in a criminal case in whose possession they are, would be unreasonable and inconsistent with the fourth and fifth amendments to the Constitution, and papers and property so obtained may not be admitted as evidence in such cases; but in those cases in which illegal seizures are made of papers or property in the possession of a party in a criminal case, to be used against him *outside of the process of the court,* the court will not consider the illegality of the seizure, but will admit the papers or property so seized, if competent and pertinent as evidence, and the party from whom the goods are taken will be left to his legal remedies in trespass or otherwise." And this general principle is applied in manner as the Georgia decision, supra, has pointed out.

The question has been to me one of some difficulty, but much of the difficulty has been removed by the realization that obiter expressions in the leading case of *Boyd v. United States*, 116, U. S. 616, are to be controlled by the more direct expressions of the Supreme Court in its later decision in the *Adams* case, supra, in which the earlier case is distinguished. The minority of courts, including, e. g., Vermont, in *State v. Slamon*, 73 Vt. 212, 50 Atl. 1097, are noted by Mr. Wigmore to have been misled by what he terms "the erroneous view" of the dicta in the Boyd decision, from which dicta, also, Waite, C. J., and Miller, J., dissented, though concurring in the concluion. 4 Wig. Ev., secs. 2264, 2183. In the supplement to his treatise on evidence, Mr. Wigmore says further: "That case, however, in later Federal opinions, has in effect been pared down, and for practical purposes repudiated (in respect to the obiter statements of the majority opinion above noted)." 5 Wig. Ev., sec. 2264.

Moreover, under the authorities, I cannot say that the search and seizure here were unreasonable and, so, unconstitutional. The authorities, on grounds of public policy, go a long way to sustain the seizure of things which may be used to prove an alleged offense. Thus, they hold that such things may be seized under a warrant authorizing search for stolen or contraband goods: *Adams v. New York*, 192 U. S. 585, 598; *United States v. Wilson*, 163 Fed. 338, 342, 343; and, even, that such things may be seized without any search warrant in the course of the arrest of the accused. *Id.*, 341. Rulings of this kind are, I believe, based on a fair reading of the history of the times which led eventually to our constitutional provision against unreasonable searches and seizures. History warrants no conclusion that the protest of our ancestors had in view the tying of our police hand and foot. In this connection a decision of Chief Justice Abbott (Lord Tenterden) may be cited for its suggestive obiter expression, contained in the following quotation:

"The warrant produced in evidence authorized the seizure of certain articles, but unfortunately some other articles also were taken. *If those others had been likely to furnish evidence of the identity of the articles stolen and mentioned in the warrant, there might have been reasonable ground for seizing them, although not specified in the warrant.* But the tin pan and sieve were not such articles. I am therefore of the opinion that the nonsuit cannot be supported. I have expressed myself in this manner in order to prevent the supposition, that a constable seizing articles not mentioned in the warrant under which he acts, is necessarily a trespasser." *Crozier v. Cundey*, (1827), 6 B. & C. 232, 108 Eng. Reprint, 439.

[2] The search warrant here directed merely a search for opium alleged to have been unlawfully imported. Though no objection was raised of any want of authority for a warrant of this kind, I at first doubted the existence of any such authority, and it may, therefore, be well to dispose of any question in that regard because of its possible bearing on the broad question at issue. The warrant recited that it was issued by virtue of sections 3065 and 3066 of the Revised Statutes, but as these sections were found in a chapter entitled "Enforcement of Duty-Laws," under a title "Collection of Duties," the recital of the warrant appeared not to justify a search for something, to-wit, opium, which was not only not dutiable but even denied importation. Thus, the authorization of a search for merchandise "imported contrary to law," Revised Statutes, section 3061, would at first appear to apply to dutiable articles imported contrary to law; but as under the preceding general title "Duties upon Imports," I find the very first section, 2491, and other sections, e. g., 2496, to treat of *prohibited* articles, it would seem as if the words, "imported contrary to law," in the chapter on "Enforcement of Duty-Laws," in the succeeding title "Collection of Duties," might be applied to

search for prohibited articles. Although sections 2491 et seq. may have been repealed by subsequent tariff acts, they may be resorted to in the construction of other provisions which were embodied in the Revised Statutes. though originally enacted at different times. See *United States v. Findlay,* post. The words of section 3061, "which he shall have reasonable cause to believe is subject to duty, *or* to have been unlawfully introduced into the United States," indicate the contemplation of non-dutiable articles "unlawfully introduced." I have not failed to observe that section 2492 provides expressly for search in case of violation of section 2491; but for cases under section 2496, for instance, there is no special provision, and the provisions of sections 3065 and 3066, in connection with section 3061, are broad enough to cover contraband opium. And considering the object of these sections of title XXXIV., chapter 10, there is no reason why the useful and necessary power there given to courts and to executives should be narrowed, but every reason for the opposite view.

The language of McGrath, C. J., dissenting, in the case of *Newberry v. Carpenter,* 65 N. W. 530, 534 (Mich.), has application here: "Police officers must be given a reasonable latitude in the pursuit of offenders, the detection of crime, and the collection of evidence." Also the language of Justice Gaynor, in the case of *Smith v. Jerome,* 93 N. Y. Supp. 202, 203, approved by the court in the case of *United States v. Wilson,* supra, 343:

"The police have the power and it is also their duty to search the person of one lawfully arrested, and also the room or place in which he is arrested, and also any other place to which they can get lawful access, for articles that may be used in evidence to prove the charge on which he is arrested. We have no statute defining this power or prescribing this duty, but the ends of justice require that they should exist, and they have been exercised under the common law from time immemorial. The authorities on this head seem to be few, but only because the thing has seldom

if ever been questioned. We have at least one such authority
in this state (*Houghton v. Bachman*, 47 Barb. 388), and
there are several in England. This right and duty of search
and seizure extend, however, only to articles which furnish
evidence against the accused. They do not, for instance,
permit the seizure of his money, unless it furnishes evidence
of his guilt, and in no other case may a prisoner's money or
other property be taken from him."

Let the petition be denied. The defendant may be permitted, however, to examine his account book and make
copies of entries therein under proper precautions for its
safety to be provided by further order of the court as may
be reasonably satisfactory to defendant's counsel and to the
district attorney.

See *Weeks v. United States*, 232 U. S. 383, 394-395; *Territory v. Hoo Koon*, 22 Haw. 597.

IN THE MATTER OF THE APPLICATION OF
CHONG SHEE FOR A WRIT OF HABEAS CORPUS.

December 30, 1911.

Aliens—Immigration—Exclusion—Chinese wife of citizen: An alien
woman whose husband is a citizen but who under Rev. Stat., sec. 1994,
cannot herself become a citizen, may be denied admission to the
country if within one of the classes excluded by the Immigration Act,
34 Stat. 878, am. 36 Stat. 263 (sec. 2).

Habeas Corpus: Hearing on return to writ.

J. Lightfoot and *G. S. Curry* for petitioner.
R. W. Breckons, U. S. District Attorney, and *C. C.
Bitting*, Assistant U. S. Attorney, for respondent.

CLEMONS, J. The woman, Chong Shee, in whose behalf this writ of habeas corpus was issued, is of Chinese descent, the wife of a citizen of the United States of America, to whom she was married in China about four years ago. She has never been in the United States, and on now coming to the port of Honolulu is denied a landing by reason of being afflicted with trachoma, a dangerous contagious disease. The writ was prayed for on the ground that she is entitled to enter the country as being the wife of a citizen of the United States and having her legal domicile here.

Though this woman's domicile is, in law, the same as that of her husband (Jacobs, Domicile, sec. 209), the principle appears to be established for this jurisdiction by our superior circuit court of appeals, that where an alien Chinese woman is not returning from a temporary absence after having once been in the country and established a residence here (see *United States v. Nakashima*, 160 Fed. 842), she cannot, even though the wife of a citizen, be admitted if she is within one of the classes inhibited by section 2 of the Immigration Act (except as therein otherwise provided, e. g., persons admitted upon giving bond in certain cases). *Looe Shee v. North*, 170 Fed. 566. The basis of the ruling in the latter case, not adverted to, however, in the opinion, lies in the fact that the woman, though married to a citizen, still remains an alien because of her incapacity for naturalization. Bouve on Exclusion of Aliens, 385, note 10a, states such to be the ruling of the Supreme Court in *Low Wah Suey v. Backus*, 225 U. S. 460, and in spite of the suggestion of the reporter Id., 461, syllabus, that the decision only raised a *quaere* on this point, Bouve's statement is borne out by the result of the court's ruling, if not by the direct expression of the court's opinion. Id., 473-474. 476. See also, *In re Nicola*, 184 Fed. 322; *Leonard v. Grant*, 5 Fed. 11; *United States v. Sprung*, 187 Fed. 903, 913.

In considering the *Looe Shee* decision, the fact has not been overlooked that the marriage of Looe Shee was alleged by the answer of the immigration commissioner to have been a sham marriage; but this allegation was not established (170 Fed. 568), and even if it had been, the fact of a sham marriage does not appear to have had any weight in the decision (Id., 571). Though the appellate court does not directly answer the contention of privilege arising from the citizenship of the husband (Id.), and might well have been explicit in that regard, the inference is clear enough that the court regarded the woman's being within one of the inhibited classes as conclusive against her, irrespective of her marriage to a citizen. It surely should not be assumed that the court determined the case on the ground of there being no marriage: for in view of the fact that by reason of the contention made in the women's behalf (Id., 571). the question was necessarily raised whether she was the wife of a citizen, the court would not have disposed of the case adversely to her on this vital question, without some express statement to such effect. In spite, however, of the question so raised, the court passed it, apparently as immaterial; and proceeded to determine the case on the fact of her being within one of the inhibited classes. It may be said. that the fact of the woman's having been already in the country, does not serve to distinguish that case, for she belonged to the special class of those who, when found practicing prostitution within three years after arrival here. are in effect presumed to have been prostitutes at the time of arrival, and, therefore. deportable as being unlawfully in the country. Id., 571.

This view of the matter is supported by section 37 of the immigration act. which provides that "whenever an alien shall have taken up his permanent residence in this country, and shall have filed his declaration of intention to become a citizen. and thereafter shall send for his wife or minor children to join him. if said wife or any of said children shall be found to be afflicted with any contagious disease. such wife or children shall be held, . . . until it shall be determined whether the disease will be easily curable, or whether they can be permitted to land without danger to other persons; and they shall not be either admitted or deported until such facts have been ascertained; and if it shall be determined that the disease is easily curable or that they can be permitted to land without danger to other persons, they shall, if otherwise admissible, thereupon be admitted." The inference is, that if the disease is not easily curable, or is dangerous, the wife may not be admitted, even though her husband is an inchoate citizen; in other words the fact of the husband's status is immaterial.

Though the *Looe Shee* case was a flagrant one of prostitution, while the case at bar is not one involving moral turpitude, but is one of the mere misfortune of physical affliction, still the principle of the latter case seems to be the same as that of the former, which this court is bound to follow. If the citizenship of the husband can not avail the wife in that case, it is not seen how it can avail the wife in this case. See *Zartarian v. Billings,* 204 U. S. 170, wherein the citizenship of the father, a naturalized alien, was held not to avail the daughter born abroad and remaining abroad until after her father's naturalization. Also see *Low Wah Suey v. Backus,* 225 U. S. 460, 473-476.

Section 1994 of the Revised Statutes, providing that the wife of a citizen shall herself be deemed a citizen, does not, of course, apply in aid of the writ of habeas corpus; by the very terms of the statute, those women, like the Chinese woman here, who are not themselves eligible to become naturalized, do not gain citizenship from their husbands' status. See 22 Stat. 61, sec. 14, act of May 6, 1882.

The court regrets the hardship, or temporary hardship, that this ruling may cause, but feels, as expressed in the decision in *United States v. Williams,* 132 Fed. 894, 896, that: "If the law . . . works hardship, application should be made to amend it. Judicial legislation, under the guise of a construction of unambiguous words, is an imperfect remedy, and one which courts—certainly courts of first instance—should be slow to adopt." See also *Low Wah Suey v. Backus*, 225 U. S. 460, 476. Because of the hardship of separating wife and husband, it is hoped that a way may be found to have the woman held for treatment, so that if possible the disease may be cured and her disability removed.

Let the writ be dismissed and Chong Shee remanded to the custody of the immigration inspector in charge at the port of Honolulu.

IN THE MATTER OF FRANCIS LEVY OUTFITTING COMPANY, LIMITED, AN ALLEGED BANKRUPT.

February 6, 1912.

Bankruptcy—Process, subpoena—Return day: In determining the return day of the writ of subpoena, it is erroneous to exclude intervening Sundays in counting the fifteen days prescribed by the Bankruptcy Act, sec. 18, subdiv. a.

In Bankruptcy: Motion to quash service of subpoena.

C. F. Peterson for the motion.
Thompson, Wilder, Watson & Lymer for petitioning creditors.

CLEMONS, J. The respondent, having been served with subpoena returnable on a date seventeen days after issuance, appears specially and moves to quash the subpoena and service thereof on the ground that the subpoena was not made returnable as required by law and that therefore the court has no jurisdiction of the cause or of the respondent. The only order of the court was that process issue as prayed for; there was no special order fixing the return day for a time longer than the statutory fifteen days distant, but, as it is understood,the clerk in reckoning the time excluded two intervening Sundays and counted only the business days of the week,—a method of reckoning contrary to the usual rule. See *Patchin v. Bonsack,* 52 Mo. 431, 434.

The statute provides that process "shall be returnable within fifteen days, unless the judge shall for cause fix a longer time." Bankruptcy act of 1898, sec. 18, subdiv. a, 30 Stat. 551. In passing, the error may be noted, of Mr. Collier's work on bankruptcy, cited by counsel, in quoting this provision with substitution of the word "shorter" for "longer." 8 ed. (1910), page 343; 7th ed. (1908), page 343. The word "within" in the phrase "within fifteen days," fixes the return day at some time before the expiration of fifteen days. See *Hower v. Krider,* 15 Serg. & R. (Pa.) 43. There is no question that such is the ordinary, and probably exclusive, meaning of the word. In speaking of linear measure, for example, it is clear that "within fifteen feet" does not mean more than fifteen feet, or necessarily, exactly fifteen feet, but means any distance of fifteen feet or less.

The requirement of the court's special order for any extension of the period, emphasizes the intent of Congress to fix the return day as a rule at not over fifteen days distant.

The subpoena is, therefore, not within the provisions of law. The motion to quash is, accordingly, granted.

The granting of the motion does not, however, dispose of the petition, over which the court still has jurisdiction, and the court, in the absence of any showing of prejudice to the respondent, will entertain a motion for issuance of a new summons and order to show cause, returnable on the next customary day of the week for the hearing of bankruptcy matters, which would be four days from date hereof. This procedure avoids obvious technical difficulties which would arise from attempting to amend the process,—for the return day could not, for instance, be fixed for a day which is now past, the statutory fifteen days from date of issuance, and it could not, under the statute, be fixed at a future day more than fifteen days from issuance without "cause" and a showing of cause. The power of the court to amend is given by statute: Revised Statutes, sec. 948; *Norton v. Dover*, 14 Fed. 106; and the issuance of a new subpoena amounts to practically the same thing, and is within the court's power apart from the statute of amendments. *Adams v. State*, 9 Ark. 33, 36; *Barndollar v. Patton*, 5 Colo. 46; *McAlpin v. Jones*, 10 La. Ahn. 552, 553.

It may be well, also, while considering the subject of return day, to suggest here as safe practice that where it is desired to fix the return day at a time *less* than fifteen days distant, the special order of the court be had, thus avoiding any question whether the clerk who issues the process has any discretion in such case.   See *Hower v. Krider*, supra.

⸱ ———

Reported, 29 Am. B. R. 13.

See *In re Angus P. McDonald*, post, regarding return day as the day of the marshal's return of process.

———

IN THE MATTER OF FRANCIS LEVY OUTFITTING COMPANY, LIMITED.

November 27, 1912.

1. *Bankruptcy—Attorneys fees of creditors' counsel, how determined:* The fees of attorneys for petitioning creditors in proceedings in involuntary bankruptcy are to be determined by the condition of the estate, as one of the main considerations,—i.e., by the results effected, the assets saved.

2. *Same—Same—No fees for services necessitated by own negligence:* Attorneys for the creditors are not entitled to a fee for arguing in opposition to a motion to quash growing out of an error of the clerk of court in fixing the return day, which error might by due diligence have been mitigated by the attorneys' early efforts. Nor are they to be allowed a fee for effecting amendments to the petition necessitated by their own oversight. Nor for arguing a motion due to their neglect to file a replication.

3. *Same—Attorney's fees of bankrupt's counsel—For contesting proceedings—For attending creditors' meetings:* The attorney for an involuntary bankrupt is not allowed a fee for contesting a petition for adjudication of bankruptcy. Nor is he allowed a fee under the circumstances of this case for merely attending a first meeting of creditors where it does not affirmatively appear that his presence was of any aid to the bankrupt in performing the duties prescribed by law. Bankruptcy Act, sec. 64, applied.

In Bankruptcy: Petition for attorneys' fees.

F. E. Thompson (Thompson, Wilder, Watson & Lymer with him) for petitioning creditors.

C. F. Peterson, attorney for bankrupt, in person.

CLEMONS, J. Two petitions for attorneys' fees are before the court, one by the attorneys for the petitioning creditors, the other by the attorney for the bankrupt.

The services of the creditors' attorneys have been:

"Drawing and filing creditors' petition;

"Appearance in court and argument on motion to quash subpoena and service;

"Drawing and filing motion to amend petition;

"Appearance in court and argument on motion to amend petition;

"Appearance in court and argument on motion to vacate and set aside special warrant and motion for order for dismissal of suit;

"Drawing and filing replication;

"Drawing and filing notice to admit facts;

"Drawing and filing motion to amend notice to admit facts;

"Drawing and filing further notice to admit facts;

"Drawing and filing petition for sale of perishable property;

"Appearance in court and argument on petition for sale of perishable property;

"Appearance in court at adjudication."

These services, excepting the items noted below, are proper foundation for an attorney's fees. In support of the petition the testimony is that they are worth $250 in view of the care and time involved, but that in view of the condition of the estate $100. would be fair and reasonable. The trustee's report shows "accounts collectable" of the nominal value of about $2,000. and of the appraised value of $300, being in small amounts and many so old that their actual value is questionable; diligent efforts, which appear to have about exhausted the possibilities, have yielded only $126.40 net above expenses of collection. This report shows the bankrupt's choses in possession to have yielded at auction sale net proceeds of $144.40, and the bankrupt's cash in bank now in the hands of the trustee to be $224.10. These assets, less expense of preserving the estate. aggregate $451.90, out of which must come court costs and other expenses amounting to $144, incurred in procuring the adjudication, leaving $307.90 for the creditors, subject to deductions for attorneys' fees, commissions of referee and trustee, and small expenses of closing the administration. The aggregate of proved claims is $1,912.27, distributed among sixteen creditors, the minimum claim being $15.79 and the maximum $458.80.

[2] The services of the creditors' attorneys are all worthy of compensation out of the estate, with the exceptions of the second, third, fourth and fifth items, supra. The services under item second, argument of motion to quash. may not be charged against the estate, as the motion was held well taken, ante, p. 84, over the objection of the creditors' attorneys. because of an error for which these attorneys are technically responsible although it grew out

of the miscalculation of one of the clerks of court in reckoning the return day: an attorney may, fairly, be presumed to know the return day written in the process by the clerk, and knowing the day to have been erroneously fixed, he is responsible for its prompt amendment so as to avoid dilatory motions of the opposition. However, it is not intended hereby to lay down any general rule, that the attorney may in no case charge for services for defending attacks made upon faulty proceedings due to the error of a clerk or officer of court to whom the attorney has entrusted a matter for action within the authority of the clerk or officer; but only to hold that where, as here, the attorney in the usual course of diligence must know what has been done by the clerk or officer, and can mend matters by slight effort, he may not suffer the disease to run its course and then have a fee for its belated and expensive cure. Under the palliating circumstances, these observations, though called for, are more for the guidance of the bar to a high degree of responsibility in future than in criticism of counsel here.

The services in amendment of the petition, items third and fourth, may not be paid for out of the estate, as the amendment was necessitated by an oversight of the attorneys themselves. Similarly, the services under item fifth, argument on motion to vacate, grew out of their failure to file replication, and cannot be allowed for.

[1] In spite of adverse conditions and the bankrupt's keen and technical opposition, the prompt and persistent action of the creditors' attorneys have been successful in saving what assets there are, and, so far as appears, no other assets could have been saved. With the testimony that, considering purely the care and time involved, the services are worth $250, I do not agree—at least in any practical view; for such fees must depend upon the condition of the estate, as one of the main considerations—i. e., upon the results effected, the assets saved. 2 Remington on Bankruptcy, secs. 2047, 2048. But I am willing to agree with the tes-

timony that $100 would be a fair and reasonable fee for
the services itemized in the petition of creditors' counsel,
and deducting the items for which, as held above, no compensation is allowable, items two to five inclusive, the fee
of these attorneys is fixed at $85.

[3] • The attorney for the bankrupt may be allowed only
for services in aid of his client's "performing the duties
. . . prescribed" for an involuntary bankrupt by the
statute. Act of 1898, sec. 64, 30 Stat. 563. *In re Stratemeyer*, 2 U. S. Dist. Ct. Haw. 269; 14 Am. B. R. 120; Collier on Bankruptcy, 9th ed., 844; 2 Remington on Bankruptcy, secs. 2078-2088. Wherefore, the items, which make
up most of the list, of services in opposing the petition for
adjudication of bankruptcy and the general progress of the
proceedings prior to adjudication, are disallowed.   The
services are itemized in the petition as follows:

"Drawing special appearance and motion to quash, copy
and service;

"Attendance and argument of same; (decision sustained
motion and new subpoena issued);

"Drawing appearance for bankrupt, copy and service;

"Drawing demurrer, copy and service;

"Argument of same (note: the demurrer was practically
confessed by petitioner's motion to amend);

"Argument at motion to amend petition;

"Drawing answer, copy and service;

"Drawing demand for jury trial, copy and service;

"Drawing motion for order of dismissal, copy and service;

"Attendance and argument of same (note: this motion
was formally denied but at expense of petitioners, who were
permitted to file a replication);

"Drawing admission of facts, copy and service (note:
this saved delay and expense of depositions);

"Attendance and argument on petition to sell perishable
property;

"Drawing admission of facts and stipulation waiving
jury;

"Attendance at dates set for hearing on petition to adjudi-
cate (all except last);

"Attendance before referee at first meeting of creditors."

Of these items the only one which could possibly be considered is that of "attendance before referee at first meeting of creditors." As to that item, there is no showing that the bankrupt's attorney rendered any services of value to the estate by his presence at the meeting; particularly, it does not appear that he there aided the bankrupt in any way in "performing the duties . . . prescribed" by the statute. See *In re Kross,* 96 Fed. 816, 819-820; 3 Am. B. R. 187, 191-192. And it does appear from the referee's minutes in this matter that nothing was done at this meeting but the election of the trustee and the fixing of his bond and that the meeting adjourned to a day certain for the important unfinished business of examining the president of the bankrupt corporation: at this meeting the bankrupt's attorney did not appear, nor on the day to which a further adjournment was had, when this examination finally took place. Had the attorney secured the preparation of the bankrupt's schedules of assets and liabilities, which have not yet been filed, and which the statute requires to be filed by an involuntary bankrupt "within ten days, unless further time is granted, after the adjudication," Act, sec. 7, 30 Stat. 548, that would have been a work of some value to the estate. and assistance of this kind is noted as a good example of what the statute intended in allowing a fee to the bankrupt in "performing the duties . . . prescribed" by law. All that could be allowed for attending the first meeting of creditors in a short session, such as here, and where the attorney was, so far as appears, of no assistance, would be a nominal fee. But under the circumstances, where the attorney did not stay out the meeting through its adjourned session at which important business was had, and has not. so far as appears, done anything to facilitate or encourage the performance of the bankrupt's first and most important duty (next to the physical discovery and delivery of assets) of filing his schedules, I do not feel justified in allowing any fee whatever. His diligence clearly entitles him to a fee, but he was serving his client the bankrupt and its officers and to them alone must he look for his reward. 2 Remington on Bankruptcy, sec. 2085.

Accordingly: the petition of the bankrupt's attorney is denied; and the petition of the creditors' attorneys granted save as to the items above excepted, and the trustee is directed to pay to the latter from the funds of said estate, the sum of $85.00 as a fee for their services herein.

Reported, 29 Am. B. R. 8.

PAUL MARTIN *v.* THE AMERICAN BARK FORT GEORGE.

August 24, 1912.

1. *Depositions—Disinterestedness:* Section 863 Rev. Stat. requires a deposition *de bene esse* to be taken before one not interested in the case. The reason for disinterestedness in an examiner under the admiralty and equity rules of the Supreme Court is equally imperative.

2. *Same—Reasonable notice:* What is reasonable notice to the opposite party of the time of taking a deposition, when there is no statutory time, depends on the circumstances, the main things to be considered being distance, number of witnesses, facility of communication and proper representation.

3. *Same—Irregularity—Waiver:* The presence of counsel for the opposite party and his participation in the examination, is a waiver of any existing irregularity in the taking of a deposition.

4. *Same—Reference to take and report testimony:* Admiralty rule 44, providing for reference of "any matters arising in the progress of the suit to one or more commissioners, to be appointed by the court to hear the parties and make report therein," includes authority to appoint commissioners or examiners to take and report testimony.

5. *Same—Certain requirements—Admissibility—Waiver:* A deposition not reduced to writing under the direction of the examiner, and not read to the deponent or signed by him, is inadmissible as evidence unless such requirements are waived.

In Admiralty: Motion to strike a deposition from the record.

G. A. Davis for libelant.
Holmes, Stanley & Olson and *R. W. Breckons* for libellee.

DOLE, J. The libelant, claiming to be an American citizen, complains of injuries received on board of the libellee while at work with others of the crew, whereby he was unable to use his left hand thereafter and would be incapacitated for work for sixty days from the date of the libel, and whereby he had suffered great pain and was compelled to employ medical and surgical aid at a large expense, and to spend money and incur liability for his maintenance and other necessary expenses, and he prays for process of attachment against the libellee, which was issued, and for judgment for three hundred and forty-three dollars.

Upon the showing of libelant, he was permitted to proceed *in forma pauperis.*

Exceptions to the libel were filed by the master and overruled and he thereupon filed his answer denying the American citizenship of libelant and the alleged injury and the alleged consequences thereof, alleging that whatever disability he was laboring under in regard to his left hand was due wholly to a disease contracted by him prior to his engagement with the libellee.

On the return day, on motion of the proctor for libelant, the proctors for libellee being present and objecting, an order was made that the testimony of libelant be taken that day at two o'clock p. m. before U. S. Commissioner F. L. Hatch, to which order the proctors for libellee excepted. At the hearing before U. S. Commissioner Hatch, the libellee was represented by counsel, who, before the witness was sworn, questioned the commissioner as to any interest he might have in the case; he admitted that he had no way of getting his fees if the case should go against the libelant;

the proctors for the libellee thereupon objected to the swearing of the witness on the ground that the commissioner was not a disinterested person as required by law.

[1]   The law requires judges and jurors to be disinterested in relation to any case they may try; the same rule should apply to commissioners and examiners taking testimony, although the necessity for it may be less vital than in the case of judges and jurors, especially in the case of reference to examiners, who are required only to take and report testimony without findings, as is the case here. Section 863 Rev. Stat.. providing for the taking of the testimony of witnesses in civil cases pending in district or circuit courts by deposition *de bene esse,* requires the deposition to be taken before a person not interested in the event of the cause. Mr. Hatch, U. S. commissioner for the district of Hawaii, who took the testimony, being interested in the outcome of the case, to the extent of his fees, would have been clearly disqualified from taking the deposition under provisions of the Revised Statutes referred to, and although the deposition in this case was not taken under the provisions of section 863 Rev. Stat. and following sections, but under the admiralty and equity rules of the Supreme Court, the reason for disinterestedness in the examiner is equally imperative.

"A commissioner to take testimony should be a person who has no bias or prejudice in reference to the litigants or the cause." *McLean v. Adams,* 45 Hun 189, 190; *Lloyd v. Rice,* 28 Texas 341, 343; *Tillinghast v. Walton,* 5 Ga. 335; *Whichner v. Whichner,* 11 N. H. 348.

[2]   Objection was also made at the same time to the taking of the testimony "on the ground that no notice such as is required by law" had been served on the proctors for the libellee. At the taking of the testimony, the libellee was represented by counsel who cross-examined the witness; no objection to the taking of the testimony of libelant is recorded on the ground of inconvenience.

One hour's notice was held to be sufficient in the District

of Columbia. *Nicholls v. White,* 18 Fed. Cas. 182, No. 10,-235; *Leiper v. Bickley,* 15 Fed. Cas. 265, No. 8,222; and one day's notice in the same place, in *Bowie v. Talbot,* 3 Fed. Cas. 1070, No. 1732. Reasonable notice where there is no statutory time, depends on the circumstances of the case. Under section 863, Rev. Stat., "the chief features to be considered in determining whether a certain notice is or is not reasonable are distance, number of witnesses and facility of communication and to obtain proper representation." *Am. Exch. National Bank v. First Nat. Bank,* 82 Fed. 961, 964.

[3] The court regards the notice of the taking of the deposition as sufficient, and, in any case, the presence of counsel for the libellee and their taking part in the examination, was a waiver of any existing irregularity. *Northern Pacific R. R. v. Urlin,* 158 U. S. 271, 273-274.

The case came up for hearing on the deposition May 9, 1912, when the reading thereof was "objected to for the reason that it was not taken in conformity with any statute or rule of court," and that it was not certified to by the examiner and there was no waiver of such certificate; that it does not appear to have been reduced to writing in the presence of the examiner and read to the witness and subscribed by him, and there was no waiver of any of such requirements. The case was continued for an opportunity to procure the certificate of the said F. L. Hatch, then living on the mainland and no longer connected with this court.

[4] At the next hearing, July 9th, a certificate by Mr. Hatch was attached to the deposition. The proctors for the libellee moved to strike the deposition from the record on the ground that it is not signed by the deponent, that there is no certificate by the examiner that it was reduced to writing in his presence, and that there is no authority in the United States for taking testimony in admiralty outside of court except by deposition. The motion to strike was denied but later the question was reopened and discussion allowed.

Admiralty rule 44 authorizes the courts when "expedient

or necessary for the purposes of justice," to refer any matter arising in the proceedings to commissioners appointed by the court to hear the parties and report. Such commissioners are given the powers possessed by masters in chancery in matters referred to them. The proctors for the libellee raise the question here whether rule 44, while providing for commissioners who may take testimony and make findings, provides also for commissioners to take and report testimony alone. I find that it does. It seems to be a clear instance where the greater includes the less; moreover, section 862 Rev. Stat. provides that proof in equity and admiralty "shall be according to rules now or hereafter prescribed by the Supreme Court, except as herein specially provided," which exception appears to refer to the several sections following section 862 in which provisions for taking "the testimony of any witness . . in any civil cause depending in a district or circuit court by deposition *de bene esse*," are made. The words "civil cause" apply equally to admiralty cases as well as to those at common law. *The Samuel,* 14 U. S. 9; *The Argo,* 15 id. 286; *Stegner v. Blake,* 36 Fed. 183, 184. Although these statutory provisions for taking testimony outside the court do not apply to this case, the conditions for taking it, such as the case of a witness being bound on a voyage to sea, or about to go out of the United States, or out of the district in which the trial is pending, etc., not appearing in the record, yet as they provide for the taking of the testimony without findings, it may be presumed that Congress contemplated such taking also in conferring upon the Supreme Court the authority to prescribe rule on the subject.

[5] We have then to consider the objections that it does not appear that the deposition was reduced to writing or typewriting under the direction of the examiner or that it was read to the deponent or signed by him; and that there is no waiver of such requirements. All of these requirements are to be found in the 67th equity rule of the

Supreme Court.   Their omission is fatal to the deposition.
Cook v. Burney, 78 U. S. 659, 668-669.   General federal
authorities referring to the requirements of section 864 Rev.
Stat. lay down the rule that they must be strictly followed
to render the deposition admissible as evidence.   These
authorities, by analogy, support an equally strict rule regarding the requirements prescribed by the rules of the
Supreme Court.   The reason for the strict policy followed in
regard to the requirements of the statute in the taking of
these depositions is briefly stated in *Bell v. Morrison*, 26
U. S. 350, 356, as follows:

"We think, in a case of this nature, where evidence is
sought to be admitted, contrary to the rules of the common
law, something more than a mere presumption should exist, that it was rightly taken.   There ought to be direct
proof, that the requisitions of the statute have been fully
complied with."

Also, in *Shutte v. Thompson*, 82 U. S. 151, 161.

With the deposition ruled out, there is nothing left to the
case, the subsequent evidence being introduced solely in
rebuttal of matters stated in the deposition.

The libel is dismissed, and, as the libelant was allowed
to bring his suit *in forma pauperis*, there will be no order
regarding costs.

IN THE MATTER OF THE APPLICATION OF TSURU TOMIMATSU FOR A WRIT OF HABEAS CORPUS.

September 17, 1912.

1. *Right of alien to land claimed on the ground of domicil—Denial
on a question of law—Habeas Corpus:* Where the right of an alien
to enter the United States is claimed on the ground of domicil, a denial

thereof by the immigration officers on a question of law, may be reviewed on an application for a writ of habeas corpus.

2. *Jurisdiction of immigration officers—Habeas corpus:* When proceedings before immigration authorities show that they have acted without jurisdiction, relief may be had by writ of habeas corpus.

3. *Domicil—Residence—Intention:* Residence in a certain locality for a period of years with one's family and the conduct of regular employment there, will prevail on the question of domicil, over any floating purpose such person may entertain to return at some indefinite future time to a former place of residence to reside.

4. *Same—Married woman—Temporary residence away from home:* Temporary residence of a married woman away from home cannot, in ordinary circumstances, be set up against the presumption of law that the domicil of the husband is the domicil of the wife.

5. *Resident alien returning to United States after temporary absence:* An alien who has acquired a domicil in the United States cannot be treated as an immigrant on his return to the United States after a temporary absence not involving a change of domicil.

6. *Construction of statutes as affected by revision or amendment:* Authoritative construction of a statue holds good as to a revision or amendment thereof when the features which have been so construed remain substantially unchanged and do not suggest, in the revision or amendment, any intention of the legislature to change them.

Habeas Corpus: Petition for writ, and order to show cause.

G. S. Curry for petitioner.

R. W. Breckons, U. S. District Attorney, and *C. C. Bitting,* Assistant U. S. Attorney, for respondent.

DOLE, J. Upon the filing of the petition an order was made for the respondent, Richard L. Halsey, alleged immigration inspector at the port of Honolulu, to show cause why the prayer of the petition should not be granted. The respondent admitted in his return that he was such immigration inspector and that the petitioner arrived in Honolulu, as alleged in her petition, June 10, 1912, in the steamship Mongolia from Japan, and further stated that the petitioner was found to be afflicted with the disease known as trachoma, and the matter was then referred to the board of special inquiry, which board took testimony upon the question "whether or not the said Tsuru Tomimatsu had returned to Japan with the intention of returning to Hawaii," and thereupon reached the conclusion that she "was an alien immigrant afflicted with a dangerous contagious disease, and that some four or five years prior to the date of the said hearing she . . . had gone from the Territory of Hawaii to Japan with the intention of remaining in Japan and not with the intention of returning to the Territory of Hawaii; and did thereupon duly and regularly order that the said Tsuru Tomimatsu be deported." The respondent further stated that the petitioner took an appeal to the Secretary of Commerce and Labor, and, through her attorney, submitted a brief in the proceedings on appeal on the question "whether or not she was an alien immigrant within the meaning of the immigration laws of the United States;" and that the Secretary of Commerce and Labor sustained the finding of the board of special inquiry.

The exhibits attached to the return include a copy of the oral testimony of the petitioner and of her alleged husband, taken before the board of special inquiry. No other testimony appears to have been received except the certificate of the medical examiner that the petitioner was afflicted with trachoma, which in his opinion could not have been detected at the port of embarkation by a competent medical examination and could not be cured in sixty days. The testimony of the petitioner and Kotaro Tomimatsu, her alleged husband, tells a story of an industrious and thrifty family coming to this country about ten years ago in order to improve their financial opportunities, leaving two children in Japan. Two more children were born here, or, according to the recollection of Kotaro, one was born here and another after the wife reached Japan upon her return there five years ago, at which time she made the trip because, as she says. "I wanted to see my children who were in Japan.

My husband's parents also wanted to see me and wanted to help me in the instruction of my children." On the question whether or not the petitioner was an alien immigrant, the testimony is as follows: Tsuru Tomimatsu: Q. "When you first came to Hawaii did you expect to go back to Japan?" A. "Yes. I expected to go back to Japan again." Q. "If you are landed now is it your intention to remain in Hawaii always, or do you expect to return to Japan again?" A. "I expect to stay here and work for ten years and then return to Japan again." Q. "Do all of your children expect to come to Hawaii sometime?" A. "Yes, they all expect to come." Q. "You have said that when you went to Japan four years ago you intended to return again to Hawaii. How long did you intend to stay in Japan?" A. "One or two years." Q. "You have now staid four years. Why did you not return sooner?" A. "I waited for Giichi to get through the grammar school." Kotaro Tomimatsu: Q. "Do you expect to remain permanently in Hawaii, or do you expect to go back to Japan sometime to live?" A. "I intend to go back to Japan, my native land, again." Q. "When you go back, do you expect to take your wife with you?" A. "Yes." Q. "Has that been your intention ever since you came to Hawaii?" A. "Yes. After we saved money enough it has been my hope to go back to Japan." Q. "When your wife went back to Japan was it your intention for her to come back again to Hawaii?" A. "Yes. She intended to come back to this country after a short visit in Japan." Q. "How long did she intend to stay in Japan?" A. "Two or three years. I intended to bring the children here after they had grown." Q. "You say your wife intended to stay in Japan two or three years. It has now been four or five years. Why did she not return sooner?" A. "The children were too small." There is considerable other testimony. I have given that portion which bears most directly upon the point at issue. In the rest, not given, there is nothing that is inconsistent with the above. Upon the testimony

IN THE MATTER OF TSURU TOMIMATSU 101

and the medical certificate the board of special inquiry rendered the following decision:

"Edwin Farmer: The applicant in this case, according to the testimony, formerly lived in Hawaii, but went back to Japan about four or five years ago with the intention of again returning to Hawaii after an absence of two or three years in Japan. Her husband has been in Hawaii ever since he came to these islands, ten or eleven years ago, with his wife. If applicant's intention of sometime returning to Hawaii no matter how many years she may have remained in Japan, her husband still being in Hawaii, makes her a resident of Hawaii, it would seem that the intention of both husband and wife to ultimately return to Japan to live would, according to the same reckoning, make them both residents of Japan. I therefore move the applicant be denied admission and returned to Japan, the country whence she came, this decision being based on the certificate of the examining surgeon that she is afflicted with a dangerous disease, and that she be allowed to appeal to the Department on the question as to whether or not she is a returning resident and therefore exempt from the immigration laws. By Inspector Moore: I second the motion. Harry E. Brown: It is so ordered."

[1] It is recognized by all the authorities that a court having jurisdiction in proceedings for writs of habeas corpus may not interfere with the decisions of a board of special inquiry or of the Secretary of Commerce and Labor on appeal from such board, in cases touching the right of aliens to land in the United States whenever such board is dealing with issues of fact within its jurisdiction, and the alien has had an opportunity to be present at the hearing and to introduce testimony. *Chin Yow v. United States,* 208 U. S. 8, 13; *United States v. Sprung,* 187 Fed. 903, 906; *United States v. Ju Toy,* 198 U. S. 253, 262. Where, however, the right of a person to enter the United States is claimed on the ground of citizenship or domicil and is denied by the immigration officers, it may be reviewed by such court on application for a writ of habeas corpus, when it depends upon a question of law. *United States v. Williams,* 173 Fed. 627; *Davies v.*

Manolis, 179 Fed. 818, 822; *School of Magnetic Healing v. McAnnulty,* 187 U. S. 94, 107-108.

The petitioner does not contest the statement of the medical certificate that she was afflicted with trachoma. Her claim of a right to land is based upon the testimony given above of the established domicil of herself and her husband in Hawaii some ten years before of her return to Japan four or five years before in relation to the welfare of her children with the intention of returning to Hawaii. The answer recites that the board of special inquiry took testimony "as to whether or not the said Tsuru Tomimatsu had gone to Japan with the intention of returning to Hawaii," and thereupon and with the statement of the medical certificate, determined that she was an alien immigrant afflicted with a dangerous contagious disease, that four or five years prior thereto, she had gone to Japan with the intention of remaining there, and ordered her deportation to Japan. The decision of the board of special inquiry, exhibited, admits that the petitioner went to Japan with the intention of returning to Hawaii in two or three years, and decides for her deportation upon the following curious reasoning: "If applicant's intention of sometime returning to Hawaii, no matter how many years she may have remained in Japan, her husband still being in Hawaii, makes her a resident of Hawaii, it would seem that the intention of both husband and wife to ultimately return to Japan to live would, according to the same reasoning, make them both residents of Japan."

[2] With this disposal of the case by the board of special inquiry upon a question of law, the authority of this court to review its decision, under habeas corpus proceedings, accrues.

"It remains, therefore, the sole duty of the court to determine whether or not the proceedings for the deportation of the relator have been according to law. If they have, he must be remanded. If they have not, he must be released." *United States v. Sibray,* 178 Fed. 144, 147.

[3] The testimony, which is not only uncontradicted but unquestioned by the petitioner, shows that husband and wife had acquired a domicil in Hawaii. Acts indicative of an intention of one to take up his abode in a certain locality for a period of years, together with his actual residence in such locality, "must prevail over any secret purpose which he may have entertained to return at some indefinite future time" to a former place of residence and make that his home. *Wright v. Schneider*, 32 Fed. 705, 706; *Holmes v. Green*, 73 Mass. 299, 301.

[4] Under such circumstances, the temporary return of the wife to Japan, obviously for family reasons, could not destroy her domicil in Hawaii. That such visit was of a temporary nature is shown both by the testimony and her return to Hawaii.

"Actual residence—residence in point of fact, signifies nothing in the case of a married woman, and shall not, in ordinary circumstances, be set up against the presumption of law that she resides with her husband." *Warrender v. Warrender*, 9 Bligh N. S. 89, 104; 5 Eng. Reprint, 1227, 1233; *Re Daly's Settlement*, 25 Beav. 455; 460; 53 Eng. Reprint, 711, 713; *Dolphin v. Robins*, 7 H. L. C. 390; 11 Eng. Reprint, 156.

[5] If this reasoning is correct the petitioner comes under the rule established in many Federal decisions to the effect that "an alien who has acquired a domicil in the United States, cannot thereafter, and while still retaining such domicil, legally be treated as an immigrant on his return to this country after a temporary absence for a specific purpose, not involving change of domicil." *Rodgers v. United States, ex rel. Buchsbaum*, 152 Fed. 346, syl. (1907), and *United States v. Aultman Company*, 143 Fed. 922 (1907).

[6] Although the act "to regulate the immigration of aliens into the United States," approved March 3, 1903, 32 Stat. 1213, was repealed, except as to section 34, relative to another subject, by the act of February 20, 1907, 34 Stat. 898, bearing the same title, the decisions under former sta-

tutes upon this point apply as well to the later statute, whose object as expressed by the title is to regulate the immigration of aliens into the United States. This object is borne out by the consistent expression of the statute throughout, and by the constant appearance and repetition of words and sentences that are inconsistent with any other purpose. For instance, the taxes collected from aliens entering the united States are constituted a permanent appropriation called the "immigrant fund," to be used for the "expenses of regulating the immigration of aliens into the "United States." Sec. 1. The "immigrant fund" is also referred to in sections 19, 20, 24 and 39. Section 3 relates to the importation of any alien woman or girl for the purpose of prostitution. Sections 4, 5 and 6 deal with the "importation or migration" of contract laborers. Section 7 forbids transportation companies from soliciting or encouraging the "immigration of any aliens." Section 8 provides punishment for anyone who may land any alien not admitted by an "immigrant inspector" in the United States. Sections 12, 14, 19, 22, 24, 25, 32, 36 and 40 refer to the "Commissioner General of Immigration," who by virtue of section 22, has charge of all laws relating to the "immigration of aliens." Sections 12, 14, 15, 16, 17, 18, 22, 24 and 25 refer to "immigration officers." Section 24 refers to "immigrant inspectors and other immigration officers." Section 25 provides for boards of special inquiry "for the prompt determination of all cases of immigrants detained . . . under the provision of law." Sections 30, 31 and 40 refer to "immigrant stations," and authorize the President to negotiate treaties for regulating the "immigration of aliens to the United States." Section 40 provides for a "division of information in the Bureau of Immigration and Naturalization . . . to promote beneficial distribution of aliens admitted into the United States among the several States and Territories desiring immigration." Section 42 treats of the accommodation to be given "immigrant passengers" on vessels bringing them to the United States. The word "alien" is used substantially as it is used in the previous statutes; only once is the phrase "alien immigrant" used in the act of 1891, and not at all in the act of 1903.

There appears little room for argument that the numerous authorities that support the construction that the restrictive measures of the acts of 1891 and 1903 do not apply to alien residents of the United States, do not support the same construction of the act of 1907.

[2b] An additional ground of jurisdiction of this court in this case is suggested by the case of *Ex parte Watchorn*, 160 Fed. 1014, 1016, in which the court says, "Doubtless the determination of the immigration authorities upon all questions of fact, even if made upon legally incompetent or inconclusive evidence, is final, but when the proceedings before them show indisputably that they are acting without jurisdiction, relief may be had by writ of habeas corpus;" and refers to *Gonzales v. Williams*, 192 U. S. 1.

The writ prayed for may issue.

Appeal dismissed, Circuit Court of Appeals, under Sec. 3 of Rule 22. See *Lapina v. Williams*, 232 U. S. 78 (1913), holding contra to paragraph 5 of the syllabi, supra.

IN THE MATTER OF THE PETIT JURY FOR THE OCTOBER, 1912, TERM.

September 18, 1912.

Jurors—Summoning—Service of wrong party: Where a person not drawn as a juror, but having the same name as a person on the jury list, has by error been served with summons to appear, the court may set the service aside and direct the marshal to summon the proper party.

Per Curiam (Judges Dole and Clemons): In executing the writ of venire facias for trial jurors for the October Term, 1912, which writ summoned, among others, one Manuel Andrade, the marshal served a man of that name, who appeared before one of the judges at chambers, and satisfied the judge not only of his exemption from jury service as being over age, but also of his disqualification as to citizenship, he being a subject of the Republic of Portugal, and of his disqualification as to ability to "understandingly speak, read and write the English language." The judge thereupon told Mr. Andrade that he would be excused on the above grounds, and directed the deputy clerk to notify the marshal to that effect. It now satisfactorily appears, however, that the Mr. Andrade who was served is not the person intended by the jury commissioners in placing the names in the jury box.

The question then arises should the service be regarded as a nullity and an effort be made to serve the person who was intended, it being possible to identify that person both from statements made by the clerk of the court (who is also one of the jury commissioners) at the time of drawing the jurors under this venire, and heard by the other judge of this court who presided at the drawing, and also from the fact that, as the records of the commissioners show, this particular name was that of the certain Mr. Manuel Andrade who is registered as a voter in Honolulu and whose name was lately taken from the register of voters for the purpose of being placed in the jury box. As between these two men, the presumption of law would, of course, be that a *qualified* person of that name was intended by the commissioners.

The writ in no way indicated what person of the name of Manuel Andrade was to be summoned, and it was no fault of the marshal that a person was served who happened to be disqualified.

To the mind of the court, the case is not to be distinguished from one where a wrong man of different name was served. There would not seem to be any doubt that in such case the service would be a nullity, and that the right man could thereupon be summoned. In other words, the writ is not "exhausted," so to speak, by service upon the wrong man of different name. And we can see no reason, in principle, why the case would be any different because of service upon a wrong man of the same name as the juror drawn.

In a community made up so largely of races whose members to so great an extent bear similar names, particularly among the Portuguese, to which race the person served belonged, it would be well for the jury commissioners, by consulting directories and voting registers, and otherwise, to ascertain whether a name to be placed in the box is a common one, and if so to designate the person to a certainty, by his occupation, residence, or otherwise.

In this case, then, the service of the writ was made in error, and is a nullity. The writ should now be served upon the man intended, whose identity may be ascertained from the clerk.

While there appear to be no decisions directly in point, reference is made to the case of *Goodwin v. State*, 15 So. (Ala.) 571, 573, and *Gregory v. State*, 37 So. (Ala.) 259, 262, especially the former, as having some bearing on this question.

J. D. SPRECKELS & BROS. COMPANY *v.* THE BRITISH SHIP LOCH GARVE.

October 3, 1912.

1. *Salvage—Distribution of salvage fund:* The old rule of allowance of one-third of the salvage fund to the owners and two-thirds to

the crew "in ordinary cases" of salvage performed from sailing vessels, radically changed with the advent of steam vessels. Prevailing allowance being from one-fourth to one-third to the officers and crews; preponderance of ordinary cases favoring the one-fourth allowance, and one-fifth and one-sixth being sometimes given.

2. *Same—Same—Consideration of special services:* Special consideration is given to special services, like carrying a line attached to a hawser to a stranded vessel a hundred fathoms away, by boat in a dark and squally night.

3. *Same—Same—Person specially engaged for the salvage enterprise:* A person engaged specially for the salvage enterprise, included in the distribution of salvage money, the chance of making something by way of salvage in addition to his pay, having been held out to him by the master in engaging him.

4. *Same—Same—Disposition of amount not claimed:* The master not claiming salvage money the amount he would otherwise have received inures to the owners.

5. *Same—Same—Deck hands:* Favorable consideration of claims of deck hands discussed.

6. *Costs—Expenses—Transcript of testimony:* Cost of a transcript of testimony furnished to counsel as the trial proceeded and to enable them to handle the case to best advantage, approved as a necessary expense of litigation.

W. T. Rawlins for claimants.

Holmes, Stanley & Olson for J. D. Spreckels & Bros. Company.

DOLE, J. The above case was consolidated for trial with that of the *Inter-Island Steam Navigation Company, Limited, v. The Loch Garve,* and judgment rendered for the libelants in both cases, four thousand dollars being the amount of the judgment in this case.

Distribution having been made to the officers and crews of the steam vessels of the Inter-Island Steam Navigation Company, Limited, upon the report of the company, the officers and crew of the Intrepid, except the master, have come into court for such distribution as they may be entitled to, the owners of the Intrepid having so far failed to report thereon. Further testimony was taken and the matter submitted on briefs.

The case of *Sonderburg v. Ocean Tow Boat Co.*, 22 Fed. Cas. 795, No. 13,175 (1878), cited by counsel for the officers and crew, refers to the rule of dividing the salvage money equally between the owners on one part and the officers and crew on the other part, adopted in the circuit to which the court belonged. The circumstances of salvage vary so greatly in different cases that a fixed rule to be followed, even in "ordinary cases," as laid down by that authority, would seem to be sometimes unfair to the owners, especially when the salving vessel is a steamer.

The case of *The Pomona*, 37 Fed. 815 (1889), is a much more recent case than the *Sonderburg*, and the judge allowed one-fifth of the salvage to the officers and crew; this rating being on the ground that the salving ship was a steamer and there being "no danger or risk, or extra trouble to the crew."

[1]   The old rule of allowing one-third of the salvage to the owners and two-thirds to the crew "in ordinary cases" (*The Blaireau*, 6 U. S. 143, 161,—1804; *The Camanche*, 75 U. S. 448, 473,—1869; *The Barque Island City*, 66 U. S. 121, 129,—1861), had begun to give way to the pressure for a larger proportion to the owners of salving vessels propelled by steam, even as far back as the trial of the last cited case, *The Barque Island City*, the decision whereof admits that in some of that class of cases the court might be justified in departing from the rule, although the point was not fairly raised in the pleadings in that case. It is perfectly obvious that with the application of steam power to vessels as a propelling agent, the rules of distribution of salvage awards must have become radically changed. Where formerly the main portion of the work in salvage cases was necessarily performed by the crews in windlass work, boat service, and, in some cases, navigating a partially disabled vessel into port, steam vessels now do all of this except the boat service, and do it much more effectively with their towing ability and their donkey engines. With this change in condi-

tions, the deck hands have much less to do than formerly, often but little outside of the necessary boat work, while the officers may have more or less according to circumstances. Thus the rule then recognized in France, England and the United States, and approximately followed, of one-third to the ship and two-thirds to the officers and crews, has become fairly obsolete. The much larger share is now generally given the owners of the salving ship and of the cargo, when the latter has been exposed to risk. Kennedy's Civil Salvage, 150-151; *The Enchantress*, Lush, 93, 96.

"The apportionment of the salvage will be influenced by the degree in which the ship on the one hand, and the personal services of the master and crew on the other, were instrumental in achieving the final result." Williams & Bruce, Adm. Jur. & Pr., 3rd ed. 171-172.

From one-fourth to one-third of the salvage fund represents the prevailing allowance to the officers and crews of salving steam vessels, with a preponderance of cases, perhaps, giving the one-fourth allowance, since 1883. Id. 172, note (s). *City of Paris*, 35 Shipping Gazette, Weekly Summary, 378 (1890); Kennedy's Civil Salvage, 154. Here and there are cases of allowance as low as one-fifth and one-sixth.

[2]   The work of the Intrepid consisted of the six and a half hours' trip at full speed to the Loch Garve and return to Honolulu, taking a line aboard the Loch Garve, adjusting the hawser, and pulling at the Loch Garve about seventeen and a half hours. The salvage work was performed mainly by the Intrepid; her officers, engineers and firemen having the burden of operating her. It does not appear that the rest of the crew had very much to do beyond boat work and handling the hawser. The man who carried the line attached to the hawser to the Loch Garve a hundred fathoms away, in the middle of a dark and stormy night, deserves special consideration.

An allowance of one-fourth of the salvage money is made to the officers and crew of the Intrepid. Deducting the aggregate expenses of $1384.95 for the legal proceedings incurred by J. D. Spreckels & Bros. Company from the amount of the judgment of $4,000 in its favor, we have a balance of $2,615.05. One-fourth of this amount is $653.76, which is distributed as follows:

Name	Position	Monthly Wages.	Distribution.
Captain Olson	Captain	$200.00	$190.00
Harry Gahan	Pilot and mate	150.00	110.00
Scott W. Ross	First deck hand and harbor mate	75.00	55.00
James Delaney	Chief engineer	150.00	110.00
John Sass	First assistant engineer	100.00	75.00
J. Johansen	Fireman	50.00	20.00
W. Widemeyer	Fireman	50.00	20.00
Tony Erickson, who carried the line to the Loch Garve	Deck hand	45.00	20.00
Andrew Knudsen	Deck hand	45.00	13.00
Mike McAvoy	Deck hand	45.00	13.00
Jim Sawata	Cook	65.00	20.00
Japanese Boy (name unknown)	Mess boy	30.00	7.76

[3]   Counsel for the owners objected to any distribution to Harry Gahan, on the ground that he was employed for this special salvage trip and knew what services would be expected of him.   It appears, however, from his testimony taken in the matter of the distribution, that Captain Olson· in engaging him for the trip, said, "There's a show to make a piece of money for all hands." This is not rebutted. Whatever his regular pay was to be,—and there is evidence to the effect that that was five dollars a day,—the chance to make salvage money was part of the inducement offered to and accepted by him.

[6]   Counsel for the crew objected to an item of $431.50, paid for transcript of testimony by the owners, and charged as part of the expenses of the litigation, on the ground that it was unnecessary, the testimony being set forth in the apostles.   But the explanation of counsel for the owners shows this expense to have been incurred during the trial here, to enable counsel to refer to the evidence as the case proceeded and so to handle the case to the best advantage. The item is properly deducted, with other expenses, from the amount of the judgment.

[4]   As the master makes no claim for distribution, the amount set apart to him enures to the benefit of the owners.

[5]   Although the allowance of one-fourth of the net salvage to the officers and crew, gives on the whole a larger proportional distribution than in the one-fourth distribution already made to the officers and crews of the Inter-Island Steam Navigation Company's boats engaged in the salvage of the Loch Garve, it is necessarily so from the fact that the award to the Inter-Island Steam Navigation Company was cut down on appeal.   There is no doubt that the crew of the Likelike and the three sailors of the Iwalani who brought the end of the four and a half inch hawser from the Loch Garve to the Iwalani, were much more entitled to consideration than the deck hands of the Intrepid, who are not reported as having done anything in particular, and

they have received a little more. It is not easy to adjust distribution in these cases with strict conformity to other cases. Conditions diverge, the salvage awards differ in amount, and those to be benefited vary in number and quality of merit. Although there is some room for argument from the distribution to the other crews, that the crew of the Intrepid should not receive a fourth of the net salvage fund, I do not see my way to reduce it. There is a still stronger argument that the other crews should have received a larger allowance than one-fourth, which might possibly have been the result had they been represented by counsel and had pushed their case. While deck hands do not have the opportunity on steam vessels engaged in salvage operations that they had on sailing vessels, yet the policy of treating them with generous consideration is one to be followed, in view of its stimulating influence upon their course of action when the occasion arises.

UNITED STATES OF AMERICA *v.* A LOT OF SILK GOODS AND OTHER MERCHANDISE (Mrs. S. Kataoka, claimant).

November 15, 1912.

1. *Jury—Waiver:* Jury may be waived by proceeding to trial in the absence of, and without demand for, a jury.

2. *Customs duties—Fraudulent attempt to import:* A fraudulent attempt to import or bring in dutiable merchandise is not reached by Rev. Sat., sec. 3082, which is directed only against actual importation or bringing in.

3. *Same—Fraudulent attempt to enter or introduce—Completed fraud:* To constitute a fraudulent attempt to enter or introduce merchandise into the commerce of the United States in violation of the customs administrative act, June 10, 1890, c. 407, sec. 9, 26 Stat. 135,

as amended by the tariff act of Aug. 5, 1909, c. 6, sec. 28, subsec. 9, 36 Stat. 97, it is not necessary that the government actually be deprived of revenue, but only that the acts of attempt be of a character calculated to work such deprival.

4. *Same—Same—Use of fraudulent devices—Forfeiture:* Though mere intent to fraudulently introduce merchandise into the country by devices of concealment, is not within said subsection 9; yet where the incoming passenger is actually making use of such devices, the merchandise is forfeitable under the statute.

5. *Same—Same—Forfeiture:* The said amendatory subsection 9 applies to goods attempted to be imported or introduced by means of fraudulent devices of concealment, and for a violation thereof by such an attempt a forfeiture of the goods, or their value, follows.

6. *Same—Dutiable merchandise in baggage—Sufficiency of declaration or entry:* The importer of dutiable merchandise fraudulently concealed in his baggage, does not by merely remaining passive fulfill the obligation of at least putting the customs officers on inquiry as to such merchandise; but the disclosure must be direct or fairly equivalent to a direct disclosure.

7. *Same—Declaration and entry—Customs regulations and procedure:* The fact that an anomalous, or an extraordinary, procedure is being pursued, by the customs officers, of getting merchandise through the customs line, affords no excuse to a passenger who attempts by devices of concealment to introduce merchandise into this country in violation of subsection 9 aforesaid.

8. *Same—Same—Same—Locus poenitentiae:* In such case there is no *locus poenitentiae*, extending until the customs officer shall pursue the regular, or the usual, course; but the goods intended to be unlawfully entered or introduced may be seized as forfeited at any time after the concealment is discovered when once the passenger has started the goods through the customs line with intent to use the devices of concealment to evade duties.

9. *Same—Entry of imported merchandise—Time for completing entry:* The fifteen day limit within which to complete entry of imported merchandise, under Rev. Stat., sec. 2785, does not apply to the case of a passenger's taking his goods with him immediately through the customs line, so as to afford a *locus poenitentia* to an importer who has concealed articles in his baggage with intent to evade duties; nor do Customs Regulations, 1908, article 1092, providing that certain goods shall be sold if not entered within one year, give a *locus poeni-*

tentiae or a privilege of making complete entry at any time within that period.

   10. *Same—Smuggling—Forfeiture—Circumstantial evidence:* In a forfeiture proceeding under said subsection 9, letters found in a passenger's baggage, indicating a plan to smuggle goods for purpose of sale, may be sufficient circumstantial evidence to sustain a finding, against the passenger, of a fraudulent attempt to enter or introduce, so as to satisfy that part of the statute requiring entry or introduction to be an entry or introduction into the *commerce* of the country; even though the passenger is not himself the addressor or the addressee or referred to in the correspondence.

   11. *Same—Forfeiture—Burden of proof—Measure of proof:* In case of probable cause for an information in rem for forfeiture under subsection 9 aforesaid, the burden is placed on the claimant by Rev. Stat., sec. 909; and the government is not, in any event, required to prove its case by anything more than a preponderance of the evidence.

   12. *Statutes—Construction of forfeiture provisions:* Though the statutes authorizing forfeiture for violations of the law of customs administration, are subject to strict construction, they are also to be construed reasonably and so as to give effect, if possible, to every word thereof.

In Rem: On information for forfeiture.

C. C. Bitting, Assistant U. S. Attorney, for the United States.

G. S. Curry and *A. K. Ozawa*, for claimant.

CLEMONS, J. This is an information *in rem* praying for the forfeiture to the United States of a lot of silk goods and other merchandise, seized by customs officers at Honolulu and now held by the collector for that port, for alleged violations of the customs revenue laws. The claim of forfeiture is based on three alleged grounds: (1) That "lately before the time of the said seizure" the said merchandise, being dutiable, was "fraudulently and knowingly imported and attempted to be brought into the said United States contrary to law, that is to say, without the payment of . . .

duties,"—i.e., a violation of Rev. Stat., sec. 3082. (2) That at said time one Mrs. S. Kataoka, "the importer, owner, or agent of the importer or owner, . . with the intent to defraud the revenue of the said United States, did knowingly and unlawfully attempt to bring in and make a landing of, and attempt to introduce into the commerce of the United States, said imported merchandise at the port of Honolulu by means of a fraudulent device, or of fraudulent devices and fraudulent appliances, . . . consisting in part of a bag so constructed that a part of the said merchandise, so attempted to be introduced into the commerce of the United States, might be and was concealed in said bag from the customs officers of the United States, . . . and consisting also in part of the packing of another part of said merchandise by folding and sewing in such a manner that the said other part of said merchandise might be and was concealed in said other articles of clothing from the customs officers of the United States,"—i.e., a violation of sub-section 9 of section 28 of the tariff act of 1909. 36 Stat. 97. (3) That at said time the said person did "knowingly, willfully and unlawfully neglect, fail and omit with intent to defraud the revenue of the United States, to disclose and declare to the proper officers of the customs at said port of Honolulu, the true character, nature, quantity, intended use and destination of said merchandise, by means whereof the said United States was then and there deprived of the lawful duties accruing upon the merchandise aforesaid,"—i.e., a further violation of said subsection 9.

[1]   The case was submitted to the court for determination without the intervention of a jury,—there having been no formal waiver, but the parties having proceeded to trial in the absence of, and without demand for, a jury and having continued with the trial, although the want of a formal waiver was called to their attention at the hearing. See *Kearney v. Case*, 12 Wall. 275 *Madison County v. Warren*, 106 U. S. 623; *United States v. Harris*, Id. 635; *Perego v.*

Dodge, 163 U. S. 166. From the evidence the facts appear as hereinafter set forth.

Upon arrival of the steamship Korea at the port of Honolulu, on July 8th, 1912, the baggage of a third class or steerage passenger, Mrs. Shigeno Kataoka, who here intervenes as claimant of the seized property, was taken to the immigration station for inspection, under a practice whereby the usual declaration in writing is not required of third-class passengers coming to Honolulu from the Orient, as it is of the first and second classes, but it is left to the customs inspectors to ascertain without the aid of such declaration what if any articles brought by the third class passengers are subject to duty. It may be noted, that the practice has been adopted, it is understood, to alleviate the condition, that this class of passengers coming from the Orient is made up largely of persons who bring nothing dutiable, who are more or less illiterate and speak only a foreign language, and who come in such numbers as to make a written declaration for each one impracticable under all the circumstances, particularly that of the want of a force of interpreters and other officers adequate to the prompt preparation of such declarations. A similar practice obtains at the Canadian and Mexican frontiers, in case of free goods or goods upon which the duty does not exceed five dollars. Customs Regulations, 1908, art. 192 and marginal citations.

The claimant pointed out to a customs inspector a trunk which apparently contained only kimonos and other garments. The weight and thickness of kimonos lying in the middle and lower part of the trunk aroused suspicion, and upon the opening of one of them a bolt of silk was disclosed sewed into a sleeve in such manner as to prevent its falling out on the lifting of the kimono. Sewed into the sleeve of another kimono were five unmade obis or sashes in rolls. Sewed into the inside of a woolen skirt were three pieces of new crepe silk, each about a foot wide and a yard and a half long. The inspector then made no further examination, and closed the trunk. A basket disclosed similar conditions; for instance, pieces of new crepe silk were sewed into the sleeves of kimonos. Having ascertained this fact, the inspector closed the basket without further search. There was next brought a large cloth bag in which were found seven new silk obis in a roll with the edges of the outside obi sewed together so as to conceal the others. The inspector then came to what appeared to be the bottom of the bag, but what was discovered to be a false bottom, securely stitched in, about six inches above the real bottom. Upon tearing open the false bottom, there were seen below eighty new silk collars each mounted on pasteboard as if for commercial display. There was also in this bag a bundle of letters, or papers which bore writing, all in the Japanese language. In one of the containers were four pieces of new crepe silk, each thirteen inches wide and all of the aggregate length of fifty-six feet, sewed inside of an old silk obi,—in the top of the bag, as the inspector says ,or in the trunk· as the claimant insists. So far as this insistence is an argument for her consistency in having placed valuable material in the trunk which contained clean goods, rather than in the upper part of the bag with food and soiled clothing, the argument is not worth much attention in view of the undisputed evidence that she left in the upper part of the bag the roll of seven new silk obis, which would be as liable to injury as the crepe silk which, she insists, was, for its protection, placed elsewhere. Two large pieces of baggage, one containing bedding and the other wearing apparel, and some small pieces of hand baggage, all bore nothing dutiable and were passed.

The trunk, basket and bag, together with their contents, were thereupon seized by customs officers. The examiners and appraisers, through whose hands the seized merchandise passed in due course, found the articles listed in detail in the information (including the concealed articles which were all dutiable), consisting mainly of goods in the piece.

and of the aggregate appraised value of $1,093.13. This list contained, among other things, 30 pieces of silk cloth, 263 silk woven belts, 90 silk woven collars, 62 silk woven sleeves. 40 silk kimonos, 74 part wool kimonos, 8 raincoats.

The character of the concealed goods and the manner in which they were packed (see *United States v. One Bag of Crushed Wheat*, 166 Fed. 562, 565, 567), as well as the uncommon number and quantity of certain articles as mere baggage or as articles merely for personal use, all force the conclusion, under all the circumstances, of an intent to secure by fraudulent means their introduction into this country without payment of duty. And the letters and papers found in the baggage are incriminating circumstantial evidence of a plan to defraud the government. Over claimant's objection, they were admitted in evidence on the authority of the ruling of Judge Robertson of this court in the case of Lum Yan, unreported, affirmed in *Lum Yan v. United States*, 193 Fed. 970, 972-973. One of the letters, dated "April 30th" (without giving the year), addressed to "My dear Shigeno" and signed "Your husband," reads in translation:

"Send your goods by the first steamer. And in order to escape paying the customs duties, I would advise you to handle and wrinkle the kimonos, so that they would appear worthless. I would like you to buy some silk goods and send them along with an iron, with which I can iron the wrinkled part of the kimonos, after their arrival here. In that way, the kimonos and the goods will appear fine and orderly. Bring these goods as if they are your own wearing apparel, ready for wear. Ask your friends to help you in this matter."

The next to the last sentence should be noted for its circumstantial bearing on the vital question, of the intended use of these goods. The following letter signed "Kenichi Kataoka" (which the claimant testified was her husband's name), addressed to "Dear parents Katsunai," and undated, has, circumstantially, a bearing, adverse to the claimant, on the question whether the concealed goods were intended to be introduced into the "commerce of the United States:

"The goods bought at Osaka are cheap and reasonable, and those bought at Kioto are costly; but their quality is much superior to those obtained at Osaka. Personally I think it is better for you to buy goods at Kioto, because. after their arrival in Honolulu, the price, though high, will bring in good income."

Another letter, unsigned, unaddressed and undated, says. *inter alia:*

"Should you succeed in getting 700 yen for Okada, you can get materials valued at 2050 yen, after deducting the passage money and other incidental expenses. As soon as I can raise some money, I will send it to you."

This letter speaks in some detail of plans for borrowing money for these purchases. It is significant that the claimant, while endeavoring to explain other suspicious circumstances, made no offer to account for these letters. Also the fact is of considerable significance. that this was her fourth passage, within a period of six years, through the customs line at the port of Honolulu; wherefrom some knowledge of customs practice and of the obligations of incoming passengers, may fairly be inferred; such an experience would ordinarily teach the policy of avoiding any circumstance in the least likely to raise suspicion. *The Robert Edwards,* 6 Wheat. 187, 190-191.

In reaching the conclusion of an intent to evade payment of duty,—an intent not abandoned but continuing down to the time of the inspector's discovery of concealment,—we have not failed to give full consideration to the testimony in behalf of the claimant; but, in view of all the evidence, not only direct but circumstantial, her defense is not convincing. The explanation of the bag's false bottom is. that it was designed to protect only the articles below (and for which there was no room in the trunk or elsewhere) from food and soiled clothing carried above; and the explanation of the concealment of silk within the sleeves of cotton kimonos and in other places, is a purpose only of protecting the more valuable material against fumigation by health authorities at various parts of the way. It is fair, to note that the cloth used for the false bottom is not as well adapted to concealment as it might be, for it is considerably more faded and worn than the lining of the bag and different in color, being of a dull blue ground bearing inconspicuous checks made up of narrow white lines, while the lining is of a dull brown ground bearing narrow inconspicuous stripes of other dull colors. But the crude manner in which this part of the plan was carried out does not weaken the conviction of the plan's existence. And it is noticeable, that the cloth used for the false bottom is so porous and worn, even worn through in small spots here and there, that it is not more adapted to the asserted purpose of protection from the food and soiled clothing above, than it is adapted to a "good job" of concealment. It is also to be noted that the food there found (and none other was described by witnesses) was not in its nature "dirty," being dried beans in a cloth sack and other food in tins. The conflict of testimony as to whether the inspector himself discovered and tore open the false bottom, or whether the claimant called the inspector's intention to it by herself tearing it open, might make the case somewhat more difficult, if other evidence in favor of the government were wanting; but on the whole, more confidence is felt in the observation and memory of the Federal customs inspector (despite his interest in the proceeds of the forfeited goods), as well as of the officer of the Territory of Hawaii engaged in inspecting baggage for infected fruit, who both had active concern with the examination of this baggage, than in the observation and memory of the two "runners" for a Japanese hotel, who were mere bystanders except for their interest in a possible patron of their house.

[2] From the evidence, the court finds for the government on the second count of the information, alleging a vio-

lation of the first part of subsection 9 aforesaid by an attempt to enter or introduce imported merchandise into the commerce of the country by false or fraudulent practices or appliances. As to the third count, alleging a violation of the last part of subsection 9 aforesaid, by an omission "to disclose and declare to the proper officers . . . the true character," etc., of the concealed goods "by means whereof the United States was . . . deprived of the . . . . duties," strictly, the proof has failed, for an actual deprival of duties is alleged and none is proved. Though the statute covers both prospective deprival and consummated deprival, yet when the latter is alleged such allegation would seem to contemplate, within the statute, that the goods should have actually passed the customs line,—e.g., a case of successful smuggling accompanied by a "willful omission," etc., would satisfy the actual allegation of count three, while an attempt to smuggle would not. The use of the words "shall or may" in said subsection 9 (quoted at length in foot note, post) supports this view. It must be admitted that the matter of the proof under count three involves questions of difficulty (not raised in argument but apparent on study), which it would be unprofitable to consider, in view of the extended discussion of the second count, below, upon which count alone the evidence is clearly sufficient to sustain the information. The above observations on count three may, therefore, be taken only as suggestive of probable conclusions.

As to the first count, alleging a violation of section 3082 aforesaid, in that merchandise was "fraudulently imported and attempted" to be "brought into the United States . . . without the payment of duties:" This statute does not reach attempts. *Keck v. United States*, 172 U. S. 434 444. 445. Therefore, the allegation of an "attempt to bring in," is an unauthorized allegation; and the proof, as here, of only an attempt to "import . . . without the payment of . . . duties," is, likewise, vain. And apart from what the statute authorizes, the pleading of an importation is, of course, not satisfied by the proof of an attempt to import.

Before concluding, some contentions of the claimant should be noted as worthy of special attention. A summary of these, with the cases relied upon in their support, and our view thereof, now follows:

(i). Even admitting, for the sake of argument only, a fraudulent intent, still as the United States has not yet been deprived of any duties on these goods and there is no possibility of such deprival by reason of the claimant's acts alone, there can, as the claimant contends, be no forfeiture under subsection 9 of section 28 of the tariff act of 1909, 36 Stat. 11, 97; citing *United States v. Twenty-five Packages of Panama Hats*, 193 Fed. 438 (applying this very subsection) and *United States v. Ninety-nine Diamonds*, 139 Fed. 961, 2 L. R. A. (N. S.) 185 (applying a corresponding provision of the customs administrative act of 1890, 26 Stat. 131, 135, 136, thereby repealed).

[3] The contention cannot prevail in the face of the fact that this provision of the statute of 1909 is directed not only against acts whereby "the United States shall . . . be deprived of the lawful duties," but also against acts whereby the government "*may* be deprived" of such duties. Subsection 9 aforesaid.* So far as the *Panama Hat* case, supra [subsequently reversed, 231 U. S. 358], is concerned, if the decision there were not plainly controlled by

---

*"That if any consignor, seller, owner, importer, consignee, agent, or other person or persons, shall enter or introduce, or attempt to enter or introduce, into the commerce of the United States any imported merchandise by means of any fraudulent or false invoice, affidavit, letter, paper, or by means of any false statement, written or verbal, or by means of any false or fraudulent practice or appliance whatsoever, or shall be guilty of any willful act or omission by means whereof the United States shall or may be deprived of the lawful duties, or any portion thereof, accruing upon the merchandise, or any portion thereof, embraced or referred to in such invoice, affidavit, letter, paper or statement, or affected by such act or omission, such merchandise, or the value thereof, to be recovered from such person or persons, shall be forfeited, which forfeiture shall only apply to the whole of the merchandise or the value thereof in the case, or package containing the particular article or articles of merchandise to which such fraud or false paper or statement relates. . . . ."

the fact of the claimant consignee's innocence of the fraud
and undervaluation of the consignor—which is enough to
distinguish it from the case at bar wherein the element of
innocence is wanting,—still the use of the word "may" in
the phrase of the new law "shall or may be deprived," would
compel the conclusion of the clearest intent to reach cases
not reached by the law which had hitherto been in force
(act of 1890, supra) and which was applied in the case of
the Ninety-nine Diamonds, supra, wherein the language of
the corresponding phrase of that act, "shall be deprived."
was held inefficient to reach a case in which the government
was not actually deprived of the duties. Id., 965. See *United
States v. Boyd*, 24 Fed. 692, 695, holding that the word
"shall" in the former law might be taken in a broad sense,
of potentiality.

[4a]   To further distinguish the *Diamonds* case from
the present case in which an attempt is alleged: Had the
information in the *Diamonds* case contained a count based
on an attempt, the court there would, of course, have been
in no way concerned with the government's ultimate deprival of its revenue,—at least, if any effect at all is to be
given to the use of the word "attempt" in the statute: indeed, this word was plainly calculated to cover culpable
cases of failure to effect such deprival—culpable cases as
distinguished from cases, such as those of *United States v.
One Trunk* (Gannon, claimant), 175 Fed. 1012, syll. 1, and
United States v. One Trunk (McNally, claimant), 171 Fed.
772, syll. 3, in which the party takes some preliminary steps
in the unlawful enterprise but, repenting before the "eleventh hour," makes no use of his fraudulent devices. As the
facts are found in the case at bar, the claimant made all the
use that she could of the devices of concealment, to effect a
purpose to evade payment of duties. *United States v. Boyd*.
24 Fed. 692, 694-695.

Another means of distinguishing the *Diamonds* case is
found in the later addition to the statute of the word "intro-

duce," by the phrase "enter or introduce," thus curing the
narrow scope of the former law wherein the word "enter"
alone was used,—a word of such technical meaning in customs procedure as to make the application of the former
statute very limited. See the *Panama Hat* case, supra, 195
Fed. 438, 439.

In *Sixty-six Cases of Cheese,* 163 Fed. 367, 368,—holding that under the statute of 1890 it is not essential that
there should be a completed fraud upon the United States,
but that it is enough if the act or attempt is of a character
calculated to deprive the United States of duty,—District
Judge Chatfield concludes from certain language of the
court in the *Diamonds* case, that "the entire decision is
directed to the point that an actual defrauding of the government must be involved in the consequences of the fraudulent act,"—and "involved" *either* as a pregnant possibility
or as an actual result. The decision is good authority
against the contention, supra, that there was "no possibility
of such deprival;" for the devices of concealment were, as
fully shown in the discussion of the evidence herein, "of a
character calculated to deprive the United States of duty."
See also the opinion of the same judge in *United States v.
Twenty Boxes of Cheese,* 163 Fed. 369, 372.

(ii). Even admitting an attempted concealment, there
can be no forfeiture under the first part of said subsection
9, which applies only to goods the importation of which is
not concealed: citing *United States v.* 218½ *Carats of
Loose Emeralds,* 153 Fed. 643, 645.

[5] No reason is seen, even under the rule of strict
construction, for giving the words "practice" and "appliances" so narrow a meaning. A device, or a method or
means, of concealment, such as was used here, is certainly
a "practice" or an "appliance" within the fair, and common,
scope of these words. "Practice" is defined by the Century
Dictionary as: "action; exercise; performance; the process
of accomplishing or carrying out; performance or execu-

tion as opposed to speculation or theory;"—also: "an
tion; act; proceeding;"—also: "*artifice, treachery, a plot;
stratagem.*" "Appliance is defined by the same authoril
as "*something applied as a means to an end,* either ind
pendently or subordinately; that which is *adapted to t
accomplishment of a purpose;* an instrumental means, aic
or appurtenance: as, the appliances of civilization, or of
trade; mechanical. chemical, or medical appliances (tool:
machinery, apparatus, remedies, etc.); an engine with i
appliances." (The italics above are ours.)

If the opinion in the *Emeralds* case, supra, of the non
applicability of the statute, is based upon the use of th
adjectives "false" and "fraudulent" as qualifying the word
"practice or appliance," then we must dissent. In our viev
the use of a "practice" or an "appliance" calculated to con
ceal (the purpose of defrauding the government being as
sumed as present), is a "false or fraudulent" act within th
reasonable intent of language. The Century Dictiona
thus defines "false": "containing or conveying deceptio
falsehood or treachery; adapted or intended to misleac
said of things." And "fraudulent" is by this authority d
fined as: "involving or characterized by fraud; proceedin
from or founded on fraud; deceitful; as a fraudulent bar
gain;"—also: "planning or using fraud; given to the prac
tice of fraud." It may be noted that the decision in th
Emeralds case was affirmed, 154 Fed. 839, but on ground
not involving the special point made by the court below
153 Fed. 643, 645. and relied on by the claimant here.

As suggesting light on this contention, reference is mad
to the decision in *United States v. A Cargo of Sugar,*
Sawy. 46, 25 Fed. Cas. 288, 290, No. 14,722, from which th
inference seems to be justified that the court regarded th
applicability of a provision of statute, 12 Stat. 737, 738
similar to (and the predecessor of) said subsection 9. as no
depending upon concealment or non-concealment.

(iii). As the claimant freely pointed out the baggage and without attempt at concealment removed articles from the trunk and other containers, there was a sufficient disclosure to put the customs officer upon inquiry, or notice of the dutiable character of the goods, and, therefore, no forfeiture could arise: citing *United States v. One Pearl Necklace*, 111 Fed. 164, 170; *United States v. One Trunk* (McNally, claimant), 184 Fed. 317, 318.

[6] The evidence does show that the claimant freely pointed out her baggage and without any active attempt at concealment removed articles from the trunk and other containers, but it also shows, for instance, that in removing kimonos and spreading them out on the table she only unfolded them but did not open them so as to disclose the inside or "wrong" side—which may be characterized as passive concealment, or "bluff." Indeed, as the fact is here found, she pointed out and opened up nothing that was concealed. But, in any event, the argument of the magic effect of "putting an officer on inquiry," cannot justly be invoked when it amounts to the curing of an attempt to smuggle by the mere fact of its successful concealment, whether accomplished through the skill of the smuggler or the want of acuteness of the inspector. In our view of the statute, the smuggler cannot escape by merely leading the inspector up to where the goods are concealed and doing everything short of opening them to view. Otherwise, the game would be one in which the dishonest importer could not lose. The statute is hardly capable of an application so contrary to its object. The "putting on notice," to be effective, must be bona fide, not mere bluff,—something actually, and fairly, equivalent to a direct statement declaratory of the goods in question. The "putting on notice" is measured not by the inspector's astuteness, keenness of scent (or the lack of it), but by the importer's good faith and real intention to make a fair declaration either by a direct statement or its equivalent. The language of Judge

Hoffman, in the case of *A Cargo of Sugar,* supra, 25 Fed. Cas. 288, 290, is pertinent:

"If the party has used those means he is clearly guilty of the offense, whether the collector knew of the commission of the offense at the time it was committed, or only discovered it afterwards. In either event the statute operates, and confiscation follows as a consequence of the employment of the fraudulent means to effect an entry of the goods. Nor does the character of the device, whether flimsy or transparent, or readily or with difficulty to be detected, provided it be fraudulent, affect the question. The degree of skill, ingenuity, or cunning with which the fraud is contrived, can make no difference."

And see Id., 289, col. 2, imposing a high degree of good faith in informing the customs officers.

(iv). Inasmuch as it was impossible for the claimant to make an entry of the goods because of their "premature seizure," there could be no violation of the law: or in other words, the inspector having, by seizure of the goods without request of a formal entry as required by law, deprived the claimant of the right to "change her mind" (*locus penitentiae*) which she had up to the time of entry, she cannot be held for any failure to declare these goods: citing *United States v. One Trunk* (Gannon, claimant), 175 Fed. 1012, 1015; *United States v. One Trunk* (McNally, claimant), 171 Fed. 772, 774; *United States v. One Pearl Chain*, 139 Fed. 510, 512; s. c. 513, 515, 516; also subsection 7 of section 28 of the tariff act of 1909, permitting an entry to be corrected.

[8a]   No decision is known which holds that in a case of attempt as distinguished from mere intent or mere preparation for an attempt (see the case of *One Pearl Chain*, 139 Fed. 515; 1 Words and Phrases, 623, col. 2), there is any *locus poenitentiae* for the dishonest importer when once his fraudulent concealment is discovered "after the goods (have) reached this country," and he has begun "that series of acts through which, by application to the customs officials, he gains possession of his goods." See the case of *One Trunk* (McNally, claimant), supra, 171 Fed. 774;

United States v. 28 Packages of Pins, Gilp. 306, 28 Fed. Cas. 244, No. 16,561. In the *Trunk* cases, (Gannon, claimant, and McNally, claimant), supra, the goods were found to have been entered as imported merchandise and not as personal baggage (175 Fed. 1015, 1016; 192 Fed. 913, 914-915, and 184 Fed. 318-319). In each case the importer there indicated to the customs officer that the goods were to go to "public stores." i. e., for examination and appraisal as imported merchandise, and in each case there was no attempt to conceal the articles themselves, for they were all itemized though undervalued, in the invoices which were submitted to the customs officials, in the *Gannon* case directly (175 Fed. 1014-1015) and in the *McNally* case indirectly through the consul (171 Fed. 773). In the case of the *Pearl Chain*, supra, the steamship passenger before landing filled out the printed blank form of declaration furnished her by the customs officer, which placed the special item "jewelry" under the general heading "wearing apparel." 139 Fed. 514-517; s. c., 123 Fed. 371, 376-377. As this declaration did not provide for an itemized list of the dutiable articles but contemplated a later, detailed entry, 123 Fed. 378, it was held that a seizure based on the mere failure of this declaration to specify the pearl chain and made before it became the duty of the passenger to complete the entry by enumerating the items of her jewelry, was unwarranted. The *Pearl Chain* case is clearly distinguished by the decisions in *Dodge v. United States*, 131 Fed. 849, 852, and *Rogers v. United States*, 180 Fed. 54, 60, 61. Why should the dishonest importer be given the benefit of a *locus poenitentiae* which he may use or not as it suits the exigencies of the occasion,—i.e., according to the probability of discovery? The mere fact of his being deprived of an opportunity to repent, is nothing which he can set up to relieve him when his fraud is detected. The doors are not to be held open for the dishonest importer. See *United States v. One Bag of Crushed Wheat*, 166 Fed. 562,

567. If the claimant here was to "change her mind" she should have done so when the inspector came to make his examination and she should then have somehow expressed her desire to declare the goods which were concealed as well as those which the trunk, bag and basket purported to contain. But having deferred disclosure, and her concealment having been discovered, it was then too late for repentance.

Subsection 7 aforesaid affords the claimant no aid. It allows amendment of the written entry, only by correcting misstatements as to value of a declared article, and not by supplying items of which the claimant has failed to make any declaration whatever. It applies to items which are stated but whose value is incorrectly given,—not to items which are not stated at all, but which it is the claimant's duty to state. The distinction is suggested in the case of the *Bag of Crushed Wheat*, supra, 166 Fed. 567.

"A crime once committed, may be pardoned, but it cannot be obliterated by repentance. Therefore, if a man resolves on a criminal enterprise, and proceeds so far in it that his act amounts to an indictable attempt, it does not cease to be such though he voluntarily abandons the evil purpose." 1 Bishop's New Criminal Law, sec. 732. See Id., sec. 728.

(v). Owing to the claimant's being in the custody of the immigration officers up to the time of the examination of her baggage, and owing to the absence then of any qualified customs officer before whom an oath could be taken, it was impossible for the claimant to make entry prior to seizure of the goods; and until the time expired within which she might make entry, she could lawfully abandon any fraudulent intent (if she had any) and make proper entry.

[7] This is practically the same as contention (iv) supra, and the same authorities were cited in its support. So far as concerns the fact of the absence of any officer qualified to administer an oath, it is true that the only customs officer present was not so qualified, but this, in our

view, is immaterial. The fact that an extraordinary "short," practice was adopted cannot excuse an attempt which had been carried as far as the claimant could carry it, a design which was calculated to defraud the government, and which was actually set in motion and well under way,—particularly when that practice of the local customs house was adopted quite as much for the convenience of the incoming passenger as for the customs officials themselves, and was being acquiesced in by the claimant, who is presumed to have known the laws as well as anybody is, and who might, in theory at least, have demanded the privilege, under the law, of making a formal entry in the usual way. This point may well be emphasized in the language of Judge Thomas, in the case of *United States v. Rosenthal,* 126 Fed. 766, 761: "The dishonest importer . . . ought not to be heard inveighing against anomalous methods."

(vi). As the goods were of more than $500. in value, a regular entry was required, for the making of which the Customs Regulations, 1908, articles 615, 1092, give one year, the seizure was "premature" and no forfeiture can follow.

[8b] This treasury regulation applies to "unclaimed merchandise" which "if not . . . entered within one year, . . . should be sold at public auction." The merchandise seized here is not within the class thus provided for. While it is the government's policy to extend time in the case of innocent delinquents, its favors are not given in order to afford a *locus poenitentiae* to the dishonest importer who has been discovered in an unlawful effort to introduce goods through the customs line.

(vii). That section 2785 of the Revised Statutes gives the claimant fifteen days within which to make the entry in writing, and no forfeiture can here arise, as the goods were seized without allowing any opportunity for this advantage.

[9] The fifteen-day privilege may not be used to shield a plain violation of subsection 9. It is a forced and un-

reasonable application of this time extension, to say that
one who has done what is clearly an attempt to evade the
law may invoke this privilege when his attempt is discovered in the very course of the goods through customs inspection and after he has done all in his power to effect his
object. Whether through ignorance of her privilege of making a written entry—and the law is no respecter of ignorance,—or whatever the reason, the claimant was actually
pursuing a different course in accordance with local practice.
The court should not go out of its way to find excuses for
the importer who if she had been pursuing one of the
ordinary courses of getting goods through the customs line.
might have been entitled to an extended time to complete
the entry.

Moreover, the fifteen-day provision seems to apply not
to articles brought in the baggage but only to merchandise
brought in the cargo. The case of the *Pearl Necklace*, supra.
111 Fed. 164, 168-169. At least, it does not apply to goods
brought in the baggage and to be taken immediately away;
for "until . . . . entry has been made, the baggage
cannot be landed." Id. 169.

(viii). Merely "a cause of forfeiture plus arrival of the
goods in the United States" is not enough to sustain this
proceeding,—the goods not having been entered, and there
having been no introduction, or attempt at introduction,
into the commerce of the United States; citing the *Panama
Hat* case, 195 Fed. 438, 439-441, and the case of the *Diamonds*, 130 Fed. 965.

[4b] The contention is disposed of by the fact that this
is not a case of "mere arrival in the United States;" for the
goods were already on their way through the hands of the
customs inspector. If the goods had not gone so far on their
course, there might be more room for argument in claimant's behalf,—though this suggestion is not meant as a ruling that her own "death-bed" disclosure would work immunity for acts already complete as an attempt. Here, by non-
disclosure when it was her duty to disclose, there was not

only a purpose to conceal, but the claimant was actually carrying·out that purpose. Indeed, at the time of the discovery, she was "lying low" as a part of her scheme of deception and in the hope of its successful consummation. See *United States v. Mescall,* 164 Fed. 587, 588-589. In the decisions the making of a fraudulent invoice is not of itself held to be an offense, until followed up by an actual attempt to *use* it for the purpose of entry. In the case at bar not only were these fraudulent devices calculated for concealment, but the claimant was actually making use of these devices. See *United States v. Twenty-eight Packages of Pins,* supra, 28 Fed. Cas. 250. Fortunately, the present case is relieved from any border-line difficulties. See the cases of *One Trunk* (McNally, claimant), supra, 184 Fed. 317, and of *A Cargo of Sugar,* supra, 25 Fed. Cas. 288-289.

(ix) The government has failed in its proof, for want of any showing of an attempt to enter or introduce the goods *into the commerce* of the country; citing the *Panama Hat* case, 195 Fed. 438.

[10] There is no direct evidence of an intent to introduce the concealed goods into the commerce of the country, but the circumstantial evidence of such a purpose is by no means insignificant. The bearing on this point of two of the letters found in the claimant's baggage has already been pointed out. There can be no question that this alone was evidence sufficient to sustain a finding so far as this element of the case is concerned.

(x). Mere acts of concealment, such as here attempted to be shown, are not sufficient to work a forfeiture: citing *Keck v. United States,* 172 U. S. 434; *United States v. Harts,* 131 Fed. 886.

While mere acts of concealment were held in the *Keck* case, supra, not to work a forfeiture, the statute there involved was not broad enough to cover attempts. Id., 434, 444. The statute now in force expressly covers attempts. The *Keck* decision itself points out the distinction between attempts and accomplished acts, and is far from holding that "mere acts of concealment" may not be attempts. Id. 445. The claimant here had done all that she could to effect her purpose, the success of the enterprise then depended only upon the want of acuteness of the inspector. In the language of Judge Hopkinson in the case of *Twenty-eight Packages of Pins*, supra, 28 Fed. Cas. 250, "the machinery was ready;" its further use depended upon another and innocent person, the inspector. At all events, the claimant's acts were not mere, innocent, acts of concealment but acts of concealment growing out of a fraudulent intent; the case is thus distinguished from the *Harts* case in which the intent was not fraudulent. *United States v. Harts*, 131 Fed. 886, syll. 3; s. c. 140, Id. 843.

(xi). The testimony shows the customs officer to have been proceeding under sections 2799, 2801 and 2802 of the Revised Statutes, and, therefore, until entry there could be no forfeiture; also following the case of the *Pearl Necklace*, 111 Fed. 164, 131 Fed. 849, the procedure under these sections was the proper, and only, procedure, and, therefore, section 3082 in particular (upon which the first count of the information is based) has no application.

(xii). The goods being in the baggage, the "baggage" statutes, sections 2799-2802 aforesaid, apply, and there must be an entry (i.e., in writing) and failure to disclose certain articles, before those articles can be forfeited: citing the *Pearl Necklace* case, supra.

(xiii). But if the goods do not come within the "baggage" statutes, supra, then the "trunk" cases, supra (wherein the goods were regarded as merchandise and not baggage, although found in trunks), apply, and the importer has fifteen days within which to make entry.

The question is not, what was the procedure followed by the inspector, but what was the statute, if any, infringed by the claimant? See discussion under contention (v) supra. So far as section 3082 is concerned, if counsel mean, by contention (xi), supra, that it has no application because there could be no importing "contrary to law" (sec. 3082) when there still remained a *locus poenitentiae,* then nothing more need be said than already said in the discussions of contentions (iv), (v), (vi), (vii), supra. The matter of the fifteen-day privilege has been disposed of elsewhere.

(xiv). Guilty intent must be proved, which proof is wanting here; citing *United States v. One Silk Rug,* 158 Fed. 974; and the burden of proof in such case is on the government. Id.

[11a]   So far as the government is concerned, the requirements of proof have been fully met. As to the burden of proof, the court has found the existence of "probable cause" for the prosecution of the information. Wherefore, under Rev. Stat., section 909, this burden lies upon the claimant. See the cases of the *Pearl Chain,* supra, 139 Fed. 510-511, and of the *Bag of Crushed Wheat,* supra, 166 Fed. 568.

(xv). The government must establish the allegations of the information by proof to a moral certainty and beyond any reasonable doubt: citing *Chaffee & Co. v. United States,* 18 Wall. 516; *Boyd v. United States,* 116 U. S. 616; *Clifton v. United States,* 4 How. 242.

[11b]   A proceeding *in rem* to forfeit is a civil proceeding, and the ordinary rule of preponderance of evidence applies: *Lilienthal's Tobacco v. United States,* 97 U. S. 237, 271-272; *The Good Templar,* 97 Fed. 651-653. See *The Three Friends,* 166 U. S. 1, 50-51; 23 Ops. Atty. Gen., 63, 64, syll.

(xvi). The statutes involved are to be strictly construed; citing the *Panama Hat* case, 195 Fed. 438, 439, 440; and such construction makes for the claimant.

[12]   Though these statutes, being penal in character, are to be strictly construed, they are also to be construed reasonably and so as to give effect to every word, including the word "attempt," and including the word "may" in the phrase "by means whereof the United States shall or may be deprived of the lawful duties," this word being used in the act of 1909 by way of amendment of the act of 1890,—

an amendment which may well have been made in contemplation of rulings such as that in the case of the *Diamonds,* supra. See *In re Suekichi Tsuji,* ante, p. 52; *In re Nakashima,* 3 U. S. Dist. Ct. Haw., 168, 175; *United States v. Aultman,* 143 Fed. 922, 928; also dissent of Judge Ward, in the *Panama Hat* case, supra.

Under subsection 9 aforesaid, the forfeiture is "not limited to the mere goods in relation to which [the] fraudulent practice is used," but extends to "the whole of the merchandise . . . in the case or package containing the particular . . . articles to which such fraud . . . relates." Wherefore, the prayer for forfeiture of all the goods found in the trunk, bag and basket, is well founded

The technicality of the law of customs administration, and some degree of inflexibility and unwieldiness in the statutes, and in particular, some improvident generalizations in the decisions, all affording plausible arguments in behalf of tariff evaders, have made the contentions of claimant's counsel "easier to overrule than to answer" (Jeremiah Black, Essays, &c., 207), especially on the question involved in most of their argument, of *locus poenitentia,* or the "recall" of attempts. This may excuse a more extended consideration of facts and law than would otherwise have been indulged.

Let judgment be entered pursuant to the government's prayer, with costs against the claimant.

Reported, 23 Treasury Decisions, 31 (T. D. 33019).

UNITED STATES OF AMERICA *v.* A LOT OF SILK GOODS AND OTHER MERCHANDISE

(Mrs. S. Kataoka, Claimant).

December 24, 1912.

1. *Judicial sales* (forfeiture sales under customs laws)—*Marshal's fees and expenses:* In the marshal's bill of fees and expenses in a judicial sale (under decree of forfeiture of goods for violation of customs laws), the statute (Rev. Stat. sec. 829), providing a fee for service of writs, does not allow a charge for delivering a copy of the notice of sale to the advertising medium designated in the decree, nor for delivering to the auctioneer a certified copy of the decree.

2. *Same—Same—Auctioneer's charges as expense of sale:* In the marshal's bill of fees and expenses in a judicial sale, he is allowed (by Rev. L. Hawaii, sec. 1889, adopted under Rev. Stat. sec. 829, subdiv. 6) certain commissions, from which he must pay any auctioneer engaged; but, with consent of the parties in interest, the marshal may be allowed something extra required to compensate an auctioneer whose just charges amount to more than these statutory commissions.

In Rem: On information for forfeiture. Motion to allow marshal's bill of fees and expenses of sale.

C. C. Bitting, Assistant U. S. Attorney, for the United States.

E. R. Hendry, U. S. Marshal, *pro se.*

CLEMONS, J.: The marshal submits for approval his account of fees and expenses in the matter of the sale conducted by him under the decree of forfeiture herein.

[1]   In this account are included the cost of advertising notice of sale and the following other items:

"Service notice of sale [upon] 'Pacific Commercial Advertiser'; 'Hawaii Shinpo Sha'; 'Nippu Jiji' and 'Hawaiian-Japanese Daily Chronicle'—4 services @ $2.00 each $8.00

"Serving decree [upon auctioneer] 2.00

"Marshal's commission for collecting $1751.50; 5%
 on first $500.00 and 2½% on $1251.50 .... 56.28
"City Auction Co. paid 5% commission for selling
 goods; 5% on $1751.50 .... 87.55"

Although there is, as pointed out by the marshal, precedent for these charges in approved accounts in earlier
forfeiture cases in this court, these precedents are in error
as regards the above quoted items of "service of notice of
sale" and "serving decree;" and they are in error as regards
the expense of auctioneer's services, at least in the absence
of consent of the parties in interest (*The John E. Mulford*,
18 Fed. 455, 456; *Wallis v. Shelly*, 30 Fed. 747; *United
States v. Fitzsimmons*, 50 Fed. 381), or perhaps of an order
of court contemplating not only the marshal's having the
aid of an auctioneer but also the auctioneer's being paid
either in part or in whole, out of the sale proceeds, in addition to the marshal's having his statutory commissions for
effecting the sale (Rev. Stat. sec. 829, subdiv. 6; Rev. L.
Hawaii, sec. 1889.   In case of the precedents for approval of similar accounts here, no written opinions were
rendered, and undoubtedly such approval would not have
been had if those accounts had been questioned.

[2]   As to the item of auctioneer's commissions: Under
the law applying to the Territorial courts of Hawaii, adopted
as the law of this Federal court (Rev. Stat. sec. 829, subdiv.
6), the local sheriff receives a commission of five per cent. on
the gross sale proceeds up to five hundred dollars and two
and one-half per cent. on any excess, Rev. L. Hawaii, sec.
1889, pp. 743-744; and, by the well-settled practice under
this statute, where the sale is conducted by an auctioneer,
the sheriff must pay that agent out of these stated commissions, and may not be allowed anything in addition
thereto for the expense of the auctioneer's services.   This
practice of the Territorial courts is a sound application of
the local law. *The John E. Mulford*, supra; *Wallis v. Shelly*,

supra; *United States v. Fitzsimmons*, 50 Fed. 381, 389-390;
see *Galbraith v. Drought*, 24 Kans. 590, 591-592. For, the
rule is that these fees and expenses, in order to be allowed,
must be strictly justified by statute. According to the authorities, the sale commissions allowable to the sheriff or
marshal are intended as the sole compensation for effecting
the sale, and if he sells through the agency of an auctioneer,
the officer must himself compensate his agent and may not
be allowed in his accounts for any expenses incurred beyond
the amount of his statutory, official commissions.

An exception has been made, however, where the parties
in interest consent to the hiring of the auctioneer at the expense of the sale proceeds. *The John E. Mulford,* supra;
Wallis v. Shelly, supra. On the strict principle of the authorities with regard to matters of fees and expenses in such
cases, and of court costs generally, it would not be just to
stretch this exception so as to give the marshal his commissions for effecting the sale and also allow him for the entire
compensation of an agent, auctioneer, whom he engages to
do his work for him. Here, the goods having been forfeited
to the United States, the only party in interest now remaining, so far as the sale proceeds are concerned, is the government; and that party by its attorneys and by its special representative, the collector of customs, has expressly, though
informally and not in writing, given its approval and consent in the engagement of an expert auctioneer to conduct
the sale on the customary basis as to compensation. The decree also provides that the sale should be held at this auctioneer's place of business, a provision to some extent cor-
roborating the evidence of this consent, though not establishing its proof. Wherefore, the item of the marshal's commission of five per cent. and two and one-half per cent., is
allowed, with the understanding that it is to go toward payment of the autcioneer; and the court approves of the extra
expense incurred, i.e., the difference between the two and
one-half per cent. commission to the marshal on proceeds

above five hundred dollars and the five per cent. charged by the auctioneer.

Let it be understood, that this extra expense is approved only because (while also consented to by the parties) it is reasonable, and not as establishing a precedent for a flat rate of five per cent. to auctioneers on any and all sales, regardless of the nature of the thing sold, or of the amount of the proceeds, or of the labor involved. Here, e.g., the auctioneer expended more time and effort in selling these goods, which were nearly all single-piece goods and each of comparatively small worth, than he would in selling a valuable piece of real property, which could be "knocked down" in a few minutes. In the latter case a downward sliding scale of commissions, or a very low rate, would be the only fair compensation, while in the former case a higher, flat, rate would be reasonable. Also, let it be understood, that this opinion is not intended as a broad-cast discouragement of the employment of auctioneers by the marshal. In these days the use of the expert is as a rule highly economical. Here, e.g., the auctioneer has been able to promote the sale to an effective extent impossible for even the efficient marshal: his list of clients, his knowledge of the buying public, and his own private means of advertising (the use of which in this case is covered by the commissions charged) are to all parties in interest well worth the extra cost. Moreover, it is apparent, that the marshal and his deputies could not themselves very very well do the work here involved, in addition to their other duties. The practical suggestion is, then: if any extra expense is to be allowed for auctioneer's fees, let the parties agree or consent thereto. For the ordinary case, in the absence of such agreement or consent, or of a proper order of court, if the marshal's statutory commissions, for which he must sell or engage an auctioneer to sell, are inadequate, the statute should be amended to keep pace with present conditions.

The matter for which "service of notice of sale" is

charged, is delivery of a copy of the notice of sale to the newspaper advertising mediums named in the decree. Acts of this kind are not contemplated in the marshal's statutory fee bill, which provides only for service in a peculiarly technical sense of the word, e.g., delivery of some mandate of the court, or of some notice emanating from the court, the receipt of which charges the recipient with certain legal consequences. See law dictionaries, tit. "service." Although these newspapers were designated in the decree, yet the decree was obviously not directed to them but only authorized the marshal to use these mediums as means of advertising the sale. This item is, accordingly, disallowed.

The item, "serving decree," does not show the nature of the service, but, as I am informed by the deputy marshal, covers delivery to the auctioneer of a certified copy of the order of sale. Undoubtedly it was proper, indeed, commendable practice, to see that the auctioneer had a true copy of the decree for his guidance; but, as in case of the item just discussed, the delivery by the marshal's deputy of such a paper to the marshal's agent, the auctioneer, is not "service" in the technical sense in which that word is used in the statute. Thte item is therefore disallowed.

The item of expense of advertising in the designated newspapers, is allowed, being expressly provided for by the local statute adopted in this court. Rev. Stat., supra; Rev. L. Hawaii, supra.

The marshal having already deposited with the clerk the net proceeds of sale and the amount of fees for service of papers and the marshal's commissions as charged in his proposed bill of account, it will be necessary that the clerk segregate these moneys in accordance with this opinion. As the auctioneer's compensation has already been deducted from the gross sale proceeds, the suggested error of double charge of marshal's sale commissions, may be cured by simply transferring the amount of his statutory commissions to the net proceeds fund. The other disallowed items may be disposed of in the same manner.

But, it has been suggested, that as the United States treasury eventually gets all this money anyway, the marshal's service fees and sale commissions being deposited by the clerk with the local United States depositary to the credit of the treasury, and the net sale proceeds going to the treasury through he collector, any segregation of the moneys on the basis of the above rulings would practically be vain, and that, therefore, the account might just as well stand as submitted. With this suggestion I disagree. Apart from any possible interest of the "detecting and seizing officer" or informer in these proceeds (Customs Regulations, 1908, arts. 1289 et seq. and citations), which, through an improper charge in the fee bill, would be prejudiced by a reduction of the net sum returned to the collector, that official is entitled to the credit of himself reporting the true net proceeds to the treasury in the regular routine; and on general principles it would be unsystematic and confusing to permit an error, even though technical, to stand uncorrected merely because in spite of it the money would finally find its way to the credit of the Federal treasury.

IN THE MATTER OF THE CITY CONTRACTING & BUILDING COMPANY, A COPARTNERSHIP, AN ALLEGED BANKRUPT.

December 17, 1912.

Bankruptcy—Partnership petition—Non-joining partner—Notice: In a proceeding in which one of the members of a copartnership petitions for the adjudication of the firm as a voluntary bankrupt, the adjudication is vacated upon it appearing that one of the partners did not actually authorize, or consent to, the petition made for and in his behalf, and was not given notice either of the filing of the petition or of the hearing thereon.

In Bankruptcy: On motion to vacate order to file schedules.

Lorrin Andrews for petitioning partner, Wong Hong Yuen.

F. Schnack for partners Chun Ping and Lau Chung.

J. W. Russell (*Thompson, Wilder, Watson & Lymer* with him) for partners Au Tin Kwai and Au Ne Chong.

I. M. Stainback (*Holmes, Stanley & Olson* with him) for Allen & Robinson, Ltd., and Hoffschlaeger Company, Ltd., creditors.

E. W. Sutton (*Smith, Warren & Hemenway* with him) for the trustee.

CLEMONS, J. The petition of four members of this co-partnership, for adjudication of the firm as a voluntary bankrupt, was signed by one of them with the words "For City Contracting & Building Company" written below his name; it was also verified by him in behalf of the company though in a form not approved for a case of this kind because, if verification by proxy be allowable at all, the showing of authority to verify for the other members was not distinct and unequivocal. Annexed to the petition were schedules of the assets and liabilities of the copartnership, but not of the individual members. After adjudication and upon motion of the creditors to require the alleged members (and others who, they averred, were also actually members of the firm and should be brought into the administration) to file schedules of their own personal assets and liabilities as contemplated by official form No. 2 prescribed by the Supreme Court, it appeared that one of the partners had not actually authorized, or consented to, the petition, and

moreover had not been served with subpoena or with a
copy of the petition, or given any notice either of the filing
of the petition or of the hearing thereon. At the hearing
on the petition the court understood that all the partners
named in the petition had authorized the petition and consented thereto, though not signing it or joining in the verification. Counsel's statement of his understanding of such
consent and authority given by all four partners together
present in his office when the financial condition of the firm
was under discussion and bankruptcy was advised by him,
is evidently the truth, but he was clearly negligent in not
getting the written consent of all, or, best, having all join
in the petition and verification thereof (especially as misunderstanding was easy through the fact that the partners,
some or all, spoke only a foreign language); or at least
there was negligence in not seeing that a subpoena, together
with a copy of the petition, was served upon all members
other than the one who signed the petition. And the present judge confesses his own negligence in taking the understanding of counsel expressed in open court instead of
insisting that, in accordance with the ordinary practice,
every member of the firm actually join in the petition by
endorsement and verification, or else be duly served with
a copy thereof and with subpoena.

To adopt the ruling of Judge Coxe in a similar case, *In re
Altman*, 95 Fed. 263, 2 Am. B. R. 407, let the adjudication
of bankruptcy be vacated. See 1 Remington on Bankruptcy,
sec. 68. Also let the order appointig a trustee be set aside.
Moreover, it appearing that the trustee has taken possession
of assets of this firm, a motion will be entertained for his
appointment as receiver under a proper bond to hold and
preserve these assets and any other firm assets pending a
new hearing of the petition upon due notice thereof to the
non-joining partner—the other partners who did not actually sign the petition having meantime appeared in open
court and expressed their consent thereto and one of them

having since filed his individual schedules. It is, also, suggested that an amended petition of the consenting partners be prepared for service, following official form No. 2 and Collier's supplementary form No. 117, Collier on Bankruptcy, 9th ed. 1226, with the individual schedules as well as the firm schedules annexed.

Reported, 29 Am. B. R. 171.

IN THE MATTER OF THE CITY CONTRACTING & BUILDING COMPANY, A COPARTNERSHIP, BANKRUPT.

May 15, 1913.

1. *Bankruptcy—Schedules, requirements:*   A statement of assets and liabilities which does not furnish a direct and full answer as to each item of the official form of schedules adopted by the Supreme Court, 172 U. S. 668-679, 89 Fed. xvi.-xxvii, is insufficient.

2. *Same—Partnership—Non-bankrupt partners—Schedules:*   In a partnership bankruptcy, a firm member who is not himself adjudged bankrupt is not required to file schedules of his individual assets and liabilities; for the reason, in the main, that his individual estate may not without his consent be administered in the firm proceeding.

3. *Same—Same—Adjudication of firm and members in one proceeding—Fees:*   On petition of a partner for adjudication of his firm as bankrupt, any of the respondent partners who appear at the hearing and ask to be adjudged bankrupt as individuals in the same proceeding, may be so adjudged, and without payment of separate filing fees,—but with payment, however, of expenses of advertising notices to individual creditors.

4. *Same—General orders, construction:*   The general orders in bankruptcy prescribed by the Supreme Court are not to be taken as enlarging the statute, but must if possible be construed consistently with it; and so far as they cannot be so construed, they must be disregarded.

In Bankruptcy: On adjudication; and on motion for schedules of firm members.

Lorrin Andrews for Wong Hong Yuen, petitioning partner.

F. Schnack for partners Chun Ping and Lau Chung.

J. W. Russell (*Thompson, Wilder, Watson & Lymer* with him) for partners Au Tin Kwai and Au Ne Chong.

I. M. Stainback (*Holmes, Stanley & Olson* with him) for Allen & Robinson, Ltd,, and Hoffschlaeger Company, Ltd., creditors.

E. W. Sutton (*Smith, Warren & Hemenway* with him) for the trustee.

CLEMONS, J. On the petition of Wong Hong Yuen, a member of the City Contracting & Building Company, a copartnership, praying "that the said firm may be adjudged . . . to be bankrupts" (as concludes Form 2 adopted by the Supreme Court: 172 U. S. 681, 89 Fed. xxvii.), this copartnership, composed of the petitioning partner and the respondents Chung Ping, Wong Gock, Au Hang Hing, Au Tin Kwai, Lau Chung, and Au Ne Chong, was adjudged a bankrupt. The respondents had all appeared and admitted service, and thereafter upon the day set for hearing, they all, excepting Au Hang Hing, expressly consented to the adjudication of the firm as prayed. Au Hang Hing entered no demurrer, plea, answer, motion, or objection, but "stood mute," except to state in open court that eight days before the petition was filed he had withdrawn from the firm by sale of his interest to the copartner Wong Gock. See Black, Law Dic., 2d ed., 818, tit. "nihil dicit;" *Buena Vista Freestone Co. v. Parrish*, 34 W. Va. 652, 654, 12 S. E. 817, 818; *Wilbur v. Maynard*, 6 Colo. 483, 485; *Falken v. Housatonic R. Co.*, 63 Conn. 258, 27 Atl. 1117, 1118-1119. See, also, *In re Solomon & Carvel*, 163 Fed. 140, 20 Am. B. R. 488, 489; Brandenburg, Bankruptcy, 3d ed., sec. 133. The adjudication having been ordered, the firm members, with the exception of Wong Hong Yuen, Au Hang Hing and Wong Gock, by their attorneys in open court, asked to be adjudged bankrupts as individuals.

Subsequently, upon motion of certain creditors and after due notice, the firm members were all ordered to file their individual schedules of assets and liabilities,—in the court's reliance upon the authorities of Collier, Bankruptcy, 9th ed., 1059, par. viii., and 3 Remington, Bankruptcy, sec. 477½. The petitioning partner complied with this order. And the respondent Chung Ping has since filed schedules, but they do not conform with the full requirements of Form 1 established by the Supreme Court, 172 U. S. 668-679, 89 Fed. xvi-xxvii.,—being merely a bare list of certain chattels, on the one hand, and on the other of certain debts whose nature is not specified. And the respondents Au Tin Kwai and Au Ne Chong have filed affidavits of "no [individual] assets excepting property exempt" by law, but no statement as to their individual liabilities. The respondents Wong Gock and Au Hang Hing have yet filed no schedules.

[1] Although not strictly required by this opinion, in view of the ruling presently to appear, the opportunity is taken to declare, that this court will countenance nothing but a strict and full compliance with the statute, rules and practice with regard to schedules. The Supreme Court in the forms prescribed has seen fit to provide that these sworn schedules shall give detailed information on definite points. A bare statement of assets and liabilities is not enough: the party must go through every item of the schedules and show the facts relating thereto,—nothing is to be left to inference. We are not to accept, e. g., his short answer, that he has nothing and owes nothing, but his verification affidavit must cover every item which the Supreme Court has considered of enough importance to designate in these specific forms.

[2a] As to the delinquent respondents Wong Gock and Au Hang Hing, it being evident that they, who were in court

and, on at least one occasion, were expressly requested to file their schedules, and who, on special motion of creditors for an order compelling them to do so, were thereafter served with a copy of the court's express order to that end, are not disposed to comply with the order, their attitude is assumed to be founded on the advice of there being no lawful authority for an order directing a non-bankrupt partner to file schedules in a proceeding in bankruptcy of his firm. Inasmuch as there are authorities directly or impliedly supporting this position, the order under discussion contrary to these authorities, and made on an uncontested presentation of the motion, calls fairly for reconsideration. And, also, any decision on so mooted a point should have some discussion, as was not then had, of the reasons which induced it.

This is one phase of the constantly recurring and unsettled question of the status of the firm members in a partnership bankruptcy, and of the intent of Congress in changing the status of the firm itself from an association not distinct from its component members to an entity entirely separate and distinct.

Although, by nearly unanimous opinion, the firm is held to be an entity under the act of 1898, yet the administration of the act in pursuance of the entity doctrine is by no means established, and by no means clear. Indeed the confusion of authorities is so persistent and in various phases the breach so widening, even between judges of the same court (see, e. g., *In re Bertenshaw*, 157 Fed. 363, 19 Am. B. R. 577, 17 L. R. A., N. S., 886), as to call for legislative remedy.

And it is, specially, because of this variance of authorities on the question whether in cases of partnership bankruptcy the estates of the firm members are necessarily drawn into the administration, and, so, whether the solvent, or non-bankrupt, member can be compelled to file schedules of individual assets and liabilities, that it becomes worth while to state the reasons leading to my own matured conclusion:

for the power, if any, of the court to require the filing of schedules of individual members, rests, it would seem, upon the very same foundation as the right to draw the estate of the partner into the administration, at all.

There is no direct provision of the statute, and as I am now satisfied, no warrant even for an inference, that the bankruptcy court has any such power, desirable though it may be. And my conclusion has not been reached without recognition of the fact that there are provisions of section 5 of the act, relating to the title "partners," e. g., clauses "d," "e," "f," and "g," 30 Stat. 547-548, which are well adapted to the administration of the estates of all the individual firm members, but which for want of clear authorization cannot be used to that particular end without some regard to the condition of the estates of those members as to solvency; nor have I failed to note that there are some grounds of criticism of the leading judicial authority to sup-support my conclusion, the majority opinion by Circuit Judge Sanborn in the matter of *Bertenshaw*, supra.

Thus, that opinion errs in resting its conclusion to any degree on plausible, and in any event not controlling, considerations of policy: see 157 Fed. 367-368, 19 Am. B. R. 582-583; for it makes much too good a case for the "shrewd and able" solvent partner,—in spite of whose shrewdness and ability, however, his firm has fallen into insolvency. When a partnership has reached this point,—when its creditors are compelled to go begging for their money,—it is useless to urge any such argument as, "Why should not the solvent partner administer the partnership property and his own and pay the partnership debts free from the delay and expense of a trustee?" 157 Fed. 368, 19 Am. B. R. 583. For the solvent partner has, with his fellow partners, already had the opportunity to pay the firm debts, as it may be said to have been in a sense his legal duty to do, the firm obligation being by the law of partnership his as well as that of the firm and of the other partners. But in spite of the member's solvency, and in spite of his "shrewdness" and his "compentent[cy] to manage the individual property and the property of his firm" better than any trustee, 157 Fed. 369, 19 Am. B. R. 583, he has permitted his firm to fall into a condition in which bankruptcy is sought by the unsatisfied creditors as a way toward, though not to, complete relief. It is only by the intent of the law as written, and not by any regard for the solvent partner in such case, that the court's ruling must be justified.

Also the majority opinion takes a view of the application of clause "h" of section 5, 30 Stat. 548, 157 Fed. 366-368, 19 Am. B. R. 582-583, with which not one of the decisions construing this clause has been found to concur. Though agreeing with the court's final ruling in that case, I deem Judge Hook's dissenting opinion to express the true view of clause "h"." 157 Fed. 379-380, 19 Am. B. R. 599-600. See, also, *In re Junck & Balthazard*, 169 Fed. 481, 482-483, 22 Am. B. R. 298, 299-300; *Francis v. McNeal*, 186 Fed. 483, 485, 26 Am. B. R. 557, 560. The object of this clause,—in which there is no intimation of its application to a firm bankruptcy,—would seem to be to make it clear, by way of final proviso after clauses "a" to "g" applying to partnership administration, that the property of a firm itself is not to be administered merely because of the bankruptcy of one of its members. It may be noted, that the illuminating article of Professor J. D. Brannen of the Harvard Law School, on "The Separate Estates of Non-Bankrupt Partners in the Bankruptcy of the Partnership," 20 Harv. Law Rev., 589, published a few months earlier, while characterizing this clause as "somewhat ambiguous," Id. 591, mentions only the use which Judge Hook's dissent found for it. Id. 595. The majority opinion argued that "if the property of a bankrupt parnership cannot be administered . . . without the consent of the solvent partner who has not been adjudged bankrupt, a fortiori the latter's individual property cannot be." 157 Fed. 367, 368, 374-375, 19 Am. B. R.

582, 583-584, 593. Even assuming, as does the majority opinion, that clause "h" applies to cases in which a firm is sought to be adjudged, is this a fortiori conclusion a, necessary one? Can Congress, for aught that appears in the statute, be held to have left to mere inference so important a matter of administration? It is not easy to believe that Congress, with the end in view which the majority opinion holds, intended by this clause "h" any such short-cut legislation; for the logic of the majority opinion is, that Congress having in view two things, viz., (1) the non-administration of partnership property in the bankruptcy of a firm member, and (2) the non-administration of a firm member's property in the bankruptcy of the firm, expressly provided for only one and left the other wholly to inference. In other words, it is enough to say, by way of criticism, that other grounds than one of bare inference, should be looked to for a solution of the question,—especially where the inference is from "somewhat ambiguous" language. See *Easton v. Childs*, 67 Minn. 242, 244, 69 N. W. 903, 904; 20 Harv. Law Rev. 591. And that there are sufficient other grounds, will presently be shown.

Again, the majority opinion's discussion of clause "c" of this section, 30 Stat. 547, is not altogether convincing. 157 Fed. 366, 367, 374-375, 19 Am. B. R. 581-582, 593. And the asserted "unavoidable inference" from this clause, 157 Fed. 366, 19 Am. B. R. 581, is not an inference upon which it would be safe to found a general rule,—not an inference helpful to a clear understanding of the clause's meaning in the more common case where one at least of the partners is insolvent. It is worthy of note, though of course not conclusive against Judge Sanborn's position, that the text-book authorities put clause "c" to quite different uses: see Collier, Bankruptcy, 9th ed., 161-162; Brandenburg, Bankruptcy, 3d ed., secs. 152 (and note 13), 153.. And 2 Remington, Bankruptcy, sec. 2233, cites clause "c" for the proposition that "the trustee elected by the partnership creditors becomes, by virtue of his office, trustee of each of the individual estates of the several partners,"—which is little more than a quotation of the statute. Also, the text of Loveland, Bankruptcy, 3d ed., 303, sec. 98, does nothing more than to quote the statute, though it cites in the notes a decision opposed to the ruling in the *Bertenshaw* case.

In the criticism of the majority opinion's discussion of special clauses of section 5, I have refrained from quotation of the opinion, merely referring thereto, in order to save space and because, as will presently be seen, this criticism plays but a minor part in my decision; it would not be ventured at all, except that I do not endorse the entire course of reasoning even of an opinion which has probably done more than any other to place the entity doctrine upon a firm. and it is to be hoped, final basis. The majority opinion, in spite of its above .noted misconceptions, as I respectfully deem them, and in spite of the very able and useful dissent of Judge Hook, has given a severe blow to a theory contra, which had' the distinguished support of Judge Lowell. *In re Forbes*, 128 Fed. 137, 11 Am. B. R. 787.

And, also, despite the foregoing minor criticisms, Judge Sanborn firmly establishes his court's ruling by pointing out the principle that the trustee has title to nothing but the estate of the bankrupt, i. e., the partnership entity. 157 Fed. 368-369, 371-372, 19 Am. B. R. 584-585, 588-589, and by showing the significant omission, from the new act, of the provision of the corresponding section, 36, of the act of 1867, 14 Stat. 534, Rev. Stat. sec. 5121, that "all the joint stock and property of the copartnership and also *all the separate estate of each of the partners* shall be taken and administered," 157 Fed. 374, 19 Am. B. R. 592; and also, by reciting as a reductio ad absurdum the parallel case of a surety.—for, as the surety of an insolvent principal cannot be brought into the bankruptcy of that principal, neither can the non-bankrupt partners here, who are "to

CITY CONTRACTING &c. CO., BANKRUPT. 153

a limited extent . . . sureties for the debts of the partnership," 157 Fed. 368, 371, 19 Am. B. R. 584, 586, be drawn into the bankruptcy of their firm. Or, in other words, the analogy is perfect between the surety of a bankrupt principal on the one hand and on the other the firm members, who in the language of the Scots law (whereunder the firm is an entity, the same as under this act) are "cautioners for the company rather than principal debtors," 20 Enc. Britt., 11th ed., 875, tit. "partnership," or, whose liability is, as stated by the Scotch commentator, "a *guarantee* by each to third parties of all the engagements legally undertaken in the social name," 1 Bell,Principles of the Law of Scotland, 9th ed., 242, sec. 351. And see adverse review of *In re Perley & Hays,* 138 Fed. 927, 15 Am. B. R. 54, in 19 Harv. Law. Rev., 615-616.

The language of the concluding portion of clause "c" is difficult to dispose of before reaching the result of the majority opinion in the *Bertenshaw* case, but it must be disposed of; and this opinion, notwithstanding its admirable dialectic qualities, is weakened by its failure to discuss a provision of the statute affording probably the most cogent basis for an argument in support of the drawing of the estate of every individual partner in all cases into the administration in a firm bankruptcy. The language referred to is: "The court of bankruptcy which has jurisdiction of one of the partners may have jurisdiction . . . of the administration of the partnership and *individual property.*" My conviction is that this provision applies solely when the partner is drawn into the administration, either because he is personally subject to adjudication, or, perhaps, because he consents,—for mere consent would not give jurisdiction without some underlying authority to take jurisdiction, wherefore, for one reason, the enactment of this provision of clause "c". And attention is directed to the significance of the use, in this clause, of the potential mood and the auxiliary verb "may," instead of the indicative mood and the auxiliary verb "shall;" for surely if the administration of a partner's estate is independent of his solvency or insolvency, the indicative mood would seem to be absolutely required. Administration of the individual property was not inevitable, or the word "may" would not have been used. It must be confessed, though, that the words "individual property" are here ambiguous and their effect not carefully thought out by the lawmakers. See 20 Harv. Law Rev., 591. But, apart from the merit of such an argument from the use of the potential mood, it may suffice to suggest in brief outline a few less technical and perhaps more practical considerations which, though indirect, outweigh, to my mind, the more direct force of the words "and individual property," standing alone in this clause and possibly seeming to call for the administration of such individual property in any and every case of a partnership bankruptcy.

A comparison of the former act with the present act, is helpful to a view of things in their true light. There has already been noted, as having been emphasized by Judge Sanborn, the signal omission from the act of 1898 of the provision of the act of 1867 for administration of both firm and individual estates in a partnership bankruptcy.

It may now be noted, too, that the provisions of the act of 1867 applied only to individual partners who were insolvent, and were so found in the firm proceeding, inasmuch as the firm could be adjudged bankrupt only upon the insolvency of all its members. Parsons, Partnership, 4th ed., 479, sec. 385. See *In re Penn,* 19 Fed. Cas. 151, 154, No. 10, 927, 5 Ben. 89, in which Judge Blatchford holds, or implies, that all the partners should be adjudged bankrupt. See also, as suggestive, *In re Burton,* 4 Fed. Cas. 863, 865, No. 2,214, 9 Ben. 324, *In re Bennett,* 3 Fed. Cas. 209, 210, No. 1,314, 2 Lowell, 400, and Lowell, Bankruptcy, sec. 119. This is the strongest kind of an argument to support the majority opinion in the *Bertenshaw* case, that the trustee

of a partnership has no title or right to the estate of the
non-bankrupt partner and that the court of bankruptcy
can give him none. The estates of solvent partners could
not, ex natura rei, be administered under the former act.
And does the mere change from the "aggregate" doctrine
to the entity doctrine require or even permit the administration of such estates against the will of the solvent owners?
The creditors, under the entity doctrine, have all the
remedies to be justly expected from the courts under the
statute, unless the courts are themselves to legislate,—for
some cases of which, on this very subject, there has been
severe criticism. 20 Harv. Law Rev. 595, 600.

If it be said, as one court declares, *Francis v. McNeal*,
186 Fed. 484, 26 Am. B. R. 559, and as Judge Hook,
dissenting in the *Bertenshaw* case, 157 Fed. 376, 19
Am. B. R. 595-595, suggests, that it is not to be
supposed that bankruptcy, a remedy of creditors as
well as of debtors, was to lose its remedial efficiency,
upon our discarding the old theory for the new
entity doctrine, it may be replied, that under the old law
all the members could be reached, as the almost unexceptionable rule at least, only when all the members were
insolvent, but that now under the new law the very same
thing can be done under the very same condition of universal insolvency and, in addition, the courts can reach the
firm as an entity if it has jurisdiction of only one member,
—which is one phase of the application of the above discussed clause "c." See *In re Dunnigan*, 95 Fed. 428, 2 Am.
B. R. 628, reflecting the practice under the former statute:
see *In re Bertenshaw*, 157 Fed. 372, 19 Am. B. R. 589. The
certainty may. be observed here, in passing, that Congress
adopted the entity principle in order to remove some weakness of the former law, to supply something which should
give the creditor a more direct, speedy, and effective remedy
against the firm and its members. 2 Sutherland, Stat.
Constr., 2 ed., sec. 471. The defect in view would seem to

be, that as a rule at least, under the former law the creditors could, as just suggested, do nothing with the firm unless or until they could get every single member into court or unless every single member was bankrupt. The attendant difficulties may be imagined. See, e. g., *In re Meyer*, 98 Fed. 976, 979-980, 3 Am. B. R. 559, 563.

In Judge Hook's dissent, 157 Fed. 376, 19 Am. B. R. 595, so much is made of the matter of discharge as determinative of the question, as to call for a caution against surprise at any discovery of the new statute's incapability of wholly harmonious or absolutely consistent application. Too much should not be expected of the entity doctrine, nor should there be any felt necessity of working the doctrine to extremes or holding it up to impracticable tests. Thus, for a very extreme instance, the entity doctrine is not to fail because of the fact that the court cannot send the entity to jail for contempt. It must be remembered, too, that the entity status was created for benefit of creditors as well as of debtors,—and creditors are not necessarily concerned with the debtor's discharge, while, in any event, all natural insolvent parties ultimately liable or liable as sureties, guarantors, or cautioners, i. e., the firm members, may have their discharge for the trouble of submitting to bankruptcy administration. This matter of discharge has proved somewhat of a stumbling block in another case. *In re Forbes*, 128 Fed. 137, 139-140, 11 Am. B. R. 787, 790.

Finally, the essential purpose of bankruptcy should have great weight in the determination of the question. That purpose is, not to get satisfaction of the creditor's claims, but to take out of the hands of the dishonest or inefficient insolvent debtor a business or an estate going bad and likely to go from bad to worse,—a business or an estate equitably charged with these claims,—and to conserve it and the debtor's assets with the view of an ultimate division among the claimants pro rata. A solvent partner, on the other hand, is in quite different case; his financial condition is presumably not becoming shaky; the creditors are presumably in no danger of losing or of seeing impaired the security of their legal claims against him, against whom and whose property they still continue to have ample remedies. There is no need of the court's taking his property out of his hands and placing it in the hands of a trustee, and no reasonable hope of a trustee's being able to manage it any better in the interests of creditors. But this consideration is based, not so much on any regard for the solvent partner of a bankrupt firm, though he is entitled to regard, as upon a sense of the creditors' obligation to exhaust their ample ordinary remedies against such partner so far as they may choose to look to him at all. The majority opinion in the *Bertenshaw* case may lean toward this view, but is hereinabove criticised for going too far in the interest of the solvent partner, even to the extent of giving to him the administration of the insolvent firm's estate. 157 Fed. 369, 19 Am. B. R. 583.

The views of Professor Brannen are added by reference and adopted as my own. 20 Harv. Law Rev. 594-597, 598-603.

[4] Before leaving this subject, it is worth while to, independently, dispose of two leading decisions which might be cited in support of my order for the schedules of all partners, *In re Ceballos*, 161 Fed. 451, 20 Am. B. R. 467, and *In re Solomon & Carvel*, 163 Fed. 140, 141, 20 Am. B. R. 488, 490. These decisions are founded on General Order viii of the Supreme Court, 172 U. S. 655, 89 Fed. vi, Collier, Bankruptcy, 9th ed. 1058-1059. But, on reflection and by reason of considerations already suggested, this general order would seem to be without authority, so far at least as applying to any other firm member than one adjudicated bankrupt in a partnership bankruptcy. The only arguable basis therefor apparent in the statute is clause "c" above discussed, providing that, "The court of bankruptcy which has jurisdiction of one of the partners may have jurisdiction of

all the partners and of the administration of the partnership *and individual property.*" So far as concerns any power
to make rules, derived from section 2, clause 15, of the act,
30 Stat. 546, as a basis for the possible wide scope of this
General Order, it is to be observed that the power
to made rules is not the power to legislate:
rules may enforce the statute but not enlarge it.
And so far as concerns any policy of liberal construction to
effect the remedial purpose of the act, it is not to be overlooked that to construe liberally is not to read into the
statute something which its own terms do not clearly express or imply. See Collier, Bankruptcy, 9th ed., 572-573,
and notes; 1 Remington, Bankruptcy, sec. 26; Anderson,
Law Dic., 911-912, tit. "rule." It is likely that the Supreme
Court in General Order viii has followed too closely General
Order xviii of the law of 1867. See Collier, Bankruptcy, 9th
ed., 1058, note; 20 Harv. Law Rev. 591.

[2b]   Now, as regards the jurisdiction given by the act
over "individual property:" we cannot predicate upon clause
"c" of section 5, or any other apparent provision of the act,
a power to require schedules, any more than we can predicate thereupon a power to require the solvent partner to
turn over to the court for administration those individual
assets and and liabilities of his own which his schedules
would disclose. While the power to require schedules, and
the advantages to the creditors of having schedules, might
exist independently of the existence of any power to require
the solvent partner to turn over his assets for administration, nevertheless inasmuch as the trustee has under the act
no right or authority that has been discovered, for proceeding in any way against the solvent partner or the solvent
partner's property, I fail to see any reason for the requirement from the partner of schedules of matters with which
the trustee has, thus, legally not the slightest concern.

If, as is the law, the trustee has no control over the
property of the non-bankrupt partner and, as would seem

on principle, no right to sue such partner on account of his individual liability to the creditors, why require schedules? The creditors have, still, the right to look to the solvent, or to the non-bankrupt, partner for satisfaction, and strictly they would seem to be the only ones who can sue such partner on his liability. Judge Sanborn and Professor Brannen before him have pointed out the availability and efficiency of the creditors' common remedies, so well as to make undesirable anything more than a mere reference to their discussions, and so well also as to dispel all fears and all considerations of policy in the interest of creditors as against the liable individual partners and their personal estates. 157 Fed. 368, 369, 19 Am. B. R. 584, 585; 20 Harv. Law Rev. 595, 596. See, also section 16 of the act, 30 Stat. 550, by which the individual partner's liability as a surety or "cautioner" would be preserved even after the discharge of the bankrupt firm.

And it is suggested, though by no means a conclusive point, that while the court requires the bankrupt firm or a bankrupt member to file schedules as of the date of the filing of petition (see *In re Harris*, 2 Am. B. R. 359, 363; act, sec. 1, clause "10;" see, also, act, sec. 70, clause "a"), yet thereafter the court has no concern with the bankrupt's assets or liabilities, the bankrupt being freed from all liabilities of subsequent incurrence, subject always, of course, to the consummation of his discharge, act, sec. 14, clause "a." But with the non-bankrupt partner, the case is quite different: the liability which would bring him into the bankruptcy proceeding at all, his so-called in-solido liability, continues even after the basic date, so that from him schedules would ever be called for with every change of his financial condition. Such difficulty or inconsistency may not be crucial, however.

Although not directly involved, there must be disposed of in advance any argument that, as the in-solido liability of the partners is one of the "resources"—I do not recall having seen them described as "assets"—of the firm, from which the trustee can realize by suit if necessary, therefore he and the court in bankruptcy are entitled to such knowledge of the nature and condition of each partner's estate as the schedules would afford.   The decisions in *Dickas v. Barnes*, 140 Fed. 849, 851, 15 Am. B. R. 566, 568, and *In re Junck & Balthazard*, 169 Fed. 481, 484, 22 Am. B. R. 298, 302, declare this personal liability to be a "resource" of the firm; and Professor Brannen observes that "under an ideally developed entity theory of partnership, the partners would be looked upon as contributories bound in virtue of the partnership relation to contribute to the firm, in case of its insolvency or bankruptcy, enough to make up any deficiency in partnership assets to pay firm debts," and that "the trustee as the representative of the firm in bankruptcy would then be entitled to sue the partners for such contribution." "But," he continues, "the enactment by Congress of a provision for adjudication of the firm as bankrupt cannot change the nature of the partner's liability. That is fixed by the law of the States and remains the same, namely, an obligation directly to the creditors;" though he then says, "It might, however, seem dogmatic to assert that there could not also be, alongside of and in addition to the direct liability to the creditors, another liability to the firm, enforceable in case of the insolvency or bankruptcy of the firm—a liability to contribute to the payment of debts after the exhaustion of the partnership assets,—but no direct authority has been found." 20 Harv. Law Rev. 603. [Set *Selig v. Hami Hon*, 234 U. S. 652, 661, par. "(1)".]

This may all be true,—as no denial is here called for,— and yet it is hard to see how any such consideration would give the court the right to require from a non-bankrupt or solvent partner who at best under this theory of entity is merely debtor to the firm, a disclosure such as the schedules would afford of intimate details of his personal business affairs. The unreasonableness and injustice of such requirement of schedules and, a fortiori, the oppression and un-called-for injury from a seizure of his property and the administration of his personal estate, all against his will, are so apparent as to need no further discussion.

The most that could be predicated of this in-solido lia-bility as a "resource" of the firm upon which the trustee could realize, would seem to be a right in a court of equity to an accounting from the individual partners; and, in this connection, Professor Brannen has a suggestion which it may be pardonable to note in anticipation as worthy of con-sideration, though he is obviously indicating what "the court should have jurisdiction to order," rather than what the court has jurisdiction to order. See 20 Harv. Law. Rev. 603-604, citing *Jordan v. Miller*, 75 Va. 442, 454, a suit for dissolution of partnership and for an accounting, wherein each partner was ordered to contribute pro rata towards the deficiency resultant upon application of firm assets to firm debts. Whether this court as a court of bankruptcy has it-self any such equity powers, the narrow limits of the point under discussion do not require me, nor am I quite prepared, to determine here,—though confessing doubt of the posses-sion of those powers by a court of bankruptcy as such, what-ever be the soundness of any possible suggestion that the trustee may have a remedy in State or Territorial, as distin-guished from Federal, equity courts.

Wherefore, let the order herein made requiring schedules from the non-bankrupt partners, be set aside. In view of the fact that these partners, of the Oriental laboring class, ignorant of our laws and even of our language, have been better advised than the court in this matter of schedules, no order will be made citing them for contempt for their delinquencies or even for their disregard of what until now stood as the court's order, and until now appeared to re-quire from them obedience and respect,—and probably no such citation could be made consistently with my ruling herein. See *In re Sawyer*, 124 U. S. 200, 221-222, and note dissent of Waite, C. J., at 223; 7 A. & E. Enc. L., 2d ed., 56-57.

Since the firm adjudication, the partner Lau Chung has presented to the clerk of court for filing, his separate petition for adjudication as an individual, with schedules in due form.

[3a]   The question, then, arises, whether these partners who desire to be adjudged bankrupt may be so adjudged in this partnership proceeding, and, also, the incidental question raised by the clerk, whether separate costs and fees are to be paid by each bankrupt partner.

Although the courts are not entirely agreed, as to whether a firm should be adjudged bankrupt without adjudication of all its individual members: Collier, Bankruptcy, 9th ed.. secs. 147, 148, 152, 158, and notes; 1 Remington, Bankruptcy, secs. 60, 61; 3 Id. sec. 60; *Mills v. Fisher*, 159 Fed. 897, 899, 20 Am. B. 237, 239, Lurton, Circuit Judge; *In re Forbes*, supra, Lowell, District Judge; yet apparently no court holding a firm to be subject to adjudication without adjudication of its members, would deny that, in a firm proceeding, all the partners or any partner might also be so adjudged. 1 Remington, Bankruptcy, sec. 64; *In re Springer*, 199 Fed. 294, 298, 29 Am. B. R. 96, 100-101. There seems to be no reason why those members who here appeared in response to summons and then in open court asked to be adjudicated, should not be granted that privilege in the firm proceeding. An order to that end would, really, amount to nothing more than an amendment of the petition, which unquestionably could be granted, by way of allowing the prayer to include not only the firm but its members. See General Order xi, 172 U. S. 657, 89 Fed. vii.; Collier, Bankruptcy, 9th ed., 21, par. "b;" Fletcher, Eq. Pr., secs. 53, 378; Story, Eq. Pl., 10th ed., sec. 884. Such an order would facilitate the administration. To that end the member's voluntary surrender of his assets should be encouraged. It is, surely, within the broad equity powers of a court of bankruptcy, with reference to practice, to so order. See Collier, Bankruptcy, 9th ed., 21-22. Another reason for this view is that, in my opinion, as above intimated, the estate of the individual partner who is adjudged insolvent, or who consents, may be drawn into the administration of the firm's affairs. Moreover, even if the individual adjudication be an entirely separate matter from the firm adjudication, still the two proceedings could properly be consolidated. See Lowell, Bankruptcy, sec. 119. So that to raise objections to the adjudication of the member in this proceeding would be to "strain at gnats." His adjudication is only a helpful circumstance and quite proper in the present proceeding.

The partner Lau Chung may, therefore, be adjudged bankrupt in the firm bankruptcy. Let his petition be filed herein. As to the other partners who at the hearing expressed the desire to be adjudicated, an adjudication will be made herein upon their filing forthwith their separate petitions with schedules in due form. See Collier, Bankruptcy, 9th ed., 144, par. "b." Each such petition should be entitled, as the major title at least, in the matter of the individual partner himself and not in the name of the firm; in order, partly, to insure or facilitate notice to the creditors of the partners as distinguished from the creditors of the firm, and the clerk, referee and trustee will see that all notices to the partners' individual creditors are entitled accordingly. See *In re Gorman,* 2 U. S. Dist. Ct. Haw. 439, 15 Am. B. R. 587.

[3b]   On the question of the necessity of separate costs and fees in case of each partner adjudged bankrupt, the courts are, also, divided. 1 Remington, Bankruptcy, sec. 289 and note 165; Collier, Bankruptcy, 9th ed., 682-683 and notes. With the most fully considered decision, however, *In re Barden,* 101 Fed. 555, 4 Am. B. R. 31, I do not agree. Here, again, are plausible considerations of policy invoked to sustain a ruling and, more erroneous, the seizing upon minor details of the statute and emphasizing them beyond any dream of the law-maker. From a single instance, of

the use of the word "estate," an argument is built up of what the law possibly ought to be, rather than of what it actually is. It requires something more than the mere use of the word "estate" in one single place in the statute,— and that not the first place, providing for fees, where, if this word were so important, its use would naturally have been called for,—in order to support the conclusion reached by the court in the *Barden* case. Why should the law-makers have been so careful to use the word "estate" in case of the clerk, act, sec. 52, clause "a," while using only the colorless word "case" with reference to the referee (act, sec. 40, clause "a"), and the trustee (act, sec. 48, clause "a"), the duties of each of whom are far more onerous and responsible than those of the clerk whose duties are largely routine,—the duties of referee and trustee often calling for a high degree of initiative, discretion, and good judgment?

And the fact, as it seems, that no such double fee system was provided or in operation under the act of 1867, even when all the partners were, as a rule, adjudged in one proceeding, may be worthy of consideration in this connection. See Rev. Stat. sec. 5124; Id. sec. 5121; G. O. Supreme Court, Oct. Term, 1874; Bump, Bankruptcy, 9th ed. 868-871; Id. 785-788.

The rulings in the cases of *In re Langslow*, 98 Fed. 869, 3 Am. B. R. 529, note, and *In re Gay*, 98 Fed. 872, 3 Am. B. R. 529, though barren of discussion are, in my opinion, sound, and the fully considered ruling in the *Barden* case, and in the case of *In re Farley*, 115 Fed. 359, 8 Am. B. R. 266, which follows it, unsound. It is therefore held, that separate costs and fees need not be paid by each involvent partner who is adjudged bankrupt in this proceeding and whose estate is drawn herein for adjudication with the estate of the firm; except, however, for the requirement from each such partner of a deposit of the customary amount to cover costs of advertising notices to his individual creditors,—such expense being not, of course, covered by the deposit already made for advertising notices to the firm creditors. But, in order that this advantage may be enjoyed, the petition and schedules of each partner must be filed herein forthwith.

In conclusion, if any excuse for the length of this opinion be in order, it must be assigned to the unsatisfactory state of the precedénts, and if any excuse for that unsatisfactory condition be desired, then, the discriminiating Professor Brannen may again be quoted: "But the possibility of finding such apparent contradictions between different clauses of the section [act, sec. 5], as well as the reenactment by section 54 of the old rule of distribution of the partnership and individual estates, indicates that the scheme of treatment of partnerships in bankruptcy was not fully thought out by the draftsmen to its logical conclusion. The theory was a new thing, and the changes necessary to the application of the theory seem not to have been carefully considered." 20 Harv. Law. Rev. 591. And another, and earlier, commentator in the same publication, 19 Harv. Law. Rev. 615-616, observes justly, "This unwarranted result of administering in a firm proceeding the estates of non-bankrupt partners indicates a failure to appreciate fully the legislative innovation in partnership law, and shows an unconscious adherence to the older law."

Surely, a statute lending itself to such differences of opinion—differences both major and minor and of all degrees—and to such varied construction by men so learned and experienced as the differing judges, calls loudly for amendment. It is not fair, that the courts should be put to such vast but preventable labor as a conscientious judge feels obliged to give to a case like the present.

———

Reported, 30 Am. B. R. 133. *Overruled*, as to question of administration of individual estate in firm proceeding (syllabus, par. 2, supra): *Francis v. McNeill*, 228 U. S. 695, May 29, 1913.

UNITED STATES OF AMERICA *v.* JAMES F. FIND-LAY, T. CLIVE DAVIES AND W. H. BAIRD .

January 20, 1913.

1. *Evidence—Parol evidence rule—Extrinsic evidence to show bond's legal object:* In a suit on a bond, though the bond may be capable of being read as contemplating an unauthorized arbitration, yet when extrinsic facts would show the intent of an authorized submission to a government officer for remission of penalties under Rev. Stat. sec. 5294, as amended, such facts are admissible in evidence, in order to effectuate the bond when that may be done without varying its terms.

2. *Public officers—Power and authority—Submission to arbitration:* United States officers have no authority, in the absence of statute, to submit to arbitration a controversy as to the fact of violations of law.

3. *Same—Same—Penalties—Remission proceedings—Requirement of bond from applicant:* The Secretary of Commerce and Labor has authority, under Rev. Stat. sec. 5294, as amended, to exact or accept from an applicant for remission of statutory penalties, a bond to secure payment thereof in case of the application's disallowance.

4. *Estoppel—To deny public officer's authority—Penalty-remission proceedings:* A ship's master violating the Passenger Act of 1882, 22 Stat. 186, as amended, who on his own request and for his own advantage obtains clearance of his vessel under bond for payment of "such penalties as may be determined by the Department (Secretary) of Commerce and Labor to have been incurred," on submission of the facts, and whose pursuant submission admits the violation but sets up alleged extenuating circumstances, is estopped to deny the submission to be an application for remission of penalties within the Secretary's power under Rev. Stat. sec. 5294, as amended, when, otherwise, the master and his ship would escape satisfaction of such penalties.

5. *Statutes—Revised Statutes—Conflict with preexisting laws:* In interpreting the Revised Statutes, resort may not be had to original antecedent acts of Congress except in case of ambiguity of the revision.

6. *Penalties—Remission proceedings—Bond:* As above, paragraphs 1, 3, 4.

7. *Shipping—Violation of regulations—Remission of penalties:* As above, paragraph 4.

At Law: Action of debt on bond.

R. W. Breckons, U. S. District Attorney, for plaintiff.

C. H. Olson and *I. M. Stainback (Holmes, Stanley & Olson* with them) for defendants.

CLEMONS, J. This is an action of debt to recover $7,960, on a bond of the defendant Findlay, master of the British steamship Orteric, as principal, and the defendants Davies and Baird as sureties, conditioned upon the payment to the United States of America through the collector of customs at the port of Honolulu, of such penalties as, in the language of this instrument, should "be determined by the Department of Commerce and Labor to have been incurred by the said master" by reason of alleged violations of the Passenger Act of 1882 as amended (hereinafter referred to as the Act), 22 Stat. 186; Act of Feb. 14, 1903, sec. 10, 32 Stat. 829; Act of Feb. 9, 1905, 33 Stat. 711; Act of Dec. 19, 1908, 35 Stat. 583. By stipulation in writing the case was submitted to the court for determination without a jury. From the evidence the facts appear as hereinafter set forth.

On arrival of the British steamship Orteric at the port of Honolulu, April 13, 1911, on a voyage from Oporto and Gibraltar, carrying passengers composed mainly of Portuguese and Spanish immigrants destined for Hawaii, an examination of the vessel was made by customs officers assigned to that duty by the collector pursuant to the provision of the Act, section 11. This inspection resulted in a report of April 17, disclosing violations of the following sections of the act: 2, relating to berths; 3, light and ventilation; 4, food; 5, hospitals; 6, discipline and cleanliness; 7, posting of notices prohibiting ship's company from visiting steerage quarters. Immediately the collector gave written notice to the master of his liability to penalties in respect to the ship Orteric for these violations, specifying them in detail, and also for violations of section 9 relating to passenger manifests. Moreover, this notice stated the maximum penalty in each instance, offering an opportunity to "present any statements desired," and directed attention to section 13 of the act providing a lien upon the offending ship for these penalties. Thereafter the local agents of the Orteric directed to the collector a letter dated April 22, requesting him to cable to the Secretary of Commerce and Labor (hereinafter called the Secretary) for permission to grant clearance to the Orteric "upon a satisfactory bond being furnished for the payment of any penalties which may be imposed in respect to the alleged violations of the Passenger Act by that steamer, . . . full particulars regarding the matter to be furnished to the Department of Commerce and Labor for their determination of what shall be done in connection therewith." On the same day the agents had already directed another letter to the collector, making "application for clearance of the said steamer for Virtoria, British Columbia," and "in view of the alleged violations" offering to "furnish an adequate bond covering the same, providing that the facts concerning such alleged violations be submitted to the Secretary . . . for determination." The collector, by cable, notified the Secretary of the application for clearance "under bond covering alleged penalties" and recommended "favorable consideration," to which the acting Secretary replied by cable of April 22, "With approval United States attorney clear Orteric, fifteen thousand dollar bond." The bond in suit, for this amount, was thereupon executed and by the United States attorney was "approved as to form and sureties." The bond recites, by way of introduction, the collector's notice to the master of the latter's having "incurred certain penalties on account of alleged violations" of the act, and the department's authority to the collector to grant immediate clearance upon the furnishing of an approved bond "to insure the payment of such penalties for such violations aforesaid as shall be determined by the department . . . to have been incurred by the said master after the presentation within a reasonable time, by. the said master, or his agents or attorneys, and the officials of the United States at Honolulu, of the facts, to said department." The condition of the bond is the payment by the master to the United States through the collector, of "the amount which the Department of Commerce and Labor of the United States shall, upon such presentation of facts, determine that the said principal is liable for on account of such penalties so alleged to have been incurred." Upon delivery of the bond to the collector, on April 23, clearance was granted forthwith.

Thereafter the Honolulu attorneys for the master sent to the collector, a letter dated April 27, in which "in order to preserve the rights" of their client, they "formally protest against the imposition of the penalties aforesaid and all penalties whatsoever that may be imposed on account of alleged violations" of the act, but promise to file with the collector as soon as possible "a full statement of the facts concerning the said alleged violations, to be submitted to the Department of Commerce and Labor in order that it may arrive at a proper determination of the matter."

After some extention of time granted to the master for his submission of facts, the collector, on June 14, received from the Honolulu attorneys a letter "submit(ting) for presentation to the Department of Commerce and Labor," the affidavits of the master, the chief officer, the ship's doctor, and one of the nurses of the Orteric, and "copies of notices in the English, Portuguese and Spanish languages, which were posted according to the above mentioned affidavits as required by said section 7 of the Act, and which the master's attorneys state were "obtained" by them "on board the S. S. Orteric from the captain and chief officer thereof." Also, this letter promised an endeavor to have the owners furnish the department with a copy of the ship's plans and specifications referred to in the master's affidavit, and asked permission to submit a supplementary presentation of facts

concerning the alleged violations of section 3, as to ventilating apparatus, by affidavit or affidavits to be secured immediately upon the return of a Mr. Campbell who was to
arrive in Honolulu on June 16, and who was expected to
establish the fact of inspection and approval of the ventilating apparatus at the port of clearance by emigration officers. There is no evidence before the court, however, that
any submission of the plans and specifications, or any supplementary presentation of facts as to ventilating apparatus, was ever made. A summarization of the affidavits
follows.

Section 2, Berths: The master admits the violation of
section 2 of the act in that all single male passengers were,
after March 5, not berthed in the fore part of the vessel in
a compartment separate from the space or spaces appropriated to other passengers, but on account of a riot between
the Spanish and Portuguese male passengers it was "in
order to maintain discipline and prevent bloodshed . . .
deemed mandatory to segregate the Portuguese passengers
from the Spanish passengers, and therefore the affiant removed said Portuguese male single passengers from said
compartment in the fore part of the said vessel aft."

Section 3, Light and Ventilation: The master does not
attempt to show the ship's provisions for light and ventilation to have conformed with the requirements of the act
but deposes to his "belief that ventilating devices in each
compartment occupied by passengers . . . were equal
in capacity and utility to the ventilating specifications set
forth in section 3 of the Act, . . . as will be more particularly shown by a copy of the plans now in possession of
. . . the owners of said steamship, and the specifications attached thereto, to be supplied for use in connection
with this affidavit" (but, as above stated, not supplied).
On the contrary, the master attempts to bring the case
within the concession made by this section of the Act, that
"in any steamship the ventilating apparatus provided, or

any method of ventilation adopted thereon, which has been approved by the emigration officers at the port or place from which said vessel was cleared, shall be deemed a compliance with the foregoing provisions." In this behalf, he deposes, "that on the 21st day of February, 1911, the said steamship was cleared from the port of Oporto in Portugal, . . . ; that on the day preceding about 10 Portuguese officials, among whom affiant believes were included Portuguese emigrant officials, carefully inspected the said steamship, . . . with reference to construction, equipment, food supply and ventilation, and [the said steamship] was approved in all such respects and otherwise by all of said officials." As to water closets the master deposes "that there were sufficient closets in number in proportion to the number of passengers according to the requirements of said section 3, . . . all enclosed, some of which were located on one side of the upper deck . . . and the others on the other side of said upper deck." Nothing is said as to the closets being "properly enclosed and located" or "kept and maintained in a serviceable and cleanly condition throughout the voyage," within the provisions of the Act, though these were subjects of complaint by the collector, and though the point to which the affidavit is especially directed, sufficiency in number of closets, is not made by the collector at all but is conceded by his letter of April 17, and therefore called for no reply or statement in behalf of the ship. Moreover, the benefit of official inspection is not by the above exception extended to the matter of closets.

The affidavit's introductory statement should here be noted, "that on the 24th day of February, 1911, the said steamship left Gibraltar with about 1,500 Spanish and Portuguese emigrant passengers aboard whose destination was Honolulu, . . . that about 550 of said passengers were Portuguese and the remainder Spanish;" and it should be noted that nothing is said as to whether some of these passengers were taken on at Gibraltar—in which case a new and favorable inspection would be required, to bring the case within the benefit of the above exception. The above-mentioned report of the inspectors was in the hands of the Secretary for consideration in this case; it shows that 1,000 of the passengers were taken on at Gibraltar after there had been taken on at Oporto, three days before, but 300 passengers, and at Lisbon, two days before, only 252 more. So the master, while claiming exemption, has failed to show that he is within the proviso of section 3,—indeed, has apparently attempted to mislead the Secretary by such a suppression and perversion of facts as would imply an inspection after *all*, instead of about a third of, the passengers had been taken aboard.

Section 4, Food: The master here also deposes by way of concession and justification, or confession and avoidance, "'that while milk for infants and children was served regularly only twice a day, nevertheless mothers of such infants and children were at all times supplied upon application with condensed milk at other times, and often served at irregular times without application."

Section 5, Hospitals: The master deposes that the hospital compartments were "ventilated by large skylights and portholes," but does not meet the complaint that the ventilation was insufficient. He also deposes to the utilization as hospitals of two large compartments aggregating more than 1,500 square feet, but gives details showing that the access of air was not direct and was cut off in rough weather. On this point the affidavit appears to dodge the question of the suitability of the regular hospital and to attempt to divert attention therefrom to two special make-shift hospitals.

Section 6, Discipline and Cleanliness: The master makes no denial of the alleged filthy condition of the ship, but deposes that he, the chief officer, the ship's doctor, and an interpreter, almost every day, and one or more of them every day, inspected the ship and passengers and "warned and directed the passengers to keep themselves in a cleanly condition and to stay on the upper deck as much as possible," and "directed said passengers to air their baggage and bedding whenever the weather would permit, but with few exceptions the said passengers refused to do so, stating that they feared their belongings would be stolen;" and he deposes that on account of the great number of passengers, the crew could not air the bedding and baggage without the passengers' assistance, and that at all times the crew "was engaged in cleaning the decks and compartments and did all in that respect that could reasonably be done." The master thus, in effect, regards the statutory duty of the ship as performed by its officers merely directing the passengers to maintain cleanliness The ship's condition of disorder and filth on arrival at Honolulu is attributed to excitement of the passengers in view of the approach of land and end of the voyage,—who threw the remnants of their breakfast about the floors and decks, instead of overboard as they had customarily done theretofore, and also to the tearing of cloth from mattresses in order to make bags for their belongings, with consequent scattering of the mattress-stuffing.   And it is stated, that it was at the collector's direction that the ship was left in this condition for several days after docking,—a precaution, by the way, which enabled the inspectors, and the grand jury who also visited the ship, to see conditions in statu quo.

The master then deposes to the posting of copies of section 6 of the Act, in the Portuguese and Spanish languages, in all of the companionways and in various parts of the vessel; but states that in the course of the voyage many of them were torn down by passengers, and that such notices were again posted about two weeks before reaching Honolulu; also that very few of the passengers could read,—as if the Act made this posting at all dependent upon the literacy of the passengers.

Section 9, Passenger Manifests: The master admits that

"the shifting of the passengers in order to segregate the Spanish from the Portuguese, resulted in some confusion, making it impossible for affiant to include in the list of passengers the exact compartments and spaces occupied by them thereafter."

The affidavit of the chief officers "confirms . . . in all respects" the affidavit of the master, as does the affidavit of the ship's doctor. The doctor also deposes that all compartments and decks were swept not less than twice daily, and were treated daily with a suitable disinfectant; that he would not permit the washing of apartments occupied by passengers because in his opinion and from the experience of physicians in charge of emigrant vessels, such washing results in unavoidable dampness highly detrimental to health. He deposes that "any and all accumulations . . . were rendered physically harmless and innocuous by disinfectants," and "the sleeping apartments were scraped with shovels every day and swept," and "most of the litter found on board . . . at Honolulu, was the result of food and rubbish and the contents of mattresses being thrown or strewn about the deck by the passengers in their excitement and haste to land." He says that "the temporary or additional hospital quarters . . . were, in the opinion of the affiant, well suited to that purpose considering the circumstances," but though deposing that he "directly superintended all of the sanitation and sanitary measures," he says nothing about the regular hospital and its ventilation. "The mortality on board said vessel," he attributes "very largely to the concealment by parents of the ailments of their children and their refusal to submit them to medical treatment." "While," as he says, "milk was served regularly only twice a day, nevertheless condensed milk was served at irregular times each day to the mothers for the use of such children, both upon application and without application;" "constant inspection was made by affiant, and milk supplied in all cases where it was found necessary," and "a quantity" (stating it) of condensed milk was provided "ample for the requirements of the children and nursing mothers." "The water supply for bathing and washing of said passengers was unlimited, and the usual accommodations for washing existed."

One of the nurses deposes that "she assisted throughout said voyage in caring for the passengers who were ill and for infants; that milk was served twice daily régularly . . . and at irregular times in addition whenever desired by the mothers of infant children and also whenever it appeared necessary to the hospital staff; that affiant believes that milk in ample quantities was served at all times." Her statements as to hospitals and ventilation are the same in substance as that of the master, whom she also confirms as to the riot and the consequent segregation of Portuguese and Spanish.

The collector thereupon, on June 17, forwarded to the Secretary, the master's showing of affidavits and copies of posted notices, and the collector's own showing which consisted of the bond in suit, the above-described letters and cablegrams (by original or copy), also the inspector's report of the vessel's condition, and a letter of the collector to the United States district attorney at Honolulu dated April 17, transmitting this report and calling attention to the violations of the Act, a letter (copy) of April 18 of the Portuguese consul at Honolulu to the governor of Hawaii protesting against the insanitary conditions of the vessel, the report (copy) of the grand jury for the April, 1911, term of this court adverse to the master on the same points as covered by the above-described letter of the collector to the master. And a few merely formal and immaterial letters of acknowledgment and of transmission between the collector and other officials were included among the papers presented to the Secretary. He also had before him a letter directed to the department by the Washington attorney for the owners, dated April 22, but not received until two days later, and perhaps of no bearing on the question of the object of a bond the negotiations for which had already been consummated by others, and the leading, attorneys in the matter at Honolulu, but which in fairness to the respondents should nevertheless be mentioned as possibly not so equivocal as the bond and the preceding Honolulu correspondence, and as more clearly capable of being read as contemplating some kind of an "adjudication," i. e., arbitration, by the Secretary. Though, under all the circumstances, the conclusion is inevitable that, even if this letter did imply an arbitration, it would not express the actual object of the negotiations. This conclusion is borne out by several considerations. In the first place, the Washington attorney had no part either in the preparation of the bond, or of the submission pursuant thereto, i. e., of the matter which the bond was intended to cover and which would indicate the bond's purpose; and it may be fairly found from the evidence, direct and circumstantial, that any light of his statements would be at most no more than dimly reflected light. Even giving his use of the word "adjudication" a strict sense, certainly not called for by any controlling fact or presumption of fact or of law (but quite the contrary), he, still, was not in as good position to characterize the proceedings as were those others who were active in the actual negotiations and on the field, and whose request for clearance discloses that the object of the proposed submission of "full particulars regarding the matter," was the Secretary's "determination of *what shall be done in connection therewith*" (agents' letter of April 22, above). Furthermore, while it might be a possible, though it is by no means a necessary, nor even the probable or reasonable, inference from the Washington attorney's letter of April 22, that it was he who had the first advice and direction from the owners of the vessel and so himself initiated the proceedings; still it is important to repeat that the Honolulu attorneys were the ones on the ground and that it was really their application for clearance, or that of the local agents under their guidance, which was acted upon, and not the application of the Washington attorney, whose letter, as suggested above, did not reach the department until two days after the vessel had cleared,—sent on a Saturday and not received until the following Monday (as shown by the department's receipt stamp on the face of the letter). Also, after the submission to the Secretary this attorney, though specially requesting by letter of July 11, further time for presentation of a "written brief of his contentions" to be "supplement(ed) . . . by a verbal presentation" of "the points which he desires the Department to consider," nevertheless failed to present any defense of the master or any argument in support of a defense,—indeed, did not appear at all, as he would naturally have done if the consideration of the Secretary had been quasi-judicial instead of executive, i. e., in the nature of judgment on disputed facts rather than of pardon for admitted acts.

This letter of April 22 recites the vessel's detention for alleged breaches of the Act, the details of which are unknown, and in view of the time required for this attorney and the Secretary to fully ascertain the facts and of the urgent importance of minimizing delay (as a cargo waited at Seattle), requests the department to instruct the collector by cable to report by cable "the cause of the detention with such details as may be necessary to enable the department to act on the owner's request, which is that permission be granted to the vessel to proceed on her voyage "upon her master or Honolulu agent entering into bond for the making good of any penalty found to be due either by the vessel or the master, and that upon the coming in of a formal report of the matter the questions involved be then adjudicated upon after a hearing."

The collector, in his letter of June 17 transmitting the papers in the case, reported penalties aggregating $7,960, as follows: "Section 2, $5 for each statute passenger,—1,242

@ $5,—$6,210; section 3, penalty of $250; section 4, ·misdemeanor reported to United States attorney; section 5, penalty of $250; section 6, penalty of $250; section 7, misdemeanor reported to United States attorney; section 9, penalty of $100." And it will be observed that in the consideration of the case, no action was taken as to the violations of a criminal nature, alleged in the collector's letter notifying the master of his liability, namely, breaches of sections 4 and 7 of the act, which are misdemeanors.

On December 4, 1911, the acting Secretary directed to the collector a letter in this matter, which he characterizes as "the application of James Findlay, master, for relief from the penalties incurred in the case of the steamer Orteric for violations of the Passenger Act," namely, sections 2, 3, 5, 6 and 9, but not sections 4 and 7 involving misdemeanors. After reviewing at length the report of the grand jury, the acting Secretary concludes:

"From the papers submitted it is evident that this vessel with 1,242 [statute] passengers was navigated on a voyage of eight weeks under all conditions of weather in violation of practically all of the provisions of the Passenger Act having to do with the health, comfort, and well-being of the passengers. The death of 57 children during the voyage marks this as the worst case ever submitted to the Department. The sexes were not properly segregated during a large portion of the voyage, the master stating that the confusion was such that it was impossible for him to state in the manifests the exact compartments and spaces occupied by the various passengers. The ventilation of the ship appears to have been wholly inadequate, this lack of ventilation in the opinion of the grand jury, increasing the rate of mortality. Ill ventilated hospital facilities without adequate equipment were furnished; the manifest of the vessel was not completed, and the sanitary conditions of the vessel were inexcusable. The Department concurs in the following extract from the report of the grand jury:

" 'We cannot emphasize too strongly the necessity for the observance of the regulations requiring vessels to be kept in a clean and sanitary condition. When poor immigrants, perhaps accustomed to modern methods of sanitation, are brought into a tropical climate such as Hawaii, not only their own good, but the good of the community in general is subserved by a rigid insistence on compliance with the law.'

"In the opinion of the Department, penalties aggregating $7,960 were incurred in this case for violation of the sections enumerated and it declines to intervene in behalf of the offenders."

Due notice of this determination was given to the principal and sureties and demand made for payment of $7,960 covering the above penalties, but such payment the obligors have refused and neglected to make.

[1a] When the action came on for hearing, the evidence first submitted consisted merely of the execution and delivery of the bond, the determination of the acting Secretary, notice thereof to the obligors and demand for payment, and the breach of the bond's condition,—all on the theory that the undertaking was in any event valid as a common-law obligation. After study of the case as thus submitted, I came to the conclusion that the bond could not be sustained on its face, so far as concerned the possibly apparent (but not necessarily exclusive) nature of the condition as one for the payment of such sum as the department, or its chief officer, should determine on an *arbitration;* in other words, the bond on its face seemed capable of the implication, and this the first apparent or natural implication, of such action by the Secretary as would amount to the exercise of judicial functions: i. e., an arbitration between the United States and the master of the Orteric, in which, also, the arbitrator was an executive officer not only of the government but of the department particularly interested. Accordingly, at the court's suggestion, the government moved to reopen the case for the introduction of further evidence, to show the exact nature of the whole transaction between the representatives of the vessel and the officers of the government. Also, in the consideration of the evidence,

a suspicion arose, from the opening statement of the acting
Secretary's letter of December 4, characterizing the proceedings as an "*application for relief* from penalties incurred," as well as from his concluding statement of "*de-
clin(ing) to intervene* in behalf of the offenders," that the
bond contemplated not an arbitration of any controversy,
not a quasi-judicial determination of disputed liability for
penalties, but a proceeding for remission of penaltes, or at
least for relef from the legal effect of admitted acts, done,
however, under alleged extenuating circumstances.

In fairness, it should be said, here, that any conclusions of
this opinion, as to the character of the proceedings, are
based entirely on what was done therein by the master and
his witnesses and attorneys, their "practical construction,"
and not in the least on the acting Secretary's characterization of the proceedings in his letter of December 4,—which
characterization is, for our purposes, assumed to be mere
irrelevant opinion, or hearsay; though without committing
myself to an opinion either way, it is possible that something could be said in support of its evidential value. No
contention is made on behalf of the obligors that the collector ever regarded the proceedings as anything but a submission for mitigation; and any such contention would be
contrary to the express language of his letter of June 17,
transmitting to the department the showing in behalf of
the respective parties.

The motion to reopen was granted, and over the objection of defendant's counsel on the ground of violation of
the parol-evidence rule,—the facts other than those proved at
the first hearing were disclosed as above set forth. This
extended review of the whole transaction has seemed necessary in fairness to all parties, and also advisable in order to
make the reasons for my conclusions fully understood.

This course of hearing further evidence was taken deliberately, and seemed an enlightened application of the parol-
evidence rule, within the rational limits marked by Mr.

Wigmore. See Wigmore on Evidence, sec 2462, pp. 3476, 3477; sec. 2463, p. 3488; sec. 2465, pp. 3490, 3492; sec. 2470, p. 3499; 5 Id., sec. 2462, note 8. In the language of Mr. Wigmore's Pocket Code of Evidence, "The ultimate standard of interpretation is the sense employed by the party or parties doing the legal act," sec. 1958, rule 222, and in resorting to the "species of usage" which may be employed "in ascertaining this ultimate standard," the court may adopt even "a sense variant from that of general usage," upon being "persuaded (1) that such sense exists in some special or personal species of usage and (2) that the party was employing that other species of usage," secs. 1959-1960; and "the sense supplied by general usage, and provisionally adopted," —["as a means of attaining (not of supplanting or of competing against) the ultimate standard, namely, *the sense actually used by the party or parties* to the act,"]—"must be rejected, as soon as it is made to appear that there exists some other sense in a special or personal usage which was followed by the party or parties in the particular case," sec. 1961, with sec. 1960 interpolated. Indeed, Mr. Wigmore in his edition of Greenleaf on Evidence, uses the language of Professor Thayer to suggest as "natural" a " 'free and full range among extrinsic facts in aid' " of "the process of interpretation." 1 Greenleaf on Evidence, 16th ed., sec. 305 j; and see Id., sec. 305 k. By this test, it appears to my satisfaction that the parties did not intend a submission in the sense in which the words of the bond might naturally be first taken, i. e., a submission of facts with the object of a determination of the master's guilt or innocence of the law's violation,—an arbitration, but that the parties had in view a submission of facts with the object of a remission of the penalties to which the actual violation of the law had made the master confessedly liable. And not only do the facts, admitted over counsel's objection, support this reading of the bond, but also the presumption of right-acting (the most universal presumption of life) leads me to disregard

the superficial or first-apparent sense of the bond's language. For, to posit an arbitration is to read the bond as
contemplating an unauthorized act. *Hobbs v. Mcean,* 117
U. S. 567, 575-576; *Delaware &c. R. Co. v. Kutter,* 147 Fed.
51, 62; *United States Fidelity, &c. Co. v. Board of Com'rs.,*
145 Id. 144, 148-149; 17 A. & E. Enc. L. 2d ed. 17-18. And
see *Cooke v. Graham's Admr.,* 3 Cranch, 229, 235, in which
Chief Justice Marshal declares that in "many cases on the
construction of bonds, . . . the letter [even] of the
condition has been departed from, to carry into effect the
intention of the parties."

[2] As a general rule in the absence of an enabling statute, public officers are without authority to submit to arbitration a controversy in which the government is a party.
In support of this proposition, a mere reference must suffice, to the following authorities as in point or suggestive:
Jones v. Howard, 4 Mich. 446, 448-449, for the general principle that "officers who are created by statute must confine
their acts within its provisions;" Mechem on Public Offices
and Officers, sec. 511 and n. 5, secs. 505-507; the valuable
decision of Circuit Judge Woodbury in *United States v.
Ames,* 1 Woodb. & M. 76, 24 Fed. Cas. 784, 789-790, No.
14,441, applying this principle to an arbitration-submission;
Morse on Arbitration, 30; *Child v. United States,* 4 Ct. Cl.
176, 184; *District of Columbia v. Bailey,* 171 U. S. 161, 176,
in which Mr. Justice White, though viewing liberally the
contractual capacity of certain officers as implied from other
recognized powers, yet holds that the "mere absence of a
statutory inhibition" is in general no justification for the
exercise of the power of submission, but that the officer
must first have his authority from that legislative body
(municipal, state, or national) which is his guardian if not
his parent; *Benjamin v. United States,* 29 Ct. Cl. 417, 419;
Child v. United States, supra. See *Brannen v. United
States,* 20 Ct. Cl. 219, 224. (It is worth while to note in
passing that the value of the Court of Claims reports as a

source of authority on many phases of the powers of public officers, has apparently been overlooked by the courts and law-book writers.)   And the reasoning of the decisions on the power of public officers to compromise, would seem to add some support to the principle, applied in the above-cited cases to the power to arbitrate,—regardless of distinctions between compromise and arbitration.   See, e.g., the opinion of Judge Benedict in *United States v. George*, 6 Blatchf. 406, 25 Fed. Cas. 1277, 1279-1280, No. 15,198.

It may be observed by the way that the violations of statute out of which the mooted transaction arose, though close to the border-line of the quasi-criminal, are nevertheless the subject of a civil action for recovery of the penalties incurred (*Jacob v. United States*, 1 Brock. 520, 13 Fed. Cas. 267, No. 7,157; *Stearns v. United States*, 2 Paine, 305, 22 Fed. Cas. 1188, No. 13,341; *Boyd v. Clark*, 13 Fed. 909; 16 Enc. Pl. & Pr. 231-239), especially if the parties so choose to regard them (see *Moller v. United States*, 57 Fed. 490, 495); so that the bond would not be held invalid on the score of a prohibited arbitration of a subject of criminal prosecution (2 A. & E. Enc. L., 2d ed., 557-558; 3 Cyc. 595; 5 Enc. L. & P. 38).

Also, it should be noted that, assuming an arbitration for purpose of discussion, the fact of the arbitrator's being practically one of the very parties, or at least the agent of a party, does not in any way control my view of the bond on its face; for the principal under the bond has waived any objection of disqualification for interest, because he has, of course, entered into the obligation with full knowledge of the arbitrator's being an agent of the government.   2 A. & E. Enc. L. 2d ed. 637; 3 Cyc. 619; 5 Enc. L. & P. 88.   See 3 Cyc. 617, n. 48.

Furthermore, even if there were plausibility in the argument made in behalf of the obligors, that the giving of a bond was enforced by circumstances (the urgent importance of getting the ship away for its waiting cargo, etc.), i. e., the claim of duress, involuntariness, such argument is quite untenable under the facts of the case, for it was the obligors themselves who proposed and urged this very procedure, and for their own convenience.

But we now come to the points which are more seriously regarded as vital. The district attorney insists that, in any event the bond, even if it contemplated arbitration and not penalty-remission, is good on its face as a common-law obligation, and maintains that the granting of clearance of the vessel, at the request of the master, constitutes a good consideration to support this obligation. This argument cannot be permitted to stand in the face of the rule that public officers are without authority to submit to arbitration. It is illogical, futile, to lay down such a rule of restraint, and then hold that, in spite of any want of power, an unauthorized act may be given effect by the officer's exaction or acceptance of a bond covering that act. This appearing to be a sound, indeed the only possible, application of the rule, the mere fact of there being a just consideration, in the grant of the requested clearance, cannot be urged to the rule's undoing. An extreme illustration may make this more clear: if the fact of a *quid pro quo* in the grant of clearance may justify an unauthorized submission to arbitration in these "civil" infractions of the Passenger Act, it might equally well justify a submission to arbitration of alleged criminal breaches of this statute punishable by imprisonment, e. g., under section 4. And, of course, the argument is not sound, according to one of the most elementary principles of the law of contracts. Anson's English Law of Contracts, 2d Amer. ed., by Huffcut, 12, sec. 10, subd. 5; Harriman on Contracts, 2d ed. sec. 228. The argument overlooks the distinction between subject-matter (or object) and consideration; validity of the latter cannot cure illegality of the former. See 1 Page on Contracts, sec. 325.

Moreover, in this argument counsel seems to overlook the fundamental policy of the law relating to the powers of public officers,—to lose sight of the broad principle of policy in his zeal to see justice done in this particular case. Indeed, there is a conflict of policies here,—the policy of securing in this particular case punishment of the offending ship and master, and the policy in general of not countenancing an abuse of power by a public officer even in a good cause. The former is a matter of insignificance compared with the latter. See Sir Courteney Ilbert's "Legislative Methods and Forms," pp. 38-40; A. Lawrence Lowell's "Governments and Parties in Continental Europe," p. 44; Jeremiah Black. Essays, etc., p. 598; also Letters of Mayor Gaynor, late justice of the Supreme Court of New York, American Magazine, January, 1913, p. 49.

As to the suggestion of an estoppel against the obligors to deny a power in the collector or his superior officer to submit to arbitration (i. e., viewing the bond according to an intention possibly apparent on its face, of an arbitration), it must be remembered that, "estoppel of whatever kind is subject to one general rule, that it cannot override the law of the land: for example, a corporation cannot be estopped as to acts which are ultra vires." 9 Enc. Britt. 11th ed. 801, tit. "Estoppel." And see the pregnant language of *Collins v. Benbury*, 3 Ired. L. (No. Car.), 285, 38 Am. Dec. 722, 726, to the effect that what is merely void cannot estop. It would be of doubtful wisdom as a precedent, though it might be fair enough to the obligors in this particular case, to hold that parties by estoppel can create a power not possessed by a public officer, to submit to arbitration.

[4] The finding has already been intimated, of a submission for the purpose of obtaining remission of the penalties alleged by the collector to have been incurred by the ship and master. Though the submission was somewhat informal,—lacking even a regular petition with prayer for relief, yet I feel satisfied of the truth of the conclusion of fact that the proceeding was intended with a view to obtain-

ing the exercise of leniency.   Such is the only reasonable, satisfactory, answer to the questions: If the master's show- ing of facts was not a submission for the purpose of obtain- ing remission of the alleged penalties, why did he set up extenuating circumstances?   If it was an arbitration of disputed facts which was contemplated, why did the master not show facts in defense, instead of facts in mitigation?

Here is a real estoppel. If the master has, as I find, actually regarded the proceeding covered by the bond, as a submission for remission of penalties, or led the govern- ment's officers from the beginning to so understand his in- tent, then why seek a principle of law to support a contrary intent? Furthermore, it is undeniable that the master and his attorneys were endeavoring to avoid liability by reason of alleged extenuating circumstances; and so, in any event, even though it be possible that such circumstances might, as the defendants claim, be adapted to a defense under an arbitration,—though it does not appear that it was ever urged *as a defense*, the department was justified in treating the submission as it did, i. e., as a submission within the authority of the Secretary to consider and pass upon under section 5294 of the Revised Statutes as amended.   Any estoppel in the case lies here; and the fact that the govern- ment permitted the vessel to clear and go beyond the reach of its courts and of the local grand jury, supplies the ele- ment of "prejudice" or "injury" which would follow denial of such estoppel. 11 A. & E. Enc. L. 2d ed. 436-438; 15 Cyc. 744. In passing, the grand jury's statements may be noted, that an indictment would have been found but for "the action of the owners of the vessel in frankly submitting the facts to the Department of Commerce and Labor for its determination and agreeing to abide by whatever decision that department might make."

(1b) The objections, made in this court, in behalf of the defendants, to the evidence submitted to the Secretary by the collector, as being hearsay and immaterial, are, it would seem, untenable. According to my theory of the case, it was proper to see just what was before the Secretary, just what was submitted to him by the parties, so that from the matter submitted a finding might be made as to the character of the submission. See authorities on evidence, supra; also Wigmore's Code, secs. 1969, 1972; *Merriam v. United States,* 107 U. S. 437, 441; *Rock Island Railway v. Rio Grande Railroad,* 143 U. S. 596, 609. Objections might technically be well taken not only to the inspector's report, the grand jury report, the official letters, etc., submitted by the collector, but also to the affidavits, the copies of posted notices and the attorneys' letter verifying the source and contents of these notices and the fact of their posting, submitted by the master. But it would be an unwarranted refinement of technicality to give heed now to the complaints of the master who had himself initiated the proceedings and throughout had made no objection but had countenanced their informality. See *Duvall v. Sulzner,* 155 Fed. 910, syll. 2, 917-918. If I were called upon in this suit to pass upon the soundness of the Secretary's admission of evidence precedent to his ruling on the submission for leniency, I would still hold that the admission of everything submitted by the collector was harmless error, and that the master stood "convicted out of his own mouth" in the affidavit which he himself swore to and presented to the department.

[5] But on this aspect of the case, counsel for the defendants argue that the power of the Secretary to remit is wanting, quite as much as the power of the collector or the Secretary to submit to arbitration; and the earnest contention is that the provision of the Revised Statutes, sec. 5294, as amended, upon which is founded the Secretary's power to remit, does not apply to any other subject than those within the purview of the power of remission given by he original act of Congress, 16 Stat. 458, embodied in this section of the Revised Statutes, to-wit, "any fine or penalty

provided for in this act," etc.   Now this original act, of
February 28, 1871 (of which section 5294 of the Revised
Statutes represents section 64, entitled "An act to proviae
for the better security of life on board of vessels propelled
in whole or in part by steam, and for other purposes," excepted from its provisions "vessels of other countries," Revised Statutes, sec. 4400, act of 1871, sec. 41, 16 Stat. 440.
And, so, if we must be guided not by what the present statute, Revised Statutes, sec. 5294, says on its face, but by
what the original statute says, then it is conceded that the
power to remit does not apply to the Orteric, which is "a
vessel of another country."   But the argument overlooks
the provisions of section 5595 and 5596 of the Revised
Statutes, which declare that these Revised Statutes "embrace the statutes . . . in force on the 1st day of December, 1873, *as revised*," and that "all acts of Congress passed
prior" to said date, "any portion of which is embraced in
any section of said revision are hereby repealed, and the
section applicable thereto shall be in force in lieu thereof."
See *United States v. Tucker*, 122 Fed. 518, 523.   Accordingly, in *United States v. Bowen*, 100 U. S. 508, 513, the
Federal Supreme Court held "that the Revised Statutes
must be treated as a legislative declaration of what the
statute was on the 1st of December, 1873, and that when
the meaning was plain the courts could not look to the
original statutes to see if Congress had erred in the revision,"—which "could only be done when it was necessary
to construe doubtful language."   *Viethor v. Arthur*, 104 U.
S. 498, 499; *Arthur v. Dodge*, 101 Id. 34, 36; *Deffeback v.
Hawke*, 115 Id. 392, 402, in which Mr. Justice Field holds
that "no reference can be had to the original statutes to
control the construction of any section of the Revised Statutes, [even] although in the original statutes it may have
had a larger or more limited application;" *Cambria Iron Co.
v. Ashburn*, 118 Id. 54, 57; *Hamilton v. Rathbone*, 175 Id.
415, 419-420; *The Brothers*, 10 Ben. 400; 4 Fed. Cas. 318,

No. 1,968; *United States v. Sixty-five Vases*, 18 Fed. 508,. 510. The suggestion of Judge Blatchford to the contrary in *The L. W. Eaton*, 9 Ben. 289, 15 Fed. Cas. 1119, 1123, col. 2, No. 8,612, has thus been overruled. See, also, 1 Lewis' Sutherland on Statutory Construction, 2d ed., sec. 271; 2 Id. sec. 450. It is sometimes quite a violent presumption that everyone "knows the law;" and to insist that where the law has been revised the average man shall know not only the law as embodied in the revision but also as contained in all the precedent statutes, would be to make law revision a burden instead of a help. Chancellor Zabriskie some years before had expressed the germ of this truth when he said in *Keyport Steamboat Co. v. Farmers' Transportation Co.*, 15 N. J. Eq. 13, 24, "The only just rule of construction, especially among a free people, is the meaning of the law as expressed to those to whom it is prescribed, and who are to be governed by it." See, also, *In re Suekichi Tsuji*, ante, p. 52. In the statute here in question the language is not doubtful; and, so, we may not look elsewhere, but must read the provision as applying to the remission of penalties under laws relating to vessels, irrespective of the nationality of the vessel concerned. It may be noted that section 5294, as amended, is even broader than originally, now applying to penalties relating to "vessels" instead of "steam-vessels." 28 Stat. 595; 29 Id. 39.

[3] Finally, counsel for the defendants would at all events save their case by the contention, that "even if the Secretary could remit a fine, that would not give him or the collector of customs the power to impose a fine." They say, "no penalty can be imposed upon the master until there has been a judicial determination of his liability,"— and in spite of the bond, the parties are left just where they started. But, we need not take the time to determine whether the collector or the Secretary has the power to "impose" a penalty. See 17 Ops. Atty. Gen. 282, 283–284; 24 Id. 583, 588. Here we have an admission by the master

·of alleged violations of statute: see summary of his affidavit submitted, and discussion thereof, supra; and where a party admits his wrong, as he necessarily must in making an application for remission of penalty (*The Princess of Orange*, 19 Fed. Cas. 1336, 1339, 1340, No. 11,431; *United States v. Morris*, 10 Wheat. 246, 295), I can see no reason nor justice in giving him this extra "bite at the cherry" so that he may have two chances to clear himself instead of the one chance of the usual fair trial by his peers.   A reasonable and just view, seems to me to be this: Where the Secretary has the power to remit, he may in order to prevent the wrongdoer's playing fast and loose with him, exact a bond as an assurance of good faith and to secure, · in case of denial of remission, full satisfaction of the penalty incurred by him and from which he asks to be relieved. This view finds support in the following cases, among many: *United States v. Garlinghouse*, 23 Fed. Cas. 1258, 1260, No. 15,189; *Neilson v. Lagow*, 12 How. 97, 107-108; *United States v. Hodson*, 10 Wall. 395, 405-408, 409; *United States v. Mora*, 97 U. S. 413, 419-421, 422; *Rogers v. United States*, 32 Fed. 890; *Great Falls Mfg. Co. v. United States*, 18 Ct. Cl. 160, 195. If the case were one of appeal from an admitted judgment of a lower court, but the statute made no provision for an appeal bond, there would not, I think, be the slightest hesitation by any court to hold that it had power to make a rule requiring the appellant to give a bond to secure performance in case of an affirmance of the judgment from which he sought relief.   The case here is no different: the power to accept or require such an undertaking is an administrative power fairly and reasonably incident to the power to remit, or refuse to remit, upon consideration of facts presented as the basis for desired remission.

The contention that "no penalty can be imposed" without "a judicial determination of liability," is contrary to the opinion of the highest authority, judicial and executive, holding that the powers of the Secretary with reference to remission of penalties may be exercised either before or after judgment. *The Laura,* 114 U. S. 411, 416; *United States v. Morris,* 10 Wheat. 246, 295-296; *Peacock v. United States,* 125 Fed. 583, 588; 17 Ops. Atty. Gen. 282, 283-284. See 24 Ops. Otty. Gen. 583, 588.

Wherefore, I find for the plaintiff. Let judgment be entered acordingly.

Affirmed on appeal: *Findlay v. United States,* 225 Fed. 337. On the particular point of the validity of the bond in suit, the affirming opinion, however, sustains the conclusion of the lower court by a different ground from that taken by the latter, i. e., as a common-law obligation rather than as a "penalty-remission" bond.

UNITED STATES OF AMERICA *v.* JAMES F. FINDLAY, T. CLIVE DAVIES AND W. H. BAIRD.

May 13, 1913.

Suretyship—Construction of bond—Surety's liability: Though the liability of a surety is a matter *strictissimi juris,* yet his undertaking is to be construed by the same rules as other contracts and gauged by the fair scope of its terms,—and, if possible, so as to be upheld.

At Law: Motion in arrest of judgment.

R. W. Breckons, U. S. District Attorney, for plaintiff.
I. M. Stainback (*Holmes, Stanley & Olson* with him), for defendants.

CLEMONS, J.   The defendants move in arrest of judgment, "on the ground that the declaration does not state facts sufficient to constitute a cause of action."

In this behalf it is contended, that the word "alleged" in the condition of the bond, contemplating a determination of "penalties so alleged to have been incurred," implies *disputed* liabilities and, so, can refer only to an arbitration, which the department' has no authority to make.

This point is disposed of at length in the decision in question, in which it was held that the bond was intended to apply to a penalty-remission proceeding and that such intent prevailed in spite of the use of the word "alleged."

Also, it is contended, that, from the standpoint of the sureties, as to whose contract the rule of strict construction applies, there can be no liability under this bond; counsel citing *Miller v. Stewart*, 9 Wheat. 680; *Legget v. Humphrey*, 21 How. 66, and *Long v. Pike*, 27 Ohio St. 498.

These authorities support the rule that "the contract of a surety is to be construed strictly, and is not to be extended beyond the fair scope of its terms," and that "a surety may stand on the terms of his undertaking." My decision had in full view the "fair scope" of the bond's terms, and applied the distinction, overlooked by counsel, between the rule of the surety's strict liability on the one hand and rules of construction on the other. This difference is so well expressed by a leading American work on suretyship, that scarcely more than a mere reference need be made thereto: 1 Brandt, Suretyship, 3d ed., sec. 107. The contract of the sureties here is "to be construed by the same rules as other contracts are." The rules of evidence and the rule of estoppel and the other rules applied in my decision against these sureties, have full force,—and not the least, the rule that in construing an agreement, such a meaning will be applied to its language as to uphold it if possible. See Id., sec. 103 and notes. Also, Stearns, Suretyship, secs. 18, 19.

The motion in arrest is denied.

UNITED STATES OF AMERICA *v.* JAMES F. FINDLAY, T. CLIVE DAVIES AND W. H. BAIRD.

December 15, 1913.

Trial—Trial by court—Special findings: The court having tried an action at law jury waived and having entered judgment including a general finding in favor of plaintiff, it declines to entertain a motion for special findings at a subsequent term.

At Law: Motion for special findings.

I. M. Stainback (*Holmes, Stanley & Olson* with him), for the motion.

R. W. Breckons, U. S. District Attorney, opposed.

CLEMONS, J.   The defendants have moved "that a special finding of the facts in said cause with the conclusions of the court thereupon, conformably to the opinion of the court heretofore filed in said cause, be made   .   .   .   and filed *nunc pro tunc* as of the April, 1913, Term of the above entitled court and as of a date prior to the 17th day of June, 1913, the date of the making and entry of the judgment." At the hearing on the motion, counsel for the defendants, taking the position that the opinion or decision of the court really constituted findings of fact and that all that was required was an amendment of the decision by entitling it "decision and special findings of fact," asked specially that the object of their motion be effected by the court's allowing an amendment of that kind.

In behalf of the motion were cited *Aetna Insurance Co. v. Boon*, 5 Otto (95 U. S.) 116, *and Joline v. Metropolitan Securities Co.*, 164 Fed. 650.   In the former case it was held that "where the court tried the issues of fact and its opinions embodying its findings and the conclusions of law therefrom, was filed concurrently with the judgment, but there was no formal finding of facts, and the court at the next

following term, . . . made an order that a special finding, with the conclusions of law conformable to that opinion
so filed, be entered *nunc pro tunc*, and made part of the
record as of the term when the judgment was rendered,"
such order was within the court's discretion. In that case
"there was no formal finding of facts, when the judgment
was ordered. It is to be inferred, it is true, from the judgment and from the entry of the clerk, that the issue made
by the pleadings was found for the plaintiffs, but how,
whether generally or specially, does not appear." 5 Otto.
124. In the case at bar, on the other hand, nothing was left
to be "inferred," but the judgment embraced not only the
judgment proper, reading: "It is therefore adjudged by
the court that the United States of America recover of" the
defendants the sum of $8,962.30 with costs, but also em-
braced in its first paragraph a general finding, which after
reciting a hearing upon waiver of jury, says: "And the
court having heard the evidence and argument of counsel.
finds the issues joined in favor of the plaintiff, and that the
defendants . . . are and each of them is justly in-
debted to plaintiff, . . . principal and interest to the
present date in the sum of $8,962.30." This judgment (and
finding) was signed by me as judge and "approved as to
form" by the endorsement of defendants' counsel thereon.
Though not labelled "finding of facts and judgment," it is
in form both, it being like a combination of the form of
finding set forth in the decision in the case of *Humphreys v.*
Third Nat. Bank, 75 Fed. 852, at 854-855, and of the form of
judgment set forth in the same decision at 855. That finding, "general in its form," and almost identical with the
finding set forth in the judgment in the case at bar, was
held by Judge Taft, speaking for himself and Judges Lurton
and Hammond, not to be entitled to consideration as a special finding, but as a general finding. Id. 855-856. It will
be noticed that the judgment set forth in *Dickinson v.*
Planters' Bank, 16 Wall. 250, at 254-255, includes a finding

in form similar to that included in the judgment here, but the court regarded it as a general finding and not a special finding. Id., 257, 258. In *Wilson v. Merchants' Loan & Trust Co.*, 183 U. S. 121, 123, the judgment entered was in form like that here, and the finding embraced therein was held to be general, Id., 127; so also in the case of *Streeter v. Sanitary District of Chicago*, 133 Fed. 124, 125, 127. In the *Joline* case, 164 Fed. 650, it appears that the judge had not yet filed findings of any kind, either general or special. See Id., 652, at conclusion. So that although he had rendered an opinion and entered judgment (Id., 651), it was, as in the *Boon* case, proper to file formal findings which the judge could make special if he deemed best.

In the case at bar, I have, as shown, signed and filed a general finding and judgment, with the written approval of defendants' counsel,—not a judgment merely *reciting* that a finding had been made. And I do not feel that I can do otherwise than leave the record just as it stands. The case of *Marye v. Strouse*, 5 Fed. 494, supports this view, and distinguishes the *Boon* case by pointing out that it was determined on the fact of there being a defect in the record, which the filing of special findings *nunc pro tunc* supplied. There is, as seen, no defect in the record here.

As to the suggestion of supplying what is contended to be an omission (but which, as above noted, is not), by labelling the decision as a "decision and special finding of facts" without disturbing what I have herein described as the general finding embraced in the judgment, such action would be unwarranted. The decision, or opinion, though necessarily finding facts upon which its conclusion is based, is not itself a special finding. *United States v. Sioux City Stock Yards Co.*, 167 Fed. 126, 127; *York v. Washburn*, 129 Fed. 564, 565-566; and see in connection therewith the respective decisions of the courts below involved therein; 162 Fed. 556; 118 Fed. 316; also *Keeley v. Ophir Hill Mining Co.*, 169 Fed. 598, 600. "The finding must be 'either general or special.' It cannot be both." *British Queen Mining Co. v. Baker Silver Mining Co.*, 139 U. S. 222; *Marye v. Strouse*, 5 Fed. 498; *Insurance Co. v. Tweed*, 7 Wall. 44, 51; *Dickinson v. Planters' Bank*, 11 Wall. 250, 256, 257; *Insurance Co. v. Boon*, 5 Otto (95 U. S.) 117, 140. Therefore, such an attempted amendment, with the formal general finding still extant, would be a vain act. *Corliss v. Pulaski County*, 116 Fed. 289, 290-291. So, if the amendment were to be effected at all, it would have to be preceded by an order setting aside the formal general finding embraced in the judgment,—and also stated at the conclusion of the decision finding for the plaintiff and ordering judgment. See Id., 291. But, the only finding in the record,—i. e., the only finding which can be regarded, according to the *Boon* case, supra, 124—being the formal finding, and *the judgment being technically based upon it* (*Streeter v. Sanitary District of Chicago*, 133 Fed. 124, 125, 127), I do not see my way clear to making the amendment asked, especially after the expiration of the term at which the judgment was rendered,—this being, indeed, the second term thereafter, a special term having intervened. It is certain that, as a rule, the judgment could not itself be amended at this subsequent term, and where as a matter of fact the formal finding on which the judgment was based, is general though, it is true, itself based on what might be termed special findings, some direct and some inferential only, I doubt the court's power to now substitute for that general finding, findings which are special. See Black on Judgments, 2d ed., sec. 306, and United States cases cited.

The question of whether the findings should be general or special would seem, in any event, at this stage, as well as at earlier stages, to be within the court's discretion. *Insurance Company v. Folsom*, 18 Wall. 237, 249-250; *School Dist. No. 11 v. Chapman*, 152 Fed. 887, 894-895; Fed. Stat. Ann., 2 Supp. (1912), 1372. And as the decision was not intended as a special finding, though its conclusion is of course based on special findings; and as these findings are to some extent argumentative and inferential, and not made with any view of their being considered as formal findings; and as counsel's delay to move for special findings has left only the very briefest time, before the expiration of the six months' period for taking appellate proceedings, within which to solve·the difficult problem of making up proper findings which may pass muster in the appellate court; and as a formal finding was entered with defendants' approval, I am disposed to let the record stand as it is.

The matter of framing special findings is not without difficulty (see the *Joline* case, supra, 651,652; *Wilson v. Merchants' Loan & Trust Co.*, 183 U. S. 121, 123, 126 et seq.); and findings improperly framed might prejudice a judgment otherwise valid. It would hardly be justifiable to incur this risk for the slight advantage, if any, which might accrue to the defendants from special findings. See *York v. Washburn*, 129 Fed. 566; *Chicago, B. & Q. Ry. Co. v. Frye-Bruhn Co.*, 184 Fed. 15, 16, 23; see also *The City of New York*, 147 U. S. 72, 76, par. 1, apparently justifying an inquiry, on appellate review of special findings of fact, only as to whether the special facts found support the judgment (Rev. Stat. sec. 700), but not as to the sufficiency of the evidence upon which the facts found are themselves based,—the Federal practice in this regard being different from that of some of the States under statutory provisions.

While running through the authorities, in making up this opinion, I came upon the case of *Supervisors v. Kennicott*, 13 Otto (103 U. S.), 554, 556-557, in which the court regarded a general finding stated in the judgment as "no more than a declaration that the court found the law to be in favor of the plaintiff on the case as stated," but that was where the obvious intent of the parties was to submit the agreed facts to the court for the court's conclusion of law thereon. How strictly this ruling is applied may be seen in *Lehnan v. Dickson*, 148 U. S. 71, 73, 74.

It is to be regretted that counsel may not have now what might have been secured by a timely request made in the manner pointed out by Judge Taft in the case of *Humphreys v. Third Nat. Bank*, 76 Fed. 852, 855-856, in which he warns against the pitfalls of practice in case of waiver of jury under Rev. Stat., section 700. See also practice indicated by *Martin v. Fairbanks*, 112 U. S. 670, 672-673, and *United States Fidelity, etc. Co. v. Board of Commissioners*, 145 Fed. 144, 151.

The motion is denied.

UNITED STATES OF AMERICA *v.* A. W. CARTER.

February 8, 1913.

1. *Census—Schedule—Unauthorized question—Refusal to answer—Penalty:* A refusal to answer a question set forth in a census schedule, which question is not authorized by the statute, does not subject the person so refusing to the statutory penalty provided for such of the designated persons who "shall refuse or willfully neglect to answer" the questions in the schedules.

2. *Tenure—Construction:* The word "tenure" in the phrase "tenure of home," required by the statute (36 Stat., p. 1, s. 8) to be placed in the census schedules relating to population, refers to the manner and upon what terms and conditions the same is held, and not to the strictly technical meaning of the word relating to feudal rights in land.

3. *Same—Mortgage of real estate:* A modern mortgage of real estate is a charge upon the mortgaged property in the nature of a lien,—a mere security for a debt, and as such does not affect the tenure.

Information under "An act to provide for the thirteenth and subsequent decennial censuses," approved July 2, 1909, 36 Stat. 1. Plea of "not guilty," and jury waived.

R. W. Breckons, U. S. District Attorney, for plaintiff.

A. A. Wilder (Thompson, Wilder, Watson & Lymer with him), for defendant.

DOLE, J. The offense charged in the information is that the defendant unlawfully and willfully refused and neglected to answer a certain question asked him by the special agent of the census office of the United States relative to the tenure of his home in April, 1910. The case is submitted on an agreed statement of facts. The defendant submits the following grounds of defense:

1. That the statute does not make it an offense to refuse to answer this particular question.

2. That the statute does not authorize this particular inquiry to be made.

3. That the statute is unconstitutional in so far as it seeks to compel a person to disclose whether his home is mortgaged.

The schedule of subjects upon which information is desired by the government, includes a division entitled "Ownership of Home." This is subdivided into the following parts, upon each of which the proper persons are expected to furnish what information they are able. "Owned or rented. Owned free or mortgaged. Farm or house. Number of farm schedule." Mr. Carter refused to answer the second question, to-wit: "Owned free or mortgaged?" It is admitted that he owned his home at that time.

The provisions of law relating to the issue made by the agreed statement of facts are to be found in "An act to provide for the thirteenth and subsequent decennial censuses," approved July 2, 1909, 36 Stat. 1. Section 8 provides "that the thirteenth census shall be restricted to inquiries relating to population, to agriculture, to manufactures and to mines and quarries. The schedules relating to population shall include for each inhabitant the name (of such inhabitant) . . . and tenure of home."

[2] Although the word "tenure" has a strictly technical meaning relating to feudal rights in land, yet it has come to be used in a more general way as expressing the manner or upon what conditions and terms land may be held (Tiedeman on Real Property, c. 3), and also other kinds of property and even immaterial things, i. e., tenure of office. Undoubtedly Congress used the word in this general sense in the expression "tenure of home," and was so understood by the director of the census, who, in making up the form of the schedule for population, used the words "ownership of home" for the statutory phrase "tenure of home."

[1a] When the defendant answered the first of the above questions, to-wit: "owned or rented," he conformed to the statutory requirement relative to supplying information called for regarding the tenure of his home. He answered that he owned his home. Was he required also to answer the question whether he owned his home free or was it mortgaged? This leads to the consideration of the further question whether a mortgage of real estate enters into and becomes an element of the tenure of the mortgaged property.

[1b] [3] The law of mortgages has generally changed since the time when, under the common law, the mortgagee was entitled, upon default, to take possession of the mortgaged property and hold it to his own use and benefit, even though it may have been worth much more than the mortgage debt. The equity of redemption became established, and equity construed a mortgage to have the effect of a lien, instead of vesting in the mortgagee a defeasible estate in the land. A lien is a charge upon the thing. "A lien is not, strictly speaking, either a *jus in re* or a *jus ad rem;* that is it is not a property in the thing itself, nor does it constitute a right of action for the thing. It more properly constitutes a charge upon the thing." Story's Eq. Jur., 13th ed., sec. 1215; *Conrad v. Atlantic Ins. Co.*, 26 U. S. 292, 335.

In the Oregon case of *Teal v. Walker,* 111 U. S. 242, the issue was whether the mortgagee was entitled to the rents and profits of the mortgaged premises after default of payment and refusal to deliver possession, as agreed in the mortgage, which appears also to have contained a power of sale. The court decided against the contention of the mortgagee, saying on page 251, "The case against the right of the defendant in error to·recover in this case the rents and profits received by the owner of the equity of redemption is strengthened by section 323, chapter 4, title 1, General Laws of Oregon, 1843-1872, which declares that 'a mortgage of real property shall not be deemed a conveyance so as to enable the owner of the mortgage to recover possession of the real property without a foreclosure and sale according to law.' This provision of the statute cuts up by the roots the doctrine of *Moss v. Gallimore, ubi supra,* (1 Dougl. 279) and gives effect to the view of the American courts of equity that a mortgage is a mere security for debt, and establishes absolutely the rule that the mortgagee is not entitled to the rents and profits until he gets possession under a decree of foreclosure. For if a mortgage is not a conveyance, and the mortgagee is not entitled to possession, his claim to the rents is without support." See also *Wood v Toask,* 7 Wisc. 484, 486.

It appears from this decision that it is the opinion of the Supreme Court that the Oregon statute is in harmony with what was already the doctrine of American courts of equity. Another American authority which I am unable to cite, holds that it is not essential to a mortgage of real estate that the instrument should contain the word *heirs* in the habendum clause.

From these considerations it would not appear that the tenure of real property is affected by a modern mortgage. It follows then, that if the question "owned free or mortgaged," is not pertinent to the requirement of the statute that the schedule relating to population shall include the subject "tenure of home", and there being admittedly no other subject in the statute calling for such a question, it is clear that it is not authorized by the statute; and although section 23 of he act provides a penalty for such of the designated persons as shall refuse and willfully neglect to answer correctly to the best of their knowledge, the questions "on the census schedules" applying to them, it is obvious that a refusal to reply to an unauthorized question, which the director of the census has permitted to appear in the schedule form, cannot subject the one so refusing to punishment.

This sufficiently disposes of all of the points raised by the defense. The defendant is found to be not guilty and is discharged.

See, also, *Allen v. Lucas*, 15 Haw. 52, nature of mortgage.

IN THE MATTER OF THE APPLICATION OF SAMUEL D. HAUSMAN, FOR A WRIT OF HABEAS CORPUS.

February 11, 1913.

1. *Warrant of arrest, mittimus—Sufficiency, requirements not technical:* Warrants of arrest, and of commitment, are not to be tested by the same technical standards as those by which an indictment is tested, but are sufficient if they disclose even by general language or statement of conclusions, a prior lawful basis therefor.

2. *Constitutional law—Police power—Opium:* The statute entitled "An act to prohibit the importation and use of opium," 35 Stat. 614, is a valid exercise of the police power of Congress.

3. *Habeas corpus—Practice and procedure—Preliminary order to show cause:* In habeas corpus proceedings, the issuance of a preliminary rule *nisi* is proper practice, and the usual practice, where the petition does not show a prima facie case of merit, or, at least, where some exigency does not require the immediate issuance of the writ.

Habeas Corpus: Petition for writ; and Motion to reconsider order discharging rule *nisi*.

George A. Davis, A. D. Larnach, and *E. A. C. Long,* for petitioner.
C. C. Bitting, Assistant U. S. Attorney, for respondent.

CLEMONS, J. Counsel presented to me at chambers a petition for writ of habeas corpus, alleging the petitioner's arrest on a warrant of the United States district attorney charging the petitioner with having on February 7, 1913, at and within this district, "unlawfully, knowingly and feloniously conceal(ed) and facilitate(d) the concealment of certain opium and preparation and derivative of opium, which . . . was subsequent to the 1st day of April, A. D. 1909, brought in and imported into the United States from some port to the affiant unknown," and "charg(ing) that said acts were in violation of the act of Congress approved February 9, 1909." 35 Stat. 614. The petition further alleged the petitioner's unlawful imprisonment and restraint of liberty at the hands of the marshal under said warrant, basing the ground of illegality upon the fact that this act of Congress is "indefinite, uncertain, unconstitutional and void." With the petition was also presented by petitioner's counsel an order to show cause why the writ should not issue. This order was granted.

At the hearing on the rule *nisi*, which for the convenience of petitioner's counsel was held within a few hours after the filing of the petition, the marshal, for lack of time, made no formal return in writing but merely presented the warrant of arrest with complaint attached, and the temporary mittimus issued by the commissioner. The warrant and mittimus recite, respectively, the complaint of, and arrest for, "violation of the act of Congress . . . of February 9, 1909, in that the said Samuel D. Hausman did unlawfully, knowingly and feloniously conceal and facilitate the concealment of certain opium unlawfully brought into the United States of America,"—the understanding being that there should be filed as soon as possible a return setting forth the complaint, warrant of arrest, and mittimus and the marshal's custody of the petitioner thereunder.

[1] In behalf of the petitioner it was contended that the writ of habeas corpus should issue, first, because of the failure of the mittimus, as well as the warrant of arrest, to show the petitioner's knowledge of any opium's having been imported contrary to law. This ground is not set forth in the petition, but it may, for sake of argument, be regarded as supplied by amendment. The reference made to Church on Habeas Corpus, 2d ed., secs. 94, 277, 286, to the effect that a warrant of arrest or of commitment may, by habeas corpus, be "impeached for any radical defect," or for failure to state the offense "with reasonable certainty," gives no support to this contention. These warrants of arrest and of commitment, which are merely the direction of the court to the marshal, and presuppose prior lawful basis therefor, are not to be tested by the same exact standards as the fundamental matters of pleading and procedure. The technical rules of pleading as applied to indictments, have no place in determining the sufficiency of a court's order to its officer, which, though important enough, is still merely incidental to a basic order which must itself be sufficient in any event and, until specially shown to be insufficient, may fairly and safely be presumed to be so. The opinion of the circuit court of appeals (Lurton, Circuit Judge, Severens and Clark, District Judges) in *Howard v. United States*, 75 Fed. 986, 988-990, suggests the reasonable view of the function and requirements of a mittimus and, also, of a warrant of arrest.

[2] The argument in behalf of the main contention, of unconstitutionality of the statute, 35 Stat. 614, is so plainly untenable as to require no discussion. The first so-called constitutional point is that this statute "invades the police

power of this Territory and therefore is contrary to the
Constitution," it being urged that Hawaii was by the Organic Act, 31 Stat. 141, given, to a large degree and so far
as consistent with a Territorial status, the enjoyment of the
same rights, powers and privileges as are held by the
States,—a point which overlooks the fact that Hawaii is
a being whose present life is subject to the will of Congress, which has not in this statute relating to opium,
enacted subsequent to the enactment of the Organic Act,
shown any intent to exempt Hawaii in particular from the
operation of a law of peculiar beneficence under conditions
in these islands. The array of authorities including
Equitable Life Assurance Society v. Brown, 187 U. S. 309,
and others marshalled in the brief of plaintiff in error in
Wynne v. United States, 217 U. S. 234, 236, does not justify
counsel's idea of Hawaii's status.

That the statute is an unconstitutional exercise of police
power, is also urged: that the mere concealment of opium
cannot constitute a crime and to make it such is to deprive
one of his constitutional liberty. In this argument a dissenting opinion in the case of *Territory v. Ah Lim*, 1 Wash.
156, 9 L. R. A. 895, is referred to. Also, it is contended, that
by the opinion in *Re Ah Jow*, 29 Fed. 181, the concealment
of the drug is consistent with a valid use, to-wit, for medicinal purposes. Id. 182-183. It is enough to say, so far
as the latter decision is concerned, that it passes by a claim
of this kind to determine the case on another point. Id.
183. The particular theory of police power here involved
has been so fully threshed over by both the Federal and State
courts, and our local Territorial Supreme Court,—and settled
adversely to this contention,—that no further discussion
would be helpful here. The attitude of Congress toward
the traffic in, and use of, opium, particularly opium prepared for smoking, reflects "a widespread conviction,"
"founded upon the experience of human conduct," of the
danger of promiscuous possession of this drug,—so wide-

spread a conviction that no court would hesitate to deny its propriety as the basis of police legislation. In the language of Justice Holmes, perhaps the highest authority on this branch of constitutional law, the police power "may be put forth in aid of what is sanctioned by usage, or held by the prevailing morality or strong and preponderant opinion to be greatly and immediately necessary to the public welfare." *Noble State Bank v. Haskell* (Oklahoma Bank Case), 219 U. S. 104, 111. The Federal Supreme Court has often made manifest its reluctance to declare void on this ground legislation otherwise valid. Late expressions of this attiude appear, for instance, in *Central Lumber Co. v. State of South Dakota*, 226 U. S. 157; *Eubank v. City of Richmond*, 226 U. S. 137; *Oklahoma Bank Case*, supra, 111. In this connection, the discussions of Freund on Police Power, secs. 21, 455, 635, 636, are enlightening.

In behalf of the contention that the statute is "indefinite," counsel has contented himself with assertion. Possibly the language of this statute is somewhat difficult to comprehend at first reading, and it might have been better for the sake of directness if, as in the local Hawaiian statute formerly in force, Penal Laws, Hawaii, 1897, sec. 1635, possession had been made the offense (substantive law) instead of evidence thereof (adjective law); but the statute is not indefinite or uncertain.

An argument is also based on the query, "Where is the corpus delicti of the alleged crime as disclosed by this complaint?"—a point not evident from the petition for the writ, or even from the complaint or any other paper before the court. And counsel contends that "if there was any importation into the United States it was into California and not here in Hawaii." Even admitting that the goods in question came here after having first been imported into the United States at another port, I cannot see that the fact would make the alleged act any less a violation of the statute.

[3] It may be noted that the Supreme Court draws the lines closely against the use of the writ of habeas corpus, especially where the objections upon which it is urged might have been raised by motion to quash or otherwise. and even where constitutional questions are raised. See *Riggins v. United States*, 199 U. S. 547; *Johnson v. Roy*, 227 U. S. 245. Upon the discharge of the rule to show cause, and the denial of the writ, counsel very strongly insisted that this form of order, this practice, would deprive the petitioner of his right to appeal; that the proper practice, in order to insure such appeal, is to issue the writ and then dismiss it. I said at once that any such practice struck me as unsound, illogical; that I was not disposed to cut off the right of appeal by following any particular method of procedure, but that my first impression of the proposed practice was decidedly unfavorable,—it struck me as insincere and vain to grant an order which, I was convinced, the petitioner was not, or would not eventually be, entitled to, only to at once set it aside. See *Soga v. Jarrett*, 20 Haw. 120, 121, citing *Ex parte Terry*, 128 U. S. 289, 301. But at all events, that an order denying the writ is appealable, see *Ex parte Snow*, 120 U. S. 274, 280-281. And the language of Rev. Stat. sec. 763, providing for an appeal "from the final decision . . . upon an application for a writ or upon such writ when issued," leaves no room for doubt of the proposition. See, also, Organic Act, sec. 86, 31 Stat. 141, 158; 35 Stat. 838.

The argument is also made, that the writ is "a writ of right," and Rev. Stat. sec. 755 makes its issuance imperative except in rare cases. This must be conceded, but the section carries the proviso, "unless it appears from the peti tion itself that the party is not entitled thereto;" and, over-looking the fact that the original order made herein followed the form of an order to show cause proposed by counsel himself, the writ does not issue as of course, or at all unless the petition makes this showing of merit. *In re*

Haskell, 52 Fed. 795, 797 (Taft, Circuit Judge) and cases cited; *Re Eaton*, 51 Fed. 804, 806 (McKenna, Circuit Judge); *Ex parte Vallandingham*, 28 Fed. Cas. 874, 920, No. 16,816; *In re Boardman* (Durant case), 169 U. S. 39, 43; Re King, 51 Fed. 434, 435; *Ex parte Terry*, 128 U. S. 289, 301. "If it is apparent upon the petition that the writ if issued ought not, on principles of law and justice, to result in the immediate discharge of the accused from custody, the court is not bound to award it as soon as the application is made." *Ex parte Royall*, 117 U. S. 241, 250. Such has been the rule since the time of Chief Justice Marshall. *Ex parte Watkins*, 3 Peters 193, 201. So here, it was, to me, apparent that for want of the slightest showing of the party's right to his liberty, the writ ought not to issue. His own showing was inadequate, as to the insufficiency of the warrants of arrest and of commitment; and the validity of his constitutional, and other, points was not apparent, but they consisted in mere assertion of conclusions of law. *Re Cuddy*, 131 U. S. 280, 286; *Craemer v. Washington*, 168 U. S. 124, 128-129; *Whitten v. Tomlinson*, 160 U. S. 231, 242; *Ex parte Milligan*, 4 Wall. 2, 110-111. See *Portland Ry. &c. Co. v. City of Portland*, 200 Fed. 890, 892.

Finally, counsel now urges that my refusal to grant the writ, would leave the petitioner in an unfortunate and unjust position, because of the fact that the rules of the Circuit Court of Appeals for this ninth circuit, provide that, in such a case, "the custody of the prisoner shall not be disturbed," and that "pending an appeal from the final decision of any court or judge discharging the writ *after it has been issued*," the prisoner may be "enlarged upon recognizance." Rule 33, May 22, 1912, which is the same as Supreme Court rule 34, Dec. 22, 1911. I take it, however, that this rule has to do only with procedure, and that, even conceding the power of any appellate court to say what the substance of a lower court's order shall be in a given case, this rule was not intended as a diplomatic means of any such supervision in the matter of petitions for writs of habeas corpus. If the intent had been such as counsel's argument would imply, the higher courts would most certainly not have expressed their object with such indirection. Considerations of policy and of justice argue, rather, for an intent to discourage appeals in cases of so little merit, apparent to the court below, that the lower court "declined to grant the writ." Rule 33, supra, subdiv. 1. While, of course, the very fact that the rules of the appellate courts have undertaken to distinguish between such cases and cases in which the court discharged the writ after issuance, Id., subdiv. 2, indicates clearly enough that the higher courts contemplated just such plainly unmeritorious cases as I deem this present petition to disclose.

The suggestion having been made that counsel realized his tactical mistake in presenting to the court for issuance an order to show cause rather than an order allowing the writ, and might, therefore, bring another petition, it will be well to point out for our guidance in future, that the issuance of a preliminary rule *nisi* is the common practice of the Supreme Court, except possibly, where some exigency requires the immediate issuance of the writ: *Ex parte Yarbrough*, 110 U. S. 651, 653; and has been since an early day: *Ex parte Watkins*, 7 Peters, 568, 570-571; *Ex parte Milburn*, 9 Peters, 704, note (Marshall, C. J.),—though, it is true, the statute now embodied in Rev. Stat., sec. 755, had not then, nor until 1867, been enacted. And see 9 Enc. Pl. & Pr. 1024-1025, and notes. Chief Justice Shaw regarded this as "the ordinary course" in habeas corpus proceedings. *Sim's Case*, 7 Cush. (Mass.) 285, 291-292. See *Soga v. Jarrett*, 3 U. S. Dist. Ct. Haw. 502, 504, 505; *In re Wong On*, ante, p. 59; *In re Tsuru Tomimatsu*, ante, p. 97.

The final order will stand as made: the order to show cause is discharged and the petition for the writ denied.

UNITED STATES OF AMERICA *v.* SAMUEL D. HAUSMAN.

March 25, 1913.

1. *Criminal law—Evidence—Confessions—Inducement:* In support of a motion to dismiss indictment, it was deposed that the district attorney, having informed the defendant of suspicions of his having opium concealed in his possession, asked if there was any objection to an examination of his trunk, and that the defendant, replying in the negative, invited the attorney to his room, whereupon the attorney said he would "make it as light as possible," would "use his influence and make the offense as light as possible," and would "do all he could" for the defendant. *Held,* that such circumstances, if true, would not of themselves alone render an immediately subsequent confession of possession of opium, at once followed by its discovery, incompetent as the basis of an indictment: the defendant having already consented to open the trunk to examination of what its contents might disclose, a subsequent suggestion of favor or leniency, though precedent to the examination, is not such an inducement of hope of favor as to render involuntary and incompetent as evidence a confession made at, or before and near, the time of such examination.

2. *Indictment—Motion to dismiss—Affidavit:* In support of a motion to dismiss indictment on the ground of its being based on the admission of an incompetent confession in evidence before the grand jury, an affidavit which shows only the confession and not the fact of its having been presented to the grand jury nor the fact of its being the basis of the indictment, is insufficient, even though those facts be stated in the body of the motion itself; such facts should be verified by oath.

3. *Indictment—Motion to quash—Grounds supporting motion:* On motion to quash indictment, an objection based on a circumstance (res gesta) involved in the act charged but not apparent on the face of the indictment, is untenable.

4. *Indictment—Sufficiency—Allegations of place:* An indictment charging violation of the "opium" act (35 Stat. 614, Feb. 9, 1909) in the defendant's having received, bought, sold, and concealed smoking opium, "theretofore imported and brought into the United States from some foreign country to the grand jurors unknown," is sufficient against a motion to quash for want of allegation of the country whence the opium was brought.

5. *Constitutional law—Due process of law—Evidence; possession as prima facie evidence of crime:* The constitutional guaranty of due process of law is not infringed by the provision of said act, that possession of contraband opium "shall be deemed sufficient evidence to authorize conviction unless the defendant shall explain the possession to the satisfaction of the jury."

Indictment: Motion to dismiss; Motion to quash; Demurrer; and Plea to jurisdiction.

Indictment under act of Congress of February 9, 1909 (35 Stat. 614).

C. C. Bitting, Assistant U. S. Attorney, for the United States.

George A. Davis and *E. A. C. Long* for defendant.

CLEMONS, J.   The defendant moves to dismiss the indictment on the grounds, in substance (I) that it was "found upon evidence not competent or legal testimony against the accused, in that the evidence consisted principally of a confession and admissions made by him in the presence and hearing of the United States attorney and the collector of customs, which confession and admissions were induced and obtained by and through certain inducements held out and extended to the defendant by the United States attorney;" (II) that "the indictment was obtained by confessions and admissions of the defendant . . . not voluntary and made by reason of certain inducements and representations made to him by the United States attorney;" and (III) that "said indictment was not presented and found upon legal and competent testimony but upon testimony obtained by improper means, and said indictment for said reasons is invalid and should be dismissed."

In an affidavit in support of this motion, the defendant deposes to the following facts (in paraphrase):   The United States attorney, on the afternoon of February 7, 1913, in the lobby of a Honolulu hotel, approached the de-

fendant and presented a card bearing the defendant's name
and place of business in Seattle.   Whereupon the attorney
said he had reasons to believe defendant had opium concealed in his trunk and asked if he had any objections to
his examining it.   The defendant replied that there were
no objections and invited the attorney to the defendant's
room upstairs.   Whereupon the attorney said "that he
would make it as light as possible; that he would use his
influence and make the offense as light as possible, and
would do all he could for" the defendant.   The defendant
and the attorney, accompanied by the collector of customs,
then went to this room, and after entering the defendant
said, "it was a sad day for him, he had just received a letter
from his wife congratulating him on his birthday, which
letter he handed to the attorney, who asked to be allowed
to take it home to read and [said] that he felt deeply
touched about it and the defendant had his sympathy."
After conversing with the collector he also said "he saw no
reason in sending this man to jail, let him remain here
under guard."   The collector acquiesced and again in the
same room the attorney told the defendant "he would make
it light for him and do all he could for him."   "Any confession or admission" which the defendant "may have then
made was induced and brought about" by the aforesaid
"conduct, representations, and inducements" of the attorney, and was "made of and concerning the opium which
was found in the defendant's trunk by the attorney and the
collector, and which the defendant after opening said trunk
himself told them was inside said trunk, were not free and
voluntary admissions and confessions of his doings in,
about, of, and concerning said opium."   The attorney did
not tell the defendant, or in any way warn him, that any
admission or confession then made would be used in evidence against him, either before the grand jury or upon his
trial.   And on the next day, the attorney called him from
the United State's marshal's office into the attorney's office

and, by reason of the inducements and representations made to the defendant on the day before, the defendant made certain other statements and answered certain other questions propounded by the attorney, and all of said statements, admissions, and answers were made while laboring under the effect of the inducements and representations so made to him by the attorney in the hotel lobby and in his room in the hotel, and but for said inducements and representations he would not have answered any of said questions propounded at the attorney's office. And the defendant was not warned that any said answer would be used against him to obtain any indictment or upon his trial.

The motion concludes with a prayer that the proceedings before the grand jury "may be fully inquired into," and that the district attorney be "orally examined in this court as to said proceedings, and as to what witnesses were examined, and as to what evidence was given" before the grand jury.

[1] Fear was clearly not the inducement to any confession made by the defendant. We may, therefore, for sake of argument, assume the indictment to have been founded on "hope of favor," and consider only whether the facts stated constitute such an inducement of hope as to make the confession incompetent evidence of guilt. Now, the only statements of the district attorney upon which a hope could have been founded are: (1) "That he would make it as light as possible and that he would do all he could for" the defendant; the affidavit failing to explain the meaning of the word "it" in the phrase "make it as light as possible," though the inference that it means "punishment" is probably clear enough. (2) "That he would make it light" . . . "and do all he could for" the defendant. The first statement was made by the attorney *after* the defendant, in response to the attorney's having said he had reasons to believe opium was concealed in the

trunk and his having asked if defendant had any objections to its examination, had disclaimed any objections and invited the attorney to come to his room.   The attorney's offer, immediately subsequent, of "making it light," and "using his influence," and "doing all he could," was, therefore, if made, purely gratuitous; it could not, in the nature of things, be called an inducement.   The second statement, also, was made *after* the defendant had said he had no objections to an examination of the trunk, and had invited the attorney to his room, but perhaps (though the point is left unexplained) not before the defendant's actual opening of the trunk and disclosure of its contents.   It may be, that defendant's counsel would have it inferred, that the mere presence of these officers of the law induced a fear or a hope of favor such as to stamp any consequent confession as involuntary.   Any inference of that kind would be an application of the law of confessions more in accord with the "excesses of by-gone practice" than suited to the present common-sense view.   1 Wigmore, Evidence, chap. xxviii, at length; Id., sec. 865, 867; 2 Wharton, Criminal Evidence, 10th ed., sec. 705, par. 2, (a) and (e).   At all events, anything the district attorney may have said to raise defendant's hope of favor, was the sequel and not the inducement of his confession: the defendant had already said in effect, in reply to the suggestion of there being opium in his trunk, "you may examine my trunk; come to my room and see whatever its contents may disclose."   Its contents disclosed the possession of opium, which mere possession is enough to justify an indictment.   And this disclosure was only the carrying out of what the defendant had himself already, and *voluntarily*, suggested.   Accordingly it is held that the defendant's affidavit does not make out a case of an incompetent confession.

[2] Though the motion is thus untenable even on the assumption, in defendant's favor, of a confession's having actually been in evidence before the grand jury, still it

should be noted that in any event the affidavit fails to show this fact,—which appears only in the list of grounds annexed to the motion. The ground that the grand jury based its finding "principally" upon evidence of a confession, is, therefore, left wholly unsupported by oath: an oversight which may possibly explain the special prayer of the motion for the court's aid in finding out just what evidence was adduced before the grand jury.

Under this view of the matter, the propriety of the motion's peculiar prayer for disclosure of the grand jury's proceedings need not concern us here; nor is the district attorney called upon to make any counter affidavit or other disclosure.

The object of the rule as to confessions is the arrival at truth, or at least the avoidance of untruth, quite as much as the protection of a particular class of persons, or the discouragement of questionable practices of public prosecutors and their allies in discovery of what the truth may be. See 1 Wigmore, Evidence, sec. 822, 823. And on the truth-object theory, there may be some room for argument that the affidavit does not make it sufficiently clear, whether the indictment might not have been justified by evidence (and whether such were not the only evidence before the grand jury) of "inculpatory facts discovered through an inadmissible confession." See 1 Wigmore, Evidence, secs. 859, 856-858; 2 Wharton, Criminal Evidence, 10th ed., secs. 677 a, 677.

By determining the motion on the merits of the alleged supporting facts, it is not intended to intimate any opinion, as to how far it may be permissible to inquire into the evidence upon which an indictment is founded.

Let the motion to dismiss, together with its special prayers, be denied.

There is next interposed by defendant a motion to quash the indictment, on grounds which are now disposed of below:

(I) That the statute involved ("Opium" act), 35 Stat.
614, is "unconstitutional and void," in that (a) the "act is
indefinite," (b) "in violation of the Constitution" (without
specifying how), (c) "usurps the functions of the legislature of the Territory of Hawaii by legislating upon subjects
beyond the powers of Congress," and (d) "in connection
therewith is an attempt to deprive citizens of their property and rights under the Constitution without due process
of law and a violation of the right to life, liberty, and the
pursuit of happiness guaranteed by the Constitution."

(II) That the act is "unconstitutional and void because
in violation of Article V of the Amendments of the Constitution."

(III, IV) Practically the same as ground (I, c) above,
adding, specially and by way of explanation, that "the Territorial legislature, under the police power, have the sole
right and power under the Constitution of the United
States and Organic Act of this Territory to legislate upon
such a subject and to regulate the buying, receiving, selling, . . . etc. of opium after it is brought into the Territory of Hawaii."

The preceding grounds of objection, (I) to (IV) inclusive, are disposed of by the decision in the habeas corpus
case arising out of the defendant's arrest herein. *In re
Hausman*, ante p. 202.

(V) That the act applies only to States of the Union and
not to Territories, and so is not applicable here in Hawaii.

The act is directed against the importation or bringing
of opium "into the United States," and any assistance in
its importation, as well as the receipt, concealment, etc. of
"such opium . . . knowing the same to have been imported contrary to law," and provides that "possession of
such opium shall be sufficient evidence to authorize conviction" unless explained.

[3] This ground of objection, as argued, would seem to
assume that the opium referred to in the indictment was im-

ported or brought into some place other than a State of the Union, the defendant's counsel presumably referring to the Territory of Hawaii. The indictment does not on its face permit any such inference, but is entirely consistent with an unlawful importation into some State of the Union. The opium may, for instance, have been unlawfully imported into the State of California and then unlawfully "received, bought," etc., here in this Territory,—which receipt, purchase, etc., would be subject to this statute, whether the statute applied to original importation into States of the Union and Territories or strictly to importation into States of the Union alone. That is to say, the objection, if tenable, can properly be raised at trial upon an offer by the government of evidence of an importation into the Territory and not into a State of the Union.

It may be noted that under the statute's peculiar provision relating to possesion, the fact of such possession would alone justify a conviction, without regard to where the unlawful importation was made, whether into a State of the Union or into a Territory of the United States.

So far as concerns the general application of the statute to this Territory, apart from any construction of its language ("States," etc.), the court would have jurisdiction under Judicial Code, sec. 24, subdiv. "second."

(VI) That the "indictment is misleading and does not inform the defendant of the nature and cause of the accusation."

(VII) That "it is impossible under said indictment, for the defendant to plead to the same, because seven distinct and separate offenses are charged in the same count , . . and no particulars of time, place, or circumstances . . . are set out, and said defendant is not able . . . to make his defense to the same."

These two objections have been overruled in the cases of *United States v. Ah Foo*, 3 U. S. Dist. Ct. Haw. 487, 490; *United States v. Fong Hing,* ante, p. 69, on one phase (ground VI above), and *United States v. Leau Hung*, 3 U. S. Dist. Ct. Haw. 552, on the other (ground VII above).

(VIII) That the provision of the act making possession of opium sufficient to authorize conviction, unless explained to the jury's satisfaction, is "unconstitutional and a violation of the fundamental principles of jurisprudence, and especially the presumption that every person . . . shall be presumed to be innocent until his guilt is established beyond a reasonable doubt by competent evidence;" being in contravention of Article XIV of the Amendments to the Constitution, as a deprival of life, liberty or property without due process of law.

[5] The highest authorities approve the principle that a law-making body has power to enact, even in criminal cases, that proof of certain facts shall be prima facie evidence of the main fact in question, if the fact proved has some fair relation to, or natural connection with, the main fact. *Meadowcroft v People*, 163 Ill. 56, 45 N. E. 303, 305, 54 Am. St. Rep. 447, 452-453, 35 L. R. A. 176. See Cooley, Constitutional Limitations, 7th ed., 526, note (2). It is common to apply this principle in support of statutes which make possession prima facie evidence of crimes involving the use of inhibited or contraband articles. 2 Wharton, Criminal Evidence, 10th ed., sec. 945; *Com. v. Smith*, 166 Mass. 370, 375-376, Holmes, J.; *Com. v. Yee Moy*, Id. 376, note.

(IX) That the said provision also violates Article IV of the said Amendments.

This was disposed of in the habeas corpus case, *In re Hausman, supra.*

(X) That the said provision is further "unconstitutional and invalid in that it makes the person guilty of crime irrespective of and in the absence of any criminal intent."

The discussion of ground (VIII) applies here.

(XI) Practically the same as ground (VII) above,— that "the indictment charges the defendant with seven distinct and separate offenses in connection with the receiving, buying, selling, concealing and facilitating the purchase, sale, receipt and concealment of smoking opium and opium prepared for smoking, alleging [an additional circumstance] that the same was imported and brought into the United States from some foreign country . . . unknown, and because said indictment does not allege . . . from which foreign country the said opium has been brought into the United States."

The principle noted in *United States v. Ah Foo*, 3 U. S. Dist. Ct. 487, disposes of the additional circumstance, i. e., place of importation, mentioned above.

[4] And that this objection is untenable may be made clear by an extreme illustration.—Such illustrations are often illuminating tests.—Suppose the defendant to have been in possession of opium of source unknown picked up on the high seas and carried to San Francisco, at which port it was "imported" or (an even broader word) "brought" into the United States. Such a case the allegations of this indictment would properly cover. Indeed, it is quite immaterial under the broad terms of the statute, where the inhibited drug may come from, provided it is imported or brought in: whatever its foreign source, it is contraband. In other words, the indictment charges an importation (or bringing in) from some unknown foreign country, and the fact that the particular foreign country cannot be described, does not make the importation any less a crime under the statute. It would seem superfluous to say that an immaterial circumstance does not require pleading.

(XII) That "it is not a crime under the act . . . to bring into the Territory of Hawaii from the United States opium . . . as charged in the indictment, and that possession is no evidence that the opium . . . was unlawfully imported or brought into the United States, and that therefore that portion of said act which provides that the possession of such opium shall be deemed sufficient to authorize a conviction is unconstitutional and void."

The latter part of this ground is disposed of above.   The first part is untenable, for the reason suggested under discussion of ground (V).

(XIII) That the indictment charges an offense with reference to opium "imported and brought into the United States from a foreign country, whereas in fact said opium which said defendant had in his possession or under his control was brought from the port of San Francisco . . . to the port of Honolulu."

This ground, involving a matter of fact not apparent on the record, has no place in a motion to quash.   The objection might be raised at trial in a proper case.

(XIV) After repeating other grounds above set forth,— that (a) the act is "unconstitutional and void, because in violation of Articles V, VI, X and XIV of the said Amendments, and that (b) the indictment and proceedings thereunder are "illegal . . . because the act makes the possession of such opium . . . evidence against a defendant and authorizes a conviction even though such possession had been acquired innocently."

These grounds have already been disposed of, either above, or in the habeas corpus proceeding.

Let the motion to quash be denied.

The foregoing opinion disposes of the defendant's plea to the jurisdiction and of his demurrer, which are accordingly overruled.

IN THE MATTER OF ANGUS P. McDONALD, AN ALLEGED BANKRUPT.

February 26, 1913.

1. *Bankruptcy—Subpoena to respondent—Service by publication:* Requisites of order and notice, under bankruptcy act, sec. 18, 30 Stat. 551, am. 32 Stat. 798, discussed.

2. *Same—Same—Same—Publications, number and time of:* The provision of said section 18 for publication of subpoena "not more than once a week for two consecutive weeks" is satisfied by two publications, one on a certain day of the week and another on the same day of the week following.

3. *Same—Same—Return day:* The words "return day," as used in said section 18, refer to the day fixed as the latest limit for the marshal's, or other serving officer's, return of the writ of subpoena into court.

In Bankruptcy: Motion for service by publication.

E. W. Sutton (*Smith, Warren & Hemenway* with him) for petitioning creditors.

CLEMONS, J. [1a] On petition of creditors for an adjudication of involuntary bankruptcy, alleging that, by reason of the respondent's absence from the jurisdiction, personal service of subpoena cannot be made upon him, the question arises as to the form and substance of the necessary order and notice of publication. Bankruptcy act, sec. 18, clause "a," 30 Stat. 551, as am. 32 Stat. 798.

Mr. Collier's form No. 121, Collier, Bankruptcy, 9th ed. 1233, is suggested, which reads in substance, after recital of respondent's absence: "It is ordered: That service of such subpoena be made by publishing this order, together with said subpoena, in ...., a newspaper published at ...., in said district, once a week for two consecutive weeks, the last of such publications to be on the .... day of ...., 19...;

and by mailing a copy of this order and said petition and subpoena to the last known place of abode of the said ...., in said district, on or before the day of the first publication."

Publication of this form of order, with the subpoena, would doubtless be efficient and in compliance with the requirements of the bankruptcy act, sec. 18, *provided* the clerk issuing the subpoena be careful to fix the day of respondent's personal appearance, not for the ordinary appearance day (sec. 18, clause "b"), but for a day *fifteen* days after the last publication—i. e., reckoned as five days after the return day (Id.), which in turn is ten days after the last publication (sec. 18, clause "a"). This aggregate fifteen days' period will not, of course, be confused with the "fifteen days" specified earlier in the same clause, and referring to the ordinary case of service upon a respondent who is within the district. See *In re Levy Outfitting Co.*, ante, p. 84, 29 Am. B. R. 13.

However, this form is not favored. It is useless, cumbersome, and conducive to misunderstanding if not error, to advertise an order of publication, and also a subpoena, which is really another order, i. e., an order to appear,— when a single order would do as well, and would save repetition of title and attestation and other matters lengthening the advertisement and nearly doubling the expense.

It is provided in section 18: that "in case personal service cannot be made, then notice shall be given by publication in the same manner and for the same time as provided by law for notice by publication in suits to enforce a legal or equitable lien in courts of the United States, except that, unless the judge shall otherwise direct, the order shall be published not more than once a week for two consecutive weeks, and the return day shall be ten days after the last publication unless the judge shall for cause fix a longer time" (clause "a").

Now, the ordinary practice in the Federal courts outside

of bankruptcy matters, is, in case of service of summons by publication, indicated by a form given by Mr. Loveland, a man of wide experience as clerk of a Federal court having much business. 1 Loveland, Forms Fed. Proc., 503 (No. 334), 82 (No. 65). This form furnishes an order complete in itself and avoiding the weaknesses above suggested as characterizing Mr. Collier's form.   There is no such virtue in official form No. 5, Subpoena to Alleged Bankrupt, 172 U. S. 683, 89 Fed. xxx, as to render it indispensable in case of summons by publication, to which use it is not adapted, or to render its repetition necessary, as with Collier's form; but, on the other hand, Mr. Loveland's form contains in substance everything found in official form No. 5. That this recommended form of Loveland's only reflects common practice, see Hagar & Alexander's Bankruptcy Forms, 79 (No. 42).

[3a] As to the matter of appearance day, the fixing of which is above referred to as requiring care: there has been in some cases misapprehension of the intent of the words "return day" as used in section 18; for instance, where they were taken as meaning answer day or appearance day. And it is understood that in one of the eastern districts, the court had fallen somewhat into confusion over these words, by having the subpoena note a day certain for the respondent's personal appearance and then holding the case open for answer or other pleading for a period of five days' grace thereafter, as if such were the intent of clause "b" read in connection with the preceding clause "a" of section 18. On an assumption of these words' meaning day of appearance, such result might be logical enough. Although the definition of Blackstone, e. g., gives an important part to the respondent in the matter of return day, still the leading part would seem to be that of the sheriff, 3 Black. Com. 275; and, historically, or in origin, the words would appear to refer to the officer serving the writ rather than to the person served. In common modern practice,

at least, the words have the meaning of "the day appointed by law when writs are to be returned and filed." *Bankers' Iowa State Bank v. Jordan,* 111 Iowa, 324, 82 N. W. 779, 780.

In any event, it is clear that "return day" as used in this section can refer only to something else than appearance day and to some other person than the respondent. Thus only is it possible to give a reasonable construction to clause "b," which reads: "The bankrupt, or any creditor, may *appear* and plead to the petition within five days *after the return day,* or within such further time as the court may allow." See *In re Wing Yick Co.,* 2 U. S. Dist. Ct. Haw. 257, 13 Am. B. R. 360.

This view is manifested in Form No. 4 of the official forms adopted by the Supreme Court. This order to show cause upon creditors' petition, after noting a day certain upon which the respondent is to appear, further orders that a copy of the petition, etc., be served on the respondent *"at least five days before* the day aforesaid." See Collier, Bankruptcy, 9th ed., 1111 (No. 27). This special provision bears a good suggestion, in the use of the words *"at least* five days," to-wit, that the appearance day be fixed at, say, the sixth day; for the use of official form No. 5, or any form ordering appearance *at an hour certain,* might be the occasion of avoidable controversy, if not of error, in case anything less than five calendar days, or at least complete days of twenty-four hours each, were counted in fixing the day of appearance. See 2 Black. Com. 141; 8 A. & E. Enc. L., 2d ed., 738.

[2] The provision of section 18 for publication of subpoena "not more than once a week for two consecutive weeks" is satisfied by two publications, one on a certain day of the week and another on the same day of the week following. Though in the local Territorial courts similar provisions as to advertising of notices have been construed to intend a third publication, i. e., an extra publication at

the end of the second week, the word "successive" is, in my opinion, intended only to preclude any possibility of two publications in weeks not successive, and, in any event, so long as a full week intervenes after the second publication (as it does under the ten days' provision of clause "a"), no question can be raised.

[1b] As to the necessity of a return of non est inventus as a prerequisite to the issuance of the order, and of a recital of such return in the order, it would be safe practice to secure a return of this kind: but its necessity has been denied. *Forsyth v. Pierson*, 9 Fed. 801, 803; *Easton v. Childs*, 67 Minn. 242, 69 N. W. 903 (Minn., divided court), overruling *Corson v. Shoemaker*, 55 Minn. 386, 57 N. W. 134, q. v.; also *Bronson v. Keokuk*, 4 Fed. Cas. 220, 221, No. 1,928, 2 Dill. 498.

[3b] The provision as to "return day" may be criticised as cumbersome, and serving no useful purpose,—only giving ground for confusion and error. The common order requiring a respondent to appear or answer within a certain number of days after service of summons, (and, as is sometimes, and desirably, added: "in default whereof the petition is to be taken as confessed," or "default will be entered," or "judgment will be entered against the respondent"), would have been simpler. And such practice is almost, if not quite, universal. For instance, the provisions of equity rule XII is in accord, though the word "returnable," as therein used cannot be applied here. *In re Wing Yick Co.*, supra. In these days of rapid transit, there is no reason why the sheriff should not, and every reason why he should, return the writ into court at the earliest possible moment. Such practice would make for promptness, orderliness, system, and the early discovery and cure of error. Conditions influencing the early common-law practice, if such it was, to make appearance day and return day the same, have no weight now. Slow and difficult transportation might then have made it advisable and rea-

sonable to give the sheriff as much time to get the writ, with his return endorsed thereon, back to "the King's Justices at Westminster" even "from the most remote part of the Kingdom," as was given to the defendant to appear or answer. See Blackstone, supra.

So far as concerns any fancied necessity of statutory enactment in order to hold the marshal or the serving officer up to a high degree of promptness and efficiency by establishing a certain definite limit for the day of the return of his doings under the order of summons,—or of securing from those officers as early a report as possible of the respondent's presence or absence or place of abode, it need only be said that the provision savors of legislative officiousness: the rule of official promptness in case of marshals and their deputies is so well established as to make any such legislation superfluous,—and the courts can always, and better, control their process by special orders as required.

Let the desired order conform with the foregoing suggestions.

Reported, 30 Am. B. R. 120.

IN THE MATTER OF THE APPLICATION OF KOICHI MAEKAWA FOR A WRIT OF HABEAS CORPUS.

March 13, 1913.

1. *Domicil—Proof—Intent—Acts:* Mere evidence of intent is insufficient to prove domicil. Acts indicative of purpose are essential.

2. *Habeas corpus—Return—Conclusions—Facts:* The return to the writ of habeas corpus must be explicit as to the grounds of the detention. A statement of the conclusions of a board of special inquiry

without giving facts upon which such conclusions were based is insufficient.

3. *Same—Consideration of grounds of detention—Facts—Law—
Bona fides—Jurisdiction:* While avoiding any retrial of the case on
the facts the court must consider the facts as questions of law may be
raised by them and also as to the genuineness and bona fides of the
hearing, in order to ascertain whether the court has jurisdiction.

Habeas Corpus: Demurrer to return.

J. Lightfoot for petitioner.
C. C. Bitting, Assistant U. S. Attorney, for respondent.

Dole, J.   The petitioner is a Japanese alien, who alleges
that he has been domiciled in the Territory of Hawaii from
July 1906 to September 1908; and that he then returned
to Japan on a visit intending to return to Hawaii, and did
so return January 28, 1913, to the port of Honolulu, Hawaii,
when he was refused a landing by the respondent.

The return to a writ of habeas corpus granted him upon
his application directed to the respondent, states that upon
his arrival he was examined as to his physical and mental
condition and also as to his right to land as an alien domiciled in Hawaii, and that the board of special inquiry
found, upon the certificate of the duly appointed officer of
the United States marine hospital service, that the petitioner was afflicted with a dangerous contagious disease
known as unciniarisis; and "also received and heard evidence as to whether or not the said" petitioner "had returned to Japan with the intention of returning to Hawaii;"
and also whether he "had returned from Japan with the
intention of permanently remaining in the United States;"
and thereupon did determine that he "was an alien immigrant afflicted with a dangerous contagious disease," and
that he "was not a *bona fide* resident of the Territory of
Hawaii at the time of his return to Japan, and did not, on
returning to Hawaii, intend to take up a permanent resi-

dence therein;" and thereupon ordered his deportation. The return further alleges that such decision had been sustained by the Secretary of Commerce and Labor on appeal to him by the petitioner.

The petitioner has demurred to the return on the general ground that the same is not sufficient in law to discharge the writ. In his argument on the demurrer, counsel for the petitioner laid special stress upon the failure of the return to state facts relative to the question of domicil of the petitioner in Hawaii.

As recited above, the return shows no facts pertaining to such question, but states conclusions, merely, of the board of special inquiry, which are, that he was an alien immigrant, was not a *bona fide* resident of Hawaii at the time of his return and did not on returning intend to take up a permanent residence therein. The doubt as to the sufficiency of the return arising from the absence of facts is not lessened by the nature of the examination of the petitioner by the board of special inquiry as there set forth, substantially as follows: The board also received and heard evidence as to whether or not the said alien "had returned to Japan with the intention of returning to Hawaii;" and also whether he "had returned from Japan with the intention of permanently remaining in the United States."

[1] [2a] Something more than evidence of intent is necessary to prove domicil. If the board of special inquiry merely procured such testimony without seeking for testimony of acts indicative of purpose, its examination on this point was defective. The return exhibits nothing more than this and leaves the court without the means of passing on the sufficiency of such examination. "No case can be found where the domicil of a party has been made to depend on a bald intent, unaided by other proof. The *factum* and the *animus* must concur in order to establish a domicil." *Holmes v. Greene*, 73 Mass. 299, 301; *Wright v. Schneider*,

Matter of Tsuru Tomimatsu, ante p. 97. In this particular the return is insufficient.

"The return should show and express a certain course of commitment; and it is said in general that upon the return of the writ of habeas corpus the cause of imprisonment ought to appear as specifically and certainly to the judge before whom it is returned as it did to the court or person authorized to commit." Church on Habeas Corpus, 2d ed., sec. 148, p. 225.

In *The King v. Lyme Regis*, Doug. 150, Justice Buller, speaking of returns to mandamus in which he said the same certainty was required as in returns to writs of habeas corpus, says:

"It is one of the first principles of pleading that you have only occasion to state facts; which must be done for the purpose of informing the court whose duty it is to declare the law arising upon those facts, and to apprise the opposite party of what is meant to be proved in order to give him an opportunity to answer or traverse it." Hurd on Habeas Corpus, 2d ed., p. 255.

" 'Minute correctness' is not required; but 'the facts necessary to warrant the detention must in substance be alleged. They will not be presumed." Hurd on Habeas Corpus, 2d ed., pp. 256, 257.

[3] It would seem that the statutory provision that in these cases the decision of the board of special inquiry, and, if appealed from, that of the Secretary of Commerce and Labor, shall be final, makes certainty and specificness in the return even more important than in other habeas corpus cases; for it is the somewhat delicate duty of the court, while avoiding any retrial of the case on the facts, to consider the facts as questions of law may be raised by them, and also to consider them as to the genuineness and *bona fides* of the hearing, and thus, with due precaution, to arrive at a solution of the preliminary question,—whether the court has jurisdiction.

"The decision of the department is final, but that is on

the presupposition that the decision was after a hearing in good faith, however summary in form. As between the substantive right of citizens to enter and of persons alleging themselves to be citizens to have a chance to prove their allegation on the one side and the conclusiveness of the commissioner's fiat on the other, when one or the other must give way, the latter must yield. In such a case something must be done, and it naturally falls to be done by the courts." *Chin Yow v. United States*, 208 U. S. 8, 12.

[2b] In order to do this duty fully, the return should be explicit. Church on Habeas Corpus, supra. This requirement is emphasized by the right of the court, formerly more in use than now, to require the production of the record of the hearing upon which the petitioner is detained. Church on Habeas Corpus, secs. 263, 264.

Under the foregoing considerations the demurrer is sustained.

IN THE MATTER OF THE APPLICATION OF KOICHI MAEKAWA FOR A WRIT OF HABEAS CORPUS.

August 12, 1913.

1. *Alien—Domicil—Dangerous contagious disease—Admission:* An alien immigrant owning land in his own country, who comes to the United States for work leaving his wife at home, and after a couple of years returns home, remaining there four years or more during which time a child is born to him, and then returns, without his family, to the United States and is found on applying for admission to be afflicted with a "dangerous contagious" disease, is properly denied the right to land, as under the circumstances he has acquired no domicil in the United States.

2. *Jurisdiction—Dangerous contagious disease:* The court in habeas

corpus proceedings is without jurisdiction to review a finding of the board of special inquiry that an alien applying for admission to the United States is afflicted with a "dangerous contagious" disease.

Habeas Corpus: Demurrer to return, and motion to discharge.

J. Lightfoot for petitioner.
C. C. Bitting, Assistant U. S. Attorney, for respondent.

DOLE, J. In this case the petitioner first came to Hawaii in August 1906, leaving his wife in Japan. In September 1908 he went back to Japan with the intention as he says of returning to Hawaii. He remained in Japan until January 1913 when he returned to Hawaii, again without his family. During this visit to Japan a child was born to him and was between three and four years old when he came back. He owns land in Japan upon which his family lives, and has no property in Hawaii. The board of special inquiry found that he had not acquired a domicil here and that he was afflicted with unciniarisis, a dangerous contagious disease, and ordered that he be deported to Japan. He took an appeal and the ruling of the board was confirmed. He thereupon applied for a writ of habeas corpus which was issued directed to the inspector in charge and he was brought into court. The return of the inspector was demurred to, and a motion that he be discharged, and a traverse were filed by the petitioner.

The traverse raises the question of the completeness of the medical examination of the petitioner, and denies that he is afflicted with unciniarisis, and that it is a dangerous contagious disease.

[2] The court does not consider, as at present advised, that it has jurisdiction to review the decision of the board as to the rejection of the petitioner on the ground of his having the said disease, the provision of the statute making

such decision, based upon the certificate of the examining medical officer, final. 34 Stat. 901, sec. 10.

[1] The only issue therefore which the court may consider is the question of the petitioner's domicil here, and I am unable to find in the record any facts calling for a conclusion that the petitioner had in his first stay in Hawaii, acquired a domicil. On the contrary all the facts and circumstances strongly support the proposition, that the petitioner, owning land in Japan and leaving his wife residing thereon, only came to Hawaii temporarily—not to establish a home here but to earn money. This view is borne out by his return to Japan after a two years' stay here and settling down there with his wife on his own land for over four years and giving his attention to the cultivation of his farm; and from the further circumstance that on his return to Hawaii thereafter to earn money, the opportunities for doing so being better here than in Japan, he left his wife and child, then nearly four years old, to occupy the Japan residence, as on the occasion of his first departure. There is nothing to show that he abandoned his Japan domicil, but rather that he has retained it and intended to do so.

The demurrer is overruled and the motion for petitioner's discharge is denied, and he is remanded to the custody of the immigration officers, and ordered to pay costs.

IN THE MATTER OF THE APPLICATION OF RYUZO HIGA FOR A WRIT OF HABEAS CORPUS.

April 12, 1913.

1. *Domicil of alien—Presumption of law:* An alien coming to Hawaii as a farm laborer continued that occupation for four years and then returned to his own country and, after a visit of eight months, returned to Hawaii, bringing his wife with him for the purpose of resuming his former occupation in the same locality as before. *Held,* that the facts relating to his first coming created a presumption that he thereby acquired a domicil in Hawaii, and that presumption is fortified by his temporary trip to Japan and return with his wife to resume his occupation and residence in Hawaii.

2. *Same—Change of domicil—Presumption of law:* Any expectation by him to return to Japan after a further stay in Hawaii of about ten years, standing alone, would not affect such domicil, which once established is presumed to continue until actually changed.

3. *Domiciled alien—Alien immigrant—Immigration Act—Jurisdiction of board of special inquiry:* The facts showed the petitioner to be a resident alien, and as the statute of 1907, 34 Stat. 898, under which the proceedings occurred, provides only for the deportation of alien immigrants, the board of special inquiry was without jurisdiction to deport him.

4. *Habeas corpus—Jurisdiction of court:* Relief by habeas corpus may be granted when the evidence is uncontradicted and shows without doubt that the case is beyond the statutes and not covered by them.

Habeas Corpus: Petition for writ.

G. S. Curry and *G. A. Davis* for petitioner.
C. C. Bitting, Assistant U. S. Attorney, for respondent.

DOLE, J.   This is an application for a writ of habeas corpus.   The applicant, Ryuzo Higa, arrived at the port of Honolulu in the Territory of Hawaii, January 28, 1913, with his wife, and was refused a landing by the board of special inquiry on the ground of his having a dangerous contagious disease, to-wit, unciniarisis, and ordered to be de-

ported. It also appears incidentally that another ground
of the decision of deportation was the finding of the board
that he was not a resident of the Territory,—supposedly
meaning that he had no domicil there. He appealed to
the Secretary of the Department of Commerce and Labor,
who sustained the findings of the board of special inquiry.

The writ was granted and the applicant produced in
court.

It is not denied that the applicant formerly came to the
Territory of Hawaii in May 1908, and remained here until
May 1912, when he left for Japan, returning as stated
above. The petition alleges that upon his first arrival here
he had his domicil on the island of Hawaii, where he worked
as a farm laborer, and that his departure for Japan in 1912
was for a temporary visit with the intention of returning
and continuing to reside on said island of Hawaii, and he
claims the right to land on that ground,—i. e., that he is
a resident alien and not an immigrant alien. The report
of further testimony taken at the hearing before the board
of special inquiry, which is made a part of the return, bearing directly on the question of domicil is as follows:—

"Q. Where did you live when you first came to Hawaii?
A. Wainaku, Hawaii. Q. How long did you live there?
A. Four years. Q. Then where did you go? A. Waiakea,
Hawaii. Q. How long did you live there? A. When I
came to Hawaii the first I went to Waiakea and lived six
months and then I went to Wainaku. Q. What did you do
in Hawaii? A. Farm laborer. Q. What is your object in
coming to Hawaii now? A. Farm laborer. Q. How long
do you expect to live in Hawaii? A. About ten years.
Q. Then where do you expect to go? A. Then I will go
back to Japan. Q. Where do you consider you have a
residence? A. Wainaku, Hawaii. Q. How do you make
that out? A. Because my brother lives there. Q. Your
parents, together with two of your brothers and two of your
sisters, live in Japan, do they not? A. Yes. Q. Who told

you to testify that you have a residence in Hawaii?   A. No one.   Q. Was it your intention when you left here in May of last year to return?   A. Yes.   Q. If you are landed, where do you expect to go?   A. Wainaku.   Q. Why did you bring your wife to Hawaii this time?   A. To work with me on the plantation.   Q. What is your intention in coming to Hawaii now, to live here and make a home here, or is it your intention to work here, you and your wife, and save money and then return to Japan?   A. I want to go back to Japan.   Q. Do I understand you correctly that you brought your wife here to work on the plantation with you so that you could make and save more money?   A. Yes.   Q. Have you anything further to say?   A. No."

The investigation shows no effort to draw out information as to the status of the applicant after his first arrival. Beyond ascertaining where he had resided and that he was a farm laborer and that he had no property here and no money invested here, there were no further questions pertinent to his then status or his intentions in regard to his stay in Hawaii, but the examination was diverted, as appears above, to ascertaining his present intention as to his future stay here and as to returning to Japan.

The real question at issue was, not what were his present intentions as to his movements ten years hence, but what was his status previous to his visit to Japan, as might be gathered from his acts and his plans during such stay here.

"The place where a person lives is taken to be his domicil until facts adduced establish the contrary, and a domicil when acquired is presumed to continue until it is shown to have been changed."   *Anderson v. Watt*, 138 U. S. 694, 706; *Mitchell v. United States*, 88 U. S. 350, 352; *Desmare v. United States*, 93 U. S. 605, 609.

[2] So far as can be learned from the somewhat scanty record of the return, and the special attention given to the present plans of the petitioner, the board reached the conclusion that the residence in Hawaii acquired previously by

him had been lost by his present intention to return to
Japan after about a ten years' further stay in Hawaii. If
I am right in this, the board has mistaken the law of
domicil, inasmuch as when a domicil is acquired it is pre-
sumed to continue until it is shown to have been changed.
Anderson v. Watt, supra.

"Two things must concur to effectuate a change of domicil: (1) An actual change or removal of residence.   (2) An
intention to make such change or removal permanent."
Doyle v. Clark, 7 Fed. Cas. 1029, No. 4053; Story, Conflict
of Laws, sec. 46; *Marks v. Marks*, 75 Fed. 321, 328.

These two things do not concur here.

[1] There is no dispute about the facts that petitioner
arrived in Hawaii in May 1908, and after a stay of six
months in Waiakea, settled in Wainaku and lived there as
a farm laborer until May 1912, when he went to Japan
with the intention of returning and did return in January
1913, bringing his wife with him, with the intention of resuming his former occupation of farm laborer, and with the
expectation of returning to Japan in about ten years.   The
above dates are exactly admitted in the return.   The presumption that he acquired a domicil in Hawaii is supported
by his visit to Japan and return with his wife to resume his
former occupation in his former place of residence,. Wainaku.   Upon these facts the conclusion of law must be that
the petitioner acquired a domicil in his first residence in
Hawaii, and that nothing has occurred or has been done
by him since, to change it.

While the case of *Ex parte Petterson*, 166 Fed. 536, 540-
541, rules that the cases decided under the provisions of the
immigration act of March 3, 1891, 26 Stat. 1084, should be
given little weight in considering cases brought under the
immigration act of March 3, 1903, 32 Stat. 1213, because
in the latter act the word "immigrant," which was contained in the former act as qualifying the word "alien," was
omitted.   Such conclusion, even if correct (*Rodgers v. United*

States, ex rel Buchsbaum, 152 Fed. 346, 351), applying to the immigration act of 1903, does not appear to apply to the immigration act of February 20, 1907, 34 Stat. 898, under which law this case is brought, inasmuch as the statute, besides its title which is in words "An act to regulate the immigration of aliens into the United States," contains repeated expressions which could hardly have been used unless Congress had intended to limit the scope of the statute to "alien immigrants." For instance the words "immigrant fund" are used in sections 1, 19, 20, 24 and 39; section 7 forbids transportation companies from soliciting or encouraging the "immigration of any aliens;" sections 12, 14, 15, 16, 17, 18, 22, 24 and 25 refer to "immigration officers;" sections 12, 14, 19, 22, 24, 25, 32, 36 and 40 refer to the "Commissioner General of Immigration" who, by virtue of section 22, has charge of all laws relating to the "immigration of aliens;" section 25 provides for boards of special inquiry "for the prompt determination of all cases of immigrants detained . . . under the provision of law;" sections 30, 31 and 40 refer to "immigrant stations," and authorize the President to negotiate treaties for regulating the "immigration of aliens to the United States;" section 40 provides for a "division of information in the Bureau of Immigration and Naturalization. . . . to promote beneficial distribution of aliens admitted into the United States among the several States and Territories desiring immigration;" section 42 treats of the accommodation to be given "immigrant passengers" on vessels bringing them to the United States. Only once is the phrase "alien immigrant" used in the act of 1891, and not at all in the act of 1903.

[3] It would appear from these references that the act of 1907 does not apply to resident aliens, and that the board of special inquiry was without jurisdiction to order the deportation of the petitioner, upon the facts of the case.

[4] A writ of habeas corpus may be properly granted

"when the evidence produced before such (immigrant) official, and upon which he assumes to act, is wholly uncontradicted, and shows beyond any room for dispute or doubt
that the case in any view is beyond the statutes and not covered or provided for by them." *Ex parte Petterson*, 166
Fed. 536, 539; *Ex parte Watchorn*, 160 Fed. 1014, 1016;
Ex parte Long Lock, 173 Fed. 208, 215.

The return was demurred to and an amended return and
second amended return were filed, whereupon the petitioner
filed a motion that he be discharged. For the reasons and
under the considerations above set forth, the motion is
granted.

Overruled, as to the holding that the Immigration Act
does not apply to domiciled or resident aliens, *Lapina v.
Williams*, 232 U. S. 78.

IN THE MATTER OF THE APPLICATION OF YOUNG CHOW YEE FOR A WRIT OF HABEAS CORPUS.

April 18, 1913.

1. *Impeachment of witnesses—Use of impeaching statements not
referred to in trial as affecting regularity of proceedings and jurisdiction of District Court in habeas corpus:* At the hearing of the question
of a person's right to land in the United States, claiming to be an
American citizen by birth, two of his witnesses had previously given
testimony in another case which the acting inspector in charge considered contradictory to the testimony they gave at the hearing, but
which was not referred to at the hearing, but was examined privately
afterwards by him. Upon this and the other testimony taken, the inspector ordered the deportation of such person. *Held*, on habeas
corpus proceedings, that the use of such alleged contradictory testimony without giving such two witnesses an opportunity of meeting

and explaining it, was irregular and deprived the person claiming the right to land of the fair and lawful hearing to which he was entitled, and gave jurisdiction of the case on its merits to the District Court.

2. *Rehearing of case before inspector—Authority of District Court having acquired jurisdiction:* A court in habeas corpus proceedings is without authority to order a rehearing before the inspector of an issue involving a person's right to land in the United States, but if it has acquired jurisdiction of the case on its merits, it may, in case the applicant had not established his right to land before the inspector, try such issue and allow the parties to introduce further testimony.

Habeas Corpus: Traverse to return.

G. A. Davis and *A. L..C. Atkinson* for petitioner.
C. C. Bitting, Assistant U. S. Attorney, for respondent.

DOLE, J.   This is an application for a writ of habeas corpus on the ground that the applicant is a citizen of the United States, born in the Hawaiian Islands in August 1891, and is refused landing at the port of Honolulu and ordered to be deported upon a hearing before the acting inspector in charge at such port, which the applicant alleges was not a bona fide hearing but was conducted in an illegal and improper manner, and that the order of deportation was made without authority of law and in excess of the jurisdiction of such acting inspector in charge.   The writ was issued and the acting inspector filed his return which was traversed by the petitioner upon substantially the same grounds as those alleged in the petition.   Upon the allegations of the traverse, a hearing was had, and the acting inspector in charge, Harry B. Brown, and the petitioner, Young Chow Yee, examined.

[1] It appeared from the examination of Mr. Brown that after the hearing before him as acting inspector was over,— two days afterward in fact, he referred to the record of testimony of two of the witnesses, i. e., Young Kuen (or Quan)

Shoon and Leong Hoy Ting, taken in 1910 in another case, and found it, in his opinion, to be contradictory to the testimony which they have given in this case. No reference was made to this contradictory testimony at the hearing, and no opportunity given to the said two witnesses whose testimony was thus sought to be impeached to meet and explain the same in view of their present testimony. Under the universally accepted rule in common law countries, such impeaching testimony may not be even introduced at a hearing without first informing the witness whose testimony it is intended to impeach, of the circumstances under which the impeaching declarations were made and giving him full opportunity of explanation, denial or admission. In this case no attempt was made to introduce the impeaching evidence, but it was privately referred to after the case was closed and the witnesses had departed; and upon it and the testimony taken in the case the petitioner was denied a landing.

"The rule is well settled in England, that a witness cannot be impeached by showing that he had made contradictory statements from those sworn to, unless on his examination he was asked whether he had not made such statements to the individuals by whom the proof was expected to be given. This rule is founded upon common sense, and is essential to protect the character of a witness. His memory is refreshed by the necessary inquiries, which enables him to explain the statements referred to, and show they were made under a mistake, or that there was no discrepancy between them and his testimony." *Conrad v. Griffey*, 57 U. S. 38, 46; *The Charles Morgan*, 115 U. S. 69, 77; *Mattox v. United States*, 156 U. S. 237, 246; *Barton v. Shull*, 70 Neb. 324, 329.

[2] Under this showing the petitioner has not received the benefit of a fair and lawful hearing to which he was entitled. *The Japanese Immigrant Case*, 189 U. S. 88, 101. Although the Secretary of Labor has authority to order a rehearing, when circumstances justify such action (Id., 102),

I am not aware that this court has any such power. As the petitioner, however, has not as yet established his right to enter the country, and as, under the above showing, the matter is now under the jurisdiction of this court, it would appear that the matter is before this court to try upon its merits and to take such additional testimony as the parties may wish to present. *Chin Yow v. United States*, 208 U. S. 8, 13.

The case may therefore be continued to such time as may be arranged between the parties for a further hearing.

IN THE MATTER OF THE APPLICATION OF YOUNG CHOW YEE FOR A WRIT OF HABEAS CORPUS.

May 16, 1913.

1. *Immigration—Habeas corpus—Exhaustion of remedies:* In immigration cases, a petition for writ of habeas corpus should be denied unless the petition contains an allegation of appeal from the decision of immigration officers denying the right to enter the United States, and of the confirmation of such decision.

2. *Same—Same—Same—Exceptions to rule:* A petitioner for a writ of habeas corpus had noted his appeal from the decision of the inspector denying his right to enter the United States, but, upon applying for the writ, had withdrawn such appeal. The writ was issued and at the hearing upon the return, it appeared that after the preliminary hearing, the inspector had discredited two of the petitioner's witnesses by referring to their previous statements in another case, without confronting them with such statements or giving them an opportunity of denying or explaining them or admitting them to be true. The court thereupon, deeming that petitioner had not had a fair and lawful hearing, authorized a hearing on the merits of the petitioner's claim of a right to land on the ground of citizenship. At the close of

the evidence, which satisfactorily proved the petitioner's citizenship, the point was raised that the writ was improperly issued on the ground that there had been no confirmation of the inspector's decision on appeal. *Held*, that the circumstances created a proper ground for an exception to the rule.

Habeas Corpus: Objection for failure to exhaust remedies.

· *G. A. Davis* and *A. L. C. Atkinson* for petitioner.
  C. C. Bitting, Assistant U. S. Attorney, for respondent.

DOLE, J. In this case the applicant claimed the right to land on the ground of citizenship, and introduced witnesses to prove his Hawaiian birth, and upon the denial of his right to land, by the inspector, took an appeal and then applied for a writ of habeas corpus and withdrew his appeal.

[1a] The point is made by the respondent, that an application for a writ was not in order until after appeal and confirmation.   There is apparently much support for this in *United States v. Sing Tuck*, 194 U. S. 161, in which the court says, at page 170, "before the courts can be called upon, the preliminary sifting process provided by the statutes must be gone through with."   That was a case in which the petitioners said they were born in the United States but refused to answer questions by the inspector or to give information to support their claim.   Under such a showing, the denial of their right to land was obviously correct.   Upon the issuance of the writ no denial was made or attempted of the facts stated in the return.   It would seem that under the circumstances, there was nothing left for he court to do but to dismiss the writ; the decision was, however, reversed by the Circuit Court of Appeals, "on the ground that the parties concerned were entitled to a judicial investigation of their status," on the question of citizenship.   Id. 166.   The Supreme Court, however, sustained

the ruling of the lower court, saying, "We are of opinion that the attempt to disregard and override the provisions of the statues and rules of the department and to swamp the courts by a resort to them in the first instance must fail. We may add that, even if it is beyond the power of Congress to make the decision of the department final upon the question of citizenship, we agree with the Circuit Court of Appeals that a petition for habeas corpus ought not to be entertained, unless the court is satisfied that the petitioner can make out at least a prima facie case. A mere allegation of citizenship is not enough. But, before the courts can be called upon, the preliminary sifting process provided by the statutes must be gone through with." The burden of the decision appears to be the failure of the applicants to present a case for consideration. They really had no grievance, no basis of a claim to land except an unsupported allegation. Does the ruling apply to this case?

[2] I do not take the language quoted to lay down an imperative rule to be followed in every case regardless of circumstances. The case of *Minnesota v. Brundage*, 180 U. S. 499, 502, recognizes exceptions to the general rule as proper in cases of urgency, such as the discharge of persons in custody under State authority involving the authority and operations of the general government, or the obligations of the United States to or its relations with foreign nations, or to bring them into a court of the United States to testify as witnesses.

Does the present case present circumstances of urgency? The applicant, after a denial of his right to land, upon a prima facie showing by him, took an appeal to the Secretary of Commerce and Labor and then, upon applying for a writ of habeas corpus, withdrew such appeal. It is unfortunate that the point was not made by the respondent at the inception of these proceedings. The petitioner has been at the expense and trouble incident to a hearing on the merits, having to bring witnesses from the other side of the island,

and suffering the delays necessarily connected with litigation. A hearing was had upon the return, the burden of which was the question whether the applicant had a legal hearing before the inspector. This was decided in the negative on the ground that the inspector discredited two of the witnesses by referring, after the hearing, to their statements in a former case, without confronting them with such statements or giving them a chance of explaining or denying them or admitting them to be true; and the court thereupon authorized a further hearing on the merits of the applicant's claim of his right to land on the ground of citizenship. At such hearing, after the evidence was in, the point was raised by the respondent as set forth above.

In my opinion the applicant satisfactorily proved his citizenship at such hearing, and it appears to me that it would be carrying the rule, which is admittedly subject to exceptions, to an extreme length, if the court should now, under the circumstances, remand to the custody of the inspector, a person who has proved that he is a citizen of the United States, necessitating a renewal of his appeal from the original ruling of the inspector, and new proceedings for a writ of habeas corpus in case of the confirmation of the inspector's decision on such appeal.

Under these considerations, I feel that the petitioner should be discharged and so order.

[1b] This court, in support of the rule referred to, will in the future require petitions for writs of habeas corpus in immigration cases, to contain allegations of appeal from decisions of immigration officers denying the right to land, to the appellate authority, and of his confirmation of such denial.

IN THE MATTER OF THE APPLICATION OF
YOUNG CHOW YEE FOR A WRIT OF HABEAS
CORPUS.

.January 16, 1915.

1. *Appeal; writ of error—Time when appeals and writs of error
may be taken or sued out:* The time when appeals or writs of error for
review in the Circuit Court of Appeals may be "taken or sued out," begins to run on the date when the judgment, order or decree is filed.

2. *Draft of judgment, order and decree by winning party:* The winning party should, without unnecessary delay, present draft of judgment, order or decree for signing and filing.

Habeas Corpus: Motion to compel petitioner to file final
judgment.

Jeff McCarn, U. S. District Attorney, for the motion.
A. C. L. Atkinson contra.

DOLE, J. On the 16th day of May 1913, the court discharged the petitioner under the writ of habeas corpus,
subject to a bond of $250 on appeal.. On the 16th day of
December 1914, motion was filed by the assistant United
States district attorney to the effect that the petitioner
through his attorney be required to file a final order and
judgment. At the hearing on the motion, the petitioner's
counsel contended that the decision of the court discharging
the petitioner and the filing of such decision was sufficient.

[1] The practice on this point appears to vary somewhat
in the different circuits, although the most general usage is
that the date of the filing of the judgment or decree is the
time when the period in which appeals may be perfected
begins to run.

"The judgment which we are asked to review by this writ
was entered in the Circuit Court of La Crosse County, May
24, 1882. It is signed by the judge on that day, and is expressly dated as of that day, and it is marked filed on that
day over the signature of the clerk of that court. This is

the judgment—the entry of the judgment—and on that day the plaintiff in error had a right to his writ, and on that day the two years began to run within which his right existed. . . . It is the record of the judicial decision or order of the court found in the record book of the court's proceedings which constitutes the evidence of the judgment, and from the date of its entry in that book the statute of limitations begins to run." *Polleys v. Black River Co.*, 113 U. S. 81, 83-84 (1885).

"The record shows that the only judgment ever entered upon the verdict was that signed by the judge and filed on November 20, 1895. This is the judgment,—'the entry of the judgment,' in the language of the Supreme Court, in *Polleys v. Black River Improvement Company*, 113 U. S. 81, 83,—and on that day the plaintiffs in error had a right to their writ, and on that day the six months began to run within which their right existed." *Marks v. Northern Pacific Railroad Co.*, 44 U. S. App. 714, 718-719. (1896).

"We cannot doubt that the entry of the 28th of November was intended as an order settling the terms of the decree to be entered thereafter; and that the entry made on the 5th of December was regarded both by the court and the counsel as the final decree in the cause. We do not question that the first entry had all the essential elements of a final decree, and if it had been followed by no other action of the court, might very properly have been treated as such. But we must be governed by the obvious intent of the Circuit Court, apparent on the face of the proceedings. We must hold, therefore, the decree of the 5th of December to be the final decree. It appears to have been entered 'as of the 28th of November.' But this circumstance did not affect the rights of parties in respect to appeal. Those rights are determined by the date of the actual entry, or of the signing and filing of the final decree. That test ascertains, for the purpose of appeal, the time of rendering the decree, as the 5th of December, 1866." *Rubber Company v. Goodyear*, 73 U. S. 153, 155-156. (1867).

[2] It also appears that "the time to be taken as when the judgment or decree may be said to be rendered or passed may admit of some latitude and may depend somewhat upon the usage and practice of the particular court." *Silsby v. Foote*, 61 U. S. 290, 295. The usage in this dis-

trict requires the winning party to present a draft of the judgment or decree which, when signed by the judge and filed, fixes the date when the time for perfecting appeals begins to run; yet the case of *Silsby v. Foote*, supra, is authority for the recognition of the date of the decision in simple cases with no special terms to be settled, and where there is urgency for such action, as the date when the time should begin to run.

There is no urgency here; the practice is the other way; and the neglect of petitioner's counsel to furnish a draft for a judgment has given some justification to the respondent for the delay in the matter of the appeal and evidently accounts for it. The petitioner is not in a position to claim that the time for appeal has lasped.

The motion is allowed and the petitioner is required to submit a draft of judgment within four days.

IN THE MATTER OF WILLIAM F. DESHA AND GEORGE W. WILLFONG, EACH IN HIS INDIVIDUAL CAPACITY AND AS PARTNERS COMPOSING THE PARTNERSHIP OF DESHA AND WILLFONG, ALLEGED BANKRUPTS.

May 27, 1913.

Bankruptcy—Insolvency—Burden of proof: The burden of proving solvency under section 3, clause "d" of the bankruptcy act, 30 Stat. 546, is not shifted from the alleged bankrupt to the petitioning creditors merely by reason of the fact that the respondent's books, papers, and accounts are in the custody of the marshal under an order to seize and hold.

In Bankruptcy: Petition for adjudication.

C. S. Carlsmith for petitioning creditors.

C. W. Ashford for respondents William F. Desha and
the firm Desha and Willfong.

CLEMONS, J. This is a creditors' petition for adjudication of bankruptcy of William F. Desha and George W.
Willfong as individuals, and of the firm of Desha and Willfong, or as sometimes called in the papers herein "Willfong
and Desha," which they compose.

The respondent Willfong is in default for want of answer
or appearance. The respondent Desha made an issue of the
fact of insolvency both of himself and of the firm and demanded a jury trial thereof, which demand was waived on
call of the case for hearing and the issue submitted to the
present judge.

The allegation having been conceded at the hearing that
there was a preference constituting an act of bankruptcy,
to-wit, the suffering of a levy of execution on a judgment
of the district court of South Hilo, without satisfying such
execution at least five days before the sale thereunder, I
shall raise no question as to that fact, though it now appears
from the sheriff's return attached to the writ of execution
placed in evidence by the creditors, that the sale was never
consummated, but was adjourned from time to time because of the pendency of this bankruptcy proceeding, and
finally the property seized under the execution was released therefrom for the same reason. But the fact of an
actual sale would seem to be immaterial in any event. *In
re Rome Planing Mills*, 96 Fed. 812, 3 Am. B. R. 123;
Bogen & Trummel v. Protter, 129 Fed. 533, 534, 12 Am. B.
R. 288, 289-290; *In re National Hotel & Cafe Co.*, 138 Fed.
947, 15 Am. B. R. 69; 1 Remington, Bankruptcy, 123-124,
sec. 141; 3 Id. 53-54, sec. 141; Collier, Bankruptcy, 9th ed.,
96-97 and notes; also *In re Lederer*, 1 U. S. Dist. Ct. Haw.
288.

At the hearing, counsel for the petitioning creditors called the respondent Desha as a witness, and examined him as to his books of account; wherefrom it appeared that this respondent had made no effort to bring into court the books, papers and accounts either of himself or of his firm, and that, as he testified, "he left it in the hands of his lawyer and he did not advise asking anyone for the books." It appears, so far as the firm is concerned, that Desha was the mechanic of an automobile repair and supply business, and Willfong the bookkeeper and the only one who knew very much about the finances and affairs of the company. The court also takes judicial notice of its own special warrant to the marshal to seize and hold "all the estate, real and personal" of the respondents Desha and Willfong, and of the marshal's return showing the "attachment of the machine shop, garage and contents, of Willfong and Desha;" and although the return does not specify the seizure of books of account, that fact is inferable from a stipulation of petitioners and respondent Desha, giving this respondent and certain others access to the "books and accounts of said Desha or (and) of the partnership" for purpose of "inspection" and of taking "a trial balance of said books and accounts." Also, creditors' counsel has treated this as a fact, in his brief and oral argument. It does not appear where those books are, but it is practically conceded and may fairly be inferred from the record herein that they are with the other seized property in Hilo, on another island of this district some 200 miles away, and in charge of a special custodian representing the marshal.

It is worth while, in passing, to emphasize the advantage, if not propriety, of a more detailed showing in the marshal's return, of the items of property seized: here there is nothing which can be termed an inventory.

The issue now made by opposing counsel is this: The burden of proving solvency being admittedly cast upon respondents by section 3, clause "d," of the act, 30 Stat.

546-547,—by reason of the fact of an admitted preference, under section 3, clause "a," subdivision "(3),"—is this burden satisfied so far as concerns the firm and the respondent Desha, by that respondent's presence and the excuse made by his counsel that the books (meaning presumably his own books and those of the firm) are in the custody of the marshal and so in the court's custody?—i. e., as much within the control of the court and of the creditors, as within his own control? Clause "d" provides:

"Whenever a person against whom a petition has been filed as hereinbefore provided under the second and third subdivisions of this section takes issue with and denies the allegation of his insolvency, it shall be his duty to appear in court on the hearing, with his books, papers, and accounts, and submit to an examination, and give testimony as to all matters tending to establish solvency or insolvency, and in case of his failure to so attend and submit to examination the burden of proving his solvency shall rest upon him."

Congress has deemed it wise to provide this rule governing the burden of proof in such cases. It is a just rule, because the solvency of an alleged bankrupt is a matter peculiarly within his own knowledge, or almost always within his power to show more easily than it can be shown by anyone else. See 4 Wigmore Evidence, 3525, sec. 2486; 2 Chamberlayne, Evidence, 1154-1156, sec. 978; Jones, Evidence, 2d ed., sec. 181 (179). Are we, then, to raise an exception to that declared rule of policy merely because, in a case like this, it is as convenient for the petitioning creditors (or for the marshal or the judge), as it is for the respondent himself, to get ᵧthe respondent's books into court? The question answers itself. The statute having made it the respondent's duty to appear with his books, the burden must remain and is not to be shifted by the mere consideration of convenience or inconvenience. The contesting respondent Desha could have secured the presence of the books by a subpoena d. t. or by other proper order of court, and it was his business to do so.

Furthermore, apart from the presence or absence of the books of account, clause "d" makes it his duty not only "to appear . . . with his books, papers and accounts, and submit to an examination," but also to "give testimony as to all matters tending to establish solvency or insolvency." He gave no such testimony, but declared himself entirely ignorant on the question at issue. Such ignorance is of itself so uncommon in business life as, fairly, to require explanation, and is itself a circumstance,—though it is not necessary to hold it controlling,—adverse to the special defense of solvency. The respondent Desha has not sustained the burden either as to himself or as to his firm. See Collier, Bankruptcy, 9th ed., 114, and cases cited.

Let the firm be adjudged bankrupt; and let its members as individuals be each so adjudged.

It may be of advantage in future cases, to point out that the delays in this proceeding have been intolerable. As the court is informed, expenses have been incurred approaching the disproportionate aggregate of one thousand dollars. Such expenses are in large measure avoidable. Counsel on both sides appear to have been too complaisant toward expense and delay. For one thing, the stock in trade might, it would seem, have been packed and locked up to avoid the hiring of a special custodian for all these five months.

Let the schedules of the partners as individuals and of the firm be filed within ten days (act, sec. 7, clause "a," subdiv. 8): no extension of time will be granted therefor, save under the most extreme necessity.

Reported, 30 Am. B. R. 130.

IN THE MATTER OF K. L. WONG (OTHERWISE CALLED WONG TIN), A BANKRUPT.

May 31, 1913.

1. *Bankruptcy—Discharge—Concealment of assets, preference:* A bankrupt is refused discharge under the following circumstances: Pressed by creditors and desiring to go into bankruptcy, he packs for shipment to out-of-town correspondents about $65 worth of his merchandise, to be by them sold as a means of obtaining the deposit of $40 required by court on filing petition. Later, on the same day, the store is closed by arrangement between his attorney and the creditors' attorneys, whereby he is to go into bankruptcy as soon as schedules can be prepared, and meantime preserve his merchandise stock intact. Ten days thereafter, he ships the packed goods as planned and immediately files petition, paying the deposit with money borrowed from a friend. Ten weeks or more later, the goods are returned unsold and the bankrupt sells them for about $48, paying therewith the loan of $40 and small charges for freight and cartage, and keeping the balance of about $5, without accounting therefor to the trustee: though the bankrupt alleged his regard of these goods as security for the loan and disclaimed intent to defraud creditors, in the face, however, of the facts, that the only understanding with the lender was that repayment be made within two months, and that the lender was not mentioned in the schedules as a secured creditor, or these goods mentioned as the bankrupt's own subject to lien.

2. *Same—Attorney's fees, attorney for voluntary bankrupt:* Attorneys for voluntary bankrupts should, as a rule and in the absence of extraordinary circumstances, be allowed only a small fee for services in aid of preparing schedules; and the same policy applies to services for attending meetings of creditors. For preparing petition for discharge, and attendance at hearing thereon, no fee is allowed under the foregoing circumstances. The mere fact that the bankrupt's accounts are voluminous is not, under the above rule, an extraordinary difficulty calling for legal services commanding more than a nominal fee; the attorney is not to be compensated on any basis of even common legal skill or knowledge for matters which require merely the routine services of a clerk or bookkeeper.

In Bankruptcy: Petition for discharge; petition for attorney's fees.

I. M. Stainback (*Holmes, Stanley & Olson* with him) for the petitioning creditors.

E. A. Douthitt (*Douthitt & Coke* with him) for the bankrupt.

CLEMONS, J. [1] On opposition of the creditors to the bankrupt's petition for discharge, the following facts appear: The bankrupt, a Honolulu dry-goods merchant, hard pressed by creditors through legal proceedings and otherwise, desired to go into bankruptcy, but, as he claims, was unable to raise the necessary deposit of $40 required by the court on filing petition. Finally, according to his statement, he packed for shipment to correspondents on the Island of Kauai about $65 worth of merchandise from his stock, to be by them sold, in order that he might secure the means wherewith to pay this deposit. Later on the same day, his store was closed, by arrangement between his attorney and the attorney for the creditors, whereby he was to go into bankruptcy as soon as schedules could be prepared, and meantime preserve his stock intact. Ten days thereafter, he shipped the packed goods as planned, and immediately, i. e. in the same forenoon, filed his petition in bankruptcy, paying the deposit, or filing fee, with money then borrowed from a friend. Ten weeks or more thereafter the goods were returned unsold, and thereupon the bankrupt sold them for $47.84, paying therewith the loan of $40 and small charges for freight and cartage, and keeping the balance of $5.27, without accounting therefor to the trustee, meanwhile appointed, or without having mentioned these goods in his schedules. The bankrupt alleges that he regarded these goods as security for the loan and disclaims any intent to defraud creditors;—though he himself testified to no understanding with the lender other than that the loan should pe repaid within two months, and though the lender is not mentioned in the schedules as a secured creditor, or at all so far as this loan is concerned, and though these goods are not mentioned therein as being the bankrupt's property subject to lien.

The inexplicable discrepancies appearing in statements of the bankrupt made here in court, made at a hearing before the referee, and made to those who testified here, it would be unprofitable to set forth. It need only be said, that the testimony and the record force the conviction, that the bankrupt, if not intending to deal unfairly toward his creditors with regard to these particular goods, is at least reasonably chargeable with such an intent under all the circumstances. If he did not know better, he should with his education and experience have known better than to act as he did. His acts were a plain violation of the spirit of the statute, sec. 7, clause "a," subdiv. (8), sec. 60, clause "b," sec. 70, clause "a," 30 Stat. 548, 562, 565, and directly within the contemplation of section 14, clause "b," subdivs. (1), (4), 30 Stat. 550. See Collier, Bankruptcy, 9th ed., 335-340, 342-343, 356-357.

As junior counsel for the creditors wisely argues: Of what force as against designing debtors is the bankruptcy law, if we are to let a bankrupt merchant decide what he is to do with his goods, at what price he is to dispose of them pending bankruptcy proceedings, and to whom he is to pay the proceeds by way of preference, if he thinks best to sell them,—all in the face of his own attorney's express instructions (as is the fact here) not to disturb his goods when his store is closed in contemplation of an agreed bankruptcy?

Let the petition for discharge be denied.

As to the duty of the bankrupt and the right of the trustee, with reference to the money realized from the sale in question, these are matters for the consideration of the trustee and of the bankrupt, hardly calling for any further suggestion from the court.

[2] The attorneys for this voluntary bankrupt move for

allowance of a fee, and in support thereof show by affidavit an estate comprised of $550 in cash and merchandise valued at $2,350 (though it is not stated whether this is the value as appraised), and show services consisting of preparation of schedules "which took the greater portion of one week," involving "a careful examination of the books, accounts, papers and documents" of the bankrupt "and the segregation and classification thereof," also the attendance "at the meeting when the trustee was elected", also the preparation of "petition for discharge of the bankrupt . . . with the order of publication thereof," and attendance in court at the hearing on this petition.

The petition was heard after notice to referee and trustee, but not to creditors,—as none seems to be required except by rule: *In re Stotts*, 93 Fed. 438, 1 Am. B. R. 641; 2 Remington, Bankruptcy, 1275-1276, sec. 2053; and as none has ever been required under the practice here, so far as the present judge's considerable experience in local bankruptcy practice informs him.

The matter of fees to attorneys for the bankrupt in voluntary cases is such "as the court may allow," act, sec. 64, clause "a," subdiv. "(3)," 30 Stat. 563, am. 32 Stat. 800, sec. 14, am. 34 Stat. 267. This gives the court a wide discretion but still a discretion to be exercised with due regard to the spirit of the statute. Collier, Bankruptcy, 9th ed. 845, and n. 71; 2 Remington, Bankruptcy, 1293, sec. 2089. See Id., 1296-1298, sec. 2097. "The maximum fee in voluntary procedings, where there is no unforeseen litigation or extraordinary services" is fixed by rule of the court for the district of North Carolina, at $50. *In re Morris*, 125 Fed. 841, 11 Am. B. R. 145.

A fee for services in the preparation of schedules is allowable: *In re Stratemeyer*, 2 U. S. Dist. Ct. Haw. 269, 14 Am. B. R. 120; *In re Hitchock*, 3 U. S. Dist. Ct. Haw. 138, 17 Am. B. R. 664; *In re Levy Outfitting Co., ante*, pp. 86, 91, 29 Am. B. 13; but insofar as these services are, though laborious, merely the work of a bookkeeper or "mainly clerical" (*In re Mayer*, 101 Fed. 695, 697, 4 Am. B. R. 238, 241), and do not require the knowledge or discretion of one learned in the law, the court is disposed not to allow to the attorney any considerable compensation therefor.

In the eastern district of Wisconsin, the "customary allowance for services in drafting schedules is from $25 to $50, according to the extent." *In re Mayer*, supra. In *In re Carolina Cooperage Co.*, 96 Fed. 950, 3 Am. B. R. 154, where there had been no litigation and where the services to the bankrupt had not been onerous, an allowance of $75 was held excessive and was reduced to $25. See *In re Meis*, 18 Am. B. R. 104, 108.

No reason is apparent why the advising in an ordinary case,—and this case, so far as concerns the necessity for legal advice and aid in the matter of schedules, does not seem to be extraordinary,—should call for more compensation than the above minimum of $25, and this sum is hereby allowed for such services; though this figure is not approved as being the minimum to be observed in the practice of this court, for the preparation of schedules in most cases involves no more care, and requires no greater amount or quality of legal advice, than, e. g., the drawing of the simplest deed of conveyance.

As to attendance at meetings of creditors, there being no showing of the extent or of the value, if any, of the attorneys' services, no more than a nominal fee of $5 is allowed.

A fee for preparation of petition for discharge, order of publication of notice of the hearing, and attendance at hearing, has been allowed by this court in the case of *Hitchcock*, a voluntary bankrupt, supra, and in the case of *Stratemeyer*, an involuntary bankrupt, supra.

Though this view has been doubted (see Collier, Bankruptcy, 9th ed. 844-845 and notes; 2 Remington, Bankruptcy, secs. 2087, 2090, 2097; Loveland, Bankruptcy, 3d ed. 161 and n. 23), and the question is, I think, an arguable

one, I am 'not disposed to doubt the correctness of the view
of Judge Brown of New York, as to the law as it is written,
if not as to the law as it should be,—adopted by Judge Dole
of this court in the matter of *Hitchock*, supra.

But in view of the circumstances, and in view of the
ruling on the petition for discharge, based, it is true, on
acts of which the bankrupt's attorney was innocent and
ignorant and which were committed even contrary to his
instructions, no fee is allowed in this matter of discharge.

A larger fee might have been allowed had there been a
showing of particulars requiring special or extraordinary
advice in the matter of schedules, or had there been a showing that the creditors' meeting was something more than
the usual routine affair of a few minutes only, or had there
been a showing of services "beneficial to creditors" in addition to services "in assisting the bankrupt to perform his
statutory duties." 2 Remington, Bankruptcy, 1294, sec.
2090; Id. 1295, sec. 2091; Collier, Bankruptcy, 9th ed., 844-
845. The court, in making this award, errs, if at all, on the
side of moderation, keeping in view an established and safe
policy. See Collier, Bankruptcy, 9th ed., 845, and n. 77.
And see *In re Kross,* 96 Fed. 816, 819, 3 Am. B. R. 187, 191.

Let the attorneys for the bankrupt be paid by the trustee
out of the funds of this estate the sum of $30 as a fee for
their services herein.

———— .

Reported, 30 Am. B. R. 125.

IN THE MATTER OF THE APPLICATION OF LEE LEONG FOR A WRIT OF HABEAS CORPUS.

June 2, 1913.

1. *Habeas corpus—Return—Practice:* Attack on the sufficiency of a petition for a writ of habeas corpus should under the settled practice be made by motion to quash or vacate, and not in the return to the writ.

2. *Immigration—Aliens—Birth certificate under S. L. Hawaii, 1911, Act 96 as evidence of citizenship:* The Federal immigration officers are justified in refusing admission to the country to a person of Chinese descent, claiming to be a citizen by virtue of birth in Hawaii and presenting a certificate of the fact of such birth, issued by the Secretary the Territory under Session Laws of Hawaii, 1911, act 96, when circumstances appear which overcome the prima facie effect of such certificate as evidence.

Habeas corpus: On return to writ.

Andrews & Quarles and *G. S. Curry* for petitioner.

C. C. Bitting, Assistant U. S. Attorney, for respondent.

CLEMONS, J.   A writ of habeas corpus issued on the allegation of the petitioner Lee Leong's unlawful detention in the custody of the respondent, the immigration inspector in charge at the port of Honolulu, for the purpose of deportation, the petitioner being entitled to land as a citizen by virtue of birth in Hawaii on or about the 21st day of January, 1888, of parents then domiciled here and lawfully married, and he being now on his return to Hawaii after having at the age of four years been taken to China by his parents with whom he has since resided there.   The petition for the writ alleged as the basis for the inspector's detention of the petitioner, a mere semblance of a hearing,—an unfair hearing,—in that no consideration was given by the immigration officers to a certificate issued by the Secretary of the Territory of Hawaii under the great seal of the Terri-

tory, dated the 21st day of November, 1912, to the effect
that the petitioner was born in Hawaii on the 21st day of
January, 1888, and in that no consideration was given to
"the uncontradicted evidence of numerous witnesses who
testified as to the identity of the petitioner and to his birth
in Hawaii." The petition also showed an appeal to the
Secretary of Commerce and Labor from the inspector's finding of want of birth in Hawaii, and an affirmance of the
inspector's decision and order of deportation.

A return to the writ was sustained on exceptions, because, as it appeared to me, it showed that the respondent
held the petitioner by virtue of a determination made by
competent authority and duly affirmed; and further because at that stage there was in the respondent's return no
admission of the identity of the petitioner with the person
named in the birth certificate. The court took occasion,
however, to criticise the prolix and repetitious character of
both the return and the petition. [1] It may be noted also
that the exception to the return for its embodiment of a
demurrer to the petition is well taken; for, the writ having
issued, any attack on the sufficiency of the petition should
have been made by motion to quash or vacate. 21 Cyc.
317; Church, Habeas Corpus, 2d ed., sec. 169. "The return
should be responsive to the writ, and not to the petition
upon which it is based." Church, Habeas Corpus, 2d ed.,
sec. 160.

Finally, on a traverse to the return, issues were raised as
to the following facts: 1. The petitioner's being of the
excluded class of aliens; 2. The abandonment or surrender
of his right to enter or reside in the United States; 3. The
issuance of the Hawaiian birth certificate; 4. The fairness
and impartiality of the hearing; 5. The consideration by
the immigration officers of the birth certificate and of uncontradicted evidence in behalf of the petitioner; 6. The
rendition of a judgment and determination of the inspector
after his admission of further evidence on reopening.

A hearing was then had in which it was shown that the inspector had given consideration to the birth certificate,—which would be presumed in any event (*Ex parte Wing You,* 190 Fed. 294, 297), unless it be for the issue made on that point under the pleadings. But of course the question of law still remained whether the consideration given was due consideration.

At the hearing the fact of the issuance of the certificate and the identity of the petitioner with the person whose photograph is annexed thereto, were admitted by the government. It also appeared that the inspector had ample evidence to establish preliminarily that the petitioner was the son of Chinese parents of the excluded class.

The point of expatriation need not concern us. Even assuming that under the circumstances shown by the evidence the petitioner by remaining away for some years after having reached his majority, impliedly renounced his nationality and allegiance as an American citizen (if he was such), still as the determination of the inspector did not raise any question of expatriation,—did not rest upon any ground of expatriation, but rather on the failure to show birth in Hawaii,—no such question was open here.

It also appeared that the petitioner on appeal had the benefit of the supplementary evidence adduced on rehearing and that although there was no other formal judgment than the original decision, still the memorandum of the inspector, "after consideration of the record I see no reason to change the opinion already formed," reaffirms the former decision or adopts it by reference.

The fairness and impartiality of the hearing on the question of his birth in Hawaii, which includes the question of the consideration given the birth certificate, i. e., its due consideration as a matter of law, is, then, the only point remaining.

The petitioner's essential point was that the certificate of birth was made prima facie evidence of the facts therein stated, by Session Laws of Hawaii, 1911, act 96, sec. 3, and must be given full faith and credit under Revised Statutes, sec. 906, in spite of which, as he contended, the immigration officers gave no consideration to this certificate and none to the petitioner's witnesses.

But prima facie evidence stands only until overcome by "controlling evidence or discrediting circumstances." *Kelley v. Jackson*, 31 U. S. (6 Pet.) 622, 631-632. And the immigration officers were, in my opinion, at liberty to find from the evidence discrediting circumstances if nothing more.

Assuming the birth certificate to be entitled to credit as prima facie evidence,—though the view of this court seems to have been otherwise in *In re Su Yen Hoon*, 3 U. S. Dist. Ct. Haw. 606, 609, 610, applying a statutory provision similar to that now reenacted in the session laws of 1911,—there were also before the immigration officers matters which they were at liberty in their province as weighers of evidence to regard as casting doubt upon the fact of birth. There was the discrediting circumstance that the petitioner produced before the immigration officers ten witnesses besides himself, offering them as persons who had knowledge of facts which would establish his birth in Hawaii, but whose testimony shows an absence of such knowledge,—testimony, either the barest hearsay, or inconsistent and untrustworthy, or insufficient when pieced together to connect the immigrant with the person born in Hawaii, taken to China at four years of age and now returning. Hereinafter the words "the boy Lee Leong" will indicate the boy born in Hawaii as distinguished from the word "petitioner" which will indicate the petitioner holding the birth certificate on the claim of being the same Lee Leong.

The reports of immigration officer Moore (marked "U. S. Exhibit 1," introduced by petitioner on cross-examination of the inspector, being letters of March 17th and April 2nd, 1913) point out this untrustworthiness in detail.

The witness Lee Yet, a relative of the petitioner (Petition, Exhibit A) and—not a neglible circumstance,—the man who applied for the birth certificate (see Id., and see birth certificate) connected the boy Lee Leong with a person who had an uncle (father's brother) Lee Ming, and who had no child, but the petitioner says that his father had no brother, that he did not know any Lee Ming, and that he himself had a child (Petition, Exhibit A). Lee Yau, who claimed to have known the boy Lee Leong at least since the latter was 4 or 5 years old (Id.) and who saw him often and visited his house often until he was 8 or 9 years old, and who saw the petitioner in 1910 some 13 years afterwards, could not identify the petitioner as the boy Lee Leong. Lee Sau, who claimed to be well acquainted with the boy Lee Leong and with his family and visited them immediately after their arrival in China (in 1892) and again in 1907, and used to teach him, was unknown to the petitioner either by face or name. Lee Lung, who knew the boy Lee Leong from the time of the latter's arrival in China, and who came to Hawaii when the boy Lee Leong was about 9 years old (1897) and was in China again in 1910 and stayed for 9 months in the village of Sun Chin, where the boy Lee Leong is alleged to have resided, was unable to identify the petitioner as the boy Lee Leong. Lee Lau, who testified to seeing the boy Lee Leong in China when the latter was 4 or 5 years old, and who lived in the same village of Sun Chin until 1900 (Petition, Exhibit A), i. e., until the boy Lee Leong was 12 years old, admitted that he never saw the *petitioner* until 1911 (Id.).

It was within the discretion of the immigration officers, who saw the witnesses and observed their demeanor when testifying, to give weight as a discrediting circumstance to the fact that none of the witnesses could identify the petitioner as the boy Lee Leong, although some of the witnesses had known him and his family very well for differ-

ent periods of time, some short and others longer, and
that the petitioner could not identify witnesses who knew
the boy Lee Leong (e. g., Lee Keau and Lee Sau, and see
Petition, Exhibit A.; U. S. Exhibit 1, letter of April 2,
1913).

When persons who ought to know, and whom the petitioner offers as witnesses who do know that petitioner is
who he claims to be, prove not to know the petitioner to
be the boy alleged to have been born in Hawaii and who
at the age of 4 went to China and to whom the certificate
is alleged to apply, that fact certainly may raise a question
whether the petitioner, though identified (by admission of
the government) as the person whose photograph is annexed to the birth certificate, was really the person who
was born in Hawaii and who went to China and for whose
birth the certificate is alleged to have issued. If the petitioner had relied only on the birth certificate and if this
certificate must be given prima facie credit as evidence, then
of course in the absence of other evidence, it alone would
be sufficient to entitle him to land. But when he offers the
certificate and in addition asserts that he was a boy who
was born in Hawaii and who at the age of 4 went to Sun
Chin village and lived there until the age of 25, and that
the certificate applies to that boy, and when he produces
witnesses who claim that they had an opportunity to know
the boy Lee Leong and his family very intimately there
in that small village continuously from 1 year to 8 years,
or until the boy was 12 years old, but are shown by their
own testimony not to have been able on return visits to
China, and not now to be able here to identify the petitioner
as that boy, and when the petitioner himself cannot identify
some of these witnesses, surely a doubt is cast upon
the fact of the petitioner's being the same person as the
boy Lee Leong, and so a doubt also upon the certificate
which he claimed to apply to that boy and to prove that
boy's (and his own) birth in Hawaii. If the circumstances

above set forth do not directly discredit the certificate itself, they indirectly do the same thing by raising a doubt as to the truth of the fact in issue, the petitioner's birth in Hawaii which the certificate is offered to prove.

Also, a minor circumstance may be noted in the discrepancy of one month between the date of birth as given in the certificate and as claimed by the petitioner in his testimony.

It may not unfairly be said, that a certificate issued, as this was, not until 25 years after the party's birth and upon an ex parte hearing then had, would, even though prima facie evidence, still not be entitled as against other evidence to such weight as, e. g., a certificate based upon a report of birth, marriage or death made contemporaneously by an attending physician or clergyman.

There appear in the record two statements which may be termed "gratuitous" (or at least the second may), but which should have passing notice. First, in the report of officer Moore to the inspector (U. S. Exhibit 1, letter of March 17, 1913), it is stated that "there is no record of the departure of the applicant." This report was not regarded as a part of the record but as in the nature of a memorandum or brief on the case (Tr., pp. 4, 5, 6, 7) and it is not to be presumed that anything in it was considered as evidence either at the original hearing or on the appeal. Though, possibly, under the decision in *Tang Tun v. Edsell*, 223 U. S. 673, 681, it may have been proper to have considered it in any event; the court taking judicial notice that at the time of the alleged departure passenger lists were required to be filed with officers of the Hawaiian government before clearance of vessels. Penal Laws of Hawaii, 1897, sec. 1177, embracing the law in force in 1892. No point, or objection, was made on account of this report by petitioner's counsel in argument at the hearing. Second, the inspector in his testimony at the hearing on traverse to the return, says, "You will find that the people who made the affidavits are witnesses in the case." This referred clearly enough to the fact that the witnesses who gave testimony before the Secretary of the Territory as a basis for the birth certificate, were witnesses at the hearings before the immigration officers; from which an inference might be justified that the weak testimony, the want of knowledge, of these witnesses here would discredit the certificate founded on their testimony there. But it does not appear, and cannot be presumed that this stated fact was considered by the inspector in reaching his decision, or by the Secretary of Commerce and Labor on the appeal: it was entirely new matter, brought out for the first time at the hearing here. And no point, or objection, was there made on account of it by petitioner's counsel. These two items should not, therefore, be considered in determining the fairness of the proceedings before the immigration officers. They serve only to suggest the question whether, even in spite of any unfairness in the hearing before these officers, the petitioner would be found on a full and fair hearing to be entitled to land. See *Chin Yow v. United States*, 208 U. S. 8, 13.

The writ is discharged and the petitioner remanded to the custody of the respondent.

Affirmed: Lee Leong v. United States, 217 Fed. 48.

IN THE MATTER OF THE APPLICATION OF TOME TANNO FOR A WRIT OF HABEAS CORPUS.

June 2, 1913.

1. *Immigration—Alien immigrant, fiancee of domiciled alien:* A woman, resident of a foreign country, with whom a domiciled alien has entered into an agreement to marry upon her arrival, is not a "non-immigrant" alien, but is subject to the provisions of the immigration act, 34 Stat. 898.,

2. *Same—Finding of immigration officers, finality of:* The finding of a board of special inquiry of the immigration service that a woman has admitted the commission of an offense involving moral turpitude, within section 2 of the immigration act, cannot be set aside, so long as the finding is based on a fair hearing, and no abuse of authority, or mistake of law, appears.

3. *Same—Exclusion of alien for commission of crime—Adultery:* The commission of adultery is a ground of deportation under section 2 of the immigration act, this being an offense "involving moral turpitude."

4. *Statutes—Foreign law—Evidence—Presumption of continuity:* When under the law of a foreign state adultery is shown by a decision of its highest court to have been a crime in 1903, it will be presumed that it continued to be a crime there in 1905.

Habeas corpus: Demurrer to respondent's return.

J. Lightfoot for petitioner.
C. C. Bitting, Assistant U. S. Attorney, for respondent.

CLEMONS, J.   This case is before the court on petitioner's demurrer to respondent's return to a writ of habeas corpus, from which return it appears that the respondent as United States immigration inspector at the port of Honolulu, holds the petitioner, an alien (Japanese) female as deportable, pursuant to the finding of a board of special inquiry, for commission of a crime or misdemeanor involving moral turpitude and for admission of guilt of such misconduct, to-wit, in the finding of the board, the "living for

several years with a man not her husband in open and
notorious adultery." The return, dated April 14th, 1913,
also shows the petitioner to have, on March 10th, 1913,
waived her right of appeal from the board's decision, and
to have at no time since then taken an appeal. See *In re
Yim Kwock Leong*, 1 U. S. Dist. Ct. Haw. (Estee) 66; *In
re Koon Ko*, 3 U. S. Dist. Ct. Haw. 623, 625. This failure to
appeal, admitted by the demurrer, would alone, suffice to
dispose of the case, apart from the substantial points hereinafter discussed. *In re Young Chow Yee*, ante, p. 241. [In
the traverse to the return, later filed, the allegation of failure to appeal was denied, and that denial was not contested
by the respondent.]

The return exhibits a transcript of the proceedings before
the board. The only direct evidence shown thereby from
which a conclusion could be drawn, of an admission of guilt
of a crime or misdemeanor involving moral turpitude, is
her own testimony that, having left her husband for his
failure to provide sufficient food for herself and small child,
she went from Hawaii to a "saw-mill" village near Seattle,
with a man whom she characterized as "her sweetheart at
that time" and who paid her transportation, and there
lived with him for two years and two months "*the same as
if she were his wife*,"—he working in the saw mill and she
washing clothes for Japanese and American laborers in the
small village of about one hundred people, mostly of her
own race, circumstances more or less relevant to the question of the notoriety of their relations. Her sweetheart thereafter paid her passage back to Japan,
where she was divorced from her husband. And
she now returns to Hawaii as a "picture bride," i. e., a
woman engaged by correspondence for a marriage to take
place upon her admission to this country. The board had
at first some suspicion that the petitioner might be identical with a woman deported from Seattle as a prostitute,

but could not ascertain the fact, and did not base their decision on such suspicion.

[1] The petitioner by her attorney (brief on demurrer) disclaims any domicil here by reason of her former residence, "since it is not claimed that she left with the intention of returning or that she has maintained her domicil" in Hawaii, but submits that since, as is a fact, her present husband is domiciled here, it follows that this is her domicil also, and so she does not come within the class of immigrant aliens.

The contention is unwarranted. It does not appear that the immigrant is married to a domiciled alien. On the contrary, according to the woman's testimony before the immigration inspector, her marriage to such an alien was only "by correspondence." The court recognizes no such marriage. The most that could be said of the transaction is that it is merely an unconsummated agreement to marry upon landing.

[2] It is also contended that the words of her testimony above set forth "do not amount to an admission of having committed the crime of adultery."

A case in which a woman is held to have admitted the commission of a crime involving moral turpitude, merely by saying that she had "lived with" a man to whom she was not married, "the same as if she were his wife," may seem close to the border-line of a fair hearing of the facts in evidence; but yet, even under this contention, it would be clearly one of those cases characterized by Justice Holmes as of mere erroneous judgment of a tribunal having jurisdiction and not to be upset by another tribunal of even higher grade, or whose judgment may be better. *Chin Yow v. United States*, 208 U. S. 8, 13. The words by which she described her relations with this man, have in common usage such a well known meaning of sharing bed as well as board, that I cannot say that they did not as here spoken of a "sweetheart" not her husband, under all the circumstances including that of the witnesses' demeanor (which cannot be viewed by me), fairly convey a meretricious meaning. The proceding before the immigration officers, being a civil rather than a criminal one, it might·be said,—though it is not necessary for me to go that far,—that, under the circumstances, this woman was called upon to give these words of her own choice any other innocent sense, of living with her "sweetheart" as housekeeper, nurse, or otherwise in a wifely capacity outside of the sharing of his bed. But my ruling is placed on more solid ground.

The hearing accorded to the immigrant was fair, no abuse of authority or mistake of law is apparent; therefore the decision thereupon cannot be set aside. *United States v. Ju Toy*, 198 U. S. 253; *Chin Yow v. United States*, 208 U. S. 8; *Tang Tun v. Edsell*, 223 U. S. 673; *In re Chop Tin*, 2 U..S. Dist. Ct. Haw. 153; *In re Pang Kun*, Id. 192; *In re Nakashima*, 3 Id. 168, 176; *In re Su Yen Hoon*, Id. 606; *In re Koon Ko*, Id. 623.

[3] And, finally, it is contended, that even if there is "an admission of an adulterous relation" between the petitioner and her former "sweetheart," "that is not the admission of a crime involving moral turpitude within the meaning of the immigration laws,"—there being emphasized incidentally the fact of her former husband's negligence and failure to provide for herself and child, "compelling her to seek . . . necessaries of life by wrongdoing," the fact that it is difficult for a woman with young child to obtain employment, and the fact that her relations, whatever they may have been, with her former sweetheart, "were terminated and the woman is now honorably married to a man able to supply her with the necessaries of life," whom she now seeks to join here.

Whether the woman's wrongdoing be adultery, no discussion should be necessary to establish to the mind of anyone of moral sense, according to standards to which social policy can admit no exceptions, that her questioned

act was one of moral turpitude. See *Pollard v. Lyon*, 92
U. S. 225, 228; also *United States v. Bitty*, 208 U. S. 393,
401; *United States v. Uhl*, 203 Fed. 152, 154; *Gomes v.
Hawaiian Gazette Co.*, 10 Haw. 108, 111. But the statute
is directed only against "*a felony, or other crime or misdemeanor* involving moral turpitude." 34 Stat. 898, sec. 2.
And, of course, if the admitted act was criminal, it must, we
will assume for the purposes of this case at least, have been
so by virtue of the law of the place where committed, i. e.,
the State of Washington; for neither adultery nor fornication were indictable at common law, unless by reasons of
such openness and notoriety as effected a public nuisance.
Com. v. Putnam, 1 Pick. 136, 140. *State v. Lash*, 16 N. J.
L. 280, 284, 32 Am. Dec. 397, 398; 1 Bishop, N. Cr. L., sec.
38; 2 Enc. L. & P. 273-274; 1 Cyc. 952; 1 A. & E. Enc.
L. 2d ed. 747; 19 Cyc. 1434-1435; 13 A. & E. Enc. L. 2d ed.
1119.

[4] And it seems that these offenses are criminal
under the statutes of that State. At least, adultery was a
crime under the Code of 1881, sec. 944, Huntley's Penal
Code (1893), sec. 2374, 2 Hill's Ann. Stats. (1891), 705, sec.
193; though, apparently, fornication was not, unless open
.and notorious (as was the character of the act here: finding
of board), Huntley's Penal Code (1893) sec. 2378; 2 Hill's
Ann. Stats. (1891) 705, sec. 192. Such I shall assume to
have continued to be the law of Washington on May 15,
1905, when this woman went to Seattle and for the two
years and two months thereafter when she "lived with"
her "sweetheart" in that vicinity,—in view of the case of
State v. Nelson, 39 Wash. 221, 81 Pac. 721, decided on July
18, 1905, one month after she began "living" with this man
as his "wife." This decision, involving an offense committed in 1903, and that of *State v. Keith*, 48 Wash. 77, 92
Pac. 893, rendered in December, 1907, but not giving the
date of the offense involved, both refer to Ballinger's Annotated Codes and Statutes, defining adultery and fixing its

punishment as a crime.   In the absence of a complete set of the statutes covering the period in question, the presumption of continuity, or the inference against change, may be applied.   2 Chamberlayne, Ev., sec. 1030; 4 Wigmore, Ev., sec. 2530; Jones, Ev., 2d ed., sec. 58.

Let the demurrer to the return be overruled.   The petitioner may have one week within which to file traverse to the return.

IN THE MATTER OF THE APPLICATION OF TOME TANNO FOR A WRIT OF HABEAS CORPUS.

October 18, 1913.

1. *Statutes—Construction—Exceptions to letter of law:* An exception to the letter of a statute may not be raised on the ground that a matter is not within its spirit, unless the reason for the exception be imperative or at least reasonably clear.

2. *Aliens—Immigration—Wife of resident alien:* The wife of a resident alien is subject to the immigration act, 34 Stat. 898, am. 36 Stat. 263.

Habeas Corpus: Hearing on traverse to return.

J. Lightfoot for petitioner.
C. C. Bitting, Assistant U. S. Attorney, for respondent.

CLEMONS, J.   A sufficient preliminary statement of this case appears in the decision overruling the demurrer to the return, ante, p. 266.   A traverse to the return was thereafter filed which, aside from its attempted renewal of the demurrer, raises an issue as to the "full [ness], complete [ness] and fair [ness]" of the hearing before the board of special inquiry. On this issue the case was set for hearing, but in reply to the court's request there was then no offer to prove anything outside of what already appeared in the record of the hearing before the board, except further matters in mitigation of the alleged adultery and further matters in support of the petitioner's alleged marriage.

In a brief subsequently filed, the petitioner again raises the question of the moral turpitude of the petitioner's alleged adultery and attempts to justify it by the circumstance of her former husband's failure to furnish her with the necessities of life. The ruling on the demurrer settles this question: the acknowledged commission of the act is what excludes the alien; there are no exceptions on the ground of circumstances,—at least save such circumstances, absent here, as the law would recognize as depriving the act of its voluntary character.

[1] The point is also made, in argument, that the principle of the decision in the case of the *Church of the Holy Trinity v. United States*, 143 U. S. 457, 472 (summarized in *Tsoi Sim v. United States*, 116 Fed. 920, 926-927) should be applied to prevent the application of the act in question (34 Stat. 898, am. 36 Stat. 263) to a woman whose admitted crime was committed some eight years ago, as is the fact here, and under stress of circumstances, and who having now married is presumed to be disposed to observe her marital obligations,—in other words, is presumed to have repented and reformed. That decision raised an exception to the letter of the law because the court conceived the excepted case not to be within its spirit. But I see no reason for regarding the present case as beyond the spirit of the statute. Courts should be slow to raise exceptions to the letter of the legislative will, unless the exception be imperative or at least reasonably clear.

[2] The petitioner, in her brief, argues also the question of the sufficiency of her alleged marriage to a resident alien. But the question is not open. She offered what testimony

she had—which was merely the say-so of herself and her alleged husband that she had been married by "correspondence." Apparently the board did not believe the evidence on that point.   But in any event, the element of marriage would seem to be immaterial.   For the petitioner's position as the wife of a resident alien could be no stronger than that of the non-naturalizable immigrant wife of a citizen, whom both the Supreme Court and the Circuit Court of Appeals for the ninth circuit have held to be subject to the immigration act.   *Low Wah Suey v. Backus*, 225 U. S. 460, 473-474, 475-476;   *Looe Shee v. North*, 170 Fed. 566, 571. See, also, the present court's ruling in the case of *Chong Shee*, ante, p. 80.   The conclusion in the cases just cited is supported by the decision in *Zartarian v. Billings*, 204 U. S. 170, applying the immigration act of 1903, 32 Stat. 1213, and holding that a minor child of a naturalized citizen, born abroad and remaining abroad until after her father's naturalization, is excluded from admission if afflicted with a dangerous, contagious disease.   The basis of that decision is the child's want of citizenship, her alienage;   just as alienage is the basis of the decision in the case of *Low Wah Suey*, supra.

One is conscious of a conflict of policies with regard to the application of section 2,—on the one hand, the unwritten policy that husband and wife should not be separated (*Tsoi Sim v. United States*, 116 Fed. 920, 923, 925) and on the other the letter of the law as here written.   But the courts have nothing to do with the fact that this statute is capable of working harshly.   *Low Wah Suey v. Backus*, 225 U. S. 476; *In the Matter of Chong Shee*, ante, p. 80.   See *Zartarian v. Billings*, 204 U. S. 175.   And this court cannot refuse to apply to section 2 the principle applied by the Supreme Court to section 3 (case of *Low Wah Suey*, supra) and to the corresponding section of the immigration act of 1903 (case of *Zartarian*, supra), merely because the principle may seem of doubtful application to one or more of the extended list of inhibited conditions attending alien immigrants: especially, in the case at bar, the court may not, if it would, enforce its own idea of what is more desirable,—to keep husband and wife (if there be a marriage here) together at all events, or to keep from our country a wife who has committed a crime involving moral turpitude. In such case a married woman may be as objectionable as a single woman. *Low Wah Suey v. Backus,* supra, at 476 [*Lapina v. Williams,* 232 U. S. 78, 92].

Aside, then, from the fact that all the evidence which the petitioner had to offer was heard by the immigration officers, the court need here receive no further evidence which she could now produce either as to circumstances mitigating her adultery or as to the fact of her marriage.

The findings of the board of special inquiry that the petitioner is an alien immigrant and that she had admitted the commission of a crime involving moral turpitude, were had after a fair hearing, and are based upon evidence legally sufficient, in my opinion, to justify the conclusions reached. Therefore, let the writ be discharged and the petitioner remanded to the custody of the respondent.

IN THE MATTER OF THE APPLICATION OF TOME TANNO FOR A WRIT OF HABEAS CORPUS (SECOND PETITION).

April 23, 1915.

1. *Aliens—Immigration—Denial of landing—Appeal—Authority to determine:* Whoever challenges the authority of an Acting Secretary of Labor to determine an appeal from a decision of an immigration

board denying the landing·of an alien, assumes the burden of proving it clearly.

2. *Habeas corpus—Accident and mistake as grounds for—Pleading:* A petition for writ of habeas corpus which alleges as one of its grounds the failure through accident or mistake to perfect an appeal in a former similar proceeding before the same court, must state fully and explicitly the manner in which the accident or mistake occurred.

3. *Same—Pleading—Sham or frivolous allegations:* Sham or frivolous allegations are to be discountenanced and especially in an extraordinary proceeding such as habeas corpus.

4. *Same—Same—Verification:* It should appear distinctly either from the verification or from the verification taken in connection with the petition for the writ, what allegations are made on personal knowledge and what on information and belief.

5. *Same—Successive applications for writ:* Where appeals have been provided for in habeas corpus cases, it has come to be the rule, either as one of law or practice, that a judgment remanding the petitioner is conclusive on a subsequent application for the writ, the petitioner being left to his remedy by appeal.

6. *Same—Same—Necessity of subsequently occurring events as new grounds:* A second application for writ of habeas corpus will not be considered, as a general rule, unless there are as a basis for the writ new facts which did not exist when the first application was presented.

Habeas corpus: On traverse to return to order to show cause.

J. Lightfoot for petitioner.
Jeff McCarn, U. S. District Attorney, for respondent.

CLEMONS, J.   The language of this court in its opinion in the case of *Denjiro Yokoda*, post, decided December 29, 1914,—referring to a decision of Judge Dooling of California,—would I think apply here, to the ground of this petition most strongly relied upon, that the petitioner, appealing to the Secretary of Labor from a decision of an immigration board of special inquiry, had not had his appeal determined by a competent officer, but by a so-called "Acting Secretary," unauthorized to act.   Also, the case of *Tang Tun v. Edsell*, 223 U. S. 673, would have some appli-

cation. In the latter case it was held that the decision
on appeal was none the less the decision of the Secretary
of Commerce and Labor, because communicated by the Assistant Secretary by telegram. [1] The part of the *Denjiro
Yokoda* decision to which I refer, in which Judge Dooling's
ruling is adopted, reads: "Moreover, . . . 'whoever
challenges his [the Acting Secretary's] right to act assumes
the burden of proving it clearly.'" *Ex parte Tsuie Chee,*
218 Fed. 256, 257. Regarding this telegram, signed merely
"Daniel J. Keefe" and communicating to the immigration
inspector at Honolulu, the fact that the alien was to be
deported, and upon which counsel relies as an implication
of the appeal's having been heard by an unauthorized person, it may be enough to say that under the presumption
of right-acting, of regularity, it is to be presumed here that
the telegram emanated from the. Secretary or from some
one authorized to act. In line with the principle and.spirit
of Judge Dooling's ruling the burden upon the petitioner
has not been sustained. The telegram may here be noted;
it is in code, meaning: "Secretary (or Assistant Secretary,
or Acting Secretary) has affirmed excluding decision Board
(or your excluding decision) [referring to the Board of
Special Inquiry] case alien(s) named and directs deportation. (Signed) Daniel J. Keefe."

[2] Here the petitioner swore to a fact, as to the presence of the Secretary of Labor, and his consequent duty
to act in the appeal, of which she and, it must be assumed
with greater reason, her attorney also, were not prepared to
offer the slightest proof,—for the mere unsupported circumstance of the telegram's having been signed "Daniel J.
Keefe" is insufficient. The other grounds of this second
petition are virtually mere repetitions of those already determined in this court's decision of October 18, 1913, in
another habeas corpus proceeding (No. 55) ante, pp. 266,
271, brought by the same petitioner in her own behalf and
attempted to be appealed but the appeal never perfected.

And her very failure to perfect an appeal is made a ground of this second petition: "That your petitioner noted an appeal . . . from the order . . . discharging said writ, but through accident and mistake the said appeal was not perfected." The suggestion is strong of want of good faith in respect to this allegation: this extraordinary ground is not even supported by any statement, as the case called for, of facts constituting the "accident and mistake." See Fletcher's Equity Pleading and Practice, sec. 95, reading:

"When a complainant in equity seeks relief from the effects or results of some accident or mistake, he should state in his bill, fully and explicitly, the circumstances, so as to present a clear picture of the particulars of how the complainant was misled, of the character and causes of the accident or mistake, and how it occurred."

"It is too clear for argument that it [a bill of complaint "rest(ing) on the ground of . . . mistake"] should set out . . . the manner in which the mistake occurred." *United States v. Atherton,* 102 U. S. 372, 374.

In the course of this proceeding I have expressed some disapproval not only of the flimsy grounds of the petition but of the bringing of this second proceeding at all. In justification counsel cites the following from 21 Cyc. 350:

"A decision on a writ of habeas corpus remanding the prisoner is not as a general rule in the absence of statute conclusive on a subsequent application for the writ; but in some of the states the decision is conclusive as to all points presented or which might have been presented on the first application."

[3] But this, unfortunately, is no authority for sham or frivolous allegations or for allegations which are not properly made (see Fletcher, Eq. Pl. & Pr., supra) or not properly verified, or which neither attorney nor client is prepared to support by proof. We might concede the soundness of the principle above quoted from the encyclopaedia, yet courts cannot countenance such practices by those who

under the court's license are its "officers."   In other words,
attorneys are officers of the court first, and secondarily representatives of their clients' interests: they are, like the
courts themselves, instruments in the administration of justice, virtually a part of the judiciary branch of our government under the Constitution,—and in the administration
of justice "within the bounds of the law."   See Canons of
Professional Ethics, Am. Bar Assn., preamble and Canon 15.

[4] The matter of proper verification of pleadings, above
adverted to, deserves just a word in passing; for this is an
abused field of practice.   The allegation of want of authority of Mr. Keefe is made directly and positively, though
the verification affidavit is as to the truth of all matters
except those alleged on information and belief, and as to
belief in the truth of such matters.   The practice of alleging
things positively, as is done here throughout, and then endeavoring to avoid the responsibility of such allegations by
a verification such as above, is practice to which no "officer
of the court" should be a party.   The prevalence of this
practice by members of the bar whose integrity is beyond
question, is surprising.

"If a pleading shows distinctly what allegations are made
on personal knowledge and what on information and belief,
it is sufficient for the verification to state that the pleading
is true, of plaintiff's own knowledge, except as to those matters stated on information and belief, and as to these the
affiant believes it to be true.   But this form of affidavit is
not sufficient where the pleading does not make this distinction."   31 Cyc. 542, and note 44.   See *Phifer v. Ins.
Co.*, 31 S. E. 716 (No. Car.) under statute requiring that
"the verification must be to the effect that the same is true
to the knowledge of the person making it, except as to
those matters stated on information and belief, and as to
those matters he believes it to be true."

[5] [6] But to get back now to the above-quoted statement of the encyclopaedia, relied on by counsel in support of his contention that repeated petitions may be
brought in the same court.   An examination of the cases

cited in support of the text compels the opinion that this quotation is misleading. In the light of the cases cited in the notes, the text should be modified to state a view, express or implied, or nearly all of the courts, and at least the later cases of the State and Federal courts, that may be gathered from the following language of Circuit Judge Putnam in the matter of *Ex parte Moebus*, 148 Fed. 39, 40-41:

"The petitioner made separate applications to the United States district judge for the district of New Hampshire and to the justice of the Supreme Court of the United States assigned to this circuit, each of which applications was denied. At common law, it was settled that a refusal by any judge to grant a writ of habeas corpus, or a refusal of any judge to discharge from custody a petitioner by, or in behalf of, whom such a writ has been granted, did not constitute res judicata, but that the petitioner was at liberty to apply to any other judge, and so on until the whole series of judges had been exhausted. It is, however, commonly understood that *the rule is practically otherwise in those jurisdictions where statutory rights of appeal, or writs of error, have been granted with reference to such proceedings*, and that, either as a rule of law or as a practical rule of administration, no judge would allow a writ when some other judge has refused it; but that any subsequent judge would remit the applicant to his remedy by appeal, or writ of error, unless some substantial change in the circumstances had intervened. In the present case, there has been no such change of circumstances, and, therefore, it may well be that we should have refused to consider this application at all, and should hold the applicant to his remedy by appeal under the statute, with the consequent further holding that, if the statutory time for an appeal had expired, the applicant had lost his rights if he had any. As, however, the petitioner has now for the first time applied to us formally, we have concluded to allow him to complete the circle made up of the justice of the Supreme Court assigned for this circuit, the district judge for the district of New Hampshire, and myself as the circuit judge who ordinarily attends to such matters in that district as come before the circuit judges. We do this more particularly in order that the petitioner may take out his appeal, if he desires so to do, but with the express statement that no further applications of the character now before us will be entertained by us."

The language of Mr. Justice Field in *Ex parte Cuddy*, 40 Fed. 62, 64, 65-66, may also be considered, as showing a development away from a view perhaps necessary at common law, but no longer necessary under modern provisions for appeals in habeas corpus cases:

"At the outset the question is thus presented whether it is permissible for a party to appeal from a judgment denying his application (for a writ of habeas corpus), voluntarily omitting a material portion of his case, and, after invoking the judgment of the appellate court upon the record presented, and failing therein to renew his application before another court or justice of the United States, without first having obtained leave for that purpose from the appellate court. Before passing upon this question some consideration should be given to" (another question) . . .

"I return, therefore, to the question whether the petitioner can renew his application for a writ after the decision of the supreme court on his appeal to that tribunal, without first having obtained its leave. If he can renew it on another record, which may also be in some other particular defective, and so on indefinitely whenever he fails on appeal, it is plain that the writ may often become an instrument of oppression, instead of a means of relieving one from an unjust and illegal imprisonment. The writ of habeas corpus, it is true, is the writ of freedom, and is so highly esteemed that by the common law of England applications can be made for its issue by one illegally restrained of his liberty to every justice of the kingdom having the right to grant such writs. No appeal or writ or error was allowed there from a judgment refusing a writ of habeas corpus; nor, indeed, could there have been any occasion for such an appeal or writ or error, as a renewed application could be made to every other justice of the realm. The doctrine of res judicata was not held applicable to a decision of one court or justice thereon; the entire judicial power of the country could thus be exhausted. *Ex parte Kaine*, 3 Blatchf. 5, and cases there cited. The same doctrine formerly prevailed in the several states of the

Union, and, in the absence of statutory provisions, is the doctrine prevailing now. In many instances great abuses have attended this privilege, which have led in some of the states to legislation on the subject. And, in the absence of such legislation, while the doctrine of res judicata does not apply, it is held that the officers before whom the second application is made may take into consideration the fact that a previous application had been made to another officer and refused; and in some instances that fact may justify a refusal of the second. The action of the court or justice on the second application will naturally be affected to some degree by the character of the court or officer to whom the first application was made, and the fullness of the consideration given to it. I hardly think that an ordinary justice would feel like disregarding and setting aside the judgment of a magistrate like Chief Justice Marshall, or Chief Justice Taney, who had refused an application for a writ after full consideration. In some states an exception is also ingrafted upon the general doctrine where a writ is issued to determine, as between husband and wife, which of the two shall have the custody of their children. In what I have said I refer, of course, to cases where a second application is made upon the same facts presented, or which might have been presented, on the first. The question is entirely different when *subsequent occurring events* have changed the situation of the petitioner so as in fact to present a new case for consideration. *In the present application there are no new facts which did not exist when the first was presented.* And under the law of the United States an appeal is allowed to the supreme court where the writ is refused,—a provision which would seem to have been adopted to prevent a second application upon the same facts which were or might have been presented in the first instance. I am of the opinion that in such a case a second application should not be heard, except where the judgment or affirmance by the supreme court is rendered without prejudice to, or with leave to make a new application by, the petitioner. He need not have appealed from the refusal of the district court; he could have applied to the circuit judge, and also, afterwards, to the circuit justice. He did not think proper to pursue that course, but took his appeal to the supreme court, and during the argument there no suggestion was made that the record did not fully disclose the petitioner's case; and when that tribunal decided the case, no request was made for permission to renew the application; and now the imprisonment of the petitioner under the judgment affirmed by that court is drawing to a close; it will expire with this day. This writ must therefore be dismissed."

Also, the dissenting opinion of Chief Justice Gilfillan in *In re Snell*, 16 N. W. 692, 694 (Minn.), expresses an enlightened revolt against a common-law rule, burdensome and not called for under present conditions:

"Notwithstanding some dicta in England, and some decisions in America following them, I think, when a party has been heard on habeas corpus, the decision is, until reversed, res adjudicata upon his right to a discharge on the facts then existing. There may be a reason for the contrary rule when no review can be had, but there is none in this state, when the party may always have the decision of the court of last resort by appeal, where the writ is not heard in the first instance in this court, or by certiorari if no appeal is given. If the decision be not conclusive, then the party may, as often as it is against him, even though it be the solemn decision of this court, apply again and again, either to the same court or officer rendering it, or to any other court or officer having authority to issue the writ; and upon each application, notwithstanding repeated decisions even by the same court or officer, the writ must issue."

And the following language of Circuit Justice Nelson in *Ex parte Kaine*, 14 Fed. Cas. 78, 79, No. 7,597, 3 Blatchf. 1, a case often cited for the general proposition of the propriety of the issuance of sucessive writs, indicates that no general rule contemplates the repeated resort to the same court or the same judge:

"According to that system of laws [common law] so guarded is it in favor of the liberty of the subject, the decision of one court or magistrate, upon the return to the writ, refusing to discharge the prisoner, is no bar to the issuing of a second or third or more writs, by any *other* court or magistrate having jurisdiction of the case; and

that such court or magistrate may remand or discharge the
prisoner, in the exercise of an independent judgment upon
the same matters. *Ex parte Partington,* 13 Mees. & W.
679; *Canadian Prisoner's Case,* 5 Mees. & W. 32, 47; *The
King v. Suddis,* 1 East, 306, 314; *Burdett v. Abbott,* 14
East, 91; *Leonard Watson's Case,* 9 Adol. & E. 731."

English cases cited by the encyclopaedia, supra, also cited
in greater number by Church on Habeas Corpus, 2d ed.,
sec. 386, are far from supporting the broad propositions laid
down by these works. Most of the cases cited by Church
and by the encyclopaedia are on another subject entirely,
viz., as to the want of remedy by writ of error or appeal to
review a judgment denying or discharging the writ of
habeas corpus; though such cases are pertinent in this way:
they emphasize the old conditions which justified then a
practice very different from that by which we should be
governed now. A later section of Church's book indicates
a development of the law along different lines: Id., sec. 3S9
and notes.

Statutes in same States have provided that a party can
not obtain the writ a second time after a judgment remanding him has been affirmed on appeal, see *Hibler v. State,*
43 Tex., 197; "but even where no statute exists, a court or
judge will not ordinarily in such case discharge a prisoner
on habeas corpus, unless events have subsequently occurred which have so changed the situation of the petitioner as in fact to present a new case for consideration."
Church, Hab. Corp., 2d ed., sec. 389, note at pages 580-581,
citing *In re Cuddy,* supra. Therefore, where a party has
an appeal, as here, but fails to take advantage of it, the
logical result would be the same. The attitude of the Chief
Justice in the case of *Hibler v. State,* supra, at page 204, as
to the dangers of abuse of the privilege of this extraordinary writ, is pertinent:

"Any undue means resorted to for the purpose of thwart-
ing or preventing the due execution of this duty of the State

are equally to be reprehended. This may be done by abusing and perverting the privileges of the writ of habeas corpus as well as by other means. This is a great writ of liberty, by being left unshackeled with forms and conditions in the mode of obtaining it. Therefore it can easily be obtained where there is no foundation for it in fact or in law.

"This would be an abuse of the privilege which, if frequently resorted to, might make it necessary to impose such limitations and restrictions upon the granting of it as would materially impair its efficiency. It is a privilege too dear to freedom to be endangered by intentional abuse of it by those who are connected with the administration of the laws. So it has been appreciated and acted on in times past, and, it is to be hoped, will continue to be in future.

"These remarks are made to induce caution in the exercise of this high privilege, and a conscientious resort to it only to accomplish its legitimate purposes."

I regret that press of other important duties forbids my treating the question last discussed more thoroughly and in a more orderly manner; but enough has been said to suggest that considerations applying under the common law, when no appeal lay in habeas corpus cases, have no application to conditions long existing everywhere in this country, or certainly in the Federal courts, under which the petitioner has an appeal. *Cessante ratione legis, cessat ipsa lex.* The principle and spirit of the law of res adjudicata has now, therefore, an application to such cases which it did not have before.

The constitutional questions of want of counsel, etc., have been determined in numerous decisions of this court adversely to the petitioner, and indeed, were covered by the court's ruling in the former petition (Case No. 55) in which the broad question of want of a fair hearing was raised. See, also, *In re Matsumoto*, post.

Let the order to show cause be discharged and the petition be dismissed.

ANDI MONROE *v.* THE AMERICAN SCHOONER SALVATOR.

June 14, 1913.

1. *Admiralty—Stowage of lumber—List of the ship—Fall of tier injuring seaman at work unloading it—Presumption:* A tier of lumber in the hold of the libellee fell from one end to the other in an unaccountable way and without warning, injuring the libelant who was engaged in unloading such tier. According to the evidence it should not have so fallen if it had been properly stowed, unless the fall was caused by too great a list of the vessel for facilitating the unloading. *Held*, that it would not have fallen if proper care had been given to its stowage or to the listing of the ship or to both.

2. *Same—Same—Safe place to work—Responsibility—Burden of proof:* The stowage of the lumber being under the control of the owners makes them responsible; it was their duty to have it so stowed that those who were to unload it would have a safe place in which to work. The evidence throws upon the owners the burden of showing that they used due care in loading.

3. *Same—Same—Unloading—Fellow servants:* Those loading a vessel with lumber, are not fellow servants of those who unload the same a month later at a distant port.

4. *Same—Unloading lumber—Experience—Danger—Supervision— Negligence:* It is in evidence that less skill is required for unloading lumber than for loading it, and consequently less experienced men answer for unloading than are required for loading. *Held*, in view of this and of the fact that the careening of a vessel toward the wharf to facilitate its unloading, tends to diminish the stability of the tiers in the side of the hold opposite the wharf, that absence of supervision of the unloading by the master or an expert agent was negligence.

5. *Negligence—Custom and usage:* A negligent act cannot be justified by custom or usage.

6. *Same—Rule of res ipsa loquitur:* With the evidence of the manner of the fall of the lumber and the failure of the claimant to satisfactorily show due care in its stowage, the rule of res ipsa loquitur applies.

7. *Same—Cause of injury to libelant:* Injuries received by libelant were due to a want of due care in the loading of the libellee, and to the absence of expert supervision of unloading the same at her destination on the part of the owners and their agent.

In Admiralty: Libel in rem for damages.

George A. Davis for libelant.
Smith, Warren, Hemenway & Sutton for libellee.

DOLE, J. The libel in this case alleges, substantially, that the libelant, a seaman, regularly shipped on board the libellee at the port of Aberdeen, State of Washington, for a voyage to Honolulu and other places and back to the port of discharge in the United States, at wages of $40 a month; that the libellee having taken on board a cargo of lumber, sailed for Honolulu and upon its arrival there proceeded to the discharge of such cargo, requiring the libelant to assist in such work; which it alleges was done in a negligent, careless and improper manner, in that after the lumber in the middle of the hold, beneath and forward of the main hatch, was removed, leaving the lumber at the sides unsupported, and without employing a skilled stevedore to superintend the work of unloading, but employing unskilled persons to remove the lumber, and during such work, while libelant was engaged therein, the lumber at the side of the hold fell over upon him, without negligence or fault on his part, breaking his right leg and dislocating his left thigh and doing other injuries; and alleges such conduct, on the part of the owners, to be in violation of the shipping articles and maritime contract, and claims $5,000 damages therefor; also $200 for wages to the end of the voyage and $100 for his passage money and expenses back to Aberdeen, and $250 for care, maintenance and support, and medical attendance during his illness.

The answer of the master, as claimant, admits the ship-. ping of the libelant as alleged; denies any further obligation on the part of the owners to the libelant, except as provided in the shipping articles or that there was any agreement that the libelant should be kept safely to the end of the voyage. It admits injury to the libelant and denies negligence on the part of the owners or that they employed unskilled persons to unload; denies that the injury occurred without negligence on the part of the libelant; denies that the fall of the lumber was due to any negligence or lack of skill or improper conduct on the part of the master or owners in any particular as alleged or otherwise; alleges that the libelant was taken by the master to the Queen's Hospital in Honolulu and there entered as a patient of the United States public health service and received proper care and attention without charge; that the claimant is ready to transport the libelant to a port of discharge on the Pacific coast and to pay his wages during the return voyage as contemplated by the shipping articles unless libelant refuses to remain with the ship.

After the evidence was in, libelant moved to be allowed to amend the libel, in order that the pleadings might conform to the proof made and given in this suit, and to insert a new article entitled "article 4a," alleging, substantially, that it was the duty of the owners to set to work a sufficient number of men in the hold of the vessel to properly handle and discharge the lumber and to work upon the sections and tiers and portions of tiers of said lumber, yet not regarding their duties and obligations under the contract and shipping articles, placed only one workman, to-wit, this libelant, to handle a section or portion of a tier of said lumber, and while so working alone and without fault, such portion of a tier, without warning, fell over and caused the injuries aforesaid. This motion to amend is denied, on the ground that the evidence has failed to sustain the allegations of the proposed amendment.

 The allegations of the libel as to negligence on the part of the master and owners in relation to the unloading of the lumber have not been proved by the evidence, except perhaps as to the want of expert superintendence; the weight of testimony, with hardly anything to the contrary, being that it was not the rule to support the tiers of lumber

at the sides of the hold after the lumber in line with the
hatches had been removed, except in the case of such discharge of the cargo taking place in a seaway where the
rolling of the vessel required such precaution; and also
that it was not customary to have skilled stevedores superintend the work of unloading in the hold, an officer of the
ship generally being on deck and attending to the portion
of that part of the unloading which consisted of raising the
slingloads from the hold by the donkey-engine and slinging them on to the wharf. It was generally agreed by the
witnesses, with some exceptions, however, that such sailors as were obtained on the coast from the sailors' unions
were competent to attend to the work of unloading without any superintendence, and were as good as, or better
than, stevedores; also that there was no more danger in
a man's working alone in one part of the tier of lumber,
taking down pieces of lumber by himself and making them
up into a slingload, than it would be to have two men
working together, except in the case of long and heavy
lumber, in which it would be obviously better to have a
man at each end of such pieces. The witnesses all agreed
that to have four or five men working together was an
unknown thing and out of the question, and would be of
no value and would introduce no element of greater safety;
indeed, the witness Anderson testified that "it increases
the danger of lots of men pulling on the tiers." Tr. 62.
Although he admitted, probably referring to long and heavy
pieces, that one man at each end would be less dangerous
than one handling alone, and even with one man at each
end and one in the middle he thought it would be less dangerous. Tr. 70. Jamieson testified "it all depends if it's
big lumber or small lumber. If it's a big piece of lumber
two men usually handles it sometimes, but if ordinary
lumber one man handles it all the time." Tr. 143. Captain Tauser says two men would be safer than one in handling lumber in unloading where the pieces are twenty or

twenty-four feet long. Tr. 127-130. There is no evidence, however, that the men were working on long and heavy pieces when the accident occurred, but on the contrary they were handling the small pieces.

The main point in this case is to ascertain to what was due the fall of the tier of lumber which caused the injury. If it fell because of bad stowage or because of bad stowage and the act of the master in listing the vessel so far as to promote the disaster, the owners would be liable, unless the persons who stowed the lumber in Aberdeen were fellow-servants of the libelant.

The only witness who can testify to the stowing of the lumber at Aberdeen are Henry Abenth, then the second mate of the libellee, and Captain Huhs, master of the libellee, who was in the hold three or four times most every day, and Mr Speckman. Abenth says he had to look "after all the stowage below deck." Tr. 44. Upon being asked by counsel as to stowing the lumber he endeavored, not very successfully, to explain his methods, and finally to the question "How did you do the Salvator?" he replied, "I worked the Salvator the same as I done any other vessel. I can't explain any other way. In lumber business a man knows how to stow lumber; he don't work any different in this vessel or any other vessel." Tr. 48. His testimony was substantially, to load up the lower part of the hold with small and short pieces, up to within seven or eight feet from the deck beams, and upon this floor the lumber is laid in tiers on each side of the vessel from the walls toward the center line of the vessel, the tiers about twelve inches wide and running the whole length of the hold, being about seven feet high, and leaving a space about ten feet wide running fore and aft through the center of the vessel between the tiers arranged on the sides, which space is called the trunk and which space is built forward and aft of the hatches and under the hatches with smaller lumber; and that he as second mate superintended the loading. The first tier is put on the side of the ship, a short tier, to take the "hog" out of the ship, by which I understand to take the curves out of the ship. Then a longer tier is put in next to that and another tier outside of that until the whole length of the ship is through.

M. Speckman, a witness for the libellee, was a member of the crew when the Salvator was loaded and assisted in the hold. The gist of his testimony as to building the tiers is to the effect that the first three tiers next the side of the vessel curved with the lines of the vessel and it was desirable to take out this curve, which was done by placing a 2x4 or 1x4 block or plank against the outside of the third tier against which to build the fourth tier. This he called taking the "sheer" out; after which process the rest of the tiers were straight, meaning, I take it, straight longitudinally. Tr. 133.

W. W. Jamieson, a witness for libellee, testified on cross-examination as follows:

"Q. Supposing that this placing of short lumber in between one tier and other to correct the curve should be neglected or improperly done so there is a straight tier and back of it a curved tier not filled in? A. Then we'd call that bad stowage, your Honor. Q. And would such a tier from the movement of the ship, would it be likely to be displaced? A. The one that was badly stowed? Q. Yes. A. It would be displaced if there was a space left between the tiers, naturally." Tr. 149. The following examination of Jamieson appeared on direct: "Q. Would it be possible for an inside tier to become disarranged without the disarrangement being indicated by the outside tier? A. Not in ordinary circumstances unless it was bad stowage. Q. And ordinary circumstances. why not? A. Because each tier comes right up against the next one; all the space in the hold is filled up solid." Tr. 144.

The cause of the fall of the lumber is not easy to ascertain. The attempt to prove that it was due to the manipulations of the libelant or of Olson, his fellow servant, who

was at work upon the same tier from thirty to fifty feet
away from him, has, I think, failed.   True, Gunderson says
that at the moment of the accident Olson was "tearing
down some lumber, tried to tear it down."   Tr. 71.   He was
recalled to say this after his direct and cross examinations
were closed in which he said Olson "was with one foot, and
a hand like this (above his head) carrying some small lumber down and he shouted 'look out'."   Tr. 40a.   He was
doing what he was there to do.   There is no evidence that
he was trying or intending to pull the tier down, as is sometimes done, but was taking "some small lumber down."
The evidence of Captain Huhs, master of the libellee, relating to danger in unloading, i. e., "for instance start in
the top tier, if you are not careful the whole tier will come
down; that's where the danger lies," (Tr. 101) is not borne
out by Anderson, Jamieson and Speckman.   Captain J. A.
Anderson, master of the schooner Ludlow, and Captain W.
W. Jamieson, master of the schooner Salem, called by the
libellee, both disinterested, so far as appears, agree that if
the tiers are properly stowed they cannot fall unless they
are intentionally pulled to come down.   Anderson: "If the
lumber is stowed right up and down, they could not fall
down except you·pull it."   Tr. 62.   Jamieson: "Q. Have
you ever known a tier loaded in the hold of·a ship to fall,
or part of a tier?   A. I've never known it, your Honor, except it was thrown down by one of the men.   Q. That is,
does it ever happen that a man is pulling off, that more
than he is pulling off, comes off also?   A. Yes, your Honor,
it happens sometimes.   Q. Is that dangerous?   A. To a
certain extent it's dangerous, but the man is pulling a tier
down and he sings out 'stand clear'."   Tr. 146.   M. Speckman said in answer to the following question by the court:
"Q. What I want to know is for instance supposing the tier
in front of it has been removed so that perhaps about three
feet of it is left, then the next tier, if it fell would it fall from
one end to the other or would it be a portion of it?   A. Only

a portion of it; the whole tier I never have seen that yet; never can, I don't think, because that lumber is always combined by running shorter lengths; it may be six inches or so from the tier is liable to come down if it is not watched very carefully by taking these top pieces off." Tr. 136-137.

The defense makes an ingenious argument from certain vague testimony of the libelant, construing it to mean that a plank or board projecting from the tier in front of the one that fell was partially built into such tier so that it supported a part of the weight of it and that upon Monroe's drawing it out, as he must have done as there was no one else near who could have done it, the whole tier fell. The testimony upon which this conclusion is based is as follows:

"Q. You were working alone there the same you were the others? A. She must been lying, that tier, with the plank underneath another tier a little and when we worked that a little down, that plank got loose what would hold that tier up, and when we took that tier off, that tier would fall down. Q. That is, if you took anything from off the top of the tier would make what is left fall down? A. You put a lumber, a long lumber that much underneath a tier, a lumber is underneath the block that will hold the tier steady. When we take that block out that whole tier fall down." Tr. 22-23.

This testimony is not easy of comprehension, but in any case it is clear that the defense abandoned its effort to construe it as offering, as a cause of the fall of a tier, the removal of a plank from the tier next in front, which was wedged into the tier that fell, supporting a part of its weight, for on page 29 of its brief, in arguing that the tiers were properly built up, it says: "There is no evidence that there was any room, on account of ragged or uneven edges (sides) of the tiers which would permit any dovetailing or tongued-and-groove effect between the tiers whereby one tier could work into another. The contrary is established

by the evidence that they were build solid and even."
Even if the defense is right in the construction of the above
testimony of Monroe, it would show careless construction
of the tier that fell, by allowing a part of the plank from
the tier in front of it to be so wedged in between its boards
that its removal, which would be likely to happen in dealing with the front tier, would endanger its stability.

It is clear from the evidence that two precautions favoring stability in building a tier are important; one is an
inward longitudinal curve toward the side of the ship, the
other is a departure from the perpendicular toward the side
of the ship; in other words the tiers should lean slightly
toward the side of the ship. Tr. 103. As to the longitudinal curve or sheer, as Speckman calls it (Tr. 133), it is
reduced after several tiers are put in by pieces of lumber
placed in the curve against which the next tier is built, in
order "to get the outside tiers more straight," as Speckman
puts it. Tr. 133. At this point in the operation, he says,
"after the second mate came out, he had some authority
and he said to do so and so, and the rest of them were
straight." Tr. 134. It is not easy to gather from the evidence whether or not it was the practice to retain some of
this longitudinal curve in the several tiers nearest the
middle of the ship. It looks to the court as if such a practice would be important as a measure of safety.

As to the inclination of the tiers toward the side of the
ship there is no evidence outside of that of Captain Huhs,
master of the libellee, who says, referring to the tiers on
the libellee, "they're been put in straight and only lean a
little but so they can't come down." Tr. 103. And
Abenth, the mate, who refers to "the lumber being pushed
over against the side of the ship leaning to the side," (Tr.
78) and yet says (Tr. 91), referring to the first tier, "it's
supposed to be straight up and down, that tier and the
next tier outside of that again. The master's assurance
that the work was properly done is based on the fact that

he had the second mate, "a good man" to superintend the stowing, and that he himself was down in the hold most every day three or four times. It is in evidence that the second mate came aboard on one occasion when Speckman was taking out the sheer, and took command of stowing operations. From this it would appear that he was not in the hold all the time.

There does not appear to be any testimony, except that of Captain Huhs, that would give the impression that after the sheer in the tiers is taken out as described by Speckman, the remaining tiers toward the middle of the vessel, which would include the one that fell, had any inclination toward the ship's side, but on the contrary they are repeatedly referred to as being straight up and down. If they were straight up and down, a list of the ship toward the wharf would tend to produce a condition of unstable equilibrium in those tiers in the side of the vessel opposite to the wharf. Monroe says, "the ship was leaning over and them tiers was leaning over," (Tr. 21) adding if the lumber had been properly stowed the list would not have caused it to fall.

Jamieson testified in regard to the possible effect of the list of a vessel in unloading:

"Q. With such a list and unloading the starboard side, with the port side toward the wharf, would that list tend to weaken the stability of the tier which had the tier in front of it removed? A. It would if it was a big list; it might weaken the tier because it is more liable to drop down. Q. Have you ever known that to happen? A. Not to my own experience on my own vesels." Tr. 121.

[1] The tier fell in a most unaccountable way from one end to the other without warning and without an apparent cause. It ought not to have so fallen according to disinterested and experienced witnesses if it had been properly stowed, unless the fall might have been brought about by

too great a list of the ship.   In such a case the presumption is that it would not have occurred if proper care had been given to its stowage or to the listing of the ship or both.   *Griffin v. Manice,* 166 N. Y. 188, 192.

"The fact of the casualty and the attendant circumstances themselves furnish all the proof of negligence that the injured person is able to offer, or that it is necessary to offer."   Shearman and Redfield on Negligence, sec. 59, quoted in *Griffin v. Manice,* supra, 192.

[2] The stowing of the lumber was under the control of the owners.   This is the test of responsibility.   It was their duty to have the lumber so stowed that their employees whose place it might be to unload would have a reasonably safe place in which to work.   With the evidence in the case the burden is thrown upon the owners of showing that they used due care in the loading of the libellee.

[3] Counsel for libellee argue that if there was negligence in the stowing it was the negligence of a fellow servant for which the owners were not liable.   Is it not pressing the doctrine of fellow servants rather far to say that men loading a vessel are fellow servants of the men who unload it a month later and two or three thousand miles away?

"Two persons may, indeed, work under the same master and receive their pay from the same source; but this is not sufficient.   They must be at the time engaged in a common purpose or employed in the same general business." *Northern Pacific R. R. v. Herbert,* 116 U. S. 642, 651.

The duty which the master owes to his servant, of providing him reasonably safe surroundings in which to work, he cannot delegate to an agent and thus free himself from responsibility.

"He is liable for the neglect of that other, which, in such

case is not the neglect of a fellow servant, no matter what his position as to other matters, but is the neglect of the master to do those things which it is the duty of the master to perform as such." *Northern Pacific R. R. v. Peterson,* 162 U. S. 346, 353.

[4] The allegation of negligence on the ground of the absence of skilled superintendence of the work of unloading remains to be considered. It is in evidence that skill acquired from experience is necessary for the work of stowing lumber on board a vessel and that comparatively little skill and experience are required for unloading. And although the prevailing testimony is to the effect that expert superintendence of the operations of unloading lumber in the hold is unnecessary and not customary, yet there is evidence which tends to shake one's confidence in the prevailing practice of not furnishing such superintendence, or giving that protection to the workers that the situation seems to require. Anderson says there is no more danger to the men in the hold in unloading than in other work, "the only thing you have to see what's going on;" (Tr. 58) also that in unloading lumber in the harbor of San Francisco he superintended such unloading himself. Tr. 60-61. Tauser says, "the degree of safety would be increased by reason of the fact of having a stevedore superintending the unloading of the cargo," although he added he didn't think it necessary. Tr. 128. Here is the situation. Tiers of lumber 12 inches wide are built up 6 to 8 feet high and perpendicular. The vessel in discharging is careened toward the wharf to facilitate the slinging of the lumber to the wharf. This obviously tends to create a condition of unstable equilibrium in the tiers in the side of the vessel opposite the wharf. The experience of men unloading is not required to be as great as of those who load. In other words, men who would not be satisfactory for loading a ship, answer for the work of unloading. The experienced

man who understands the requirements and methods of loading lumber would probably be able to detect a dangerous condition of a tier of lumber such as one of unstable equilibrium or being ready to fall, while the man unused to loading lumber would be likely to fail to notice it.

Under the circumstances of unloading operations in general, and the circumstances of this case as shown by the evidence, it appears to me that some supervision by the master or an expert agent, of the stability of the tiers of lumber as they are severally exposed by the partial removal of the tier next to them, is called for in relation to the safety of the men at work taking down such tiers, and the absence of such supervision is negligence on the part of the owners and their agents.

[5] "A negligent act, clearly shown to be such, cannot be justified on the ground of custom or usage." 6 Thompson's Commentaries on Negligence, sec. 7882.

The attempt to defend an act from the charge of negligence by evidence that the practice of similar methods is customary is, if the act complained of is negligent, "in effect, an offer to show, as an excuse for its negligence, a custom of others to be equally negligent." *Cleveland v. N. J. Steamboat Co.*, 5 Hun. 523, 529.

Under these circumstances I find:

[6] *First*, that the manner of the fall of the tier of lumber whereby libelant was injured and the circumstances connected with it, and the principles and methods involved in the loading and unloading of lumber, bring the case within the rule of res ipsa loquitur, and the claimant has failed satisfactorily to show due care in the loading of such lumber.

[7a] *Second*, the owners and their agents are shown to have been guilty of negligence, in their failure to have expert inspection of the tiers of lumber in the hold as to their stability as they were severally exposed by the partial removal of the tiers next outside of them respectively.

[7b] *Third*, the injuries received by the libelant by the fall of lumber in the hold of the Salvator on January 2, 1913, were due to a want of due care in the loading of the Salvator at the port of Aberdeen, and to the absence of expert supervision of the work of unloading the same in the port of Honolulu on the part of the owners and their agents.

As to the injuries received by the libelant, there is no serious conflict in the testimony. His leg was broken below the knee and his hip dislocated; there were other minor injuries, causing doubtless some pain.

The claim for wages has been settled as appears by stipulation filed herein. The claim for care, maintenance and support and for medical attendance for and during the illness of the libelant, is affected by the fact that the claimant entered the libelant immediately after his accident in the Queen's Hospital at Honolulu as a patient of the United States public health service, and that he thereafter received the necessary medical care and attendance without charge or expense to himself. The two medical witnesses agreed that he would be disqualified for seaman's work for four or five months. The balance of whatever the libelant is entitled to under his claim for passage money back to the port of Aberdeen, is included in the award herein made, which for such claim and his claim for damages on account of his injuries, is fixed at one thousand dollars. Decree will be entered for that amount in favor of the libelant, with costs.

INTER-ISLAND STEAM NAVIGATION COMPANY. LIMITED, *v.* THE BRITISH SHIP CELTIC CHIEF. MILLER SALVAGE COMPANY, LIMITED, *v.* THE BRITISH SHIP CELTIC CHIEF. MATSON NAVIGATION COMPANY *v.* THE BRITISH SHIP CELTIC CHIEF.

June 17, 1913.

1. *Admiralty—Salvage—Improper rivalry of salvors as affecting award:* The award of a salvor may be reduced or denied by reason of an improper spirit of rivalry, prejudicial to the salvage operations and particularly to the interests of the other salving agencies.

2. *Same—Same—Basis of compensation:* Salvage compensation may be based, inter alia, on the conditions of danger from which a stranded vessel is rescued, the perishability of her cargo on exposure to sea water, the value of the property saved, the undamaged condition in which it is recovered, the time consumed in the operations, the value of the salving agencies, the number of men employed, the risk to which the men and the salving agencies are subjected, and the expenses incurred and losses suffered by the salvors.

3. *Same—Same—Right to compensation—Forfeiture:* A tug went to the assistance of a steamship stranded on a reef outside the harbor of Honolulu, and for more than 50 hours, most of the time with other vessels, pulled constantly, rendering valuable service in preventing the swell from driving the stranded ship further on the reef. At the end of that time she refused the request of the master of the ship to give her place to a larger vessel, and her hawser was cut and she was discharged from further service, but continued to stand by. *Held,* that while she was properly discharged for refusing to give up her place, she did not, because of such refusal, forfeit her right to compensation for the service rendered; and she was awarded $4,000.

4. *Same—Same—Compensation—Release of stranded steamship:* Another salvor employing four vessels in assisting the stranded ship, the lowest aggregate value of the vessels employed at any one time being $240,000, and the minimum number of men employed at any one time being 97, all being used in pulling on the ship and in lightering over 360 tons of cargo, *held* entitled to a salvage award of $17,500 and allowance for certain extra expenses; the value of the ship and cargo salved being about $135,000, of which the cargo represented about

$111,000, and the service extending over three days and nights in ordinary but threatening weather, with great danger to the ship through her pounding on the reef, and great danger to the cargo because of its perishability on exposure to sea water. And another salvor, employing five smaller vessels and a large anchor and other equipment aggregating not over $22,000 in value and employing from 45 to 60 men at all times during three days and nights in pulling on a laid-out anchor and in lightering about 240 tons of cargo, *held* entitled to $8,000 and allowance for certain extra expenses; the awards aggregating $29,500, in addition to expense allowances aggregating $3,446.71.

5. *Same—Same—Same—Special awards to officers and crews:* In the above award to owners of salving ships, it is ordered that one-fourth be divided among officers and crews pro rata according to salaries or wages, except that in case of certain officers extra sums are first given for especially meritorious services.

6. *Same—Same—Costs—Penalizing prevailing libellants for excessive claims:* By reason of excessive claims of libellants, the court orders the taxable costs to be divided between them pro rata according to the amount of their claims.

In Admiralty: Libels *in rem* for salvage (consolidated for trial).

L. J. Warren (Smith, Warren & Hemenway with him) for libelants, Inter-Island Steam Navigation Company, Ltd., and Matson Navigation Company.

P. L. Weaver (Magoon & Weaver with him) for libelant, Miller Salvage Company, Ltd.

C. H. Olson (Holmes, Stanley & Olson with him) for libelee.

CLEMONS, J. Three libels *in rem*—of the Inter-Island Steam Navigation Company, Limited, claiming $35,000 as compensation for salvage services, the Miller Salvage Company, Limited, claiming $20,000 for similar services, and the Matson Navigation Company, claiming $15,000 for similar services,—against the British ship Celtic Chief, her cargo and freight, are here consolidated for the purpose of trial. During the course of the hearing, the Inter-Island company modified its claim to $25,000 and the Matson company its claim to $10,000.

Each company libelant concedes that in addition to its own efforts in the alleged salvage operations, which effected the removal of the ship from a condition of stranding on a reef, some assistance was rendered by the other libelant companies and also "some very slight assistance" by a German cruiser the Arcona, in whose behalf no claim for compensation is made.

In behalf of the ship, the claimant, her master, Captain John Henry, contends that the Miller company, though having lightered 239 tons of cargo and rendered some service with its anchor and tackle in pulling the ship away from the reef when finally afloat, or in starting her toward deep water as she neared the floating, has forfeited any reward by reason of the wilful misconduct of its superintendent, Captain F. C. Miller, in deliberately concealing from the other pulling agents, for at least two hours before the ship left the reef, his own knowledge that she was about to float free, in order that he and his company might have the more credit for her rescue. This point was not made in the claimant's answer, but is urged in his counsel's brief from certain evidence in the case. Other misconduct of the Miller superintendent, of which complaint is made, is his attitude, appearing from the evidence, with regard to the possible bumping of the Arcona by the Celtic Chief as she came off the reef,—he desiring such collision as proof that the German cruiser was not pulling. And also the commencement of the lightering operations without laying anchors to prevent further drifting aground, and the delay in bringing to the ship's assistance an available, large anchor of the Miller company until the morning of Wednesday, two days later than agreed, are assigned as negligence.

The claimant contends that the Matson company is entitled to no salvage, by reason of the want of success of the efforts of its tug the Intrepid, and of the misconduct of her master, Captain McAllister, in refusing to obey the request of the Celtic Chief's master to yield the Intrepid's position to the Arcona, a more powerful vessel.

As to the Inter-Island company, the claimant contends, that its services were of the lowest order of merit, mere towing and lightering under conditions of no danger to either the salvors or the salved ship, and requiring no high degree of skill, and in which the salvors were actually negligent in beginning to lighter without having laid out anchors to prevent further drifting aground. However, there is conceded to the Inter-Island company an award of $4,379.77, being interest at 40 per cent. per annum on the value of the property in use for the number of days each item was used, added to that company's own estimate of its expenses, $3,561.77, i. e., only $818 net for its services.

The claimant contends that, while the Inter-Island vessels and the Miller tackle did some pulling at the time the ship came off, one of the chief elements in her floating was the great strain on the lines of the powerful cruiser Arcona.

The value of the Celtic Chief, her cargo and freight money, is also made an issue. And with regard to costs, it is contended by the claimant that the three libelants should each bear one-third, in view of their exorbitant claims.

The facts, as found to be established by the evidence and by the admissions of the pleadings, are hereinbelow set forth.

At about 2:20 o'clock in the morning of December 6. 1909, the Celtic Chief, bound from Hamburg, Germany. to Honolulu, with a cargo mainly of fertilizer and a small quantity of general merchandise, ran aground on a shoal reef about one-half mile to the westward of the channel entrance to the Honolulu harbor. When off port early on the previous evening her master. Captain Henry, who was without experiential knowledge of Hawaiian waters, had been warned by Captain J. R. Macaulay, the harbor pilot, of being too close to the reef, but this advice was not heeded, whereupon the pilot immediately boarded the ship and offered further advice, which, also, was not heeded until too late. And at 9 o'clock that night the ship ran lightly aground on this reef, where she remained in a calm until 2 o'clock the next morning, when an off-shore breeze arising, she put on sail and endeavored to make the open sea, but had hardly gained headway before the breeze died down and left her in nearly the same position as before.

The reef in this locality runs east and west in ledges of coral rock, the outer ledge rising abruptly from deep water and extending back in a northerly direction on a plane of very slight grade for about a thousand feet to another ledge from two to four feet higher. The surface of the outer ledge presents patches of sand interspersed with hummocks of outcropping coral, some of them of boulder size. Though the seabottom here shows superficially more sand than coral, the dominant character of the reef is coral rock, somewhat sharp and of some degree of hardness but at its surface not hard enough to withstand grinding under the moving weight of a vessel such as the Celtic Chief.

The air continued calm until about daybreak of Monday. Thereafter a light southeasterly breeze prevailed instead of the northeast trades which blow most of the year, but the indications, indeed immediate probabilities, were of a "kona" or period of southerly winds likely to blow strong and steady for several days, not uncommonly developing into a protracted gale. See *The Chiusa Maru*, 3 U. S. Dist. Ct. Haw. 366-367. A considerable but by no means extraordinary swell was striking the ship on her starboard quarter, and a current of from one to three knots per hour was running more directly against her starboard,—in other words, the current ran more from east to west and the swell more from south to north, the former more parallel with the reef, the latter more at a right angle with the reef.

The southerly swell continued throughout the stranding, varying in height to an average maximum of about eight feet.   One of the photographs in evidence forcibly bears out the testimony on this point.   The swell broke on the reef somewhat further in than the ship, as is also shown by two of these photographs; and of course, the sudden change of elevation of the plane of seabottom on going from deep water to the reef would tend to roughen the water in the vicinity.

For some time after both the first stranding and the second stranding, signal lights of distress were burned, but without response, and it was not until after daylight that help came when at about 6:30 o'clock the Young Brothers' launch Huki-Huki appeared.   She exerted a pull on the stern of the Celtic Chief with a new 4-inch Manila hawser (Manila lines are herein measured by circumference, steel lines by diameter), but withdrew after about an hour. No claim is made in her behalf.   At about 7 o'clock there came the tug Intrepid of the libelant Matson company, which after a few minutes' inconclusive dickering for terms of compensation, gave the ship Celtic Chief a 12-inch Manila hawser about 100 feet long with a 1 1-8-inch steel wire about 300 feet long attached to it, making a line of about 400 feet clear length.   She towed more or less continuously until Wednesday noon.   The tug's position was almost astern, her line attached to the ship's starboard quarter. The intrepid's tonnage was, gross 123, net 55.   Her engines were of 350 horsepower.   No showing was made of the useful or effective thrust of her propeller.   She carried 12 men including her master.

When the first assistance came, the ship lay headed in a northeasterly direction, making an angle of about 45 degrees with the reef, with her stern on its outer edge and her bow free, her starboard anchor down.

As the current and swell inclined to move the ship further on the reef and into a broadside position, and as her starboard anchor had comparatively little holding power from the small amount of chain which was out, and which could be put out with safety as she lay, it was decided by the master and by Captain Macaulay, who remained on board throughout and was the master's chief counsellor during the stranding, to be of great advantage to get the ship at right angles to the reef so as to receive the sea as much as possible right astern. Accordingly, the starboard anchor was taken up and, with the tug and the launch holding her stern, the ship swung around to the desired position, her head pointing northerly. This position was maintained until she came off at 12:20 o'clock a. m., of Thursday.

From the moment of touching the reef, and until the arrival of the tug Intrepid, the ship was gradually altering her position, being carried forward by the swell, her tendency being toward a position broadside to the reef. After taking the tug's line, her position on the reef was easier, but in spite of the efforts of the tug and of the Inter-Island vessels which soon arrived, she kept gradually going in during Monday until on that night she was aground for her whole length, and moved about six feet still further in on Tuesday; by Wednesday morning her forward movement had ceased. In this forward movement she had been carried fully 70 feet. Her final position, solid on the reef, may be appreciated by a comparison of her draft laden to water-line, as she was on this voyage,—20 feet 10 inches forward and 21 feet aft,—with the soundings of the water around her,—16 feet forward, 18 feet amidships, and 19 feet aft.

The Inter-Island company's steamship Mikahala arrived at about 10:30 o'clock on Monday morning, and within a half hour later the Mauna Kea of the same company. The master of the Celtic Chief, upon their inquiry, expressed his desire to have all the assistance obtainable, and they at once passed lines to the ship,—the Mauna Kea a new

12-inch Manila hawser of about 600 feet length through
the ship's port quarter wharfing chock and fast around the
mizzenmast, and the Mikahala a new 8-inch Manila hawser
through the ship's starboard quarter chock to strong iron
bitts on the main-deck. The Mikahala's line was attached
to a bridle (or double line) running in through the steamer's midship chocks, port and starboard. On Wednesday
the Mikahala ran a second line of the same kind and size
from her port chock amidship to the same point of attachment on the Celtic Chief as her first line. The Mikahala
pulled by use of her propellers almost continuously thereafter until the ship was floated, having out about 400 feet of
towing line and her port anchor down about two points (a
point is 11½ degrees) east of the ship's stern, with about
thirty fathoms of chain in about five fathoms of water,—
the purpose of her anchor being principally to maintain her
in position. Her bearing from the ship was S. E. by S.
The Mikahala's tonnage was, gross 444, net 354. Her engines were of 404 horsepower. The useful or effective
thrust of her propeller was about 2.97 tons both tied up
and running free. She carried a crew of 35 men besides
her master.

The Mauna Kea dropped anchor off her port quarter,
put a heavy and steady strain on her line and, after several hours' pulling, parted it at the ship's quarter chock.
The line was again made fast, and the steamer, going full
speed ahead in a quick jump, broke it a second time, pulling so hard as to make a 1 3/4-inch dent in the steel mast
to which the line was fast. Once more she ran her line to
the ship and pulled until 7 o'clock Tuesday morning when
she left to make her regular scheduled run to Hilo with
mail, passengers and freight, and her place and towing line
were taken at 8 o'clock by the Inter-Island vessel Helene.
The bearing of the Mauna Kea was southward and a little
to the westward of the stranded ship. That "there was a
big weight on the Mauna Kea's line all the time," "that it

had a good strain on it," is admitted by the Celtic Chief's
master and first mate. The Mauna Kea's tonnage was,
gross 1,566, net 940. Her engines were of 2,400 horsepower.
The useful or effective thrust of her propellers was over
12 tons both tied up and running free. Her crew was of
60 men, besides her master.

The Helene placed her two 2,000-pound anchors for the
special purpose of effective heaving on her anchor chains,
in addition to pulling by her propellers. She lay at a distance of 635 feet from the Celtic Chief, and her starboard
anchor had out 90 fathoms of chain and her port anchor
about 60 fathoms, these anchors being two or three points
apart. Her 12-inch line was not only itself fast to the vessel, but was also attached thereto by a bridle. The Helene's
tonnage was, gross 618, net 392. Her engines were of 470
horsepower. The useful or effective thrust of her propeller
was 3.11 tons tied up and 3.26 tons running free. Her
crew was of 31 men besides her master.

On Wednesday noon the Inter-Island company's steamer
Likelike laid out her anchor ahead about two points off the
ship's stern and passed to the ship an 8-inch Manila hawser
which was made fast through the port quarter hawse-pipe
to bitts on the main deck. The Likelike's tonnage was
gross 374, net 214. Her engines were of 340 horsepower.
The useful or effective thrust of her propellers was about
2.5 tons both tied up and running free. Her crew was of
28 men besides her master.

Meantime on Monday morning at about 7:30 or 8
o'clock, Captain Miller representing the libelant Miller
Salvage Company, offered his assistance, without agreement
as to compensation, and about 10 o'clock the Miller boats,—
the schooner Concord, the gasoline motorboat Mokolii, and
the steamship James Makee,—arrived and the lightering of
the cargo began, stevedores passing out by hand bags of
fertilizer directly into these vessels which were moored
alongside the ship. After noon of Monday the Miller

lighter Kaimiloa was also brought out. The Miller company's men continued lightering until 2:30 a. m. of Tuesday. By this time they had taken out 239 tons of fertilizer, which was carried to the wharf and discharged.

On Tuesday afternoon Captain Miller came out with a so-called 7-ton anchor (actual weight 10,000 pounds) which was finally laid out astern and connected with the Celtic Chief through the starboard after chock by powerful lines and a system of triple purchase tackles rigged on the deck of the ship and worked most of the time from the ship's duplex capstan with sixteen men at the bars, and when infrequent occasion offered by the ship's winch. These lines consisted of a new 2 1/4-inch steel wire cable attached to the anchor and a new 12-inch Manila hawser shackled to this wire at about 30 feet from the ship's stern, the Manila line being reinforced by a double piece of 1 1/8-inch steel wire. The large Manila line was attached to the system of three tackles through the first, second and third triple blocks of which ran, respectively, 7-inch, 5-inch and 3 1/4-inch falls of new Manila rope. The Miller anchor lay about 900 or more feet almost directly astern of the Celtic Chief, and a little to the starboard. The Miller company employed under Captain Miller about 45 to 60 men, most of them working overtime from 5 to 11 hours in addition to a full day on Tuesday and Wednesday, and in addition to a three-quarter day on Monday. Besides the above vessels, a small gasoline launch, the Elizabeth, was used in the Miller company's operations.

At the request of the ship's master, the Inter-Island company's superintendent Captain Haglund began lightering operations at about 11 o'clock Tuesday morning, working at the main hatch until noon, and after 1 o'clock at both the main hatch and the after hatch with an increase of men, continuing all that afternoon and evening and until about 2 o'clock Wednesday morning. Men from the crews of the Mikahala and Helene and extra stevedores, about 100 in all, were thus employed. About 6 a. m. lightering was resumed and continued until about 11:30 p. m., or shortly before the ship was free. At about noon of Wednesday a floating donkey hoist was moored by an anchor and lay opposite the main hatch off the port side, as a complement to the ship's winch which was used throughout but which was inadequate for all the work required. The Inter-Island company took out about 365 tons of cargo, carrying it in surf boats to the Inter-Island steamers, whence it was discharged at the wharf.

At noon of Wednesday the cruiser Arcona, of tonnage 2,800 and horsepower 8,200, with a full equipment of anchors and lines, came out to assist the ship, at the request of her agent and of the British consul. Monday evening and again on Tuesday she had been called upon for aid, but her commander "did not relish the job," and wanted to wait a day to see if the salving agencies at work were not successful unaided. The master of the Celtic Chief desiring that the Arcona, because of her great power, should have the most favorable position, occupied by the Intrepid, requested the master of the tug to cease towing, so that his line could be cast off, but he refused to yield. The ship's master then sent a note in writing to the same effect, stating as his reason for this action the desire "to make a good berth for the man-of-war," also offering to take the tug's line "from some other part of the ship." But as the tug still stood firm, her line was cut by order of the ship's master. The Intrepid then made room for the Arcona, and continued to lay within hailing distance in case of need, though informed that her assistance would not be required further. It was a condition imposed by the commander of the Arcona that his vessel should have the Intrepid's position astern before giving any aid.

The Arcona dropped her port anchor dead astern of the Celtic Chief and a little outside the position of the Helene. After having parted her first line, of Manila, which appears to have been merely a messenger for another line, she passed a small wire line of her own to the ship and started ahead at increasing speed.   The wire broke almost immediately. This was at about high tide, between 12 and 1 o'clock. She swung around to her anchor and drifted with the swell and current down rather close to the Helene.   She hove anchor and moving further eastward and seaward, dropped her port anchor again, this time about directly ahead of the Mikahala's bow and some three or four hundred feet distant therefrom.   Her stern was then on a line directly ahead of the Mikahala's bow.   She paid out more chain and swung westward toward the Helene until she was half-way between the Helene and the Mikahala and seaward of them a little.   She then ran a wire of her own and took one from the ship, started her engines ahead, and after pulling for from five minutes to a half hour, broke the ship's wire at about 3 o'clock.   She then attempted for several hours to get a long wire aboard the Celtic Chief, but failed, and again ran two wires using the ship's broken wire which had been spliced and reinforced; between 6 and 7 o'clock she had finally made fast, and proceeded to "equalize" the wires and to then heave in on her anchor chain, not using her propellers at all.   She kept somewhat of a strain on her anchor chain thereafter until the ship floated.   About 8 o'clock she turned on her two large searchlights which afforded a favorable condition for the salvage operations during the rest of the evening.

A vast, and very much of it profitless, mass of testimony was offered on the point whether the Arcona did any pull-ing on the stranded ship,—that is, by means of her steam winch's hauling in on her anchor chain, for it was not contended that she made any use of her propellers until after the ship was free from the reef,—and if she exerted any efforts, whether they were effective.   The barrenness of the depositions of the Arcona's officers, and the fact that these witnesses were content to refer to an official report

which was not in evidence, deprived the court of most of
their knowledge on vital points. Detail and circumstance
were greatly to be desired, but these depositions were too
general and sketchy to be of much assistance, and raised
inconsistencies which a more searching examination of the
witnesses might have removed. This deficiency is not
attributed to anything more than the inherent limitations
and inefficiency of an examination on written interrogatories. The testimony of the Arcona's officers is apparently irreconcilable with that of other witnesses of undoubted veracity who were present at the time when, and
for several hours before, the ship was freed. The master
of the Celtic Chief also testifies in apparent disagreement
with others who testified to there having been little or no
strain on the Arcona's lines at that time. The testimony
of the Celtic Chief's first mate, J. J. Lowry, as to strain
upon the Arcona's lines is not to be referred to the vital
period here, for from 10 to 11:30 o'clock he was resting
below, and thereafter was busily engaged forward. His
testimony of a great strain that crushed the "strong-backs"
does not fix the time of this strain and it cannot be assumed to apply to the period in question,—when the witness was not in a position to observe. It may well, and most
likely, have applied to the time of the Arcona's first efforts,
when she was using her powerful engines to move her
propellers.

[1] No justification appears for the imputation of falsehood to the German officers and Captain Henry who testified to there having been a strain on the Arcona's lines and
to her having heaved on her anchor chain for the two or
three hours before the Celtic Chief was floated, and the
apparent conflict of testimony can be fairly attributed to
nothing more than difference of view-point, difference of
degree of intensity implied by use of such words as "tight,"
"taut," "strain," et cetera, referring to lines and anchor
chains, and perhaps, though less likely, to actual error of

The reason which at least four credible witness assign
as preclusive of the application of any power to the anchor
chain, to-wit, that if such power had been applied, the
Arcona or her lines would have run afoul of the Mikahala,
is somewhat difficult to explain away: but repeated re-
views of the testimony, and regard for the principle by
which testimony in apparent conflict is to be reconciled if
possible,—for we are not to impute untruth to anyone in
the first instance or to one witness rather than to another,—
all incline me to the belief, that such testimony of Captain Macaulay and other credible witnesses is in error. I do
not think the Arcona's anchor was as far over toward the
line of direction of the Mikahala as Captain Piltz., e. g.,
believed or supposed.

And the testimony of the Inter-Island witnesses bears
this out. Although Captain Macaulay placed the Arcona's
anchor far over on the port bow and directly, and only a
little, ahead of the Mikahala and the Mikahala's anchor
out dead ahead of the Mikahala, Captain Tullett, master
of the Mikahala, placed the anchor of his own ship about
as far over on her port bow as he, and as Captain Macaulay also, placed the Arcona's anchor with relation to that
vessel, but much further ahead of the Mikahala than Captain Macaulay. Now, again, Captain Piltz, first officer of
the Mikahala, testifies not that the anchor of his ship was
dropped dead ahead, as Captain Macaulay's diagram shows,
but "on our weather, port, bow," and that "the winches
were used, first pulling to take in slack of another chain
and after[wards] keeping tight; that was the way we lay,
with anchor chain ahead tight." So, if the Mikahala's
anchor lay on her port side and the chain was kept taut,
the result would be that the Mikahala with strain on her
chain, would be pulled as far over to port as was the Arcona with strain on her chain, and there would be no
danger of interference. To appreciate these conditions,
reference should be made to Captain Tullett's diagram,

libellants' exhibit "H." I may say here that I am not unmindful that after 1ʰ.45 o'clock the Mikahala had lost her
anchor in an effort to heave -it in, on her master's order
to get in readiness to tow the Celtic Chief. But it was
then still the Mikahala's duty to look out for the Arcona,
and it may be presumed that she did it. Another
thing, in spite of some instances of clumsiness and want of
foresight and of forethought manifested in the Arcona's
operations, it should not be inferred except as an unavoidable inference, that she would place her anchor in a position of danger to herself and to the Mikahala. It is equally
clear that the Mikahala's officers so intelligent, alert, and
experienced in salvage operations, would not have observed such action on the part of the Arcona without complaint or effort to have her take a safer position,—of which
there is no evidence. The Arcona moved her anchor from
its first position to avoid interference with the Helene on
her starboard: is it reasonable that she should have picked
up anchor only to at once place herself in danger of interference with another vessel on her port,—especially when
consideration for her own safety and great reluctance at
mixing in the operations at all, were her prime controlling
motives?

The testimony of the Inter-Island witnesses on this point
is, on the one hand, of the tautness of Manila lines and,
on the other, of the slackness of steel wire lines,—or rather
not so much a condition of slackness of lines as of lines
running from their points of exit at more or less of an acute
angle or approaching the perpendicular, as contrasted with
a condition of lines standing out more or less horizontally,
"tight as a fiddle string," as one witness, though not an
Inter Island witness, said in exaggeration. Such testimony
might be explained by differences of density of the lines
compared; the Manila line tends to float, the steel wire to
sink, and under even a fair strain a long steel line would

naturally not be as straight as a line of more buoyant material, such as Manila rope.

On the whole, though the depositions leave much to be desired on this point, I am of opinion that there was some strain on the Arcona's lines, perhaps such a strain as the power of her winch would permit, or could effect under the conditions,—it being remembered that the weight of the two long steel wires and the force of the current and swell against the comparatively large mass of the cruiser gave some resistance for the winch to overcome, aside from the resistance or inertia of her anchor and anchor chain. I do not find that the winch was being used constantly,—but, in accordance with the commander's orders, that "the hawsers were to be made taut by heaving in the chain," and "to be kept taut all the time by heaving in the chain as soon as the hawsers would slacken." Witness Mason described her lines fairly when he said, that the Arcona was "only hanging on to her anchor,"—"not pulling, but her lines were fairly taut."

However, as it is conceded by the claimant, that the Arcona was exerting force only through her winch's heaving in on the anchor chain, there seems to have been no occasion for all the contention and the great mass of testimony over so small an element of aid.

For the Helene was using her own winch in the same way and had down two anchors whose combined weight, with the combined weight of their chains, was at least about a ton and a third, and perhaps two and a third tons more than the weight of the Arcona's anchor and chain, and the Helene put all the power that she could on her winch. The Helene's two anchors were laid further out than the Arcona's anchor, one about 200 feet further and the other 30 feet further, giving her anchors better holding power. As the Helene was exerting power more effectively, as I find, in a similar way at the same time, it cannot be that the Arcona can take all the credit or any more than a share of the credit for pulling the Celtic Chief from the reef. The mere fact that the Arcona was a larger vessel than the Inter-Island boats, and her engines vastly more powerful, is immaterial. Her anchor-moving agencies cannot be presumed,—in view at least of the evidence as to the comparative size of anchors of the two vessels,—to have been any more powerful. But, at all events, I do not find that it was any pulling agencies that saved the ship from her position on the reef,—that is, primarily. But it was the lightering that put her further afloat or so nearly afloat that her moving was comparatively easy.

The pulling agencies did not keep her from going further on the reef at least until some time on Tuesday,—which is rather significant and, to my mind, speaks strongly of the force of the Helene's heavy anchors then placed, at about 8 o'clock a. m., far out ahead for the express purpose of holding. The forward movement of the Celtic Chief had already ceased a day or so before the Arcona was finally made fast to the ship. So the cruiser cannot have any credit on that score.

It may be, however, that too much credit should not be given to the Helene for the ship's final stationary position, in view of the circumstantial evidence,—afforded by the soundings above given, showing a rapidly lessening depth of water from stern to stem,—of the hard-aground condition of the ship as due to her keel's being carried forward with great force against a more sharply sloping seabottom. It may be noted, that earlier soundings had showed 19.5 feet all around the ship; also that her keel was, finally, embedded 6 inches, in Captain Macaulay's opinion, and as much as 12 inches, in the opinion of other experienced seamen. But, this might prove only the ship's stable equilibrium at low or average water, and not that the considerable holding power of the Helene's anchors would not be called for at high tide large, when the sea level was a foot and a half or more higher.   And, under all the evidence, I feel justified in giving full credit to the Helene's anchors for the ship's secure position.

The pulling agencies had accomplished nothing positive toward the removal of the ship from her stranded position to a place of safety.   Therefore it was reasonable to seek increased and more speedy lightering.   In the early evening of Wednesday, a point was reached when Captain's Macaulay and Henry were calculating that the removal of only a comparatively few more tons, about 80, would enable the ship to float at high tide large of that midnight.   Only about 40 tons were removed, however, before lightering was stopped, at 11:30, and before that time the ship had become livelier and was soon rolling in her bed.

When the Inter-Island men stopped lightering at 11:30 o'clock Wednesday night, over 600 tons of cargo had been removed by them and the other lightering agencies.   By midnight, this lightering and the increase of the tide to its flood, had, as just intimated, begun to show their effects. At about 11:45 the ship was first seen to be moving seaward, gradually, very slowly.   She seemed then to stop and her subsequent movements to have been more decided and distinct, i. e., not one gradual movement.   Her momentum then gradually increased again, and at 12:20 the Celtic Chief left the reef.   All lines other than those of the Arcona were immediately cut away except that the Mikahala kept one line fast until she had pulled the ship off to eastward away from the Arcona which she was approaching—some say dangerously close, depending upon their viewpoint.   And I am inclined to think that there was danger of bumping, though bumping did not actually occur.   The Arcona kept at first both lines, and then only one, fast and towed the ship by her stern for some distance. It was understood that the Arcona was to take the ship to an anchorage, but when a mile—and unnecessarily far—

out to sea, her commander desired to be relieved. Whereupon the Mikahala towed the Celtic Chief to a safe anchorage, and in the morning the Inter-Island steamship Maui took her into the harbor.

It is undeniable that the Celtic Chief was rescued from her unfavorable position and brought to a place of safety by efforts other than her own, and that those efforts were exercised by the tug Intrepid, the Inter-Island ships and men, the Miller anchor and tackle and the Miller boats and men, and by the cruiser Arcona. The services of all but the Arcona were substantial, indispensable; the efforts of the Arcona were not substantial, were not indispensable, and were rendered in a manner which was clumsy and slow, and which might have been a source of danger. Her services would, however, be entitled to some allowance. But not as much as if she had lent her hand "with a will;" for, if it was for any purpose that she came out there, and her presence was desired there, it was for the great power of her propelling engines and not the ordinary power of a capstan engine or winch engine. It is evident that her commander preferred to wait until daylight, which had already been wasted in a prodigal manner, when by such promptness and decision as shown by the Helene, she might have been ready to exert her pulling powers at the preceding high water at noon and thereafter. This is important only as bearing on the attitude of the cruiser as a salvor, because actually her efforts were not needed: the ship would have come free without her.

It may be noted here, that a half-heartedness characterized the efforts of the Arcona's men. They were gingerly, in a fear of damage to their vessel. At the start they used comparatively small lines, then tried to put a large wire aboard but by means which were sure to fail because of the want of a buoying agency to keep the wire's great weight afloat. Their fear of the small lines is evident, wherefore the attempt to run a large line, and fearing further breaks and the danger consequent with the smaller lines which were retained, they may not have executed quite their best efforts. The fear of fouling broken lines explains why they did not use their propeller on Wednesday night. But it seems feasible to have run the larger line, had they been persistent and only disposed to do what was necessary though inconvenient,—viz., secure a large launch (and the Arcona had one herself) or buoying agency to keep the heavier line from the sea-bottom. They used only small boats. It would seem, however, that the master of the Celtic Chief should himself have appreciated the necessity for a buoying agency,—for instance, the Intrepid was there at hand and with her small draft could get up close to the ship. It is probable that the careful and certain calculation of the ship's floating upon being relieved of a certain amount more of her cargo, made the Arcona's officers confident that the case would not be one requiring any great amount of pulling,—merely the operation of towing a floating ship.

[3] The Intrepid's services though on the whole of far less value than those of the Inter-Island and Miller companies, were of great value, were indispensable, as she arrived very promptly and gave the first efficient aid. Her master, Captain McAllister, did wrong in not giving place to the Arcona at the request of the Celtic Chief's master, especially as the Celtic Chief offered to take his line at another place. But he showed the right spirit in moving promptly out of the way immediately when his line was cut and in standing near by ready to help if required, even after dismissal by the Celtic Chief's master. Therefore I do not feel called upon to penalize the Intrepid though under other circumstances, especially a wilful disposition to hinder the operations, a reduced award would have been just.

[1a] Before determining the amounts of the awards to which the various libelants are entitled, I will dispose of

the claim that the Miller company had forfeited its rights by misconduct. The only fault I can find is, that Captain Miller had made too much out of what naturally arose from sportsmanlike rivalry between the Miller men and the Inter-Island men, and perhaps a little more than rivalry, though probably "only human," between these local men and the foreigners who came on the scene late and displaced one who had been the first to aid. If Captain Miller was guilty of anything, it was of false swearing, but I do not wish to be understood, for I do not feel so justified, as imputing deliberate falsehood to his testimony. His attitude as to bumping the Arcona is not approved. Some may excuse it as "only human," for it was clearly inspired by much the same considerations as have been intimated in our discussion of rivalry; yet it is heroic and generous qualities that are to be rewarded in case of salvage, the highest "human" qualities, and not the weaker "human" qualities. The award given to the Miller company will, therefore, not only for Captain Miller's mental attitude, but for the little he was actually doing under its impulse, be reduced by $400, being double the amount which Captain Miller himself considered would cover any possible trifling damage that might result from a bumping. The allegation of negligence in the Miller company's having begun lightering without having put out anchors comes with poor grace from the master of the Celtic Chief, who was from the very first advised by Captain Miller to put out the Celtic Chief's own extra anchor seaward or to let him get the Miller anchor which was finally put out, but who failed to act upon such advice. A mere reference to Captain Henry's own testimony will suffice to show the unfairness of this claim. The fact is, that Captain Henry was more anxious to have the Miller company lighter than to bring out its anchor. It might have done both, however, but so far as Captain Henry is concerned, that does not appear to have been urged by him. A similar claim

to reduce the award of the Inter-Island company is even
more unreasonable.   For the Helene had her anchors out
three hours before the Inter-Island began lightering.

Enough has been said to indicate that what was effected
on Wednesday night, might as well have been done at high
tide, and more safely by daylight high tide, at least a day,
and possibly more, earlier.   When the men and the ship's
engines and appliances did work, they worked with energy
and efficiency, though the pulling agents towed at reduced
speed at low water, as was advisable.   The Inter-Island
and Miller men and the men of the Intrepid were deserving
of praise for their efforts and their spirit.

[2] The element of danger was clearly present,—not the
danger of rough weather, though that was actually immi-
nent, but particularly the danger of the ship's being rapidly
pounded to pieces on the coral sea-bottom, or thrown broadside on the reef, as the testimony shows to have been the
case with other ships stranded in this vicinity.   She bumped
considerably and was violently shaken when lifted by the
swells early in her stranding.   These dangers were relieved more and more as the salving agencies came to her
assistance.   It does not take long for a vessel so heavily
weighted to open her seams when lifted and dropped upon
a resistant sea-bottom, the time of destruction being dependent upon the stress of wind and wave; and that the
weather and see conditions were so favorable was a lucky
circumstance.   The cargo was practically all of a character perishable on exposure to sea water.   The fact that
no leak resulted in these three days on the reef, shows how
effectively her early bumping was checked.   It will be said
here once for all, that the ship was saved without material
injury.   There was danger to the men who lightered cargo
into surf boats,—especially the Inter-Island men.   The case
was a different one from that of lightering from a large
vessel riding at anchor, and rising and falling with the
swell, but to some of the men presented the peril of work-

ing in a small boat close to a solid body against which the
sea was pounding, and under an overhanging sling carrying several hundred pounds' weight. The danger to the
other men engaged was nothing more than is commonly
involved in a seaman's or stevedore's work, except. of
course, the increase of danger inherent in working under
pressure and with engines and appliances strained to their
limit of safety. The success of the lightering is demonstrated by the small amount of loss in the lightered cargo,---
only $1,441.

The property saved was a ship whose value I find to
have been $25,000, accepting practically, with a little lib-
erality, the valuation of men more experienced in appraising ships than was the Inter-Island's witness whose expert
knowledge clearly did not extend to values in the present
market.

The Celtic Chief was built in Dunbarton in 1885; an
iron ship of 266.8 feet length, 39.5 breadth and 22.3 depth.
Her tonnage was, gross 1,789, net 1,709. Her condition
was first class. She was rated by Lloyds as "100 A1." The
conceded value of the cargo, including the freight thereon,
was $111,000, which less $1,441, the damage to lightered
cargo, gives a net value of $109,559. This added to the
value of the ship gives the aggregate value of property.
salved, as $134,559.

The value of the Inter-Island vessels with their equipment, and the length of service of these vessels, according
to their own witnesses, are as follows:

Mauna Kea, $325,000, engaged about 20 hours;
Helene,   100,000, engaged about 12 hours;
Mikahala,   40,000, engaged about 62 hours;
Likelike,   100,000, engaged about 12 hours.

The expenses of the Inter-Island operations exclusive of
regular salaries and wages, were $3,561.77, including over-
time of men, extra stevedores, launch hire, use of barge

and donkey hoist, extra fuel, loss and depreciation of ropes, lines, and anchor chain and anchor. Overtime cost $456 and extra stevedores $1,059.

The highest value of the Inter-Island ships engaged at any one time was $465,000, the lowest $240,000.

The values of the Miller vessels engaged were, according to Captain Miller, as follows:

Concord, $3,000; Mokolii, $8,000; James Makee, $15,000; Kaimiloa, $2,000; Elizabeth, $4,000.

The value of the Miller anchor and tackle was claimed to be $12,000. The aggregate of these values is $44,000. The values were shown, by comparison with tax returns and purchase prices and other data, to be so exaggerated, that they can be safely discounted to one-half and still be very liberal.

[4] [5] In consideration of the foregoing views, I find that the services of the salving agents are reasonably worth $30,000—which is about 17½ per cent. of the value of property salved, plus interest at 6 per cent. for the 3½ years since the services were rendered: see *The Chiusa Maru*, 3 U. S. Dist. Ct. Haw. 361, 371, for it is only just and equitable that allowance be made for the great delays, most of them at least unavoidable. Deducting $500, which though small, is all that can be allowed for the services of the Arcona, which is not suing for an award, there remains $29,500, which is apportioned as follows:

To the Intrepid and her men, $4,000, to be divided 3/4 to her owners the Matson Navigation Company, and 1/4 to her master and crew, pro rata according to their salaries or wages and the number of hours of their service, there first being deducted, however, an award of $175, in place of any pro rata aforesaid, to Captain McAllister, whose award might have been somewhat more but for his attitude toward the request of the Celtic Chief's master.

[1b] To the Miller Salvage Company, Limited, and men, $8,000, to be divided 3/4 to the company and 1/4 to the men, pro rata according to their salaries or wages and the number of hours of their service, less $500 which would have been awarded to Captain Miller but for his attitude above discussed. That is to say, the 1/4 is to be reduced by $500 to $1,500. And, as above determined, the 3/4 is to be reduced by $400 on account of the matter of the bumping of the Arcona. The contention that the Miller company should have all the award and its men nothing, is not favored. It is urged that the men were mostly at least hired for this special work, and that the rule contended for applies also where men are in the regular employ of a company engaged in salving as a business. It is not shown with any clearness or conclusiveness, if at all, that the men were to waive any rights to a share in the award. This fact, and considerations set forth by Judge Benedict in *The Cetewayo*, 9 Fed. 717, 719, 720, influence my view of the contention.

To the Inter-Island Steam Navigation Company, Limited, and her men, $17,500, to be divided 3/4 to the company and 1/4 to the officers and crew, pro rata according to their salaries or wages and the number of hours of their service. The award to the men is to be first applied as follows: $500 to Captain Haglund, superintendent of the Inter-Island operations, $250 each to Captain Tullett of the Mikahala and Captain Nelson of the Helene, $150 to first officer Piltz of the Mikahala, and $75 to Captain Naopala of the Likelike, all these special awards to take the place of the pro rata shares of these officers in the general award to the men.

Captain Macaulay whose services were of special value, and who was on duty throughout and was the guiding spirit in the operations, and whose testimony has been helpful in a full view of conditions at all times, makes no claim. But it would not be just to pass his services without special commendation.

As to the claims for expenses, the Inter-Island company's claim of $3,561.77 is allowed, except as to $1,515 for overtime and extra stevedores, which are covered by the general award; and the claim of the Miller company is allowed in the sum of $1,400, being the amount claimed in its libel (the actual proof was $65.26 more, but no amendment to conform to the proof is asked for, and while the court's equitable powers may permit the presumption of an amendment, this seems not a case for the exercise of such powers at this stage, unasked). The Miller company's claim of $726.30 for regular wages of men is disallowed as covered by the general award.

The court is indebted to Mr. Warren, of counsel for libelants, for his very thorough, well arranged and on the whole fair synopsis of the vast mass of testimony. Such briefs are most helpful, though it must not be understood that the court has not itself given the case full and conscientious attention or that briefs of other counsel were not able and helpful.

[7] As to the costs, the court considers the claims aggregating $70,000 excessive, and orders that the libelants divide the taxable costs herein, hereafter to be taxed, between them pro rata according to the amount of their original claims set forth in the first paragraph of this opinion. See *The Manchuria*, 3 U. S. Dist. Ct. Haw. 150, 168.

Affirmed, with modification of awards in cases of Inter-Island Steam Navigation Company and Miller Salvage Company: *The Celtic Chief*, 230 Fed. 753.

THE CELTIC CHIEF.

May 31, 1916.

1. *Appeal—Mandate—Allowance of interest in modified decree in admiralty:* A mandate of an appellate court reducing a salvage award in admiralty but making no provision for interest, is to be carried out by entry of a decree for the substituted award without interest.

2. *Same—Same—Subsequent decree of lower court—Amendment of mandate:* In entering decree pursuant to the appellate court's mandate after determination of an appeal, the lower court's "duty and function are ministerial rather than judicial," and it can only execute the mandate. Any amendments of the mandate, even in the interest of justice, are to be secured by application to the appellate court.

Admiralty: Entry of decree pursuant to mandate of appellate court.

L. J. Waren (Smith, Warren & Sutton with him) for the Inter-Island Steam Navigation Company, Limited, and the Matson Navigation Company.

P. L. Weaver for the Miller Salvage Company, Limited.

C. H. Olson (Holmes & Olson with him) for the Celtic Chief.

CLEMONS, J. The mandate of the Circuit Court of Appeals has been filed herein reading in part as follows:

"It is now here ordered, adjudged and decreed by this Court, that this cause be, and hereby is remanded to the said District Court with directions to reduce the award made to the Inter-Island Steam Navigation Company, Limited, to the sum of $12,500.00 plus its expenses amounting to $2,046.77, and to reduce the award made to the Miller Salvage Company to the sum of $6,500.00,—the costs in this court to be apportioned two-thirds against the appellees because of the large amount of unnecessary matter put into the record, and one-third against the appellant."

The libelant Inter-Island Steam Navigation Company, Limited, now presents its final decree providing inter alia for interest on the aggregate award of $14,546.77, above, at six per cent. per annum from the date of the lower court's decree. And to such allowance of interest the libellee objects, relying on the case of *The Haxby*, 83 Fed. 720, and on rule 30 of the Circuit Court of Appeals providing, in section 4, that, "in cases in admiralty, damages and interest may be allowed, *if specially directed by the court*,"—referring to "cases where a writ of error is prosecuted" in that court "and the judgment of the inferior court is affirmed." Id. sec. 1. It is to be noted that in cases other than admiralty the provision is, that "interest shall be calculated and levied from the date of the judgment below." Id. The latter provision is significant, and in connection with section 4 of the rule, enforces the independent holding of the courts, that interest is not a matter of course in salvage cases. See *Hemenway v. Fisher*, 20 How. 255, 260.

In the *Haxby* case the "district court awarded to the salvors the sum of $27,000." (with interest from the date of the completion of the salvage services, s. c., 83 Fed. 717), and upon appeal this award was reduced to $16,666.66, and on receipt of the mandate from the appellate court, "the district court entered a decree for libelants in the sum specified, with interest from . . the date of the completion of the salvage services," but upon a "second appeal assigning error in respect to the court's action in allowing interest," the court above "without filing any written opinion, thereupon reversed the decree below, and remanded the cause, 'with instructions to enter a decree . . . for the sum of $16,666.66, with interest thereon from the 3d day of November, 1897,' this being the date of the decision on the prior appeal." Id. 720; Id. 715. The contention of the libellee here is, therefore, that the date of the upper court's decision January 10, 1916, is the basic date in the calculation of interest.

The libelant relies on the case of *Hagerman v. Moran,* 75 Fed. 97, and *The Glenochil,* 128 Fed. 963. All that the former holds, however, is that "when a decree making no provision for interest is affirmed by a mandate which is silent on the point, the lower court has no power to allow interest." 75 Fed. 101. And the latter case, in admiralty, is to the same effect, holding that where on appeal a decree in which no allowance of interest is specially directed "is simply 'affirmed with costs' by the circuit court of appeals, the district court thereafter is without authority to allow interest on the final decree; and no interest can be recovered thereon unless the circuit court of appeals so modifies or amends its affirmatory decree as to include interest." The most that could be said of these rulings is, that they are not necessarily against the libelant's claim. It does not follow at all, as contended, that because the upper court does not allow the lower court to add interest where it was not added originally, it impliedly does here allow the lower court to maintain a provision for interest in an original decree which the upper court has modified by reduction of the award to a specific sum without any provision for interest. For the mandate is not in terms one of affirmance of the original decree pro tanto, but in the view of the decisions presently to be quoted, must be regarded as one of substitution. See *Hemenway v. Fisher,* 20 How. 255, 260.

On account of the delay in the final determination of the case, my inclination has been favorable to the allowance of interest, and there is something to be said in behalf of its allowance, particularly on the suggestion of the Chief Justice of the State of Washington in the case of *Fairhaven Land Co. v. Jordan,* 34 Pac. 142, 143: "Upon the argument . . . the question of interest was not raised. No error of the court below in allowing interest was assigned, and it cannot be raised now for the purpose of construing the opinion of the court, which was written without an investigation of that question or without reference to it." It is fair to note that there was in our case an assignment of error covering interest, but it may be doubted if it was narrow enough to cover the point now raised. That assignment of error was: "That the court erred in awarding interest to libelant from the time of the completion of its salvage services." Error 15.

[2] But the distinct ruling of the Supreme Court in *In re Washington and Georgetown Railroad Co.*, 140 U. S. 91, compels a different view from that urged by the libelant here. In that case, it is true, nothing was said about interest in the original judgment of the trial court, but in modifying a judgment entered upon presentation of the mandate of the Supreme Court and containing a provision for interest from the date of the original judgment, the appellate court said, "The *principle* has been well established. in numerous cases, that on a mandate from this court, containing a specific direction to the inferior court to enter a specific judgment. the latter court has no authority to do anything but execute the mandate." Id. 96.

The cases of *Boyce v. Grundy*, 9 Pet. 275, and *Green v. Chicago, etc. R. Co.*, 49 Fed. 907. are similar. In the latter case it is said. at page 909, "Under a mandate from the Supreme Court in cases like the present." the inferior court's "duty and function are ministerial. rather than judicial, in such cases, inasmuch as it is executing the judgment or decree of a higher court, instead of its own judgment or decree." In *Kimberly v. Arms*, 40 Fed. 551, the authorities on this subject are cited. They establish that under a mandate from the supreme court the inferior court cannot vary in any way the decree of the former. or give other or further relief, but is limited to the execution of the mandate."

In the case of *Boyce v. Grundy*, supra, it is said, at pages 289-290:

"By the rules of the supreme court . . . [similar to part of Rule 30 of the Circuit Court of Appeals] "in cases where the suit is for mere delay, damages are to be awarded at the rate of ten per centum per annum on the amount of the judgment, to the time of the affirmance thereof. And in cases where there is a real controversy, the damages are to be at the rate of six per cent. per annum only. And in both cases, the interest is to be computed as part of the damages. It is, therefore, solely for the decision of the supreme court, whether any damages or interest (as a part thereof) are to be allowed, or not, in cases of affirmance. If, upon the affirmance, no allowance of interest or damages is made, it is equivalent to a denial of any interest or damages; and the circuit court, in carrying into effect the decree of affirmance, cannot enlarge the amount thereby decreed; but is limited to the mere execution of the decree, in the terms in which it is expressed. A decree of the circuit court, allowing interest in such a case, is, to all intents and purposes, quoad hoc, a new decree, extending the former decree. In *Rose v. Himely*, 5 Cranch 313, it was said, that upon an appeal from a mandate, nothing is before the court but the proceedings subsequent to the mandate; and the court refused to allow interest in that case, which was given by the circuit court, in executing the mandate, because it was not awarded by the supreme court upon the first appeal. The same point was fully examined in the case of *The Santa Maria*, 10 Wheat. 431, 442, where the court held, that interest or damages could not be given by the circuit court in the execution of a mandate, where the same had not been decreed by the supreme court upon the original appeal."

So, here, the upper court's decree is to be substituted for that of the lower court, and the lower court is to be careful not to exceed its limits. The principle of the case of the *Washington and Georgetown Railroad* and of the other similar cases is, in my opinion, against the libelant, and upon that principle the court's ruling is founded rather than upon the authority of the bare order made without any discussion whatever in the *Haxby* case. Moreover it may be said that the facts in that case are not wholly the same as those here. There the lower court on presentation of the mandate entered judgment for interest from a time back of the date of the original decree, to-wit, from the date of the completion of the salvage services which were the basis of the suit, while in our case the award, which included some allowance, though not definite, for interest in consideration of delays, was cut down on appeal to a certain sum which must be taken to exclude interest at least for any period between the rendition of the salvage services and the date of our original decree. If in the *Haxby* case there had been a specific question as to interest on the amount awarded by the decree itself, from its date, the case would be of somewhat more persuasive authority.

The proposed form of decree must, therefore, be modified by striking out all provisions for interest on the specific sums awarded. In order that there may be no possible prejudice from the court's delay in signing this decree it will be entered *nunc pro tunc* as of the date of presentation of the draft, March 28th, 1916. See *Mitchell v. Overman*, 102 U. S. 62, 64-65; 23 Cyc. 840, 841.

This case emphasizes the necessity of counsel's having the decree and mandate of the upper court settled exactly in that court within the thirty days period allowed by the rules before the mandate is sent down.

June 3, 1916.

In the matter of the decree in the case of the Miller Salvage Company, which it is claimed should contain a provision for the expenses of $1400. originally allowed by this court: Although from the written opinion of the appellate court I can see no reason why the Inter-Island Company should be allowed its expenses and the Miller Salvage Company should not, nevertheless, although the mandate originally contained no provision for expenses of any party, it was amended so as to provide for such expenses in the case of the Inter-Island Company.

And in view of that provision (*expressio unius exclusio alterius*) and following the principle there relied on (see *Washington and Georgetown Railroad case,* supra) this court can do nothing else but sign a decree without provision for the expenses of the Miller Salvage Company.

The court's present ruling is made in full appreciation of the provision of the mandate immediately following that herein above quoted at p. 325:

"That such execution and further proceedings be had in the said cause in accordance with the *opinion* and decree of this court and as according to right and justice and the laws of the United States ought to be had, the said decrees and amendment of the said district court notwithstanding."

It is hoped that it is not yet too late for the Miller Salvage Company to have the form and substance of the mandate reconsidered in the upper court. As said in the *Inter-Island* case, above, this case emphasizes the necessity of counsel's having the decree and mandate of the upper court settled exactly in that court within the thirty days period allowed by the rules before the mandate is sent down.

THE CELTIC CHIEF.

July 22, 1916.

Judgments—Modification by lower court after remand by appellate court: After remand by the appellante court fixing a salvage award at a certain sum, the lower court is without authority to make any deductions from such award, even in order to do equity between the parties. The award being in court, counsel fees may, however, be charged against it for services in the interest of all the awardees in an attempt, subsequent to the remand, to have the award bear interest from the date of the decree appealed from.

Admiralty: On motion of shipowner for allowance of certain expenses against salvage award to seamen.

L. J. Warren (Smith, Warren & Sutton, with him) for the motion.

W. T. Rawlins for Inter Island Co. seamen, opposed.

CLEMONS, J. The decision of this court directed an award of a certain sum "to be divided one-fourth to the officers and crew [of the libellant Inter Island Steam Navigation Company] and three-fourths to the company." which award was modified on appeal to $11,053.25 after deduction of costs; and the decision also allowed certain expenses, but in disallowing certain other expenses stated that the disallowed items amounting to about $1500 were "covered by the general award."

The Inter Island Company having paid into court one-fourth of the whole award, or $2,763.32, now claims that as the disallowed items represent payment for extra stevedores and overtime of crew (and a few other items) contributing to the success of the salvage operations for which the award was made, the libellant company should not bear the whole of these expenses but that the officers and crew should bear their pro rata of one-quarter. These items of expense are as follows:

Diving—Kaipo $5.00, Launch Exp. $10.00 $15.00
Extra Expense of lightering and handling cargo:—
  Overtime paid regular men on Mikahala $160
      "   "   "   " " Likelike   76
      "   "   "   " " Helene   120
      "   "   " " Mauna Kea   100 456.00

Extra Stevedores   1052.00

It has been taken for granted by the court that the only things properly chargeable now against the award to the officers and crew would be the fees of proctors and reasonable expenses of litigation outside of the costs bill, on the principle that these men, sharing in the benefit of the award, should bear their part of the burden directly incident to the litigation, particularly as the libel was brought for the benefit of all concerned. There is nothing in the decision or decree to indicate that the expenses just mentioned were to be borne entirely by the Inter-Island Company: such items were, obviously, for later consideration and adjustment.

But as to the items of expense now in question, these very items were before the court when it made its decision; and as they were not included in the list of items specially allowed, but were, in the language of the decision, "covered by the general award," the natural conclusion would seem to be that they were regarded as in the same case as the other things, not specially allowed for, which the Inter-Island Company contributed,—that the three-fourths was intended to cover everything (except specially allowed items) that the company contributed, and the one-fourth to cover what the officers and men contributed, their skill and labor. The company was primarily liable for the expenses under consideration, and in the absence of any suggestion of their being shared by the men, it seems the more reasonable view that the burden of these expenses is to stay where it first fell, charged against those originally liable.

It is appreciated that most of these items represent pay received by the men from the company for certain of their efforts in the salvage operations, and that the crew are in a sense twice paid or extra-paid for their services, if these items are charged entirely against the company; but aside from what has been above considered, it is not to be forgotten that the idea of premium or bonus is the very essence of salvage awards, particularly in case of those who have contributed to the work their minds and bodies, as distinguished from property.

If the one-fourth award to the men is unfair to the company, it is too late for correction after approval of this division by the appellate court.

The court was at first surprised at the inclusion of these questioned items in an account which it considered was only to include counsel fees and expenses of litigation outside of the costs-bill, but it is now appreciated that the contention in behalf of the presented account is not unreasonable as a ground for argument, and the endeavor has been made to view the matter from the standpoint of the Inter Island Company as well as from other standpoints. Nevertheless, the first impression remains, and the court cannot give a forced construction to the words of an affirmed decision in order to do what may now be thought to be equity. The fact still is, that what the appellate court affirmed was an award of three-fourths to the company for all that it contributed in ships, tackle, coal, supplies and men (except for certain items for which it was allowed specially) and an award of one-fourth to the men for what they contributed in skill and labor.

In the cognate case of the Miller Salvage Company the very great reduction which would result in the share of the men from adopting the view contended for here by the Inter Island Company, would also seem to lend support to the ruling now made, that the questioned items be disallowed.

The item of counsel fees for services in the matter of settling the final decree with respect to the question whether the award should bear interest, is allowed, as these services though unsuccessful, were in the interests of the officers and crew as well as of the shipowners. Other counsel fees are allowed, as above suggested. See *Trustees v. Greenough*, 105 U. S. 527, 531; *In re Gillaspie*, 190 Fed. 88, 91, par. 9; 2 Thornton on Attorneys at Law, secs. 477, 624.

IN THE MATTER OF THE APPLICATION OF KIUSUKE SOKEN FOR A WRIT OF HABEAS CORPUS.

July 5, 1913.

Alien—Domicil—Dangerous contagious disease—Admission: An alien coming to the United States, without his family, and remaining a few years for business purposes, and then returning to his native land and spending a year or more with his family and then returning to the United States for business purposes, still without his family, and who is found upon applying for admission to be afflicted with a dangerous contagious disease, is properly refused admittance, as under the circumstances he has acquired no domicil in the United States.

Habeas Corpus: Motion for discharge of petitioner.

J. Lightfoot for petitioner.

C. C. Bitting, Assistant U. S. Attorney, for respondent.

DOLE, J.   Upon this application for a writ of habeas corpus the writ was issued, and to the return made by Mr. R. L. Halsey, immigration inspector in charge, a copy of the proceedings before the board of special inquiry was attached.   This shows an examination of the applicant by the board, in which it appears that he came to Hawaii in May 1906, returned to Japan in November 1911, and returned to Hawaii in January 1913, whereupon the proceedings referred to took place at the port of Honolulu.   It also appears that he is married and has two sons and one daughter, 12, 9 and 7 years old respectively.   This family has never been in Hawaii and is still in Japan.

The applicant returned to Hawaii, as set forth above, without bringing his family here and states that his object in coming to Hawaii now is to earn money and that he expects to remain here seven or eight years and then go back to Japan.   The board of special inquiry found that he was afflicted with the disease of unciniarisis and ordered him to be deported, but gave him a right of appeal from the finding of the board that he was a non-resident, which appeal was taken and the decision of the board affirmed by the Secretary of Labor.

This court does not recognize that it has any jurisdiction or authority to review a decision of the board of special inquiry in relation to an applicant afflicted with a dangerous contagious disease, and on the other ground upon which the board was of the opinion that he is a non-resident, upon which question this court has heretofore taken jurisdiction on the ground that the point raises a question of law and therefore the court has jurisdiction as established in the *Nakashima* case, 3 U. S. Dist. Ct. Haw. 168, and other cases, the court finds that the applicant has not shown that he has acquired a domicil in this country. A man who goes to a foreign country, leaving his family at home, works for a few years and returns to his family, visits them for a period and then returns to such foreign country leaving his wife and family, cannot claim to be domiciled in such foreign country without possibly a showing of extraordinary and necessary reasons for his separating himself from his family and living in such foreign country away from them. I do not know that a claim of domicil under such conditions could be proved in any case. A man's home is where his family has its permanent residence and he cannot claim a domicil different from that. The evidence shows that the residence of the family in Japan is permanent and is so recognized by him.

The motion for discharge of the petitioner is denied.

IN THE MATTER OF THE APPLICATION OF LI CHIONG FOR A WRIT OF HABEAS CORPUS.

July 5, 1913.

1. *Habeas Corpus—Chinese resident of Philippine Islands applying for admission into the United States—Certificate—Contest by United States:* A Chinese subject, previously a resident in the Philippine Islands, applying for admission into the United States, who shall exhibit his certificate of identification and permission issued by H. I. C. M. Consul General in and for the Philippine Islands, viseed by the collector of customs at Manila, thereby establishes his right of entry into the United States unless such certificate is contraverted and the statements thereof disproved by the United States authorities.

2. *Aliens—Chinese—Life of certificate of identification and permission:* There is no rule limiting the life of such certificate except the words in the act of 1884, i. e., "who shall be about to come to the United States," and these permit reasonable delays for business and social purposes, and stoppages on the journey for the same objects.

Habeas Corpus: Application for writ.

G. S. Curry for petitioner.
C. C. Bitting, Assistant U. S. Attorney, for respondent.

Dole, J.   [1a] Upon this application for a writ of habeas corpus, the immigation inspector in charge contested the application on the ground that from the petition itself it appears that it was decided by such immigration inspector that the petitioner did not present a certificate issued by the Chinese government viseed by the diplomatic representative of the United States in China; also that the petitioner did not present a certificate as a merchant viseed by the consular representative of the United States at the port or place from which the person named in the certificate departed; also that the petitioner did not present to the proper immigration officials such a certificate as is required by the laws and treaties of the United States; also that it appears from the petition itself that the petitioner had abandoned his intention of coming to the United States subsequent to the issuance of the certificate; also that it appears from the petition itself that it had been determined by such immigration inspector in charge that the petitioner. subsequent to the issuance of such certificate, had abandoned his status as a merchant.

It appears by the copy of the certificate submitted with the petition that it was issued by His Imperial Chinese Majesty's Consul General in and for the Philippine Islands and that it was viseed by H. B. McCoy, Insular Collector of Customs at Manila.

Rule 11c of the regulations governing the admission of Chinese provides as follows:

"The governor of the Philippine Islands having, by exeutive order No. 38, of September 23, 1904, designated the collector of customs, Manila, to issue to Chinese citizens of those islands the certificate provided by section 6 of the act of July 5, 1884, and it being impracticable to require that such certificates shall be viseed, officers at ports of entry for Chinese will regard certificates issued to such Philippine citizens in the same manner as certificates issued by officials of foreign countries and viseed by American diplomatic or consular officers. Certificates issued by the Chinese Consul General, Manila, to subjects of the Chinese Empire residing in the Philippines will be viseed by the collector of customs at Manila, and when so viseed will be accorded the usual consideration."

From this it appears that the rule has been exactly followed in regard to the issue and vise of the certificate in question.

[2] As to the other points, first, that the petitioner had abandoned his intention to come to the United States subsequent to the issuance of the certificate, there is no rule or statute that I am aware of which limits the life of such certificate or provides that if not used within a certain time it shall become invalid, except the expression in the act referred to below, i. e., "who shall be about to come to the United States," which certainly allows reasonable delays for business and social purposes and stoppages on the journey for similar objects.

[1b] And as to the point that the petitioner, subsequent to the issuance of such certificate abandoned his status as a merchant, I find in section 6 of the act of 1882, as amended by the act of 1884, that "such certificate viseed as aforesaid shall be prima facie evidence of the facts set forth therein and shall be produced to the Chinese inspector in charge at the port of the district of the United States at which the person named therein shall arrive .   .   . and

shall be the sole evidence permissible on the part of the person producing the same to establish the right of entry into the United States; and said certificate may be controverted and the facts therein stated disproved by the United States authorities."

From this we find that all that the petitioner had to do was to produce his certificate. In fact he should not have been permitted to do anything more than to exhibit his certificate, leaving it to the government to controvert and disprove the same. This has not been done, except as the government may have considered the petitioner's testimony to have controverted and disproved the certificate and the facts therein stated, which cannot be said to have happened. The inspector in charge has, in the view of this court, mistaken the law of the case.

The petitioner is therefore discharged from the custody of the respondent.

Reversed: United States v. Li Chiong, 217 Fed. 45.

IN THE MATTER OF THE APPLICATION OF NOBU MITOBE FOR A WRIT OF HABEAS CORPUS.

July 5, 1913.

Habeas corpus—Jurisdiction: The case involving solely issues of fact, and appearing to have been fairly tried,—rehearing having been granted more than once for further proceedings, the court upon a petition for a writ of habeas corpus is without jurisdiction to modify or reverse the decision of the board of special inquiry denying admission to the applicant.

Habeas Corpus: Petition for writ.

J. Lightfoot for petitioner.
C. C. Bitting, Assistant U. S. Attorney, for respondent.

DOLE, J.   The petitioner in this case arrived in May of this year and is refused admittance by the board of special inquiry on the ground that she had come here, or was brought here, for some immoral purpose, and that she is likely to become a public charge; that her passage has been paid for by money of another, and that it had not been satisfactorily shown that she did not belong to one of the excluded classes; to which ruling she took an appeal to the Secretary of Labor who affirmed the decision of the board of special inquiry.

Section second of the immigration act of February 20, 1907, 34 Stat. 898, as amended by the act of March 26, 1910, 36 Stat. 263, and the act of March 4, 1913, 37 Stat. 736, provides that there shall be excluded from the United States: persons likely to become a public charge; women or girls coming to the United States for the purpose of prostitution or for any other immoral purpose; contract laborers who have been induced or solicited to migrate to this country by force or promises of employment or in consequence of agreement, oral, written or printed, express or implied, to perform labor in this country of any kind skilled or unskilled; or any person whose ticket or passage is paid for with the money of another or who is assisted by others to come, unless it is affirmatively shown that such person last mentioned does not belong to one of the foregoing excluded classes and other excluded classes mentioned in the act not germane to this case, and that the ticket or passage was not paid for by any corporation, association, society, municipality or foreign government either directly or indirectly.

The board of special inquiry went into this case, examining witnesses as to the various grounds above mentioned for exclusion, and decided as set forth above that the applicant should be refused admission.

The case as tried involves issues of fact solely and appears to have been fairly tried, giving to the applicant abundant opportunity to introduce evidence.   The case was reopened for further proceedings more than once and the views of the board of special inquiry remained unchanged after such further proceedings.

No ground has been shown whereby this court might or could assume jurisdiction in the case and it is therefore without authority to review and modify or reverse the decision of the board of special inquiry.   The application is denied.

IN THE MATTER OF THE APPLICATION OF NOBE MITOBE FOR A WRIT OF HABEAS CORPUS (SECOND PETITION).

January 17, 1916.

1. *Habeas Corpus—Second petition, based on immaterial grounds, disapproved.*

2. *Pleading—Allegations on belief:* Allegations on belief merely, without some showing of knowledge or information to support such belief, are insufficient.

Habeas corpus: Hearing on return to writ.

J. Lightfoot for petitioner.
H. W. Vaughan, U. S. District Attorney, for respondent.

Clemons, J. [1] The petition for the writ of habeas corpus which was issued in this case adds nothing to the petition for a writ in the previous case (habeas corpus No. 62), ante, p. 339, determined on July 5, 1913, by his honor Judge Dole adversely to the petitioner. For the added allegations of her employment as a nurse (to show that she is no longer likely to become a public charge, as was a ground of the order denying her admission to the country), and the added allegation of her present good moral character (to show that she was not imported for immoral purposes, as was another ground of said order), and the added allegation of her failure by "accident and mistake" to perfect an appeal from Judge Dole's said order, "therefore [as her petition reads] depriv(ing) her of her right to an appeal", are each and all not only irrelevant and immaterial, but to say the least frivolous and trifling.

[2] Nor is the sham character of the petition at all cured by the allegation of the appeal's having been heard by another person than the Secretary of Labor, when the Secretary was himself officially present in Washington and no one else could, therefore, be authorized to hear it.   For that allegation is merely one of "belief"; and it is remarkable that there is not even the usual allegation of information to support the belief.   The verification affords no clue to the source of the allegation, for it has only the common statement of generality, "that the same is true, *except as to matters and things therein alleged on information and belief,* and as to these she believes it to be true".   A mere allegation of belief unsupported by some show of knowledge or at least information, is unknown to the science of pleading.

Judge Dole's opinion in the former case shows that the finding of the board of special inquiry, affirmed on appeal to the Secretary of Labor, was justified in law, as I am inclined to believe it was justified in fact, for it should be remembered that inasmuch as there was evidence of her own witnesses showing that her passage was paid for by another

(Record of Proceedings, pages 3-9, inclusive, 14, 15), the burden was upon her of "affirmatively and satisfactorily show(ing) that" she did not "belong to one of the . . . excluded classes". Immigration Act, section 2, 34 Stat. 898, as amended. There was, therefore, justification for the conclusion of the board of special inquiry, that she was "coming or being brought to this country, for immoral purposes" and was "likely to become a public charge" (Id.), that "her passage was paid for with money of another" (Id.)' and that "it was not satisfactorily shown that she does not belong to one of the excluded classes" (Id.). And the demeanor of the alien and her witnesses was an important factor in the view of the board. See Record of Proceedings, 2, 4 and 20 (and indications of failure and hesitation of applicant as a witness, 3, 9, 14, 15), and *Fong Gum Tong v. United States*, 192 Fed. 320, 321.

Let the writ be dismissed and the petitioner be remanded to the custody of the respondent, with costs against the petitioner.

IN THE MATTER OF THE APPLICATION OF JIRO MIYAGUSUKU FOR A WRIT OF HABEAS CORPUS.

August 12, 1913.

1. *Alien—Admission to the United States—Domicil:* Where an alien who has formerly resided in the United States and having been absent on a prolonged visit to his own country, seeks again to enter the United States and is found to be afflicted with a "dangerous contagious" disease, the first question for the immigration officers to consider is whether or not the applicant had previously during his first visit acquired a domicil in the United States. If they should find that

he had, the next question to be considered would be whether such domicil had continued or had been terminated by abandonment or by the acquisition of another domicil.

1. *Same—Same—Hearing:* At such hearings where the applicant for admission is not allowed the active assistance of counsel, it is due the applicant that the immigration officers shall by questioning draw out and give him the benefit of his own knowledge bearing upon the matter at issue.

Habeas Corpus: Motion to discharge petitioner, and Demurrer to return.

J. Lightfoot for petitioner.
C. C. Bitting, Assistant U. S. Attorney, for respondent.

Dole, J. It appears from the petition and the respondent's return that the petitioner first came to Hawaii on May 7, 1907, and located in Ookala, Island of Hawaii, where he remained six months and then moved to Kohala on the same island where he remained two years and about one month, then returning to Japan he remained there working on his own land as a farm laborer for about three years, and then came to Hawaii, bringing with him his wife and daughter, the latter being eighteen years old.

The board of special inquiry at the port of Honolulu, after investigation, found, upon the certificate of the medical inspector, that he was afflicted with unciniarisis (hook worm), a "dangerous contagious disease;" that he was an alien imigrant and that he should be deported to Japan, which decision as to his status as an alien immigrant and deportation, was sustained upon his appeal to the Secretary of Commerce and Labor.

A writ of habeas corpus directed to the inspector in charge was issued upon his petition therefor and he was brought into court. The return of the respondent contained a report of the proceedings before the board of special inquiry, including a copy of the written testimony. This return was demurred to by petitioner as insufficient. He also filed a traverse to the return, to the effect that the examination of petitioner by the officers of the marine hospital service, was incomplete and not in accordance with the immigration laws; that he was not afflicted with unciniarisis; that unciniarisis is not a dangerous contagious disease within the meaning of the immigration laws; that the examination by the board of special inquiry of petitioner's status on the question of whether he was an immigrant or a domiciled alien, was unfair and incomplete and that a fair and complete examination would have shown that he had established a domicil in Hawaii and that the same had remained unchanged. A motion was filed to discharge the petitioner from custody, based on the pleadings and the decision of this court in the matter of *Ryuzo Higa*, ante, p. 233.

[1] It appears from the return that, beyond ascertaining the length and location of petitioner's former residence here, the board of special inquiry made no effort to obtain information from the petitioner or any one bearing upon the question of his domicil. In such cases the board of special inquiry appears more keen to obtain from candidates for admission, an expression as to their present plans of remaining here, than to gather information as to their previous residence,—their acts and their intentions as relating to their settlement here bearing on the question of domicil. The first question for the board to consider is, whether or not the applicant for permission to land has previously acquired a domicil in Hawaii and if they should find that he had so acquired a domicil the next question is whether such domicil has continued, or has been terminated by abandonment and the acquisition of another domicil.

[2] It is not to be expected that these people as ignorant of the law of domicil as other laymen, will be able to conduct their own cases before the board of special inquiry without the active assistance of counsel, which they are not

allowed under the statute. Something is due them from the board in the way of assistance. At the least, the board should as a matter of simple justice, by questioning, give them the benefit of their own knowledge bearing on the issue. This has not been done in this case. The petitioner cannot be said to have had the benefit of a fair hearing before the board. The motion for the discharge of the petitioner cannot, however, be granted at the present stage of the proceeding, as there is no showing in the record that he had previously acquired a domicil in Hawaii. Under the authority of *Chin Yow v. United States*, 208 U. S. 8, 12-13, cited by this court in the case of *Young Chow Yee*, ante, p. 238, the court will hear testimony on the question of domicil, which under the circumstances, as above outlined, is the only issue in which this court has jurisdiction.

NOTE: On a subsequent hearing on the question of domicil, petitioner was admitted September 17, 1913.

Overruled, as to holding that the Immigration Act does not not apply to domiciled aliens: *Lapina v. Williams*, 232 U. S. 78.

IN THE MATTER OF THE PETITION OF JOAQUIM GOMES DA SILVA FOR NATURALIZATION.

August 29, 1913.

Aliens—Naturalization—Qualifications—Conflict between applicant's religious beliefs and possible civic duties: An applicant for naturalization is not disqualified for citizenship by reason of religious scruples against war or against the taking of life in defense of country,—in view of the exemption extended by Congress, 32 Stat. 775, to adherents of religions teaching such scruples.

Naturalization: Hearing on petition.

R. W. Breckons, U. S. District Attorney, for the United States.

Joaquim Gomes da Silva, petitioner, *pro se*.

CLEMONS, J. At the hearing on this petition for naturalization, it appeared that the petitioner was a Seventh-Day Adventist and reluctant, if not opposed, to doing jury duty on Saturday, and also opposed to capital punishment and to the taking of human life even in defense of one's country,—though in the latter regard his opposition was rather to personal service in an army enlisted to destroy life if necessary, than to such service by others of his countrymen who had no conscientious scruples in the matter.

The petitioner in his brief insists that in spite of his own scruples of conscience and their possible conflict with civic duties, he is entitled to naturalization. He affirms, "I shall do everything to uphold and defend the Constitution and all constitutional laws of the United States on any and every day of the week, provided, however, that by so doing my natural and inalienable right to worship God according to the dictates of my own conscience is not lost but vindicated," and he argues, that as under Article VI of the Constitution, no religious test may be required as a qualification for any office "on this ship of State," so much the less is "a common fellow passenger" required to submit to any religious test; and that questions as to his willingness to perform jury duty on his Sabbath-day, or to take life in defense of the country, are as improper as would be questions directed to a Presbyterian's scruples against Sunday labor or a Hebrew's scruples against pork as a food or a Roman Catholic's scruples against eating beef on Fridays.

The observation is made in argument that: "What the learned district attorney. . . . has sought to interject into this controversy is the matter of the conscience of this petitioner as to whether wars are right or wrong. This question is not embraced within the naturalization laws and there is no requirement therein that an applicant for citizenship or naturalization shall promise to be ready to enlist in the army or navy of the United States. If such were the case, women would be debarred from citizenship, as would men too old to serve in the army or navy." The petitioner asks, should "many good American citizens, to the manor born, and others who have been naturalized and proven good and worthy citizens," and who "are as opposed, on religious convictions, to war as I am," be "deemed traitors to their country, or be deprived of their citizenship?" And he calls attention, also, to the fact that under 32 Stat. 775, act of January 21, 1903, his age, over fory-five years, precludes his own enlistment for military service against his will, and that even if it did not, he would be exempt under section 2 of this statute for the benefit of those "whose religious convictions are against war or participation therein."

The government's able brief cannot, says the petitioner, "escape the conclusion that the applicant is reserving to himself the right to determine in what manner he shall perform his duties of citizenship assumed by him,"—"it matters not whether a law of the United States be declared constitutional by the highest court of the land; from that decision he reserves the right of appeal to his own conscience." The district attorney contends, that "the very existence of a government carried on along these lines would be immediately imperiled. Refusal to perform either civil or military duties on a given day of the week because perchance a citizen entertained religious scruples about performing duties on that day would likewise justify a refusal of those duties on other days. Conditions would become chaotic. The government would soon come to depend on the mere whim of the individual members of that government."

In the petitioner's brief in reply to that of the district

with performance of civic duty, is now removed from the controversy by the unequivocal declaration, that "in a case where your petitioner should be called to sit on a jury, and the trial should run into Saturday, your petitioner, while regretting the necessity, would be willing to act as a juror on Saturday, as it would be necessary . . . within the rule taught by Christ when he gave the lesson of pulling the ox out of the ditch on the Sabbath." The only question remaining is, therefore, that of the conflict of scruples as to the taking of life, with the sworn duty of the citizen to "defend the Constitution against all enemies, foreign and domestic."

I must confess to a first impression of sympathy with the district attorney's argument, but with no disposition to criticise the petitioner for his scruples,—only an intellectual sympathy on purely technical grounds of principle. For there is weight in the consideration that he who desires the benefits of our Constitution should be ready to bear his share of all possible civic burdens. And the inclination was, to view the petitioner's case as one of misfortune, that he could not be both a good citizen and a good Christian at the same time, and to regard it as incumbent upon him to make his choice between two things, of which he could not consistently have both.

But Congress, in the statute cited in petitioner's behalf has granted an exemption to those who are already citizens, and so long as the statutes bear this declaration that such religious scruples are not deemed inconsistent with good citizenship, even though some others less scrupulous have to do any necessary fighting "for our altars and our fires," I do not feel that I should deny this application for admission to citizenship.

It seems inconsistent to seek citizenship in a country whose defense one is willing to leave to others in case of attack by "enemies, foreign or domestic." But Congress has clearly expressed its policy, and so long at least as those

ity, I am not prepared to question, nor is it a judge's business to question, the policy of this legislation. And this policy is well established: the statute merely expresses a public sentiment which has been growing stronger ever since the case of Pringle. See Atlantic Monthly, February, 1913, vol. 111, page 145, title "The United States vs. Pringle: the Record of a Quaker Conscience." Wherefore, it is proper not to deny citizenship to one otherwise well qualified, as is this petitioner, simply because of something which is made a ground of exemption in case of those who are already citizens.

This decision is, of course, not based on the petitioner's claim of right to worship deity according to the dictates of his own conscience. For there is no such absolute, supreme, right under the Constitution. See Freund, Police Power, secs. 467-470.

Let the petition be granted.

IN THE MATTER OF THE APPLICATION OF TANESABURO MATSUYE FOR A WRIT OF HABEAS CORPUS.

September 10, 1913.

1. *Habeas corpus—Order to show cause:* The return, under an order to show cause, exhibiting testimony supporting the warrant of deportation, and there appearing no evidence of illegality or error of law in the proceedings leading up to the warrant, the court is without jurisdiction. Petition denied.

2. *Aliens—Deportation of aliens unlawfully in the United States, under section 3 of act approved March 26, 1910, 36 Stat. 263:* The provision of section 3 of an act approved March 26, 1910, to amend an act to regulate the immigration of aliens into the United States, approved February 20, 1907, for the deportation of aliens found to be unlawfully in the United States, "in the manner provided by sections 20 and 21" of the amended act, is not deprived of its force through the pro-

visions of such sections 20 and 21, which provide for the deportation
of aliens found to be unlawfully within the United States within 3
years after landing; as the reference to such sections in the amending
act is limited simply to the manner of the deportation therein provided.

Habeas Corpus: On order to show cause.

J. *Lightfoot* for petitioner.
C. C. *Bitting*, Assistant U. S. Attorney, for respondent.

Dole, J.   It appears that the petitioner came here from
Japan with his wife Kami over 12 years ago, and after trying various occupations in different parts of the Territory,
settled in Honolulu, where, over 3 years ago, he engaged
with others in fishing with a gasoline boat, which, after
about a year, became disabled.   He then worked as a stevedore for a while, and then,—about 2 years before his arrest
January 23, 1913, engaged in fishing again, having procured
a small row boat for that purpose.   For some time before
his arrest, approximating 3 years, the wife Kami had been
practicing prostitution in Honolulu while still living with
petitioner.   The petitioner was arrested and examined under
the provisions of section 3 of an act to regulate the immigration of aliens into the United States, approved February
20, 1907 (34 Stat. 898) as amended March 26, 1910 (36
Stat. 263).   This section provides that "any alien . . .
who shall receive, share in, or derive benefit from any part
of the earnings of any prostitute . . .   shall be deemed
to be unlawfully within the United States, and shall be deported in the manner provided by sections 20 and 21" of
the original act.   In the course of such examination, testimony was taken to the effect that petitioner had not consented to the practice of prostitution by his wife, and had
expostulated with her in regard to such conduct; that she
had not contributed any part of her earnings toward the
household expenses but had paid for her own clothing from

her earnings in such business; that when he expostulated with her in regard to such conduct on her part, she had replied that his earnings were not enough for the household; that the petitioner had replied to the question, whether his wife had his tacit consent to practice prostitution, "exactly, I don't give my consent, but at the same time I shut my eye so there is nothing to see;" that he sometimes attended to the business of forwarding her money to her parents; that she denied that he ever sent money for her to her parents; that petitioner testified that his wife sometimes sent money to his mother; that she denied this, and also denied that she had ever given her husband anything for his use or purchased any food or paid any of the household expenses out of her earnings as a prostitute. Another witness testified that petitioner was "not a regular fisherman, fishing just for pleasure; if he catches a few extra, he sells them."

Following this examination the examining inspector transmitted his recommendations with his opinion that Tanesaburo Matsuye was an alien and that he had shared in and derived benefit from the earnings of a prostitute, to the Secretary of Commerce and Labor, who thereupon, through the Acting Secretary of Labor, issued a warrant for the deportation of Tanesaburo Matsuye to Japan, on the ground that he was unlawfully within the United States, in that he has been found receiving, sharing in, and deriving benefit from the earnings of a prostitute.

A copy of the testimony which was taken at the hearing before the immigrant inspector, covering some 33 pages of typewriting, was attached to the petition for the writ as Exhibit B, and upon such exhibit the case was argued.

[1] The hearing before the immigrant inspector appears to have been conducted with fairness toward the petitioner, whose counsel was present during a part of the proceedings and assisted in the examination of the petitioner and his wife.

The issue was simply one of fact, and, as may be seen by
. the testimony referred to above, there was evidence tending
to support the charge against the petitioner, to-wit: that
he had received, shared in, or derived benefit from the earnings of a prostitute.

This court is without jurisdiction in this case to weigh
the evidence as on an ordinary appeal and to decide according to the weight of evidence. It is not its function to
retry the case, but to investigate the legality of the proceedings which have resulted in the detention of the applicant for the writ.

"The question brought forward on a habeas corpus, where
the commitment is under legal process, is always distinct
from that which is involved in the cause itself." *Ex parte
Bollman & Swartout*, 4 Cr. 75; Hurd on Habeas Corpus,
2d ed., 140.

Counsel for the petitioner raised the point that because
the warrant of arrest of the petitioner stated that it appeared that the alien Tanesaburo Matsuye was found in the
United States in violation of the statutes, "for the following among other reasons," then giving the charge mentioned
above, the petitioner was prejudiced by such statement,—
in which the "other reasons," were not set forth. There is
nothing in this contention, the words referred to being entirely negligible so far as the interests of the petitioner are
concerned.

[2] The petitioner's counsel also raised the point, that
inasmuch as sections 20 and 21 of the act of February 20.
1907, supra, which are referred to in the amending act of
March 26, 1910, supra, in the following words, "shall be
deported in the manner provided by sections 20 and 21" of
the original act, still contain the provision for deportation
of aliens within 3 years after landing if they are found
in the United States in violation of law, the authority of
such sections cannot be invoked for the deportation of an
alien who has been in the country over 3 years,—as in this

case. This contention has been disposed of in *Bugajewitz v. Adams*, 228 U. S. 585, 591, in the following words:

"We are of the opinion that the effect of striking out the three-year clause from section 3 [of the amended act] is not changed by the reference to sections 20 and 21 [of the amended act]. The change in the phraseology of the reference indicates the narrowed purpose. The prostitute is to be deported, not 'as provided' but 'in the manner provided' in sections 20 and 21. Those sections provide the means for securing deportation, and it still was proper to point to them for that."

As there is nothing in the return that gives jurisdiction to this court, the petition for a writ of habeas corpus is denied, with costs to the respondent.

IN THE MATTER OF UNCLAIMED MONEYS ON DEPOSIT IN THE REGISTRY OF THE COURT.

September 18, 1913.

1. *Courts, unclaimed moneys in registry of—Deposit in Federal Treasury after five years:* Balances of assets in bankruptcy cases deposited with clerks of court by trustees or referees on closing the estates instead of having been distributed with the final dividends, as they should have been, should after remaining unclaimed for five years be transferred from the registry of the court to the account of the United States Treasury, under Rev. Stat. sec. 996, as amended by act of March 3' 1911, 26 Stat. 1083. . Deposits to cover awards in admiralty cases, remaining unclaimed for five years, should be disposed of in the same way; also a tender paid into court in behalf of a libellee but not withdrawn although the tender had not been accepted, the suit had gone to judgment and the judgment had been fully satisfied.

2. *Same—Other miscellaneous cases of unclaimed deposits considered.*

On request of clerk for instructions as to disposition of unclaimed moneys in registry of court.

A. E. Murphy, clerk, *pro se*.

CLEMONS, J. An auditor of the Department of Justice in his report respecting the accounts of the clerk of this court notes:

"That certain items, amounting to $71.80, in admiralty and bankruptcy cases, have remained in the registry of the court for more than five years, and that certain other items, amounting to $217.36, in deceased seamen cases have remained in the registry for more than six years."

Upon this report, the Assistant Attorney-General in charge of such matters asks the clerk for advice "whether or not the above-mentioned amounts have been deposited to the credit of the Treasurer of the United States in accordance with law."

As transfers of moneys from the registry of the court to the credit of the Treasury in such cases are made only on order of a judge, the question is one for the court. Rev. Stat. secs. 995, 996, am. act of March 3, 1911, 36 Stat. 1083; Rev. Stat. sec. 4545.

[1] In the bankruptcy cases contemplated by the above report, the referees, by reason either of ignorance of their duties or of carelessness, have closed (or attempted to close) the estates, leaving as high as $16.39 (In re Geo. C. Stratemeyer, No. 69) unadministered and in most instances small amounts, as low as $1.55, and have themselves turned these moneys over, or permitted them to be turned over by the trustees, to the clerk of court by whom they have been held on deposit in the court registry for more than five years in each case. In all of these cases the dividends paid were insufficient to satisfy creditors. In none of them do the balances on deposit represent dividends awarded to definite creditors but remaining unpaid or un-

claimed,—in which case their disposition in the manner suggested by the department's inquiry, above, would be more clear than it is here.

The law governing the matter is Rev. Stat., sec. 996, as amended, 36 Stat. 1083, which provides inter alia:

"In every case in which the right to withdraw money so deposited has been adjudicated or is not in dispute and such money has remained so deposited for at least five years unclaimed by the person entitled thereto, it shall be the duty of the judge or judges of said court, or its successor, to cause such money to be deposited in the Treasury of the United States, in the name and to the credit of the United States: *Provided,* That any person or persons or any corporation or company entitled to any such money may, on petition to the court from which the money was received, or its successor, and upon notice to the United States attorney and full proof of right thereto, obtain an order of court directing the payment of such money to the claimant, and the money deposited as aforesaid shall constitute and be a permanent appropriation for payments in obedience to such orders."

In order then that moneys may be transferred from the registry of the court to the United States Treasury under this statute, there must exist "the right to withdraw" the money either because the right "has been adjudicated" or "is not in dispute." There may be conditions or circumstances in which no judgment or order has been made awarding or otherwise disposing of the money but in which, nevertheless, a transfer to the Treasury would be proper; for the words of the statute, "the right to withdraw [which] . . is not in dispute," present an alternative to the words "the right to withdraw [which] . . has been adjudicated," and would cover, e. g., as later noted herein, the deposit of a tender, which the depositor might, upon stipulation or upon satisfaction of judgment, withdraw at will, or, e.g., a deposit for any purpose followed by a discontinuance.

The moneys in these bankruptcy cases may in a loose sense be regarded as "adjudicated," or at least they are "not in dispute," as belonging to the creditors—at all events indirectly as cestuis que trust; but the question is, whether there exists the precedent "right to withdraw" them.

These are cases of undistributed assets which are not chargeable with further costs or expenses and which should have been distributed pro rata among the creditors who have proved their claims. In other words, these balances *belong* to the proved creditors, and a judge would, it seems, be authorized to order their withdrawal by the parties entitled thereto—as, indeed, in spite of any right to withdraw, the judge's order for their withdrawal is made necessary by this very section of the statute.

Wherefore, it is held that the quoted provision of the statute applies, and these moneys will be ordered transferred to the Treasury.

In the admiralty suit of Robert R. Hind v. The Brigantine "Consuelo," No. 11, there has been an adjudication which covers the balance of ten dollars of the judgment paid into court over five years ago and remaining unpaid to and unclaimed by the person having the right to withdraw it, an awardee named Hupo. This case falls within the provisions of the statute above quoted, and the court will order the money on deposit therein to be transferred to the Treasury of the United States. In the admiralty suit of K. Imada v. The Steamship "Stanley Dollar," No. 60, the facts are the same as in the case of the "Consuelo," and the court will order the balance of $122.49 transferred to the Federal Treasury.

In the admiralty suit of Thomas J. Ford v. Oceanic Steamship Company, No. 86, there remains in the registry of the court unclaimed fifteen dollars deposited therein more than five years ago by the attorneys for the libellee company as a tender of satisfaction of the libelant's claim. This tender must have been refused, for the suit proceeded to judgment in favor of the libelant and its full satisfaction appears from the record. So it is clear that the tender having fulfilled its purpose, the libellee (or its attorneys) has "the right to withdraw" the same, and this right cannot be, and is not "disputed." The case is therefore also within the provisions of the statute above quoted, and the court will order transfer of the deposit therein to the Federal Treasury.

The numerous cases of moneys arising from the unclaimed wages and effects of deceased seamen, which moneys have remained in the registry of the court for more than six years, are controlled by Rev. Stat. sec. 4545, as amended, 29 Stat. 689, providing inter alia:

"When no claim to the wages or effects or proceeds of the sale of the effects of a deceased seaman or apprentice, received by a circuit court, is substantiated within six years after the receipt thereof by the court, it shall be in the absolute discretion of the court, if any subsequent claim is made, either to allow or refuse the same. Such courts shall, from time to time, pay any moneys arising from the unclaimed wages and effects of deceased seamen, which in their opinion it is not necessary to retain for the purpose of satisfying claims, into the Treasury of the United States, and such moneys shall form a fund for, and be appropriated to, the relief of sick and disabled and destitute seamen belonging to the United States merchant marine service." These provisions apply, also, to cases of deserting seamen. See Rev. Stat. sec. 4604.

Although the statute thus places the matter, of the payment of such moneys into the Treasury, in the sound discretion of the court, and the six-year period provided does not fix an absolute limit at which it becomes the duty of the court to forthwith order the transfer from the registry to the Treasury, still in view of the fact that in each case, excepting two, over seven years, and in the excepted two very nearly seven years, have elapsed but no claimants have appeared. it seems a reasonable exercise of the court's discretion to at once order such transfer into the United

States Treasury, and an order to that end will be made in these cases.

An anomalous case, in bankruptcy, may be noted, In re Fred L. Schmidt, No. 255, in which the referee has within the past year paid into the registry of the court two dollars. If the facts are, as they are understood, that no creditors proved claims, and that this sum is an unexpected balance of assets, this money should be forthwith paid over to the bankrupt by whom it was originally deposited, and it will be so ordered.

It may be said in conclusion, with reference to the bankruptcy cases first above discussed, that referees and trustees in bankruptcy should in each case be very careful to see that the declaration of a final dividend, or other final disposition, disposes of every cent in the estate.

HOFFSCHLAEGER COMPANY, LIMITED, v. THE GERMAN BARK PAUL ISENBERG.

October 7, 1913.

1. *Admiralty—Seaworthiness—Stormy weather—Leaking of ship:* The fact that the hatches and hatch coamings of a ship on the high seas, are injured by the violence of waves sweeping over the deck, and deck seams are sprung from the straining of the hull from gales and accompanying heavy seas of unusual severity, whereby sea water leaks into the hold and injures the cargo, does not necessarily show the vessel was in an unseaworthy condition at the beginning of the voyage.

2. *Same—Stowage of cargo a part of which on being dissolved by sea water, reaches and tends to injure other goods:* Under such circumstances, where the cargo is mainly sulphate of ammonia, which on becoming wet was partially dissolved by the sea water, the fact that

such solution reaches metal goods and bales of school bags made of vegetable fiber, tending to injure the same, does not necessarily show that there was a defective stowage of the cargo.

2. *Same—Stowage of goods liable to be injured by the fumes arising from other goods when wet by sea water:* Under the same circumstances, the fact that fumes arising from the combination of sulphate of ammonia with sea water would have a corrosive action on certain goods stowed near the sulphate of ammonia, would not be evidence of bad stowage where the metal goods were separated from the sulphate of ammonia by a bulkhead and two feet of air space, and the school bags were stowed on the sulphate of ammonia but separated therefrom by proper dunnage.

4. *Same—Damage from fumes arising from portions of the cargo without the presence of sea water—Assumption of risk—Difficulty of apportioning such damage from the actual damage received:* With the same cargo and the probability that the metal goods would be damaged by fumes arising from the sulphate of ammonia without the presence of sea water, and the admission of the owner of the goods from its past experience that such damage would take place to such goods stowed with sulphate of ammonia; *Held,* that the owner had assumed the risk; also that it was impossible to differentiate between the damage that would have been caused without the presence of sea water, and the actual damage received.

5. *Same—Neglect of master on turning aside from his course, to care for goods which had been exposed to injury from sea water and from the corrosive effects of solutions and fumes from other parts of the cargo—Liability of the ship:* A vessel turning aside from its course to a port for survey and repairs, after the cargo had been exposed to such damage, and which remained in such port three and a half months pending repairs, during which time no effort was made by the master to save the goods from further injury and deterioration that would be likely to result from their then condition during the continuation of the voyage, is liable for the damage found to be existing at the end of the voyage, six months later.

In Admiralty: Libel *in rem* for damages.

Holmes, Stanley & Olson, and *R. W. Breckons* for libelant. *Thompson, Wilder, Watson & Lymer* for libellee.

DOLE, J. It is established in this case that the libellee,

lying at the port of London, about the 20th day of July
1905, shipped on board merchandise received in good order,
well conditioned, and free from damage, to be carried to
the port of Honolulu and there delivered to the libelant,
the bill of lading therefor making exceptions for all and
every damage and accident of the seas and navigation of
whatsoever nature and kind,—one exception among others
being for any loss or damage caused by the prolongation
of the voyage. The libellee arrived in Honolulu May 6,
1906, and delivered to the libelant the said packages of merchandise, which upon delivery were discovered to be damaged, such merchandise consisting of galvanized tubs and
buckets packed in nests, and bales of school bags made of
some kind of vegetable fiber.

The libelant complained that such damage was due to
the unseaworthiness of the libellee, bad stowage, the want
of proper dunnage and to the negligence, carelessness, improper conduct and want of attention of the master and
crew, and claims damages to the amount of $968.06.

It is alleged by the libellee that the ship was at the beginning of the voyage tight, staunch, strong, seaworthy, and
in every way properly fitted, equipped, manned and found
in every requisite for the voyage, and that in the stowage
of the cargo every precaution was taken for the protection
of the same, it being properly dunnaged and matted and
after it was taken on board, the hatches were battened
down and covered with tarpaulins and properly secured and
fastened. The libellee further alleges that after leaving
London and reaching the open sea she met incessant stormy
weather during September and October, with occasional
short periods of fair weather; that such stormy weather
was of unusual violence, heavy seas swept the ship and constantly filling the upper deck with sea water caused great
injury to the upper works, such as the deck house, the rail
and the hatches; that the tarpaulins of the hatches were
torn away, the hatch coamings wrenched and bent out of

their proper shape and many of the hatches broken with the violence of the waves and the weight of sea water; that during this stormy weather several of the seams of the deck were sprung and became leaky in consequence thereof, and because thereof and the injury to the hatches and hatch coamings considerable water leaked through and around the hatches into the hold; the rigging was damaged, a large and considerable portion of the sails blown away; that on at least two occasions when the weather was good, the hatches were opened and the cargo examined and found to be damaged by sea water. The evidence shows that the ship was in such a damaged condition from such stormy weather that upon passing the Falkland Islands, it was considered necessary to proceed to Port Stanley, on such islands, for repairs, where she arrived about November 1st. An official survey was at once made and repairs were proceeded with according to the recommendations of such survey. The delay at Port Stanley occupied three and a half months, during which period the cargo was left intact and the hatches, after having been opened and the cargo examined by the board of survey, were shut down and remained so for the rest of the stay.

[1] The burden of proof as to the seaworthiness of the ship and good stowage of the cargo is upon the libellee and I consider from the testimony that it has satisfactorily demonstrated that the ship was in reasonably seaworthy condition at the time the cargo was shipped in London. The testimony of the officers and of the log showed that the stormy weather experienced by the libellee was of unusual violence and that the leakage of sea water into the hold as a result therof was such as would be likely to happen to any sailing ship in good order under the circumstances.

There is one feature of the testimony, however, which might point to some defective construction of the vessel whereby sea water reached the hold in consequence of such construction. I refer to the stanchions of the ship's rail

which were made of iron and were so connected with the
interior of the ship and a runway of cement along the edge
of the deck as to open a way to the hold upon being bent
and wrenched by the violence of the seas which swept over
the ship.   There is very little evidence on this point except
as to the fact, and it is not easy under the circumstances to
pass upon the question of defective construction, but it
appears to the court that no such intrusion of sea water
into the hold should have been possible from any injury
to the said stanchions.   For want of more definite testimony on this point, however, I will not consider that these
facts point to an unseaworthiness of the ship due to a
defect in its construction.   Moreover it does not appear
that the sea water that reached the hold in this way caused
the damage complained of.

[2] [3] As to the libelant's allegation of defective stowage, it appears from the evidence that the cargo in the
main was ammonaic, or sulphate of ammonia, between 1400
and 1600 tons of that material being stowed between decks
and in the lower hold "pretty near" up to the fore hatch;
that the general merchandise including the galvanized ware
and cases of liquor were stowed under and forward of the
fore hatch,—that being the driest part of the ship, and were
separated from the ammoniac by a bulkhead which reached
as high as the goods, and by two feet of open space.   This
does not include the school bags which were placed on the
ammoniac in the same hold and separated therefrom by
dunnage.   There was no shifting of the cargo occasioned
by the stormy weather.   With so large a proportion of ammoniac in the cargo, it may have been, and probably was,
impracticable to stow it all in the lower hold or all between
decks, both for want of space and for the proper and safe
trimming of the ship.

There is some evidence as to the propriety of stowing
some of the tubs and buckets right side up whereby they
were in a position to catch the sea water that leaked through

the deck and the hatches, and did receive a considerable quantity. The testimony,—what there is of it on this point, supports the practice. Of course the decks are supposed not to leak, and it is obvious that in stowing parcels of an irregular shape such as packages of tubs and buckets would be, in order to have them fit each other firmly so that there would be no movement or sliding with the motions of the vessel, some would be stowed right side up, some bottom side up and some on the side.

I am of the opinion that the libellee has shown the stowage of the cargo to have been reasonably free from defect.

[4] One ground of the claim of the libelant for damages is based on the testimony that there was defective stowage of its goods, in that they were stowed in the same hold with sulphate of ammonia, which exposed them to the corrosive effect of the gases which would arise from the sulphate of ammonia in a close hold even though no water reached them, the point evidently being that even though the greater injury caused by the presence of the sea water should be allowed by the court as an exception due to the perils of the sea, yet there was injury without the presence of the sea water and in spite of it, due to stowage of the goods in the same hold adjacent to the sulphate of ammonia.

Mr. Angus, a witness for libelant, testified as follows: "I have never known a shipment [of buckets and tubs where the sulphate of ammonia has been included as a part of the cargo] to come out in a first class condition. Part of them could probably be passed, but the majority would be touched. On a total shipment I should say it [depreciation] would run from 35 to 60 per cent. others would run more than that." This statement was repeated by Mr. Angus in other words. Mr. Lange, manager of the libelant company, also testified to the same effect, placing the ordinary depreciation of such goods resulting from such shipments at about 40 per cent. From these admissions it is apparent that galvanized goods would be injured where a part of the cargo is sulphate of ammonia regardless of their position in the ship and that the libelant knew of this probability from its experience. It must be taken therefore to have assumed such risk. Moreover, it is impossible in this case to draw a line between the injury which would have been caused without the presence of sea water and the actual injury which the goods have received.

The sea water which entered the hold wet the sulphate of ammonia, dissolving a portion of it and the solution dripped, or ran, in and over the tubs causing a corrosion of the surface which was the main cause of the injury to them. Mr. Shorey, a chemist who testified in the case, explained how a solution of sulphate of ammonia would destroy such ware, would corrode all metals except gold, silver and platinum, and that the evidence of such corrosion was found extensively on such ware upon its arrival in Honolulu. His testimony as to the injury to the school bags was, that on the outside of the burlap cover of the bales there was a deposit, a sample of which he took, which deposit showed 80 per cent. of sulphate of ammonia; he also examined the inside one of the bales and found on the inner wrapping of the bale 28 per cent. of sulphate of ammonia. The bale from which he took these samples was similar to the other bales as to the appearance of a similar deposit on them. He testified that the effect of the deposit on the school bags would be to alter the structure of the vegetable fiber in the course of time and weaken it. He stated that the effect of dissolving sulphate of ammonia with water would be a solution of sulphate of ammonia containing some free sulphuric acid and the action of the free sulphuric acid on the sea water would generate in small amounts a free hydrochloric acid gas which would have a corrosive action on material subject to corrosion, which might be in close proximity to it: such gas would have more effect upon metals than upon the bags,—would have very little on the latter. He also stated that sulphate of ammonia, independent of the effect which would result upon being dissolved by sea water, would, in a close hold where the free air is not permitted to circulate, develop smaller amounts of hydrochloric acid gas than in case of being wet with salt water; the result would be of the same nature but different in degree. In his opinion the deposit referred to developed from gas generated either from the sweating of the sulphate of ammonia in the close atmosphere or the sweating accelerated by dampness or water. The 80 per cent. deposit on the bales must have come from the combination of the sulphate of ammonia with water. It is clear from the testimony of the chemist that although in a close hold there might be considerable corrosive gases given off which would be injurious to galvanized ware and to a lesser degree to vegetable fiber, yet the amount of such injury would be less than where such gas was developed by the combination of salt water and sulphate of ammonia.

In the examinations of the cargo which were made on two occasions in good weather before the vessel reached Port Stanley, Jentzen, the second mate, says there were no signs of ammoniac inside the tubs and buckets, the whole deposit being on the outside; the whole top of the bags was wet. He didn't see any white stuff on the bags. Abelt, the first mate, said in reference to the same inspections, "water was in the tubs and pails, wet on top of the cargo, 'tween decks wet, cases was wet and ammoniac was wet too." "We took the water out of them: the tubs were damaged by sea water, and then the ammoniac melted wet by the water coming down and running along the beams."

The report of the surveyors who examined the ship and cargo at Port Stanley has this reference to the injury: "Cargo in the vicinity of main and No. 3 hatch slightly damaged by sea water." No. 3 hatch is testified to be the after hatch. The log under date of November 1st recites: "Surveyors found cargo under and around the hatches damaged by sea water." I find no such entry in the report of the surveyors. Their report, as above quoted, places the damage to the cargo as in the vicinity of the main and after hatches. The evidence therefore of the injury existing on November 1st, when the vessel reached Port Stanley and the hatches were opened, tends to the belief that the cargo was but slightly injured at that time. The injury as shown by the report of the appraisers in Honolulu is 75 per cent. on the galvanized ware and 80 per cent. on the school bags, and the sale of the goods at auction in Honolulu shows a depreciation of about 58 per cent., or a loss of $750.

[5] It appears from the testimony that the master of the ship made no attempt at Port Stanley to do anything to prevent the cargo in question from further deteriorating through its condition at that time from having been wet with salt water, exposed to the fumes and the drippings of a solution of sulphate of ammonia. There was certainly a great opportunity of making an effort to save these goods from further deterioration in consequence of the condition that they were in at that time. Mr. Shorey testifies that when the bags were opened in Honolulu they were damp and in a heated condition. As regards the tubs and buckets having already been exposed to the action of the solution referred to and to the fumes, does it not seem likely that an examination of their condition, perhaps removing them to the deck and exposing them to the wind and sun. thoroughly drying them out, might not have checked the corrosive action which must have been begun at that time? No such attempt was made, apparently no thought was given to the subject. Now if these goods received their main injury through being left through this period and for the rest of the voyage in statu quo, it was damage not within the exceptions of the third section of the Harter act (27 Stat. 445) or of the exceptions of the bill of lading.

"Losses by perils which have no peculiar connection with the sea, or the navigation, though they may occur during the voyage, do not fall within the exception. For example, damage . . . by the heating or sweating of the cargo; or by fumes arising from other goods, although the several parts of the cargo may have been well stowed." Carver, Carriage by Sea, 5th ed., sec. 86, p. 117.

"Faults or errors in taking care of the cargo, apart from any working of the vessel are probably excused under section 3rd of the Harter Act." Id., sec. 103 e, p. 152; *Rowson v. Atlantic Transp. Co.*, 9 Asp. M. C. 347.

"I think that the words 'faults or errors in the management of the vessel,' include improper handling of the ship as a ship which affects the safety of the cargo." *The Rodney*, 9 Asp. M. C. 39, cited in *Rowson v. Atlantic Transp. Co.*, supra.

The Rodney case turned on the construction of the Harter act.

It appears to be established that the exceptions of the Harter act would not include a neglect by the master to take care of the cargo by which the cargo is injured while the ship is lying in port, or where such neglect has no connection with the navigation or the management of the ship.

It might be contended that one of the exceptions of the bill of lading would make such injury developing after the arrival of the libellee at Port Stanley a matter of exception. The exception is as follows: "Nor for any loss or damage caused by the prolongation of the voyage." I am of the opinion that that does not affect this case. That refers to a prolongation of the voyage which might be caused by circumstances as have happened to the libellee in which certain goods would have suffered from having been long on board but could hardly include a damage resulting from the negligence of the master in taking care of the goods although the injury arising therefrom might be enhanced by the prolongation of the voyage.

In the case of *Pearce v. The Thomas Newton*, 41 Fed. 106, 108, judgment was rendered against the ship for neglect by the master in doing something or allowing something to be done for the preservation of the goods after they were injured.

"But no overpowering force prevented them from doing what was necessary for the preservation of the goods after they were injured. Admit that they had no means of drying them. The owner asked for them, and they should have given him an opportunity of doing what they could not, or did not, do themselves. For the damages resulting from the fact that the goods remained uncared for from Monday until Friday . . ,. libelant is entitled to a judgment in rem against the steamer."

I do not think the claimant can complain if the libellee is called upon to pay the whole loss to the libelant, for he had it in his power to avoid all liability by doing what could have been done at Port Stanley to save the goods from the deterioration that was very evidently likely to take place from their condition if nothing should be done to avert such deterioration.

There is no evidence definitely showing that the goods were damaged at the time the hold was opened at Port Stanley, November 1st. The survey refers only to the cargo in the vicinity of the main and after hatches, and reports that as "slightly damaged by sea water." The goods under consideration in this action were beyond question in a condition in which they would suffer damage if left in the hold of the ship without some immediate attention. The galvanized ware had some kind of deposit on the outside, probably sulphate of ammonia or zinc salts, or both. The bags were wet. The first knowledge of the officers that some of the seams had sprung and that the vessel was leaking in consequence thereof was on October 18th, fourteen days before the hatches were opened in Port Stanley. On October 19th the uppermost tarpaulins on the hatches were torn by the sea. On October 23rd the log reports tarpaulins of main and after hatches washed away and the hatch coamings bent inwards and several hatches broken. It would appear from the evidence that the injury to the hatches was confined to the main and after hatches.

It is improbable that the serious injury of the goods which was discovered when they were discharged at Honolulu could have developed during the fourteen days between October 18th and November 1st, when no real damage was discovered by the board of survey. According to Shorey the injury to the bags that would be caused by a deposit of sulphate of ammonia would require a period of time. It is obvious that the damp condition of the bags just before the ship reached Port Stanley, would in the course of time if not remedied create serious injury. The hatches were opened for about an hour at Port Stanley and then closed permanently, so far as the record informs us, leaving the wet bags and the galvanized ware with its deposit of corrosive salts, to swelter for the next six months in the close hold of the ship in company with the ammoniac which had been wet and partially dissolved by salt water

A decree may be entered in favor of the libelant in the sum of seven hundred and fifty dollars ($750.00), being the amount of its loss as shown by the auctioneer's return of the sale of the goods in question at public auction, filed herein, with interest from May 29, 1906, and costs.

These proceedings were begun in this court May 29, 1906, but it was not until October 8, 1912, that the case was finally submitted.

IN THE MATTER OF THE APPLICATION OF RYONOSUKE SAKABA FOR A WRIT OF HABEAS CORPUS.

October 8, 1913.

Aliens unlawfully in the United States—Habeas Corpus—Remedies before the inspector in charge: An alien under arrest for being unlawfully in the United States may not have the benefit of a writ of habeas corpus until he has exhausted his remedies before the inspector in charge.

Habeas corpus: Motion to dismiss petition and order to show cause.

Andrews & Quarles for petitioner.
C. C. Bitting, Assistant U. S. Attorney, for respondent.

DOLE, J. The applicant for the writ of habeas corpus is under detention as being an alien unlawfully in the country. He has had a private hearing before the immigration officers and was then entitled to a further hearing assisted by counsel; this, through his counsel, he has declined.

I have tried to consider as favorably as possible the petition for the writ. The defect in the petitioner's case is that he did not exhaust his remedies before the inspector in charge. This court has no means of knowing that the proceedings before the inspector were unfair. The counsel has had the advantage of discussing the matter with his client and hearing his client's statement. The court, however, has to take it for granted that the work of the officials of the government is *bona fide* and honest until the contrary is proved, and on a showing like this cannot presume that the petitioner did not have a fair hearing, that the interpreter was dishonest, and that the statement by the respondent of the examination before him is untrue. Although the petitioner was not told at that time that he had a right to inspect the warrant and to a copy of all the proceedings that led up to the warrant, yet the proceedings were not finished; they were *in mediis rebus,* and it was to be expected that before the determination of such proceedings the petitioner and his counsel would have been informed, and would have been given an opportunity to inspect such papers, failing which, there would have been good reason for asking for a writ of habeas corpus on the ground of unfairness.

There is more liberality toward persons arrested in these proceedings, as regards their assistance by counsel, than there is in proceedings for the detention and deportation of persons desiring to land in the United States, where they are not allowed counsel who may take any part in the proceedings, and it is to be expected that with such opportunity, complaints of unfairness and illegality will be few, and based only upon definitely probable grounds.

To make a precedent that would favor a practice of applying for writs of habeas corpus before petitioners have exhausted their remedies before the immigration officers, would be embarrassing to the court, and productive of no benefit to applicants.

The motion to dismiss the petition and the order to show cause is allowed, with costs to the respondent.

IN THE MATTER OF THE APPLICATION OF CHING LUM FOR A WRIT OF HABEAS CORPUS.

IN THE MATTER OF THE APPLICATION OF WONG YUEN FOR A WRIT OF HABEAS CORPUS.

IN THE MATTER OF THE APPLICATION OF SUI JOY FOR A WRIT OF HABEAS CORPUS.

October 25, 1913.

1. *Habeas corpus—Delay of writ until remedies below exhausted*: On a petition for habeas corpus the court will not usually grant the writ, except under peculiar and urgent circumstances, until the petitioner has exhausted his remedies before the authority detaining him and on appeal therefrom.

2. *Immigration acts—Detention of persons charged with violation thereof*: Temporary detention of persons charged with offenses under the immigration acts, pending inquiry, is valid.

3. *Arrest—Probable cause*: Arrest of persons without probable cause, unauthorized.

4. *Same—Grounds*: Upon arrest of a person, he or his counsel should be informed of the grounds thereof.

Habeas corpus: Demurrer to petition.

Thompson, Wilder, Watson & Lymer for petitioners.
C. C. Bitting, Assistant U. S. Attorney, for respondent.

DOLE, J. The petitions in these cases claim that the persons in whose behalf the petitions are made are unlawfully restrained of their liberty and prevented from being at large by R. L. Halsey, inspector in charge of immigration; also that the said Halsey had stated that such persons were being held for investigation by the immigration authorities of the United States in and for the Territory of Hawaii; and further allege that such persons are not now and have "not been charged with the commission of any crime or offense against the laws of the United States relating to immigration."

[1] The precedents in habeas corpus cases in the United States courts, particularly in the Supreme Court, emphasize and reiterate the practice that although a Federal court with power to grant a writ of habeas corpus, may grant such writ and discharge the accused in advance of his trial under an indictment, it is not bound to exercise that power immediately upon the application being made for the writ, but may await the result of the trial, and in its discretion as the special circumstances of the case may require, put the petitioner to his writ of error from the highest court of the State. *Ex parte Terry*, 128 U. S. 289, 302.

In the case of *Whitten v. Tomlinson*, 160 U. S. 231, 242, and citing many cases in the Supreme Court, the court says:

"But, except in such peculiar and urgent cases previously mentioned the courts of the United States will not discharge the prisoner by habeas corpus in advance of a final determination of his case in the courts of the State; and, even after such final determination in those courts, will generally leave the petitioner to the usual and orderly course of proceeding by writ of error from this court."

The court has followed this practice and in the recent case of *Ryonosuke Sakaba*, ante, p. 372, dismissed the petition for a writ on the ground that the applicant had not exhausted the remedies before the immigration officers, and still more recently the court refused to make any order on the petition for the writ, because the usual proceedings before the immigration officers had not taken place. This practice is, I think, a reasonable one both for clients and the court. The exhausting of remedies below will tend to prevent cases from being brought which ought not to be brought, and to put the court in a position to hear petitions on the basis of a clear understanding.

[2] It is "clear that detention, or temporary confinement, as part of the means necessary to give effect to the provisions for the exclusion or expulsion of aliens would be valid. Proceedings to exclude or expel would be vain if those accused could not be held in custody pending the

inquiry into their true character and while arrangements were being made for their deportation."

Accused of what? This expression "those accused," in the above citation from *Wong Wing v. United States*, 163 U. S. 228, 235, implies that the person held in custody is accused of something. In other words, has been arrested, in the words of the Constitution, "upon probable cause."

For the purposes of this demurrer the allegations that the persons arrested are not now and have not been charged with the commission of any crime or offense against the United States relating to immigration, must be taken as true. It cannot be argued that they might have been arrested for some other offense not relating to immigration, inasmuch as a previous allegation which must also be admitted to be true, refers to the statement of the respondent that such persons were being held for "investigation by the immigration authorities of the United States in and for the Territory of Hawaii," thus limiting the possible grounds of arrest to offenses under the immigration laws.

IN THE MATTER OF THE APPLICATION OF CHING LUM FOR A WRIT OF HABEAS CORPUS. (ALSO, IN THE MATTERS OF WONG YUEN, SUI JOY, AND KIMI YAMAMOTO.

August 2, 1915.

1. *Immigration—Deportation—Entering the United States:* An alien who came to the Hawaiian Islands previous to their annexation to the United States, and was living there at the time of such annexation cannot be said to "have entered the United States" within the

meaning of section 3 of the act of February 20, 1907, as amended by the act of March 26, 1910, 36 Stat. 263.

2. *Same—Same—Same—Actual landing subject to statutory conditions:* The provisions of the said statute for the deportation of aliens found "to be unlawfully within the United States", presume an actual landing of such aliens, subject to the conditions as to conduct set forth in the statute.

3. *Habeas Corpus—Newly discovered evidence in behalf of respondent, basis for in pleadings; laches:* A motion of respondent for leave to show that the alien though originally coming to Hawaii before annexation, later visited China and returned again to Hawaii, is denied, as there is no basis for such testimony in the pleadings and no showing that the alleged fact is newly discovered, and as such evidence, if existing, was within the reach of the respondent during the pendency of the proceedings.

Habeas corpus: On demurrer to return.

Thompson, Wilder, Watson & Lymer for petitioners Ching Lum, Wong Yuen and Sui Joy.

J. W. Cathcart for petitioner Kimi Yamamoto.

Jeff McCarn, U. S. District Attorney, and *J. W. Thompson,* Assistant U. S. Attorney, for respondent.

DOLE, J. In the first three of the above cases demurrers to the petitions were overruled, whereupon the respondent filed his returns which were demurred to by the petitioners, the fifth ground of demurrer being as follows: "That it does not appear in the said return that the said Sui Joy is an alien who has ever entered the United States within the meaning of the law herein provided." In the fourth case, the petitioner filed a traverse to the return of the respondent, in which, among other things, she raised the same point as raised on the fifth ground of the said demurrers, to-wit, that she was not subject to the immigration laws of the United States, having come to the Hawaiian Islands while they were under the jurisdiction of the Republic of Hawaii.

The argument on this point is, briefly, that the petitioners, having come to the Hawaiian Islands previous to annexation, as alleged, and being domiciled residents here at the time of annexation, the statute does not apply to them, such persons, although aliens, not having "entered" the United States.

The following is the immigration rule applying to these cases:

"The application must state facts bringing the alien within one or more of the classes subject to deportation after entry. The proof of these facts should be the best that can be obtained. The application must be accompanied by a certificate of landing (to be obtained from the immigration officer in charge at the port where landing occurred) or a reason given for its absence, in which case effort should be made to supply the principal items of information mentioned in the blank form provided for such certificates. Telegraphic application may be resorted to only in case of necessity and must state (1) that the usual written application has been made and forwarded by mail, and (2) the substance of the facts and proof therein contained." Immigration Rule 22, subdivision 2.

The statute under which the petitioners are held is a part of section 3 of the act of February 20, 1907, as amended by the act of March 26, 1910, 36 Stat. 263. It is as follows:

"Any alien who shall be found an inmate of or connected with the management of a house of prostitution or practicing prostitution *after such alien shall have entered the United States,* or who shall receive, share in, or derive benefit from any part of the earnings of any prostitute, or who is employed by, in, or in connection with any house of prostitution or music or dance hall or other place of amusement or resort habitually frequented by prostitutes,or where prostitutes gather, or who in any way assists, protects, or promises to protect from arrest any prostitute, shall be deemed to be unlawfully within the United States and shall be deported in the manner provided by sections 20 and 21 of this act."

The demurrers are allowed on the fifth ground. It is obvious from a reading of division 2 of Immigration Rule 22, above quoted, that the Commissioner General of Immi-

gration and the Secretary of Labor, who are authorized by the Immigration Act of February 20, 1907, sec. 22, 34 Stat. 898, to establish rules for carrying out the provisions of the act, have construed the act on the point referred to, as meaning an actual entry or landing in the United States. The said division 2 of the 22nd rule, in providing for an application by the immigration officers to the Secretary of Labor for authority to arrest an alien suspected of being unlawfully in the United States, requires, among other things, that the application "shall be accompanied by certificate of landing (to be obtained from the immigration officer in charge at the port where the landing occurred) or a reason given for its absence." Of course this can refer to nothing else than an actual landing in the United States. This construction is rendered still more positive by the "certificate of landing," required by the rule to accompany the application. The blank form provided by the Secretary of Labor and the Commissioner General of Immigration under the authority of the statute, is as follows:
"Form 564.

Certificate as to Landing of Alien
(To accompany application for warrant of arrest.)

DEPARTMENT OF COMMERCE AND LABOR
Immigration Service

...., 190

I hereby certify that I have examined the records of the immigrant station at ....with reference to the record of the landing or entry of ...., an alien, and that the following facts relative to such landing or entry are disclosed by said records.

(1)   Name of alien,..................; age,.... ....; sex................;

(2)   Race, ...; country whence alien came,........ ....

(3)   Exact date and port of arrival in the United States,

....

(4)   Name of vessel and line,...

(If alien arrived via Canada or Mexico, so state.)

(5)   Destination, ...

(6)   Occupation, ...; money brought, $............
(7)   By whom passage paid, ...
(8)   Whether ever in United States before, ...
(9)   Whether inspected at time of arrival, ...

(If held for special inquiry, so state.)

Remarks: ....

(Signature) ....
(Official title) ...."

Such construction, being authoritative and official, is entitled to great weight. Endlich's Interpretation of Statutes, sec. 357.

Counsel in the Sui Joy, Ching Lum and Wong Yuen cases, set forth somewhat exhaustively the constitutional argument that Congress derived its powers to legislate as to immigrant aliens after being admitted, solely from section 8 of the first article of the Constitution of the United States, which gives it the power "to regulate commerce with foreign nations." Quoting from the brief, "the theory is that commerce with foreign nations includes not only an exchange of commodities, but also the importation or incoming of passengers. The proposition that Congress has no power to regulate the affairs of individual persons in the United States except as an incidental to some one of the powers expressly given to it by the Constitution, is fundamental." It follows therefore that whereas Congress may permit an alien immigrant to land under certain conditions as to conduct thereafter while in the country, involving forcible deportation upon his failure to conform to such conditions, it may not deport alien residents for similar conduct, with whom there has been no such conditional entry into the United States. In other words, an alien resident of the United States in regard to whom there was no condition as to his conduct during his residence, that was made the basis of his landing or entry into the country by a then existing statute, is not within the scope of section 3 of the immigration act of February 20, 1907, 34 Stat. 899, as amended by the act of March 26, 1910, 36 Stat. 263. Plainly the law does not affect persons who have not *entered* the United States previous to doing the acts charged. These petitioners all claim to have been living in Hawaii before and at the time of annexation. In matters of immigration the world *enter* has not acquired a technical meaning. It would appear that these cases might well have been disposed of on their inception, on the ground that the statue is too clear to require interpretation. *"Absoluta sententia expositore indiget."* Potter's Dwarris, 128; Vattel's first rule, id. 126.

As the ruling on this ground of the demurrer disposes of the cases, the court need not consider the other grounds.

It is not clear whether there remains a question of fact to be decided. The returns in the first three cases do not specifically deny the allegations of residence in Hawaii before annexation, but make a general denial of all further allegations and averments of said petitions necessary to be denied. The return in the fourth case accepts the allegations of the petition in that case that the petitioner arrived in Hawaii in the year 1897, as correct. She (Kimi Yamamoto) is, therefore, under the foregoing conclusions, entitled to her discharge under the writ, which is hereby ordered.

If the respondent desires to contest the allegations of residence in Hawaii in the first three cases, an opportunity will be given, otherwise such petitioners will be discharged.

August 4, 1915.

[3] On the afternoon of the day the foregoing decision was given in open court, counsel on both sides filed the following stipulation:

"It is hereby stipulated and agreed by and between the United States of America through J. W. Thompson, its assistant district attorney of the District and Territory of

Hawaii, and Sui Joy, Ching Lum and Wong Yuen, by their attorneys, Thompson & Milverton, that each of said petitioners were residents of the Hawaiian Islands for a period of more than five (5) years prior to the 15th day of June, A. D. 1900."

By which stipulation it would appear that the said petitioners were resident here for over three years before the annexation of Hawaii to the United States, which took place August 12, 1898. The court was thereupon prepared to order the discharge of the petitioners, according to the conclusions of the foregoing decision, but before such order was effectuated the assistant district attorney, acting for the respondent, moved the court for an opportunity of showing that the petitioners severally visited China after annexation and returned again to Hawaii.

Such motion must be denied, inasmuch as the cases contain no pleadings which would form a basis for such testimony and there is no showing that such information is newly discovered and as such information, if it exists, obviously has been, during the pendency of these proceedings, within the reach of the respondent.

The writs are made absolute and the petitioners discharged.

Reversed: United States v. Sui Joy. 240 Fed. 392; *United States v. Kimi Yamamoto,* 240 Fed. 390.

IN THE MATTER OF THE APPLICATION OF MASUICHI TANAKA FOR A WRIT OF HABEAS CORPUS.

November 8, 1913.

Aliens—Immigration—Birth certificate as evidence of status: Held,

under the evidence before the board of special inquiry of the immigration service, that the board was justified in regarding the prima facie
weight of a certificate of Hawaiian birth, issued by the Secretary of
the Territory of Hawaii, as having been overcome.

Habeas corpus: On return to writ.

J. Lightfoot for petitioner.
C. C. Bitting, Assistant U. S. Attorney, for respondent.

CLEMONS, J.   The petitioner, Tsuneichi Tanaka, on arrival from Japan at the port of Honolulu, was found by a
board of special inquiry to be an alien afflicted with trachoma, a dangerous contagious disease, and was denied a
landing.   His appeal to the Secretary of Labor was dismissed and the order denying a landing confirmed.   In order
to secure his release from the custody of the respondent
(the inspector in charge of the immigration station at this
port), the petitioner applied for a writ of habeas corpus,
on the ground that he is in fact an American citizen, by
virtue of his birth in Hawaii, and that he offered to prove
before the board of special inquiry that he had a certificate
of Hawaiian birth (issued by the Secretary of the Territory)
and to prove his identity as the person named in the certificate, but that the hearing before the board was "unfair,
unjust, unlawful, and irregular, in this, that petitioner was
not allowed to show by the said Hawaiian birth certificate
and otherwise, that he is a citizen of the United States of
America," and was not allowed to show that he is the same
person "referred to" in this certificate, though there designated Masuichi Tanaka instead of Tsuneichi Tanaka.   The
writ issued, and before any return thereto a supplementary
petition was filed substantially the same as the original
petition except that it annexed thereto, in accordance with
the practice indicated in *Low Wah Suey v. Backus*, 225 U.
S. 460, 472, a transcript of the proceedings before the immigration officers.

The petition and supplementary petition, together with the transcript of proceedings attached thereto and made a part thereof show not only a hearing but a rehearing, the latter had after the affirmance by the Secretary of Labor of the board's finding upon the first hearing, and at the rehearing the introduction of the birth certificate, a transcript of the evidence upon which it was obtained, and oral testimony in addition thereto in petitioner's behalf.

The transcript of the rehearing proceedings shows that the petitioner then indicated his desire to appeal, but nothing appears in the record to show that an appeal was had. The petitioner makes no objection of having been denied an appeal or of being refused the hearing of any evidence which he had to offer, but rests his case solely upon the contention that the board did not give due weight to the birth certificate or to the other evidence in his behalf.

The respondent's return amounts to a demurrer to the petition, by referring thereto and particularly to the transcript of the proceedings incorporated therein, as justification for the alleged unlawful detention of the petitioner in the custody of the respondent. A demurrer attacked the return on the general ground of insufficiency.

As this demurrer is a demurrer to what is in effect another demurrer (the answer), the whole record is open to examination. Andrews' Stephen on Pleading, 2d ed., 268-269, sec. 140.

It is very clear that the petitioner was given every opportunity to make what case he could, and it is equally clear that the discrepancies in the testimony, and the doubts which they raise, pointed out by inspector Moore in his statements appearing at pages 16-17 and 29-30 of the transcript annexed to the supplementary petition, are ample to overcome any prima facie weight of the certificate as evidence of the petitioner's birth in Hawaii. *In re Lee Leong,* ante p. 258. The board's finding is so clearly justified by the evidence before it, as to make any discussion of this evidence unprofitable.

Moreover, the testimony appearing in the transcript attached to the birth certificate, being the testimony upon which the certificate was issued, would seem to indicate that the certificate had been issued upon an insufficient showing, resting as it does upon the testimony of the alleged father and of Tomizo Munesato, the former of whom had not, so far as appears, seen his alleged son, now of the age of eighteen years, since the son was three years old, and the latter of whom had not, so far as appears, seen the son since the son was less than two months old. Zenkichi Ouye and Tomizo Munesato, in affidavits attached to the application for the certificate, depose to having "frequently seen the said child, often at daily intervals and often at intervals not exceeding weekly," and having "noticed the child grow from infancy to its present age;" and each deponent gives as "the reason of the frequent observation," "the fact that this deponent lived as a neighbor of Umematsu Tanaka" (the father) and he visited at the house frequently and became a very intimate friend of Umematsu Tanaka. But the alleged father appears to have resided in Hawaii since his return from Japan in 1898, Ouye to have resided in Hawaii since 1890 and Munesato since 1892, while the alleged son has resided in Japan since 1895. So, even though neighbors of the father's, the two deponents were not in a position to "notice the child grow from infancy to its present age." Ouye did not testify at all before the Secretary of the Territory, and Munesato's testimony does not show that he ever saw the child after his departure for Japan. But quite apart from any suggestion that the issuance of the certificate was unwarranted, the board of special inquiry was fully justified in regarding the certificate as discredited by the evidence before it.

Let the writ be discharged and the petitioner remanded to the custody of the respondent.

As supplementing this decision, and in explanation of the record, it may be said that through inadvertence, an order to show cause issued upon the filing of the supplementary petition. The return, nominally a return to the order to show cause, has, therefore, been regarded herein as a return to the writ, which had originally been issued in the case. I may say that the practice which has lately become a rule of this court, to issue in the first instance an order *nisi* instead of a writ, had my approval in *In re Hausman*, ante p. 202, and I am convinced that such practice would, under the showing made by the transcript annexed to the supplementary petition, have been justified in this case.

UNITED STATES OF AMERICA v. SIMON POPOV, ALIAS CHARLES W. BOYD, AND GREGORY GUSTOHIN.

November 8, 1913.

1. *Post offices—Deposit of obscene matter in the mail—Principal; accessory:* One who prepares for another person an obscene communication with the knowledge that the other is to deposit it in the post office for mailing and delivery to a third person, may by virtue of Penal Code, sec. 332, be indicted and convicted as a principal under Penal Code, sec. 211.

2. *Criminal law—Accessory before the fact:* Penal Code, sec. 332, authorizes the charging of an accessory before the fact as a principal.

3. *Same—"Aid", "abet":* Definitions of, discussed.

Indictment: On motion in arrest of judgment.

S. E. Hannestad for the motion.
C. C. Bitting, Assistant U. S. Attorney, contra.

CLEMONS, J. The defendants, Simon Popov and Gregory Gustohin, were indicted on a charge of depositing, and causing to be deposited, in a post office obscene matter for mailing and delivery. Penal Code, sec. 211. Gustohin plead guilty. Popov plead not guilty and on trial by a jury was convicted. He now enters a motion in arrest of judgment, based on the same grounds as an earlier motion for a directed verdict of acquittal, viz: that according to the evidence he had nothing to do with the admitted fact of the deposit of such non-mailable matter in the mails, but only at Gustohin's dictation and because Gustohin could not write, wrote the obscene matter on a postal card, already bearing a printed picture of an extremely lewd and indecent nature, and wrote on the envelope in which the card was enclosed the name and address of a young woman to whom it was mailed, and to whom he then knew it was to be mailed,—in other words, that Popov's acts were not the acts of a principal but at most were nothing more than those of an accessory before the fact. The assistant district attorney contends that, even on this statement of Popov's, he was properly indicted as a principal within the provisions of Penal Code, sec. 332, which reads:

"Whoever directly commits any act constituting an offense defined in any law of the United States, or aids, abets, counsels, commands, induces, or procures its commission, is a principal."

[3] There are authorities which might afford foundation for an argument in support of the motion, but I am convinced that they "originated at a time when criminal lawyers puzzled their wits and taxed their ingenuity to invent metaphysical shades of distinction." See language of Manning, J., in *State v. Poynier*, 36 La. Ann. 572, 1 Enc. L. &

P. 238, n. 4. The argument that the word "abet" colors all its associate words in section 332 with the idea of assistance at the time and place or at least contemporaneous assistance, seems to me unreasonable It is true that authorities are at hand to support various shades of meaning of the word "abet" and its associate "aid," some of them in line with the defendant's contention. For instance, the words "aid" and "abet" have been held to be "pretty much the synonyms of each other, . . . comprehend [ing] all assistance rendered by acts, words of encouragement or support, or presence, actual or constructive, to render assistance, should it be necessary:" *Raiford v. State*, 59 Ala. 106, 1 Enc. L. & P. 106, n. 22; while these words have elsewhere been held not to be synonymous: that "to abet is to encourage, counsel, incite, or instigate the commission of a crime, the word indicat(ing) the act of an accessory before the fact; to aid is to support, the word describing an accessory after the fact." *State v. Empey*, 79 Iowa, 460, 44 N. W. 707. Still other authorities seem to hold that the word "abet" connotes such participation as formerly made one an accessory *at* the fact: these are the numerous expressions appearing to make "presence" an essential factor. Thus Cowell, also Fleta, as cited by Black, Law Dic., 2d ed., 7, tit. "abettor", says, "The distinction between abettors and accessories is the presence or absence at the commission of the crime." Black, ubi sup., also cites American decisions for the proposition, that "presence and participation are necessary to constitute a person an abettor."

[1] [2] Enough has been said to indicate the confusion of authorities, and, also, to suggest a possible reason for the enactment of section 332, above, making certain persons all principals. Moreover, the only prior statutes known to the court, relating expressly to accessories before the fact are Rev. Stat. 5323, reading:

"Every person who knowingly aids, abets, causes, procures, commands, or counsels another to commit any murder, robbery, or other piracy upon the seas, is an accessory before the fact to such piracies, and every such person being thereof convicted shall suffer death,"

and Rev. State. sec. 5427, reading:

"Every person who knowingly and intentionally aids or abets any person in the commission of any felony denounced in the three preceding sections, or attempts to do any act therein made felony, or counsels, advises, or procures, or attempts to procure, the commission thereof, shall be punished in the same manner and to the same extent as the principal party."

Now, these provisions are both repealed by the Penal Code, sec. 341, and there is enacted section 332 above quoted, which enlarges the provisions of these repealed sections of the Revised Statutes, so as to make them of general application, though, it is true, without any direct expression to indicate that accessories before the fact are thereby intended. Moreover, while the Penal Code makes here, or elsewhere so far as I have found, no specific provision as to accessories before the fact, it provides in the very next section for acessories after the fact, sec. 333, and later, sec. 341, repeals the sections comprising the chapter of the Revised Statutes relating to punishment of accessories after the fact, Rev. Stat. secs. 5533-5535, the new provision being such an enlargement of the repealed sections as to be of general application. The intent would seem to be to cover the whole ground, to provide for all accessories, both those before the fact as well as those after the fact, the former by section 332 and the latter by section 333. Such was the intent deduced from a similar but even narrower enactment of the State of Kansas, the provision there being that "any person who counsels, aids, or abets, in the commission of any offense may be charged, tried, and convicted in the same manner as if he were a principal." From this language the Kansas supreme court held, "The intention of the legislature . . . is obvious. It authorizes the charging of an accessory before the fact as a principal." *State v. Cassidy,* 13 Kans. 550, 555, Brewer, J.

Independent of this very high authority, there is no reason why we should give the word "aid" the qualified meaning of "then and there aid," especially as the associated words "induce" and "procure" and perhaps also "counsel", are words which aptly and primarily, philologically, denote antecedent action as contrasted with contemporary action. The language is broad enough, in my opinion, to include the furnishing, as Popov did here, of the means of committing an offense. There are, I am informed, some decisions taking a very narrow view of the word "deposit," in the phrase "deposit in the mails," or similar expressions, used in the statutory definition of offenses against the postal service. Under the peculiar language of the statute, such rulings may be plausible, but if they are sound, we might just as well say that on a charge of injury to letter boxes, under Penal Code, sec. 198, by Gustohin's having exploded dynamite therein, Popov's participation by furnishing the means of committing the offense,— by preparing the explosive for use by Gustohin for the special purpose by Gustohin intended and by Popov known, would not be the rendering of "aid" within the meaning of section 332.

The interesting opinions of then Circuit Judge Van Devanter in the cases of *Demolli v. United States,* 144 Fed. 363, 365-366, and of *Burton v. United States,* 142 Fed. 57, 62, go a long way to support an indictment for participation as an accessory and are authority for the contentions of the assistant district attorney, but, in my view of the facts of the case at bar, it is not necessary to go so far as the court went in those cases just cited, and for that reason, if not for the reason that I am not quite prepared to approve their conclusions on the facts there, those authorities have no influence in my present ruling. The strong dissent of Circuit Judge Hook in the *Demolli* case may be noted.

The foregoing discussion may well be concluded with the context of the above-quoted language of Judge Manning:

"The distinction between principals and accessories before the fact is in most cases a distinction without a difference, and often requires nice and subtle verbal refinements to express it. In some of our states it has been abolished by statute; in others judicial decisions have attenuated it until it is perceptible only by a close mental effort. The fact is, it is not a creature of statutory law, but wholly of judicial construction, the origin of which is so vague and indeterminate that the text writers have not found out where to place it. It is supposed to have originated at a time when criminal lawyers puzzled their wits and taxed their ingenuity to invent metaphysical shades of distinction, such for instance as that between principals and accessories *at* the fact, which once existed, and is now exploded. The distinction between principals and accessories before the fact is fast following its kindred technical refinement." *State v. Poynier,* 36 La. Ann. 572; 1 Enc. L. & P. 238, n. 4.

But conceding that if the question were to be determined solely on Popov's version of the facts, it would be one upon which lawyers might disagree, nevertheless, it is to be noted in the evidence that the witness McDuffie, chief detective of the Honolulu police, testified to this defendant's confession, "I sent that picture" (meaning the card bearing the printed picture and written matter, above described), made in answer to the direct question, "Who sent that picture?" There is also to be noted, the testimony of post office inspector Jarvis, that this defendant confessed to him that "both [Popov and Gustohin] prepared the card and both went to the post office to mail it," though Popov himself testified here that Gustohin went alone to the post office and that Popov went elsewhere This evidence was for the jury, and if believed by the jury would warrant their finding Popov to have been a principal within a narrow definition of that term, even if he were not a principal under the broad provision of section 332 of the Penal Code. It certainly would not be for the court to say that Popov's testimony is true, making him merely one who participated in preparation of the objectionable matter for the mail, and that McDuffie's testimony to Popov's confession of having himself "sent" it and Jarvis's testimony to Popov's confession that he and Gustohin both "went to the post office to mail it," are untrue.

By reason of the foregoing considerations, the motion should be overruled. It is so ordered.

IN THE MATTER OF T. K. OGINO, A BANKRUPT.

November 21, 1913.

Bankruptcy—Attorney's fees for services in interest of estate: A fee is allowed to attorneys for services in the interest of the estate rendered in an examination of the bankrupt and witnesses at six hearings before the referee: overruling the conclusion of the referee that the attorneys having as attorneys for certain creditors filed their claims against the estate and it not appearing that the trustee expressly directed such examination, it must be presumed that their attendance at the hearings was pursuant to their employment as such attorneys; the court basing its allowance of a fee partly on the fact of a previous general retainer by the trustee and on the fact that the examination was in line with the trustee's duty to discover the assets of the estate.

In Bankruptcy: On review of order of referee.

J. W. Russell for petitioning attorneys, *Thompson, Wilder, Watson & Lymer.*

G. S. Curry, Referee in Bankruptcy. contra.

CLEMONS, J. The referee has certified to this court for review the following question raised by the petition of the attorneys for the trustee,

"Whether counsel for the trustee, having been previously retained as attorneys for certain creditors in the filing of their claims, can be given an allowance for services in attending upon the referee in the examination of the bankrupt and witnesses when such examination was conducted by them without the express direction of the trustee."

The referee's certificate has the following "summary of the facts" on which he based the order of disallowance which it is desired to have reviewed:

"Counsel admitted that the trustee did not expressly authorize or direct them to conduct the examination of the bankrupt or the witness before me; that previous to the time of said examinations they had been formally retained by the trustee as his attorneys, and that at the first meeting of creditors as attorneys for M. Philips & Co., Isadore Rubenstein and C. Neuman & Co., creditors, they filed claims against the bankrupt, in the following respective amounts: M. Phillips & Co. $1,414.37, Isadore Rubenstein $324.00 and C. Neuman & Co. $577.21, aggregating the total sum of $2,315.58; that the total amount of the claims of said bankrupt, as appears by his schedules is $11,377.00."

The referee's order is as follows:

"Counsel for the trustee, having as attorneys for M. Phillips & Co., Isadore Rubenstein and C. Neuman & Co., filed their respective claims against the bankrupt, and said claims constituting a substantial portion of the liabilities of said bankrupt, it must be presumed that counsel's attendance upon me in the examination of the bankrupt and witnesses was in pursuance of their employment as such attorneys for said creditors and not as counsel for the trustee; it not appearing that the trustee expressly directed said examination; and I, therefore, feel that I am without power to allow the claim of said counsel of the item: 'To services—Attendance upon referee, re examination of bankrupt and witnesses, 6 days, viz: Jan. 22nd, Jan. 23rd, Jan. 30th, Jan. 31st, Feb. 13th and Feb. 15th, $60.00,' and must accordingly disallow the same, and it is so ordered."

The affidavit of counsel in support of the claim says:

"That the items of disbursement as set forth in the said statement were actually incurred in behalf of said trustee in the administration of said bankrupt's estate, and the items of services as set forth in said statement were actually performed in the proper administration of said estate and for and in behalf of said trustee, and the deponent verily believes the charges made therefor as therein set forth are reasonable and fair.

"Deponent further says that said services were not performed by virtue of any retainer of any person or corporation, other than said trustee and that no compensation has been received for any of said services or any charge made therefor to any person or corporation other than said trustee."

There is no doubt that the services were such as should have been paid for if specially requested by the trustee, and that they were services rendered in the interests of the estate and of all the creditors. The referee having conceded this, it seems to me that the presumption of the attorneys' being in the employment of the trustee, who had retained them for the general purposes of the bankruptcy administration, is more natural than the presumption upon which he bases his order of disallowance,. viz.: that they were representing only the petitioning creditors. The adjudication having been secured, the fruits of any examination of the bankrupt were for the benefit of all the creditors.

It was the trustee's first duty to discover all the assets of the estate, and the aid which counsel gave him in that behalf, even though not especially requested, was for the benefit of all concerned and should be paid for out of the general fund administered. Therefore, from considerations of equity, the principles of which guide courts of bankruptcy, this claim for attorneys' fees should, being reasonable, be allowed.

The following cases, cited in behalf of the petition, may be referred to as bearing on the question: *In re Berko-*

witz, 22 Am. B. R. 236; *In re Fidler & Son*, 23 Am. B. R. 16; *In re Stotts*, 93 Fed. 438; *In re Fixen*, 96 Fed. 748; *In re Hart & Co.*, 3 U. S. Dist. Ct. Haw. 73; *In re Hitchcock*, 3 U. S. Dist. Ct. Haw. 138.

The case is remanded to the referee for further proceedings in conformity herewith.

IN THE MATTER OF P. D. KELLETT, JR., A BANKRUPT.

December 4, 1913.

Bankruptcy—Discharge—Debt created by embezzlement: A bankrupt is not deprived of his right to a general discharge, by reason of the fact that a debt due one of the creditors was created by embezzlement; but such debt is not to be affected by the discharge, being excepted from the order of discharge by Bankruptcy Act, sec. 17.

In Bankruptcy: On objection to discharge.

J. A. Magoon, objecting creditor, *pro se.*
R. J. O'Brien (E. C. Peters with him) for the bankrupt.

CLEMONS, J. A creditor of the bankrupt objects to the bankrupt's discharge, assigning the ground that the whole of the debt due this creditor was "created by fraud, embezzlement and misrepresentation while acting in the fiduciary capacity as provided by section seventeen of the Bankruptcy Act of 1898 as amended," and alleging that this creditor, on June 13, 1908, had as surety for P. D. Kellett, Jr., guardian of Kan Yee, a minor, in a matter pending in the Circuit Court of the First Judicial Circuit,

Territory of Hawaii, made the said Kan Yee whole for his loss of about $2,344, suffered through the said Kellett's failure to faithfully perform his duty as said guardian, to-wit, the said Kellett's appropriation of said moneys to his own use. The bankrupt interposes a traverse to the creditor's objections, in which he makes a general denial of the allegations of the creditor and proffers the records and files of the Circuit Court in the matter of the guardian-ship. These records and files show, however, everything above alleged except the fact of misappropriation and the fact of payment by the surety, but the latter excepted fact has been conceded as also the fact that Kellett was ac-countable to the estate of his ward for some $2,344 which, as the records show, a judge of the Circuit Court had on April 23, 1907, ordered Kellett to pay, after having removed him as guardian because of his inability to produce that sum, or to "give any satisfactory statement as to where the same is now lying."

The creditor's objections have been argued orally, and in briefs, on the question of the bankrupt's right to a dis-charge solely on the merits of the above facts. See *Halli-burton v. Carter*, 55 Mo. 435 (1874); also *Cromes v. Crome's Adm'rs.*, 29 Gratt (Va.) 280 (1877).

A reading of the statute, section 17, makes it very clear that the objections are vain at this time, and do not entitle the creditor to an order denying the discharge. Section 17 has declared what debts are not to be "affected by a dis-charge," and no order of mine could add anything to it: if this debt is "provable" and is "created by the bankrupt's fraud, embezzlement, misappropriation, or defalcation while acting as an officer or in any fiduciary capacity," then the law ipso facto operates to except it from the discharge, just the same as it does in case of taxes, alimony, etc., speci-fied in the same section. Moreover, it will be noted, as leading to this conclusion, that section 14 of the act, in specifying the facts for which the judge shall deny a dis-

charge, does not give fraud, embezzlement, etc., as grounds
for such denial. And any order on this petition for adjudication must necessarily be without prejudice to the rights
of the objecting creditor arising under section 17 from the
facts above alleged.

Let the petition for discharge be granted.

IN THE MATTER OF THE APPLICATION OF CHIUGI YOSHIDA FOR A WRIT OF HABEAS CORPUS.

December 5, 1913.

*Immigration—Conclusiveness of findings of immigration officers as
to right of alien to landing, discussed.*

Habeas Corpus: On motion to dismiss petition for writ.

J. Lightfoot for petitioner.

C. C. Bitting, Assistant U. S. Attorney, for respondent.

DOLE, J. (Orally).   I have listened attentively to the
argument of counsel for petitioner and he has given us a
great deal of excellent law. His discussion of the question
would, to my mind, be more appropriate before the immigration officers than here, because it is not a review of
the case in the ordinary sense. Many of these cases would
be, I think, without a standing in court if it were not for
the copy of the proceedings before the board of inspectors
attached to the petition. I feel that the mere allegation
of unfairness,—of a semblance of a trial,—or of illegality,
is not sufficient to justify the court in using this great power
of habeas corpus. Such allegation should be followed by
an explanation stating wherein there was unfairness, alleg-

ing certain facts of unfairness or illegality. In these cases
such allegation is generally founded upon a copy of the
proceedings before the board of inspectors. I believe it
would be a good practice to state such explanation briefly in
the petition.

The simple question before this court is whether there
has been shown unfairness or illegality, either of which definitely shown would give this court jurisdiction. It is within
the discretion of the immigration officers to weigh testimony and to act thereon according to their judgment, if
there is anything to act upon.

The former case in which this court made the ruling
which counsel for petitioner has cited with a good deal of
satisfaction, and which I feel was a sound ruling, was a case
in which the question of domicil was vital and absolutely
no question relating to domicil had been asked, and the
ignorant applicant for admission, not knowing anything
about the law of domicil, was simply left in the lurch,
stranded so to speak, for want of that little help which I
felt that the government was bound to give him.
In re Jiro Miyagusuku, ante p. 344. In making that
ruling, I even felt that it may have been somewhat radical, and was not sure that it would be sustained
on appeal. I am not sure now. But the case before the
court is a case in which the immigration authorities did
go into the question which was at issue, which was the
question whether this applicant had participated in the
earnings of a prostitute. Now they went into that to a
considerable extent and there was testimony which they
had a right to consider. The applicant on being asked
whether he had received any aid from his wife since she
had been practicing prostitution, said, "Well, I can't say
entirely no aid from her; I had some," and she said, on
being asked what the reason was that she took up that
practice, "I tell you my husband turned to sickness and I
wanted to endeavor to cure him of his illness and need

money for the doctor." Now, there is an admission from the husband,—the applicant, and testimony from the wife, which the inspector had a right to consider.

Counsel for petitioner very properly argues that there was evidence which would tend to show that all this happened before she took up this practice. Of course the inspector had a right to decide that the uncertainty in their testimony in regard to time did not neutralize or overweigh this pretty significant testimony as to the fact of his receiving such aid. Counsel argues that the aid was very slight, probably assistance a wife would naturally give. I do not think this court has the jurisdiction to say that such aid should have been substantial aid; for instance you cannot draw a line between slight aid and substantial aid. You cannot draw a line in the matter of testimony as to its sufficiency in a case like this. The case to which I have referred, in which the court ruled that there was nothing which justified the immigration officers in their decision, is very different from this case in which there is testimony, and I think you will see the difficulty the court will have in trying to draw a line where there is testimony which is weakened by other statements, as to how far such testimony should go before it is sufficient. An examination of this case might go on for days and become very exhaustive. And has the court a right to say that such exhaustive examination must take place before there is sufficient evidence for the inspectors to act upon? How little, how much? No two judges would have the same view as to where to draw the line. The fact is that there is testimony in regard to the issue in this case upon which the inspector weighing it decided the case. This court cannot therefore review it or take jurisdiction because perhaps if the case were tried on its merits before this court, the court would have decided differently. The possible difference of opinion in a matter of this kind is no justification for the discharge of the prisoner.

In regard to the sacredness of the right to habeas corpus, I think I agree with all that has been said and yet it is established that the United States may create its own executive officers to deprive persons of their liberty upon an examination of their own, and any argument that it is extreme and harsh and severe is hardly an argument for a right to the writ; and in any case this court has no discretion in that matter unless it comes to a question of the constitutionality of that law. We have to accept the law as it is given us and act upon it.

I have very carefully weighed the case as it went on and it seems to me unnecessary for me to write an opinion on it, but favorable to all interests to dispose of it at once. I feel that no jurisdiction has been shown, no justification for the court to take jurisdiction, and the motion to dismiss is allowed.

UNITED STATES OF AMERICA, FOR THE USE AND BENEFIT OF LEWERS & COOKE, LIMITED, A CORPORATION, ET AL. *v.* BURRELL CONSTRUCTION COMPANY, A CORPORATION, AND THE AETNA INDEMNITY COMPANY, OF HARTFORD, CONNECTICUT, A CORPORATION.

December 5, 1913.

1. *Building material—Cost of transportation—Reasonable value at place of delivery:* The cost of the transportation of building materials, furnished by sub-contractors for the construction of public works, is an element of their value at the place of delivery.

2. *Materials and labor—Tools and machines:* Tools and machines

used in the construction of buildings under an engagement to furnish
materials and labor, are not within such contract.

At Law: Action in intervention for labor and materials.

Kinney, Prosser, Anderson & Marx for Lewers & Cooke,
Limited, Bank of Hawaii, Limited, Honolulu Iron Works
Company, Catton, Neill & Company, Limited, Lucas Broth-
ers, and A. B. Johanson.

W. W. Thayer and *R. W. Breckons* for E. O. Hall & Son,
Limited.

H. G. Middleditch for The von Hamm Young Company,
Limited.

P. L. Weaver for Robert Dalziel Jr. Company.

Thompson, Wilder, Watson & Lymer for defendants.

DOLE, J.   This case was begun in this court February 5,
1908, under the provisions of an act of Congress approved
August 13, 1894 (28 Stat. L. 278), entitled "An act for the
protection of persons furnishing materials and labor for
the construction of public works," as amended by an act
approved February 24, 1905 (33 Stat. L. 811); the said
Burrell Construction Company being the party who had
contracted with the United States to construct certain public works, and the said Aetna Indemnity Company being the
surety under the statute on the bond of the Burrell Construction Company.   Besides the original petition by Lewers & Cooke, Limited, there are eight petitioners intervening in the case.   Subsequent to the institution of said suits
of intervention, Theodore H. Macdonald and J. Birney Tut-
tue, both of New Haven in the State of Connecticut, were
appointed receivers of the said Aetna Indemnity Company
in a case then pending in the Superior Court of the said
State in and for the county of Hartford, entitled Theodore
H. Macdonald, Insurance Commissioner, versus the Aetna
Indemnity Company.   After certain questions of law were

disposed of and considerable evidence was taken in the original proceedings, all of the petitioners, excepting Robert Dalziel Jr. Company, a corporation, and the said receivers filed on May 28, 1912, a stipulation, and on August 20, 1912, an agreement, it being understood between counsel that duplicates or originals of such stipulation and agreement were also filed in the said case of Theodore H. Macdonald, Insurance Commissioner, pending in the said Superior Court of the said State of Connecticut; by which stipulation and agreement, the parties thereto agreed, subject to the approval of the said Superior Court of the said State of Connecticut, that judgment as to the said petitioners should be rendered in this court dismissing this case, and by which the said receivers agreed to and did confess judgment in favor of each of the said petitioners,—parties to said stipulation and agreement, in a sum equal to twenty-five per centum of their respective claims filed herein, "that is to say in the amount set opposite the names of said claimants in schedule A attached to such agreement and made a part thereof, . . . with interest thereon as stated in such agreement and schedule, and also to pay the costs of court, reference fees and other necessary expenses as the same may be taxed" in this court.

Judgment may therefore be entered dismissing this case as to the said petitioners, upon their filing full receipts respectively for the said twenty-five per centum of their said claims with interest as aforesaid, and costs, reference fees and other necessary expenses as may be taxed by this court.

The disposition of the claims of the other petitioners being thus provided for, it remains for the court to consider the remaining claim.—that of Robert Dalziel Jr. Company.

This intervenor filed an amended petition December 1. 1911, in which it alleged that it had supplied and delivered to the said Burrell Construction Company, defendant herein, between June 20, 1905, and March 27, 1908, materials and labor at the agreed price and reasonable value of $22,428.90 which were used in the prosecution and completion of the said public works, and that neither the said sum of money or any part thereof except the sum of $6,485.71 had been paid it by the defendants, and that there was then due and owing it from the defendants the sum of $15,943.19, with interest at six per cent. per annum, from the said date of March 27, 1908. A bill of particulars was filed May 26, 1909, which agrees in its totals with the said allegations.

Upon the evidence submitted I find the claim of Robert Dalziel Jr. Company satisfactorily proved, subject however to several corrections and deductions as hereinafter set forth. No reasonable ground appears why this claim should have been contested except as to such items.

[1] Counsel for defendants moved to strike out the testimony of witness Durant relating to freight and expressage on building materials used, and to cartage of copper and drain boards from Fort Shafter to town for the purpose of having work done on them, and for cartage back to Fort Shafter. Gurney, Tr., 100-101. This motion was denied except as to such cartage of copper and drain boards, in relation to which it was allowed. The cost of transportation of materials to the place of deliverey is an element of their value at such place. *United States v. Hageman,* 54 Atl. 344, 346; *Kehoe v. Hansen,* 65 N. W. 1075, 59 Am. St. Rep. 759; *Fowler & Guy v. Pompelly,* 76 S. W. 173; *United States v. Morgan,* 111 Fed. 474, 489.

[2] The following items are disapproved and deducted from the amount claimed:

Work that had to be replaced (Gurney Tr., 89)....$ 4.50
Cartage of copper and drain boards, mentioned
   above (Gurney Tr., 82)...................... 2.00
Collection charges on draft for $1,000 (Bill of particulars 17) 35

Tools and implements . . . [including 1 mal-
let, 4 wood clamps, 2 picks and handles, 2 shovels,
2 pipe cutters, 2 pipe vises, 1 large furnace, 1 metal
pot, 9 testing plugs, 1 pipe machine, 1 box],
amounting in value to......................$113.28

There are also deducted from the amount claimed items
amounting to $137.48, representing materials furnished to
Robert Dalziel Jr. Company by Burrell Construction Company, not shown to have been paid for (Bill of Particulars 23).

Judgment may therefore be entered in favor of Robert
Dalziel Jr. Company for $15,685.58, with interest at the
rate of six per cent. per annum from March 27, 1908, and
costs.

UNITED STATES OF AMERICA, FOR THE USE AND
BENEFIT OF LEWERS & COOKE, LIMITED, ET
AL., v. BURRELL CONSTRUCTION COMPANY,
A CORPORATION, AND AETNA INDEMNITY
COMPANY OF HARTFORD, CONNECTICUT, A
CORPORATION.

December 18, 1913.

Costs—Mileage fees—Witnesses attending voluntarily: In the case
of witnesses living out of the jurisdiction of the court and more than
one hundred miles distant therefrom, whose testimony is necessary
to the settlement of the issue, and who voluntarily attend the trial
and give their evidence, their mileage fees may be taxed as costs of
court against the other side when it is the losing party.

At Law: Taxation of costs.

Thompson, Wilder, Watson & Lymer for the objection.
Prosser, Anderson & Marx contra.

DOLE, J. Two items in plaintiff's bill of costs are questioned by the defendants. These are for mileage of the witnesses H. A. Willis and R. W. Sweet, the former from Seattle to Honolulu and return, and the latter from Missoula, Montana, to Honolulu and return, the objection being that the statute provides only for mileage fees for witnesses when they have been subpoenaed; such contention being based on the acts of 1799 (1 Stat. 626) and 1853 (10 Stat. 167), and section 848 of the Revised Statutes, the wording of which is, "for each day's attendance pursuant to law," and "when a witness is subpoenaed in more than one cause between the same parties," in reference to mileage fees in such statutes. The act of 1799 provides that "compensation to jurors and witnesses, in the courts of the United States, shall be as follows, to wit: to each grand and other juror for each day he shall attend in court, one dollar and twenty-five cents; and for travelling, at the rate of five cents per mile, from their respective places of abode, to the place where the court is holden, and the like allowance for returning; to the witnesses summoned in any court of the United States, the same allowance as is above provided for jurors."

The case of *Woodruff v. Barney*, (1862), 30 Fed. Cas. 518. No. 17,986 (law), holds that the words in these acts, referring to "compensation", or "pursuant to law", or "subpoena", mean the same thing.

For a number of years the courts held that where a witness was not subpoenaed, the provision of the law did not apply to a case in which he voluntarily came and testified. The provision of section 876 of the Revised Statutes, to the effect that subpoenaes may only run to a distance of

one hundred miles where the witness is living out of the
district, was also regarded in the earlier cases as providing
a limit beyond which mileage fees would not be allowed.
The precedents in England, however, and more recent cases
in the United States, have by a very decided weight of
authority reversed this rule and adopted the policy and the
practice of allowing such fees on the ground as stated in
United States v. Sanburn, 28 Fed. 299, 302:

"A witness who, in good faith, comes to court to testify
in a pending suit, whether he comes in obedience to a subpoena or at the mere request of one of the parties, attends
pursuant to law, and while coming, attending and returning is privileged from arrest on civil process even if he
comes from abroad and has no writ of protection."

The case of *Walpole v. Alexander*, 3 Doug. 345, 99 Eng.
Reprint, 530, is cited in the above case and in which, among
other things, the rule is held as being in furtherance of
justice. This, I think, is obvious, for under its liberal
policy necessary witnesses who were out of reach of compulsion, would in many cases be in attendance, where, under
the old rule, they would be less likely to attend.

In addition to the above authorities, I refer to *Prouty
v. Draper*, 2 Story, 199; *In re Williams*, 37 Fed. 375, and
Gunkel, Costs in Federal Courts, 101. There is a large
number of cases agreeing with this conclusion which need
not be cited.

There is another point in favor of the contention of the
plaintiffs and that is under the agreement of compromise
referred to in the decision filed in this case on December 5,
1913, there was a provision for the payment by the defendants "of the costs of court, reference fees and other
necessary expenses as the same may be taxed by the above
entitled court." It is admitted by the defendants that the
appearance of the two witnesses referred to was in good
faith and there is no contention that their appearance was
not necessary. Under this agreement, therefore, without

the rule adopted above, the court would, I think, tax such mileage as costs against the defendant.

The mileage fees claimed, therefore. are hereby allowed.

H. KISHI *v.* THE BRITISH STEAMSHIP "WILLESDEN."

December 22, 1913.

1. *Maritime lien—Necessaries—Supplies of food furnished alien immigrants pending quarantine:* There is no maritime lien for the cost of supplies of food furnished to alien immigrants during their detention in quarantine on shore after they have been landed from a foreign vessel but have, technically, not yet been admitted to the country; and a suit *in rem* does not lie to recover for supplies so furnished.

2. *Aliens—Immigration—Rules and regulations under Immigration Act—Support of immigrants pending quarantine:* Rule 26 of the rules pertaining to immigration, Bureau of Immigration, Rules of Nov. 15, 1911, 3d ed. pp. 40-41, providing that "owners, masters, agents, and consignees of vessels bringing aliens shall pay all expenses [including maintenance] incident to or involved in their removal from the vessel or their detention . . . irrespective of whether the aliens removed or detained are subsequently admitted or deported", is invalid as unauthorized by and inconsistent with the Immigration Act, 34 Stat. 898, am. 36 Stat. 263. *U. S. v. Holland-American Line*, 205, Fed. 943, 946 [aff'd 212 Fed. 116], followed.

In Admiralty: Libel *in rem* for supplies.

E. C. Peters for libelant.

L. J. Warren (*Smith, Warren, Hemenway & Sutton* with him) for libellee.

CLEMONS, J. This is a libel *in rem* against the steamship Willesden, a foreign vessel, to recover compensation for meals alleged to have been furnished to its passengers, alien immigrants, at the port of Honolulu, pending their examination by the United States immigration inspector as to their admission into the country. Two causes of action are stated, one in the nature of a quantum meruit in assumpsit, based on the furnishing of meals to these passengers at the request "of the agents and servants of said ship acting for and on behalf of the owner thereof," and the other based on an obligation implied by law by virtue of rule 26 of the rules pertaining to immigration, which provides that "owners, masters, agents, and consignees of vessels bringing aliens shall pay all expenses [including maintenance] incident to or involved in their removal from the vessel or their detention . . . irrespective of whether the aliens removed or detained are subsequently admitted or deported." Bureau of Immigration, Rules of Nov. 15, 1911, 3d ed., pp. 40-41. The first cause of action alleges the meals to have been furnished to passengers "while detained" at the port of Honolulu, for the purpose of examination as to their "eligibility to admission" into the country "and until admitted," but does not state just where these meals were furnished, whether on board of the vessel or ashore. The second cause of action is for meals furnished at the immigration station at Honolulu where the passengers had been "temporarily removed for examination," during which examination these meals were furnished at "the price privileged to be charged" and "under the direction of the inspector in charge of the port," by the libelant as holder of a special license to furnish meals there.

As, under both causes of action, the meals for which compensation is sought, are alleged to have been furnished between December 22d, 1911, and February 12th, 1912, and as the same bill of particulars of meals furnished, Exhibit

"A" of the libel, is given for both causes of action, the inference is warranted that the same meals are the subject of the two causes of action, and that, as alleged under the second cause of action, they were all furnished at the immigration station where the passengers had been "temporarily removed for examination." Also, the meaning is plain, under the allegations of the first cause of action, that these passengers were finally admitted. Such pleading, the allegation of facts by indirection, is not to be encouraged, but, as no objections are raised against it, the libel is read, for the purposes of the decision, according to its obvious, though implied, intent.

The claimant's exceptions to the libel raise the following points:

1. The want of showing that the passengers were brought to the United States on the steamship Willesden in violation of law or that any of the passengers were not legally eligible or entitled to enter the United States.

2. The want of a law or of a valid rule or regulation requiring the cost of maintenance of alien immigrants not brought here in violation of law, pending their examination as to eligibilty to enter the country, to be borne by the vessel's owner or to be borne by or made a charge against the vessel, or giving a lien upon the vessel or a right to proceed against her *in rem*.

3. The want of specification by name, description, or identification of the persons brought by said vessel in violation of law or not entitled to enter, for whose maintenance the libelant has any claim or lien against the vessel.

4. The want of showing that the meals were furnished to· said vessel or for its account, use or benefit, or that they were necessary to or for said vessel;

5. Or that they were furnished by reason of any request, direction or authority of the owner or of any person having authority to request, direct, or agree for the same in his behalf.

6. The showing by the second cause of action that the meals were furnished at the special instance and request

of the inspector in charge of immigration, irrespective of and without any authority of or direction by the owner, master, or any agent of the vessel, and that the meals were not furnished on the credit of the owner, master, or vessel.

7. Inconsistency, duplicity, and multifariousness, in that the two causes of action are separately set forth, each inconsistent with and independent of the other, and based upon different grounds.

8. Defect of parties respondent, in failure to name or join the owner as respondent, without jurisdiction over whom (not here acquired) the court cannot proceed and cannot make any valid decree of condemnation against the vessel or other property of the owner.

9. Failure to state a cause of action within the court's jurisdiction.

[1a] The first two points constitute the claimant's main contention as to the second cause of action, which is that the Immigration Act (34 Stat. 898, am. 36 Stat. 263) provides only for maintenance of passengers by the owner of the vessel in case of "aliens brought to this country in violation of law" (sec. 19), and that any rule of the Department of Labor charging the vessel with maintenance of passengers not brought here in violation of law, is invalid. The same point was made in the parallel case of *United States v. Holland-American Line*, 205 Fed. 943, 946, in the southern district of New York [affirmed, 212 Fed. 116], and the decision of Judge Mayer ruled against the ship-owner's liability, after a discussion so thorough and satisfactory, that it is unnecessary to go over the same ground again here. The principle of *expressio unius, exclusio alterius*, justifies his construction of the statute.

"The act of 1907 specifies with great care the cases of instances which impose obligations or penalties upon the steamship companies. This, section 19 provides that all aliens brought to this country 'in violation of law' shall be deported on the vessel bringing them and that the cost of their maintenance while on land as well as the expense of the return of such aliens, shall be borne by the owner of the vessel. The act will be searched in vain for any provision which imposes expense upon the owners of vessels where there has not been neglect or a violation of law." Id., 946.

[2] And, further, the legislative will being so construed, it may not be set aside by a rule or regulation of an executive department of government. See *United States v. Two Hundred Barrels of Whiskey*, 95 U. S. 571, 576, in which it is held in regard to departmental regulations: "They may aid in carrying the law *as it exists* into execution, but they cannot change its positive provisions,"—"the law as it exists" being, of course, the law not only as plainly written, but as, perhaps, less plainly construed. Especially is this so when a penalty is involved, as is in effect the case here. *United States v. One Package of Distilled Spirits*, 68 Fed. 856, 858; *United States v. Three Barrels of Whiskey*, 77 Fed. 963, 965. See, also, *United States v. Hemet*, 156 Fed. 285, 287-288; *In re Kornmehl*, 87 Fed. 314.

Rule 26 was not discussed by Judge Mayer, but a ruling of the department similar to rule 26 had his attention and he noted: that there had been constant opposition thereto; that any acquiescence therein had been under duress of circumstances; and that the ruling was contrary to previous departmental rulings, thus disposing of any argument of practical construction by the department. Case of *Holland-American Line*, supra, 951.

Judge Mayer also pointed out that the statute affords ground for charging against what is known as the "immigrant fund", rather than against the carrier, such expenses as are here involved. Id. 947-949.

As to the citation, in support of the libel, of section 16 of the act, which says that "temporary removal" of alien passengers from a vessel shall not relieve "the transportation lines, masters, agents, owners, or consignees of the vessel . . . from any of the obligations which, in case such aliens remain on board, would, *under the provisions of this act*, bind said transportation lines," etc., suffice it to say that the qualifying words, "under the provisions of this act," exclude the operation of an unauthorized or invalid departmental rule. And it has already been shown that there are no "provisions of this act" charging expenses of maintenance against the carrier, except in case of aliens brought into the country in violation of law.

Accordingly, rule 26 is invalid so far as it contravenes section 19 of the act, which places the cost of maintenance upon the owners of the vessel only in case of aliens "brought to this country in violation of law." This disposes of the second cause of action.

[1b] Another fact may, however, be briefly adverted to as also disposing of that cause of action. Rule 26, if valid, would give nothing more than a remedy *in personam*, it having fixed the liability upon "the owners, masters, agents and consignees of vessels bringing aliens,"—a personal liability and not a charge *in rem* against these vessels. Even in case of aliens brought in contrary to law, their maintenance is not the foundation of a lien, but is charged to "the owner or owners of the vessels," under section 19 of the present act, although—and this is significant—an earlier statute, covering part of the same ground as the present act, and apparently superseded by it, made "such expense . . . a lien on said vessel(s)." 24 Stat. 414, 415, 3 Fed. Stat. Ann. 303, act of Feb. 23, 1887, sec. 8.

There remains, then, only the first cause of action, against which the more substantial exceptions, points 4 and 5 supra, are: the failure to show that the meals were furnished to the vessel or for its account, use or benefit, and the failure to show that they were necessary to or for the vessel. The effect of the latter exception is to challenge the procedure *in rem* for want of the essential, basic, lien. See *Mayne v. The Makura*, ante, p. 43; *The Corsair*, 145 U. S. 335, 347; *The Bold Buccleugh*, 7 Moore, Privy Council Cases,

267; s. c. Ames' Cases on Admiralty, 92, 94-95; Carver's Carriage by the Sea, 5th ed., sec. 698.

Apart from any requirement of the recent statute (not relied on by counsel here) "relating to liens on vessels for repairs, supplies, or other necessaries," 36 Stat. 604, act of June 23, 1910, which on the principle of *noscitur a sociis* applied to the language "repairs, supplies, or *other neces-saries*," would afford a lien only for such supplies as are necessary, the general maritime law had already made ne-cessity an element vital to such a lien.   See *The Grapeshot,* 9 Wall. 129, 141; *The Brigantine Nicolaus,* 4 Haw. 354, 355. See also Adm. Rule 12, and, for an interesting and valuable discussion, Abbott, Ships and Seamen, 14th ed. 177-185. By the statute cited, necessaries are presumed to have been ordered on the credit of the ship, the statute in this regard being only declaratory of the general maritime law.   *The Grapeshot,* supra, 141; *The Lulu,* 10 Wall, 192, 197, apply-ing to a case of implied hypothecation (lien) the same prin-ciple applied to an express hypothecation (bottomry bond).

This element of necessity is sometimes spoken of as finan-cial necessity, the need of credit (see *The Suliote,* 23 Fed. 919, 922); but for the purposes of pleading, it is prac-tically the necessity for something which the credit is in-tended to secure,—not for the credit itself.   Thus from the opinion in *Pratt v. Reed,* 19 How. 359, it appears that the necessity for credit is presumed if there be shown the neces-sity for the supplies and the actual giving of credit to the vessel.   *The Lulu,* 10 Wall. 202-203.   And from the court's holding in the cases of *The Lulu,* supra, and *The Grape-shot,* supra, we need consider merely the necessity for the supplies, without regard to the giving of credit to the ves-sel, for, as seen above, if the supplies are necessary, the credit of the ship is presumed.

In the law of maritime liens, the words "necessary" is of narrow scope.   While it is not essential that supplies fur-nished be anything more than useful or convenient, 19 A.

& E. Enc. L., 2d ed., 1094-1095, it is indispensable that they be necessary, useful, or convenient in aid of the business in which the ship is employed,—i. e., they must be necessary, useful, or convenient to the ship in its maritime character, as a carrier by sea. There must be an actual or apparent necessity for the supplies to effectuate the object of the voyage, i. e., here the carriage of passengers, or to secure the safety of the vessel.

The term "necessaries" was held by Lord Tenterden to include whatever is fit and proper for the service in which the vessel is engaged, or whatever would have been ordered by a prudent owner if present. *Webster v. Seekamp*, 4 B. & Ald. 352, 354, 160 Eng. Rep. (Full Reprint), 966, 967; Benedict on Admiralty, 4th ed., sec. 196; Hughes on Admiralty, 96-98; 26 Cyc. 764, n. 99. The definition of the Supreme Court in the case of *The Grapeshot*, 9 Wall. 129, 141, is substantially the same:

"Necessity for repairs and supplies is proved where such circumstances of exigency are shown as would induce a prudent owner, if present, to order them, or to provide funds for the cost of them on the security of the ship."

The supplies of food furnished here, to passengers who were removed from the ship to the immigration station and who were finally admitted to the country, do not seem to fall within the narrow limits which determine a maritime lien. If this case was one of necessity, the necessity was plainly one respecting a matter collateral to the maritime venture on which the ship was then engaged. This conclusion is based upon the "reason and spirit" of the authorities, rather than upon any decision directly in point on the facts: for there are none that I have been able to find. As suggestive of this spirit, the case of *Diefenthal v. Hamburg-Amerikanische P. Actien-Gesellschaft*, 46 Fed. 397, may be cited, in which it is held that a contract with the owners to supply their vessels for a year with all the provisions which they might require while in a certain port, is not a maritime contract.

The decision in the case of *The City of Mexico*, 28 Fed. 239, not cited by counsel, may be an authority in support of the libel. It allowed "expenses for provisions provided passengers and crew detained on board a vessel under seizure, after arrival in port, and before service of attachment under libel for forfeiture." But its use of the language, "the position of the passengers on board was different from that of *ordinary passengers* who had taken passage from port to port, and *whose voyage had terminated*," might seem to distinguish it from the case at bar. See, also, *The Augustine Kobbe*, 37 Fed. 696 (syll., par. 5), 699.

When it is considered, that the maritime lien is a secret lien, following the ship into the hands of innocent holders, it is not to be extended to cases not clearly within its purview. See 26 Cyc. 751; *Stephenson v. The Francis*, 21 Fed. 715, 720. In the language of the *Hamburg-Amerikanische* case, supra, which comes nearest to the present case of any which has been found, other, perhaps, than the case of *The City of Mexico*, supra, the alleged transaction even "though relating remotely to navigation and commerce, is separated so far from them that it did not spring from the necessities of navigation, and is not within the considerations which make it essentially and distinctively maritime." *Diefenthal v. Hamburg-Amerikanische P. Actien-Gesellschaft*, 46 Fed. 397, 399.

"It need not be held that there could not be an admiralty suit in some cases where there is no maritime lien. But where the contract is for supplies, to bring it within the admiralty jurisdiction it must come within the reason that brings material-men within the dominion of admiralty courts,—i. e., it must appear that the necessities or conveniences of ships in ports remote from home ports require that a credit should be given and a debt created which, though arising on land, are distinctively maritime, because necessary to maritime commerce as conducted by ships." Id.

It has been seen that the rules of the immigration department created no legal liability to furnish these supplies. Also, there was no liability of the ship by reason of the contract of carriage, so far as the pleadings show, to provide food for her passengers while detained at the immigration station on shore pending their examination as to eligibility to admission to the country—these passengers having been eventually landed. And no liability of the kind is implied as against the carrier. The implied contract of the carrier of passengers by sea-going vessels is to "supply the passengers with such food and other accommodations as will be necessary for his health and comfort upon the voyage and as may be usual and customary upon such vessels and upon such voyages." 2 Hutchinson, Carriers, 3d ed., sec. 1156. In other words, there was no contract necessity for the carrier to maintain the passengers who had been taken ashore by the immigration officers. The implied contract pertains only to the voyage. When the voyage has ended and the passenger is finally ashore, whether for examination or for any other purpose which concerns himself personally and not the ship in its contract capacity as a maritime carrier, his maintenance is not a matter within the contemplation of the contract,—a contract which at best is raised only by implication. The question would, admittedly, be more doubtful if the passengers had been detained on the ship, but we may give such a case as that the full force which the libelant's counsel contends for it and still not hold the ship liable when once the passengers have gone ashore,—though, it is true, they have not, strictly, been "landed" in the technical sense of that word in the immigration law. See the case of the *Holland-American Line*, 205 Fed. at 950.

In my conception of the case, the relation between carrier and passengers, had ceased to be one which may be called maritime. See the analogous case of *The Pulaski*, 33 Fed. 383, in which a contract to hold a cargo in stowage after arrival was regarded as not within the admiralty jurisdiction. And, in any event, any obligation to continue furnishing the passengers with food, was at an end when they went ashore.

It may be observed that the authoritative definitions of the term "voyage" afford little or no help. The question is not alone one of what terminates the voyage, but largely one of whether the carrier impliedly assumes an obligation not only to carry the passengers to the port of destination, but to land them there "unquarantinable," or "undetainable," and support them while in quarantine or detention,—an obligation not only to carry them overseas but to furnish, as it were, hotel accommodations for them for an indefinite time thereafter, when once they have been taken from the ship by the immigration authorities for reasons which do not involve any act or default of the carrier. I have not overlooked the fact that cases might perhaps arise,—though I am not called upon to so hold,—in which considerations of humanity might create an obligation to supply food to passengers even after landing. See *The President,* 92 Fed. 673, 675-676.

As to the exception of want of showing that the meals were furnished to the vessel, or for its account, use, or benefit: This exception is well taken. The allegation is, that "the agents and servants of said ship acting for and on behalf of the owner thereof, requested this libelant, that, pending examination by the United States immigration inspectors in respect to eligibility to admission into the United States, and while detained therefor, and until admitted by such inspectors into the United States, he maintain each alien to the extent of furnishing such alien with three meals daily." This is merely an allegation of something done "for and on behalf of the owner," and too broad to support a proceeding *in rem* against the vessel. Further, in view of the above conclusion that the contract of carriage imposed no liability, it cannot be presumed that this request of the agents and servants was authorized, as it would have been if the furnishing of the food had been a matter of contract necessity or of other necessity, in which case, under the lien law, 36 Stat. 604, sec. 2, there would have been a presumption of authority in "the managing owner, ship's husband, master, or any person to whom the management of the vessel at the port of supply is intrusted" "to procure repairs, supplies, and other necessaries for the vessel." Wherefore, all the more reason for a specific allegation that the meals were furnished for the account of the vessel.

These considerations are sufficient to dispose of the first cause of action, without discussion of other exceptions, affecting matters of form and not of substance.

For the foregoing reasons, the exceptions are sustained, without prejudice, however, to any amendment of which counsel may be advised that the libel is capable.

H. KIHI *v.* THE BRITISH STEAMSHIP "WILLESDEN".

October 31, 1914.

Maritime lien—Necessaries—Supplies of food furnished alien immigrants pending quarantine: The fact that a charter party providing for transportation of alien immigrants stipulates that the owners of the carrier, a foreign vessel, shall comply with all the laws, rules, and regulations of the port of destination with reference to immigration and quarantine, is no basis for a maritime lien or suit *in rem* for supplies of food furnished to alien immigrants so transported pending their detention in quarantine on shore at such port but before their admission to the country. Nor is the rule any different by reason of the fact that the master in behalf of the owner of the vessel requested the furnishing of such supplies.

In Admiralty: Libel *in rem* for supplies.

E. C. Peters for libelant.

L. J. Warren (*Smith, Warren, Hemenway & Sutton* with him) for libellee.

CLEMONS, J. The exceptions to the libel having been sustained without prejudice to amendment, ante p. 407, the libelant filed an amended libel in which he added to the original libel two counts.

The first of the new counts (third cause of action) shows a charter party between the Territorial board of immigration as charterers and the Britain Steamship Company as owners, which provided that the steamship Willesden would proceed to certain ports and embark certain alien passengers destined for Honolulu. The reason for bringing in the charter party appears in its special provision:

"That said Owners would comply with all the laws, rules and regulations of the United States with reference to immigration, quarantine and the carriage of passengers by sea that were in force in May, 1911, and that said Owners would in every way provide for the passengers according to the United States Passenger Act of 1882, as amended prior to May, 1911."

It is then alleged that the vessel took on these passengers and arrived at Honolulu with them on December 3, 1911, when they applied for admission into the United States. and that the master of the vessel "acting for and on behalf of the owner thereof," requested the libelant that, pending their examination as to eligibility to be admitted, the libelant should furnish them with food; whereupon the libelant accordingly, and on the credit of the vessel and for its account, use and benefit, furnished the meals alleged.

The second of the new counts (fourth cause of action) is a modification of the new count just set forth (still relying on the charter party) in reciting that the meals were furnished by the libelant "under the direction of the inspector in charge at the port of Honolulu, upon the special instance and request of the master of said steamship Willesden acting for and on behalf of the owner thereof, but upon the credit of said steamship and for its account, use and benefit."

Exceptions to the amended libel raise two new grounds of objection: (1) The want of any legal right of expectation on the part of the libelant to look to the vessel or extend credit to the vessel; as the charter party laid no foundation for extending such credit. (2) The fact that the charter party itself did not open the "necessity door" and make the supplies a legal necessity of the voyage, by virtue of which the master had any authority to order the meals on the credit of the vessel.

In arguing these exceptions, counsel for the libellee "challenge any possible claim of authority on the part of the inspector in charge, acting either on his own responsibility or at the instance (or as an agent) of the master for the owners, to create any legal liability against the owners of the vessel or to authorize a proceeding against the vessel *in rem*." Brief of claimant, p. 3.

It is not perceived that the case is strengthened by the new allegations showing the charter party stipulation. Even if the doubtful proposition be conceded, that the charter party is such a contract as would give the libelant a beneficial interest entitling him to sue thereon in his own name (see 18 Fed. 523, note by Francis Wharton; 15 Enc. Pl. & Pr. 509-517; Abbott's Justice and the Modern Law, 38 et seq.), nevertheless the fact remains that this proceeding as one *in rem* must have a right of lien for its support and such right must depend upon the furnished meals' being necessaries within the narrow meaning of that word in the law of maritime liens. Our former opinion, ante,

p. 408, holds that such supplies, furnished under the circumstances here, are not necessaries.

As supporting that opinion, the following authorities may be added to those therein cited: *The Plymouth Rock,* 19 Fed. Cas. 897, 898, (Benedict, J.) suggesting as a test, whether the article supplied "forms part of the actual and reasonable outfit for a vessel for the business in which she is engaged"; *Hubbard v. Roach,* 2 Fed. 393, 394-395, suggesting as a test, whether the things supplied "pertain to the navigation of the vessel, and are directly incidental to and connected with her navigation, that is, those things which directly aid in keeping her in motion for the purpose of receiving, carrying and delivering cargoes", or (to apply the principle to passenger carriers) of embarking, carrying and disembarking passengers.

And the special charter party stipulation for compliance with the law, above quoted from the third cause of action, adds nothing to the libelant's case. Nor is anything gained by the new allegations that the furnished meals were requested by the master of the vessel or were furnished "under the direction of the inspector of immigration at the special instance of the master". The facts stated would, at most, support no more than a suit *in personam* against the owner of the vessel,—even conceding the authority of the master to order the furnishing of meals to immigrants detained on shore under quarantine regulations, meals which neither the immigration laws nor the Passenger Act (referred to in the charter party), nor any statute which we have been able to find, required the vessel or its owner to furnish. These things are not such supplies as "a prudent owner if present" would provide. See our former opinion, ante, p. 414, also 26 Cyc. 764 and n. 99.

Further discussion seems unnecessary. See, however, *U. S. v. Holland-American Line,* 212 Fed. 116, affirming the decision, 205 Fed. 943, followed in our former opinion herein.

Let the exce tions to the amended libel be sustained.

UNITED STATES OF AMERICA *v.* TROEL SMITH.

January 15, 1914.

1. *Indictment—Description of defendant as within class of offenders contemplated by statute:* When a statute denominates as an offender any one of a certain class of persons who shall do or omit a certain act, an indictment for an offense within the statute must describe the defendant as one of that class.

2. *Same—Variance—Conviction for lesser offense embraced within greater:* Where an indictment, endorsed as covering an offense under Penal Code, sec. 291, assault by master of a vessel upon a seaman, nevertheless fails to describe the defendant as such master, but aptly describes an offense under Penal Code, sec. 276, assault upon the high seas, the case may be proceeded with as a prosecution under the latter section. Rev. State., sec. 1035 applied.

3. *Same—Endorsement varying from body in describing offense:* Where the endorsement of an indictment indicates a different offense from that described in the body of the indictment, it may be disregarded.

Criminal Law: Motion for directed verdict.

A. L. C. Atkinson for the motion.
Jeff McCarn, U. S. District Attorney, contra.

CLEMONS, J. The indictment under which the defendant was tried charged that the defendant "on the high seas . . . in and on board of a certain American vessel . . . owned . . . by . . . a corporation organized and existing under and by virtue of the laws of the State of California, did wilfully, intentionally, unlawfully and feloniously, and without justifiable or any cause, strike, beat and wound a member of the crew of said steamship . . ."

This indictment bore the following endorsement over the signature of the foreman of the grand jury: "Indictment. Assault on Seamen. Violation Section 291 Penal Code. A

True Bill." Section 291, so far as here material, reads as follows:

"Whoever, being the master or officer of a vessel of the United States, on the high seas, or on any other waters within the admiralty and maritime jurisdiction of the United States, beats, wounds, or without justifiable cause, imprisons any of the crew of such vessel, or withholds from them suitable food and nourishment, or inflicts upon them any cruel and unusual punishment, shall be fined not more, than one thousand dollars, or imprisoned not more than five years, or both."

The case has been tried on behalf of the government on the theory that the indictment covered the offense indicated by the endorsement, i. e., assault of a seaman by an officer of a vessel. The body of the indictment might indicate an intent to charge an offense under section 291, but, as will presently be seen, its language is quite as apt to charge an offense under section 276 of the Penal Code, describing various classes of assault committed by any person, without regard to whether he be an officer of a vessel or not, and including the following: "Whoever shall unlawfully strike, beat, or wound another, shall be fined not more than five hundred dollars, or imprisoned not more than six months, or both. Whoever shall unlawfully assault another, shall be fined not more than three hundred dollars, or imprisoned not more than three months, or both."

[1] At the conclusion of the government's case, the defendant's attorney moves for a directed verdict on the ground that the indictment is insufficient to charge a violation of section 291, because of failure to allege the very essential fact of the defendant's having been a master or officer of a vessel, i. e., one of the class of persons contemplated as offenders by section 291. In support of the motion, counsel cites the case of *State v. Sloan,* 67 N. C. 357. This sole case is also cited by 22 Cyc. 327, for the proposition (which is almost the identical language of the decision

there), that "when a statute enacts that any one of a certain class of persons who shall do or omit a certain act, under certain circumstances, shall be guilty of a crime, the indictment must describe the person indicted as one of that class and aver that he did or omitted the act under the circumstances making it criminal." The ruling in that case arose on a motion to quash the indictment. A similar ruling was made in the case, not cited by counsel, of *United States v. McCormick*, 1 Cranch, C. C. 593, 26 Fed. Cas. 1060. No. 15,663, which arose on a motion in arrest of judgment. Under the principle enforced by these two cases, the indictment in the case at bar is defective as a charge of an offense under section 291.

[2] However, the language of the indictment is apt to charge an offense under those portions of section 276 of the Penal Code, above quoted, relating (1) to unlawful striking, beating and wounding, and (2) to unlawful assault. And, as in spite of any deficiency of the indictment under section 291, the indictment describes an offense within section 276, and as section 1035 of the Revised Statutes allows the jury to find the defendant "guilty of any offense the commission of which is necessarily included in that with which he is charged in the indictment," this court held that it was not at liberty to direct a verdict for the defendant, but the case must be proceeded with, regarding the indictment. however, as an indictment under section 276. The jury, accordingly, were in the court's charge instructed that they could not bring in a verdict of guilty of violation of section 291 of the Penal Code but that they might, if the evidence so warranted, return a verdict of violation either of that part of section 276 directed against simple assault. or of that part of section 276 directed against assault by striking, beating, or wounding.

It is urged that in order to apply section 1035 of the Revised Statutes, it is necessary that the indictment be sufficient as an indictment of the offense of assault by a master or officer of a vessel upon a seaman. Unquestionably, this is an arguable point, but the Supreme Court has held against it, in a case in which it ruled that in spite of the fact that an indictment for murder was insufficient to support a conviction of that offense, nevertheless if the language of the indictment was apt to describe an assault, the jury might, under the authority of section 1035 of the Revised Statutes, return a verdict of the lesser offense. *Ball v. United States,* 140 U. S. 118, 121-122, 136.

[3] Moreover, it seems that the fact of the indictment's being endorsed as covering an offense under section 291, is not controlling, and that if the language of the body of the indictment is apt to charge an offense under section 291, the indictment may still stand as a sufficient indictment. See *Williams v. United States,* 168 U. S. 382, 389, holding:

"It is wholly immaterial what statute was in the mind of the district attorney when he drew the indictment, if the charge made was embraced by some statute in force. The indorsement on the margin of the indictment constitutes no part of the indictment, and does not add to or weaken the legal force of its averments. We must look to the indictment itself, and, if it properly charges an offense under the laws of the United States, that is sufficient to sustain it, although the representative of the United States may have supposed that the offense charged was covered by a different statute."

See, also, *Wechesler v. United States,* 158 Fed. 579, 583; 22 Cyc. 257.

It may be noted that the description of the offense as having been committed on the high seas and on a particular vessel, does not necessarily indicate an intent to indict under section 291, for such description would be apt, proper, and even necessary, to describe an offense under section 276. It may also be noted, that there is nothing inconsistent with the court's ruling in the case here, in the ruling in the case cited by defendant's counsel, of *United States v. Hartwell,* 6 Wall. 385, particularly at page 397 at

the conclusion of the majority opinion.   Indeed, the court
in the case at bar followed the ruling of the *Hartwell* case,
in instructing the jury that it could not find the defendant
guilty of an offense under section 291, because, to adopt
the language of the Supreme Court in the *Hartwell* case,
the indictment as a charge of violating section 291, did
not by its averments bring the defendant within that section.   See 6 Wall. 397.

The motion is denied.   The case may be proceeded with
as a prosecution under Penal Code, sec. 276.

IN THE MATTER OF THE APPLICATION OF CHOW CHIU FOR A WRIT OF HABEAS CORPUS IN BEHALF OF WONG SHE.

February 16, 1914.

1. *Immigration—Fairness of hearing before officers:* The conduct
of a hearing may be fair, but as a trial is incomplete until there is a
decision, it may be unfair if the decision is not based on the evidence.

2. *Evidence—Testimony of collateral facts as affecting testimony
of facts germane to the issue:* Slight inaccuracies of testimony as to
collateral facts cannot be used to evade conclusions necessarily arising from testimony of facts germane to the issue.

3. *Marriage, proof of:* Proof of agreement of parties to take each
other as husband and wife, followed by continuous cohabitation as
such, sufficient. *Meister v. Moore,* 96 U. S. 76, 82.

Habeas Corpus: Demurrer to petition.

Andrews & Quarles for petitioner.
Jeff McCarn, U. S. District Attorney, for respondent.

DOLE, J. The petitioner, an American citizen, applied for a writ of habeas corpus for the discharge of Wong She, a woman whom he alleges to be his wife. He complains that the hearing before the inspector in charge was not a fair hearing, in that the evidence showing the marriage of the petitioner to the said Wong She was ignored and no weight given it. They both recently arrived in Honolulu and Wong She was refused admittance to the United States and ordered to be deported upon the ground that she is a Chinese woman not satisfactorily shown to be the wife of the petitioner. An order to show cause was made and the respondent demurred orally to the petition on the ground that it is alleged therein that the immigration authorities ignored and gave no weight to the evidence adduced during the proceedings before them, in support of the marriage of the petitioner with the said Wong She, contending that the point made would, if considered, cause the court to weigh the evidence taken before the immigration authorities, as on an appeal.

[1] This raises the question whether the immigration authorities have given the claim of Wong She to be admitted a fair trial. I find that, so far as the conduct of the proceedings is concerned, the hearing has been reasonably fair. A trial, however, is not complete without a decision; and a decision on the merits, as must be the case here, must be based upon the evidence and the law applicable to the case. The following is the decision of the inspector in charge:

"This case has been re-opened and additional testimony taken and documentary evidence submitted.

I have given careful consideration to the entire record. Chow Chiu has been admitted as a citizen.

In the case of Wong She there is no marriage certificate. The woman is of unusual age for a new Chinese wife. Chow Chiu admits he lived for years in illicit relations with another woman and had children by her. Wong She and Chow Chiu show by their own testimony that they cannot be depended upon to tell the truth. There are disagreements, contradictions and discrepancies, numerous and evident and of such a character that I am not satisfied that Wong She is the wife of Chow Chiu, a citizen, and I am of the opinion that she is not. There has been a failure to prove that Wong She is a Chinese person having a status entitling her to land, she is therefore, and hereby, denied a landing in the United States and ordered deported to the country whence she came."

[2] The testimony taken from the record of the hearing shows that both Chow Chiu and Wong She testified that they were married at Lung Tow Wan, at the residence of the parents of Chow Chiu, by Chinese estimate in 1912, on the 8th day of the 8th month; that they lived there as man and wife until the time they left to come to Hawaii. There are no disagreements, contradictions or discrepancies of any importance in their testimony,—nothing to raise a suspicion as to their veracity or good faith. Chow Chiu had two children, boys, by an Hawaiian woman in Hawaii. They were in China at the time of the alleged marriage, living at the house of Chow Chiu's parents and attending school and lodging at the school, at least part of the time. Wong She at first disclaimed any knowledge of any children of her husband, but when asked if she knew whether he had children in China named Chow Chock and Chow Kee, replied, "Yes, he had three children in China," but said she didn't know their names, and that they slept and had their meals at the house where she was staying. It appeared that besides them there was a younger boy, an adopted son of Chow Chiu's brother, who she had supposed was also one of her husband's sons. It appears also from Chow Chiu's testimony that when they left China to come here his children were staying at his parents' house. There is nothing here to suggest duplicity or want of reliability as to the point at issue.

There is a divergence between the testimony of Chow Chiu and that of Chow King Ng, alias Chow Kum Cheong.

Chow Chiu said that a man named How In lived in a house opposite his father's house in front. Chow King said that *he* lived in that house and that How lived in a house across the street in the rear of the house of Chow Chiu's father. This does not weaken the veracity of Chow Chiu; it does not touch his good faith; at the most it is inaccuracy of memory on a matter not in issue that he may never have especially noticed. Chow Chiu said that Chow Min Sing lived in the house to the right of his father's house; Chow King said the person who lived in the house to the right was Chow Chung Sin. Both of these statements may be true inasmuch as Chow King arrived in China four months or more after Chow Chiu, and people change their residence sometimes.

The statement of the persons interested in regard to the marriage of Chow Chiu and Wong She, is supported, as follows: A letter dated 15th day of 9th month C. R. I. (1912) received by Lee Chuck in October 1912, from Chow Chiu, which refers to his marriage on the 8th day of the previous month, at which he states Lee Chuck's daughter was present; that he will take his family to Hawaii next autumn; asks Lee Chuck's assistance in getting two tickets for their return, and mentions enclosing pictures of himself and "wife." Lee Chuck, who says he has known Chow Chiu since he was born, says he knows he went to China to get married and that "I do not think he is a man who would bring someone who is not his wife." Chow King, the witness already referred to, says he knows Wong She is the wife of Chow Chiu because she was living in the house opposite his at Lung Tow Wan after her marriage with Chow Chiu; that he went to China in the 12th month 1912, and returned to Honolulu on the same ship with them. He and Wong She recognized each other at the hearing. The witness Yong Yin Yun, alias Yong Choy Bun, says he came to Honolulu six months ago and while in China visited the house where petitioner and Wong

She were living and that petitioner told him that they had been married in the 8th month of the year before. He also saw Chow Chiu's parents there. He identified Wong She but she did not recognize him. It is admitted that H. Hackfeld & Company, by letter of August 1st, 1913, requested its agents in Hong Kong to furnish passage to Chow Chiu and wife to Honolulu, and that in compliance therewith such passage was furnished as shown by letter of October 21st, 1913.

[3] The Supreme Court of the United States has, in the case of *Meister v. Moore*, 96 U. S. 76, 82, laid down the rule of evidence sufficient to prove marriage, as follows:

"Whatever the form of ceremony, or even if all ceremony was dispensed with, if the parties agreed presently to take each other as husband and wife, and from that time lived together professedly in that relation, proof of those facts would be sufficient to constitute proof of a marriage binding upon the parties, and which would subject them and others to legal penalties for a disregard of its obligations."

The evidence in this case shows agreement to take each other as husband and wife, a living together thereafter professedly in that relation, and long continued recognition by others as husband and wife. If there is no reason to doubt this evidence, and the record shows none, the fact that a certificate of marriage was not produced by the parties, but reported by them as existing elsewhere, is immaterial.

In the case of *Tang Tung v. Edsell*, 223 U. S. 673, 681-682, in which Tang Tun and his wife had been refused admission into the United States, and had applied for a writ of habeas corpus, it was claimed for the applicants that their evidence before the inspector in charge who had denied them admission "was of such an indisputable character that their rejection argues the denial of the fair hearing and consideration of the case to which they were entitled." This contention was examined by the Supreme Court carefully analyzing the evidence and reaching the conclusion that the point was not supported, saying, "The record fails to show that their authority was not fairly exercised, that is, consistently with the fundamental principles of justice embraced within the conception of due process of law, and this being so, the merits of the case were not open to judicial examination." The court's analysis of the evidence showed clearly that the inspector in charge had some basis for his denial of the admission of the applicants. The action of the court also shows that it was ready to consider the testimony on the question of the jurisdiction of the courts. The present case presents none of the features of the evidence in that case supporting the conclusion that the court was without jurisdiction.

Another feature of the case is some uncertainty as to the grave of Chow Chiu's Hawaiian mistress or wife. He says she died during his absence in California. The witness, Hee Leong, an acquaintance of Chow Chiu, testifies as to the death and burial of an Hawaiian woman, eight or ten years ago, who he says was the wife of Chow Chiu, and to a visit to the cemetery where he pointed out her grave, at the head of which was a wooden slab inscribed in Chinese letters, the translation of which is "Chinese girl, Ah Chut, Wong She, graveyard, 1911, died Nov. 10," and the number 21. This matter was further investigated by one of the inspectors who looked up the burial records of the Board of Health, and failed to find any death on Nov. 10, 1911, reported, but did find the record of the death on November 13, 1911, of one Ah Chut at 12 months of age, whose parents were Wong Hee and Ko She. Although the inspector in charge does not refer to this uncertainty as casting a doubt as to the alleged death of the Hawaiian woman, the district attorney contends that it is a material element for consideration. The witness Hee Leong testifies to an acquaintance with Chow Chiu and his Hawaiian family, the birth of their two children, who, he says, had gone to China, and that she died eight or ten years ago. Eight years ago would fix her death in 1905 which would be about the time of Chow Chiu's departure for California, or just after, which would, if correct, throw out of the case the above testimony as to the date on the head board of the grave in Manoa. The departure of the children for China after Chow Chiu's return from California tends to support the testimony as to her death, although it does not prove it. Although the evidence of the death of the Hawaiian woman may have given the immigration officers some ground for doubting it, the fact remains that Chow Chiu testifies that he was not married to the mother of his children, and Lee Chuck, who says that he has known Chow Chiu ever since he was born and gives the place of his birth at Waikiki, near Queen Emma's yard, says that he never had any other wife than Wong She. There is no evidence against these statements except that of Hee Leong, who speaks of the Hawaiian woman who was buried in Manoa as "the wife of Chong Chiu." This expression—the words of the interpreter—standing alone without further questioning in view of the testimony of Chow Chiu and Lee Chuck, has no bearing on the case other than testimony that she was Chow Chiu's woman.

I am of the opinion that the inspector in charge acted arbitrarily in refusing admission to the applicant's wife in the present case, and that the contention of the petitioner that he ignored the evidence in so ruling is substantially correct. It was not an abuse of discretion, but it may perhaps be described as an unconscious or unintended abuse of authority.

The demurrer is overruled.

June 8, 1914.

(On Re-hearing)

This case having been heard, a decision was filed on the 16th day of February, no brief having been filed by the respondent, the court having received the impression, in some way, that the respondent did not intend to file a brief. After the decision was filed, District Attorney McCarn, for the respondent, expressed a desire to put in a brief and the court agreed to consider the same and make such supplementary decision as might be called for. On the 5th of June the brief of respondent was filed. I have carefully examined it and find no reason to modify the decision of February 16th.

[1] [2] The evidence of the marriage of the petitioner and Wong She, in whose behalf the petition for habeas corpus was filed, is convincing and should have been convincing to the immigration authorities, there being no opposing testimony, either as to the marriage or as to the fact that they lived together and held themselves out to their friends and acquaintances as man and wife. This continued for a considerable period, up to the time they left China for Hawaii. The petitioner was a citizen of the United States, he having been born in Hawaii and having spent his life there. To refuse recognition of his alleged wife and refuse her an opportunity to join her husband, thereby separating husband and wife or compelling him to break up his home in Hawaii and return to China, would create a hardship which can only be regarded as a wrong to them, and is unjustified unless there had appeared in the case a preponderance of evidence against the marriage, or an element of unreliability in the evidence for it, which would have made it most difficult to accept the theory of the marriage. No such condition appears. The weight of evidence is all the other way.

As to the women with whom petitioner had previously cohabited in Hawaii and who had borne him two children, the evidence is that they were not married and also that she had died some years before.   No evidence appears in the case, either that they had married or that she was still living at the time of the alleged marriage of petitioner and Wong She.   The evidence on record showing uncertainty in regard to her burial place is negligible, either to prove her dead or alive.

I still feel that the petitioner and Wong She did not receive at the hearing before the immigration authorities a fair trial, and affirm the previous decision overruling the demurrer.

IN THE MATTER OF THE PETITION OF LUCY TOMSON FOR A WRIT OF HABEAS CORPUS.
IN THE MATTER OF THE PETITION OF ROSE WALTERS FOR A WRIT OF HABEAS CORPUS.

February 18, 1914.

1. *Habeas corpus—Return to writ, or order to show cause:* Upon the issuance of a writ of habeas corpus, or an order to show cause why such writ should not issue, the return should be explicit, giving facts which justify the detention.

2. *Same—Same—Allegations of admissions:* A return is not made sufficient by allegations of admissions by the petitioner of conduct which, if true, would show him to be unlawfully in the United States, when it contains no charges of such conduct.

Habeas Corpus: Exceptions to return to order to show cause.

Andrews & Quarles for petitioners.

C. C. Bitting, Assistant U. S. Attorney, for respondent.

DOLE, J. The petitions in these cases are substantially on the same grounds. They allege American citizenship; that the petitioners are illegally deprived of their liberty by the respondent, the United States Immigration Inspector in Charge at the Port of Honolulu, for being unlawfully in the United States, but were not shown any warrants for their arrest nor affidavits upon which warrants were issued, and were ignorant of their right to inspect the same. They further allege that threats were made to them by the immigration authorities to deter them from taking legal proceedings, and complain that they have not had a fair hearing upon any charge of violating the immigration laws of the United States, and, so far as they are aware, have had no hearing at all on any such charge.

The return to the order to show cause in each case is excepted to on the following grounds: (1) The said return is insufficient in law to justify the detention and imprisonment of the petitioner, and does not show that she is lawfully detained and imprisoned by the respondent; (2) The said return does not set forth and show any proceeding, lawful or otherwise, under which the petitioner is held, or has been held.

The return is largely made up of denials of the allegations of the petition, but no denial is made of the allegation that the petitioners were not shown any warrants for their arrest nor affidavits on which such warrants were issued. It affirmatively states that the petitioners have been at all times fully informed as to all the steps taken in the proceedings and the causes and consequences of the same, and that at the time of their first arrest and subsequently they were informed of the grounds thereof, but nowhere is there any statement in the return of the grounds of their arrest or of any charge against them for violation of the laws of the United States, but it is alleged that they admitted that they were engaged in prostitution in violation of the laws of the United States; neither does the return exhibit, by copy or description, the warrants under which the petitioners were arrested, nor any affidavits or other forms of evidence appertaining thereto, or warrants of deportation, nor any records of the hearings which, in immigration rule 22, are required to be held.

[1] This court has stated the rule of practice in such cases, in the case of the application of *Koichi Maekawa* for a writ of habeas corpus, ante p. 226, with a citation of the following authorities: Church on Habeas Corpus, 2d ed., 225, sec. 148; Hurd on Habeas Corpus, 2d ed., 255, 256, 257. The return must be explicit, giving facts necessary to justify the detention; the necessary facts cannot be presumed. Without such facts the court cannot deal with the question raised by the application for the writ.

[2] The allegation of the return that the petitioners admitted that they were engaged in prostitution, does not make the return good. There is nothing in the record charging them with prostitution. As far as any showing is made they may have been suspected of being unlawfully in the country for any of the other statutory grounds.

It is unnecessary for me to take up at the present time the question of their rights under these proceedings, arising from their allegation of marriage with American citizens.

I find the return to be insufficient and allow the exceptions.

IN THE MATTER OF THE PETITION OF LUCY
TOMSON FOR A WRIT OF HABEAS CORPUS.
(ALSO IN THE MATTER OF ROSE WALTERS.)

April 28, 1914.

1. *Citizenship of alien women by marriage with United States citizen:* An alien woman who might herself be naturalized on the ground of being a free white woman, becomes a citizen of the United States upon becoming the wife of a citizen, without regard to her moral character.

2. *Naturalization by marriage with citizen—Free white woman:* No other requirement than that she is a "free white" woman is necessary for her recognition as a citizen of the United States upon such marriage.

Habeas Corpus: Motion to discharge petitioners, deportable alien women, on ground of their marriage to citizens.

Lorrin Andrews for petitioners.

J. W. Thompson, Assistant U. S. Attorney, for respondent.

DOLE, J.   The circumstances in these two cases are similar, and a conclusion relating to the first will apply to the second.

The petitioner, an alien woman, was detained on the ground of having been found practicing prostitution, thereby being unlawfully in the country. A warrant of deportation was issued to the commissioner of immigration at Ellis Island, N. Y., and the inspector in charge at Honolulu, T. H., respondent, was instructed by the acting commissioner general to forward her to the commissioner of immigration at the Angel Island Station, San Francisco, California. A writ of habeas corpus was issued and a hearing came up on exceptions to the amended return of respondent.

One of the allegations of the petitioner is that she is an

American citizen, being married to an American citizen. The return contains the contention that, if petitioner has participated in a marriage ceremony with her alleged husband, the same was performed after said order of deportation was made and served, and that she was not then capable of becoming a citizen of the United States, having been adjudged of bad moral character and having admitted that she was engaged in the practice of prostitution, and that if the said marriage ceremony was performed it was done for the purpose of evading the law and was not a legal marriage. Argument was had upon this point, and upon other points at issue as well, and authorities cited.

[1] [2] The main point made for the respondent was that the provision of law admitting alien women married to American citizens to the status of citizenship when they themselves might be lawfully naturalized, is limited by the provisions excluding from naturalization and admission to the United States persons of immoral character and those who might be undesirable by reason of disease, mental deficiency, etc., as well as by the provision denying naturalization on grounds of race.

Section 1994 of the Revised Statutes, which is a restatement of the act of February 10, 1855, 10 Stat. 604, enacts as follows:

"Any woman who is now or may hereafter be married to a citizen of the United States, and who might herself be lawfully naturalized, shall be deemed a citizen."

The Revised Statutes were passed by Congress as of December 1, 1873.

The respondent contends that the expresssion, "who might herself be lawfully naturalized", refers to the requirements of the statutes of naturalization, prominent among which is the possession of good moral character, and as the admission of the petitioner is a denial of such quality and would preclude her from obtaining letters of citizenship under the provisions of the statute, she is precluded

from recognition as an American citizen through marriage
to an American citizen.

The case of *Kelly v. Owen,* 7 Wall., 74 U. S. 498 (1868),
in referring to the statute above quoted, says:

"As we construe this act, it confers the privileges of citizenship upon women married to citizens of the United
States, if they are of the class of persons for whose naturalization the previous acts of Congress provide. . . .
His citizenship, wherever it exists, confers, under the act,
citizenship upon her. . . . Its object, in our opinion,
was to allow her citizenship to follow that of her husband,
without the necessity of any application for naturalization
on her part; . . . The terms, 'who might lawfully be
naturalized under the existing laws,' only limit the application of the law to free white women."

The case of *Hopkins v. Fanchant,* 130 Fed. 839, (Circuit
Court of Appeals, Ninth Circuit, 1904). is in some ways
similar to the case before the court, in that, pending proceedings for the deportation of the petitioner, and after
the writ of habeas corpus was issued, she married a citizen
of the United States. The court said:

"The rule is well settled that her marriage to a naturalized citizen of the United States entitled her to be discharged. . . . The status of the wife follows that of
her husband. And by virtue of her marriage her husband's
domicile became her domicile."

It does not appear in the report of the case upon what
grounds she was found to be unlawfully in the United
States.

Against these cases the respondent cites two decisions;
one by a Circuit Court and the other by a District Court:
In re Rustigan, 155 Fed. 982-983 (1908, Circuit Court), *Ex
parte Kaprielian,* 188 Fed. 695 (1910, District Court).

The point made by the *Rustigan* case is that the decision in *Kelly v. Owen* was made in view of the disqualifications for naturalization of aliens under the then existing
laws, which, as the decision states, "limit the application

of the law to free white women", generally to free white persons, and adds, "the immigration laws have since added to the classes of persons who are incapable in their own right of naturalization". The *Kaprielian* case, emphasizes this point as follows: "The present act regulating immigration, passed in 1907, . . . repeals all prior acts or parts of acts inconsistent with its provisions. After a final determination according to those provisions, that a woman belongs, and belonged at the time of her entry into the country, to a class of aliens forbidden by law to enter or to remain, it cannot be said that she is capable of being lawfully naturalized."

Now let us see what the requirements of naturalization were at the time the said cases of *Kelly v. Owen* and *Hopkins v. Fanchant* were decided. In April, 1802, a law was passed by Congress requiring good moral character as one of the conditions of naturalization of aliens. 2 Stat. 153-154. The statute containing this requirement was reenacted as a part of the Revised Statutes in the session of 1873 and 1874, p. 378. As to the restrictions on immigration, we find the following: On March 3, 1878, Congress passed an act excluding women imported for purposes of prostitution, and convicts (18 Stat., part 3, 477); on August 3, 1882, an act excluding persons likely to become public charges, convicts, lunatics and idiots (22 Stat. 214); on March 3, 1891, an act excluding polygamists, felons, those having contagious diseases, insane persons, idiots and those likely to become public charges (26 Stat. 1084); on March 3, 1893, an act with similar exclusion provisions as the last (27 Stat. 569); on March 3, 1903, an act excluding, among other classes of aliens, prostitutes and those importing prostitutes (32 Stat. 1214).

It appears from these citations that when the decision in *Kelly v. Owen*, supra, was made, the Supreme Court of the United States proceeded to say, referring to the act of 1855, supra, "it confers the privileges of citizenship upon women married to citizens of the United States, if they are of the class of persons for whose naturalization the previous acts of Congress provide"; and proceeds to define such class in the following words: "The terms 'who might lawfully be naturalized under the existing laws', only limit the application of the law to free white women." And this in spite of the fact that good moral character, attachment to the principles of the Constitution of the United States, and some other conditions, are required by the previous acts of Congress. And when the decision in *Hopkins v. Fanchant*, supra, was rendered, the existing laws excluded from admission to the country many classes of persons regarded as undesirable, including prostitutes; and yet the Circuit Court of Appeals of the Ninth Circuit announced its view of the law as quoted above, and cites the case of *Kelly v. Owen*, among others, in support of it.

It thus appears that these two tribunals agree upon such a construction of the statute (Rev. Stat., sec. 1994) as limits its application to aliens being free white persons, following the original statute of naturalization, supra. The amendment of this statute, enlarging its application to Africans, does not concern this case, or those cited. This agreement involves necessarily the view that the descriptions of persons classed as undesirable from disease, morals, or pauperism, and therefore excluded, were not intended by Congress to be considered in the application of the words, "who might herself be lawfully naturalized."

In the case of *Low Wah Suey v. Backus*, 225 U. S. 460, 473, the court declined to interfere with the deportation of the Chinese wife of an American citizen, who had been found practicing prostitution, saying, "Being incapable of naturalization herself, although the wife of a Chinaman of American birth, she remained an alien and subject to the terms of the act." Also, "Under the present statute, when a woman who could be naturalized, marries a citizen of the United States, she becomes by that act a citizen herself." The woman in that case was allowed to be deported presumably because, being an alien who was practicing prostitution in the United States, she was not a free white woman, or a woman of African descent, who was the wife of an American citizen.

The exceptions on this point relating to the claims of petitioner of the status of an American citizen, are allowed, and evidence will be heard on the question of such marriage.

The same ruling as to the case of Rose Walters.

STANFORD VEINO *v.* THE AMERICAN SCHOONER BLAKELY.

February 25, 1914.

1. *Admiralty—Official log-book—Entries:* The statute requires the master of a vessel making a foreign voyage to log each offense by any member of the crew for which he intends to prosecute or enforce a forfeiture, and the name of any one who ceases to be a member of the crew otherwise than by death, with the time, place, manner and cause thereof.

2. *Same—Same—Failure to log offenses—Legal proceedings—Evidence:* In legal proceedings dealing with such offenses, the record thereof should be produced or proved, failing which the court may at its discretion refuse evidence of such offenses. In case such offenses are satisfactorily proved, it is better practice to ignore failure to produce or prove log entries thereof.

3. *Same—Discharge of seaman in foreign port:* Discharge of a member of a crew in an out-of-the-way foreign port unjustifiable, except for offenses of a very serious and aggravated character.

In Admiralty: Libel *in rem* for wages and damages.

G. A. Davis and *W. T. Rawlins* for libelant.
Holmes, Stanley & Olson for libellee.

DOLE, J.   It has been satisfactorily shown in the trial of
this case that on the 6th of March, 1911, libelant shipped
as first mate of the American schooner Blakely, at Port
Blakely, in the State of Washington, for a voyage to the
port of Tocopilla, in Chili, South America, and return to
a port of discharge in Washington, Oregon, California, or
British Columbia; that the said schooner arrived in Tocopilla on the 23rd day of May, in the same year, and lay
there until after July 3rd discharging her cargo; and that
on the 3rd day of July the master paid off and discharged
the libelant against his will and protest at the port of
Tocopilla.   The libelant alleges that such discharge was
without cause and in violation of the shipping articles entered into between him and the libellee, and claims wages
to the amount of $520, less the amount received at the end
of the voyage, and $520 for his necessary expenses during
his enforced detention at Tocopilla and Valparaiso in said
Chili, where he went from Tocopilla, and passage money
back to the port of discharge; and alleges that he faithfully and in a skillful manner attended to his duties as mate
up to the time of his discharge.

The answer denies the faithful and skillful service by
libelant and alleges that on numerous occasions he slept
while on watch, encouraged and aroused a spirit of insubordination in the crew; that libelant at Tocopilla absented
himself from the vessel without leave and in defiance of
the orders of the master, with general allegations of neglect
of duty and definitely charges him with injury to the gaff
of the schooner through neglect and inattention to duty,
and upon the master's remonstrance, with having used violent language toward him and assaulted him, and that the
libelant acquiesced in his discharge at Tocopilla.

[1] It is a noticeable feature of these proceedings that

none of the matters complained of in the defense as to neglect of duty, encouraging a spirit of insubordination among the crew, absence from the vessel without leave at Tocopilla, and the use of violent language toward the master and committing an assault on him, on the part of the libelant, were entered in the official log of the vessel. The law requires that the master of any vessel making a voyage from a port in the United States to any foreign port shall have an official log-book and shall enter therein "every offense committed by any member of his crew for which it is intended to prosecute or to enforce a forfeiture; . . . a statement of the conduct, character and qualifications of each of his crew or a statement that he declines to give an opinion of such particulars, . . . and the name of every seaman or apprentice who ceases to be a member of the crew otherwise than by death, with the place, time, manner and cause thereof." Rev. Stat., sec. 4290. Section 4596 of the Revised Statutes states the following offenses among others and sets forth the punishment that may be inflicted for them respectively: "Continued wilful neglect of duty at sea; . . . and assaulting any master or mate." Section 4597 of the Revised Statutes is as follows:

"Upon the commission of any of the offenses enumerated in the preceding section an entry thereof shall be made in the official log-book on the day on which the offense was committed, and shall be signed by the master and by the mate or one of the crew; and the offender, if still in the vessel, shall, before her next arrival at any port, or, if she is at the time in port, before her departure therefrom, be furnished with a copy of such entry, and have the same read over distinctly and audibly to him, and may thereupon make such a reply thereto as he thinks fit; and a statement that a copy of the entry has been so furnished, or the same has been so read over, together with his reply, if any, made by the offender, shall likewise be entered and signed in the same manner. [2] In any subsequent legal proceedings the entries hereinbefore required shall, if practicable, be produced or proved, and in default of such production or proof the court hearing the case may, at its discretion, refuse to receive evidence of the offense."

When the charges in such matters are satisfactorily proved, it is undoubtedly the best practice to ignore the failure of the master to make the appropriate entries in his log-book and to proceed with the trial.

"Sections 4596 and 4597 show that the failure to enter facts in any log on which deduction of wages is claimed, does not absolutely prevent proof of those facts, but gives the court a discretion to reject the evidence. No doubt the general purpose of these provisions of law is such as libelant's counsel suggests, to prevent the oppression of seamen by trumped up unfounded claims of misconduct, and ordinarily, and if the facts are left in doubt, the failure to enter the facts in the log should defeat the attempted defence." *The T. F. Whiton,* 23 Fed. Cas. 873, No. 13,849.

It is difficult from the evidence offered as to the complaints by the master against the libelant, to reach a conclusion. Under such a situation the law and the precedent cited above would seem to apply, and they will be followed. The court will not further consider such evidence.

[3] The act of the master in dismissing the libelant in such an out-of-the-way port as Tocopilla, was a severe one, and could only be justified by convincing evidence, which does not appear. So far as one may judge from the evidence, the libelant was practically marooned there, the conditions being such that he, although making reasonable efforts to find a new position as mate on some vessel leaving there or Valparaiso, for the Pacific coast, was unable to do so before about the first of January, 1912, and was without funds for paying for a passage to the Pacific coast, except possibly at the time of his discharge at Tocopilla, at which time there does not appear to have been such opportunity, and even then insufficient for a first-class passage.

"Generally speaking, the causes which justify the master in discharging a seaman before the termination of the voy-

age, and especially in a foreign port, are such as amount
to a disqualification and show him to be unfit for the
service he has engaged for, or unfit to be trusted in the
vessel.   They are—mutinous and rebellious conduct, per-
severed in, gross dishonesty, or embezzlement, or theft, or
habitual drunkenness, or where the seaman is habitually
a stirrer-up of quarrels, to the destruction of the order of
the vessel and the discipline of the crew. .   .   . Ordinarily, the law will not justify the master in dismissing a seaman for a single offense, unless it be of a very high and
aggravated character, implying a deep degree of moral
turpitude, or a dangerous and ungovernable temper or disposition.   It looks on occasional offenses and outbreaks of
passion, not so frequent as to become habits, with indulgence, and by maritime courts it is administered with lenity
and a due regard to the character and habits of the subjects to whom it applies." *Smith v. Treat*, 22 Fed. Cas.
687, 688, No. 13,117.

I find that the libelant was paid off at the time of his
discharge at Tocopilla; that his discharge was unjustifiable; that he remained at Tocopilla about four months
under a necessary expense of 697 pesos, without being able
to find a position on a vessel as first mate for return to
Washington, California, or British Columbia; that he then
went to Valparaiso where he remained about two months
at an expense of 279 pesos before finding such a position,
when he shipped as first mate on the four-masted schooner
E. B. Johnson, January 1, 1912, bound to Gray's Harbor at
$40 a month, arriving there in April, when he could have
earned $120.   While at Tocopilla he earned 60 pesos splic-
ing wire rope.   Had he continued in the˙ Blakely on the
voyage from Tocopilla to Port Townsend, where she arrived September 18, 1911, two and a half months from his
discharge at Tocopilla, his wages, at $65 a month, would
have amounted to $162.50.   Under the general prayer for
relief, I allow damages in the nature of wages at $65 a
month from the time the Blakely arrived at Port Town-.
send, September 18, 1911, to the time the libelant arrived

at Gray's Harbor, April 1st, 1912, six months and twelve days, $415.99. It is in evidence that at Tocopilla one American dollar was worth 4.68 of Chilean money. These items may be stated in the following form:

Expenses at Tocopilla and Valparaiso 976 pesos, equal to $204.27

Wages due on the Blakely from July 3 to September 18, 1911 .... 162.50

Wages as damages at the same rate from September 18, 1911, to April 1, 1912, when he reached Gray's Harbor, 6 months, 12 days................... 415.99

Wages received as first mate on the schooner E. B. Johnson..............$120.00

Amount due libelant 662.76

$782.76 $782.76

I find for the libelant in the sum of $662.76, with costs.

JAMES KAULANA v. OAHU RAILWAY & LAND COMPANY, AND McCABE, HAMILTON & RENNY COMPANY.

March 6, 1914.

1. *Negligence—Fellow servants:* As a rule the master is not liable for injury to a servant caused by the negligence of a fellow servant in the course of the master's business.

2. *Same—Incompetent fellow servant—Burden of proof:* Where exception to this rule is claimed by a servant by reason of injury resulting from the master's employment of an unskilled or incompetent fellow servant, the burden is on the injured servant to show the master's negligence in employing or retaining the unskilled or incompetent servant.

In Admiralty: Libel *in personam* for damages for personal injuries.

G. A. Davis (*W. T. Rawlins* with him) for libelant.

M. F. Prosser (*Frear, Prosser, Anderson & Marx* with him) for libellees.

CLEMONS, J.   This i s a libel *in personam* to recover damages for injuries sustained by the libelant through alleged negligent acts of incompetent and unskilled servants of the libellees. From the evidence adduced at the hearing, and the view of the locus in quo had by the court at the request, and in the presence, of the attorneys for all parties to the suit, the facts are found to be as hereinafter set forth. They are given with some detail, so as to permit of the disposition of all possible questions of the law of master and servant, whether apparent in the pleadings or suggested by the evidence, i. e., in the pleadings as existing or as amendable to conform to the proof.

Injuries as alleged were received by the libelant, a servant of the libellee McCabe, Hamilton & Renny Company, employed in the operation of loading and stowing bags of sugar in the lower hold of the American steamship Columbian at the port of Honolulu. The sugar was delivered over the side of the vessel at the upper deck by an electric elevator or endless chain carrier operated by servants of the libelee Oahu Railway & Land Company. Thereafter it was handled exclusively by servants of the McCabe company, being guided by those servants so as to slide down inclined chutes to the several decks, until finally some, or all, of it ran to the lower hold by four chutes coming from the deck immediately above. At each deck, before the sugar was diverted to different chutes to decks below, the bags ran on to a flat table so that their speed was checked and they could, therefore, be more easily handled and could be started on their new way with little momentum.

It having been found necessary to move the lower end of the chute at which the libelant was working, he signalled to two of the McCabe company's servants who were at the hatch above directing the sugar down the chute, to stop the stream of sugar bags until the end of the chute had been moved to a new position. The stream was stopped for about seven or eight minutes and before the libelant had carried the end of the chute to its final place, the servants above started another bag on its way down the chute, and although one of them shouted to the libelant to "look out," the bag struck the libelant in the leg before he could drop the chute and jump out of the way, causing the injuries which are the basis of the libel. Another servant, Kaikai, was assisting the libelant at the time, there usually having been two additional assistants but these having gone above temporarily to obtain relief from weeping eyes caused by the presence of fresh paint in the hold. It was the custom for one or two men of the gang at each chute to lay off from time to time to rest, to go to the toilet, or for other reasons, and it was testified that as the end of the chute was kept within three or four feet of where the sugar was being stowed, two men were always able to handle it. Kikapa, a fellow worker, witness for the libelant, testified that "when the sugar comes right down to where you are working [as was the case here], you don't need so many; these others can get a rest." The sugar ordinarily came aboard ship at the rate of from 18 to 20 bags per minute, but as the work was at this time being rushed, the rate was double, or about 40 per minute, the highest average rate for each of the four chutes below being 10 bags per minute. When sugar was left on the deck above, of course the rate would be lower at each of the other chutes according to the amount left on the way, and when the flow was stopped at any one chute the rate would be higher.

The libelant's affirmative answer to the questions, "Did they sing out to the fellows in the tower?" and "Did they stop the machinery?" might be taken to imply negligence on the part of servants of the railway company in again starting the stream of sugar bags before a signal had reached the tower of the elevator, that the chute below had been safely moved.   But it may be observed, that so far as concerns the libelant's testimony that the man above whom he asked to "stop the sugar on top," said "all right, they stop the sugar," and "sung out to the fellows in the tower," the libelant was not in a position to know whether any such message was passed on up through the decks above and then over the side of the vessel to the tower, which was on the wharf some distance away.—This was a point which it was incumbent upon the libelant to clear up by testimony, but we have only his own testimony above quoted, against which are the circumstances suggested, and the positive testimony of the foreman of the work, the libelant's own witness Sam Ku, that the men in the tower were not told to stop the machinery, and that such a course was not necessary.   And we see elsewhere in the libelant's testimony that his knowledge of what went on above was unreliable—not false, but mistaken; thus, at first he said that the machinery was stopped upon his request, but finally he said that "they didn't stop the machinery; we didn't hear the machinery when they stopped."   When he testified "we stopped the fellows from *pushing* sugar down," he told, from my judgment of the testimony and the circumstances in evidence, just what happened.

[1] The facts establish no negligence on the part of the railway company.   They establish, or even if they did not it may at least be assumed that they establish, the negligence of the McCabe company's servants in charge of the chute above in permitting the bag of sugar to go down the chute before the libelant had placed the lower end of the chute in the desired position.   As the negligence is that of fellow servants, the master is not liable, unless there is something in the facts to make the case an exception to

the rule. *Southern Pacific Co. v. Hetzer*, 135 Fed. 272, 275-276; *Mejea v. Whitehouse*, 19 Haw. 159, 160-161; *Silva v. Ewa Plantation Co.*, 21 Haw. 129, 130-131, 132. The only exception alleged consists in the wrong of the masters in employing unskilled and incompetent servants, but this allegation is not borne out by the facts. Indeed, the libelant is himself a witness to the experience and competency of the men immediately responsible for the injuries.

[2] Cooley states the rule to be that the burden is on the plaintiff to show the master's negligence in employing or retaining the servant whose act or omission caused the injury. 2 Cooley, Torts, 2d ed., 1155. And see *Gravelle v. Minneapolis & St. Louis Ry.*, 10 Fed. 711, holding that skill and competency are presumed.

Counsel for libelant has suggested that negligence is apparent in the McCabe company's not furnishing sufficient men for this chute, and contends that the absence of the men who had gone above left such an inadequate force below that there became a congestion of sugar bags so great that the libelant and Kaikai could not handle it. There is no evidence of the inability of these two men to handle the sugar at this chute,—indeed, the evidence is to the contrary; and the only just conclusion from the testimony is that the chute had to be moved, not because of any congestion, i. e., undue accumulation, of sugar, but for the reason merely that sufficient sugar had been stowed at the foot of the chute and it became necessary to move to another place. In any event, even if the force below had been inadequate, the proximate cause of the injury was the negligence of the fellow servants at the hatch above.

Wherefore, the court must find, and does hereby find, for the libellees. A decree in conformity with this finding will be signed on presentation.

UNITED STATES OF AMERICA *v.* JOSEPH A.
   DOYLE.
UNITED STATES OF AMERICA *v.* MAUDE SCHUR-
   MANN, ALIAS MAUDE SCHOLL, ALIAS MAUDE
   DOYLE.

April 30, 1914.

1. *Indictment—Duplicity:* An indictment charging in one count
the commission of adultery "on or about the 15th day of January,
1911, and between the 15th day of January, 1911, and the
1st day of August, 1912, at various times, the exact date
of which is to the grand jurors unknown," is bad for duplicity. Also,
an indictment charging in one count the commission of adultery "on
or about the 10th day of December, 1913, and between the 20th day
of November, 1913, and the 23rd day of December, 1913".

2. *Same—Same—Demurrer, practice on sustaining:* On sustaining demurrer to indictment upon such ground of duplicity, the court
rules that if the government will elect to proceed upon the single
offense first charged, the case may proceed upon such election; otherwise the indictment to be dismissed and the defendants discharged.

3. *Same—Adultery—Naming spouse:* In an indictment for adultery the designation of the defendant's spouse as "one ——— Scholl
whose full and correct name is to the grand jurors unknown," is not
a fatal defect.

Criminal Law: Demurrer to indictment.
Jeff McCarn, U. S. District Attorney, for the United
States.
E. C. Peters and *R. J. O'Brien* for the defendants.

CLEMONS, J.   The defendant demurs to the indictment
in each of these cases, on the ground, among others, that
"more than one offense is charged in the single count."
This objection is based upon the manner in which time is
laid.   It is clearly untenable in cases No. 950 and 953,
wherein the act is charged as having been committed "on
or about" a certain day, "the exact date of which is to the
grand jurors unknown".

And in these cases the objection is overruled.

In case No. 951, the time of the alleged offense is charged as "on or about the 15th day of January, A. D., 1911, and between the 15th day of January, A. D., 1911, and the 1st day of August, A. D. 1912, at various times, the exact dates of which is to the grand jurors unknown". The word "dates" appears to have been originally typewritten "date" and the letter "s" added by pen and ink.

In case No. 952, the time of the alleged offense is charged as "on or about the 10th day of December, A. D., 1913, and between the 20th day of November, A. D., 1913, and the 23rd day of December, A. D., 1913, at various times, the exact date of which is unknown."

In case No. 954, the time of the alleged offense is charged, as "on or about the 10th day of December, A. D., 1913, and between the 20th day of November, A. D., 1913, and the 23rd day of December, A. D., 1913, at various times, the exact date of which is unknown".

[1] Against the objection of duplicity, it is urged (1) in each case the limitation of time as between certain dates is only descriptive of the preceding temporal clause "on or about" a certain date, and (2) that at all events, so far as concerns any other offenses than that the date of which is given, those additional offenses could be proved, any way, under the indictment, just as in a recent trial in this court, wherein other acts of adultery than that alleged in the indictment were admitted in proof of intent and disposition of the parties. It is also urged (3) that the objection is technical, and that courts are now ruling against such objections.

A careful reading of the language above quoted from these indictments disposes of the first of the government's contentions just mentioned.

The government's second objection is removed by due consideration of the distinction between what may be alleged in one count of an indictment and what may be offered in proof thereof. While under an indictment for a particular act of adultery, other acts of adultery may, for example, be proved to show an adulterous disposition, nevertheless:

"Charging in one count a series of distinct offenses, each meriting a separate penalty or punishment, with a continuando or as committed at divers days and times between certain dates is certainly not in accordance with the general principles of criminal pleading and we are referred to no authority showing that it is permitted in offenses of this kind, or in any analogous cases. . . . No satisfactory reason is perceived why this case should not be subject to the general rule of criminal pleading, which forbids putting the accused on trial for a multitude of offenses charged in a single count." *State v. Temple*, 38 Vt. 37, 39.

The opinion in this case is referred to for the clear distinction made between matters of pleading and of evidence, as also for its statement of the policy of the rule just quoted and its justification of the rule by early precedents. *Commonwealth v. Fuller*, 163 Mass. 499; 40 N. E. 764, is a more recent case in support of the rule. Justice Peck, in the case of *Temple*, supra, characterizes "an indictment for assault and battery on divers times and days covering a period of two years" as "certainly a novelty" in pleading, and as calculated to bring "uncertainty and embarrassment to the mind of the respondent as to what he is called upon to meet." Ibid. 40. He also points out the unsoundness of such pleading when viewed in the light of the law of *res adjudicata*, former conviction or acquittal,—which is often made the test of good pleading: he asks, "How can it be ascertained after verdict of guilty upon this indictment, of how many offenses the respondent is convicted?" Ibid.

With such authorities, and those cited in Joyce on Indictments, sec. 408, in support of the rule, it can hardly be called technical. And though one decision has been found in which, by way of dictum merely, adultery is character-

ized as "a continuing offense", *State v. Dennison*, 60 Neb.
192; 82 N. W. 628, 629, it is believed that this characterization, which finds no support elsewhere so far as discovered, is in error, and that the express ruling contra in the
Fuller case, above cited, involving adultery, should be
followed.

Finally, Rev. Stat., sec. 1024, appears to contemplate the
joining of separate offenses in separate counts:

"Where there are several charges against any person for
the same act or transaction, or for two or more acts or
transactions connected together, or for two or more acts
or transactions of the same class of crimes or offenses, which
may be properly joined, instead of having several indictments the whole may be joined in one indictment *in separate counts.*"

The objections on the ground of duplicity are, therefore,
sustained in cases No. 951, 952, and 954.

In case No. 953 an objection is based on the fact that,
the defendant being a married woman charged with the
offense of adultery, the name of her husband is described
as "one ——— Scholl, whose full and correct name is to
the grand jurors unknown". The context describes this
person Scholl as a person "other than the said Joseph A.
Doyle", the latter having been therein above described as
the co-participant with the defendant in this offense. It is,
then, impossible to misunderstand the allegation, so far as
concerns the person "——— Scholl" and his relation to
and distinction from the other parties named in the indictment.   See *State v. Hutchinson*, 36 Me. 261, 263.   And
apart from any question of uncertainty, the better rule
seems to be that the allegation of the defendant's spouse
is unnecessary.   *Davis v. Commonwealth*, 7 Atl. 194
(Penn.); 1 Cyc. 958.   The omission of the whole of the
spouse's name would be but a formal defect, in any event,
Davis v. Commonwealth, supra; and the omission of the
spouse's Christian name even more a formal defect, and

so within Rev. Stat., sec. 1025, providing that "no indictment found and presented by a grand jury . . . shall be deemed insufficient . . . by reason of any defect or imperfection in matter of form only, which shall not tend to the prejudice of the defendant." This ground of demurrer is, therefore, overruled.

[2] In accordance with the general practice, upon the foregoing ruling, the indictments in cases No. 951' 952. and 954 should be dismissed and the defendants discharged. See 1 Bishop, New Crim. Proc., sec. 781 (2), citing Archb., Crim. Pl. & Ev., 14th Lond. ed. 116. But, inasmuch as it may be possible under these indictments for the government to make an election to proceed on only one of the offenses charged in the single count, and the allowance of such an election would work no injustice to the defendant, and would save the considerable expense of convening the grand jury to bring new indictments, the court will order that the indictments in cases No 951, 952, and 954 be dismissed and the defendants discharged, unless the government shall within two days file its election to proceed upon the single offense first charged in the count of the indictment. The time of the other offenses charged is laid with such uncertainty, indefiniteness, as not to justify an election to proceed upon any of them. Though no precedent has been found for this disposition of the matter, the court feels confident of its practicability and of its justice, and that it is in line with the present progressive spirit of revulsion from undue technicality in criminal cases, so strongly emphasized by Mr. Justice Day in the case of *Garland v. The State of Washington*, 232 U. S. 642, 646.

WALTER MUISHNECK AND ARCHIBALD SNAITH v. THE AMERICAN STEAMSHIP ST. HELENS.

May 7, 1914.

1. *Admiralty—Disobedience of seamen—Discharge:* Admiralty precedents do not favor the discharge of seamen for a single offense, unless it is of an aggravated character.

2. *Same—Same—Same—Reinstatement:* A seaman discharged for such offense should generally be given an opportunity to return to the employment of the ship, with such penalty as is reasonable under the circumstances.

In Admiralty: Libel *in rem.*

G. A. Davis for libelants.
G. S. Curry for libellee.

DOLE, J. The libel in this case complains that the libelants were discharged by the master at Honolulu, wrongfully and illegally and in violation of their contract and shipping articles, and they claim return passage money, their wages to the termination of the voyage, and one month's extra wages, and such further indemnity as the court may award.

They shipped on the libellee at Seattle, in the State of Washington, about September 19th, last year, for a voyage from Seattle to Rainier, Oregon, and thence to Honolulu and such other ports as the master might direct, and back to the final port of discharge, in Washington, Oregon, or California, at a rate of wages of fifty dollars a month, such voyage not to exceed four months.

While in the port of Honolulu the crew, with the assistance of longshoremen, were engaged in discharging lumber from the libellee. On Saturday, October 18th, at five o'clock P. M., libelants quit work, refusing to continue longer that day, whereupon the master instructed the mate to discharge them. They remained on board until Monday morning, at which time, without making any request to be reinstated, they were on hand, apparently expecting, or hoping, to be allowed to continue in the employment of the libellee. The master offered to so continue them, subject to the forfeiture of their wages for the Sunday intervening. This they refused to accept, and were paid off at the commissioner's office, under their protests.

It appears by the working rules of the Sailors' Union of the Pacific, which according to the evidence is recognized by all ship owners on the Pacific Coast, that nine hours are fixed as a day's work in loading and unloading vessels, and fifty cents an hour is allowed for working over time. In this case, during the previous days of the week, unloading had been discontinued at four o'clock P. M., after eight hours work; on the Saturday in question it was continued past that hour, notice having been given to the men during the afternoon that work was to continue that day till six o'clock.

The action of the libelants in quitting work necessitated the discontinuance of the work of unloading for that day, according to the testimony of Mr. Hanson, the mate, as their departure broke up one gang, making it undesirable to go on with the rest of the force, considering the subsequent work of fumigating and time for supper.

[1] The practice in these cases is lenient towards seamen, and does not encourage dismissal for a single offense, unless it is of an aggravated character. The act of the libelants in quitting work and refusing to go on was subversive of discipline and contrary to their contract with the ship; [2] and yet, in view of the fact that their conduct during the voyage so far had been good, as shown by the evidence, it would have been in accordance with the practice in such cases that the master should have given them an opportunity to return to the employment of the ship; and if the case showed no such opportunity offered

to these men by the master, I should be disposed to consider that the discharge was unnecessary and unjust. But as the master did give them an opportunity to return to work on Monday, subject to the loss of wages for the day before, being Sunday, I feel that he acted as reasonably in the matter as the circumstances called for; that the loss of wages for one day was not a severe punishment for their conduct, but, on the contrary, a mild one. Refusing such offer, libelants are without any substantial grievance in this case. Their conduct in quitting work, without complaint as to any hardship, without any request for a cessation of work on account of fatigue, or other good reason, and their positive language, as testified to, refusing to continue, justified the master in taking some action; and the action taken in discharging the men and later in giving them a chance to return, subject to the penalty mentioned, was, I think, within his rights and not unreasonable.

There was some testimony as to the heat of the day, the unfavorable state of things within the hold of the ship, but this evidence was not sufficient to enable the court to arrive at the conclusion that they were treated with unreasonable severity in being kept at work for so long a time during the day on which they quit.

I find for the libellee, dismissing the libel.

IN THE MATTER OF OLAF OMSTED, A BANK-RUPT.

May 19, 1914.

1. *Evidence—Judicial notice:* The court takes judicial notice of the recent tariff act, 38 Stat. 114, and of its depressing effect upon the stock market, and the sugar industry, in Hawaii.

2. *Bankruptcy—Administration; Sale of assets; Trustee's duty:* The trustee may be surcharged for loss arising from want of due diligence in reducing the property of the estate into money. In the case of assets of corporation stock, the court may surcharge for the difference between the amount actually realized from sale and a fair maximum figure reached in the open market, and justified by conditions, during the time when the stock could have been sold by the trustee.

In Bankruptcy: On trustee's petition for allowance of final accounts.

J. W. Mason, trustee, *pro se.*

CLEMONS, J. The trustee's final accounts and petition for discharge are before the court; and inasmuch as the question suggests itself, whether or not the trustee should be surcharged for the depreciation in value of certain assets of the bankrupt, consisting of fifty-five shares of the capital stock of the Olaa Sugar Company, held by the trustee for at least six years after the time when they should have been sold, the court has retained the accounts for consideration and given the usual notice to creditors of a hearing thereon, with the intention, however, of referring the matter finally to the referee at Hilo for such other action, including the declaration of dividends, as may be necessary to close the administration. No creditors or other parties in interest appeared at the hearing, and the court examined Mr. Albert F. Afong, a member of the Honolulu Stock and Bond Exchange, and a qualified witness as to values, subpoenaed by the court, as to the market value of this stock during the period since it was obtained by the trustee, to-wit, July 13, 1907, according to the trustee's statement of April 23, 1914, on file herein. Mr. Afong's testimony is that the highest price reached during this period was $9 a share (during the year 1912), and the lowest 50 cents (during the year 1913); that a good deal of the stock sold in 1912 at figures around $8 or $9; that in 1912 the lowest price was $3-7/8, and that a fair maximum figure for that year and for the period since July 13, 1907, was $7 or $8. He also testified that in 1907 the price of the stock was very steady, running from $3 to $3.50, and that in 1913 the highest price was $4.50. And his testimony showed further, that these maximum prices were justified by the general tone of the market, the high price of sugar, and the large sugar crop of the Olaa plantation, owned by this corporation.

[1] The court takes judicial notice of the recent tariff act and of its depressing effect upon the local stock market and upon the sugar industry of Hawaii. See 4 Wigmore, Evidence, sec. 2580. These considerations account for the low price of 75 cents received by the trustee when he sold in January, 1914. They do not, however, excuse the trustee's want of diligence. On May 24, 1911, this court made an order directed toward the prompt closing of estates by all delinquent trustees; that order included this trustee, who had been in office since early in 1902, and who then had as trustee a small interest in, or claim to, lands which on July 13, 1907, he exchanged for the Olaa shares,—an exchange which was later approved by the court on a petition for such approval, and for leave to sell, not filed by the trustee, however, until August 20, 1913, and then only after repeated requests from the court,— the first request made by the clerk's letter of the date of May 26, 1911, acknowledged by the trustee's letter of June 28, 1911, followed by the clerk's letter of reminder of July 7, 1911, and the judge's own letters of December 10, 1912,

April 8, 1913, May 23, 1913, and October 17, 1913. The trustee in reply always expressed the purpose of taking early action to close the estate; but the. demands of the trustee's own business were pleaded as an excuse for delay.

It seems unnecessary to cite authorities for the proposition that· one who assumes such a position of trust should be responsible for any losses arising from his want of care and diligence; the criterion in such cases being the care and diligence exercised by prudent persons in the manage- · ment of their own affairs. See *Hill v. Evans*, 114 Mo. App. 715, 91 S. W. 1022, 1024. The case of *In re M. D. Monsarrat*, a bankrupt, 3 U. S. Dist. Ct. Haw. 641, indicates the disposition of this court in cases of such neglect, and would authorize the surcharging of a negligent trustee in such a case as the present. It may also be noted in this connection, that the statute under which the trustee derived his authority, provides that trustees "shall reduce to money the property of the estate . . . and close up the estate as expeditiously as is compatible with the best interests of the parties at interest." Act, sec. 47 (a) (2). See Remington, Bankruptcy, secs. 23, 908. Here, the trustee had already taken over five years to dispose of the interest in lands by exchange for this stock, so that the delay has really been since early in 1902 instead of since the above date of 1907.

It is due to the trustee to state that his good faith has never been questioned. In fact his neglect has injured himself more than any one else, as he is a creditor having an allowed claim of $2,761.75 out of a total aggregate of $5,602.88 of claims allowed. His loss of vouchers in the San Francisco fire of 1906 embarrassed him somewhat, but he lost no data which prevented the sale of this stock. It may be noted that there are data in the files of court and the marshal's office accounting for almost all of the payments which these vouchers represent; the other payments aggregated only about $40 and would be reasonably accounted for by the course and requirements of the administration. As to the former items: the person giving the receipt for the largest item was the trustee himself, a secured creditor, who in these accounts makes further and sufficient acknowledgment; and in the case of the one other large item, the court has been assured that the secured creditor, since deceased, who is alleged to have given the receipt, actually received the money. As this assurance was given by an officer of this court, attorney for the creditor, and husband of one of the creditor's heirs, having an intimate knowledge of the creditor's estate, the court feels safe in relying upon the trustee's accounts in this particular. Furthermore, the latter secured creditor received payment through the sale of corporation stock of the bankrupt, held by himself as collateral, the details of which sale the court has ascertained from the purchaser and from others having knowledge,—all as shown by correspondence on file herein.

It will accordingly be ordered that the trustee's accounts to March, 1914, be approved, except that for the loss aforesaid, hereby found to have been due to the negligence of the trustee, the trustee be surcharged the difference between the 75 cents per share received from the sale of the fifty-five shares of Olaa stock, and the highest fair average market price of $7 aforesaid. Inasmuch as the estate will be eventually liable to the trustee for commissions of $60.66 already earned, he may deposit in bank to the credit of the estate the amount of the surcharge, $343.75, less this amount of $60.66.

The case will, as above suggested, be now referred to the referee at Hilo, for further disposition.

Reported, 32 Am. B. R. 344.

IN THE MATTER·OF SHOHICHI HOSHIDA, AN ALLEGED BANKRUPT.

June 20, 1914.

Bankruptcy—Service by publication; prerequisites: The proper basis for service by publication under Bankruptcy Act, sec. 18, 30 Stat. 551, am. 32 Stat. 798, is an affidavit showing that personal service of process upon the respondent is impracticable, because he is absent from the jurisdiction and cannot be found. The marshal's return of non est inventus is also desirable practice; but whether essential, not involved.

In Bankruptcy: Motion for service by publication.

Carl S. Carlsmith for petitioners.

CLEMONS, J.   The marshal having made a return of inability to find the respondent after due and diligent search, the question arises as to the proper foundation for an order of publication of notice to the respondent to appear and answer this petition in involuntary bankruptcy.

Is the return of non est inventus alone sufficient?   It is, according to the dictum of Judge Gresham in *Forsyth v. Pierson,* 9 Fed. 801, 803, that "the marshal's return to a subpoena, that one or more of the defendants cannot be found within the district would, no doubt, authorize the court to enter such an order."

But, for the reasons suggested by Judge Dillon in *Bronson v. Keokuk,* 2 Dill., 498, 4 Fed. Cas. 220, No. 1,928, we prefer the thorough-going practice therein pursued, of having "the complainant, or his attorney or agent, most conversant with the facts, make a showing on oath as to the residence of absent defendants."   It is to be noted that the provision of the act of June 1, 1872, 17 Stat. 198, sec. 13, there involved, for service of the warning order "upon the absent defendant, if practicable, wherever found,"

Bronson v. Keokuk, supra, 221, is continued in the new statute now in force, Judicial Code, sec. 57, superseding the act of March 3, 1875, 18 Stat. 472, sec. 8. In any event, the basis of Judge Dillon's ruling, shown in the following excerpt from his decision, would apply to the statute now in force:

"If practicable, says the statute, personal service of the order must be made upon the absent defendant, wherever found; and it is only in cases where such personal service is not practicable, that the statute contemplates that the court shall direct a publication of the order. How is the court to know whether it is practicable to make personal service? This may be ascertained by requiring the complainant, or his attorney or agent, most conversant with the facts, to make a showing on oath as to the residence of absent defendants. If from this it appears that such defendant resides in another district, service upon him may be directed to be made by the marshal of that district; and perhaps, in such a case, the court might make a special order directing or authorizing service by some other officer. If, from the showing, it appears to the satisfaction of the court that the residence of the absent defendant is not known to the complainant, or his agent or attorneys, and cannot, by reasonable diligence, be ascertained (and on this subject the affidavit should state facts, and not mere conclusions), personal service of the order may as well be said not to be practicable, and then the court may direct the order to appear and plead to be published in such manner as it shall deem most likely to give the desired notice."

See, also Collier, Bankruptcy, 9th ed., 420.

As to other details of practice in service by publication, see *In re McDonald,* ante, p. 221, 30 Am. B. R. 120.

The desired order will issue upon the petitioner's compliance with the practice hereinabove approved.

Reported, 32 Am. B. R. 451.

UNITED STATES OF AMERICA v. GEORGE A. BOWER.

June 24, 1914.

Criminal Law—Practice: application of Territorial statutes to United States District Court: A statute in force in the Hawaiian Islands at the time of their annexation to the United States and continued in force in the Territorial courts, providing that the successive disagreement of two juries in a criminal case shall operate as an acquittal, does not govern the United States District Court for the Territory of Hawaii.

Criminal Law: Motion for discharge of defendant.

Jeff McCarn, U. S. District Attorney, and *J. W. Thompson*, Assistant U. S. Attorney, for the United States.

E. A. Douthitt and *L. M. Straus* (*J. L. Coke* with them) for defendant.

CLEMONS, J. The jury having disagreed in two successive trials of the defendant on an indictment for adultery, his counsel move for his discharge on the ground of the applicability of section 2822 of the Revised Laws of Hawaii of 1905, providing in part as follows:

"The successive disagreement of two juries impaneled to try the cause, shall operate as an acquittal of the accused, and the court shall order his discharge from custody."

The defendant contends that this rule of Territorial law in force in Hawaii since 1876 (S. L. 1876, c. 40, s. 3), is made applicable to the Federal court by section 83 of the Organic Act (31 Stat. c. 339, p. 157), which provides that "the laws of Hawaii relative to the judicial department, including civil and criminal procedure, except as amended by this act, are continued in force."

This contention overlooks the obvious fact that section 83 contemplates the "judicial department" of the Territory and not that of the United States,—not only as indi-

cated by the words "judicial department" in their immediate context, but by the fact that chapter IV of the
Organic Act, in which this section occurs, relates to "the
judiciary of the Territory" (see chapter title) and "the
judicial power of the Territory" (see section 81); and by
the fact also that section 86, pertaining to the Federal
court, is placed in a separate, later chapter entitled "United
States officers", thus distinguishing them from Territorial
officers provided for elsewhere.

Moreover, the contention is contrary to the well-settled
intent of the Organic Act. "The Territory of Hawaii is in
every particular, except sovereignty, in the position of a
State; certainly in that position so far as its courts are
concerned." *United States v. Morimoto*, 2 U. S. Dist. Ct.
Haw. 396, 399; *Wilder's S. S. Co. v. Hind*, 108 Fed. 113,
116; *Ex. p. Wilder's S. S. Co.*, 183 U. S. 545, 551; *Equitable L. A. Co. v. Brown*, 187 U. S. 308, 309; *Territory v.
Carter*, 19 Haw. 198, 200, 201; *Territory v. Martin*, Id.,
201, 202-205, 213-214; *Territory v. Morita Keizo*, 17 Haw.
295, 297-299; *Bierce v. Hutchins*, 18 Haw. 511, 518. The
practice of the United States District Court must, then, be
governed in the same way as practice in the Federal courts
in the States. See Organic Act, sec. 86.

This brings us to another contention, less strongly relied
on by counsel but more difficult to dispose of, that section
2822 of the Revised Laws is effective here because in matters of practice not otherwise provided for, this court must
follow the practice existing in Hawaii at the time of annexation. In support of this contention, reliance is had upon
the ruling in *United States v. Moore*, 3 U. S. Dist. Ct. Haw.
66, and the cases therein cited.

In the *Moore* case and the more recent case of *United
States v. Marimoto*, supra, as also in the cases of *United
States v. Reid*, 12 How. 361; *Logan v. United States*, 144
U. S. 263, and *Withaup v. United States*, 127 Fed. 530,
which the *Moore* and *Morimoto* cases follow, it was held

that "the rules of evidence governing Federal courts in criminal trials are those which were in force in the State [or Territory] at the time such courts were established therein, subject to such changes as have been made by Congress." 127 Fed. 530, par. 2.

The reasoning of Chief Justice Taney in the leading case of *Reid*, supra, may seem to justify the following not only of such local rules of evidence, but of such local rules of practice in general, as were in force at the time of the establishment of the Federal court in the particular district. He says, at pages 365-366:

"Neither of these acts [the Judiciary Act of 1789, 1 Stat. 73, 88, and the Crimes Act of 1790 , 1 Stat. 112, 118] make any express provision concerning the mode of conducting the trials after the jury are sworn. They do not prescribe any rule by which it is to be conducted, nor the testimony by which the guilt or innocence of the party is to be determined. Yet, as the courts of the United States were then organized, and clothed with jurisdiction in criminal cases, it is obvious that some certain and established rule upon this subject was necessary to enable the courts to administer the criminal jurisprudence of the United States. And it is equally obvious that it must have been the intention of Congress to refer them to some known and established rule, which was supposed to be so familiar and well understood in the trial by jury that legislation upon the subject would be deemed superfluous. This is necessarily to be implied from what these acts of Congress omit, as well as from what they contain.

"But this could not be the common law as it existed at the time of the emigration of the colonists, for the Constitution had carefully abrogated one of its most important provisions in relation to testimony which the accused might offer. It could not be the rule which at that time prevailed in England, for England was then a foreign country, and her laws foreign laws. And the only known rule upon the subject which can be supposed to have been in the minds of the men who framed these acts of Congress, was that which was then in force in the respective states, and which they were accustomed to see in daily and familiar practice in the state courts. And this view of the subject is confirmed by the provisions in the act of 1789, which refers its courts and officers to the laws of the respective states for the qualifications of jurors and the mode of selecting them. And as the courts of the United States were in these respects to be governed by the laws of the several states, it would seem necessarily to follow that the same principles were to prevail throughout the trial: and that they were to be governed in like manner, in the ulterior proceedings after the jury was sworn, where there was no law of Congress to the contrary.

"The courts of the United States have uniformly acted upon this construction of these acts of Congress, and it has thus been sanctioned by a practice of sixty years. They refer undoubtedly to English works and English decisions. For the law of evidence in this country, like our other laws, being founded·upon the ancient common law of England, the decisions of its courts show what is our own law upon the subject where it has not been changed by statute or usage. But the rules of evidence in criminal cases, are the rules which were in force in the respective states when the Judiciary Act of 1789 was passed. Congress may certainly change it whenever they think proper, within the limits prescribed by the Constitution. But no law of a state made since 1789, can affect the mode of proceeding or the rules of evidence in criminal cases."

Circuit Judge Swayne, in *United States v. Ambrose*, 3 Fed. 283, 285, summarizes the ruling in the *Reid* case as follows:

"The case of the *United States v. Reid*, 12 How. 361, lays down the proposition, and maintains it unanswerably, that, as regards all criminal proceedings and jurisprudence in the courts of the United States, the courts of the United States are in no wise bound by state laws or state practice in anything."

But the rule applied in the *Reid* case, and in the cited cases which follow it, was adopted as a rule of necessity. The Supreme Court there decided that, as the Judiciary Act referred the selection and qualification of jurors in United States courts to the practice then existing in the several

States, respectively, it would seem necessarily to follow that the courts "were to be governed in like manner in the ulterior proceedings after the jury was sworn, *where there was no law of Congress to the contrary*" (it being noted that "ulterior proceedings" within the contemplation of the question before the court, related only to the competency.

other words, that as the Judiciary Act recognized the State practice at the time of the court's creation as governing the selection and qualification of jurors, the court, for rules and practice governing the trial

recognize the same convenient authority as perhaps within the intent of the act. This conclusion, although not very clearly within the act, is yet in harmony with its spirit, especially with the safeguarding words, "where there is no law of Congress to the contrary". This is about as far as the Supreme Court could go in that direction. And the *Reid* case is not, in the opinion of this court, a precedent for recognizing authority in an Hawaiian statute existing at the time of annexation, by which the freedom of prosecutions under a Federal statute is to be curtailed. Are not the acts of Congress by which this court is created and its powers given, necessarily, though impliedly, contrary to the local statutory rule? Do they not exclude it? Or, in other words, is not the local statute itself inconsistent with the Federal statutes? The *Reid* case provides for an obvious necessity, an emergency. No such element exists in the case at bar. The situation is provided for by the natural course of things: there is no obstacle to further proceedings.

It is a startling proposition that a Federal court should in the absence of legislation, be compelled to follow every rule of practice in force in the local courts at the time the district is brought under Federal jurisdiction, even, it may be, a century or more before,—as in the case of the thirteen original colonies, or of the first admitted States,—unless it be in cases of extreme necessity." And it is safe to say, that no Federal court regulates its practice in general by any such guide. No reason can be seen for giving unqualified application to a rule which arose only as a rule of necessity: let it be applied in cases of necessity, but not where its application would curtail the court's inherent powers. For instance, must this court adopt the rest of section 2822 of the Revised Laws and declare an acquittal in every case in which there is "a failure to prosecute upon an information or indictment at the term at which the same is presented against the accused, unless the venue be changed or the case be postponed by the court?"

It may be well to remove some misunderstanding of the rule which might appear from the four authorities about to be noted. In the case of *United States v. Maxwell*, 26 Fed. Cas. 1221, 1222, No. 15,750, Judge Dillon states: "Congress has never enacted a code of criminal procedure, and the States have no power to prescribe either modes of procedure or rules of evidence in prosecutions for Federal offenses. In a general way the Federal courts must be governed in these respects by the common law with the modifications pointed out by the Supreme Court. *United States v. Reid*, 12 How. 361." But Judge Dillon's reference to the *Reid* case clearly implies a qualification of the terms "the common law" to mean "the common law as modified by local law in force at the time of the court's organization" and subject to the provision, "no law of Congress to the contrary". What has just been said of the *Maxwell* case applies to the case of *United States v. Shepard*, 27 Fed. Cas. 1056, No. 16,273, q. v. at 1058.

In *United States v. Coppersmith*, 4 Fed. 198, 204–205, the broad rule just quoted from the *Maxwell* case is qualified by referring to "the laws and usages of the State when the judicial system was organized", "in all matters respecting the accusation and trial of offenders, not otherwise provided for". This concluding proviso would, if taken in a broad sense, distinguish the *Coppersmith* case, and indicate an intent to limit the application of the rule to contingencies of actual necessity.

Foster states that, as a general rule, Federal courts in the several States do not adopt the local procedure, but "follow the old practice at common law, except so far as the same have been changed by a Federal statute." 2 Foster, Federal Practice, 5th ed., 1615, sec. 483. This statement, also, may be misleading, unqualified as it stands; for the learned author, though citing the *Reid* case, notes no limitation with respect to local practice as existing at the time of the Federal court's organization, or otherwise, and fails to cite the *Logan* case, or to cite anywhere in his book Judge Van Devanter's notable opinion in the *Withaup* case.

Counsel's main reliance upon the decision in the *Moore* case, supra, lies, however, in the idea, somewhat difficult to comprehend, that inasmuch as the rule of evidence there enforced was based upon the removal of a disability existing at common law, viz., the disqualification of certain persons as witnesses, so here, as the local rule, Revised Laws of Hawaii, section 2823, removes a disability, as it were, or rather creates a privilege or right, this court must enforce it just as it enforced the right or privilege in the *Moore* case. And in this connection it is urged that section 2822 provides for matter of substance and not mere procedure. It is enough to say that this argument does not truly reflect the basis of the *Moore* decision or of the leading cases of *Reid* and *Withaup* upon which it is founded.

Another decision relied on by counsel is that of *Britton v. Thornton*, 112 U. S. 526, 534-535, holding that a "statute giving a conclusive effect to judgments in ejectment, which they did not have at common law, establishes a rule of property concerning the title to land within the State of Pennsylvania, and binds the courts of the United States as well as the courts of the State." There the statute made conclusive two successive verdicts, or two out of three verdicts, for the same party. The opinion in the leading case of *Miles v. Caldwell,* 2 Wall. 35, cited in the *Britton* case, held a local statutory provision, making "judgment in ejectment a bar to certain future suits, to be a rule of property," and Mr. Justice Miller said: "It is a matter which involves something more than a mere rule of practice. It is a question whether a matter, which is conclusive of the title to land in the State courts, shall have the same effect in the Federal courts." *Miles v. Caldwell,* supra.

Aside from the rule-of-property basis for this decision, it would have been justified by the fact that the case was civil, and governed by Revised Statutes, section 914, adopting local rules of practice, if practice were involved, or at all events by Revised Statutes, section 721, adopting local laws as rules of decision "in trials at common law . . . in cases where they apply", if substantive law were involved. See *Burgess v. Seligman,* 107 U. S. 20, 33.

Something may possibly be said,—though I am not yet persuaded of its soundness,—in justification of an argument that Revised Laws of Hawaii, section 2822, is not a rule of mere procedure at all, and, therefore, not within the rule in the *Reid, Withaup,* and *Moore* cases; that procedure provides mere means, manner, or method of reaching a judicial determination, while a statutory declaration, as here, of the effect of certain facts, partakes, rather, of the nature of substantive law. Suggestive language of Mr. Justice Holmes, in a recent decision, lends support to such an argument, to quote but a single sentence from an illuminative context: "The substantive portion of the section [of the statute of limitations as to crimes] is that no person shall be tried for any offense not capital except within a certain time." *Gompers v. United States,* decision of the United States Supreme Court, May 11, 1914 [233 U. S. 604, 611]. The logic of this view would seem to be, that the statute here in question, itself a kind of statute of limitations, is one of substantive, rather than of adjective law. The distinction is close, recalling other language of the same jurist: "Whenever we trace a leading doctrine of substantive law far enough back, we are very likely to find some forgotten circumstance of procedure at its source." Holmes, Common Law, 253.

The parol evidence rule, also, may be cited as an example of the supposed distinction. Mr. Wigmore says, "the rule is in no sense a rule of evidence, but a rule of substantive law. . . . What the rule does is to declare that certain kinds of fact are legally ineffective in the substantive law; and this of course (like any other ruling of substantive law) results in forbidding the fact to be proved at all." 4 Wigmore, Evidence, §369, sec. 2400. And see Id. sec. 2401; Harriman, Contracts, 2nd ed., sec. 61.

But it may be said, granted that the parol evidence rule is a rule of substantive law rather than of evidence, nevertheless it is applied practically as a rule of evidence. See I Chamberlayne, Evidence, sec. 1710. To this, even if true, it need only be replied, as already indicated, that the urged rule, of applying local procedure, is not regarded as binding upon the Federal courts in matters which are clearly not mere matters of ways and means but are rather matters of substance: the substantive phase is dominant. See the *Gompers* case, ubi sup. And, of course, in Federal criminal law nothing is substantive except as Congress has declared it.

But in denying the motion, without further discussion. I rely on the already sufficiently justified regard of the rule in the *Reid* case as a rule of necessity, not to be applied in this case where its application is not only uncalled for, but where its application would be inconsistent with the inherent, natural, powers of the court. The provision of section 2822 may be wise, but it does not govern this court.

Let the motion be denied.

IN THE MATTER OF W. WAYNE, WITNESS BE-
FORE THE GRAND JURY.

July 7, 1914.

*Evidence—Confidential communications; privilege of witness—Con-
tempt. Information given a journalist as the basis of newspaper
articles is not privileged; and his refusal to disclose to a grand jury
the source of such information would, in a proper case, be contempt
of court.*

*Investigation by grand jury; witness' claim of privi-
lege; contempt in refusal to answer questions.*

*E. W. Sutton (Smith, Warren, Hemenway & Sutton with
him) for respondent.*

*J. W. Thompson, Assistant U. S. Attorney, for the
United States.*

CLEMONS, J. The grand jury having voted on a matter
under consideration, its finding was reported to have become public, in advance of its being regularly reported to
the court; and on an investigation by that body as to who,
if any, of its members had violated his oath of secrecy,
W. Wayne, the city editor of a Honolulu daily newspaper,
from whom a previous witness had testified to having
obtained the information thus prematurely reported, was
called and asked the name of his informant. He declined
to answer. The foreman of the grand jury reported the
facts to the presiding judge, and in open court made a
statement thereof in substance as above. The reluctant
witness then said, in reply to the court's request for the
reason for such refusal:

"The same as would be the reason of any gentleman of
the jury against giving his private business secrets publicity. It is our source of news that we rely on to enable
us to get out a newspaper; and if we break confidence with

the source of news we would lose all of our sources and
would have no newspaper.

"It is a matter of information, was given to me in secrecy,—it is a matter of honor, aside from the newspaper's
standpoint."

In the opinion of the court, the position of the witness
is untenable. Though there is a canon of journalistic
ethics forbidding the disclosure of a newspaper's sources of
information,—a canon worthy of respect and undoubtedly
well-founded, it is subject to a qualification: It must yield
when in conflict with the interests of justice,—the private
interests involved must yield to the interests of the public.

This principle has been applied by this court in the case
of *United States v. Kekauoha*, 3 U. S. Dist. Ct. Haw. 259,
involving communications made by a church member to
church officials. In this case it was said by Judge Dole:

"No private or social or religious obligations can dispense with that universal one which lies on every member
of society to divulge all information in regard to crimes
against the public interests, except as provided by law, in
the recognition of certain communications which are privileged, because of the sentiment that to compel testimony
under the circumstances would be of more prejudice than
value to the public. These privileged communications include those made between attorney and client, husband and
wife, physician and patient, clergyman and penitent, and
some others." Id. 261.

And it is not within the power of a court to add to the
list of communications which are privileged. Even the
privilege as to communications between priest and penitent required a statute for its foundation. Id.; 4 Wigmore.
Evidence, sec. 2394.

And the principle has been enforced specifically as to
communications to newspapers and their representatives.
4 Wigmore, Evidence, 3186, sec. 2286, and note 7, citing,
inter alia, the Parnell Commission's Proceedings, and
United States v. Shriver.

"Such a rule [of privilege] would be in violation of a

sound public policy." Smith's Digest of Precedents of
Privilege of Congress (1894), 828, 848, 856, reporting the
Shriver case, supra.

Thus, in *Ex parte Lawrence*, 116 Cal. 298, 48 Pac. 124,
a newspaper reporter was held to be in contempt of legislative authority in refusing to disclose to a state senate
committee the names of persons from whom he had received information touching a charge of improper conduct
of senators then under investigation. See also *People v.
Durrant*. 116 Cal. 179, 48 Pac. 75, 86, in which was dismissed a similar claim of privilege, with the statement that
"the claim scarcely merits comment."

"For 300 years it has now been recognized as a fundamental maxim that the public (in the words sanctioned
by Lord Hardwicke) has a right to every man's evidence.
We may start, in examining the various claims of exemption, with the primary assumption that there is a general
duty to give what testimony one is capable of giving, and
that any exemptions which may exist are distinctly exceptional and are so many derogations from a positive general
rule." 4 Wigmore, Evidence, 2965, sec. 2192.

"In general, the mere fact that a communication was
made in express confidence, or in the implied confidence
of a confidential relation, does not create a privilege. This
rule is not questioned to-day. No pledge of privacy, nor
oath of secrecy, can avail against demand for the truth in
a court of justice. . . . Accordingly, a confidential
communication to a clerk, to a trustee, to a commercial
agency, to a banker, to a journalist, or to any other person
not holding one of the specified relations hereafter considered, is not privileged from disclosure." Id. 3186-3187,
sec. 2286.

The decision of the supreme court of Georgia, in the case
of *Plunkett v. Hamilton*, 136 Ga. 72, 70 S. E. 781, 35 L.
R. A. (N. S.) 583, follows the California case of *Lawrence*,
above cited, and also the New York case of *People v. Fan-
cher*, 4 Thomp. & C. 467. The court in the latter case sustained an imprisonment for contempt for refusal to give

the name of the writer of a libel published in a newspaper. In a case in the New Jersey supreme court, of a witness before the grand jury, who had testified that he knew the name of the person who furnished the information upon which he had written a certain newspaper article, but refused to give the name, for reasons similar to those advanced by Mr. Wayne, above, the privilege there claimed was characterized by the appellate court as "a privilege which finds no countenance in the law," a privilege "far-reaching in its effect, and detrimental to the due administration of the law." *In re Grunow,* 85 Atl. 1011, 1012. See 4 Jones, Commentaries on Evidence, 620-621, sec. 771.

See, also, 7 A. & E. Enc. L., 2 ed. 47-48, par 3 (a), for a valuable suggestion; and generally as to the court's control over witnesses before the grand jury; *United States v. Caton,* 25 Fed. Cas. 350, No. 14.758; 1 Cranch. C. C. 150; *In re Rogers,* 62 Pac. (Cal.) 47; *Heard v. Pierce,* 8 Cush. (Mass.) 339, 342; *In re Taylor,* 28 N. Y. Supp. 500, 501.

The Maryland statute stands alone in making such communications privileged. It is characterized by Mr. Wigmore as an "enactment . . . detestable in substance [which] will probably remain unique." 4 Wigmore, Evidence, 3187, n. 7.

In consideration of the above authorities, contrary to which no authorities have been found, the witness here must answer the proposed question; or stand committed for contempt of court.

NOTE: After the court had made its opinion as above, Mr. Wayne immediately purged himself of any possible contempt by not only giving the desired information but producing his informant as a witness before the grand jury.

UNITED STATES OF AMERICA v. MARIANO ENSENA.

July 18, 1914.

1. *Indictment—Sufficiency of allegations—Breaking into postoffice:* An indictment does not charge an offense under Penal Code, sec. 192, in alleging "the breaking and entering a certain building used in whole or in part as a postoffice," without describing the portion entered as being used for postoffice purposes.

2. *Same—Same—Statutory crimes—Allegation in language of statute:* Though it is a general rule that it is sufficient to charge a statutory offense in the language of the statute, the rule is not satisfied unless the pleading is certain and unambiguous. *United States v. Lee Kai Fai*, 3 U. S. Dist. Ct. Haw. 627, followed.

3. *Same—Same—Pleading facts by inference:* In criminal pleading an allegation of facts is not to be supplied by implication, at least where the implication is not conclusive.

4. *Same—Same—Allegation by reference aliunde:* Reference in one count of an indictment to facts stated in another count is not unavailing merely because the latter count is insufficient in law.

Indictment: Demurrer to indictment.

J. Wesley Thompson, Assistant U. S. Attorney, for the United States.

Lorrin Andrews for defendant.

CLEMONS, J. The defendant demurs to the three counts of the indictment on grounds hereinafter set forth.

The first count purports to allege a violation of Penal Code, section 192, by the act of:

"Feloniously break(ing) and enter(ing) a certain building then and there used in whole or in part as a postoffice of the United States of America, to-wit, a building at Kukuiaele, . . . with the felonious intent then and there to commit a larceny, that is, to take, steal, and carry away personal goods of another."

The objections to this count are: (1) failure to charge

an offense; (2) indefiniteness and uncertainty in not stating whether the alleged breaking took place in the portion of the building used as a postoffice; and (3) indefiniteness and uncertainty in not stating whether the building was used in whole or in part as a postoffice, or whether the intent was to steal and carry away goods from the portion of the building used as a postoffice or from any other portion of the building.

[1] Though the editors' note to section 192 of Tucker and Blood's Annotated Federal Penal Code, at page 159, hereinafter quoted, may give support to this count as drawn, nevertheless it is my opinion that the reasons which impelled the sustaining of demurrers to a similar form of allegation in the cases of *Sorenson v. United States*, 16S Fed. 785, 788-789, and *United States v. Martin*, 140 Fed. 256, would compel the same conclusion here. See, also, *United States v. Campbell*, 16 Fed. 233, 6 Sawyer 20.

The statute, section 192, reads:

"Whoever shall forcibly break into or attempt to break into any post-office, or any building used in whole or in part as a post-office, with intent to commit in such post-offile, or building, or part thereof, so used, any larceny or other depredation, shall be fined not more than one thousand dollars and imprisoned not more than five years."

This section is the same as Revised Statutes, section 5478, involved in the cases just cited, except that the words "in such postoffice or building, or part thereof, so used" are substituted for "therein." And the editorial note above referred to, says that "the present form of this section is doubtless due to a line of decisions which held that under the former wording no crime was committed unless the defendant broke into or attempted to break into that part of the building actually used as a postoffice". However, the reasoning of Circuit Judge Shelby in *United States v. Martin*, 140 Fed. 256, is applicable here, though there applied to an offense within a State, and not as hereto an offense within a Territory over which Congress has the power of legislation. Judge Shelby said, Id. 257, "A building used in part as a postoffice may have many stories and many rooms not so used, and it was not the intention of Congress, by this statute, to protect from larceny or other depredation property situated in a part of the building not used as a postoffice." Suppose a branch postoffice located in the westerly (makai) ground floor rooms occupied by the von Hamm-Young Company in the Alexander Young building in Honolulu: would this statute be violated by breaking and entering the room of a guest of the Young Hotel on the sixth floor in the extreme easterly (mauka) wing of the building?

The above-noted change in language effected by the Penal Code does not seem to make the intent any more apparent than it was before, to punish the breaking and entering of any place other than one used, or so much thereof as may be used, for postoffice purposes.

[2] Of the contention that this count is good because it "follows the language of the statute", it is enough to say that the general rule that it is sufficient to charge a statutory offense in the language of the statute, is not satisfied unless the pleading is certain and unambiguous. Where the statute makes alternative acts offense, it is of course not following the language of the statute in any sense of the rule to allege the commission of all the alternatives when they are inconsistent with each other. See *United States v. Lee Kai Fai*, 3 U. S. Dist. Ct. Haw. 627; *United States v. Cruikshank*, 92 U. S. 542, 557, 558; *United States v. Potter*, 27 Fed. Cas. 604, No. 16,077, 6 McLean, 182.

The demurrer to this count is, therefore, well founded.

The objections to the second count are: (1) failure to state any crime, and (2) untintelligibility, uncertainty, and want of sense.

A clerical mistake is evident in the striking of the words of the printed skeleton form, "do further present", from the introductory phrase "and the grand jurors aforesaid do further present", and the misplacing of these words below; leaving the names of the defendants, where they first appear, without any apparent grammatical connection with the rest of the count. They may, therefore, be disregarded as neither aiding nor vitiating the allegation. The same comment may be made as to the words in the printed form, "District aforesaid", the preceding words "in the" having been inadvertently stricken out. There then remains the statement that:

"The grand jurors . . . on or about the 22nd day of April, . . . do further present that" the defendants "on the Island of Hawaii and within the Territory and District of Hawaii, unlawfully steal, take, and carry away certain and numerous letters", etc., "out of, and from the Post Office at Kukuihaele, the same being then and there within the custody and control of the Postmaster thereof, and subject to the directions of the Post Office Department of the United States, and the postage necessary for its conveyance having heretofore been paid, and having been delivered to the aforesaid postmaster at said place for distribution to whomsoever addressed; contrary to the form of the statute", etc.

This statement is uncertain for its failure to lay the time of the offense; the date at the beginning of the count cannot avail to fix this time, for if it refers to anything at all, it is only to the grand jury's presentment.

On this ground alone the objection to the second count is well taken. Other infelicities of expression, if not inadequacies, are apparent in this count.

The third count is in the main as follows:

"And the grand jurors aforesaid . . .   do further present that Gregorio Lacruz and Mariano Ensena on or about the 22nd day of April 1914, . . .   on the Island of Hawaii, and within the Territory and District of Hawaii. . . .   did then and there . . .   feloniously . . .   destroy certain letters, packages, postal cards and wrapped newspapers, the necessary postage for the conveyance of same having heretofore been paid, and the same having been deposited and posted in various post offices, and having reached the post office at Kukuihaele for distribution to whomsoever addressed, and having been stolen and carried away as set out in another count of this indictment", etc.

The objections to this count are (1) failure to state any crime; (2) vagueness and uncertainty in the use of the words "necessary postage for the conveyance of same having heretofore been paid;" and (3) vagueness and uncertainty in the reference to "another count of this indictment."

[3] Though this count is wanting in that clearness and certainty required in good pleading, especially in criminal cases, the second objection of vagueness and uncertainty is passed for the first and third, which are more vital. The first objection appears to be well taken. Referring to that portion of the statute upon which this count is based, it will be noted that the mail matter whose destruction is inhibited, is mail matter "before it has been delivered to the person to whom it was directed". This is the only reasonable construction that we can give to the words "the same" in the phrase "or shall open, secrete, embezzle, or destroy the same." Penal Code, sec. 194. Inasmuch as "the functions of the postoffice department, and the powers of the Federal government, are at an end" upon the delivery of the mail matter to the addressee or to his authorized agent, the possibility of such delivery should be negatived,—as is not done here. For all that may be known from the indictment, the mail matter may have come into the addressee's hands before destruction. See *United States v. Sanders*, 27 Fed. Cas. 949, No. 16,219; 6 McLean, 598. This may seem a very strict view; but it is undoubtedly within the rule *fortius contra proferantem*, Joyce, Indictments, sec. 187, which includes the prin-

ciple than in criminal pleading an allegation of facts is
not to be supplied by implication or inference, at least
where, as here, the implication is not conclusive. Id. sec.
246; 22 Cyc. 293-294; *United States v. Post*, 113 Fed. 852,
854.

[4] For the third objection, it is said, that the weakness
of the count to which it refers makes its incorporation in
this count unavailing. I am inclined to disagree with this
contention, *United States v. Ridgeway*, 199 Fed. 286, 288;
but, at all events, as other considerations, as above, dispose
of this count adversely to the government, it is unnecessary to go further.

For the reasons suggested, let the demurrer be sustained.

IN THE MATTER OF THE APPLICATION OF KUME-
KICHI TSUGAWA FOR A WRIT OF HABEAS
CORPUS FOR KOZO KAWACHI.

July 20, 1914.

1. *Immigration—Contract laborer—Labor skilled or unskilled—
Salesman:* The words "contract laborers who have been induced
. . . to migrate to this country . . . to perform labor . . .
of any kind, skilled or unskilled,' in section 2 of the immigration act,
do not, under the provisions of subdivision 5 of rule 11 of immigration
rules, include salesmen.

2. *Same—Same—Salesman:* An alien applying for admission to
the United States, who has been solicited to come by offers of employment as a salesman, is not a "contract laborer" and may not be denied
admission as such, within the provisions of section 2 of the immigration act.

3. *Habeas Corpus—Jurisdiction:* The findings of the board of special inquiry created a situation under which an applicant for admission was entitled to land; the board, however, denied such right, thus
raising a question of law whereby jurisdiction was conferred on this
court under an application for a writ of habeas corpus.

Habeas Corpus: Hearing on return to writ.

Bitting & Ozawa for petitioner.
Jeff McCarn, U. S. District Attorney, for respondent.

DOLE, J.   A writ of habeas corpus was issued in this case upon the filing of the petition therefor.

[1] [2] It appears from the record of the proceedings before the board of special inquiry that Kozo Kawachi came to Honolulu from Japan at the suggestion of Iwahara, a local merchant and a connection by marriage, to work in the store of the latter as bookkeeper and salesman.

The board of special inquiry ruled that *salesmen* came within the description of persons excluded under section 2 of the immigration act.   The words of the act considered as applicable, referring to classes of aliens to be excluded, are as follows:

. . . "persons hereinafter called contract laborers who have been induced or solicited to migrate to this country by offers or promises of employment or in consequence of agreements . . . to perform labor in this country of any kind, skilled or unskilled; . . . And provided further, that the provisions of this law applicable to contract labor shall not be held to exclude professional actors, artists, lecturers, singers, ministers of any religious denomination, professors for colleges or seminaries, persons belonging to any recognized learned profession, or persons employed strictly as personal or domestic servants."

The commissioner general of immigration is required by the act, section 22, to establish such rules and regulations not inconsistent with law as he shall deem best calculated for carrying out the provisions of the act.   Such rules, so established, have the force of law.   *United States v. Sibray,* 178 Fed. 144, 147.

We find in subdivision 5 of rule 11 of immigration rules, so established, referring to the President's proclamation of February 24, 1913, excluding alien laborers, skilled and unskilled, who have passports to any other country than the continental Territories of the United States, the following:

"For practical administrative purposes, the term 'laborer, skilled and unskilled,' within the meaning of the Executive order of February 24, 1913, shall be taken to refer primarily to persons whose work is essentially physical, or, at least, manual, as farm laborers, street laborers, factory hands, contractors' men, stablemen, freight handlers, stevedores, miners, and the like; and to persons whose work is less physical, but still manual, and who may be highly skilled as carpenters, stonemasons, tile setters, painters, blacksmiths, mechanics, tailors, printers, and the like; but shall not be taken to refer to persons whose work is neither distinctly manual nor mechanical, but rather professional, artistic, mercantile, or clerical, as pharmacists, draftsmen, photographers, designers, salesmen, bookkeepers, stenographers, copyists, and the like."

This is a construction of the meaning of the words "laborers, skilled and unskilled," in the President's proclamation, and if applicable to the words quoted from the immigration act, would justify the admission of an alien bookkeeper and salesman who should come under the inducement of offers of employment. Do they so apply? The introductory note to the immigration rules of November 15, 1911, has the following:

"The act entitled 'An act to regulate the immigration of aliens into the United States,' approved February 20, 1907, is the immigration act or law referred to in the following (revised) rules."

The words "within the meaning of the executive order of February 24, 1913," appearing in the second and third lines of subdivision 5 of rule 11, do not appear to limit the application of the construction of the words "laborer, skilled and unskilled," to cases arising under such order. The construction may and should be adopted in all cases within the scope of the expression "for practical and administrative purposes", where the words appear as they do in this case, especially as such construction is supported by or is in line with Federal precedents.

"A laborer in the sense of this statute and this treaty (act of May 6, 1882, an act to execute certain treaty stipulations relating to Chinese, 22 Stat. 58) is one that hires himself out, or is hired out, to do physical toil." *In the matter of Yee Hip*, cited in *In re Ho King*, 14 Fed. 724, 725; *Church of the Holy Trinity v. United States*, 143 U. S. 457; *United States v. Laws*, 163 U. S. 258; 27 Ops. Atty. Gen. 383 (*McNair* case).

The board of special inquiry finds that the employment of Kozo Kawachi, if allowed to land, "will undoubtedly be that of salesman, and perhaps that of bookkeeper", and yet decides to deny him admission on the ground that he is a contract laborer within the meaning of the immigration act, and also that he has been assisted to come with the money of another and has not shown that he does not belong to one of the excluded classes.

[3] Here a question of law is raised, which gives the court jurisdiction, if the ruling of the board of special inquiry thereon is wrong.

"It is of course well settled by abundant authority that the writ of habeas corpus cannot be employed to perform the function of a writ of error or an appeal. There are, however, several recent decisions of the Supreme Court holding that the courts of the United States have jurisdiction to grant relief to a party aggrieved by any action by the head or one of the subordinate officials of a department, when the evidence adduced before such official, and upon which he assumes to act, is wholly uncontradicted, and shows beyond any room for dispute or doubt that the case in any view is beyond the statutes, and not covered or provided for by them." *Ex parte Petterson*, 166 Fed. 536, 539; *Ex parte Watchorn*, 160 Fed. 1014, 1016; *Ex parte Long Lock*, 173 Fed. 208, 215.

The board finds that Kozo Kawachi will work as a salesman and perhaps as a bookkeeper, if admitted. The evidence supports this finding, as it appears that he had worked for one year in his uncle's store, in Japan, in which electrical goods were handled. Under the considerations set forth above, it being established that Kozo Kawachi is an applicant for permission to land, as a salesman, it follows that he is not within the excluded classes described in section 2 of the immigration act, and the board and the Secretary of Labor had no jurisdiction to detain and deport him "by deciding the mere question of law to the contrary." *Gonzales v. Williams*, 192 U. S. 1, 15. He is, therefore, entitled to his discharge, and it is so ordered.

PUGET SOUND COMMERCIAL COMPANY *v.* INTER-ISLAND STEAM NAVIGATION COMPANY, LIMITED.

September 18, 1914.

1. *Admiralty—Evidence of position of a ship under way—Position in relation to line to landmark—Distance:* The testimony of a witness as to the position of a ship under way, in relation to a line from the witness to a conspicuous landmark, is more reliable than his estimate of the distance of such object from himself.

2. *Same—Two witnesses observing vessel from different points—Landmarks—Intersection of lines of direction to landmarks:* Where two witnesses, observing a vessel under way from different standpoints, testify that her position at a particular time is on lines from their respective standpoints to conspicuous landmarks, which lines cross each other, such point of crossing fixes the position of the vessel and, coming from credible witnesses, may be regarded as conclusive.

3. *Same—Towing sailing vessel—Safe offing—Res ipsa loquitur:* A sailing vessel without cargo or ballast was towed out to sea and let go by the tug before her crew had completed setting her sails. They had the heavy hawser to take in, the wind being baffling and changeable, and the sea against her; she attempted to gain the open sea,

tacking several times to port and starboard but losing for the most part, and finally going ashore and becoming a total loss. *Held* that the doctrine of *res ipsa loquitur* applied, and the result showing that she was left in an unsafe place,—unless it should appear that the loss was due either to the fault of those on board or to inevitable accident.

4. *Same—Same—Responsibility of master after being let go:* Under such circumstances the master was justified in persisting in the attempt to make the open sea up to the point where such persistence would expose his ship to obvious danger. At such point he had a good opportunity of giving up such attempt and running in to a safe anchorage. *Held* that he should have made the most of such opportunity, and failing to do so made the owner liable, partially at least, for her subsequent loss.

5. *Same—Liability of tug for failure to give tow safe offing and subsequent assistance, and of tow for failure of good judgment and seamanship:* Held, in view of the negligence of the tug in letting go of such vessel in an unsafe place, and her neglect to render assistance, when it became evident that she was losing ground and approaching danger in her attempt to gain the open sea, and of the failure of the master of such vessel to exercise good judgment and seamanship at such juncture, that both the owner of the tug and the owner of the sailing vessel were jointly liable for her subsequent loss.

In Admiralty: Libel for damages for negligence in towing.

J. W. Russell (*Thompson, Wilder, Watson & Lymer* with him) for libelant.

L. J. Warren (*Smith, Warren, Hemenway & Sutton* with him) for libellee.

Dole, J. It is admitted that both the libelant and libellee are corporations. It is claimed by the libelant in both the count in tort and the count in contract, that the master of the libelant engaged the master of the steamship Keauhou, belonging to the libellee, on the 9th of November, 1912, to tow the Klikitat, a barkentine, out of Hilo harbor, to a safe offing and until ready to proceed with her own sails; that, pursuant to such agreement, the Keauhou

towed the Klikitat out of Hilo harbor and cast off the towline before the Klikitat had been towed out sufficiently
clear of the land to afford her a good and safe offing and
before she had an opportunity to set sail, leaving her in a
dangerous position within about half a mile from the rocks,
and that in consequence of being left in such a position she
went ashore and was so damaged as to be valueless; that
while the Klikitat was in a position of danger the Keauhou could have rescued her by the exercise of ordinary
effort, but negligently failed to do anything in the way of
assistance; that such injury was due solely to the negligence of the libellee and its agents, and that libelant and
those on board the Klikitat were free from any fault or
carelessness contributing thereto.

The libelee admits the towing engagement to the extent
of agreeing to tow the Klikitat sufficiently clear of the land
to afford her a good and safe offing, but denies that there
was any stipulation in relation thereto that libellee should
continue to tow her until she should be ready to proceed
under her own sails, except as such a condition might be
implied in any case of the towing of a vessel to sea for the
purpose of taking her to a point sufficiently safe and distant
from land, whence she could safely proceed under her own
sails if handled in the usual and seaman-like manner; but
alleges that the Keauhou towed the Klikitat in a northeasterly direction from the whistling buoy, at the entrance
of Hilo harbor, to a point approximately three miles or
more northeast of the whistling buoy and there released
her, having given notice of intention to do so by blowing
the steam whistle and slowing down; that the Klikitat
then had practically all her sails set, and then and for some
time theretofore had good steerage way and was drawing
well away on her towline under a fresh breeze and was
ready to proceed and did proceed on her voyage. And it
denies that the wreck of the Klikitat was due to her being
cast off by the Keauhou as aforesaid or as claimed. Libellee

further denies that while the Klikitat was in a position of danger the Keauhou could, by the exercise of any ordinary effort, have saved her from destruction, and denies that the Keauhou carelessly or negligently omitted to render such assistance, and alleges that at no time except during the few minutes before said Klikitat went ashore did it appear to the Keauhou or any persons on board that the Klikitat was in a position of danger, she being at all times apparently under full control and having at all times when near shore and until a few minutes before going ashore, been over safe anchorage ground; that at all the times when the "Klikitat approached nearer land she was sailing well in a safe and free course to sail directly back into Hilo harbor, and to the observation of those on board the Keauhou, such appeared to have been her intention"; that such return could well have been effected at any time, or the Klikitat could have dropped her anchor and rode safely at anchor at any time, and no danger could have been apprehended by the servants of the libellee in time for them to have rendered assistance. Libellee further alleges that the loss of the Klikitat was due solely to the negligence and want of ordinary care and seamanship on the part of those on board, and that libellee and its agents were free from any fault or negligence contributing to such loss. The claim of the libelant as to the value of the Klikitat in the sum of ten thousand dollars, is denied by the libellee.

It is satisfactorily shown that early in the afternoon of the 9th of November, 1912, the Keauhou proceeded to tow the Klikitat out of Hilo harbor and that the time consumed in the towing was approximately 50 minutes; that the time consumed after passing the whistling buoy to the time the hawser was cast off was approximately 40 minutes; that from the start of the tow the crew of the Klikitat proceeded to set up their sails, and that at the time the hawser was cast off she was on the starboard tack with the fore-and-aft sails set, also one of the squaresails on the foremast.

Upon being cast off the crew of the Klikitat with a donkey engine, tried to take in the hawser and, finding it slow work, abandoned it for the time being in order to finish setting sail. With the light winds then prevailing it appeared to be impracticable for the Klikitat to tack, such movement being desirable because she was not heading clear of Pepeekeo point which was off her port bow, and the master decided to wear ship which took considerable time, and he came up into the wind at a place perhaps slightly more favorable for proceeding to sea. About this time the hawser was cut. It is not clear to me whether it was cut before or after the vessel wore around; the probabilities are that it was before. From then on the Klikitat beat back and forth in her attempt to gain the open sea, going to leeward and toward the shore all the time. She was finally close to the shore in the neighborhood of the place where she went ashore, still apparently trying to get out to sea. The wind was variable, swinging from easterly to northeast to north and to the west of north, blowing in squalls, with calms between. I judge that the wind was generally favorable for the return to the harbor if the master of the Klikitat had so desired; but he continued his efforts to put out to sea, losing with every tack, until finally, when perhaps he was trying to return to the harbor, there was a calm during which he dropped anchor and then was struck by a considerable squall with his sails aback; the anchor failed to hold and he was swept ashore.

The libelant's witnesses substantially agree in fixing the place where the towline was cast off at a point less than a mile from the whistling buoy and less than a mile from the shore. This, I think, is not borne out by the evidence in the case and the circumstances existing at the time. The captain of the Klikitat allows 50 minutes as the time consumed in the tow. As the distance from the start to the whistling buoy is about a mile or a little more, the distance beyond the whistling buoy of less than a mile would make an aggregate distance for the tow of approximately two miles, and it is difficult to account for the tow's consuming 50 minutes and going only about two miles although witnesses for libelant state that the two proceeded slowly, sometimes almost stopping during squalls.

Mr. Brigham, who testified for the libellee, was so far as appears, an entirely disinterested witness. He observed the movements of the tow and of the Klikitat after being cast off, from the window of his office at the shore end of the breakwater. He was interested in making a close observation of these movements from the fact that he was building a tug for the work of the breakwater, with which he expected to do some towing in the harbor of Hilo; and, as this was the first tow he had seen there, he was anxious to see how it worked and to asertain whether the tug he was building and had designed would answer the same purpose. In watching the progress of the tow, he took the line from his position to Pepeekeo point as the line from which to offset the movements of the tow and Klikitat after she was cast off. He found that the Klikatat was cast off almost exactly on this line, and fixes her position on the map, exhibit A, when cast off at a point three miles from the whistling buoy and one and six-tenths miles from the Papaikou mill. He stated that upon being cast off the Klikitat was sailing on the starboard tack inshore; then she wore ship and came around to the port tack and went offshore a short distance to a point a little outside of the line mentioned, marked on the map, exhibit A, "TWB 5", at which point the Klikitat went about and came inshore to "TWB 6", during which movement more sails were set.

Mr. Drummond, a witness for the libellee, observed the Klikitat from the same point that Brigham had been looking from. He says, "My attention was called to her being out there and I took a look at her; she was quite a distance off to the right of the line between the breakwater and Pepeekeo point, probably a quarter of a mile." He marked

the place as "1" on exhibit 4. He further said that he did
not see a tug near the Klikitat or any other vessel outside
the harbor besides the Klikitat. This corresponds with the
position fixed by Brigham at "TWB 5", as the outward
point from said line, reached by the Klikitat after wearing
ship for the first time or with "TWB 7", the second point
reached by the Klikitat outside of such line.

[1] Capt. Bruhn said that "as we passed the Klikitat on
our return, the whistling buoy was pretty near in line with
Pueo." The testimony of the witnesses as to positions
based on conspicuous landmarks, is more reliable than their
estimates of distances, especially as to distances from the
witness in a direct line away. I therefore recognize Capt.
Bruhn's statement of his alignment with the whistling
buoy and Pueo, and also Mr. Brigham's conclusion as to
the place where the tow was cast off as aligned with his
point of view and Pepeekeo point, as reliable. Adjusting
these two estimates, the place at which the hawser was cast
off must be nearer to Mr. Brigham than he estimated it.
This point is on a line between Mr. Brigham's point of
observation and Pepeekeo point and also near a line with
the whistling buoy and Pueo. Mr. Brigham's testimony
as to the position of the tow at the point the hawser was
cast off as on a line between him and Pepeekeo point, is
more to be relied on than Capt. Bruhn's testimony as to the
distance he towed the Klikitat from the whistling buoy.
and must fix the place where the tow was cast off at a point
approximately near where a line from Pueo through the
whistling buoy would cut the line from Brigham's office
to Pepeekeo point. This place, however, must be farther
north than that point for the reason that Bruhn noticed
that "as we passed the Klikitat on our return the whistling
buoy was pretty near in line with Pueo", which means that.
as the turn was made to starboard, the place where the
hawser was let go must be farther north than where the
whistling buoy and Pueo line would cut the breakwater and

Pepeekeo line.   It is not easy to fix such place but it may be approximated with the assistance of some of the other evidence.   The distance to the whistling buoy from the place where the Klikitat was anchored, which may be taken as the start of the tow, may with the varying estimates be taken approximately as one and twenty-hundredths miles. A point on the breakwater and Pepeekeo line forty-two hundredths mile north of the place where it would be cut by an extension of the Pueo and whistling buoy line, is giving as much leeway as seems justified by its departure from its line of towing made by the Keauhou in turning after cutting loose the hawser, when Capt. Bruhn testifies that they passed the Klikitat on their return about one hundred feet away, at which time he noticed that he was in line with the whistling buoy and Pueo.   Such point is two and twenty-hundredths miles from the whistling buoy, which with the one and twenty-hundredths miles from the whistling buoy to the start of the tow makes three and forty-hundredths miles; and as the speed of the Keauhou on her return was anything from seven to nine knots, or miles, an hour, she may have covered no more than three and a half knots or miles, during the half hour occupied in her return, especially as her place of anchorage is not given and, as Mullins, the assistant engineer of the Keauhou, says, "There was no particular reason for hurrying; there was plenty of time."

The speed of the tow is variously estimated at two knots, two or three miles, four or five miles, and four and a half or five knots an hour; and the time of the tow beyond the whistling buoy may be taken approximately as 40 minutes, which at a speed of three miles would give a distance of two miles; at a speed of three and a half miles would give a distance of two and thirty-three hundredths miles.   The greater speeds and longer distances testified to seem out of question in view of the testimony of Brigham and Bruhn, analyzed above.

This result is in a measure supported by the testimony of Murray, the chief engineer, and Mullins, the assistant engineer of the Keauhou.   Murray says full speed was reached by the tow half a mile before reaching the whistling buoy, and they went at full speed 45 minutes.   Mullins' testimony substantially agrees with this.   They both say the speed of the tow was from four and a half to five miles, or knots.   If we take it at four and a half miles, 6 2/3 minutes would be consumed before reaching the whistling buoy, leaving 38 1/3 minutes for the tow outside of the whistling buoy and a distance of two and eighty-seven-hundredths miles.

Capt. Bruhn says they got up full speed with the tow half way between the knuckle buoy and whistling buoy, and it took them seven minutes to reach the whistling buoy from there.   Allowing 40 minutes for the tow outside at the same speed,—four miles an hour, the distance reached was two and eighty-five-hundredths miles.

Brigham says the speed of the tow to the whistling buoy was a little under three miles an hour, and outside of the buoy four or five miles, and that the tow took a trifle over an hour.   Taking the speed outside at four and inside at three miles an hour, we have about 24 minutes consumed in reaching the whistling buoy, leaving 36 minutes for the tow outside, giving a distance outside of two and forty-hundredths miles.

So, taking conservative figures as to times and speeds from the witnesses for the libellee, we obtain distances beyond the whistling buoy supposedly reached by the tow, varying from two and forty-hundredths to two and eighty-seven-hundredths miles, and this without using the evidence of Lawson and Ahu, witnesses for the libellee, who fix the distance at one and twenty-five hundredths to one and five-tenths and two miles respectively, or the evidence of the witnesses for the libelant, Capt. Nelson, Hansen and Boswell, who estimate the distance at five-tenths, seventy-five-hundredths and sixty-hundredths mile, respectively.

A tendency is noticeable in some of the witnesses on both sides to favor the side on which they were called.   This is referred to without criticising the honesty of such witnesses, inasmuch as their observations were mainly casual, not apprehending the subsequent disaster.   Under such circumstances a good deal of guessing was unavoidable as was also the tendency, unconsciously perhaps, to guess favorably toward the side representing their respective employers.

[2] With this great divergence in the testimony on this point, I feel that it is safe to rely upon the crossing of the lines of direction fixed by Brigham and Bruhn, as outlined above, and the necessary correction thereof on account of the departure of the Keauhou from the line of the tow in turning around to the point where she was on the line through the whistling buoy and Pueo, thus fixing the point where the tow was cast off somewhere north of such crossing of lines, which the court finds to be approximately at "X Ct." on the maps,—exhibits A and B, and two and twenty-hundredths miles from the whistling buoy.

Was this point a safe locality at which to cast loose the Klikitat under all the circumstances?   The circumstances were these: Although the libellee's witnesses who were on the Keauhou generally agree that the wind was easterly, varying according to some to south of east, a very favorable direction for the Klikitat in getting out to sea, yet the weight of evidence favors the conclusion that, although varying and interspersed with calms, and squally at times, its general direction was about northeast, varying toward the north and northwest.   Hansen, a sailor on the Klikitat, who was aloft loosening sail when the hawser was cast off and therefore in a favorable position for observing, says the sails during the tow did not keep filled, kept shaking all the time, did not draw, wind was squally, and yet the tow was proceeding toward the northeast according to Bruhn or

even more northerly if the point found by the court, "X
Ct.", exhibit A, for the letting go the hawser, is correct.
Mosher, pilot and harbor master, testified that when the
Klikitat was coming in toward the harbor the wind was
north on the wharf and appeared to be north and northeast farther outside.   Murray said that after they cast off
the hawser the wind "was coming away from Pepeekeo",
which would signify a northerly wind.   At one time in
Hansen's examination, he said the wind was five or six
points on the weather bow at the time the Keauhou gave
the signal blast.   This does not agree with his testimony
as to the action of the wind on the sails during the tow
outside of the whistling buoy, and must stand for what it
is worth.   It corresponds in a way, however, with Capt.
Nelson's testimony that the wind was northeast, east-
northeast and north-northeast, blowing in all directions.
It would seem that, in view of this testimony and that of
Bruhn and Simerson, the wind sometimes on that afternoon
swung around to an easterly direction.   This must, however, have been exceptional, as the weight of the testimony
is convincing that its prevailing directions were from the
northeast around northerly to a northwesterly direction.
If the wind was northeast or northerly or northwesterly at
the point where Bruhn testifies the Klikitat was cast off,
she would have been compelled to fall away several points
to port to fill her sails, which was what happened according to the testimony of those on board.   The same would
have been the result if she was cast off at "X Ct.", exhibit
A, with the wind northeast or more northerly, in which
case she would have pointed well inside of Pepeekeo point
as was the case according to the testimony of Brigham, of
Boswell, the mate of the Klikitat, and of Nelson, the master, as she could not sail nearer than six points to the wind
according to him.   Boswell said the wind was baffling and
"heading us off to the shore" and Nelson said, in answer
to the question "What did you do then?", referring to the

time of the casting off of the hawser, "After I got my sails
on I wore the ship around as I was heading toward the
shore . . . I was headed about northwest, something
in that neighborhood", and added, in answer to a question
about the conditions of the sea, "It was a northeast swell
setting right . . . in toward the land", which is supported by Capt. Bruhn of the Keauhou, who said, "The sea
was a kind of little northerly swell . . . coming along
the land from Pepeekeo way." Nelson afterward described the swell as setting in toward the northwest. The
evidence that the swell was from a more northerly point
is borne out by the evidence as to the effect of the sea on
the Klikitat on her starboard tacks.

As to the progress made by the crew of the Klikitat in
setting its sails at the time she was let go, it is satisfactorily
shown that the fore-and-aft sails were up and one of the
square sails on the foremast. According to Capt. Nelson,
it took him three-quarters of an hour to finish making sail,
which is substantially supported by Brigham. When
asked why he wore ship, he replied, "We had to get around
to stand to seaward. Q. You couldn't tack? A. I didn't
have sails enough on her and the wind was too light to
tack." He also said she "was up in the wind and not taking the wind when the hawser was let go." Mate Boswell
said they didn't have sail enough up when cast off to navi-
gate her safely. And Otto, one of the crew, said "She was
helpless then when she was dropped . . . because she
did not have enough sails on her and at the time the hawser
was over the bow."

Another circumstance was that the Klikitat was without a load, which must have been obvious to all who saw
her. Mullins, in speaking of the speed of the tow, said.
"She was not a heavy tow, because she was light." Lawson, the cook, said, when asked if the Klikitat had any
cargo on board, "Not a thing but stores and a little dunnage wood." Capt. Nelson says she was drawing 16-6

(meaning feet and inches) when they left Port Gamble and 9-6 when they left Hilo; that they had nothing on board. "We sailed without ballast." Hansen said she was pretty light out of water, had a lot of her hull showing. A sailing vessel without a load is at a disadvantage in beating; some, however, doing better than others on account of their build. The tendency is to drift or move sideways when sailing close hauled or into the wind. It appears that from the time the Klikitat was cast off, although she was trying to get out to sea, away from the land, she steadily approached the shore where she was finally wrecked. She would point one way and move in a different direction. This was obviously due largely to the fact that she had no cargo or ballast. There was another condition, however, affecting her progress that added materially to the difficulty she had in trying to beat out to sea, and that was the northerly swell referred to above, which struck her starboard side whenever she was on the starboard tack, pointing northerly or northwesterly, tending to force her in toward the shore. Brigham's statement as to her movements back and forth, tacking and wearing,-- the most reliable testimony given on that point, shows that after being cast off she invariably lost on her starboard tacks when the sea was against her, and made fair headway on her port tacks when the sea was in her favor or at any rate not against her. To illustrate, referring to exhibit A at "TWB 3", she wore around, coming up into the wind on her port tack, that is, with the wind on her port side, on which leg she ran out to sea beyond the Pepeekeo and breakwater line above referred to, to "TWB 5"; then coming about, she sailed on the starboard tack and drifted, or "slid", as Brigham put it, inshore to "TWB 6"; wearing or tacking there, she proceeded on her port tack out to sea again beyond the Pepeekeo and breakwater line to "TWB 7"; then presumably tacking, she again drifted, or slid, on the starboard tack directly inshore to "TWB 8";

another leg on the port tack took her out to "TWB 9";
when she had to come about to the starboard tack as she
was approaching the reef toward the breakwater, and on
such starboard tack, with the swell against her starboard
side, she sailed and drifted directly to the place near where
she finally went ashore, where she luffed up and dropped
her anchor.   On her starboard tacks, although pointing
northerly or northwesterly, it appears that she moved more
or less sideways almost directly inshore, while on her port
tacks she made progress toward the open sea which was
more than lost on her starboards tacks.   While the court
does not recognize the places fixed on the map by Brigham as reliably giving the distances from his position
reached by the Klikitat for the reasons already stated, it
accepts them as approximately showing her movements
transversely to the line between the breakwater and Pepeekeo point.   Thus we have these important circumstances
existing at the time the Klikitat was cast off by the Keauhou at a point approximately two and twenty-hundredths
miles outside of the whistling buoy;—a baffling wind interspersed with squalls and calms, and blowing mainly from
the northeast and more northerly; a northerly swell; the
crew of the Klikitat engaged in making sail with a long,
heavy hawser to take in, and she without cargo or ballast.

The testimony as to the proper distance for towing sailing vessels out from Hilo harbor before letting them go
varies greatly.   It is clear, however, that what is a safe distance depends on the condition of the weather and the sea
and the sailing conditions of the vessel as to her lading.
These distances as given vary from one to five miles beyond the whistling buoy.   It is deemed essential that they
shall be left in a position from which they can clear the
heads,—Pepeekeo and Leleiwa points.

[3] I cannot avoid the conviction that the master of the
Keauhou failed to take the Klikitat out to a safe offing, in
view of the fact that she was without cargo or ballast, and

of the condition of the wind and sea then existing. Both R. Nelson and Mosher regarded the fact of the Klikitat's being light, as placing greater responsibility on the tug. The facts that the crew of the Klikitat had not completed making sail at the time she was let go and that her hawser was still to be taken in, may well be regarded as important elements of the situation that add weight to the complaint against the libellee. The doctrine of *res ipsa loquitur* may be cited in support of this conclusion, inasmuch as results showed that the Klikitat was left in an unsafe place, unless it should appear that her loss was due either to the fault of those on board of her or to inevitable accident. *The Steamer Webb*, 81 U. S. 406, 414. There is no claim on either side that the disaster was due to the latter cause; but the libellee claims that it was due to the master's neglect and bad seamanship.

[4] The testimony in regard to what was first done on board upon being let go is somewhat confusing. The witnesses from the Klikitat, including the master, agree that they first proceeded to go on with the work of making sail. They must have relinquished this before it was completed, and devoted themselves to the hawser, first, trying to haul it in, and then cutting it, as Capt. Nelson says they completed making sail three-quarters of an hour after the hawser was cut, and Brigham's testimony that she increased sail between "TWB 5" and "TWB 6" sugstantially agrees with this. I am not able to find that what was done or not done in relation to the hawser showed evidence of bad seamanship; certainly the cutting of the hawser was a sacrifice tending to favor the safety of the vessel.

The fact that Capt. Nelson made no protest by signals to the Keauhou, after being let go, affords no basis for argument against his seamanship, as he was a stranger in those waters and may well have supposed at the moment that the master of the Keauhou knew what he was about.

Wolf v. Çalkins, 2 Fed. 788, 793; *The Naos,* 144 Fed. 292, 300.

I feel that Capt. Nelson showed a want of judgment in persisting in his efforts to beat out to sea when he found he was losing ground with every tack and most emphatically so on his starboard tacks. According to all the testimony he had the opportunity, while on his last port tack across the entrance to the harbor, of sailing in with a free wind to a safe anchorage inside; to tack again to starboard and persist in the attempt to beat out to sea at that stage was a blunder. This movement took him directly to the dangerous position from which he was unable to escape by maneuvering or to render secure by anchoring. The question whether he should have taken in sail before anchoring in this predicament hardly concerns the issue. It cannot be said that if he had deferred anchoring until he had taken in sail the anchor would then have saved him. His ship would certainly by that time have drifted in nearer to the lee shore where it was wrecked. For some reason or other his anchor did not hold. Is it likely that it would have held any better if he had waited until he had taken in sail and the ship had drifted farther inshore? If it was an error to drop anchor first, which I do not believe, it was an error *in extremis* and not negligence. *The Steamer Webb,* 81 U. S. 405, 417. The anchor by all accounts was a sufficient one for the vessel. Why it dragged is variously accounted for by the wind squall, by the fact that there was no holding ground, the sea bottom there being gravel from the Wailuku river, and by the supposition that the anchor chain broke, of which there is no evidence.

He should have dropped the port anchor as soon as he found the starboard anchor was dragging, and the failure to do so, either because it was not ready or because he decided not to do it, would seem to be a failure to do all that should have been done to hold the vessel from going

ashore until relief might be had. He said he did not have
a chance to drop his port anchor. If it had been ready,
with cable laid out, it would have taken no time to speak
of. Yet it is uncertain that it would have done any good
if it had been put out.

The question arises from this showing, whether or not
both parties were responsible for the loss,—the libelant
through the mistaken judgment and defective seamanship
of its agent, the master of the Klikitat, and the libellee by
reason of the failure of its agent, the master of the Keauhou, to give the Klikitat a safe offing. Does the mistake
in judgment of Capt. Nelson, which led eventually to the
wreck of the Klikitat, relieve the libellee from liability for
its failure to give the Klikitat a safe offing, whereby she
was placed in a situation which resulted in her destruction
through the failure of her master to exercise good judgment and seamanship? The solution of this question may
be aided by first considering the point raised by the libelant, that the master of the Keauhou neglected his duty in
his failure to look after the Klikitat and assist her after he
had let her go, when it was evident from her movements
that she was losing ground in her efforts to gain the open
sea.

It appears from the evidence that after the Klikitat was
let go, the master of the tug paid little attention to her
movements and did not seem to consider that he had any
further responsibility in the matter,—"looked around once
or twice; I think I looked around at her",—and yet he did
observe that she was losing ground in her effort to gain the
open sea. Upon the return of the Keauhou to her anchorage, Capt. Bruhn noticed the Klikitat at a place marked
"B 3" on exhibit B, less than a third of a mile from the
shore by the map. From there he gives her course on the
map to "B 4, 5, 6, and 7"; the latter place being where
she luffed up and dropped her anchor and from whence she
moved ashore. He says at no time before she came around

off Honolii Gulch, which the court understands to correspond to "B 7" on the map, did it become evident to him that she might be in danger; and yet it must be obvious to any one, especially to a sailor, that from "B 3" to "B 7" she was tacking back and forth in an effort to get away from Hilo harbor, not to enter it, and losing all the time. It should have been evident to him that after tacking to starboard from "B 6", exhibit B, or perhaps more correctly from "TWB 9", exhibit A, and still beating out, she was in danger.

[5] Does the fact that the Klikitat could have reached safety by giving up her puprose for the time being of proceeding on her voyage and entering Hilo harbor, relieve the libellee from responsibility; first, for its failure to take the Klikitat out to a safe offing and, second, for its failure to render her assistance when it became evident that she could not make the open sea with her own sails? The Klikitat was bound for the mainland. The master was naturally unwilling to give up his attempt to get away from the shore, and was justified in persevering up to the point where such persistence would expose his ship to danger. This point the court finds to be the starboard tack from "B 6" to "B 7", exhibit B, or, according to exhibit A, from "TWB 9" to "TWB 10", which statement of her movements the court regards as the more reliable of the two. Deciding to go about on the starboard tack instead of giving up and running in to an anchorage in Hilo harbor was, at the worst, a mistake in judgment involving defective seamanship by one new to those waters, and who may be said to have been brought into such an emergency by the failure of the libellee to give his vessel a safe offing. I am inclined to the opinion that, having undertaken to tow the Klikitat to a safe offing and finding after he had let her go that she was losing ground in her attempt to beat out to sea and was nearing danger, considering her evident persistence in beating out to sea, it was the duty of the master

of the Keauhou, in the exercise of ordinary care and vigilance for the safety of his tow, to have proceeded to her assistance,—his contract under the circumstances not having been completely performed when he cast off her hawser, as shown by the result. *The Printer*, 164 Fed. 314.

The fact of the vessel dragging her anchor simply illustrates one of the dangers to which she was exposed by the action of the libellee.

I do not find negligence on the part of the libelant except possibly in not having its port anchor ready to drop without loss of time, but it is chargeable with bad judgment and defective seamanship in persisting in beating out to sea after tacking at "TWB 9", exhibit A, and perhaps before that time.

The libellee failed to carry out its contract to tow the Klikitat to a safe offing and consequently remained thereafter in a measure responsible for her safety, which responsibility it could have discharged by giving her timely assistance. The duty of a tug to its tow is a continuing one until the completion of the towing contract. In this case the obligation of reasonable care continued until the Klikitat was safe at sea or safe back in Hilo harbor. *The Printer*, 164 Fed. 314, 316; *Alaska v. Williams*, 128 Fed. 362.

In view of these findings, I am of the opinion that there was a division of responsibility between the parties, justifying an equal division of the loss and the costs.

As to the value of the Klikitat at the time of her loss, the testimony varies from fifty-five hundred to ten thousand dollars. The market for lumber schooners at the Sound had been dull for two years previously and was improving in 1912, especially in the fall. Two witnesses, O. A. Case and E. C. Genereaux, both of them marine surveyors, made official surveys of her in June, 1912, for purpose of sale, and both assessed her value at ten thousand dollars. J. L. Hubbard, a ship-builder, long acquainted with the

Klikitat, made the same estimate and called it a conservative one. The market in November was more favorable than in June. W. Walker, chief engineer of the Puget Sound Mill Company, which owned an interest in the Klikitat, had overhauled her thirteen years before. He said, without professing to name her market value, "If anybody wanted a vessel like her ten thousand dollars would be cheap for her." Of the witnesses testifying to a lower value were C. L. Saunders, who had not seen the Klikitat for five or six years; C. E. Wilson, a marine broker, who testified that early in 1912 she was offered to him to sell for eight thousand dollars, and that he did not act in the matter until about the time she sailed and then she had gone; and H. S. Garfield, a marine broker, who was familiar with market prices of sailing vessels in June, 1912, but was not buying or selling in November. He says she was worth six thousand dollars in November, basing such valuation on market value of other vessels estimated in June. Moreover, he had not seen the Klikitat during 1912. I consider the weight of testimony to decidedly favor the larger estimates. Considering broker's charges for selling, the fact that the Klikitat was in Hawaii at the time of her loss, and the time and expense of getting her back to the Sound on the theory of her sale, together with the receipt of one hundred and ten dollars realized at the auction sale of the wreck, I feel that a valuation of nine thousand dollars immediately previous to her loss would not be unfair to either party, and so find.

During the course of the proceedings, Capt. Nelson filed a motion for leave to intervene for loss of personal property in the wreck and afterward testified as to the articles lost and as to their first cost in some cases. In such a matter probably the fair rule is to estimate what it would cost to replace the lost articles, which were in good condition, rather than to consider their market value. By such a rule the aggregate loss would approximate one hundred dollars. Lawson's testimony as to the landing of the captain's trunk the next day, and his remark as to the contents, is too indefinite to be considered as against Capt. Nelson's testimony. There is no showing as to what part or proportion of the hundred and ten dollars that was bid for the wreck and its contents related to Capt. Nelson's personal property.

In the consideration of the complicated testimony brought out in this case, I have not referred to the question of signals in relation to the casting off of the towing-hawser, made much of by counsel, not deeming it to have any special bearing on the issue. Nor have I felt the evidence to the effect that during the tow the Klikitat at times drew up to some extent on her towline, that is, gained on the tug, showing a fair wind, to be of importance. With the varying direction of the wind, the fact that this sometimes happened does not affect the preponderating weight of the evidence as to the prevailing general direction of the wind.

The testimony in regard to distances is somewhat confused by the indiscriminate use by the sailor witnesses of the words *knots* and *miles* in testifying as to speed of the tow and of the Keauhou on her return. Although the word "knot" is a measure of rate of speed per hour, yet it indirectly gives distances in nautical miles, which are longer than the standard or statute mile. It seemed hopeless, however, to act upon the distinction between the two words; and it is believed that whatever error in regard to distances may exist in this opinion on that account is insufficient to substantially vary the results reached.

Under the considerations hereinbefore set forth, a decree may be entered, awarding the libelant the sum of forty-five hundred dollars, with interest from December 4, 1912, the date of service, and one-half the costs, and one-half the costs to the libellee, and fifty dollars to J. A. Nelson.

IN THE MATTER OF LEE LEONG, DOING BUSINESS AS THE SHANGHAI DRY GOODS CO., BANKRUPT.

October 17, 1914.

1. *Bankruptcy—Attorney's fees:* Discussion of proper allowance to attorney for petitioning creditors, whose attendance in court at a place remote from his residence, involves protracted absence from his office.

2. *Same—Referee—Review of findings:* The rule of presumption in favor of a referee's finding does not apply where the finding is based on undisputed facts set out in the record.

In Bankruptcy: On review of order of referee.

J. W. Russell, petitioning attorney, *pro se.*
C. S. Carlsmith for the trustee.

CLEMONS, J.   This matter is before the court on petition of the trustee for review of the referee's order awarding to the attorney for the petitioning creditors a fee of $750 for services to the estate, as follows:

1.   Preparing and filing petition for adjudication;
2.   Investigation of law as to questions suggested by fact that two of the respondent firm were minor children of the other member;
3.   Trip from Hilo to Honolulu involving attorney's absence of five full business days from office, for attendance upon hearing of petition;
4.   Attendance at hearing and services in securing amendment of petition to make parent sole respondent;
5.   Preparing and serving upon county sheriff, notice of adjudication and of stay of pending attachment;
6.   Advice and attention as to custody of property;
7.   Writing to bankrupt's attorney and finally threatening contempt proceedings, in endeavor to procure filing of schedules;
8.   Obtaining correct addresses of creditors for purpose of giving notice of first creditors' meeting; preparing and mailing notices to creditors, and preparing proof of notice;

9.   Attendance at first meeting of creditors, and one continuance thereof;

10.   Securing fire insurance on property in place of insurance cancelled by reason of attachment.

It will be noted that items 1 and 2 cover the same work, also items 3 and 4.   Item 10 represents services not specially mentioned in the referee's decision, but which indicate that counsel was not only diligent in the usual routine of the case, but looked after the interests of the creditors in a practical way worthy of high commendation.   Likewise, item 6 represents foresight and economy which secured such custody of the property as would be satisfactory to all concerned and save the extra expense of seizure by the marshal.

The fee of $750 does not cover transportation and hotel expenses of $126, a special bill for which was allowed by the referee without objection.

The estate, inventoried at $13,231.06, realized $6,481.04 from sales of merchandise and $192.11 from collections on book accounts of $573.59.   Proved claims aggregated $18,566.76.

Services to creditors prior to preparation of petition for adjudication, in the matter of a general assignment for benefit of creditors, and of a pending attachment by certain creditors, were not considered by the referee, and no contention is made here that they were entitled to any consideration.   See *In re Hart & Co.*, 3 U. S. Dist. Ct. Haw. 73;   16 Am. B. R. 275;   *Randolph v. Scruggs*, 190 U. S. 533, 537-538.

The case was in no way difficult—it was only unusual. The property of the bankrupt was already secure under writ of attachment of the Territorial court.   And the question which arose from the fact that the bankrupt was doing business under a firm name with his two minor children as purported partners, could not possibly have given counsel any embarrassment;   for in a petition against a firm an amendment may permit an adjudication against one of the

members alone: *In re Richardson*, 192 Fed. 50, 27 Am.
B. R. 590 (Mass.); Collier, Bankruptcy, 10th ed., 416.
As a matter of fact, in making the petition against the
father and his infant children, counsel here had as a guide,
and followed, the uniform precedents of *In re Duguid*, 100
Fed. 274, 3 Am. B. R. 794 (N. C.) and *In re Dunnigan*, 95
Fed. 428, 2 Am. B. R. 628 (Mass.). See Collier, Bank-
ruptcy, 10th ed., 124-125, 154.

On the appearance day, the petition, as in the *Richardson* case, supra, was amended so as to make the parent,
doing business under the alleged firm name, sole respondent; it having appeared upon examination of the bankrupt, that the minor children had no interest in the business and that he was sole proprietor. There was no difficulty in securing this amendment or the adjudication; the
respondent made no answer to the petition, and on the
appearance day freely admitted the fact of bankruptcy and
all other facts alleged in the petition, except that of partnership,—the error as to which his frank statement permitted to be cured by amendment. But counsel, it seems,
did not know whether the bankrupt would make opposition to the petition, and was prepared for any contest. It
is probable that the matter of the hearing could have been
attended to by associate counsel at Honolulu with entire
safety; but under the special circumstances set forth in
the application for an attorney's fee, the court has no
criticism of counsel's course in himself coming to Honolulu for the hearing.   These special circumstances were
that he had engaged an associate at Honolulu to present
the case for adjudication, and had given him careful instructions; but the Honolulu attorney had advised that
in view of the importance of the case and senior counsel's
familiarity with the facts and the law, it would be unwise
for the latter not to be present, and the Honolulu attorney
also, at the same time, informed senior counsel of his own
inability to be present at the hearing in any event. The

eleventh hour at which this advice and information were given made it questionable whether it was not best for senior counsel to go to Honolulu, as he did.

[1] The important point of controversy here is, as to how much, if anything, may be allowed for absence involved in attendance at court at a distant point, whereby counsel is detained from his office at the risk of possible, or probable, loss of other business. In behalf of the objecting creditors, it is contended that in this case the attention required in court at Honolulu could have been given equally well by an attorney of that city, and that it is not fair to charge the estate for the four extra days' absence of an attorney who came from a remote city to attend the hearing,—that as well might a San Francisco attorney have been engaged at extra expense for the two weeks or more consumed in transportation between that city and Honolulu.

We have already indicated our approval of the Hilo attorney's coming to Honolulu to attend court under the circumstances. The matter of the general retainer of Hilo counsel rather than Honolulu counsel, which has been adverted to in argument, is also approved because of the desirability of having an attorney residing near the bankrupt's place of business. Item 10 alone is suggestive of the wisdom of such action.

Now, supposing there were allowed $50 for items 1 and 2; and $300 for items 3 and 4 (being, say, $100 for the day in court, only half an hour of which was used, and $50 a day for the four other days absent), and for item 5 which covers minor services ancillary to those under items 3 and 4; and $25 for item 6; $25 for items 7 and 8; $25 for item 9 (admitting the necessity of this service); and $75 for item 10 (which is all that could be given for even this valuable service), we would have an aggregate fee of $500, which, it will be remembered, is net above expenses involved in the five days' absence. It must not be understood, however, that this estimate is intended as fixing any rigid scale of fees, especially as to attendance at Honolulu of attorneys from remote places in Hawaii. Rather, is the estimate made to demonstrate in a rough way the over-liberality of the fee of $750 allowed by the referee. In cases like this where a large part of the attorney's time is taken up by transportation, the court cannot take a highly opti-mistic, speculative, view of possible business lost through the attorney's absence from his office. Only moderate com-pensation is to be expected in such cases. See *In re Hart & Co.*, supra, involving a larger estate and more extensive and equally difficult services (save for the element of attendance at a distant point), for which a fee of only $100 was allowed; see also as to the policy of conservatism in the matter of fees, *In re Stratemeyer*, 2 U. S. Dist. Ct. Haw. 269, 271; *In re Talton*, 137 Fed. 178, 14 Am. B. R. 617; *In re Coldville Mfg. Co.*, 123 Fed. 579, 10 Am. B. R. 552, 556-557; *In re Carr*, 117 Fed. 572, 9 Am. B. R. 58, 59; *In re Mayer*, 101 Fed. 695, 4 Am. B. R. 238, 240.

In view of these considerations, no more liberal allow-ance can be made than that above supposed for the element of absence, and for the whole services it is the court's opinion that a fee of $500 is all that could reasonably be allowed. Let the referee's order be modified accordingly.

In so ruling there is no disposition to criticize a conscien-tious and efficient officer of this court. The real ground of our difference of opinion lies, we think, in the referee's hav-ing regarded the size of the estate as inventoried rather than the cash actually realized therefrom and, as already indicated, in his having allowed rather too much for the attorney's absence in attending court at Honolulu.

[2] Also, this decision recognizes the cited rule of pre-sumption in favor of a referee's finding, but must hold that the rule does not apply where a finding is, as here, based on undisputed facts set out in the record. *In re Big Cahaba Coal Co.*, 183 Fed. 662;, 26 Am. B. R. 910, 912; *In re McCrary Bros.*, 169 Fed. 485, 22 Am. B. R. 161; *Ohio*

Valley Bank v. Mack, 163 Fed. 155, 20 Am. B. R. 919;
In re McDonald & Sons, 178 Fed. 487, 24 Am. B. R. 446,
affirmed 25 Am. B. R. 948.

IN THE MATTER OF HONOLULU ELECTRIC COMPANY, LIMITED, A BANKRUPT.

October 29, 1914.

Bankruptcy—Review of Referee's finding—Practice: Where a question of law certified to the court by the referee for review, requires further examination of the relation between a creditor and the bankrupt as a basis of a determination of whether the creditor's claim is entitled to priority, the matter is remanded to the referee: the court will not in such cases determine questions of law in advance of a necessary finding of facts.

In Bankruptcy: Question for review on certificate of referee.

W. T. Carden, trustee, *pro se* (*Thompson, Wilder, Milverton & Lymer* with him).

CLEMONS, J. The referee in bankruptcy at Honolulu has certified to a judge of this court the following facts (appearing from the certificate and papers therewith filed), upon which he bases the question hereinbelow set forth:

At the first meeting of creditors, W. H. Stuart presented a claim of $385 "for salary due as manager" of the bankrupt corporation, "being a balance due of $85 for the month of March, 1914, and the sum of $150 each for the months of April and May, 1914." This claim the predecessor of the present referee approved, allowing $300 as a preferred claim and the balance as an ordinary claim.

At a subsequent meeting of creditors before the present referee, the trustee appeared and opposed the allowance of any part of this claim "as entitled to priority of payment as a claim for wages, on the ground that the president and manager of a corporation, is not such a person as is entitled to priority in the payment of a claim for wages." The former referee was present and testified that he had allowed the sum of $300 as a claim having priority.

The present referee has thereupon rendered decision that such finding of his predecessor is binding upon him; and he certifies to the judge of his opinion the question: "Is the claim of the president and manager of a corporation entitled to priority in the payment of a claim for wages?"

It is clear to me that what is required here, is not the opinion of a judge on the legal question propounded; but, rather, such a reconsideration or re-examination of the claim as is contemplated by the Bankruptcy Act, sec. 57, subdiv. k, and General Order XXI, subdiv. 6. Any opinion of the court at this time would seem to be impracticable. As the case stands, the ruling of the former referee is, as the present referee has held, still in force, and there is in the record submitted nothing new respecting this claim, except an affidavit of the claimant, filed with the referee since the latter meeting of creditors, and showing that while he was "president and manager, the salary paid to him was paid to him as manager only, the office of president being without salary and purely nominal," and "that as said manager he performed the services of a working fore-man rather than the services of a manager of the corporation." I am not prepared to hold as a principle of law that because a person may be called "manager" he is not entitled to make a priority claim, or, on the other hand, that because he is called "working foreman" he is entitled to make such claim.   And so, and in any event, inasmuch as justice requires a careful examination of the relation of the claimant to the corporation, the nature of his employment and services, the case should be remanded to the referee for such proceedings as may be desired under the practice above indicated.   To state the matter in another way: All we have before us is the trustee's objection to a claim which has been allowed by the former referee and which in the absence of evidence or of something appearing in the record to the contrary, we must presume to have been rightly allowed; and in the face of this presumption and of this want of evidence or appearance of wrong on the record itself, the question propounded is purely academic.

In consideration of the foregoing opinion, the above matter is remanded to the referee for such further proceedings as may be required.

IN THE MATTER OF HONOLULU ELECTRIC COMPANY, LIMITED, A BANKRUPT.

December 9, 1914.

Bankruptcy—Claims—Priority—Manager; Workman: **A workman who assumes additional duties as manager may have a priority claim for his services as workman in a proper case, where the latter services are substantial.**

In Bankruptcy: On review of order of referee.

W. T. Carden, trustee *pro se* (*Thompson, Wilder, Milverton & Lymer* with him).

W. H. Stuart, claimant, *pro se.*

CLEMONS, J. This matter is certified to the court for review of the referee's order disallowing as a priority claim the bill of W. H. Stuart for two months' wages as mechanic. The facts as certified are that:

"Stuart, a majority stockholder in the bankrupt corporation, up to two months prior to the adjudication, was employed by the corporation as an ordinary mechanic at a salary of $150 per month. At a special meeting of the stockholders held two months prior to adjudication the former president and manager was dismissed and Stuart elected to that office. Stuart performed the duties of president and manager and, in addition to the performance of such duties, he worked as before as a mechanic. He claims that he was allowed no salary as president or manager but that the $300 he claims is for wages as an ordinary mechanic."

Upon these facts, the referee held that, "Stuart having accepted the office of president and manager, is not entitled to priority in a claim for wages under the bankruptcy act."

This language of the referee seems to go too far, in its apparent implication that a person may not under any circumstances make a claim in the distinct capacities of manager and workman. The principle of corporate identity is recognized as permitting a claim for labor by a stockholder or director or manager. *In re Swain Co.*, 194 Fed. 749, 750; *In re Crown Point Brush Co.*, 200 Fed. 882, 889. But, of course, the burden is upon the claimant to make out his claim clearly. See the *Crown Point* case at pages 888, 889. Employment in distinct capacities is not unusual in enterprises of small extent.

The cases cited in the brief in behalf of the trustee are not opposed to this view, and most if not all of them are distinguished by the fact that the creditor made a priority claim for services as manager.

It is not a question of what the claimant is called so much as of what services he performed.

It appears that he had for some time been a mechanic of a superior grade at a monthly salary of $150, and when he took the duties of manager, which required but a small part of his time, he kept on doing the manual labor of his old position. It was "understood" that he should do this, though, unfortunately, there is no written agreement or memorandum covering the latter, and it was also not understood that he should receive any additional compensation for his new duties, or at least it was understood that he should receive nothing more for all that he did than the $150 a month. Two things only may be taken as against his claim: (1) that in his original proof of debt he described himself as manager, though he soon amended his claim to show services as a working foreman, and (2) in his testimony had before me in open court (in which I went very fully into the whole matter of his employment and of his work) he testified that he "tried to reduce expenses and so reduced the manager's salary to $150 for all the work that he did." But in spite of this, the undoubted fact is that during the work day of eight hours he spent usually seven hours of the time in the same manual labor which he had performed before. It was not a large business, and while he did whatever was required of a manager, his duties in that capacity during business hours averaged only about one hour a day and consisted in the main of (1) visits at the offices of architects, contractors, and builders for the purpose of soliciting contracts and getting copies of plans and specifications as a basis of bids, and (2) the keeping of what was called the "contract book", made up of entries of material used and labor expended in contract work; and also during business hours he took whatever time was necessary to answer inquiries involving prices on such work, and to do anything else that might be required of a manager. He did also managerial work at night, such as figuring estimates of costs as a basis of contract bids. And, he claims that, as he went to work as early as seven o'clock in the morning and stayed at work until as late as five-thirty o'clock in the afternoon, he fully made up any time lost from his laborer's day. However, the amount of this work overtime is not definitely shown. And his extra hours of service may not unfairly be presumed to have been given because of his own large interest in the welfare of the concern,—a "tottering business", as he called it, which he was endeavoring to hold on its feet.

The good faith of the claimant is shown by the fact that he took no advantage of his controlling position to pay himself any wages as workman during the two months in question. This is no case of "juggling" or of trying, as in some of the cases cited, to characterize as workman's services the incidental or voluntary efforts of a man employed as manager.

The claimant performed substantial services as mechanic, indeed, such was the burden of his work, and he is entitled to a priority claim therefor. The only question is, how much? And though it is shown that on most days the time taken as manager was not over an hour a day, there was more or less other time during work hours devoted to duties as manager. It is certain, however, that he spent very considerably over one-half a day in work as a mechanic. No better rule can be applied than that sometimes applied in admiralty cases where two claimants are entitled to an award but their services cannot exactly be apportioned: Let the claimant, then, in his capacity as mechanic and the claimant in his capacity as manager divide the compensation of $150 a month. This will permit a priority claim for one-half of the $300 in the bill and an ordinary claim for the other half.

The case is remanded to the referee for further proceedings in conformity herewith.

IN THE MATTER OF THE APPLICATION OF DEN-JIRO YOKODA FOR A WRIT OF HABEAS CORPUS.

December 29, 1914.

1. *Immigration—Deportation—Preliminary arrest, basis of:* On habeas corpus the court declines to consider the competency of testimony taken at a hearing before immigration officers in another case, which testimony led to the arrest of a landed immigrant as subject to deportation, when at all events the testimony was sufficient to arouse suspicion against the immigrant, which the evidence in the final deportation proceedings was ample to confirm.

2. *Same—Same—Finality of findings:* In deportation cases in which a fair hearing has been accorded, the findings of immigration officers are final.

3. *Same—Same—Fair hearing, self incrimination:* Claim of incrimination under duress, *held* not made out.

4. *Same—Same—Evidence—Husband and wife as witnesses:* Deportation proceedings being civil in their nature, the local rule of competency of husband and wife applies.

5. *Same—Same—Hearing—Benefit of counsel:* Where an immigrant arrested as deportable was represented by attorney if not personally present at the hearing following his arrest, and a brief in his behalf was filed by his attorney for consideration by the Secretary of Labor, it cannot be said that the immigrant was without benefit of counsel.

6. *Same—Same—Authority of Acting Secretary of Labor:* When the warrant of deportation shows the proceedings to have been determined by the Acting Secretary of Labor, the presumption is that he was authorized to act; and he who challenges this authority assumes the burden of proving its absence.

Habeas corpus: Demurrer to order to show cause.

C. C. Bitting for petitioner.

J. W. Thompson, Assistant U. S. Attorney, for respondent.

CLEMONS, J. This is a demurrer to a return to an order

to show cause why a writ of habeas corpus should not issue. The grounds of demurrer are general grounds of insufficiency, except the special ground that the return discloses that "the proceedings against this petitioner upon which his arrest was based and upon which the warrant for deportation was asked, were had upon an entirely ex parte proceeding and on an alleged inquiry to which the petitioner was not a party."

The petition for the writ shows: the arrival and landing at Honolulu of the petitioner, Denjiro Yokoda, a native of Japan who has since been a resident of this city; and his restraint upon a warrant of deportation issued by the Acting Secretary of Labor, on the ground of the petitioner's being unlawfully in the country, as having been a contract laborer at the time of his entry, induced or solicited to migrate here by an offer or promise of employment or in consequence of an agreement to perform labor in the United States, and also as having entered without the inspection contemplated and required by the Immigration Act, and having secured admission by reason of false and misleading evidence.

The petition shows a preliminary order of arrest, based upon testimony given by the wife of petitioner in her examination at the immigration station, Honolulu, upon her arrival here subsequent to her husband's arrival,—testimony which the petitioner alleges, on information and belief, to have been "based entirely upon presumptions" and "not upon facts within her own knowledge" and "irrelevant to the proper subject of inquiry". (The facts set forth in the foregoing sentence, are hereinafter referred to as Objection I). And the petition shows the taking of the petitioner before an immigration inspector, and his there being informed that his wife had made statements contradictory to statements made by him at the time of his entry into the country, and that he had been arrested upon those statements of hers.

There is also shown: the compulsion of the petitioner
to be a witness against himself and the evoking from him
under duress of incriminating testimony (Objection II),
and the compulsion of the wife to testify against him, "if
she did so testify".   (Objection III).   In connection with
the latter allegation, it is said that "the wife was used as a
witness whose testimony was the basis of the arrest and
attempted deportation, without your petitioner's being
present or in any manner having the privilege of objecting
to said witness."   (Objection IV, covered also by the special ground of demurrer, above).

Another ground of the petition is, that if false testimony
was given by petitioner at his entrance into the country,
there is no provision for deportation therefor, and that having been permitted to enter, the deportation proceeding
violates his right to indictment by a grand jury for an infamous crime, perjury, and to confrontation by the witnesses against him.   (Objection V).

The petition alleges an "appeal" to the Secretary of
Labor, but the exhibit annexed to the petition shows merely
the filing of a brief with the Secretary.   The fact is that
proceedings for deportation are original matters before the
Secretary of Labor, though he considers testimony taken by
the local immigration officers.

The return of the immigration inspector to the order
to show cause, admits the admission of the petitioner into
the country, his arrest and the warrant of deportation, and
sets up: that in the examination of the wife by the immigration officers, at the time of her application for admission, she testified that her husand, the petitioner, was a
contract laborer, working in Honolulu, for a company whose
secretary and treasurer, A. Kimura, hereinafter mentioned,
had assisted him in obtaining transportation from Japan
and had promised him a job and had given him a job, or
assisted him in securing one, with that company.   It is
also alleged that his passport presented to the immigration

officers at landing was the passport of a merchant, and was fraudulently obtained and used to gain his admission into the country.

The return shows, that the petitioner was called and gave voluntary testimony and verified the statements of his wife, much of which testimony was corroborated by Kimura, and that upon this evidence so taken the recommendation for and warrant of arrest were based; and that thereafter the petitioner and his wife testified at a hearing in pursuant to his arrest, at which hearing the petitioner was duly represented by counsel.

The return denies, among other things, that the petitioner was sworn at all when he landed in Honolulu,—thus to meet the point regarding perjury, made above by petitioner.

The transcript of the proceedings before the immigration officers is made a part of the answer. Therefore, for the purpose of the demurrer, the allegations of the return have been taken with such modifications as the transcript might require, i. e., the testimony itself is considered, rather than the respondent's or the peitioner's version of it or conclusions from it.

[1] Objection I, above, need not concern us, for in the record of proceedings, aside from the evidence given by the wife at her examination on arrival, there appears ample evidence to sustain the finding. It does not matter (even admitting it to be true), that her testimony given at the hearing in her own case was "based entirely upon presumptions" and "not upon facts within her own knowledge"; for, as a basis for the petitioner's arrest, it was sufficient to arouse suspicion against him. which the other evidence before the Acting Secretary of Labor was sufficient to confirm,—i. e., within the Secretary's power to find facts.

The following, among other, testimony may be noted as tending to support the finding made: The petitioner's repeated admission, that he was "invited" by Kimura, his

present employer, his sister's husband, to come to Honolulu (Transcript p. 3, also see Id. p. 14), taken in connection with Kimura's admission that he "wrote in the application [for the petitioner's passport from the Japanese gov-
ernment], that our soda water works [where the petitioner
has been employed] were flourishing and that he needed
another man, and the consul wrote the certificate and I sent
it to Denjiro", the petitioner (Transcript p. 6); also Kimura's testimony, that he "sent for" the petitioner because
Kimura's wife, the petitioner's sister, "wanted to send for
him", and that "I intended to make a trip to Japan and
wanted him to take charge of the business while I was
gone" (Id.). Though this testimony of Kimura was given
at the hearing before a board of special inquiry on the wife's
application for landing and before the issuance of the warrant of arrest, at which hearing it does not appear that
the husband was present, nevertheless he had under Immigation Rule 22 the right to examine this and all other evidence on which the warrant of arrest was issued, and to
offer evidence to meet any evidence theretofore presented;
and, as the record shows (Transcript p. 18), counsel for
the petitioner were at the hearing informed "that an opportunity would be offered them to present any evidence
they may have in defense and that C. Kimura would be
called, his testimony given before the board of special inquiry offered in evidence, and they would be allowed to
cross-examine him on said testimony". In reply, "the
attorneys stated that they did not desire to offer any more
evidence, that they would not recall the alien, and that
they did not wish to cross-examine C. Kimura on the testimony given by him before the board of special inquiry."
(Transcript p. 18). The wife's testimony,—given freely
and spontaneously we may presume,—at the hearing of her
own case, was that Kimura wrote to Japan to get her husband to go to Honolulu and take a position in the soda
water works; though, it is true, at the later hearing, a

week afterwards, she tried to "explain" away this testimony.

So far as the petitioner's denials go, they may be affected by his admissions of having made false statements in obtaining a passport for a merchant, or having at least made use of a passport containing a false statement, in order to facilitate his entry into this country, his status having been only that of a laborer (Transcript pp. 3, 14). His veracity may be weakened also by the fact that his testimony with regard to when he began work for Kimura is quite different from that of the latter (Transcript pp. 1, 5, 15).

[2] The cases cited by this court in the decision of June 2, 1913, in *In re Tome Tanno,* ante, p. 266, and a long list of other cases, firmly establish the finality of findings of immigration officers in cases like the present, if a fair hearing has been accorded. The specific objections of want of fairness, or of due process of law, will now be disposed of.

[3] The claim of incrimination under duress (Objection II, above) is not made out by anything appearing in the transcript of proceedings above referred to, nor does it appear that any testimony given by the petitioner was such as to tend toward incrimination, or to tend to subject him to any criminal proceeding within the contemplation of the fifth amendment to the Constitution. A consideration of the following authorities will be profitable in this connection: *Low Foon Yin v. United States Immigration Commissioner,* 145 Fed. 791, 793, et seq.; *United States v. Hung Chang,* 134 Fed. 19, syll. par. 1, also 25; see also *Li Sing v. United States,* 180 U. S. 486, 494, 495; *Fong Yue Ting v. United States,* 149 U. S. 698, 730; *Bugajewitz v. Adams,* 228 U. S. 585, 591; *United States v. Wong Dep Ken,* 57 Fed. 206, 209; *Sire v. Berkshire,* 185 Fed. 967, 969; Bouve, Exclusion of Aliens, 616, and cases cited; 2 Watson on the Constitution, 1443-1444.

[4] As to Objection III, above: The proceedings being civil in their nature, Bouve, Exclusion of Aliens, 616, the

local rule of competency of husband and wife (Rev. Laws, Haw. 1905, sec. 1950) applies.   Rev. Stat., sec. 914.

[5] As to Objection IV, above, it is enough to say that, the petitioner was present by his attorney, if not personally present, when the wife was examined at the hearing pursuant to the warrant of arrest; and under the immigration rules, he had the right to "inspect the warrant of arrest and all the evidence on which it was issued," and also to "inspect and make a copy of the minutes of the hearing [pursuant to the arrest] so far as it had proceeded and to meet any evidence theretofore or thereafter presented by the government", and to file a brief. A brief was filed here by the petitioner's counsel, and, presumably, the record was inspected for its preparation. It is not apparent that the petitioner was denied any right, or that he had anything but a fair hearing, within the uniform rulings of the courts in such cases. *Low Wah Suey v. Backus,* 225 U. S. 460, 469-470, 471-472. See also Bouve, Exclusion of Aliens, 336-338.

Objection V is without merit; for conceding the fact, denied by the return, that the petitioner's statements, made to the immigration officials at the time of his landing, were made under oath, nevertheless the deportation proceedings were not a punishment for perjury but for his being unlawfully in the country. That false statements happen to be the means by which he effected his entry, is only an immaterial circumstance.

[6] In oral argument, counsel for the petitioner makes the point that the warrant of deportation shows the proceedings to have been determined by the Acting Secretary of Labor, whereas the petitioner is entitled to have the matter of deportation disposed of by the Secretary himself. In behalf of this point, there is cited the decision of Federal Judge Dooling of California, rendered October 23, 1914, in the case of *Ex parte Tsuie Chee,* 218 Fed. 256. But that case, though holding that the Acting Secretary should not

perform any duties except in the absence of the Secretary or Assistant Secretary, also ruled that, "from the very fact of his acting the court will presume that both the Secretary and Assistant Secretary were absent, because it is only in their absence that he may lawfully perform the duties which the law casts upon the Secretary." Moreover, Judge Dooling held that "whoever challenges his [the Acting Secretary's] right to act must assume the burden of proving it clearly." As the record stands, then, in our case here, the presumption of regularity and authority must prevail against the contention.

Let the demurrer be overruled.

IN THE MATTER OF THE APPLICATION OF DENJIRO YOKODA FOR A WRIT OF HABEAS CORPUS (SECOND PETITION).

January 19, 1915.

Habeas corpus—Petition for writ—Verification: A petition for writ of habeas corpus should be verified by oath of the petitioner or of someone having knowledge of the facts upon which relief is asked, and as a general rule if allegations are made on information and belief, the source of information and belief should appear.

Habeas Corpus: Petition for writ.

J. Lightfoot for petitioner.
Jeff McCarn, U. S. District Attorney, for respondent.

CLEMONS, J.   The district attorney earnestly contends that in this case the writ should not issue in the first instance, inasmuch as the vital matter of the alleged want of authority of the Acting Secretary of Labor, which is made a ground of the petition, is stated only on information and belief, without even a showing of the source and nature of the information. The district attorney cites in his support the instance of the writ of attachment, which does not as a rule issue on bare information and belief unsupported by a showing as to the nature of the information.

This phase of form or practice is something which counsel and the court had passed over rather lightly for attention to the material ground of the petition with regard to the Acting Secretary's want of authority—the latter being the only ground of the petition regarded by the court as a proper basis for the writ, this ground appearing to be a jurisdictional point which could be raised at any time, but the other grounds being either covered by a former petition for a writ of habeas corpus lately determined by this court adversely to petitioner, or excluded within Judge Field's ruling in *Ex parte Cuddy*, 40 Fed. 62, 66, as being old matters of fact (not jurisdictional) existent at the time of the former petition.

Though the material ground for the writ above noted appeared to be well taken, within the decision of Judge Dooling in *Ex parte Tsuie Chee*, 218 Fed. 256, I had some hesitation with regard to the practice of issuing the writ in a case where the material ground is so poorly supported by oath. As a matter of ordinary pleading, it is true that bare information and belief without show of sources is allowable, and in several instances even in habeas corpus cases, the judges of this court have permitted such verification to pass and the writ to issue. But I think we have been overlooking the extraordinary nature of the writ of habeas corpus. It is at least as extraordinary as the writ of attachment, cited by the district attorney: 4 Cyc. 480, and as extraordinary as the writ of injunction: 22 Cyc. 926, in both of which a foundation by affidavit is required as to material allegations. Thus, "an injunction cannot be granted in the first instance upon an allegation of this character." *Brooks v. Hare,* 8 Fed. 529, 532. The cited requirement as to attachment may be to some extent statutory, but the rule is certainly a reasonable one, and a guard against abuse. He who invokes such special relief, should bear the burden of the showing indicated.

The new equity rules of the Supreme Court recognize the distinction above noted, in providing that "if special relief pending the suit be desired, the bill should be verified by the oath of the plaintiff, or someone having knowledge of the facts upon which such relief is asked." Equity Rule 25.

These considerations impel me to issue merely an order to show cause instead of a writ of habeas corpus at this stage of the proceeding. Upon being satisfied as to the truth of the allegation, of the Acting Secretary's having determined the appeal from the immigration officers in question instead of the Secretary of Labor himself having made the determination, although actually present, I shall be disposed to allow the writ to issue, following the case of *Tsuie Shee,* supra.

IN THE MATTER OF THE APPLICATION OF WONG KUM WO FOR A WRIT OF HABEAS CORPUS.

December 24, 1914.

Habeas corpus—Demurrer to petition: It is not proper practise to demur to a petition for a writ of habeas corpus after the writ has issued.

Habeas corpus: On motion to strike demurrer to petition, the writ having issued.

F. E. Thompson, (Thompson, Wilder, Milverton & Lymer with him) for the motion.

Jeff McCarn, U.S. District Attorney, contra.

CLEMONS, J. The authorities are almost unanimous in holding against the practice of demurring to a petition for a writ of habeas corpus after the writ has issued. See especially *Simmons v. Georgia Iron Co.,* 117 Ga. 229, 305, 43 S. E. 780, 61 L. R. A. 739; also Church, Habeas Corpus, 2d ed., sec. 160; 9 Enc. Pl. & Pr. 1035; and a majority of authorities hold that the result intended by the demurrer may be reached by a motion to quash. See, e.g., *In re Taylor,* 23 Fed. Cas. 728, 729, No. 13,744.

The Federal statutes, Rev. Stat. secs. 750, 757, however, appear to contemplate that the respondent shall make a prompt return showing the *true* cause of the detention,—which is a different thing, for instance, from showing by demurrer what is not necessarily the true cause of detention but only a cause admitted to be true for the purpose of the demurrer. It has been pointed out that these Federal statutes are intended to forestall delays; and in view of this intent and of the practically unanimous rulings against demurrers in cases like the present, the motion to strike will be granted. *Ex parte Baez,* 177 U. S. 378, 388-389.   The suggestion occurs to me, that matters of demurrer, i. e., objections to the sufficiency of the petition, might, if desired, be raised in connection with the return as they are in the new equity practice in connection with the answer,—such objections amounting to a motion to quash.

Motion granted.   Let the respondent have five days within which to file return.

IN THE MATTER OF THE APPLICATION OF WONG KUM WO FOR A WRIT OF HABEAS CORPUS.

January. 14, 1915.

Habeas corpus—Return, scope of: A return to a writ of habeas corpus is not limited to a narrow compliance with Rev. State. sec. 757, requiring the return to show "the true causes of the detention," but may answer specific allegations of the petition for the writ.

Habeas Corpus: On exceptions to return.

F. E. Thompson and *W. T. Carden* (*Thompson, Wilder. Milverton & Lymer* with them) for petitioner.
Jeff McCarn, U. S. District Attorney, for respondent.

CLEMONS, J.   The petitioner for a writ of habeas corpus, in exceptions to the respondent's return, moves to expunge as scandalous and impertinent portions of the return which do more than attempt a bare compliance with the statutory requirement of a showing of "the true causes of the detention," Rev. Stat. sec. 757, namely, those portions of the return which meet squarely allegations of the petition giving particulars of a want of due process of law in proceedings before immigration officers.   The theory of the motion to expunge is based (1) on the rule that the return is to the writ and not to the petition and (2) on the statutory requirement, above mentioned, as to what the return shall show.

In support of the motion are cited decisions holding that the respondent is not required to make any issue on the petition; the contention being that these decisions suggest by analogy the necessity of disregarding the petition entirely, once the writ has issued.   *In re Moyer*, 35 Colo. 159, 85 Pac. 190, 192. 117 Am. St. Rep. 189, and *Ex parte Durbin*, 102 Mo. 100, 14 S. W. 821, the latter involving a statute similar to Rev. State. sec. 760, which provides that

the petitioner may deny any of the facts set forth in the
return or allege any other fact that may be material in the
case.   In the *Moyer* case, the court says:

"It is urged by counsel for petitioner that certain averments in the petition for the writ are not controverted by
the return.   The latter is not treated as an answer to the
application, but rather as a response to the writ itself.   The
averments of the petition are made for the purpose of obtaining the writ, and the respondent, in his answer thereto, simply seeks to relieve himself from the imputation of
having imprisoned petitioner without lawful authority, and
this he does, or rather, is required to do, under the law, by
statements in the return from which the legality of the
imprisonment is to be determined, without regard to the
statements of the writ.   In short, he is not required to
make any issue on the petition for the writ, but to answer
the writ.   *In re Chipchase*, 56 Kan. 357, 43 Pac. 224; *Ex
parte Durbin* (Mo. Sup.), 14 S. W. 821; *Simmons v.
Georgia Iron & Coal Co.* (Ga.), 43 S. E. 780, 61 L. R. A.
737."

The motion is urged as logically following the court's
order, made at a prior stage of the present case, striking a
demurrer to the petition interposed after the writ had
issued.   But this is the logic of a narrow view of the rule
that the return should respond to the writ and not to the
petition; for this rule arises from the summary nature of
the proceeding of habeas corpus and not from any idea
that the petition, once acted upon in the granting of the
writ, is out of the case for all purposes.   See *In re Depue*,
77 N. E. 798, 800 (N. Y.); 2 Spelling on Extraordinary
Remedies, sec. 1317.   The court in issuing the writ is in
theory supposed to pass upon the sufficiency of the petition (see *Simmons v. Georgia Iron Co.*, 117 Ga. 229, 61
L. R. A. 739, 43 S. E. 760, 782, 783); and, the writ having
issued in response to the petitioner's prayer, the petition
becomes to some extent functus officio.   But the allowable
practice of moving to quash the writ, affords an instance
of the fact that the petition is not entirely to be disre-

garded; for a motion to quash though directed against the writ itself, is still grounded upon the insufficiency of the petition. See *In re Taylor*, 23 Fed. Cas. 728, 729, No. 13,774; *McGlennon v. Hargrave*, 90 Ind. 150, 153; *Milligan v. State*, 97 Ind. 355, 356, 357. The distinction between a demurrer, attacking the petition directly, and a motion to quash, attacking the petition indirectly, is of course technical, but it is none the less recognized. See the Indiana cases, supra.

However, the question before us may be considered on more practical, less technical, grounds. We cannot ignore the fact that in nearly every, if not every, case the real subject of controversy is the very thing alleged in the petition. It is only fair to presume that the detailed showing of want of due process, made by the petition in this case, is what the petitioner is going to rely upon at the final hearing. Is it not, then, impracticable to defer the joining of issue to a later stage by ignoring what is already apparent? Is it not carrying a theory too far, to say that the respondent may, e. g., show that the petitioner is held by virtue of a warrant of deportation, but may not show that the petitioner is held by virtue of such a warrant based upon a hearing conducted duly and fairly in certain specified particulars in regard to which the petitioner's claim of unfairness and want of due process of law, is evident in the record?

To anticipate or meet in the return the petitioner's stated position, may at least be justified on the ground of practicability; it effects the arrival at an immediate issue, just as does the charging part of a bill in equity, still permissible under the new equity rules. See Hopkins' Fed. Eq. Rules, 159, note to rule 25; see, also, 2 Rose's Fed. Proc., sec. 1689, regarding habeas corpus as in the nature of an equitable proceeding.

At all events, the Federal Supreme Court has firmly established a rule, inconsistent with the motion before the

court, that "in a petition for a writ of habeas corpus, verified by oath of the petitioner, as required by Rev. Stat.
U. S. sec. 754, facts duly alleged may be taken to be true,
unless denied by the return or controlled by other evidence." *Whitten v. Tomlinson,* 160 U. S. 231, 242; *Kohl
v. Lehlback,* 160 U. S. 293, 296; *Kentucky v. Powers,* 201
U. S. 1, 34. The New York court of appeals takes the same
view. *In re Depue,* 77 N. E. 798, 800. And Spelling on
Extraordinary Remedies, sec. 1317, states that "while,
strictly speaking, owing to the summary character of the
proceeding, there are no pleadings in habeas corpus, yet for
all practical purposes the petition is treated as the complaint, and the return as an answer in an ordinary civil
action."

To meet the suggestion made in argument that the petition is no part of the record, see rule 126 of our own court,
following Rev. Stat. sec. 765. There may be some question whether this section has been repealed by the circuit
court of appeals act of 1891 (c.. 2 Rose's Fed. Proc. 1379-
1380 with 26 Stat. 826-830); but I have no doubt that our
rule is merely declaratory of what would be the rule independently of the statute.

The exceptions are overruled and the motion to expunge
denied.

IN THE MATTER OF THE APPLICATION OF WONG KUM WO FOR A WRIT OF HABEAS CORPUS.

Ferburary 8, 1915.

Aliens—Admission of Chinese—Habeas Corpus—Bail: **Under the**
provision of sec. 5 of the Chinese exclusion act of May 5, 1892, 27 Stat.

25, that on an application to any court or judge of the United States in the first instance for a writ of habeas corpus by a Chinese person refused admission into this country, no bail shall be allowed, bail is not allowable upon the issuance of the writ, or before a final hearing on the merits after return to the writ.

Habeas Corpus: Motion for bail.

W. T. Carden (*Thompson, Wilder, Milverton & Lymer,* with him) for the motion.

Jeff McCarn, U. S. District Attorney, contra.

CLEMONS, J.   The petitioner's motion to be released on bail, after the issuance of the writ of habeas corpus and before the determination of the case on its merits, presents for consideration the meaning of section 5 of the Chinese exclusion act of 1892, 12 Stat., 25, which reads:

"On an application to any judge or court of the United States in the first instance for a writ of habeas corpus by a Chinese person seeking to land in the United States, to whom that privilege has been denied, no bail shall be allowed, and such application shall be heard and determined promptly without unnecessary delay."

The words "in the first instance," the meaning of which is specially in controversy on this motion, are not as clear an expression of intent as is desirable.   See *Ex parte Tsuie Shee,* 218 Fed. 256, 259.

The first impression given by the statute is that of an intent to forbid bail until the petitioner has by proof made good his allegation of an illegal restraint.   And such is the uniform construction given by the few judges who have had this statute before them in reported cases.   It is true, that in two of the three cases bearing on the question, the construction of the court might be regarded as in the nature of dictum, for these cases have to do with bail at a later stage of the proceedings, i. e., after a hearing on the merits. *In re Chin Yuen Sing,* 65 Fed. 788 (N. Y., Lacombe, J.);

In re Jem Yuen, 188 Fed. 350, 355-356 (Mass., Dodge, J.). But in the first case the dictum, if it be such, of Judge Lacombe is worthy of great weight, as a link in the chain of the court's reasoning:

"It would be a singular exercise of discretion which would release an immigrant on bail after the court has decided that he should not be permitted to enter the country, *when the statutes require that he shall not be released on bail before the court has so decided,* and when there is still a possibility that its decision might be favorable to him."

The second case adopts Judge Lacombe's opinion without discussion. In the later case of *In re Ong Lung,* 125 Fed. 813, 814, Judge Lacombe reaffirms the construction given by him in the decision above cited. Though the scant statement of facts in the subsequent case does not show the stage of the proceedings at which bail was moved for, the inference is conclusive that it was at a preliminary stage, from the fact that the decision on the merits was not had until a later date. See second opinion in the case, 125 Fed. 814. Judge Lacombe's ruling, 125 Fed. 813, is, therefore, directly in point here. Though it may, it is true, be urged against the weight of all these three decisions in the matter of bail, that they state a conclusion without a discussion.

But the reason and spirit of the law, and contemporary history (see, e. g., *United States v. Fan Chung,* 132 Fed. 109, 110, though a case considerably later than the statute), support the view of Judge Lacombe and Judge Dodge. A remedy was called for and the statute should be so construed as to effect a remedy, if it may be done without arbitrariness. See 1 Blackstone, Comm., *87. And the words of the first clause of the statute "on an application for a writ of habeas corpus" are apt enough to describe the whole habeas corpus proceeding down through the hearing on the merits, for while the application is determined in a preliminary way when the writ issues, it is not substantially, finally, disposed of until after the hearing on the merits; and inserting in the phrase just quoted the words "in the first instance" serves to emphasize the distinction between the preliminary stage when the petitioner's showing of facts is by mere allegation and the "final instance" when the showing must be by proof.

The only thing that might be urged against Judge Lacombe's construction is, that the statute being in restraint of liberty, and also being discriminatory against one particular nation, should be strictly construed: with such a principle in view, the concluding provision of this statute, that "such application shall be heard and determined promptly without unnecessary delay," might possibly be read as referring to a preliminary hearing and determination whether the writ should issue, and the narrow application of the last clause of the statute might be then contended as giving color to the first clause. Such a conclusion is plausible when it is considered that if these words of the concluding clause do not contemplate a preliminary stage of the proceedings, then Congress has here made the most general kind of a provision for promptness in the final hearing on the merits, when the most explicit kind of a provision had already long existed. Rev. Stat., sec. 759.

However, it is unwise to infer too much from any presumption of Congress' having had clearly in mind all the details of the existing habeas corpus law, Rev. Stat., chap. 13. And the improbability of Congress' unconsciousness of the definite existing provisions of Rev. Stat., sec. 759, is balanced somewhat by the fact that so far as preliminary stages of the proceedings are concerned, the law had already provided for the usual run of cases (i. e., cases in which the petitioner shows a good case in his petition: see *In re Jordan*, 49 Fed. 238, 246),—Rev. Stat., sec. 755, insuring the issuance of the writ "forthwith" unless it appears from the petition that the party is not entitled to it. As regards this large proportion of cases, it would seem absurd for Congress to take the trouble to enact this statute, for the period of inhibited bail would be only the very brief period between the presentation of the petition to the judge and the issuance of the writ.

Against this, on the other hand, it may be argued that the hearing on an order to show cause would be a case, not already specially provided for, to which the concluding clause of the statute could aptly apply.   The argument loses force, however, when the summary character of habeas corpus proceedings is considered; for the universal practice is, not to defer the hearing on an order to show cause any longer than the hearing on a return to the writ.   And the time in such cases, also, is so brief as to make the demand for such a statute as this is contended to be, little less impracticable than in the case where the writ has forthwith issued.

It would seem that Congress in enacting this statute of 1892, did so with little or no regard to the details of the existing habeas corpus law.   If these details had been in mind, it is likely that the present question would have been obviated by more definite provisions,—the new law and the old would have been better co-ordinated.

But, after all, we are construing the words "in the first instance," of the first clause of the statute,—these are the important words,—and it would at least be as well to read the last clause of the statute in the light of these words as to read these words in the light of the last clause, or, rather, to endeavor to fit these words to a narrow meaning of that last clause.   And it may be, even, that the last clause could refer to a preliminary hearing and still the words "in the first instance" of the first clause be unaffected thereby; for it would not be unreasonable to read the whole statute as meaning that there shall be no bail at any time before the *final* instance, of the petitioner's making good his claim by proof, and that at the same time in order to make against delay there shall be a speedy preliminary hearing as to whether the writ shall issue, as well as the speedy hearing on the merits after the writ has issued, already guaranteed by Rev. Stat., sec. 759.

The cases cited, showing a liberal disposition to allow release on bail pending appeals from orders dismissing the writ, such, e. g., as *In re Chin Wah*, 182 Fed. 256, and *United States v. Fah Chung*, 132 Fed. 109, do not help us; for they are deportation cases, involving aliens already in the country, as distinguished from habeas corpus cases involving aliens seeking to enter the country, for which cases the special rule now before the court was provided.

That bail has been allowed in this court and in other courts, in other similar instances, upon the issuance of the writ or before final hearing, has been due to want of opposition (see unreported Vermont case, cited in *In re Jem Yuen*, 188 Fed. 350, 356) or to want of consideration (see *In re Ong Lung*, 125 Fed. 813, 814, and *In re Jem Yuen*, supra).

This discussion will indicate the difficulties which have made me hold this motion under advisement. But these difficulties do not justify overturning the precedents above cited.

Let the motion be denied.

IN THE MATTER OF THE APPLICATION OF WONG KUM WO FOR A WRIT OF HABEAS CORPUS.

November 24, 1915.

1. *Aliens—Immigration—Unfair hearing—Bias of immigration in-*

spector: Claim of bias as shown in an alleged assault by an examining immigration inspector upon a witness for the immigrant, *held* not made out.

2. *Same—Same—Finality of finding of fact by immigration officer:* A finding of fact by immigration officers on a hearing to determine an immigrant's right to land, is final as a rule.

3. *Evidence—Experts—Qualifications:* In order to qualify as an expert witness competent to give an opinion as to the nationality of a certain person, it is not necessary that the witness should be learned in the science of ethnology, but it is sufficient if he have long experience and familiarity with people of the race to which the person in question is contended to belong.

4. *Habeas corpus—Basis of petition: prejudicial omissions in record not remedied before the original tribunal:* It is no ground for relief by writ of habeas corpus, that the record on appeal to the Secretary of Labor from a decision of immigration officers denying an immigrant a landing, is not absolutely complete, at least in cases where the immigrant has a reasonable opportunity to have the defect remedied before the original tribunals, and where the defect is not calculated or intended to work prejudice.

5. *Aliens—Immigration—Fair hearing—Representation by counsel:* The mere fact that an immigrant is without counsel in hearings before immigration officers as to his right to land, does not make such hearings unfair.

Habeas Corpus: Hearing on return to writ.

W. T. Carden and *C. S. Franklin* (*Thompson, Milverton & Cathcart* with them), for petitioner.

Jeff McCarn, U. S. District Attorney, and *J. W. Thompson*, Assistant U. S. Attorney, for respondent.

CLEMONS, J.   This writ of habeas corpus is based on a petition alleging an unfair hearing before officers of the immigration station at Honolulu respecting the right of the petitioner Wong Kum Wo, an immigrant from China, to land in the United States.

He claimed this right because of his alleged birth in Hawaii—in the year 1892, of a Chinese father and an Hawaiian mother. The unfairness of this hearing is rested on eight grounds:

(1) "Gross bias" of the examining immigration inspector "exhibited by an unprovoked and brutal assault upon a witness presented by the attorneys for your petitioner on his behalf in an examination on the 1st day of September, 1914, to-wit, an assault upon his aged and infirm father, Wong Sai Quin;"

(2) The inclusion "in the records of the case [of] a materially and wantonly false translation of two documents written in the Chinese language, attempting thereby to impute fraud to your petitioner;"

(3) The inclusion "in the records of the case [of] a statement of the examining inspector that one of the two documents aforesaid, was in his opinion not in the handwriting of the applicant, your petitioner;"

(4) The inclusion by the examining inspector "in his finding of facts in the records of the case, [of] a materially false statement as to the finding place of the aforesaid two documents by which false statement a material and unwarranted inference of fraud was drawn against your petitioner;"

(5) The receiving "as expert witnesses as to the nationality of your petitioner [of] divers persons utterly unqualified, incompetent, and unfit to render opinion as expert witnesses as to the nationality of your petitioner;"

(6) The "malicious and wrongful" failure of "the examining inspector, by his stenographer, to take down and transcribe the entire testimony" given by a material witness in petitioner's behalf, and "instead thereof taking down and reporting only the parts thereof which to him, the stenographer, did seem important;"

(7) The denial to the petitioner by the inspector in charge of "the right to be represented by counsel at the various purported hearings had and held to determine the question of your petitioner's right to land at the port of Honolulu;" and the denial to the petitioner of "the right to be present by counsel at the examination of persons called by the inspector in charge as expert witnesses, or to be informed of the calling of such persons or to attack the qualifications of unqualified, incompetent, and unfit per-

sons so called by the inspector ín charge as expert witnesses;"

(8) The denial of a landing to your petitioner "as a Chinese alien withtout any evidence whatsoever that he was a Chinese alien, and contrary to the conclusive proof produced by your petitioner that he is a citizen of the United States and of the Territory of Hawaii."

[1] It was upon ground (1) that the petitioner's counsel mainly relied, and the evidence as at first submitted afforded them some basis for argument that at a hearing in the immigration office the petitioner and his alleged father, when approaching to greet each other, had been pushed apart by one of the inspectors with such abruptness and force as to cause the father to lose his balance. The father was infirm from locomotor ataxia, and in any event it would not have taken more than slight force to upset him; but apart from that fact, I became entirely satisfied from the testimony of the petitioner himself, whom of my own motion I ventured to call as a witness after the case had been heard and argued, and who, rather strangely, had not been called as a witness by either party, that there was no element of viciousness or brutality or even of force in any technical assault that might have been made by the examining inspector or any other person. The petitioner, questioned then not only by the court, but by the district attorney, and by his own counsel, testified clearly and unqualifiedly against any such happenings as were charged in the petition.

It may not be without significance, that no claim was ever made of any bias manifested by an assault, until such claim was here made a basis of the petition for this writ of habeas corpus. The alleged assault might well have been called to the attention of the Secretary of Labor on appeal. See discussion of ground (6), post.

[2a] Grounds (2), (3) and (4) relate to two documents in the Chinese language, found beneath the canvas cover

of the petitioner's trunk, under circumstances and conditions which led the examining inspector to conclude that they had been concealed there, and that (as translated by the official Chinese interpreter of the immigration station) they were in the nature of a quiz, with questions and answers, one in the petitioner's handwriting and the other in the handwriting of some one else,—the first item in each document being, respectively:

"When asked your name answer Wong Kum Wo." This is noted by the inspector in the record as being "in the applicant's handwriting."

"When asked how old you are, answer 23 years, 6th month, 6th day" (Note by inspector in the record: "This latter is evidently to be given as the date of his birth, as that is the way he answered"). This is noted in the record as being in the handwriting of another person.

Counsel for the petitioner claim, however, that the natural translation is, to take a single example, "Q. How old are you? A 23 years June 6th"; that the papers are both in the same handwriting, and that they are merely "the writer's recollection of what had happened previous to his writing of it," as shown in several instances by the words 'again asked,' "—in other words merely memoranda of testimony given.   To dispose of the contentions on this point, it is enough to say: (1) that so long as it appears, as it does appear, that two translations may be possible, one in the ordinary "Q" and "A" form of transcripts of testimony, and the other in the form "when asked, answer," the finding that the meaning was in accordance with the latter form rather than the former, is in the nature of a finding of fact which should not be disturbed, for anything that appears in the record; and (2) that the original papers in the Chinese language were forwarded to the Secretary of Labor on appeal, and the petitioner had the advantage of having them available there for examination, and also had the advantage of the statement of the official interpreter of

the immigration station included in the record an appeal
at page A 25) that "so far as the wording of his translation
of the papers found in the applicant's trunk is concerned,
it could have been written after the same questions were
asked him [as well] as before. Instead of translating 'when
asked' and 'answer',—as it is,—it could be made to read,
'asked' and 'answered'."

The conclusion from the evidence and circumstances that
these papers were concealed, was well within the inspect-
or's province as a finder of facts, as was also the conclusion
that they were each in the handwriting of different persons, though as to the latter point, if, as claimed, the examining inspector at some time subsequent to the hearing had
expressed to one of petitioner's counsel some doubt if after
all the writings were made by different persons, I do not
see any ground for setting aside the finding that the applicant was not shown to have been born in Hawaii; for, the
applicant, having neglected to place the inspector's change
of opinion, if any, before the Secretary of Labor on the
appeal, should not be heard to say here and now that the
inspector's suggestion of the different handwritings should
have been changed in the record, to comply with his final
change of opinion.   See discussion of ground (6), post.
And it may be noted, that it was shown here that the Secretary of Labor did not consider these two documents at
all, but rested his decision on appeal on other sufficient
grounds.

[3] As to ground (5), the witnesses heard by the immigration officers on their own motion may fairly be regarded
as qualified experts, though not ethnologists; for they had
resided many years in Hawaii and had had much experience with the Chinese and with the Hawaiians, and with
mixtures of these races. As ethnologists the witnesses produced by petitioner's counsel were more learned, but I
doubt very much if they were practically any more competent.   One of the former, Dr. Felix von Luschen, professor

of anthropology in the University of Berlin, himself admitted with reference to a person who had lived for a long time among Chinese, Hawaiians, and Chinese-Hawaiians, but was uneducated (i. e., supposedly, not highly educated): "Education makes no difference. If he is intelligent and careful, his opinion would be worth just as much as that of an anthropologist." (Record, page A 3).

[4] As to ground (6), the most that appears to have been omitted from the record is an explicit showing of the fact that Dr. von Luschen examined for shape et cetera the heads of various persons of the pure and of the mixed races involved, including the petitioner, and also compared their complexions with standard test complexion-tints. This omission, so far as there was any, is a matter which it was counsel's duty to have remedied at the time of taking his appeal. It cannot be presumed that the opportunity unusal in proceedings on appeal would not be afforded for a fair, full and complete record. Counsel who countenance an incomplete record cannot be heard to complain of unfairness in that regard. Counsel, however, are free from any charge of wilful acts or omissions, here or elsewhere in the case, calculated to cause "error in the record"—acts or omissions forbidden by a high standard of legal ethics not always observed in practice.

If there is any merit in the rule, established in this court (see, e. g., *In re Hatsuyo Kobayashi*, post, and local cases cited), that the petitioner in habeas corpus who bases his petition on an unfair hearing before immigration officers must exhaust his remedies by appeal to the Secretary of Labor before moving for that extraordinary writ, then there is merit also in a rule, to be applied generally at least, that the petitioner who complains of any particular act or omission of the immigration officers in a hearing before them, should try to have the cause of complaint remedied at the first opportunity and by the officer or board making the act or omission complained of, at least where the defect is not calculated or intended to work prejudice.   See *In re Can Pon.*, 168 Fed. 479, 480, syllabus, par. 3.

But the contention may be disposed of by the clear showing in the reported testimony of Dr. von Luschen and in the transcript of proceedings, that his opinion was based upon just such an examination and comparison as the petitioner's counsel contends should be in the record: the fact that such examination and comparison are stated with generality instead of with particularity could not have worked any prejudice here.   The record shows (page A 2) an examination and consideration of the petitioner's color, eyes, nose, back of head, chin, and height.   And finally, all that Professor von Luschen would say was, "A man has been examined by me to-day, who does not look absolutely like a Chinese.   I think he might be a halfcaste, Chinese and Hawaiian."

[5] As to the alleged denial of the right of representation by counsel, ground (7), it seems that counsel were given every consideration by the immigration officials, though the latter were somewhat too sensitive to counsel's repeated exceptions and earnest efforts to preserve the rights of their client, and that counsel had every advantage recognized by the weight of authority as the due of their client in such cases.   It has been held by some courts, as, e. g., apparently in *Ex parte Ung King Ieng*, 211 Fed. 119, 121, that the presence of counsel should be permitted at such examinations before immigration officers, with an opportunity for cross-examination then and there, but the view of the Supreme Court and of the majority of lower Federal courts is otherwise.   See *In re Can Pon*, 168 Fed. 483; *United States ex rel. Buccino v. Williams*, 190 Fed. 479, 483; *United States ex rel. Buccino v. Williams*, 190 Fed. Fed. 1001; *United States v. Sing Tuck*, 104 U. S. 161, 169; ·*Low Wah Suey v. Backus*, 225 U. S. 460, 469, 470.

[2b]   Ground (8) is untenable.   Though having found, as I do, that the hearings before the immigration officers

were fair, and being therefore without jurisdiction to review their finding so long as there was some evidence to justify it, I may still say that the evidence is ample to warrant the conclusion of the petitioner's failure to show himself to be a citizen by birth. Inter alia, the difference is very marked between the ears in the photograph of the petitioner taken at arrival and those in the photograph of the son of Wong Sai Quin taken for registration purposes just before his departure from Hawaii fourteen years before; and also the general features suggest no identity; furthermore, there is the noteworthy failure of petitioner's alleged relatives, father, mother, and grandparent, to identify him at the immigration station; though, as it is admitted and as may be an excuse, they had not seen him for fourteen years or since he was eight and one-half years old, and two of them had "poor eyesight" which might explain their failure to recognize so near a blood relative.

Let the writ be dismissed and the petitioner remanded to the custody of the respondent, inspector in charge of the immigration station at Honolulu.

W. TIN YAN, TRUSTEE OF THE ESTATE OF L. AH CHAP, A BANKRUPT, *v.* L. AH CHAP, CHONG MEU LAN AND LEU LEN SHIN.

July 21, 1915.

1. *Resulting trust—Transfer of property by husband to wife:* Defendant husband took lease in his own name; afterward defendant wife made advances for rent, expenses and improvements of leasehold on his promise to transfer improvements to her after completion. Before such advances, husband defendant advertised the lease for

sale because he did not have money enough to build, and she would not advance money because the lease was not in her name. *Held*, no foundation for resulting trust in favor of the wife. "Such a trust must arise at the time of purchase; it cannot arise by after advances."

2. *Transfer of property by insolvent husband to wife:* Transfers of property to a wife by insolvent husband are viewed with distrust by courts. Substantial testimony besides that of husband and wife, essential.

3. *Bankruptcy—Settlements of results of mutual enterprise on wife—Rights of creditors:* An attempt to make a voluntary settlement of the results of a mutual enterprise for the family benefit, in favor of the wife, the husband being insolvent, is in derogation of the rights of creditors.

4. *Contracts and agreements between husband and wife:* Agreement by husband to transfer property to wife in consideration of advances of money by her for improving the same, void as against creditors.

5. *Equitable interest of wife in mutual venture for family support, or otherwise:* A husband being solely responsible for the support of the family, wife entitled to advances made by her to family venture as a creditor in equity of her husband; also so entitled to contributions to mutual business investment.

6. *Admissions:* An admission of a respondent to a petition for adjudication in bankruptcy, of an allegation charging him with a conveyance of property with intent to hinder, delay, and defraud his creditors, is sufficient, without explanaion, for the cancellation of such conveyance.

In equity: Bill to set aside fraudulent conveyance.

W. B. Lymer for complainant.
J. Lightfoot for respondents.

DOLE, J. The defendant, L. Ah Chap, as Ah Chap doing business as the American Dry Goods Company, was adjudicated a bankrupt in this court on the 15th day of April, 1914, on the petition of M. Phillips & Company, H. Hackfeld & Company, Limited, and Theo. H. Davies & Company, Limited, who in their petition alleged as an act of bankruptcy, that the said Ah Chap, within four months preceding the filing of the said petition, to-wit, on the 18th day of March, 1914, and being then insolvent, conveyed to his wife, Chong Meu Lan, a certain lease, with intent to hinder, delay and defraud his creditors.

The present action was brought May 23rd, 1914, by W. Tin Yan, the trustee of the estate in bankruptcy of the said L. Ah Chap, against him, the said bankrupt, and Leu Len Shin, the intermediary assignee of the said lease, and the said Chong Meu Lan, to whom the said lease was assigned by the said Leu Len Shin, as the bona fide grantee, praying that the said assignment and another previous assignment to the same effect, executed but not delivered, the consent of the lessor thereto not having been obtained, be cancelled as fraudulent and that the said leasehold estate be decreed to be vested in such trustee.

The answer of L. Ah Chap admits the transfer of the lease to his wife but denies that it was done with intent to hinder, delay and defraud his creditors. He alleges that the improvements on the leasehold cost approximately four thousand dollars of which his wife contributed about fifteen hundred dollars, and that he had further used the rents rendered available by reason of the new buildings for payment of the debts due on account of the construction thereof. He further answers that, being in debt to Allen & Robinson, Limited, for goods, wares and merchandise sold to him and used in the said buildings, in the amount of eight hundred dollars, he borrowed that amount from the Honolulu Dry Goods Company giving therefor four promissory notes in the amount of two hundred dollars each and with such funds paid his debt to Allen & Robinson, Limited; that the the said Chong Meu Lan, his said wife, had endorsed the said promissory notes.

The respondent contends in his answer, that by reason of such facts the said leasehold, although in his own name, was of right the property of his said wife, and that in executing the said assignment to his said wife he did not intend thereby to hinder, delay or defraud his creditors but merely to place the property in the name of the "actual" owner thereof.

The answer further denies that the defendant Leu Len Shin acted in the matter of the said assignment with the purpose of aiding the said L. Ah Chap in the accomplishment of any fraudulent purpose; and he further denies that he had any fraudulent intent in relation to the said transaction of which the other defendants had knowledge.

The other respondents answer formally, denying any fraudulent intent in relation to the said transaction of which the other defendants had knowledge.

The other respondents answer formally, denying any fraudulent intent or any knowledge of any fraudulent quality in the assignment of said lease.

It appears that at the hearing of the petition for adjudication in bankruptcy, April 15, 1914, counsel for L. Ah Chap asked that paragraph seven in the petition be stricken; counsel for the petitioner then consented to the withdrawal of this paragraph, upon the admission by counsel for the alleged bankrupt of the other act of bankruptcy alleged in the petition and, generally, all of the other allegations. This was agreed to by the latter. The following is a copy of the paragraph so withdrawn:

"That within four months preceding the filing of this petition, namely, during the month of March, 1914, the said Ah Chap, while insolvent, committed an act of bankruptcy in that he transferred, removed and concealed and permitted to be removed, transferred and concealed, and is now attempting to transfer, remove and conceal certain of his property with intent to hinder, delay and defraud his creditors."

The other act of bankruptcy referred to as admitted. is paragraph six of the petition, and is as follows:

"That within four months preceding the filing of this petition, viz., on or about the 18th day of March, 1914, the said Ah Chap, while insolvent, committed an act of bankruptcy, in that he caused to be transferred and conveyed from himself to his wife, Chong Meu Lan, by himself conveying to one Leu Len Shin, and causing and procuring the said Leu Len Shin to convey to his said wife, Chong Meu Lan, with intent to hinder, delay and defraud the creditors of the said Ah Chap, certain of his property of great value, to-wit, that certain leasehold from Mary P. Puuiki, dated June 17, 1911, for the term of twenty-five (25) years from said date."

This incident is testified to by Mr. O. P. Soares, the official reporter who was acting as such upon the occasion mentioned, and is further supported by the endorsement of the presiding judge, Hon. Charles F. Clemons, upon the margin of the petition in bankruptcy, opposite the said paragraph seven. The introduction of this incident into the evidence was followed by a motion to strike which was not allowed.

No immediate advantage was taken of such admission by counsel for the petitioner, and the court proceeded to hear further testimony.

The evidence introduced in behalf of the respondents was aimed, mainly, to substantiate the theory of a resultant trust to the wife or, in the alternative, to show that the assignment of the lease to her was the execution of an agreement therefor as the consideration of the money received.

It appears from the testimony of the wife that before she advanced any money on account of the lease, L. Ah Chap had procured the lease in his own name. Then after he had promised to make it over to her, "after it is complete," referring probably to proposed improvements on the leasehold, she began to make advances; first, one hundred and fifty dollars for rent and expense, and later other amounts. The lease was executed June 17, 1911, and was to go into effect, according to its provisions, July 1, 1911. It is in evidence that on the 7th day of July, 1911, L. Ah Chap advertised the lease for sale in a Chinese newspaper. He explains that he did this "because I didn't have enough money to build and she wouldn't advance me the money because she said the lease wasn't in her name. I can take the lease and go out and sell it."

[1] There does not appear in this transaction any foundation for a resulting trust in favor of the wife. The husband took the lease in his own name. Later he advertised his lease for sale, and then when his wife agreed to make advances of money for matters relative to such lease he gave up his plan of selling it. "Such a trust must arise at the time of the purchase; it cannot arise by after advances." *In re Wood,* 5 Fed. Cas. 443, 446; *Olcott v. Bynum,* 84 U. S. 44, 59; 1 Perry on Trusts, 5th ed., secs. 124, 133.

With this conclusion the question arises whether the assignment of the lease to the wife may be supported as the execution of an agreement therefor for which the money advanced by her was the consideration; or is she only a creditor entitled to her pro rata with other creditors; or were her advances of money merely contributions to a common enterprise for the benefit of both husband and wife as a family? There is no support in the evidence to the theory that such advances were gifts to the husband.

In their testimony both L. Ah Chap and his wife try to show that the lease was the wife's enterprise from the beginning and that the husband was only concerned in it as an agent for her. He says, in reference to fifteen hundred dollars which his wife paid him to "help along", as he said at first, in the matter of improvements on the leasehold, that "I don't borrow any money from her. She gave me this money to attend to her own business." His testimony appears to become more definite, from day to day, as the case progresses, in the direction of the theory that it was solely his wife's enterprise. Some light is thrown upon this development in his mind through his testimony given before the referee in bankruptcy in May, his testimony here having been given in July and August. The objection of his counsel to the admission, in the trial, of his testimony before the referee was overruled. In such testimony he said that the lease belonged to him but his wife also had a money interest in it; that she put fifteen hundred dollars into it and that he put in more than a thousand dollars. He admitted that he transferred the lease to his wife in order to protect her in her investment of the fifteen hundred dollars which she had put into it. In answer to the question, "And it was this fifteen hundred dollars she put into the building that you wanted to secure her in by this assignment?", he said, "When I borrowed the money from her, she wanted me to sell the property to her, or buy it in her name, but I did not pay any attention to her because she is my wife."' He further said in such testimony in May, that he borrowed eight hundred dollars from the Honolulu Dry Goods Company for the building expenses and mortgaged the lease to secure it. In his testimony in this court in July he said he was acting for his wife when he signed the notes for the eight hundred dollars. As stated above, he said in May that he had put more than a thousand dollars into the building fund, in addition to the fifteen hundred dollars advanced by his wife, whereas in July he testified that outside of the fifteen hundred dollars, the money was procured by borrowing from loan associations and giving notes, some of which were signed by his wife and endorsed by her, he acting for her.

Some further light is obtained by reference to the schedules sworn to by him April 28, 1914, and filed in the bankruptcy proceedings of L. Ah Chap, May 5, 1914. In "Schedule A (2), creditors holding securities", is the following entry:

Names of creditors	Residence	Description of securities	When and where contracted	Value of securities	Amount of debts
Honolulu Dry Goods Co.	Honolulu	Mort. on lease from Mary Kahai Puuiki and Mary Kahai, dated June 17. 1911, to me	Nov. 21, 1911, at Honolulu	$4,500.	$800.

Mary Kahai Puuiki, the landlady, who has no interest in the present issue, as far as appears, says that Ah Chap first came to her in March, 1914, to ask her to consent to the assignment of the lease to his wife, and that he came more than four times. On his first visit he gave as a reason for the proposed assignment, that he was going to China, to be absent a year. At his second visit he urged the immediate execution of the assignment because the vessel on which he was to embark for China was to sail the following week. She also said the papers he brought for her to approve were not the same as Exhibits 5 and 6 for the respondents, shown to her in court; also, contrary to testimony of Ah Chap, that he had not visited her in regard to the assignment before March, 1914.

Five witnesses were introduced to support the theory that the improvements on the leasehold were in Mrs. Ah Chap's interest. The first, Wong You, said in reply to the following question, "I'll ask you if in the month of November, 1911, you had any business dealings with Mrs. Ah Chap?", "She was building some buildings that year, and she said she didn't have enough money, and asked me for a loan", which he says he gave her. Plaintiff's Exhibit D is a note for four hundred dollars in favor of Wong You, signed by Chong Meu Lan—the wife, and endorsed by Liu Chap—the husband. On cross-examination, he says it was Ah Chap who told him that Mrs. Ah Chap was building. Also that in 1911 and 1912, he was lending money to Ah Chap but couldn't say how much he loaned Ah Chap for himself and how much for his wife. Then on redirect he could not remember that he loaned Ah Chap any money in 1911. The next witness, Liu Dai, after the following question, "Do you know anything about a money loan association in the year in August, 1911, in which Mrs. Ah Chap was interested?", said she heard Mrs. Ah Chap speak to her (Liu Dai's) husband about borrowing money for a building she had started. The third witness, Ching

Kim Chong, was asked this question: "Do you know anything about a money loan association in which Mrs. Ah
Chap was interested in the year 1911, month of August?"
The interpreter asked the counsel before the witness replied, "Is it Ah Chap or Mrs. Ah Chap's loan?" Counsel
answered, "Mrs. Ah Chap." The witness then said, in answer to the original question, "I do." On being asked if
she acted for herself or through her husband, the witness
replied, "His wife spoke to my wife; my wife asked me
about it, then I decided to assist them for this purpose
of building a house." On cross-examination he said that
"when they got the money", Mrs. Ah Chap came and said
she wanted the money to build a house. Respondent's
Exhibit 3 was produced and identified as the note of Chong
Meu Lan (Mrs. Ah Chap) in favor of Ching Kim Chong
for the first loan of fifty dollars. The note is endorsed L.
Ah Chap. The next witness, Chun How, in answer to the
question, "In the month of December, 1911, did you have
any business dealings with Mrs. Ah Chap?", and following questions, said that he did and loaned her four hundred dollars on her asking for it to build a house, and she
gave her note for it, which was produced as plaintiff's Exhibit E, a note for four hundred dollars in favor of Chun
How, signed Chong Mew Lan and endorsed Liu Chap. · Witness further said the building in question was not then begun, then that he thought it was begun, then, when told that
Ah Chap had testified that the house had been finished in
September, that he did not know when it was begun or finished but that he did know that she came to borrow money
for that purpose. The note is dated December 1, 1911.
The note was paid by Ah Chap in instalments. It was
brought out on cross-examination that witness and another
were endorsers of a note signed by Ah Chap for four hundred dollars, and that the time of payment was two months
later. In regard to advertising the lease for sale, he said,
"They didn't have any money to build the house on it,

then Mrs. Ah Chap she didn't want to sell it and he thought he could borrow money to build on it." L. Seu Chun, the last witness in support of Mrs. Ah Chap on this point, has been the manager of the Honolulu Dry Goods Company since it started. He said that when he saw the advertisement of the lease for sale he expostulated with Ah Chap, who said, "He got no money he want ask his wife get money to build." He then went to Mrs. Ah Chap and upbraided her for not furnishing the money. She said, "That lease sign to Ah Chap." Witness replied, "That's all right, you dig up money, by by pay up he sign to you just the same." He also testified to the loan of eight hundred dollars to Ah Chap in relation to the building, and that he received therefor from Ah Chap four notes of two hundred dollars each, secured by a mortgage of the lease. These notes and mortgage were dated November 21, 1911; the notes were endorsed Chong Mew Lan (Mrs. Ah Chap), March 19, 1914.

[2] I have quoted thus largely from the testimony, as transfers of property to a wife by an insolvent husband are viewed with mistrust by courts.

"In transactions between husband and wife, which are impeached as fraudulent, it requires less proof to sustain the impeachment, and more and stricter proof to repel it, than would be required if the transaction were between strangers. A transfer of property, either directly or indirectly, by an insolvent husband to his wife, is justly regarded with suspicion; and unless it is clearly shown to be entirely free from an intent to withdraw the property from the husband's creditors, or the presumption of fraud be overcome by satisfactory affirmative proof, it will not be sustained." *Zinn v. Law et ux.*, 9 S. E. 873.

Substantial testimony, besides that of the husband and wife, is considered essential in such cases. The case, *In re Teter*, 23 Am. B. R. 228, 229, emphasizes this in efforts to establish a resulting trust in favor of the wife, but the rule applies equally to the case before the court in its present phase.

Goo Peang, a witness for respondents, according to his story, was the one who first informed the Ah Chaps that the place in question was for lease, and went with them to see the lot. He said further that in about a month after the lease was obtained, Ah Chap wanted to sell it. In answer to the question, "Was there anything said as to who the leasehold was to belong to?", Goo Peang, after stating that the lease was made to Ah Chap, said, "How they settled afterwards and understood each other, I do not know". Goo Peang was an old acquaintance of Ah Chap's and appeared to hold the position of a confidential friend. He it was to whom the lease was assigned in 1913 by Ah Chap, in order that he should assign it to Mrs. Ah Chap, which he did. This assignment does not figure in the case as evidence of title in Mrs. Ah Chap, it not having been endorsed by Mrs. Kahai, the landlady, but merely to show previous intention on the part of Ah Chap.

Taking all of the evidence together, there is much that is conflicting on the question of an agreement by Ah Chap to transfer the leasehold to his wife. The wife did not make the mortgage of the lease to the Honolulu Dry Goods Company, as she says she did; and the notes that were secured by this mortgage she did not endorse until March 19, 1914, the day after the lease was assigned to her, as complained of in the bill. Was her endorsement of such notes made in consideration of the assignment of the lease to her? Evidently Ah Chap was not telling the exact truth when he said in July that he was acting for his wife when he signed the four notes to the Honolulu Dry Goods Company; otherwise he would not have included them as one of his debts in his bankruptcy schedule in April, together with his mortgage of the lease ; and evidently he was not telling the truth when he said in July, "I didn't borrow any money from her (Mrs. Ah Chap). She gave me this

money to attend to her own business"; otherwise he would
not have said in May before the referee that the lease "belonged to myself but my wife had money invested too.
. . . My wife put up fifteen hundred dollars and I put
up more than one thousand dollars and I borrowed some
money from other people. . . . When I borrowed the
money from her, she wanted me to sell the property to her,
or buy it in her name. . . . She growled me every day,
so this year I do what she talked to me." Again in July,
apparently forgetting for the moment his plan of defense,
he gave as a reason to the court for his assignment of the
property to his wife, that, "I had sometimes ago borrowed
a little over a thousand dollars from my wife and built a
house", and wanted to secure her so that she would not
lose the thousand dollars she had advanced. Then there
is the allegation of his answer to the complaint, in which
he says that he borrowed the eight hundred dollars from
the Honolulu Dry Goods Company to pay Allen & Robinson for goods, etc., sold to him and used in the buildings
under consideration.

Much more might be done in analyzing the testimony
for the defense. The further it is investigated the more
defective it appears. Counsel for the defense, admitting
the weakness of Ah Chap's testimony, appeals for a favorable view for the testimony of the wife. But her husband's testimony in May, and his acts in April, in relation
to his bankruptcy, not only have undermined his testimony
in this court, but have greatly tended to weaken hers. Her
supporting witnesses with the exception of L. Sen Chun,
have nothing whatever to say about any agreement between
husband and wife. These agree, with almost parrot-like
unanimity, that she was looking for money with which to
build a house. L. Sen Chun speaks of the advertisement
of the lease for sale, upon seeing which he expostulated

with Ah Chap, who said he had no money for improving
the leasehold, and wanted witness to talk with Mrs. Ah
Chap about getting money; witness did so and blamed her
for not furnishing money. She excused herself on the
ground that the lease was made to Ah Chap. Witness encouraged her to furnish the money with the expectation
that when, as I understand his testimony, the improvements were paid for, Ah Chap would transfer the lease to
her. Here is no evidence of an agreement.

[4] Mrs. Ah Chap's notes, introduced in evidence as
vouchers of money raised for this enterprise, are uniformly
endorsed by Ah Chap; and his four notes in favor of the
Honolulu Dry Goods Company were endorsed eventually by
her. These notes, except those in favor of the Honolulu
Dry Goods Company, have all been paid by Ah Chap out
of the rents of the improved leasehold. The undertaking,
under all the circumstances disclosed by the evidence, looks
like an enterprise mutually entered into by husband and
wife for the family benefit, to be managed by the husband.
If it was a part of this scheme to have the business carried
on in the name of the wife, it was in derogation of the
rights of the creditors of the husband, as it was an attempt
to make a voluntary settlement of the results of his business management and of a portion of his property as well,
in favor of his wife. The decision in the case of *Glidden,
Murphy & Company v. Taylor*, 16 O. St. 509, 521, comments upon a somewhat similar project as follows: "The
principle of the arrangement would be the same whether
it embraced property which he had already acquired or only
his future acquisitions; and if the arrangement be valid
as against creditors for the period of about four years that
elapsed from the time of its date to the time of the trial
it may be continued during the joint lives of the parties, if
they so elect."

Of course a husband and wife are disqualified from entering into partnership relations with each other. 1 Bates

Laws of Partnership, sec. 140; *Lord v. Parker,* 85 Mass. 127, 129. An attempt to enter into such partnership, and the investment of funds by the wife in the supposed firm, would make her a creditor of her husband or of the firm, if there were other partners, at least in equity. *Lord v. Davison,* 85 Mass. 131, 133. And yet by our statutes a married woman may not enter into a contract with her husband, (Rev. Laws, Haw. 1915, sec. 2951) nor sue him or be sued by him (Id., sec. 2954). This would seem to neutralize any contract or agreement which may have been made between them, as to her advances of money on account of improvements to the leasehold and a promise by him, in consideration thereof, to transfer the leasehold to her, even if the evidence sustains the contention of the existence of such agreement, which it cannot confidently be said to do. As the case stands, it fails both on the facts and the law to sustain the contention of Ah Chap and his wife that she is entitled to hold the lease as the real and equitable owner thereof.

Having acquired jurisdiction, the court will proceed under the rule, to dispose of the whole case as it has developed under the pleadings and evidence, and particularly to determine the rights of Chong Meu Lan in relation to the leasehold, the transfer of which to her is complained of as fraudulent.

[5] The question remains whether Mrs. Ah Chap has in equity a rightful claim for the advances she has made toward the improvement of the leasehold? It appears to be well established by the evidence that she advanced from her own money sixteen hundred and fifty dollars, Upon the theory suggested, that the lease affair was an enterprise for the benefit of the family, she was not required to contribute to such venture, the husband being solely responsible for the support of the family, Rev. Laws, Haw. 1915, sec. 2956. In the *Glidden* case, referred to above, the court

says, after adjudging the settlement as to the wife to be void, "The only remaining questions, in this aspect of the case, is as to the extent of the equity of the wife in the property. As the plaintiffs are, in equity, seeking to divest her of the title, she is, as against them, entitled to protection to the extent of her right; and, as we have already remarked, the most favorable position she can claim to occupy is that of a creditor in equity of her husband, and, as such, entitled to her money and interest." In that case the profits of the venture were used both for the support of the family and for further investments. Whether the venture in this case was for family support or was merely a business speculation, Mrs. Ah Chap is entitled to the money she put into it as a creditor in equity of her husband.

[6] I have dealt with this case upon the main issue as exhibited by the pleadings and the evidence in general, leaving out of consideration the extraordinary admission made by the counsel for the bankrupt, referred to in the early part of this opinion; which in itself was sufficient as it stood, without explanation, had the plaintiffs counsel pressed it, to have justified the cancellation of the assignments complained of.

An attempt was made by the defense to show that Ah Chap's testimony before the referee which is inconsistent with his testimony before the court, was due to the interpreter, who used a different Chinese dialect than the one most familiar to Ah Chap. This has failed, and partly so through Ah Chap's own testimony on the point, in addition to the testimony of others.

I find that the prayer of the complaint, that the two assignments of the lease in question be cancelled and that the leasehold estate therein described be decreed to be vested in complainant, should be granted; and also that a claim of sixteen hundred and fifty dollars should be allowed against the said bankrupt estate in favor of the said

Chong Meu Lan, the wife of the said bankrupt, costs to
be divided equally between the complainant and Mr. L. Ah
Chap.

IN THE MATTER OF THE APPLICATION OF KIKU YU FOR A WRIT OF HABEAS CORPUS.

August 12, 1915.

1. *Conflict of laws—Divorce according to Japanese procedure:*
Divorce by Japanese procedure is not recognized in the United States.

2. *Marriage by correspondence:* Marriage by correspondence between parties living one in Hawaii and the other in Japan, is not
recognized in the United States.

3. *Immigration—Board of special inquiry:* A board of special
inquiry under the immigration laws, made up of the immigration
inspector, who makes a preliminary examination of an alien desiring
to land and detains him for examination before such board, and two
other immigration inspectors, is not a legal board, and is without
jurisdiction to decide such alien's right to land.

4. *Same—Decision of incompetent board refusing landing to alien
—Status of alien under such decision:* An alien refused landing by
a board so constituted, may not be detained in custody awaiting the
determination of the respondent's appeal, or a new trial of his right
to land by a competent board, but may be discharged under bond to
appear in case their decision should be reversed on appeal, and a new
board of special inquiry be constituted to try the case.

Habeas Corpus: Hearing on traverse to return.

G. S. Curry for petitioner.
J. W. Thompson, Assistant U. S. Attorney, for respondent.

DOLE, J.   The petitioner applied for a writ of habeas

corpus, which was issued and she was brought into court. It appears that one Rihei Yu came to this country a number of years ago, with his wife, Tsuya; that after living here a short time his wife deserted him and finally lived with another man; that a divorce between them, according to Japanese procedure, was obtained, whereupon the said Rihei Yu and the petitioner were married by correspondence—she then living in Japan—according to Japanese procedure. The petitioner was detained from landing on the ground that Rihei Yu was still a married man and that her coming to Hawaii to live with him would involve her in bigamous relations with him, and therefore that she was brought here for immoral purposes and was not entitled to land.

[1] [2] The court does not recognize a marriage of the kind alleged, nor does it recognize a Japanese divorce as alleged, of parties resident in Hawaii.

After the arrival of the petitioner here, on June 7, 1915, and after the issuance of said writ of habeas corpus, on July 9th, it appears that a legal divorce was otained in the courts of the Territory by Rihei Yu, divorcing him from his former wife. Evidence also was given of the issuance of a license to marry to the said Rihei Yu and Kiku Yu, about the 15th day of June, after the issuance of the writ of habeas corpus. Evidence of the divorce and license to marry was admitted, not as affecting her right to land on the ground of the removal of all obstacles to their union, as they were obtained subsequent to the issuance of the writ of habeas corpus, but as bearing on the question of the purpose with which Kiku Yu, the petitioner, came to Honolulu.

It is clear to me that, although when she arrived in Honolulu she could not have legally married Rihei Yu without a subsequent decree of divorce, yet both she and Rihei Yu, in their ignorance of the marriage laws of Hawaii and their confidence in the effectiveness of the Japanese laws of marriage and divorce, as affecting their status, arranged her coming entirely free from any conscious immoral purpose, but that they both intended and expected that they should and would be man and wife here.

. The board of special inquiry have decided otherwise, and I do not feel that its decision on this point is a matter that this court might interfere with, it being a decision of fact, were this the only point to be considered. The traverse to the return, however, raises another point, and that is that the detention of the petitioner is illegal for the reason that the board of special inquiry which decided that she should be sent back to Japan was without jurisdiction and its decision void, inasmuch as Jackson L. Milligan, one of such board, was the inspector who detained the petitioner for examination as to her right to land before the board of special inquiry.

It appears that Mr. Milligan acted as the examining immigration inspector at the preliminary examination of the petitioner, with other passengers who had arrived with her on the same vessel from Japan, and detained her for examination before a board of special inquiry. Thereafter the said Kiku Yu was examined by a board of special inquiry, of which board the said Milligan was a member.

[3] Counsel for Kiku Yu, in his traverse to the respondent's return, contends that a board of special inquiry including as one of its three members the inspector who had detained an arriving alien for examination before such board, as one not clearly entitled to land, was not such a board of special inquiry as is required by the immigration laws and regulations, and was without jurisdiction to try the petitioner's right to land. The statute;—Act of 1907, s. 25, 34, State. 898, 906, provides that such board "shall be selected from such of the immigrant officials in the service as the Commissioner General of Immigration, with the approval of the Secretary of Labor, shall from time to time designate as qualified to serve on such board: *Provided*, that at ports where there are fewer than three immigrant in-

spectors, other United States officials may be appointed."
The case of *United States ex rel. Pasos v. Redfern, Com.
of Im.*, 180 Fed. 500, which is parallel to this on this point,
is cited by petitioner's counsel in support of his contention.
The opinion in that case holds that the words "fewer than
three immigrant inspectors" should be construed to mean
fewer than three immigrant inspectors eligible to serve, and
continues as follows:

"It is fundamental in American jurisprudence that every
person is entitled to a fair trial by an impartial tribunal, and
a board of special inquiry constituted as in this case is at
least open to suspicion.   I do not believe the law contemplates that the inspector who makes the preliminary examination shall serve on the board of special inquiry, and I
must hold in this case that the board which denied to petitioner the right to land was illegal and without power."

The construction adopted in the cited case seems to follow the rule that "all laws should receive a sensible construction.   General terms should be so limited in their application as not to lead to injustice, oppression or an absurd consequence. . . . The reason of the law in such cases
should prevail over its letter." *United States v. Kirby*, 74
U. S. 482, 486-487.   The spirit of the law requires a fair
hearing for arriving immigrants in regard to whom there is a
doubt as to their right to land   It would hardly be contended that the letter of the law would be strictly carried
out if one of the inspectors was a near relative of the arriving immigrant, or a partner in business with him.   The
examining inspector in these cases may be said to be like
a committing magistrate who, by general opinion, is dis-
qualfied from sitting with another court in a case committed
by him to such court; and a law which would allow such
jurisdiction would be generally regarded as defective legislation.   The record of the examination of petitioner before
the board of special inquiry contains an incident which sug-
guests the danger of the practice.   At the close of the examination Mr. Milligan made a motion that petitioner be

denied admission and be returned to Japan, which was seconded by another member and concurred in by the third. Of course in cases where the examining inspector has reached a conclusion unfavorable to the immigrant, his presence on the board would be likely to be an element unfavorable to an impartial hearing. The leading part that Mr. Milligan took in the final decision of the board may have had no significance, or it may be the straw indicating a desire on his part to carry the decision of the board in support of his previous ruling. Whatever may have been his exact attitude, his presence raises suspicions unfavorable to the status of the board as an impartial tribunal.

I am disposed to follow the precedent of the *United States ex rel. Pazos v. Redfern,* 180 Fed. 500, and hold that the board of special inquiry as constituted in this case was not a legal board under the statute.

[4] Under this ruling, what is the status of the petitioner? The case of *Chin Yow,* 208 U. S. 8, appears to apply and yet that was a case in which a person claiming to be a citizen of the United States was alleged to have been deprived of a fair hearing. The court ruled that upon proof of such unfair hearing, the trial court was authorized to try the case on the merits. The decision, however, contains language which might limit such authority in cases where the question of citizenship was an issue, to-wit, "As between the substantive right of citizens to enter and of persons alleging themselves to be citizens to have a chance to prove their allegation on the one side and the conclusiveness of the commissioner's fiat on the other, when one or the other must give way, the latter must yield. In such a case something must be done, and it naturally falls to be done by the courts." With this doubt in my mind, I will take the clearer way. See *ex parte Tsuie Shee,* 218 Fed. 256, 259. The petitioner may not be indefinitely detained awaiting a determination of an appeal by the respondent or a due hearing of the question of her right to land by a

competent tribunal. It is ordered that she be discharged from custody upon giving bond in the sum of one hundred dollars, conditioned that she will surrender herself to the immigration officers in case this decision shall be reversed on appeal, or in case a new board of special inquiry shall be constituted to try her right to land.

IN THE MATTER OF THE APPLICATION OF LOOK WONG BY LOOK SAY, HIS FATHER, HIS NEXT FRIEND, FOR A WRIT OF HABEAS CORPUS.

August 30, 1915.

1. *Aliens—Chinese Exclusion Act—Admission of minor son of resident merchant, born of a polygamous marriage*: The minor son of a resident Chinese merchant, the issue of a marriage contracted by the father in China when the father had a lawful wife living in Hawaii, is not entitled to admission to this country, unless on other grounds than that of being the son of such resident, even though the prior marriage was dissolved subsequent to the son's birth.

2. *Conflict of laws—Foreign marriage—Polygamous marriage and issue thereof*: A marriage lawful in China will not be recognized here, so far as to warrant the admission as an immigrant, of the minor son of a Chinese resident merchant, the issue of such marriage, when the marriage was entered into during the existence of a prior lawful marriage contracted in Hawaii between the father and a woman other than the mother of the immigrant—except on another ground than the mere relation of father and son.

Habeas Corpus: Hearing on return to writ.

W. T. Carden and *C. S. Franklin (Thompson, Milverton & Cathcart* with them) for petitioner.

Jeff McCarn, U. S. District Attorney, for respondent.

CLEMONS, J. This is a petition for a writ of habeas
corpus in behalf of an immigrant, Look Wong, denied a
landing at the port of Honolulu, for having "failed to prove
a status which entitles him to admission." The order of
the immigration inspector denying admission was affirmed
on appeal to the Secretary of Labor. In the testimony on
which the order was based, the following facts appear:

The immigrant, a minor, male, was born in China August
3, 1898, of Chinese parents. His mother was a resident
of China, and was married to his father there in 1891. At
the time of the marriage the father who was, had for some
time been, and is now, a resident merchant of Hawaii, had
here an Hawaiian wife, to whom he had been married for
twenty years or more but from whom he was divorced by
decree of the Circuit Court of the First Circuit of the Republic of Hawaii, dated February 21, 1898. In 1898 the
father returned to Hawaii, after a year's absence in China,
and in 1903 again went to China, where he lived with the
immigrant's mother until 1913, then returning to Hawaii.

The inspector's decision in full follows:

"It is a maxim that the law favors matrimony. This is
based on public policy. The present case presents peculiar
conditions, and, in common with others, I have an aversion
against doing violence to human feelings. However, a careful consideration of the record in this case leads me to conclude that the applicant, Look Wong, is the natural and
not the lawful son of Look Say, whose mercantile status is
satisfactorily established. The fact of cohabitation raises
a presumption of marriage only in cases where the cohabitation is not meretricious and the subsequent cohabitation
with a woman with whom a man had illicit relations would
not of itself constitute a common law marriage as it would
if the first cohabitation were free from former marital impediment. This matter is comprehensively discussed in the
case of *Randlett v. Rice*, 141 Mass. 385. The applicant is
a minor.

"Look Wong is hereby denied a landing as a Chinese
person who has failed to prove a status which entitles him

to admission to the United States and he is ordered deported to China, the country whence he came."

[1] [2] As to the basis of that decision, two arguments may be possible, (1) for a finding of illegitimacy from want of marriage of the parents, and (2) even if such marriage existed, for a finding of illegitimacy by reason of the existence of a prior marriage. A finding such as the former, being a finding of fact, would be conclusive and preclude review by this court; a finding such as the latter, so far as it is a conclusion of law, would not be conclusive if erroneous. *De Bruler v. Gallo*, 184 Fed. 566, 570. And see Bouve, Exclusion of Aliens, 530-535.

In support of an argument for a finding of no marriage, (1) supra, the presumption in favor of the validity of official acts might be invoked And so it might be supposed that although the testimony tended to prove marriage, the inspector, who was the judge of the credibility of the witnesses, was not convinced—especially as under the regulations of the bureau of immigration governing the admission of Chinese, the inspector should "in every instance" require "exacting evidence of the relationship claimed." Rule 9 (a), (b). Moreover, the language of the decision might be taken to indicate that the inspector did not regard the marriage as established; for it reads: "the fact of cohabitation [i.e., apparently, with the Chinese wife before the divorce of the Hawaiian wife] raises a *presumption* of marriage only in cases where the cohabitation is not meretricious, and the *subsequent* cohabitation [i. e., after the divorce] with a woman with whom a man had *illicit* relations would not of itself constitute a common law marriage as it would if the *first* cohabitation were free from marital impediment."

However, in view of the fact that the decision may not be so definite as to preclude the possibility of the two arguments above stated, as also in view of the fact that, while the only direct evidence of the marriage was the say-so of the immigrant's father and the bare say-so of the immigrant himself and two others, there were still no inherent inconsistencies in the testimony on this point and no contradiction of it, and in view of the fact that the examining official made no effort to test the witnesses as to the basis of their conclusion of marriage and as to their means of knowledge, etc. (see *In re Jiro Miragusuku*, ante, p. 344), it is more fair to assume that the inspector would not have made a finding of fact so contrary to what evidence there was (weak as it may be) and a finding of fact absolutely determinative of the case, without a definite statement of such finding,—especially as it is not an unreasonable contention that the immigrant was entitled to an express determination of the fact of the alleged marriage upon which his right to enter is based. See Bouve, Exclusion of Aliens, 517, also Id. 510. For these reasons, as well as because it is possible to view the decision as a finding of illegitimacy, based on the existence of the father's prior marriage, we shall consider the case in the latter aspect, and then endeavor to determine whether the inspector's decision would be valid as a matter of law. In other words, admitting the fact of the second marriage, would the child of such marriage be entitled to enter the United States?

It may be said here that in spite of the above suggestion, of the use of the words of the decision last quoted as an argument for a finding of no marriage, the word "cohabitation", as first used in the quotation (in reference to the relation between the father and mother before the dissolution of the prior, Hawaiian, marriage), might imply merely that, because of the existence of the prior marriage, the relation based upon the alleged marriage in China could not be called a valid marriage relation, but only a state of cohabitation. With that sense of the word "cohabitation" as applied to the marriage in China, the only question is one of law. (2) supra.

It is urged that the marriage, being lawful in China where entered into (as appears from the certificate of the Chinese consul at Honolulu submitted to the Secretary of Labor on the appeal), is lawful here and everywhere, and that the immigrant, born of that marriage and being legiti- mate there, must be regarded as legitimate here; also, that if the immigrant is legitimate by the law of his domicile, it is immaterial how he came to be so; also, that in applying considerations of policy against polygamy, the court should look no further than the immediate parties, father and mother, and should not look to those one degree removed, who are innocent parties.

Of course, the inspector's decision would be in error in broadly characterizing as illegitimate the issue of such a marriage valid in China. But in the opinion of the court the effect of the decision is essentially sound; for an excep- tion to the rule of recognition of a foreign marriage arises when the marriage contravenes the spirit and policy of our laws and institutions. This polygamous marriage in China is within such exception, and the immigrant here whose status is derived from this marriage must be governed ac- cordingly.

Story says:

"The general principle certainly is that between persons *sui juris*, marriage is to be decided by the law of the place where it is celebrated. If valid there, it is valid everywhere. . . . The most prominent, if not the only known ex- ceptions to the rule, are those marriages involving polyg- amy and incest; those positively prohibited by the public laws of a country from motives of policy; and those cele- brated in foreign countries by subjects, entitling themselves under special circumstances to the benefit of the laws of their own country. . . . In respect to the first excep- tion, that of marriages involving polygamy and incest, Christianity is understood to prohibit polygamy and incest, and therefore no Christian country would recognize polyg- amy, or incestuous marriages." Conflict of Laws, 7th ed., secs. 113, 113 a, 113 b (and note 3), 114. See also secs. 89, 114 d.

Minor says:

"If one having a consort living and undivorced marries again, though the subsequent marriage should take place ih a barbarous state where marriages are valid, it will not be upheld in any civilized country." Conflict of Laws, sec. 75.

Wharton says:

"It is agreed that an act valid when done by a person in his own country is to be regarded as valid in foreign countries, even though in such foreign countries he is treated as incapable of performing such act. . . . At the same time a status held by the *lex fori* to be immoral, or to contravene public policy, will not be enforced although established by a foreign state in conformity with its own jurisprudence." Conflict of Laws, 3d ed., sec. 125. See also Id., secs. 126, 130, 131 a, 175.

Judge Cooley says:

"Polygamous and incestuous marriages celebrated in countries where they are permitted, are nevertheless treated as invalid here, because they are condemned by the common voice of civilized nations, which establishes a common law forbidding them." *Hutchins v. Kimmell*, 31 Mich., 126, 134.

To the same effect are: *Commonwealth v. Graham*, 31 N. E. 706, 707 (Mass.), Field, C. J.; *Ross v. Ross*, 129 Mass. 243, 247, Gray, C. J.; *Commonwealth v. Lane*, 113 Mass. 458, 463, Gray, C. J.; *True v. Ranney*, 21 N. H. 52, 53 Am. Dec. 164, 166; *Pennegar v. State*, 10 S. W. 305, 306-307 (Tenn.); *State v. Ross*, 76 N. C. 242, 22 Am. Rep. 678, 680-681; *Jackson v. Jackson*, 33 Atl. 317, 318-319 (Md.); *Van Voorhis v. Brintnall*, 88 N. Y. 18, 26; *Succession of Gabisso*, 44 So. 438, 441 (La.), and *Campbell v. Crompton*, 10 Fed. 417, 424, Wallace J.; *State v. Tutty*, 41 Fed. 753, 759-760; *United States v. Rodgers*, 109 Fed. 886, 887. See *State v. Ross*, 76 N. C. 242, 22 Am. Rep. 678, 682.

Wharton on Conflict of Laws, 3d ed., sec. 250 a, extends to the offspring of a polygamous marriage the principle above applied by Story and others to such marriage itself:

"As a general principle, the issue of a marriage valid

where celebrated, will be deemed legitimate for the purposes in question, though the marriage would have been invalid and the children therefore illegitimate, tested by the *lex rei sitae* or *lex domicilii decedentis.* The only exceptions to this rule are cases in which the marriage itself, for some reason, comes within an exception to the general rule that a marriage valid where celebrated is valid everywhere."

This rule is applied in *Fenton v. Livingstone*, 5 Jur. N. S. 1183, 3 Macq. H. L. Cas. 497, 556; 3 Wharton, Conflict of Laws, 3d ed., p. 547, n. 4.

The language of Robertson, C. J., in *Sneed v Ewing*, 5 J. J. Marsh. (Ky.) 460, 489, 22 Am. Dec. 41, 68, is pertinent:

"Counsel . . . insist that as Mrs. Ewing was legitimate in Kentucky, she could not have been illegitimate in Indiana or elsewhere. This argument is inconclusive when applied to the facts in this case. As issue is one of the objects and fruits of marriage, and as it is a general rule that the incidents follow the law of marriage itself, the argument would have been more formidable if it had been shown that the marriage in this case had been legal. But, even then, it would not have been conclusive, for although marriage, like other civil contracts, must be regulated by the *lex loci contractus*, it is not every marriage which may be valid by the law of the place where it was consummated, that will be recognized as legal everywhere else. Every sovereign state is the conservator of its own morals, and may nullify incestuous or polygamous contracts."

Any application of the rule of universal recognition of a foreign marriage cannot be tolerated which would give to men who marry in countries where polygamy is lawful, as it is conceded that it was lawful in China, privileges which are denied to our own citizens. Our own citizens do not here gain any privileges, but quite the contrary, *by virtue of a polygamous marriage*, either with respect to their polygamous wives or their children by such wives, and certainly, therefore no subject of a foreign country may come here and *by virtue of a polygamous marriage* valid there be free to bring with him his polygamous wife and her children, the fruits of such polygamous marriage. This immigrant must come into the country on his own merits and not by virtue of a relation which we recognize as valid in China but disapprove as contrary to our own institutions.

The distinction here is suggested by Lord Justice Turner in *Hope v. Hope,* 8 De Gex, M. & G., 731, 3 Beale's Cases on Conflict of Laws, 468, 471:

"When the courts of one country are called upon to enforce contracts entered into in another country, the question to be considered is not merely whether the contract sought to be enforced is valid according to the laws of the country in which it is entered into, but whether it is consistent with the laws and policy of the country in which it is sought to be enforced."

See *In re Bethell,* 38 Ch. D. 220, as summarized in 3 Beale's Cases on Conflict of Laws, 31, note. That this distinction is valid when applied to status as well as when applied to contracts, see the decision of Judge Ware in the case of *Polydore v. Prince,* 1 Ware 402, 19 Fed. Cas. 950, No. 11,257, 3 Beale's Cases on Conflict of Laws 2-7, 9. The argument in that case is similar to the argument in the present case. 3 Beale's Cases, 2-3. See also *Somerset v. Stewart,* Lofft, 1, 3 Beale's Cases on Conflict of Laws, 1, Mansfield C. J., holding that the status of slavery, though then recognized as legal in Virginia, "is so odious that nothing can be suffered to support it [in England] but positive law."

And so the court in *Van Matre v. Sankey,* 148 Ill. 536, 3 Beale's Cases on Conflict of Laws, 53, 55, says: "The status of appellee having been established under and by virtue of the *lex domicilii,* is to be recognized and upheld in every other State, unless such status or the rights flowing therefrom are inconsistent with or opposed to the laws and policy of the State where it is sought to be availed of." See also Story, Conflict of Laws, sec. 87; *Shick v. Howe,* 137 Iowa, 249, 114 N. W. 916; *Finley v. Brown,* 122 Tenn. 316, 123 S. W. 359, 364; *In re Williams' Estate,* 102 Cal. 70, 82, 36

Pac. 407, 410, and, as to the general basis of public policy,
Black, Judicial Precedents, 163.

In view of the foregoing authorities, the regulations of
the bureau of immigration governing the admission of Chinese, in providing for the admission of the "lawful wife and
minor children," may be taken to have intended the word
"lawful" to apply to the minor children as well as to the
wife, and to have intended that word to mean such children as are the fruits of a marriage which it is our policy
to recognize./ Rule 2; Rule 9 (a); see also Rule 9 (b).

The policy above suggested disposes of the following
argument of counsel, even though it be an argument plausible and of merit:

"At the time of its inception the marriage in China was
not recognized as valid here because of a former marriage
here still binding, but as soon as the former marriage is
dissolved the cause of the failure to recognize here the second marriage is removed. Immediately upon the granting
of the divorce the husband returns to his status of a single
man and the courts of this jurisdiction are in a position to
recognize the marriage in China, which had not been recognized before because of the prior undissolved marriage."

The Hawaiian case of *Kekula v. Pioeiwa*, 4 Haw. 292,
throws light on the question raised by the argument just
quoted, if not on the question of how far the public policy
above expressed by Justice Story and other authorities may
be extended. In that case a daughter was born of parents
who were cohabiting pending the existence of the father's
marriage to another woman.. On the death of the lawful
wife, the father and mother were married, and the legiti-
macy of the daughter was claimed under a statute reading,
"All children born out of wedlock are hereby declarel legitimate on the marriage of the parents with each other, and
are entitled to the same rights as those born in wedlock."
This claim was overruled, the court holding that "any other
construction of the act would be subversive of good morals."

The effect of this decision has its application here,—which seems to be that where from policy the court cannot recognize the relation of the parents, it cannot recognize the offspring of that relation.

Let the writ of habeas corpus be dismissed.

IN THE MATTER OF THE GRAND JURY FOR THE SPECIAL AUGUST, 1915, TERM.

September 2, 1915.

Jurors—Venire—Amendments: The venire for grand jurors bore the name of F. S. F. when the person shown by the court records to have been intended and whose name was drawn for service in accordance with Judicial Code, sec. 276, was F. B. F.   Upon the marshal's return of service showing that no such person as F. S. F. could be found, it is ordered that the venire be amended to correct the name to F. B. F. and the marshal be directed to summon him to appear forthwith.

Venire for grand jurors: Amendment.

Jeff McCarn, U. S. District Attorney, for the United States.

CLEMONS, J. It appearing that the name of Frank B. Freitas, who was drawn in accordance with Judicial Code, sec. 276, for service as a grand juror, was incorrectly stated in the venire as Frank S. Freitas, and the marshal's return of service showing that no such person as Frank S. Freitas can be found, the question arises whether the court may amend the venire and have the intended party summoned.

No obstacle to the amendment is apparent: such amendment is a reasonable practice and could not possibly prejudice any one. Also, it would seem to be authorized by the statute of amendments, Rev. Stat., sec. 954.

No opportunity has been afforded for more than a glance at the authorities.   While no decisions directly in point have been found, the propriety of the amendment is suggested by this court's decision in *In the Matter of the Petit Jury for the October, 1912, Term*, ante, p. 105, and by the cases therein cited of *Goodwin v. State*, 15 So. (Ala.) 571, 573, and *Gregory v. State*, 37 So. (Ala.) 259, 262.

There is here in the record "something to amend by" (1 Enc. Pl. & Pr. 509), for the certificate on file herein of the judge and clerk as to the regularity of the drawing of this grand jury shows the true name of the juror. The clerk's record of names in the box from which the jurors were drawn, and the slip bearing the juror's name, which was preserved by the clerk, and the court stenographer's notes are also available, to confirm such certificate.

Let the venire be amended accordingly, and let the marshal summon the juror to appear forthwith. Pending service of such summons the grand jury will be sworn and proceed to business without this juror, who is meantime excused.

IN THE MATTER OF THE PETITION OF JACOB KAHN FOR NATURALIZATION.

October 2, 1915.

Naturalization—Witnesses—Posting: The requirement of section 5 of the Naturalization Act of June 29, 1906, 34 Stat. 596, that the names of the witnesses whom the applicant for citizenship expects to summon in his behalf, shall be posted with the notice of his petition for ninety days, applies equally to such substitute witnesses as he may desire to summon in place of original witnesses who cannot be produced at the final hearing.

Naturalization: On motion to substitute witness.

Jacob Kahn, petitioner, *pro se.*
Jeff McCarn, U. S. District Attorney, for the United States.

DOLE, J. This case was called and heard, and continued for decision on the question whether the testimony of Leon M. Straus, a substituted witness, could be received until his name had been posted for ninety days, under the requirements of sections 5 and 6 of the act of June 29, 1906, "to establish a bureau of immigration and naturalization and to provide for a uniform rule for the naturalization of aliens throughout the United States," 34 Stat. 596. Section 5 of such act requires the clerk, immediately after filing a petition for naturalization, to "give notice thereof by posting in a public and conspicuous place in his office or in the building in which his office is situated, under an appropriate heading, the name, nativity and residence of the alien, the date and place of his arrival in the United States, and the date, as nearly as may be, for the final hearing of his petition, and the names of the witnesses whom the applicant expects to summon in his behalf." Section 6 provides that the final action *on such* petitions "shall be had only on stated days, to be fixed by rule of the court, and in no case shall final action be had upon a petition until at least ninety days have elapsed after filing and posting the notice of such petition."

It sometimes happens that a witness whom the petitioner has expected to summon in his behalf and whose name has been posted as required, as set forth above, is not obtainable for the final hearing because of his death, absence, or other adequate cause. Section 6 provides for such emergency in the words, "but in case such witnesses cannot be produced upon the final hearing other witnesses may be summoned." The question before the court is, in case another witness has to be summoned for failure of one of the expected witnesses, whose name has been posted according to law, to appear, must the name of such new witness be posted for ninety days before the final hearing can take place?

What is the object of the requirement that the names of the witnesses who are expected to testify at the final hearing shall be posted with the notice of the case for ninety days? Is it not that the representatives of the government may, upon being informed of the petition by such notice, have full opportunity to investigate the status of such witnesses as to their bona fide ability to testify to the residence and character of the petitioner? If this is not the object, what purpose can be gained by such public notice with the long delay in the proceedings? Among the several Federal cases which hold that the names of substitute witnesses need not be posted for ninety days if at all, only two attempt to define the object of the posting of the witnesses' names. The decision in *In re Schatz*, 161 Fed. 237, 239, says:

"The purpose of this provision . . . to insure publicity of the proceeding and, among other things, to inform the public as to the names of the witnesses by whom the applicant expects to establish his right to be admitted to citizenship."

The case of *United States v. Doyle*, 179 Fed. 687, 689, offers the following:

"If a posted witness is not present the applicant has the burden of satisfying the court that he cannot be produced. If any suspicion should arise that the posted witnesses had been run off, or that the tendered witnesses were not reliable, the court, on motion, should allow the government ample time in which to investigate, and a denial might be deemed an abuse of discretion for which a naturalization order should be reversed."

Has not the statute fixed ninety days as "ample time"?

The cases of *In re O'Dea*, 158 Fed. 703, and *United States v. Thomas Daly*, 32 App. D. C. 525, both holding that the names of substitute witnesses should be published for ninety days before the final hearing, account for the reason of the law requiring, as set forth, the posting of the names of the two persons first intended by the applicant to be summoned and so, necessarily, including substitute witnesses. The *O'Dea* case says:

"The very object of posting the names of the witnesses is to give the government opportunity for a full investigation conducted by its own officers, without having to depend solely on the cross-examination of persons of whom it never heard until the cause comes up for final disposition."

The decision in *United States v. Daly* was given by the court of appeals of the District of Columbia, reversing the judgment of the supreme court of the District of Columbia. Referring to the *O'Dea* case, the decision in *United States v. Daly* proceeds as follows:

"With the views expressed in this opinion we fully agree. To hold otherwise would furnish an avenue through which one of the chief safeguards of the law could be evaded. It would place it within the power of a designing applicant to escape giving notice of his witnesses altogether. He could on filing his petition give the names of two witnesses whom he knew could not qualify, or whom he had no intention of having present at the hearing, and at the trial produce substitutes unknown to the court or to the officers of the government, and thereby secure his admission by totally evading one of the most material requirements of the statute. This law was evidently intended to throw every protection possible around the government, to prevent, if possible, disqualified aliens from becoming citizens; and it is the duty of the courts to hold applicants to a strict compliance with its provisions."

To my mind these two cases have satisfactorily construed

a somewhat vague phase of the statute and given the two sections of the act referred to an intelligible and logical status; for what possible guarantee to the government as to opportunity of informing itself about witnesses favoring an applicant for the rights of citizenship exists in a provision for publication of names which may only cover a part or none of the witnesses who are to appear?

Apropos of this discussion, is a letter of Richard K. Campbell, Chief, Division of Naturalization, dated June 16, 1909, to William S. Gregg, Assistant United States Attorney, Philadelphia, Pennsylvania, which, correcting a misapprehension of the *Daly* case on another point, confirms its ruling upon the question which concerns the case before the court in the following words:

"Clerks of courts should therefore be directed to advise all petitioners . . . that a petitioner may not introduce other witnesses in his behalf at the time of hearing than those whose names have been posted for the required ninety days."

The name of the substituted witness, Mr. Straus, or whoever else the applicant may desire to summon as a witness in his behalf at the final hearing, must be posted for ninety days before such hearing.

UNITED STATES OF AMERICA *v.* AH SING AND FANNIE GUERRERO. UNITED STATES OF AMERICA *v.* WILLIAM DUNN.

October 2, 1915.

1. *Penal statutes—Definition of crime—Adultery, fornication*: The statute, Penal Code, secs. 316, 318, sufficiently defines adultery and

fornication in merely providing that those offenses, naming them without further description, shall be punished in a certain manner.

2. *Same—Construction by aid of common-law*: When the name of an offense is used in a statute instead of a full description of it, the common law may be looked to in determining the legislative intent, provided, of course, the common law affords a certain definition.

3. *Indictment—Fornication—Joinder of participants*: One participant in fornication may be indicted without joining the other, though the statute, Penal Code, sec. 318, provides that "each" participant shall be punished.

Criminal Law: Motion to quash.

G. A. Davis and *C. S. Davis* for defendants Ah Sing and Guerrero.

J. W. Cathcart (*Thompson, Milverton & Cathcart* with him) for defendant Dunn.

Jeff McCarn, U. S. District Attorney, for the United States.

CLEMONS, J. In the indictment in the first case, an unmarried man and a married woman, having a husband then living other than her co-defendant, are charged, under Penal Code, 316, with adultery, in having had "carnal knowledge of the bodies of each other."

In the indictment in the second case the defendant, an unmarried man, is charged under Penal Code, sec. 318, with fornication in having had "carnal knowledge of the body of . . . an unmarried woman."

In these two cases motions to quash are interposed, which include the grounds that the acts charged are not offenses under the laws of the United States; and that there is no law of the United States defining adultery or fornication.

[1] [2] The basis of these motions is the contention that the statutes do not define adultery in the one case or fornication in the other, but that their only effect is in each case to fix a penalty for an undefined offense. The principle relied on is expressed in the following quotations from

decisions of the Supreme Court:

"Laws which create crime ought to be so explicit that all men subject to their penalties may know what acts it is their duty to avoid . . . Before a man can be punished, his case must be plainly and unmistakably within the statute." *United States v. Brewer,* 139 U. S. 278, 288.

"It is axiomatic that statutes creating and defining crimes cannot be extended by intendment, and that no act, however wrongful, can be punished under such a statute unless clearly within its terms. There can be no constructive offenses and before a man can be punished, his case must be plainly and unmistakably within the statute. *United States v. Lacher,* 134 U. S. 624; Endlich on the Interpretation of Statutes, sec. 329, 2d ed.; Pomeroy's Sedgwick on Statutory and Constitutional Construction, 280." *Todd v. United States,* 158 U. S. 278, 282.

See also *United States v. Wiltberger,* 5 Wheat. 76.

It is urged that the Penal Code does not define adultery or fornication, but merely declares a punishment therefor when it provides in the one case (Penal Code, sec. 316):

"Whoever shall commit adultery shall be imprisoned not more than three years; and when the act is committed between a married woman and a man who is unmarried, both parties to such act shall be deemed guilty of adultery; and when such act is committed between a married man and a woman who is unmarried, the man shall be deemed guilty of adultery;"

and in the other (Penal Code, sec. 318):

"If any unmarried man or woman commits fornication, each shall be fined not more than one hundred dollars or imprisoned not more than six months."

And, it is contended, the court cannot supply a definition of the words "adultery" and "fornication," for the reason that adultery and fornication were not crimes at common law, and that they had no certain, definite meaning either in the common law at the time of the Declaration of Independence or at the time of the enactment of the statutes here involved.

There can be no doubt that where a crime is of a "settled and determinate nature," the law-making body may be taken to define such crime in providing that the offense, merely naming it, shall be punished in a stated manner. So held Justice Story, in considering a statute fixing a punishment for "piracy as defined by the laws of nations." *United States v. Smith*, 5 Wheat. 153, 160-161. So also held the Massachusetts supreme court in the case of *Commonwealth v. Call*, 21 Pick. 509, wherein it is said, at pages 510-511:

"If questions arise in such cases as to what constitutes the offense, recurrence is to be had to well-established definitions sanctioned by books of authority and adopted by long usage, and with reference to which it may be supposed the legislature have acted in the enactment of the law punishing the offence."

So, also, Judge Dole, in the case of *United States v. Lee Sa Kee*, 3 U. S. Dist. Ct. Haw. 262, says:

"Although the section on adultery [the same provision as now contained in the Penal Code] is somewhat clumsily drawn, adultery is a word whose meaning is fully adjudged and settled so far as to express an act of sexual intercourse between a married person and another person not his or her husband or wife. It further defines the offense as not applying to an unmarried woman who may have sexual intercourse with a married man."

The decision in the case of *Lee Sa Kee*, supra, is directly in point on the motion here in the *Ah Sing* case involving adultery. Counsel, however, desire to have it reviewed now, in view of the suggestion of the opinion in *Commonwealth v. Call*, supra, and of what they claim appears from the dictionaries and other sources, that one cannot look to the authorities for any invariable or certain definition of the word. In that opinion it is said:

"It so happens, that on the present question we derive less aid than usual from the lights of the common law, the crime of adul   not bein   izable b the tem oral courts in England as a public offence, but only as a private injury; and hence we have not that distinct character of this crime, well defined and made familiar to us by the books of common law, that would be found to exist in relation to other offenses." 21 Pick. 511.

A careful reading of the context, however, will prove this decision to be a strong, as well as a very interesting, authority against the contention of defendant's counsel. Id., 510-513.

The supreme court of New Jersey happens to have passed on the sufficiency of both the words "adultery" and "fornication" to express a definite, certain idea. In *State v. Lash*, 1 Harrison (16 N. J. Law), 380, 32 Am. Dec. 397, construing a statute which provided a punishment for adultery without defining the offense, the court admitted a difference of opinion among "professional men" as to "what adultery is," but declared it to have arisen from a difference of the codes of law which were in the view of those holding such differences—on the one hand the common law and on the other the ecclesiastical law, and it was held in that case that "sitting as a court of common law" the court must with "no hesitation" follow the common law as its "constitutional guide," 32 Am. Dec. 398, though courts of chancery follow the ecclesiastical law, Id., 398-399. See *State v. Searle*, 56 Vt. 516, 518. And it was found that adultery, though not a crime at common law, was the subject of civil actions and had a well known legal meaning, namely, unlawful sexual intercourse between a man, whether married or unmarried, and a married woman (other than his wife), Id., 400-403, citing Black. Com. 139; Buller, N. P. 26, and the early American commentators, Swift and Reeve. The New Jersey court seems to regard fornication at common law as unlawful sexual intercourse between a man, whether married or unmarried, and an unmarried woman.

The same court in the recent case of *State v. Sharp*, 66 *Atl.* 926, has held that under a statute making fornication "a misdemeanor", an indictment is sufficient which uses the word "fornication" as "descriptive of the act", without further description or detail,—that the word has "a well-settled meaning," implying "an act with an unmarried woman." Id., 927.

The Indiana supreme court (in the first sentence about to be quoted) goes further than we need to, but its opinion fairly supports the cases just cited. It says:

"Our statute does not define fornication or adultery; but crimes, as we have seen, need not be defined by the statute, and, consequently, the court must judicially declare the definition. Fornication is sexual intercourse between a man, married or single, and an unmarried woman. Adultery is sexual connection between a married woman and unmarried man, or a married man other than her own husband. These definitions are not in accordance with some authorities, but they are with others, and, we think, the better; and they appear to us to be in harmony with the reason of things. We will limit the discussion of this topic to the question of adultery; as when we show what that is, we necessarily show what fornication is, an unlawful sexual intercourse that is not adultery is fornication." *Hood v. State*, 56 Ind. 263, 26 Am. Rep. 21, 24-25.

The Iowa supreme court in *State v. Hasty*, 121 Ia. 507, 96 N. W. 1115-1116, in construing a statute which merely names the crime without further definition, says:

"Adultery at common law was not denounced as a crime. As the basis of a civil right of action it consisted only of a man having sexual intercourse with a married woman other than his wife, thereby introducing the danger of spurious issue of the marriage. Connection with a single woman, though fornication, was not adultery. The same rule seems to have obtained under the Roman law but was radically modified by the ecclesiastical courts, which denounced the offense as the sexual violation of the marriage relation, regardless of whether the offender were male or female. And the definition of the canonical law, according to Wharton, was accepted by every Christian state at the time of the colonization of America and 'is no doubt a part of the common law brought with them by the colonists of all Christian nationalities.' 2 Wharton on Crim. Law, sec. 1719."

It may be noted that in the *Lash* case, supra, 32 Am. Dec. 400, the court adverted to the fact that the constitution of New Jersey "adopted the common law as a guide." Of the other states whose courts are cited above, the common law is adopted and declared to be in force in Vermont and Indiana, 1 Stimson, Am. Stat. L., 135-136, but it seems not in Massachusetts or Iowa, nor in Alabama, whose court is hereinafter cited. Id. In any event, in none of the foregoing decisions does it appear that the adoption of the common law influenced the conclusion that was reached The common law is looked to only because, or if, it affords a ready and freely accepted definition of these words "adultery" and "fornication"—and the common law rather than the ecclesiastical law, because common law courts are the courts which have jurisdiction of criminal matters, and such courts are the prototypes of the Federal court, so far as its criminal jurisdiction is concerned.   That equity may follow the broader definitions of the ecclesiastical courts in order to do justice in civil cases is natural, but it is just as natural, and in accord with the theory and policy of criminal law, that a court in the exercise of criminal jurisdiction should take a stricter view; and it cannot be seen that the fact of the difference between the view of the two systems militates at all against a Federal court's seeking the aid of the common law in such a case as the present.

In the opinion of this court, each of the words "adultery" and "fornication," as well shown in the *Lash* case, supra, has a definite meaning in the common law; and the definitions above given are to be looked to in arriving at the intent of Congress here. However, in spite of its clumsy work in this statute (see *United States v. Lee Sa Kee*, 3, U. S. Dist. Ct. Haw. 263), Congress has shown a clear purpose to widen the limits of the offense of adultery, by providing a punishment for "the act"—which can only mean sexual intercourse—when "committed between a married woman and a man who is unmarried," Penal Code, sec. 316. The common law definition is, therefore, to be modified accordingly. In Vermont, also, an enlargement of the common law definition of adultery has been effected by legislation. *State v. Searle*, 56 Vt. 516, 517-518.

Furthermore, at the time of the original enactment of the statute, March 3, 1887, 24 Stat. 635, 636, the term "adultery" with reference to the criminal law, had acquired the well settled import, as pointed out in the *Hasty* case, supra, of "such sexual intercourse as violates another man's bed— as may entail a spurious issue upon a defrauded husband," *Smitherman v. State*, 27 Ala. 23, 25, though in divorce the term was to be taken in the broader canonical sense, embracing "the infidelity of the husband to the wife." Id. The former definition, in which the "adulteration" of the issue of a married woman, is made the test, is in accord with the common-law definitions above set forth. Beyond doubt, the term "fornication" had at the time of the original enactment of the Federal legislation against sexual immorality, also acquired a well-settled import. And as the term "adultery" had become crystallized, the meaning of the term "fornication" was to be inferred as "sexual intercourse that is not adultery." *Hood v. State* supra.

There remain for consideration the additional grounds of the motion to quash in the case of Dunn defendant, "that the crime attempted to be punished by said section 318 is a joint and not a several crime;" and "that defendant is indicted severally and not jointly with the unmarried woman named in said indictment." These grounds are based on the use of the word "each" in section 318 of the Penal Code, which reads: "If any unmarried man or woman commits fornication, *each* shall be fined," etc.

In overruling a similar ground of objection to an indictment, under a statute that "every person who shall commit the crime of adultery shall be punished," etc., the court said, in *State v. Searle*, 56 Vt. 516, 519:

"The other ground of objection that it is necessary to join both parties in the indictment is not well taken.   The provision that both parties shall be punished, etc., does not import that both must be joined in the indictment. *State v. Brown*, 49 Vt. 440; Bish. Cr. Proc. ss. 263, 264, 266; *State v .Davis*, 2 Sneed, 273; Vermont Justice, p. 719."

So, in *State v. Davis*, 2 Sneed (Tenn.) 273, cited by the Vermont court, a statutory provision, that all persons engaged in the same offense shall be embraced in the same indictment, was held to be directory only and to afford no basis of defense to one of several co-offenders who is indicted alone.

[3] The legislative will that "each shall be fined," is directed to the discretion of the prosecuting authorities, and is not a matter of concern to a defendant who is indicted alone for the offense of fornication; it is not a matter of pleading.

"The doctrine is, that since all participants in a crime are severally liable the same as if each had done the whole together, all or any number of them may be charged together, in one count, or each may be indicted separately, at the election of the prosecuting power. Thus, it will not impair an indictment that, of many participants in the crime, only one, or any number less than the whole are made defendants." 1 Bishop's New Crim. Proc., sec. 463.

Though "the peculiar nature of some crimes [as, e. g., conspiracy and riot] is such as to require the indictment to charge guilt on more than one, whether they are made defendants or not," Id., sec. 464, nevertheless it is conceivable that in sexual intercourse one of the parties might be acting "in perfect good faith and without guilty knowledge," and so could not be subject to indictment at all. See *Delany v. People*, 10 Mich. 241, 245 (a case of adultery, however). See, also, *People v. Plyler*, 53 Pac. (Cal.) 553, 554.

There is nothing in the nature of this offense requiring the participants to be joined in an indictment. See, aside from the authorities just cited, 22 Cyc. 373; 9 Enc. Pl. & Pr. 645; also 1 Enc. Pl. & Pr. 308; 2 C. J. 20.

The motion to quash is denied in each case.

IN THE MATTER OF THE PETITION OF HATSUYO KOBAYASHI FOR A WRIT OF HABEAS CORPUS.

October 9, 1915.

Habeas Corpus—Exhaustion of remedies: An immigrant cannot obtain by habeas corpus relief from an order of immigration officers denying a landing, before exhausting his remedy by appeal to the Secretary of Labor.

Habeas Corpus: On application for writ.

G. A. Davis for petitioner.
Jeff McCarn, U. S. District Attorney, for respondent.

DOLE, J.   The applicant has had a hearing or hearings, before the immigration officers, who have decided that she is not entitled to land and have ordered her deportation. Without appealing to the Secretary of Labor, she has applied to this court for a writ of habeas corpus, and her counsel has offered in support of such application the cases of *In re Ah Tai*, 125 Fed. 795; *United States v. Fah Chung*, 132 Fed. 109, and *United States v. Wong See Foo*, 108 Pac. 488.

. The point in these three cases is concerned with the right of appeal of a Chinese refused a landing and for being unlawfully in the country, the law providing (28 Stat. 8) that an order of deportation made by a United States commissioner or judge shall be executed by the marshal, and pending execution of such order the Chinese person shall remain in the custody of the United States marshal and shall not be admitted to bail.

The case of *In re Ah Tai* correctly construes this section to mean that the refusal of appeal shall apply only where such order of deportation is final and open to immediate execution, but where an appeal is taken from such order the Chinese person may be admitted to bail. The other cases referred to adopt this construction.

But these rulings do not affect the question before me, which is, whether the court shall grant a writ of habeas corpus to an alien denied landing by the immigration officers, where he has taken no appeal therefrom to the Secretary of Labor. This matter has been threshed out in this court, adopting the authorities of *United States v. Sing Tuck*, 194 U. S. 170, and *Minnesota v. Brundage*, 180 U. S. 499, 503. This court has considered that the reasoning of the authorities mentioned applies equally to questions of aliens applying for writs who are detained by immigration officers. See *In re Young Chow Yee*, ante, p. 241; also, *Ryonosuke Sakaba*, ante, p. 372; also, *Chung Lum, Wong Yuen and Sui Joy*, ante, p. 376.

The *Sing Tuck* case, above referred to, has the following:

"Before the courts can be called upon, the preliminary sifting process provided by the statutes must be gone through with."

The point made by counsel that the case of his client is one of urgency does not appeal to me; for although undoubtedly the petitioner is greatly inconvenienced by being detained, the same is true of every alien who applies for admission to this country and is refused. The practice is important and necessary. To quote from the decision in the above-mentioned case of *Chung Lum, Wong Yuen and Sui Joy:*

"This practice is, I think, a reasonable one, both for clients and the court. The exhausting of remedies below will tend to prevent cases from being brought which ought not to be brought, and to put the court in a position to hear petition on the basis of a clear understanding."

The application for the writ must be denied.

IN THE MATTER OF THE PETITION OF HAT-SUYO KOBAYASHI FOR A WRIT OF HABEAS CORPUS.

January 14, 1916.

Aliens—Immigration—Benefit of counsel at hearing before immigration officers: In the absence of any showing of request for counsel, the finding of immigration officers, as to an immigrant's right to land, should not be set aside merely because he had no counsel at the hearing in his case before such officers.

Habeas Corpus: Hearing on return to writ.

G. A. Davis for petitioner.
H. W. Vaughan, U. S. District Attorney, for respondent.

CLEMONS, J. The petitioner having made a showing supplementary to her petition and to overcome the objection of his honor Judge Dole, in the opinion rendered on October 9, 1915, ante, p. 591, the writ of habeas corpus issued.

This case is one in which the court has no right to interfere with the action of the board of special inquiry as a body authorized to find facts. There was, in my opinion, evidence to sustain its conclusion at least as to the admission of the commission of a crime involving moral turpitude. See Transcript of Testimony, pages 2 and 3, and note that although the petitioner's husband may not have been heard from for over seven years (raising the possible presumption of death), the petitioner had committed the offense of adultery with a man with whom she had lived. ostensibly as wife, during a period beginning "about nine years ago" (Id., 2),—a date which may be verified by her testimony in the same context that it was "two or three years" after her husband left her (Id.), which was two years and seven months after she first came to Hawaii (Id.), which was in 1901 (Id.). All this time she was undivorced from her husband (Id., 1, 2).

The justness of the board's finding that the petitioner was likely to become a public charge, is not so clear, though in my opinion it is still a finding that cannot be set aside by this court.

So far as concerns the ground of deprivation of counsel, the petitioner claims that this case is distinguished from those like *Low Wah Suey v. Backus*, 225 U. S. 460, 470, in which the applicant had counsel at *some* stage of the proceedings; because in the present case it appears that the benefit of counsel was not had at all. But it seems to me that in the absence at least, as here, of any showing of request for counsel, the finding of the board of special inquiry should not be set aside now. See Bouve, Exclusion of Aliens, 291; *United States v. Sing Tuck*, 194 U. S. 161, 170. The complaints of want of counsel and of violation of the constitutional guaranty against self-incrimination, have both been disposed of by recent rulings of this court. *In re Ko Matsumoto, post*, determined Dec. 4, 1915, and see *In re Ryonosuke Sakaba*, ante, p. 372.

Let the writ be discharged and the petitioner be remanded to the custody of the respondent.

UNITED STATES OF AMERICA *v.* C. KAM MOON.

October 29, 1915.

1. *Obscene publications*: Question of obscenity of published words or pictures, dependent on their suggestion. If that tends to make the procreative functions of men and women subjects of levity, the law is violated.

2. *Same—The test*: The impression such publications make upon a community of average men and women as to their decency, and as to their probable effect upon the young.

3. *Same—Knowledge as to nature of publication*: One exhibiting words and pictures is chargeable with knowledge of their character if he understands the words. In the case of nude figures accompanied with words, it is the duty of the exhibitor to acquaint himself with the meaning of the words in relation to the pictures before exposing them.

4. *Same—Combination of words and pictures:* Where words and pictures are combined, it is the impression of men as a whole that is to be considered. It is no defense that the words or the pictures taken separately are unobjectionable, if their combination suggests indecency of conduct or calls forth impurity of thought.

Indictment: Charge to jury.

Jeff McCarn, U. S. District Attorney, for the United States.

Lorrin Andrews for the defendant.

DOLE, J. (Charging the jury.) The statute under which this indictment has been found provides that, whoever shall in any manner exhibit or otherwise publish any obscene writing, print, picture, drawing, or other representation is liable to the punishment set forth in said statute.

[1] In the human body, evolution has reached its highest attainment in physical life. It is the worthy residence of the soul and as such is entitled to the greatest respect and consideration. To think of the human body as shameful is an unfortunate misapprehension of its intrinsic purity

and dignity. Nothing but a superficial and imperfect view
of the inherent nature of licentiousness could lead one to
such a conclusion as to the moral status of the human
body. Sexual relations between men and women in their
normal condition are of unexceptionable rectitude and importance. The profanation of such relations, or of the
procreative powers of men and women, by coarse allusions
or pictures, making such relations and powers the subject
of levity, of ribaldry, of low suggestions, is a sacrilege deserving of legal interference and punishment. If all men
were gentlemen and all women of corresponding quality,
there would be no occasion for legislation of such character.

An obscene writing or print or picture is one that is
offensive to decency, indelicate, impure, as one unbecom-
ing, immodest, unfit to be seen in public, and tending to
corrupt the mind and subvert respect for decency and
morality.

[2a] I instruct you that laws of this character are made
for society in the aggregate. The test is, what is the judgment of the aggregate sense of the community? What is
the probable, reasonable effect of these words and pictures
on the sense of decency, purity, chastity of society, extending to the family, made up of men and women, young boys
and girls,—the family, which is the common nursery of
mankind, the foundation rock upon which the State reposes.

The question for you to determine is, how would the
pictures, and words accompanying them, impress and affect
the average man and woman of intelligence and sensi-
bility? What is the probable effect upon society in general? How would such pictures, language and matter impress a public assembly of decent men and women?

The question for you, as jurors, to determine is, whether
the tendency of the matter is to deprave and corrupt the
morals of those whose minds are open to such influences,
and into whose hands or before whose eyes such prints
and sentiments may fall? And in this connection you

should consider the question as to whether these prints and sentiments are likely to fall into the hands of young boys and girls, or to be observed by them, and what would be the effect on young minds that are open to influences of such pictures and sentiments?

[2b] [4] In passing on the question as to whether these pictures and words are obscene or not, it is of no consequence that the language employed, or even the pictures shown, when taken separately, may be pure and innocent. It is a question as to what the combination of the language and picture conveys. What was in the mind of the person preparing the pennant and what was intended to be conveyed by it, as well as the real impression that it makes on the average mind, should all be considered by you, and if in your opinion it was intended to convey an indecent or impure thought, and, as a matter of fact, does have that effect, it would fall within the statute and should be suppresed. The law has relation as well to the subject as to its dress. Both the subject and its treatment must be free from obscenity. The most debasing topic may be presented in the choicest language. In such garb it is the more dangerous. Impure suggestion clothed in pleasing attire allures and corrupts, when bald filth would disgust and repel.

Any matter is obscene if it is calculated to lower the standard which we regard as essential to civilization; if it is calculated to excite those feelings pertaining to the sexual relations which, in their proper field, are legitimate, but which, transcending the limits of that proper field, play much of the mischief in the world.

If in your opinion these pictures and words contain matter which in the hands of a young boy or girl, or of any susceptible or inexperienced person, would have a depraving and demoralizing or a corrupting influence upon him or her, then this is such matter and is prohibited from exhibition by this statute. If in your opinion these pictures and words drawn and printed upon these pennants, falling into the hands of an inexperienced boy or girl or other person, would incite in him or her improper thoughts and indecent ideas, it is indecent. If the matter as presented by these pennants is offensive to delicacy, expressing or presenting to the mind something which delicacy, purity and decency forbid to be exposed, it is offensive and indecent, and you should so find.

The jury are instructed that the law presumes the defendant innocent in this case, and not guilty as charged in the indictment, and the presumption should continue and prevail in the minds of the jury until they are satisfied by the evidence, beyond all reasonable doubt, of the guilt of the defendant; and acting on this presumption the jury should acquit the defendant unless constrained to find him guilty by the evidence convincing them of such guilt beyond all reasonable doubt.

The defendant has testified that he has never been convicted of a criminal offense. This has not been rebutted. You have the right to take this evidence into consideration in connection with the presumption of innocence, of which you have already been instructed; and if from all the evidence in the case, including this testimony, you are not convinced beyond a reasonable doubt of his guilt, you should acquit him.

The indictment in this case is of itself a mere accusation or charge against the defendant, and is not of itself any evidence of the defendant's guilt, and no juror in this case should permit himself to be to any extent influenced against the defendant because or on account of the indictment.

The burden of proof rests upon the prosecution to make out and prove to the satisfaction of the jury, beyond all reasonable doubt, every material allegation to the indictment, and unless that has been done the jury should find the defendant not guilty.

To warrant a conviction of the defendant, he must be proved to be guilty so clearly and conclusively that there is no reasonable theory upon which he can be innocent, when all the evidence in the case is considered together.

If you find from the evidence in this case, beyond a reasonable doubt, that the acts, or one of them, charged against this defendant in this indictment were committed as therein alleged, then I charge you that it is not necessary that you should look for any motives for such acts. The prosecution is not bound to prove a motive for the commission of a crime.

[3] If you find that the defendant in this case exhibited the pictures in question you need not inquire whether or not he knew that they were obscene; it is enough if he knew the contents, that is, the words and the pictures. Having such knowledge, he is chargeable with knowing whether they are or are not obscene. That is, if you find that the pictures, or any of them, with the words going with them, are obscene, all you have to find outside of that is that he exhibited them, and knew their contents, and you are not to trouble yourselves with any question as to what his view of the contents was; but in order to convict the defendant, you must not only find that the pennants or banners, exhibit 1 and exhibit 3, related to counts 1 and 2, offered in evidence by the prosecution, are of an obscene nature, but you must further find that the defendant was so well acquainted with the English language that he understood the meaning of the words thereon and, if you find that he did not know sufficient English to understand the meaning of the words upon said pennants, even if you find the same were obscene, then it is your duty to acquit him on these two counts, 1 and 3.

In the case of the two pennants exhibiting figures of nude women, exhibit 2, count 5, and exhibit 4, count 4, I charge you that the nude figures put the defendant on his guard as to the nature or meaning of the pictures in view of there being words connected with them. In was incumbent upon him, if he did not understand the meaning of the words, to find out in some way the meaning of the whole design, including the words, before exhibiting them; and if you find that those two pictures, with the words belonging to them, are of an obscene nature, and that he exhibited them, he should be found guilty.

It is not the exhibition of pictures or description of the human body that is obscene, but it is an exhibition that includes such poses or allusions that suggest the sexual organs and their function with a view of ribaldry, levity or low jesting.

[2c] If any banner referred to in the different counts, as exhibited in the window of defendant, is obviously obscene in the impression that it must naturally produce upon the average person, the defendant, if found to have exhibited the same as alleged, is guilty.

You are instructed to return a verdict of acquittal on the second count. In regard to the other four counts, you are at liberty to find a verdict of either acquittal or conviction upon each one according as you shall find the evidence requires.

A verdict of acquittal or conviction requires a unanimous vote of the jury.

FARM CORNN v. JUSTUS S. WARDELL.

November 2, 1915.

Removal of causes—Suit on account of act done by officer under color of office: A suit for damages for falsely charging the plaintiff with being a crook and an opium smuggler, such charge being made in the presence of others, by the Surveyor of the Port of San Francisco, an officer of the Customs of the United States, while investigating in Honolulu alleged unlawful importation of opium by persons other than and unknown to the plaintiff, is removable from a Circuit Court of the Territory of Hawaii to the United States District Court for the Territory of Hawaii, on the ground within 36 Stat. 1097, sec. 32, Act of March 3, 1911, of being a suit against an "officer appointed under or acting by authority of [a] revenue law of the United States . . . on account of [an] act done under color of his office or of any such law, or on account of any right, title or authority claimed by such officer . . . under any such law."

Removal of Causes: Motion to remand.

E. C. Peters and *R. J. O'Brien* for the motion.
Jeff McCarn, contra.

DOLE, J.   This case was begun in the Circuit Court of the First Circuit of the Territory of Hawaii. Before the time for answer had expired, the defendant filed a petition in said court for removal of the cause to this court, on the ground that the case "involves a question as to whether a Federal officer, while engaged in an investigation for alleged or suspected violations of the Federal law, has the right to express his opinion after having come into possession of certain facts with relation to the guilt or innocence of one suspected of violating the Federal statutes, the enforcement of which is submitted by law to his care", and filed the bond required by the statute in proceedings for removal of such causes, and notified counsel for plaintiff of

the time in which the motion would be made for an order
of removal.

Hearing was had and an order made by the judge of said
court for removal of said cause to this court; whereupon a
certified copy of the proceedings in said Territorial court
was filed in this court.

The plaintiff in his complaint alleged that the defendant,
while in Honolulu, on the 2nd day of September, 1915, as
an officer of the customs of the United States, to-wit, Surveyor of the Port of San Francisco, investigating alleged
unlawful importation into the United States of opium prepared for smoking, by persons other than and unknown to
the plaintiff, falsely charged the plaintiff, in the presence
of others, with being a crook and opium smuggler, and the
plaintiff claimed to be damaged in his good name to the
extent of five thousand dollars. The said certified copy
of the record was filed in this court on the 1st day of October, 1915. On the same day, counsel for plaintiff filed a
motion for remand of the cause to said Territorial court
upon the ground that neither by the complaint of the
plaintiff nor the petition of the defendant for removal was
there disclosed any facts sufficient to warrant the removal
to or the assumption of jurisdiction by this court of said
cause.

The law provides that:

"When any civil suit or criminal prosecution is commenced in any court of a State against any officer appointed under or acting by authority of any revenue law
of the United States now or hereafter enacted, or against
any person acting under or by authority of any such officer, on account of any act done under color of his office
or of any such law, or on account of any right, title or
authority claimed by such officer or other person under
any such law . . the said suit or prosecution may, at
any time before the trial or final hearing thereof, be removed for trial into the District Court next to be holden
in the district where the same is pending, upon the peti-

tion of such defendant to said District Court." 36 Stat. 1097.

The law of which the above quotation is a part is an act to codify, revise and amend the laws relating to the judiciary, approved March 3, 1911, 36 Stat. 1087.

Sections 28 and 29 of the act provide that causes of which the District Courts have original jurisdiction may be removed to the United States District Court at any time before the defendant in such case is required to answer or plead to the declaration of the plaintiff, by petition and bond, as has been done in this case.

The question on the motion for remand is, whether there are disclosed in the proceedings any facts sufficient to warrant the removal to or the assumption of jurisdiction by this court of the cause.

The practice in such matters requires that somewhere in the proceedings, either in the original petition or petition for certiorari, it shall appear "that the act for which the defendant is sued is in fact in the performance of a necessary duty imposed on him by law, having some relation to the collection of revenue for the government." *People's United States Bank v. Goodwin*, 162 Fed. 945. This decision was rendered before the act relating to the judiciary, above referred to, was passed, which provides, besides the proceedings for removal, as provided in section 643 of the Revised Statutes, proceedings as set forth above for petition for removal before the expiration of the period fixed for answer to be filed. It follows that, if either in the original petition or in the petition for removal of these proceedings, it shall appear that the act for which the defendant is sued was done in the performance of an official duty imposed on him by law and having some relation to the collection of revenue for the government or under color thereof, the showing would be sufficient.

The original petition alleges that the conduct complained of occurred while the defendant was an officer of the customs of the United States, to-wit, Surveyor of the Port of San Francisco, investigating alleged unlawful importation into the United States of opium prepared for smoking. The petition for removal alleges that the plaintiff's petition shows that the suit arises under the laws of the United States providing for the appointment of a surveyor of customs of the United States and defining his duties as such officer, and further, that he was then and there an officer of the customs of the United States, to-wit, Surveyor of the Port of San Francisco, investigating the alleged unlawful importation into the United States of opium prepared for smoking.

Does this description bring the cause for removal within the statute which provides, as cited above, that a civil suit begun in any court of a State against an officer appointed under or acting by authority of any revenue law of the United States, on account of any act done under color of his office or of any such law, or on account of any right, title or authority claimed by such officer under such law, is ground for removal?

If the defendant, as an officer of the customs of the United States, a Surveyor of the Port of San Francisco, investigating unlawful importation of opium into the United States, charged the plaintiff in the presence of others with being a crook and an opium smuggler, it cannot be denied that he was acting under color of his office or of some authority claimed by him under the revenue laws under which he was appointed or by authority of which he was acting.

The motion for remanding the case is denied, and the defendant is required to answer to the complaint within ten days.

FARM CORNN *v.* JUSTUS S. WARDELL.

December 23, 1915.

1. *Removal of causes—Jurisdiction of parties—Residence:* A non-resident defendant who secures removal to this court of a suit brought against him in an Hawaiian Territorial court, cannot then have the suit dismissed for a United States court's want of jurisdiction of non-residents, under Judicial Code, section 51.

2. *Courts—Jurisdiction—General appearance on removal of cause:* In a cause so removed the defendant waives any right of objection to this court's jurisdiction of the person by entering into stipulation here extending time to answer.

At Law: Motion to dismiss for want of jurisdiction of person of defendant.

R. J. O'Brien (*E. C. Peters* with him) for plaintiff.
Jeff McCarn for defendant.

CLEMONS, J. The defendant moved the present cause to this court from the Circuit Court of the First Circuit of Hawaii, and my associate Judge Dole, on plaintiff's motion to remand, held, ante, page 601, that the cause was properly here, inasmuch as the defendant was sued for alleged slander uttered by a Federal official acting *colore officii* in the performance of statutory duties. The defendant now moves to dismiss the case altogether on the ground that he is not a resident of this district where served with process but is, as the complaint itself shows, a resident of the Northern District of California.

[1] The laws relating to removal of causes were extended to the district of Hawaii by our Organic Act, sec. 86 (31 Stat. 141, 158; am. 33 Stat. 1035; am. 35 Stat. 838); and although the defendant could be sued in a United States court originally only in the district of his residence (Judicial Code, sec. 51), still he was acting consistently in hav-

ing the suit removed from the Territorial court to this, "the next district court of the district where . . . pending" (Judicial Code, sec. 31). See *Cowell v. City Water Supply Co.*, 96 Fed. 769, par. 1.

And according to the decision just cited, the defendant, having "formally requested that this suit be placed within the jurisdiction of this court," has "thus waived the provision of the statute" requiring a defendant to be sued in the district of his residence. To the same effect, see *O'Donnell v. Atchison, etc. Ry. Co.*, 49 Fed. 689, 692.

The defendant's counsel, however, contends that the plaintiff's position is absurd: to let the plaintiff still stay in this court, says counsel, is to override the statute requiring the defendant to be sued in a Federal court only in the district of his residence. The answer is, that the defendant had a perfect right to sue in the Territorial court—the Federal court's jurisdiction being not exclusive, but only concurrent. See *Pittsburgh, etc. Ry. Co. v. Wood*, 84 N. E. 1009 (Ind. App.) as quoted in 34 Cyc. 1216, n. 1. It was because of the very fact that the Territorial court had jurisdiction that the defendant there sought to remove and not to dis-. miss. It is this concurrence of jurisdiction, that distinguishes the present case from that relied on by counsel, of *Wabash, etc. Ry. Co. v. Brow*, 164 U. S. 271, in which the cases cited in Black's Dillon on Removal of Causes, sec. 283, n. 24, are overruled, and in which neither the Federal court nor the local court had jurisdiction of the defendant's person. And it must be remembered, the right of removal is purely a creature of statute: 34 Cyc. 1215-1216; and if removal *under its terms* does not happen to put the defendant in the same position, as to place of trial, as if sued in the Federal court in the first instance, it cannot be seen why the plaintiff should, therefore, be deprived of his right to resort to a Territorial court of concurrent jurisdiction on the one hand, or on the other why the defendant should in excess of the removal remedy, be given the advantage of throwing the plaintiff out of the court to which the defendant has removed the cause and of forcing the plaintiff to bring a new suit in the Federal court where the defendant resides.

[2] Moreover, defendant through his counsel has submitted to this court's jurisdiction in entering with counsel for the plaintiff into the written stipulation on file, "that the defendant Justus S. Wardell, may have to and including the 30th day of November, A. D., 1915, within which to answer or otherwise plead herein." Under a well settled rule of practice, this stipulation operates as a general appearance of the defendant, and is an added reason for the denial of his motion. 2 Enc. Pl. & Pr. 633-634, 639-642, 644; 3 Cyc. 522-523; *Briggs v. Stroud*, 58 Fed. 717-719; *Waters v. Central Trust Co.*, 126 Fed. 469, 471 (Townsend and Lacombe, Circuit JJ.) And see *Stonega Coal, etc. Co. v. Louisville, etc. Ry. Co.*, 139 Fed. 271, 272.

Let the defendant's motion to dismiss be denied.

UNITED STATES OF AMERICA *v.* AH POI.

November 12, 1915.

1. *Criminal law—Former conviction—Similarity of offenses:* A conviction in the District Court of Honolulu for the unlawful possession of opium under the Territorial statute, R. L. Hawaii, 1915, sec. 2075, is no bar to an indictment in this court for the receipt, purchase, sale, concealment, etc., of opium under the Federal statute, 35 Stat. 614, am. 38 Stat. 275.

2. *Same—Evidence—Burden of proof—Possession of opium:* This is true even though the Federal statute makes possession prima facie evidence of receipt, purchase, concealment, etc., of opium.

Indictment: Demurrer to plea of former conviction.

Jeff McCarn, U. S. District Attorney, for the United States.

G. K. French for defendant.

CLEMONS, J.   The defendant is indicted for unlawfully receiving, buying, selling, transporting and concealing, and facilitating the purchase, sale, receipt, transportation and concealment of smoking opium and opium prepared for smoking—the charge following the language of the statute, as in *United States v. Fong Hing*, ante, p. 69; *United States v. Ah Foo*, 3 U. S. Dist. Ct. Haw. 487; *United States v. Leau Hung*, Id. 553.

[1] The defendant files a plea of former conviction, from which it appears that prior to the indictment he was duly sentenced by the District Court of Honolulu to pay a fine of twenty-five dollars and costs,—which sentence was duly satisfied,—on a prosecution based upon facts which are "identical [with the] facts upon which this indictment has been found and filed".   In that prosecution the charge against the defendant was the unlawful possession of opium or preparations thereof, which was then a misdemeanor under Revised Laws of Hawaii, 1915, sec. 2075, amended by Act 143 of the Session Laws of Hawaii of 1915, making it an offense to "use or smoke opium or any preparation thereof, or to have the same in possession", though permitting an exception in cases of persons receiving medical treatment, etc., but under strict regulations of the board of health.

The present case is now for consideration on the government's demurrer, which, in substance, lays the grounds that it appears from the plea:

(1) That the offense now charged here is a different offense in law from the offense heretofore charged in the Territorial court;

(2) That the defendant has not hitherto been indicted, tried, convicted or acquitted, nor placed in jeopardy by the United·States, the sovereignty offended by the offense here charged;

(3) That the defendant in the same act has committed an offense against both the United States and the Territory of Hawaii.

The defendant relies upon the case of *United States v. Perez and Walsh,* 3 U. S. Dist. Ct. Haw. 295, and the case therein followed of *Grafton v. United States,* 206 U. S. 333. In the *Grafton* case the principle is established:

·"That a person tried for an offense in a tribunal deriving its jurisdiction and authority from the United States and acquitted or convicted cannot be tried again for the same offense in another tribunal deriving its jurisdiction and authority from the United States." *United States v. Perez,* supra, 298.

In the case of *Perez and Walsh* the application of the rule announced in the *Grafton* case is clear, for the defendants there were "charged with adultery and plead(ed) in bar an acquittal in a Territorial court on the same charge and covering the same period." 3 U. S. Dist. Ct. Haw. 295.

But does the present indictment embrace "the same charge" as that made against the defendant in the District Court of Honolulu?

The question, "What constitute former jeopardy?" is, in the language of Mr. Bishop, "in its nature difficult and intricate". And, he continues, "it is rendered more so by much conflict in the decisions". 1 Bishop, New Crim. L., sec. 1012. See *Roberts v. State,* 14 Ga. 8, 58 Am. Dec. 528, 531; 17 A. & E. Enc. L., 2d ed., 597. A wide and thorough search of the authorities impresses me that many of them fail to give a convincing answer to this question. Indeed, it may be doubted if any authority has laid down a general rule which in practice will solve all cases. The majority opinion of Justice Hartwell, as well as the dissent of Chief Justice Frear, in the case of *Territory v. Schilling,* 17 Haw.

249, afford illuminating discussions of the subject. Yet the division of that able court as to the application of the law only illustrates and emphasizes the difficulty.

The decision in *State v. Elder*, 65 Ind. 282, 32 Am. Rep. 69, 71-72 (affirmed in *State v. Gapen*, 47 N. E. 25), may be referred to as an able attempt to lay down clear-cut rules and tests. In that case, it is said by Judge Biddle:

"We believe the true rules deducible from both principle and authority to be,

1. When the facts constitute but one offense, though it may be susceptible of division into parts, as in larceny for stealing several articles of property at the same time, belonging to the same person, a prosecution to final judgment for stealing a part of the articles will be a bar to a subsequent prosecution for stealing any other part of the articles, stolen by the same act.

2. When the facts constitute two or more offenses, wherein the lesser offense is necessarily involved in the greater —as an assault is involved in an assault and battery with intent to commit a felony, and as a larceny is involved in a robbery—and when the facts necessary to convict on a second prosecution would necessarily have convicted on the first, then the first prosecution to a final judgment will be a bar to the second.

3. But when the same facts constitute two or more offenses, wherein the lesser offense is not necessarily involved in the greater, and when the facts necessary to convict on a second prosecution would not necessarily have convicted on the first, then the first prosecution will not be a bar to the second, although the offenses were both committed at the same time and by the same act."

See also the case of *Roberts v. State*, 14 Ga. 8, 58 Am. Dec. 528, 531, wherein the court, citing other courts of high authority, says:

"Of the sufficiency of the plea of former acquittal or conviction, the following is said to be the true test, viz.: whenever the prisoner might have been convicted on the first indictment, by the evidence necessary to support the second; or in other words, where the evidence necessary to support the second indictment would.have sustained the first".

This rule is regarded by 17 A. & E. Enc. L , 2d ed. 597, as of almost universal application. That authority states the test in this language: "Whether the facts required to support the second indictment would have been sufficient if proved to have procured a conviction under the first indict-.ment. If they would be, the offenses are identical." Id.

The rules given by Mr. Bishop and quoted in Rawle's edition of Bouvier's Law Dictionary are worthy of attention; seeming to cover the ground as well as any rules, unless perhaps it be those of Judge Biddle, supra:

"The constitutional guaranty is against two trials for the same offense, and the decisions as to what constitutes identity of offenses are not uniform. They are collected in 1 N. Cr. L. secs. 1048-69, by Mr. Bishop, who lays down the following rules as sustained by just principle: 'They are not the same when (1) the two indictments are so diverse as to preclude the same evidence from maintaining both; or when (2) the evidence to the first and that to the second relate to different transactions, whatever be the words of the respective allegations; or when (3) each indictment sets out an offense differing in all its elements from that in the other, though both relate to one transaction,—a proposition of which the exact limits are difficult to define; or when (4) some technical variance precludes a conviction on the first indictment, but does not appear on the second. On the other side, (5) the offences are the same whenever evidence adequate to the one indictment will equally sustain the other. Moreover (6) if the two indictments set out like offences and relate to one transaction, yet if one contain more of criminal charge than the other, but upon it there could be a conviction for what was embraced in the other, the offences, though of different names, are within our constitutional guaranty, the same.' The author considers the test to be, 'whether if what is set out in the second indictment had been proved under the first, there could have been a conviction; when there could, the second cannot be maintained; when there could not, it can be.' Id.

sec. 1052, and cases cited in notes." 2 Bouvier L. D. (Rawle's ed.) 5-6.

The oft-cited opinion of Justice Gray in *Morey v. Commonwealth*, 107 Mass. 432, affords a valuable discussion of former jeopardy. It holds:

"Although proof of one particular fact is necessary to a conviction under either of two statutes, yet, if each statute requires proof of an additional fact which the other does not, an acquittal or conviction under either is no bar to prosecution and punishment under the other" (syllabus; and see p. 434).

A broader, more liberal rule is possibly suggested in *State v. Cooper*, 1 Green, L. (N. J.) 361, 25 Am. Dec. 490, 492:

"A first inquiry . . . in this case will be, whether there is such identity in these offenses, that according to the rule laid down, and *the spirit which pervades the administration of criminal justice,* they shall be considered one for the purposes of this plea."

Since this opinion was drafted, defendant's counsel has called attention to the following noteworthy language in *Morgan v. Devine*, 237 U. S. 632, 641:

"As to the contention of double jeopardy upon which the petition of habeas corpus is rested in this case, this court has settled that the test of identity of offenses is whether the same evidence is *required* to sustain them; if not, then the fact that both charges relate to and grow out of one transaction does not make a single offense where two are defined by the statutes. Without repeating the discussion, we need but refer to *Carter v. McClaughry*, 183 U. S. 365; *Burton v. United States*, 202 U. S. 344, 377, and the recent case of *Gavieres v. United States*, 220 U. S. 338."

The case here does not fall within the first class described by Judge Biddle in the *Elder* decision supra. Nor does it fall within the second class there described, viz., "when the facts constitute two or more offenses, wherein the lesser offence is necessarily involved in the greater;" for the charge here made, of having bought, sold, received, and concealed, and facilitated the purchase, sale, receipt, and concealment of opium is not "necessarily" involved in the charge made in the Territorial court, of having possessed opium,—except, perhaps, as to the allegation of receiving, which will have special attention presently.

For the defendant might have either bought, sold, or concealed opium or facilitated the doing of any such act without having been in possession of that drug, or he might have possessed it without having done any of the other things just mentioned. However, as to the offense of "receiving", it is not so easy to say that the word "possession" is not broad enough to cover the idea of "receipt". In the criminal law in the case of receiving stolen goods, and in the common law in the case of the sale of goods, the word "receipt" implies a change of possession; that is, there cannot be receipt without a change of possession. See 34 Cyc. 517, and Brown, Stat. Frauds, 5th ed., sec. 317.

[1] [2] But though receipt and possession may be thus intimately connected, they are not the same. Receipt is merely the getting of possession. The Federal statute, though bent upon preventing all manner of traffic in opium, evidently intends to say that a man shall not be punished for mere possession (which is made only prima facie evidence of any of the specific offenses: section 2 of the Act), but shall be punished for attempting to get possession. The distinction may at first appear technical, even trivial, far-fetched, unreasonable; yet, of course, it is entirely reasonable that Congress should have regarded an attempt to get possession, an act which involves wilfulness, a positive disposition to disregard the law, as worthy of special inhibition, whereas not regarding mere possession, which does not necessarily involve receipt or even any degree of wilfulness whatever or anything more than mere passiveness, as being worthy of any other effect than to raise a prima facie case of purchase, sale, concealment, receipt, etc. And in any case of possession, if there be any degree of wilfulness it would seem to involve some one of these

offenses of purchase, concealment or receipt, or facilitating the purchase, etc.

At all events, in view of the use of the word "possession" in the same section as here in question, section 2 of the Act, it would seem that the words "possession" and "receipt" are different and not coextensive in meaning.   At least so far as the offense of receiving is concerned, it would be vain to enact that proof of possession might be taken as equivalent to proof of receipt, if receipt and possession were regarded as actually and exactly the same thing. However, under the Territorial law wherein possession is itself alone made an offense, such possession must of course be wilful, i. e., with criminal responsibility. See Bl. Comm. 21; Kenny, Outlines of Crim. Law (Webb's Am. ed.), 45, et seq.

It would not be unreasonable to suppose that such a "possession" as raises a prima facie case under the Federal statute is any possession, no matter what the knowledge or intent—the purpose being merely to throw upon the defendant the burden of explaining any possession; while the "receipt" which is made an offense is something wilful.

It may be said, by the way, that it is apparent that possession by being made prima facie evidence of guilt of any or all of the various offenses enumerated in the statute, is not thereby made an offense (substantive law) as it is in the Territorial statute: in the Federal law the provision as to possesion is only a provision of procedure (adjective law).   If possession were here made an offense, of course the Territorial proceeding would be a bar. See 2 Wig. Ev., sec. 1353, par. 1; *United States v. Yee Fing*, 222 Fed. 154, 155-156, and *United States v. Woods*, 224 Fed. 278, 279-280; *United States v. Wilson*, 225 Fed. 82, 84.

That the offenses here charged are different from that charged in the Territorial court, makes it unnecessary to consider any question arising from the fact that the former are felonies and the latter only a misdemeanor, under the statutes above cited. See *State v. Campbell*, 32 Pac. 752 (Wash.) and *State v. Durbin*, 73 Pac. 373 (Wash). both cases, however, being governed by peculiar statutory provisions. See, also, *State v. Cooper*, 1 Green L. (N. J.) 361, 25 Am. Dec. 490, 494.

. It may be noted in passing that the evident object of the two statutes, Federal and Territorial, being the same, viz., the destruction of the opium traffic, there is no room for an argument against the plea, based on any difference of intent of the two statutes (see *State v. Gapen*, 43 N. E. (Ind.) 678, 679), although the Territorial statute is a part of a chapter of the Revised Laws of Hawaii, 1915, devoted to licenses and, in a way, to the raising of revenue, to-wit, by imposing a fee for license to sell poisonous drugs, c. 121, sec. 2071. The context indicates a clear legislative policy against the use and smoking of opium (Id. secs. 2072, 2075, as amended as above), though in general neither the language of the statute nor the means adopted to carry out its intent are nearly as forcible as in case of the Federal act.

The case appears to fall within the third class enumerated by Judge Biddle, q. v., supra, inasmuch as the alleged offenses of receiving, buying, selling concealing, or facilitating the receipt, purchase, sale, or concealment of opium, are not, any of them, "necessarily" involved in the broader Territorial offense of "possession". Mr .Bishop's third rule, q. v., supra, might also cover the case.

And so it may be, as it is by the government's demurrer, admitted "that the facts upon which the prosecution" in the Territorial court "was founded and upon which judgment was duly entered, . . . are the identical facts upon which this indictment has been found and filed" (plea, supra), but still the possession, of the Territorial law, and the receipt, purchase, etc., of the Federal law, are separate and distinct offenses.

In view of the foregoing considerations, let the demurrer to the plea in bar be sustained. It is so ordered.

UNITED STATES OF AMERICA *v.* CYRIL GEER.

Novmber 22, 1915.

Criminal law—Jeopardy—Mistrial on one count of indictment, acquittal on another: Where under an indictment of two counts charging violation of the White Slave Traffic Act, 36 Stat. 825, and of one count charging adultery, there is an acquittal on the two former counts of white slavery and a mistrial as to the count of adultery, the defendant has not been in jeopardy on the latter count, and a new trial may be ordered as to that.

Indictment: Plea in bar.

Jeff McCarn, U. S. District Attorney, for the United States.

G. A. Davis for the defendant.

DOLE, J. The defendant was acquitted on two counts of the indictment, while, in regard to the third count, the jury was unable to agree. The first two counts are charges under what is known as the "White Slave Act", alleging the transportation of a girl from one place to another in the Territory of Hawaii, for certain immoral purposes. The third count, upon which there was a mistrial, charges the defendant with adultery.

Counsel for defendant contends that the acquittal on the first two counts amounts to an acquittal on the whole indictment. A number of authorities have been cited, and I have looked up other authorities. There is no case among them all which is parallel to this case, that is, no case in which a verdict has been rendered on some counts in the indictment and a failure to reach a verdict upon another count through a mistrial. The authorities agree that where a verdict is rendered on some one or more counts in an indictment, and no action is taken in regard to another count in the indictment, it amounts to an acquittal of the count not considered. This is because:

"When a jury is empaneled the State must proceed with the prosecution; there can be no non-suit, as in civil actions. If the accused cannot be convicted, he is entitled to a verdict of acquittal." *State v. Schuchardt,* 18 Neb. 454, 25 N. W. 722.

That is, where the trial of a case before a jury has been entered upon, the defendant is entitled to a conclusion of such trial. A discharge of the jury without sufficient legal cause amounts to an acquittal.

But these authorities do not apply to a case where there has been a mistrial. A mistrial of an indictment containing but one count is recognized as not bringing the prisoner into jeopardy, and a new trial is had as a matter of course.

Counsel refers to an Alabama case in support of his contention that the verdict in this case of acquittal on two counts means an acquittal on the third, on which there was a mistrial. This case is *State v. Standifer,* 5 Porter 531. The decision says:

"Cases exist in which a minor offense may be discharged by the acquittal of the individual charged, on an indictment for a major offence; but these are cases in which the jury, trying the case, could have lawfully returned a verdict for the lesser crime."

This was an indictment for murder, upon a trial of which the defendants were acquitted. They were thereafter indicted for assault and battery with intent to commit murder, of which charge some of the defendants were acquitted and others were acquitted of an assault and battery with intent to murder, but found guilty of an assault and battery. The court found on writ of error that there was no bar; that the "offenses have no appearance of identity . . . and the evidence which would produce an acquittal of the one might produce a conviction of the other." In the course of the opinion, the paragraph quoted above appeared. This dictum of the court evidently refers to cases in which, as in the case before that court, the indictment includes but one count charging the greater offense, like murder, which would be a bar to an indictment for the same act on a charge of manslaughter or assault and battery, for the reason that the jury would have the discretion, if justified by the evidence, in returning under such an indictment a verdict of manslaughter or assault and battery.

In the case before the court, it becomes pertinent to answer the question whether, under an indictment charging only white slavery, the jury could under any evidence return a verdict of guilty of adultery. If such question is answered in the negative, it would seem that the dictum of the court in the Alabama case, above quoted, would be inapplicable.

The charge of white slavery is a charge of certain acts otherwise innocent, with a malicious or unlawful intent or for an unlawful purpose. The charge of adultery is a charge of an unlawful act. The proof of neither one would prove the other.

"As to the contention of double jeopardy upon which the petition of habeas corpus is rested in this case, this court has settled that the test of identity of offenses is whether the same evidence is required to sustain them; if not, then the fact that both charges relate to and grow out of one transaction does not make a single offense where two are defined by the statutes. Without repeating the discussion, we need but refer to *Burton v. United States*, 202 U. S. 344, 377, and the recent case of *Gavieres v. United States*, 220 U. S. 338." *Morgan v. Devine*, 237 U. S. 641.

The United States has been liberal as to the freedom with which its grand juries may include different charges in the same indictment, and giving the courts discretion even to try separate indictments at the same trial, only requiring as the conditions where this may be done that the several charges against any person are for the same act or transaction, or for two or more acts or transactions connected together, or, thirdly, for two or more acts or transactions of the same class of crimes or offenses, which may be properly joined; thus adopting a broad policy which might render some of the precedents of the several States inapplicable.

Under an indictment for white slavery alone, it is my opinion that the jury could not return a verdict of adultery. Therefore, under the reasoning of the cases referred to, an acquittal on the counts for white slavery would not acquit the defendant on the count charging adultery, on which count the jury failed to find a verdict.

There are two opinions as to what constitutes jeopardy, the opinion more favored being that, when in a criminal trial, the jury is sworn and all the preliminary things of record are ready for trial, the prisoner has met with the jeopardy in the repetition of which our constitutional rule protects him. The other view is that jeopardy begins only after verdict, or at or upon a verdict of conviction or acquittal.

In a case in which there is a mistrial, no jeopardy has been created, as is evidenced from the universal practice that there may be at least one more trial. It would seem, therefore, that in such a case the question of jeopardy is undecided up to the time of the verdict, and that the finding of the verdict fixes the point of time in which his jeopardy is created; but that, in case of the failure of the jury to find any verdict, no jeopardy is created, and this because there has been no conclusion of the case.

The plea in bar is overruled.

UNITED STATES OF AMERICA *v.* NG YEE CHOUNG.

December 1, 1915.

1. *Indictment—Counts:* Where a statute sets forth a series of acts, either of which or all together constitute an offense, fixing the same penalty for one or all of them, the commission of two or more of them may be alleged in one count of an indictment if conjunctively charged.

2. *Practice:* If all such alleged acts are committed by one person at the same time and place, they are parts of the same transaction and constitute a single offense.

3. *Same—Indictments—Counts:* Several alleged distinct offenses under different Acts of Congress, of the same class which may be properly joined, may be set out in separate counts in the same indictment, or if they are charged in several indictments, the court may order such indictments to be consolidated.

4. *Same—Same—Same—Offenses of different kinds charged in same indictment:* If an indictment contains counts charging offenses not only under different statutes, but also of different classes or grades, requiring different punishments, the practice is to require the prosecution to elect.

Indictment: Motion to quash.

H. W. Vaughan, Assistant U. S. Attorney, for the United States.

G. A. Davis for the defendant.

Dole, J. The motion to quash may be divided into two parts; first, that the indictment is bad in that two or more offenses are set out in the same count of the said indictment; second, that there are several distinct offenses and crimes set out in the said indictment under different acts of Congress, the punishment for the violation of which is different, involving separate counts in which such distinct offenses are separately charged.

[1] [2] As to the first division, it is a feature of the statutes against opium that a number of offenses are charged

disjunctively in the same act, and sometimes in the same paragraph. For instance, the statute forbidding the importation into the United States of smoking opium or opium prepared for smoking, uses the following language: "or shall receive, conceal, buy, sell, or in any manner facilitate the transportation, concealment or sale of such opium", evidently describing several offenses, under which statute, with the proper indictment, any of such acts, if proved may be punished.

It is the practice here and in other jurisdictions, however, to follow the words of the statute in a single count of an indictment, but instead of setting them forth disjunctively, or connected by the word "or", they are set forth conjunctively, or connected by the word "and." This charges them as constituting a single offense, and authorizes a verdict of guilty if there is proof of any of such acts.

The case of *Morganstern v. Commonwealth*, 26 S. E. 403, a Virginia case, has the following:

"Where the legislature, for the purpose of suppressing a vice or preventing a wrong, has, by statute, made the vice or wrong a criminal offense, and, in defining the offense, has specified a series of acts, either of which separately or all together may constitute an offense, and has prescribed, as here, the same penalty for the commission of one or all of the acts, it is well settled that the commission of any two or more of them may be alleged in the same count of an indictment, if conjunctively charged. Although each act by itself may constitute an offense under the statute, yet, if they are all committed by the same person at the same time and place, they are to be considered as parts of the same transaction, and collectively constitute a single offense."

See also *State v. Malone*, 35 N. E. 198; *State v. Fidler*, 47 N. E. 465, and *State v. Dawson*, 78 N. E. 353; all Indiana cases.

The indictment in this case charges in the first count that the defendant did unlawfully import opium, and in the second count that he did "feloniously receive, conceal, buy and sell, and facilitate the transportation, concealment and sale of certain opium". In the third count, that he did "then and there unlawfully produce, import, manufacture, deal in, dispense, sell, distribute and give away opium", etc., without registering his place of business as required by law, and without having paid the special tax required by law.

In these three counts the offenses respectively charged, are charged conjunctively and come within the precedents cited above.

I am of the opinion that the rule established by such authorities is sound and not unfair to the defendant, and overrule that part of the grounds of the motion to quash.

As to the ground of the motion to quash, that there are several distinct offenses and crimes set out in said indictment under different and separate acts of Congress, punishment for which upon conviction thereof is different, section 1204 of the Revised Statutes has the following:

"When there are several charges against any person for the same act or transaction, or for two or more acts or transactions connected together, or for two or more acts or transactions of the same class of crimes or offenses which may be properly joined, instead of having several indictments, the whole may be joined in one indictment in separate counts; and if two or more indictments are found, in such case the court may order them to be consolidated."

The second provision of this law, providing that where there are several charges against any person for "two or more acts or transactions connected together", appears to the first three counts of this indictment. The first count charges felonious importation of opium, or assistance in so doing; the second count charges, among other things, dealing with opium after the importation thereof; the third charges importation and manufacturing, among other things, without registering and without having paid the special tax required.

A case in 10 Mich. 54, 95, entitled *McKinney's Case*, has the following:

"Where the several offenses charged, though distinct in point of law, yet spring out of substantially the same transaction or are so connected in their facts as to make substantially parts of the same transaction, or connected series of facts, the defendant cannot be prejudiced in his defense by the joinder, and the court will neither quash nor compel an election."

[3] This authority applies to the second division of the statute as above cited, where there are several charges against any person "for two or more acts or transactions connected together, instead of having several indictments all may be joined in one indictment in separate counts"; and it would appear also that the first division of the statute would apply, "where there are several charges against any person for the same act or transaction". If these different charges were made in separate indictments, it would seem that under the same statute they might, at the discretion of the court, be consolidated for trial.

The fourth count charges the manufacture of opium for smoking purposes, without filing with the collector of internal revenue the notices and inventories and bonds required by the regulations prescribed by the commissioner of internal revenue, and failing to render a return of material and products as required by such regulations and failing to put up signs and the number of his factory as required by such regulations, and that the defendant did conduct his business without the surveillance of the officers and agents required by such regulations. The punishment under the statute (38 Stat. 277) of which this count charges a violation, is a penalty of not less than ten thousand dollars or imprisonment for not less than five years.

It will be seen that here is a charge not only under a

separate statute from those under which the first three counts were brought, but a statute creating an offense not in the same class or grade, but of a different character from those charged in the other counts and requiring a different punishment. In form it is in the nature of an internal revenue act, providing for a heavy tax on the manufacture of opium, making it ostensibly an act for revenue, although in its details it certainly is intended conspicuously to discourage the manufacture of opium.

"Such a joinder of incongruous charges has been made a ground for granting a new trial, because 'it can hardly be said that a party has had a full, fair and impartial trial who has been forced to defend himself on the same indictment against two inconsistent and widely different offenses.'" *State v. Fitzsimmons*, 18 R. I. 236.

In *State v. Tuller*, 34 Conn. 299, the court said:

"In England, if two different felonies are charged in separate counts, the court will quash the indictment. But that is not the practice here; the court, if two distinct transactions are joined, may direct the attorney to elect and to nolle one of the counts."

In *State v. Scott*, 15 S. C. 436, it is held:

"That if distinct felonies, not growing out of the same transaction, are charged in separate counts, the practice is to require an election, even though no motion to that effect could be made by the accused."

[4] Now, although the offense charged in the fourth count may have grown partially out of the same transaction or course of conduct as is charged in the other counts, yet the different nature of the offense and its incongruous character as compared with the charges in the other counts, justify the court in following these precedents.

The court finds that the four counts of the indictment should not be tried together, as unfair to the defendant, and requires the prosecution to elect to proceed to trial either under the first three counts of the indictment or under the fourth.   It is not necessary, under such conditions, that the whole indictment should be quashed, but it is in the discretion of the court to rule as above; and the court so rules.

IN THE MATTER OF THE APPLICATION OF KO MATSUMOTO FOR A WRIT OF HABEAS CORPUS.

December 4, 1915.

1. *Aliens—Immigration—Exclusion for offense of moral turpitude:* Adultery and perjury are offenses involving moral turpitude; and alien immigrants may be excluded from the United States therefor under section 2 of the Immigration Act (34 Stat. 898, am. 36 Stat. 263).

2. *Same—Same—Fair hearing before immigration inspectors—Benefit of counsel:* An alien immigrant who does not request aid of counsel in his preliminary examination before the immigration inspector or in the subsequent hearing before the board of special inquiry, but who thereafter has counsel and is furnished with a copy of the testimony taken at the examination and hearing, cannot complain of such want of counsel at the first stages as unfairness in the proceedings.

3. *Same—Same—Same—Interpretation of testimony:*   Qualifications of interpreters and elements of fair interpretaion considered.

4. *Constitutional law—Examination of alien immigrant before immigration officers—Self-crimimnation—Confessions:* The immigration officers may place an alien immigrant on the witness stand and any answer which he gives voluntarily may be used against him.

5. *Habeas corpus—Bail on appeal from order dismissing writ:* Under rule 33 of the Ninth Circuit Court of Appeals and rule 34 of the Supreme Court, this court in its discretion may on dismissing a writ of habeas corpus admit to bail pending appeal the person in whose behalf the writ issued.   But to guard against delay the court in such cases may require the appeal to be perfected before the appellant's release.

Habeas Corpus: Hearing on return to writ.

G. S. Curry and *E. A. Douthitt* for the petitioner.
Jeff McCarn, U. S. District Attorney, for the respondent.

CLEMONS, J. The board of special inquiry of the immigration service at the port of Honolulu denied the petitioner a landing at that port "as a person who admits having committed a crime or misdemeanor involving moral turpitude, namely the commission of adultery with one Matsumoto, in the Territory of Hawaii; also as admitting having committed perjury by giving false testimony before the board of special inquiry while under oath, and as a person likely to become a public charge."

[1a] The admission of adultery is based on the following testimony of the petitioner, in her examination before the board on October 25th of this year, after she had earlier in the same hearing distinctly denied that she had committed adultery with Matsumoto, and had at a previous hearing on October 22d testified in a manner indicating her denial of any such offense.

"Q. Do you expect us to believe that you were refused a divorce by reason of your own adultery, and that Matsumoto pleaded guilty and spent six months in jail for the same reason and yet you were innocent? A. I never tell a lie. I will tell you the truth now, *I did commit adultery with Matsumoto* and also sued my former husband for divorce. (Transcript of proceedings, page 4). . . . . Q. Did you go to his room for the purpose of committing adultery or did he persuade you to do it after you arrived? A. I never went there to do it, and he didn't persuade me; *it just happened after I got there.* Q. Any further statement to make? A. Dr. Grossman knows that I wasn't making a *practice* of living with another man. You can ask him about it." (Transcript of proceedings, page 5).

The petitioner bases the present proceedings in habeas corpus on the following broad contentions, as finally relied on in argument, though stated somewhat more in detail in the pleadings:

(1) Unfairness in failure of the board to call witnesses required by the petitioner in her hearing before it;

(2) Unfairness in her not being afforded counsel at the beginning of the hearing, or thereafter;

(3) Unfairness in the incompetence of the interpreter who translated questions and answers from English into Japanese or Japanese into English, as the case might be; particularly in that the interpreter was an Okinawa Japanese, speaking the Okinawa dialect of which the petitioner was ignorant;

(4) Denial of any admission of the commission of any crime or misdemeanor involving moral turpitude,—which includes not only (a) a denial of the fact of any such admission but also (b) a contention that what she is alleged to have admitted does not in law constitute any such crime or misdemeanor as is contemplated by section 2 of the immigration act, 34 Stat. 898, am. 36 Stat. 263;

(5) Denial that the petitioner is likely to become a public charge.

In view of my conclusion below, under ground (4), ground (5) will not be considered. I may say, though, that if this ground were determinative of the case, my conclusion would be very different.

Grounds (1), (2), and (3) I find nothing to sustain. And evidence has been adduced to make the solution of these questions very clear. Furthermore, as to ground (1), the evidence of what the two witnesses who are claimed to have been required would have testified to, was heard *de bene* because of the prospective absence of one and for the business convenience of the other, and it shows that they could neither of them say anything of any materiality in view of the petitioner's distinct admission discussed below under ground (4), or say anything except that the petitioner had been a faithful servant of each of them during her former residence in Honolulu and that they trusted her and would be glad to give her employment again. Their testimony would have been very desirable under ground (5) above, if that ground had been conclusive.

[2] Aside from the want of facts to support grounds (1) and (2), the cases of *United States v. Sing Tuck*, 194 U. S. 161, 169, 170; *Law Wah Suey v. Backus*, 225 U. S. 460, 469, 470, may be referred to, among others, as to the law governing ground (2), want of counsel. The decision in the case of *United States ex rel. Buccino v. Williams*, 190 Fed. 897, affirmed in *United States ex rel. Falco v. Williams*, 191 Fed. 1001, says:

"There is nothing in the statute which calls for the presence of counsel at the examination of aliens preliminary to admission; nothing to indicate that it was the intent of Congress that these investigations in hundreds of thousands of cases touching the qualifications of an alien seeking to enter were to be conducted as trials in court, with counsel present to represent the alien, witnesses called to testify, and elaborate examination and cross-examination of them. On the contrary, Congress relegated this question to administrative boards who might act summarily and expeditiously, and, to provide against an abuse of their discretion, accorded to the alien a right of appeal to the Secretary of Commerce and Labor. Nor do the rules provide for the presence of counsel at such examinations."

And see *United States v. Greenwalt*, 213 Fed. 901, 905; *Ex. p. Chin Loy You*, 223 Fed. 833, 838-839, also 836-838; *Ex. p. Chin Kwock Wah*, 224 Fed. 138, 139; *Whitfield v. Hanges*, 222 Fed. 745, 749, par. 3; *In re Ryonosuke Sakaba*, ante, p. 372.

[3] As to ground (3), I may express specially my confidence in the conscientiousness of the interpreter and also in his qualifications, and note that the careful reading over of the testimony to the petitioner before she signed it, together with the repeated call for her objection if everything was not correct, reduced the possibility of error to a minimum—particularly as the petitioner's admission was in effect repeated in her words last above quoted, "it just hap-

pened after I got there" ("it" referring unmistakably to adultery), and the repetition was made at a time somewhat later in her examination than the time of the more direct admission. In other words, the later admission appears to be separate and distinct from, and perhaps uninfluenced by, the first admission. The circumstance that the interpreter was born an Okinawa Japanese, does not weigh against his extensive education and experience in the Japanese language, fully tested here in court by all counsel.

As to ground (4), subdivision (a), what I have just said indicates my satisfaction that the petitioner understood the interpreter and that she was correctly interpreted as having as a matter of fact made the admission of adultery—she being at the time of the offense a married woman and having a husband living.

[1b] There remains, then, the sole question, one of law, whether or not adultery is "a felony or other crime or misdemeanor involving moral turpitude". The cases of *United States v. Sibray*, 178 Fed. 144; *United States v. Uhl*, 211 Fed. 628, and *Ex parte Isojiki*, 222 Fed. 151, are cited for the proposition that it is not.

The identical question was before me in *In the Matter of Tome Tanno*, ante, p. 266, decided June 22, 1913, when I held adultery to be an offense involving moral turpitude; though not then having the advantage of reference to the decisions of other courts above cited. I there disposed of the matter rather summarily:

"It should require no discussion to establish to the mind of any one of moral sense, according to standards to which social policy can admit no exceptions, that her questioned act [adultery] was one of moral turpitude."

I then cited, without quoting, *Pollard v. Lyon*, 91 U. S. 225, which says at page 228:

"Beyond all doubt, offences of the kind involve moral turpitude," referring to adultery, see page 227.

I also cited, without quoting, *United States v. Bitty*, 208 U. S. 393, which says at page 401, what is pertinent and suggestive:

"Was that [concubinage] an *immoral* purpose within the meaning of the statute? . . . Beyond question . . . Congress had in view the protection of society against another class of alien women other than those who might be brought here merely for the purpose of 'prostituion'."

Also, at page 403: "The statute in question, it must be remembered, was intended to keep out of this country immigrants whose permanent residence here would not be desirable or for the common good, and we cannot suppose either that Congress intended to exempt from the operation of the statute the importation of an alien woman brought here only that she might live in a state of concubinage with the man importing her, or that it did not regard such an importation as being for an *immoral* purpose."

And I cited the case of *United States v. Uhl*, 203 Fed. 152, which says at page 154:

" 'Moral turpitude' is a vague term. *Its meaning depends to some extent upon the state of public morals.* A definition sufficiently accurate for this case, however, is this: 'An act of baseness, vileness, or depravity in the *private and social duties* which a man owes to his fellow-man or to society."

Also cited without quotation was *Gomez v. Hawaiian Gazette Co.*, 10 Haw. 108, which says at page 111:

"Moral turpitude is defined to be an act of baseness, vileness, or depravity in the private and social duties which a man owes to his fellow-man or to society in general, *contrary to the accepted and customary rule of right and duty between man and man*", quoting Newell on Defamation, and ruling that to charge a person with selling opium, an offense [which may perhaps be said to be in some degree merely *malum prohibitum*] punishable by imprisonment at hard labor, is to charge him with an offense involving moral turpitude.

Also, adultery is regarded as such an offense in *Ranger v. Goodrich*, 17 Wis. 80, 82-83.

The three decisions cited by petitioner's counsel, though the conclusions of able courts, cannot prevail as against the authorities just quoted.   The court's discussion in the *Isojiki* case, 222 Fed. 151, seems unconvincing, and the court in the *Sibray* case, 178 Fed. 144, I respectfully submit, shows its misconception when it says, at page 150: "The answer is that the police power of the State of Pennsylvania must have control of those who offend against her laws." But this is not the "answer" at all; for it is not, of course, a case of Congress' administering the police power of any State but a question of Congress' right to say who may be admitted as desirable immigrants: Congress must let the State exercise its own police power unhampered, but in addition to any punishment to which an offender may be subject under such authority, Congress may punish the offender further by providing that his infraction of local laws shall make him, if an alien who has left the country, an undesirable person who cannot return.

If the decalogue, the moral precepts of the ages, and the rules of ecclesiastical law from early times, do not indicate that adultery is an offense involving moral turpitude, then our common teachings are hypocrisy.   Note the following language of *In re Hopkins,* 103 Pac. 806, 806:

"This presents a question of right conduct from a purely moral standpoint, independent of the fact that the law prescribes a punishment for the making of such false statements. 'Thou shalt not bear false witness' was not only one of the ten commandments of the Mosaic law, but finds sanction in the teachings of Jesus as a standard of right under the new dispensation.   Indeed, this standard of right seems to be a part of the moral consciousness of the race, and to be recognized by all peoples with any appreciation of moral ideals."

If we may not judge of moral turpitude by these standards, by what standards are we to judge of it?   Even though adultery was not a crime at common law,—a fact which counsel urge to be significant and controlling,—it still re-

mains true that adultery is and has for centuries been
denounced by the church and by society, and that in ecclesiastical law it was regarded as a ground of divorce, and
even at common law, though the act was not recognized as
criminal, it was held to be a cause of damages in a civil
action by an offended spouse. See 1 Cyc. 952; 21 Cyc.
1626. That Christianity, which forbids adultery, may be
looked to in determining the public sense of what is moral
turpitude, see *Holy Trinity Church v. United States*, 134
U. S. 457, 470-471; Cooley, Const. Law, 7 ed. 669, et seq.

"This element of moral turpitude is necessarily adapt-
ive; for it is itself defined by the state of public morals,
and thus far fits the action to be at all times accommodated
to the common sense of the community." *Beck v. Stitzel*,
21 Pa. 522, 524.

Any argument growing out of a difference between an
offense *malum in se* and one merely *malum prohibitum*,
would fall with any argument based on the fact that adultery was not a crime at common law. See discussion,
supra, and *Pullman Palace Car Co. v. Central Transportation Co.*, 69 Fed. 158, 164; 1 Black. Comm. (Cooley's 4th
ed.) 50-51, n. 2 (*57, *58).

From the finding that the testimony was correctly and
fairly interpreted, it follows that the petitioner committed
perjury—which would alone suffice to exclude her from the
country; for it could hardly be said that she did not by
her testimony "admit" the commission of perjury when in
her testimony admitting guilt, above quoted, she changed
her testimony of the previous hearing, denying guilt. See
20 A. & E. Enc. L., 2d ed. 872, and n. 6; 16 Id. 246-247, and
cases cited.

[4] The question which has occurred to me as worthy
of consideration in the petitioner's behalf, whether the circumstances did not make her admissions of guilt inadmissible in evidence on the principles applying to confessions, and so make the board's consideration of such

admissions a want of due process of law, or of fair trial, has been entirely removed by consideration of the very principles of the law, as it is, relating to confessions. See 1 Wigmore, Ev:, secs. 848, 849, (and n. 3, p. 971), 851; 2 Chamberlayne, Ev., sec. 1569. See, also, 2 Wharton, Crim. Ev., 10th ed., secs. 664, 669. It may be noted in this connection, that Rev. Stat.; sec. 860, which might otherwise be contended as having some bearing on the question, has been repealed. 36 Stat. 352.

The competency of the government in such cases to swear the immigrant as a witness against himself, is established by the Circuit Court of Appeals for this circuit. *Low Foon Yin v. United States Immigration Com'r*, 145 Fed. 791, 793 et seq. And the Circuit Court of Appeals for the sixth circuit (Lurton, Severens, and Richards, JJ.), in *United States v. Hung Chang*, 134 Fed. 19, holds that:

"Admissions or statements of a defendant, voluntarily made to the officers by whom he is arrested, in answer to questions put by them either before or after his arrest, are admissible in evidence against him, and the government has the right to call and examine him as a witness." Syllabus, par. 1. See, also, Id. at page 25.

[5] The writ of habeas corpus is discharged and the petitioner remanded to the custody of the respondent. However, as petitioner's counsel have noted an intention to appeal, and as the petitioner appears to be a woman whom two responsible citizens, witnesses here in her behalf, are ready to employ in their own households, and who has been trusted by one of them as faithful and steady in her work as nurse and housemaid in his family, and it is not apparent that she is a woman of vicious tendencies but had once lapsed from virtue under conditions of ill-treatment by her husband, from whom she has since been divorced, and as her paramour, if he may be so called, a steady and reliable laborer, is now to marry her and provide for her, the proposed motion of her counsel for release on bail will be enter-

tained with favor, but not, however, until after her appeal
has been perfected to the extent of the filing of a petition
and assignment of errors and execution of an approved
bond on appeal, and with the understanding that the transcript of testimony and the record on appeal shall be completed within thirty days from the time of allowance of
the appeal. This attitude of the court is a precaution,
warranted from experience, against want of good faith and
delay in appeals. The amount of the bail bond will be
$500. This order is made, in spite of the ruling cited by
the district attorney, of *United States v. Sisson*, 220 Fed.
538, 540-541, which flies in the face of rule 33, sec. 2, of
the ninth Circuit Court of Appeals, and of rule 34, sec. 2,
of the Supreme Court, made pursuant to Rev. Stat., sec.
765, and which errs,—it may be worth while to note,—in its
statement that, "a writ of habeas corpus does not put the
relator into the custody of the court." *Barth v. Clise*, 12
Wall. 400, 402; *In re Wilkins*, 71 N. H. 591, 53 Atl. 1019;
In re Grant, 26 Wash. 412, 67 Pac. 73; 15 A. & E. Enc. L.,
2d ed., 213-215. The case of *In re Kaine*, 14 How. 103, is
cited by this encyclopedia to the same effect as the later
decision of *Barth v. Clise*, supra, and is also regarded in the
same way by Judge Blatchford, *In re Hamilton*, 1 Ben. 453,
11 Fed. Cas. 319, 320, No. 5,976; and in spite of language
of Mr. Justice Curtis in the case of *Kaine*, 14 How. at page
121, Mr. Justice Nelson's view at pages 133-134, in which
the Chief Justice and Mr. Justice Daniel concur specially,
at page 148, without doubt expresses the view of the court
at that time, and later expressed in the case of *Barth v.
Clise*—in which the reporter cites in a note the earlier case
of *Kaine*. See 12 Wall. 402, note.

Appeal dismissed for non-compliance with rules 23 and
24, Circuit Court of Appeals, Ninth Circuit.

UNITED STATES OF AMERICA v. BENEGNA DAGO-MAN..

December 8, 1915.

Costs—Fees of witnesses for indigent defendants in criminal cases: Where in a criminal case an indigent defendant, by affidavit under Rev. Stat. sec. 878, as to materiality of proposed testimony, obtains subpoena for a witness who at trial proves to know nothing of matters as to which he is expected to testify, the defendant's motion for costs of process and witness fees in such case is disallowed.

Criminal Law: Motion to tax costs.

H. W. Vaughan, Assistant U. S. Attorney, for the United States.

G. K. French for the defendant.

DOLE, J. The defendant in this case filed an affidavit under section 878 of the Revised Statutes, setting forth the names of certain alleged witnesses to be subpoenaed, whose evidence was claimed to be material to the defense. After the trial, in the matter of taxing costs, it appeared that one of the witnesses named Beata Jumalon Atad, who had been subpoenaed and who attended the trial, was unavailable for the defense, not knowing anything about matters that it was expected that she could testify to. Counsel for the defendant claims that the costs incurred by the process of subpoena, and the fees of said witness, should be paid as similar costs and fees were allowed in regard to the other witnesses, and submitted several authorities.

The case of *Merriam v. Johnson*, 101 N. W. 308, a Minnesota case, and *Farmer v. Storer*, 28 Mass. 241, agree that, in cases where defendant's witnesses are summoned and not used, because, during the trial, the necessity of their testimony is obviated by admissions of fact made at the trial, or by the course of pleading, or by rulings of the court, or for any circumstance by which, on the plaintiff's theory of the case, the necessity of their testimony may have been eliminated, there is no good reason why the costs of process and their fees should not be allowed. And this is because their testimony was ready in response to allegations of the complaint and that the facts which they were ready to testify to were material to the defendant's case.

A statute in Missouri provides that:

"The judge and prosecuting attorney shall in no case tax the state or county with more than the costs of three witnesses to establish any one fact, nor with costs of witnesses unnecessarily summoned and not examined, but the costs of such surplus or unnecessary witnesses shall, in the discretion of the court, be taxed against the parties or the attorney causing them to be summoned." Ses. 4420, R. S. Mo.

This statute is in harmony with the decisions above cited, and supports the practice that fees should not be allowed for witnesses unnecessarily summoned; the cases deciding that the costs and fees of witnesses necessarily summoned and ready to give relevant testimony should be allowed.

A further authority cited by defendant's counsel in this case, *Mankato v. Craig*, 83 N. W. 983 (Minn.) is as follows:

"If a party acts in good faith, the mere fact that the testimony is immaterial or inadmissible will not deprive him of fees necessarily paid or incurred."

This authority, although extremely favorable to a defendant acting in good faith, does not support the contention of defendant's counsel, that the costs and fees of a summoned witness who knows nothing about the case should be allowed.

I feel that the best attitude of the court is to expect counsel to know that the persons whose names are furnished to the court under an affidavit for process have at least some information to offer relating to the case; and that it is too much to ask that the United States should pay costs and fees on account of alleged witnesses who attend and yet cannot furnish any information whatever, material or immaterial, admissible or inadmissible, that has some reference to the case.

The previous ruling of the court, therefore, in regard to the person, Beata Jumalon Atad, summoned as a witness herein, refusing to allow the costs of process and fees claimed on her account, is affirmed.

FRANK SULLIVAN v. THE SHIP "EDWARD SEWALL."

December 16, 1915.

Dismissal of proceedings out of court: **Agreement out of court between parties to litigation, viewed with suspicion by courts, but this suspicion may be overcome by preponderance of evidence.**

In Admiralty: Motion to strike plea in bar.

G. S. Curry for the libelant.
R. W. Breckons for the libellee.

DOLE, J. This suit was brought April 27, 1912, and answer was made May 3, 1912. The libel was for damages to the libelant in that he was injured while up aloft at sea, by the breaking of a part of the rigging of the vessel, of the crew of which he was a member, causing painful injuries to his face and hands. Libelant was allowed to bring proceedings without advancing costs, under a pauper's oath.

On the 18th day of May, 1912, the libellee filed a plea

in bar, setting forth a copy of a release by the libelant, discontinuing the case in consideration of the sum of fifty dollars and settlement of his wages. On the same day the proctor for libelant filed a motion that the release and discontinuance of the action filed by the proctor for libellee be declared null and void and stricken from the records, alleging certain reasons therefor relating to the libelant's youth and weak mental condition, which was enhanced by the injuries he had received—the basis of this action—and also that he had been given liquor by the master and some agent of the libellee, under the influence of which he had signed the release, being at the time mentally incapable of making a contract. The affidavit of the libelant was attached to the motion, and supports it in detail.

The deposition of the master, who had in the meantime left the Territory, was finally obtained and filed herein on October 1, 1914, denying generally the statements of the libelant's affidavit.

The release of the libelant stated that it was made without the knowledge of his attorneys. It does not appear that the proctors for the libellee had anything to do with said release, which is a satisfaction to the court, inasmuch as such action by members of the bar of this court, dealing with an opposite party without the benefit of the advice of his own proctors, would be considered as unprofessional.

I offer the following citations as dealing with the law relating to this plea in bar:

"Where parties have once submitted their rights to the jurisdiction of Equity, a private agreement between themselves, out of court, will not operate as a dismissal of the bill, and a stay of proceedings in the suit. Some step must be taken in court, either by motion to dismiss the bill, or to stay proceedings." Hovenden on Frauds, 83.

"Supposing Wood had applied to this court to stay proceedings, and had produced this agreement; and the other party had said, When that agreement was signed I was in the King's Bench prison, and had nobody near me but the other parties and their attorneys: would the court have acted upon an agreement of that sort? I think, undoubtedly, not." *Rowe v. Wood*, 1 Jacob & Walker 345 (37 English Reprint, 396, 404).

The case as it stands is unsatisfactory to the court, inasmuch as the libelant, in his affidavit attached to the motion for setting aside the release, states that the second mate of the libellee, whose name is Snyder, having given him two large drinks of whiskey, induced him to go to the ship, and that upon reaching the ship, the master, Captain Quick, was waiting for him and then made the propositions of settlement; the first for one hundred dollars, the libelant to remain with the ship for the voyage to New York, which was rejected; the second, an offer of fifty dollars and settlement of wages, being accepted. No testimony has been produced from this man Snyder, the real actor in the plan of creating a state of intoxication in libelant and in said condition obtaining the release in question, according to the affidavit of libelant.

In addition, however, to the deposition of the captain, I have referred to the testimony of three witnesses who were present at the execution of the release or discontinuance. These were the notary public who took the acknowledgment, Frank Fernandez; J. K. Clarke, a clerk in Hind, Rolph & Company's offices; and George McCorriston. These witnesses were examined and cross-examined on the question of the mental condition and capacity of the libelant at the time when he executed the release, and they all agree that, so far as they could judge, he was perfectly sober, and no one of them had any doubt that he was so.

With this testimony, in addition to that of the captain, although I regret not having the testimony of the mate Snyder, who was the man charged in libelant's affidavit with having furnished him with liquor, I do not feel that I can sustain the motion of libelant that the said release and discontinuance of the action be declared null and void and stricken from the record. The same is, therefore, denied and the release by libelant, discontinuing the case in consideration of the money named therein, is sustained and the suit is discontinued; the libellee to pay its own costs.

INTER-ISLAND STEAM NAVIGATION COMPANY, LIMITED, *v.* THE AMERICAN SCHOONER "HALCYON."

December 16, 1915.

1. *Salvage:* A salving vessel having towed a vessel in a dangerous position to a supposedly safe place, would lose all claims to remuneration, should it neglect to attempt to save it a second time, when the salved vessel is carried by the same tempestuous weather into a new danger.

2. *Same—Danger to salving vessel:* Remuneration to a salving vessel is enhanced through its being exposed to loss in the salvage operations.

3. *Same—Lesser danger to cargo of libellee than to libellee itself; in case of non-salvage affecting decree:* In case the libellee has not been salved but had become a total wreck upon a sand beach on the occasion of her second peril, the fair possibility that a good proportion of her cargo of lumber might be saved at some expense justifies a lesser proportionate decree against the cargo than against the vessel.

In Admiralty: Libel *in rem* for salvage.

L. J. Warren (Smith, Warren, Hemenway & Sutton with him) for libelant.

J. W. Russell for libellee.

DOLE, J. In these proceedings for salvage, the undisputed story is as follows:

The libellee had arrived in the port of Hilo, with a load of lumber, and had begun to discharge her deck-load at the railroad wharf. On the night of the 12th and 13th of January, 1914, as she was lying a little way off the wharf, moored both to the wharf and to buoys on the port side, a heavy wind came up from the north and caused her to drift, breaking a line attached to the buoy and colliding with a smaller schooner moored near her stern. Either by blue lights or communication by boat with the steamer Niihau, belonging to the libelant, she suggested assistance. The steamer immediately raised her anchor and came down the wind, near the libellee, and anchored and sent a tow line by boat to the libellee, which then had drifted close to the shore, near the mouth of the Wailoa River, the shore on the east side of the mouth of that river being rocky and that on the west being sandy. The line was connected and the Niihau towed the libellee out of this dangerous position to a place out in the bay, beyond the end of the railroad wharf; whereupon the tow line broke and the libellee, which had already lost one anchor, dropped the other anchor, the Niihau also anchoring.

In a few minutes it was evident to the master of the Niihau that the libellee was drifting again, this time toward the sandy shore on the west side of the entrance to the Wailoa River. As she approached this shore the Niihau changed her position and came close to her, reaching a position a little way to the windward. The master of the schooner, finding himself near to the breakers and still drifting, raised a signal for assistance, and about this time a boat with a tow line left the Niihau and came down the wind on a surf line from the steamer, and upon reaching her delivered the end of the tow line, which the crew of the libellee fastened to her bow; the boat then returning to the steamer and bringing another and larger line which was also fastened to the libellee. The libellee was then pulled out of this dangerous position to a safe place in the harbor, where she anchored, and, her one anchor having proved insufficient, the Niihau held on to her during the rest of that day and the succeeding night with a line.

There was apparent effort on the part of the libellee to show that she was in no special danger on either occasion and that the master of the steamer Niihau was not prompt in rendering assistance on the second occasion of relief. I am convinced from the evidence that on both occasions the schooner was in great danger of going ashore and of becoming a total loss if she had gone ashore. The wind was blowing a gale, variously estimated from twenty-five to forty miles an hour, the weight and character of the testimany favoring the latter speed. The first aid given was in the darkness of the night, the circumstances creating some danger to the salving steamer, in that she had to proceed between the railroad wharf and unlighted buoys one hundred and fifty to two hundred feet away from the wharf, and anchor and send out her tow line and proceed into the bay with the libellee in tow. The manoeuver was successfully accomplished, yet the tow line parted after the libellee had reached a comparatively safe place; and there is considerable evidence that the parting of the tow line was caused by friction with one of the afore-mentioned buoys. After the line was attached to the libellee, the Niihau sent a boat to sound alongside of the libellee, on her port side, where they found the depth of the water to be eighteen feet amidship and twelve feet near the stern, showing the libellee to be almost ashore.

The evidence of the captain of the Niihau and the members of his crew shows that as soon as those on board noticed that the libellee was drifting again, after her first relief, they immediately began preparations for assisting her, pulling up anchors and proceeding toward the drifting schooner and dropping anchors and letting out

chain until the steamer had reached a favorable position
for assisting the schooner, getting out a tow line, coiling
it in the boat, and then sending the boat down the wind
on a surf line, with a tow line for delivery to the schooner.
The evidence of the captain and members of his crew that
this boat left the steamer before the signals had been
raised by the schooner for relief was positive, it appearing
from their testimony that the signals for relief were raised
while the boat was on the way and had nearly arrived at
the schooner.

A point was made by libellee's counsel that as, according
to the evidence, about two hours elapsed between the time
of the breaking of the tow line at the first relief and the
delivery of the end of the tow line to the schooner on the
occasion of the second relief, the Niihau must have been
doing nothing during a part of this time—had perhaps
waited for signals of distress before moving. The fact as
shown by the testimony of libellee's witnesses, that the boat
from the steamer, carrying the tow line, started almost immediately after the signals were raised, shows conclusively
that the steamer was thoroughly prepared to act and had
been engaged. for some part of the two hours in making
preparations. We have to consider that when her master
noticed the schooner was drifting, fifteen or twenty minutes after the tow line parted, he had to raise his anchors
and steam out to the place where he anchored the second
time, finding the right position and dropping both anchors,
letting out the chain to an extent which would bring him
in a favorable position for assisting the schooner, all of
which, according to the testimony, took from twenty minutes to half an hour. He then prepared his boat for conveying the tow line to the schooner, coiling the tow line
of a six-inch size in the boat, fastening that to a four-inch
line for giving it sufficient length for handling, and sending
the boat in by a surf line to the ship, negotiating with his
boat's crew, who demurred to going without such surf line.

Such preparation might well have occupied an hour and a half, or more; and the testimony in regard to the time elapsed is of such a general character, merely approximating two hours, that, as a basis for inexcusable delay, it does not appeal to me as being very substantial.

The case presents itself to my mind as one of the most satisfactory cases of salvage on the part of the salvors that has appeared in this court.   The agents of the libelant, upon being informed of the danger of the libellee, promptly came to her assistance in the darkness of the night, under circumstances of some danger to its steamer, and removed her from her dangerous position to a safe one in the harbor, or which would have been a safe one if the libellee had been equipped with her two anchors.   As soon as the agents of the libelant noticed that the libellee was drifting again they began preparations for her relief, and continued such preparations until they were ready to send her a tow line the second time, at which time the libellee was in a dangerous position and, without the relief which was given her, was in prospect of becoming a total loss.

[1] I cannot find from the testimony that there was any neglect or inexcusable delay on the part of the libelant's agents.   Having once salved the schooner, they understood, or should have understood, that any neglect by which she might have been lost the second time would lose them all claims for remuneration for her first salvage, unless it should absolutely appear that the second danger and final loss was caused solely by the fault of the libellee.   The salving methods were the best, and were carried out with skill and courage and resulted in the entire deliverance of the libellee.

[2] In all these operations, there was, according to the evidence, considerable danger to the salving steamer, from the possibility of entangling her propeller with tow lines, in which case she would be helpless if her anchors should

fail to hold from any cause, whether from dragging or the parting of the anchor chains.

[3] There was considerable testimony as to the danger to the cargo in case the schooner had gone ashore and had become a loss. As the weather began to diminish in severity during the following night after the salvage, after a period of perhaps twelve hours or so, it is hard for the court to say from the testimony what the situation of the lumber would have been if the schooner had been wrecked. The evidence in the case shows that the schooner was old and in a weak condition from age and decay. It is uncertain that the ship would have been so broken up that the lumber would have escaped into the waves, and yet that might have happened. In any case, the danger to the cargo was considerable. If the ship had gone ashore and held together until the storm subsided, twenty-four hours or more afterwards, the removal of the cargo from the hull to the shore would have been attended with very considerable expense.

In view of the circumstances, as shown by the evidence, that the ship was in the greatest danger and was, to my mind, rescued from total loss, and that the danger to her cargo was considerably less, I think a decree awarding libelant one-half of the value of the schooner, the whole value of which has been admitted to be $1,500; and one-third of the value of the cargo, which has been admitted to be $6,381.85, would be reasonable. A decree may be entered for $750, as one-half of the value of the vessel, and $2,127.28, as one-third of the value of the cargo, totalling $2,877.28; all costs to be paid by the libellee.

CHARLES KARLSON, JOHN CARMICHAEL, H. B. DAVIS, NEIL MORRISON, FRANK CALVE, HENRY WILLIAMS AND WILLIAM MORRIS v. THE AMERICAN SCHOONER "J. M. WEATHER-WAX."

December 16, 1915.

1. *Costs—Marshal's fees and expenses—Service of petition:* In the marshal's bill for fees items of $2 each for serving copy of petition and copy of order for process are disallowed, and $1 allowed instead, following *Swanscott v. Remsen,* 76 Fed. 950, 951; 21 Dec. Comptroller, 439, 440 (Dec. 31, 1914).

2. *Same—Same—Service of notice of monition upon publisher:* There is no authority for the marshal's charging for "service" of the notice of monition, upon the publisher. And the marshal's act in such case does not constitute a "service." *United States v. A Lot of Silk Goods,* ante, p. 137.

3. *Same—Same—Service of release and venditioni exponas:* Item of "serving release and venditioni exponas" disallowed as covered by the sale commission.

In Admiralty: On taxation of costs.

G. A. Davis for libelants.
J. J. Smiddy, U. S. Marshal, *pro se.*

CLEMONS, J. (Memorandum opinion).

[1] In the marshal's bill, October 7, 1915, items of $2 each for serving copy of petition and copy of order for process, are disallowed, and the item of $1 under date of October 9, is allowed in its stead: See *Swanscot v. Remsen,* 76 Fed. 950, 951; 21 Dec. Comptroller, 439, 440 (Dec. 31, 1914). And the same criticism is made of item, October 9, 1915, service of similar papers on H. A. Hyland, managing director of the ship-owner.

[2] In the marshal's bill, October 8, 1915, there is disallowed $2 for serving upon the publisher notice of monition, for publication. See *United States v. A Lot of Silk Goods,* ante, p. 137.

[3] In the marshal's bill, December 15, 1915, $4 for serving release and venditioni exponas is disallowed in toto. The latter item is covered by the sale commission which is all that the marshal can get on account of a writ of execution (the venditioni exponas). See Rev. Stat. sec. 367, subdiv. 16, and cf. Id. subdivs. 1 (particularly the language "except execution") and 6. As to the former item, though the marshal did release the vessel by discharging the custodian and turning the vessel over to the purchaser, he served no process of any kind and no order of release either formal or informal was made by the court.

The Metropolitan Meat Co. bill filed with the marshal as expenses, includes food supplies furnished between October 5 and 7, both inclusive, and between October 8 and 17 both inclusive. With the deduction of twenty per cent. made by the Meat Company, I will approve the bill as a charge, first, as against any moneys of the shipowners in court to the extent of $21.26 (net after the 20% deduction) for the first period when the men were on board and still in the ship's service; second, as against any moneys of the crew in court to the extent of $29.60 (net after 20% deduction) for the second period after the men had left the vessel. The bill could not be collected here in this way without the consent, which has been given, of the crew and of the shipowner through its proctor.

The bill of J. S. Walker, notary public, is allowed under disbursements taxable as costs, to the extent of $1.75 for taking seven oaths to libel, and $1.75 for taking seven oaths to amended libel, but disallowed as to "services attending vessel to secure signatures, $2.50."

The bill of the Seamen's Institute for $235.85 (being reasonable) for meals and lodging furnished to the crew pending suit, is approved under the crew's agreement to assign judgment to cover this amount.

IN THE MATTER OF THE ACCOUNTS OF J. S. WAR-
DELL AND JOSEPH HEAD, GOVERNMENT
OFFICERS, FOR EXPENSES AS WITNESSES.

January 13, 1916.

Witnesses—Government officers—Expenses: Under Rev. Stat. sec.
850, a government officer attending as a witness for the government
at a place away from his office, may be allowed in a reasonable amount
for expenses of steamer chair; but not for gratuities or tips to stewards and waiters, the latter not being a "necessary" expense within
the statute.

Approval of witnesses' expense accounts.

J. S. Wardell and *Joseph Head*, claimants, *pro se.*

CLEMONS, J. The claimants, J. S. Wardell, surveyor of
customs for the port of San Francisco, and Joseph Head,
captain of customs inspectors for the same port, presented
for allowance their accounts for attendance as witnesses in
this court before the United States commissioner in the
case of *United States v. E. P. Winter,* each claiming among
other items the expense of rent of steamer chair on trip to
Honolulu and return, $1 each way, and the expense of gra-
tuities or tips to stewards and waiters, $6.50 each way, and
Captain Head claiming the expense of tips to table waiters while here in Honolulu, $1.75, amounting in the aggre-
gate in the case of Mr. Wardell to $15 and in the case of
Captain Head to $16.75. The accounts were both ap-
proved except as to the items above mentioned, the propriety of which was taken under advisement.

On the presentation of these accounts, I sought the advice of the Comptroller of the Treasury, to the end that I
might, in the want of a very complete library on the subject in hand, be better able to arrive at a just conclusion.
My inquiry was in part as follows:

"A question has arisen here with regard to an allowance
of items of gratuities or tips to stewards, waiters, etc., in
the accounts of traveling expenses of government officials
attending court as witnesses.

"The policy of the Treasury Department, as appears from Treasury Decisions, No. 34583, Circular No. 31, Treasury Department, June 25, 1914, and the policy of the Department of Justice, as reflected in the Blue Book, [Instructions to U. S. Marshals, etc., Apr. 1, 1904], sections 661 and 1055, are adverse; and in order that I may determine the question after a full consideration of the rulings and authorities, I would be greatly obliged if you would let me know if there is any ruling as to such items in the accounts contemplated by Rev. Stat., sec. 850. Are these items 'necessary expenses' within said section? Also, is the item 'use of steamer chair' on the trip from San Francisco to Honolulu a proper item in such an account, or otherwise, within any decisions or authorities known to you?"

To this the Comptroller replied, under date of September 22, 1915:

"Briefly stated, the rulings of this office are to the effect that gratuities such as are mentioned in your letter are not necessary items of travel expense unless expressly allowed as such by competent administrative regulation. It is well known, however, that such gratuities are, by common usage, expected of and paid by the traveling public generally, and administrative offices have, with few exceptions, made and promulgated regulations governing allowances in this respect.

"The Comptroller's office has acquiesced in this custom, and has allowed reasonable gratuities in accordance with the respective regulations, which vary in the different offices both as to character and amounts.

"It has been held by the Comptroller that actual expenses of witnesses who attend under section 850, Revised Statutes, are not governed by the regulations of the Department in which they are regularly employed, but are subject to the court's order. (18 Comp. Dec. 992; *United States v. Sanborn*, 135 U. S. 271.)

"It is for the court to determine what gratuities, if any, shall be allowed in actual expense accounts of witnesses before it, and the court's order in the premises, either general or special, will be accepted by this office, as are the regulations of administrative offices."

A similar inquiry was made by me of the Attorney General, to which Assistant Attorney General William Wallace replied under date of October 4, referring me to the "decision of the Comptroller" above quoted. This reference to the Comptroller's views might seem to give them the sanction of the Department of Justice.

The Treasury Regulations referred to my letter, 27 T. D. 19-21, after quoting as authority statutes providing for allowance of "only actual travelling expenses" of officials absent on public business, "except marshals, district attorneys, and clerks of the courts of the United States and their deputies" (18 Stat. 452, and see 38 Stat., 318), proceed to sanction, among other items, "customary fees to stewards and others on steamers as follows: For an ocean trip of 10 days or less, not exceeding $10; . . . rent of steamer chair, not exceeding $2." Marshals, district attorneys, and clerks of court are excepted, supra, because the traveling expenses of those officials are specially provided for by other statutes giving a per diem allowance or mileage. See Rev. Stat., sec. 829, par. 6, Blue Book, sec. 589; 29 Stat., 191, sec. 8, Blue Book, sec. 1039, and especially sec. 1055; Rev. Stat. sec. 828, par. 18, Blue Book, sec. 1323.

And the following similar provisions are found in the United States Army Regulations:

"Actual expenses only will be paid to officers for sea travel when traveling under competent orders. . . . .

"(4) . . . Amount of rent of steamer chair, not exceeding $1 for trips of two days or longer on each commercial steamer, and fees to cabin and other stewards not exceeding the following: . . . On the Pacific Ocean, 15 days or less, $1 a day" . . . (U. S. Army Reg., 1913, sec. 1280, am. C. A. R. No. 12, Sept. 15, 1914).

But the Blue Book of the Department of Justice, above referred to, provides that in the expenses of marshals and deputies while absent on official business "tips to waiters will not be allowed," sec. 661, and that in the expenses of travel and subsistence of United States District Attorneys "necessary porterage, not exceeding 25 cents a day, while traveling by railroad will be allowed, but no allowance will be made for tips to waiters", sec. 1055.

My attention is called by Mr. Wardell to the Treasury regulations, above, which, it is urged, are of persuasive authority as the executive interpretation of similar provisions of statute to that here involved. See *Brown v. United States*, 113 U. S. 571; *Bell Tel. Co. v. Mutual Tel. Co.*, 5 Haw. 456, 460. And note, also, the Department of Justice's construction above adverted to, of the word "necessary", with reference to 29 Stat. 181, sec. 8. But it is to be noted, that these Treasury regulations are based on a statutory allowance of "actual" expenses, which are very different from the "necessary" expenses contemplated by Rev. Stat. sec. 850. Indeed the expression "actual and necessary" expenses is often seen, in which "necessary" is distinguished from "actual". See *Mombert v. Bannock County*, 75 Pac. 239, 241, 9 Idaho, 470. "Actual" seems to imply expenses incurred, or an expenditure made, as a matter of fact; and "necessary", to imply not only an actual incurrance or actual expenditure but an incurrence or expenditure that is inevitable, as well—i. e., "impossible to be dispensed with, without preventing the attainment of a desired result." Webster, New Internat. Dic., 1913, p. 1443, tit., "necessary". In other words, a thing may be actual but not necessary.

The common characterization of tips as "gratuities" indicates that they are voluntary and not "inevitable". See 19 Comp. Dec. 218, 219 (1912). But, of course, the word "necessary" is not to be taken too strictly, i. e., unreasonably. Taking the items of transportation, e. g.: a witness, while not allowed the expense of a bridal suite on a trans-Pacific steamship, is not required to travel by a sailing vessel which might happen to be available at a lower rate of fare. That the expression "necessary expenses" is a flexible one, see *People v. Board of Supervisors*, 132 N. Y. Supp., 808, 810.

Though tipping may add to one's comfort, and may be allowed where "actual expenses" are authorized, the statutory provision "necessary expenses" does not, in my opinion, cover it. One may be sued by an ocean carrier for unpaid transportation, or by a hotel for meals, but not by a steward for making up his berth nor by a waiter for handing him his food,—there being no contractual relation whatever between the passenger or the hotel guest on the one hand and the steward or waiter on the other. Such examples seem a fair test of the necessity element here.

Considerations of policy are, of course, not to be regarded. The question is, what the statute says, and not whether it would not better tend to secure the presence of witnesses if the court were liberal. One cannot be liberal with the strict intent of this statute.

The steamer chair is fairly a necessary item of expense.

Accordingly, these accounts are disallowed except for the items of steamer chair, amounting to $2 in case of each claimant. It being apparent that claim was made in each case for steamer chair for the return trip to San Francisco, before the trip was entered upon, and that no receipt for prepayment is on file with the accounts, no order for payment will be made until such receipts, or affidavits of payment, with reasons for want of receipts, are filed herein.

See Instructions to Marshals, etc., June 1, 1916, pars. 403, 409 (g), 670, 835, for new rules as to "tips."

IN THE MATTER OF THE APPLICATION OF HO TIM FOR A WRIT OF HABEAS CORPUS.

January 15, 1916.

1. *Aliens—Chinese—Deportation—Arrest—Burden* of *proof:* An alien Chinese may not be arrested as deportable within the Act of Sept. 13, 1888, c. 1015, sec. 13, 25 Stat. 479, without a warrant based on circumstances showing him to be unlawfully within the United States; but upon such lawful arrest the burden is on him of showing his right to remain.

2. *Same—Deportation—Moral turpitude:* In considering an alleged offense of moral turpitude as a basis of deportation under the immigration laws, moral turpitude is held to mean moral turpitude according to our own standards and not according to those of alien races.

3. *Same—Same—Hearing—Aid* of *counsel:* Claim of an unfair hearing by reason of want of assistance of counsel, overruled.

Habeas Corpus: On petition for writ.

F. J. Schnack (A. S. Humphreys with him) for petitioner.
H. W. Vaughan, U. S. District Attorney, for respondent.

CLEMONS, J. [1] In deciding this case, as the court does, adversely to the petitioner, little more might be said than to remind counsel of the fact that when an alien of the Chinese race seeks to enter the country, or, as here, is lawfully arrested (see *United States v. Hom Lim,* 214 Fed. 456, par. 1, 460, also 461-462) under the provisions of the Chinese immigration laws, the burden is upon him of showing that his status is such or his qualifications are such, as to entitle him either, as the case may be, to land or to remain in the country. And although in this case of deportation of a person already in the country, the record shows some evidence of a purely hearsay character, evidence not competent, still that fact did not relieve the petitioner of the burden, above stated, which was upon her to show: (1) that she had not been found within the country in violation of section 6 of the Chinese exclusion act of May 5, 1892, as amended, being a Chinese laborer not in possession of a certificate of residence; (2) that she had not been found within the country in violation of rule 9, Chinese rules, having secured admission by fraud, and not having been at the time the lawful wife of a member of the exempt classes; and (3) that she had not entered the United States unlawfully as the wife of a domiciled Chinese merchant for the purpose of laboring in the United States and not conducting herself therein as the wife of such merchant—all in order to meet the first three charges made in the warrant of arrest of August 19, 1915, Transcript of Record, pages 59-60, and based upon "facts making the arrest presumptively lawful." See *United States v. Hom Lim*, supra. There might be, as counsel contends, some ground for a distinction, as to burden of proof, between a case of an alien not yet landed and one of an alien landed and then charged with being deportable, but the following provision of statute, 27 Stat. 25, sec. 3, May 5, 1892, nullifies any such distinction:

"That any Chinese person or person of Chinese descent arrested under the provisions of this act or the acts hereby extended shall be adjudged to be unlawfully in the United States unless such person shall establish, by affirmative proof to the satisfaction of such justice, judge or commissioner, his lawful right to remain in the United States."

See *Chin Bak Kan v. United States*, 186 U. S. 193, 200; *United States v. Hom Lim*, ubi sup.; *Yee Ging v. United States*, 190 Fed. 270, 271-273, the decision in the latter case making, at page 272, this pertinent criticism of a contra decision of Judge Grosscup in *Moy Suey v. United States*, 147 Fed. 697:

"He appears to proceed upon the assumption that a different rule of evidence should be applied to a Chinese person 'physically and politically' in the country from that applicable to such a person who is stopped at the border line and refused admission. . . . The statute makes no such distinction, nor is it to be found, so far as the Court is advised, in any case decided by the Supreme Court."

Also the suggestive language of Judge Chatfield in *United States v. Hom Lim,* supra, may be referred to:

"It must be observed that no Chinese person or person of Chinese descent may be arrested, even upon a warrant, unless *based upon circumstances showing him to be unlawfully within the United States.* Section 13, Acts of 1888. [For such showing before the above warrant of arrest, which was the second warrant, see Transcript, pages 1-58, and for such showing before the first warrant of arrest, of March 30, 1915, see Id., pages 1-18.] A person who has been lawfully 'arrested' shall be adjudged to be unlawfully within the United States unless he furnishes affirmative proof of his right to remain. It would render the law unconstitutional if it should be held to allow the arrest and deportation of a person, even where a warrant had been issued, unless the record showed some proof, at least in the way of allegations of fact, that the person arrested was a Chinese person or person of Chinese descent, and that this person was 'unlawfully' in the country and had been arrested because of some state of facts prohibited by and within the language of the law." (At page 460.)

"Unless the record shows that an order of arrest could lawfully be made, [and it does so show] then the entire case must fall for lack of right to deport. A person cannot be physically 'arrested' without some basis of fact showing unlawful presence, and then be forced into the position of proving his right to remain, when the 'arrest' is not based upon any facts making the arrest presumptively lawful." [But it is so based here.] (At pages 461-462.)

The cases embraced within the *Hom Lim* decision, supra, are distinguished from the case here by the fact of their want of anything making the warrant of arrest "presumptively lawful". 214 Fed. 461-462.

The language of Mr. Justice Holmes as quoted in *Looe Shee v. North,* 170 Fed. 571 (and see Id., 566, syllabus, par. 2) may suggest that, apart from statute, the burden of showing an alien's status of qualifications to be such as to entitle him to land may be regarded as continuing to rest upon him even after his permitted entry in case question arises as to his being lawfully in the country under the Immigration Act (the general statute as distinguished from the more strict statutes applying to the Chinese); although it is to be noted that the statute in force and considered by the justice was one creating a three-year term of probation which has since been extended to make such term unlimited in cases involving sexual immorality, 36 Stat. 825-826, —an extension which does not seem, however, to change the principle applied by Mr. Justice Holmes. And see sections 20 and 21 of the Immigration Act as to the three-year limit, still maintained in other cases.

The fact that the Assistant Secretary of Labor was justified, as I am convinced that he was, in finding a failure of the evidence to establish what was claimed for the alien here, is sufficient, then, to determine the case against her.

And so it would not be necessary to regard the additional grounds of the second warrant of arrest, as founded on the general, as distinguished from the Chinese, immigration laws. They are (4) that the petitioner has been found in the United States in violation of 34 Stat. 898, act of Feb. 20, 1907, as amended, in that she has been convicted of or admits having committed a felony or other crime or misdemeanor involving moral turpitude prior to her entry into the United States, and (5) that she has been found in the United States in violation of that statute in that she entered without the inspection by it contemplated and required, having secured admission by means of false and misleading statements (sections 20 and all sections requiring aliens to be inspected). But even the burden of proof as to these last two grounds, which is upon the government (see Bouve, Exclusion of Aliens, 533, 560), has in my opinion been sustained. At all events, under the evidence direct and circumstantial, taken in hearings which were fair, it would not be within the province of this court to say otherwise. See Id., 523, 546, and 623, citing *Chin Yow v. United States*, 208 U. S. 8.   The close connection between the general Immigration Act and the Chinese exclusion laws may here be worthy of some notice,—particularly the provision of section 21 of the former:

"That in case the Secretary of Labor shall be satisfied that an alien has been found in the United States in violation of this Act, or that an alien is subject to deportation under the provisions of this Act *or of any law* of the United States, he shall cause such alien within the period of three years after landing or entry therein to be taken into custody and returned to the country whence he came."

[2] And, for another reason, it is not necessary to go into the question, whether there was or not, a showing of the admission of an offense involving moral turpitude,—or, whether, conceding the fact of the petitioner's concubinage only, as distinguished from adultery, such concubinage would, as a matter of law, amount to an offense of moral turpitude; for this, though stated as a ground of the warrant of arrest, was not included in the warrant of deportation as a ground thereof.   Nevertheless, as the Secretary might, on the evidence and the circumstances in evidence, have included this ground in the deportation order, and as counsel for the alien gave some attention to the question, I am disposed to make the observation, in line, as I believe, with my opinions in the cases of *Tome Tanno*, ante, p. 266, and of *Look Wong*, ante, p. 568, and of *Ko Matsumoto*, ante, p. 625, that "moral turpitude" if it means anything at all must mean moral turpitude according to our own standards and not according to those of alien races. This view would set at rest the argument here made, that it is not in China immoral, and does not involve moral turpitude, to be the concubine of a married man.   But her admissions were not of mere concubinage, if there is any moral difference, but of bigamy and adultery; and these are offenses of moral turpitude. See *In re Ko Matsumoto*, supra.

The alien's counsel find in the cases of *United States* v. *Hom Lim*, supra, and *In re Tam Chung*, 223 Fed. 801, something to dispose of ground (1), supra.   But I fail to follow them in their view of these cases.

But, apart from the question of the burden of proof above discussed, it is fair to the immigration officers and to the Assistant Secretary of Labor to point out in the record matter supporting rather strongly most, at least, of the charges in the warrant of arrest of August 19, 1915, and of the order of deportation of December 6, 1915 (Transcript, pages 60-61, 70).

For inconsistencies as to fact of death of alien's father, see Id., pages 9, 12, 13, 20, 21, 30, 62, 64.

For inconsistencies, also the alien's absolute admission (the page references to the latter being *italicized*) as to the fact, or otherwise, of her first husband's death, see Id., pages 1, 7-9, 11, 12, 20-23, 24, 28, 30-32, 34-38, 40, 42, 43, *44-47*, 55-58 (alien's own witness), 63-65.

For suggestion that alien came with other intent than that of living with the merchant Goo Nam Kong, by reason of whose status as a merchant she claimed the right to enter, see Id., pages 62, 64 (she wanted to go and live with her alleged husband, but she waited first to stay with her father and "talk things over," yet though her father, after she had been with him for a little [4 months, see page 63], advised her to go back to her alleged husband), 69, (she failed to do so, but went out to work for a considerable time) 63, (and her alleged husband resorted to habeas corpus proceedings in an endeavor to get her on her refusal to go back) 45, 64-65, 69.

As to alien's suspicious change of name, see Id., pages 7, 35, 40, 67, 68; though the Chinese, especially those in business, are sometimes chameleons with regard to names. See Id., page 44.

The following complained of facts may all be disposed

of by the statutory presumption, above discussed, placing the burden upon a Chinese under arrest and investigation as the petitioner then was: that the alien when taken to the immigration station under the first warrant of arrest, that of March 30; 1915, "was informed that if she did not make a statement, a presumption might be taken against her" (Id., page 20) and that the inspector also then stated to her, "These statements are made by different people and we do not know how much of it to believe and how much of it not to believe. Therefore, we are asking you to inform us how much of it is the truth and how much of it is false. If you do not deny the statements, it will be necessary for us, in the absence of any other circumstances to show their falsehood, to believe that the statements made are true" (Id., page 21).

[3] In view of the repeated rulings of this court, e. g., in *In re Ko Matsumoto*, supra, it is useless to discuss the contention that the immigration officers at the time of her arrest under warrant of March 30, 1915, failed to accord the alien a fair hearing in the matters of assistance of counsel and cross-examination of witnesses. And the fact is, that the immigration officers were unusually liberal in regard to counsel though she had no counsel (and sought none so far as the record shows) at her preliminary examination upon her arrest; but very early in the case, after her release on bond of only moderate penalty, she was informed that she "might have a lawyer to represent her during the further proceedings" (Id., page 26) and thereafter she had two most able counsel, who presented witnesses in her behalf and cross-examined witnesses of the government. Id., pages 27-69.

Counsel for the alien make some capital out of the fact that two warrants of arrest were issued, one of March 30, 1915, and the other of August 19, 1915; claiming that the first warrant was discharged, wherefore the evidence must have been insufficient to establish the grounds thereof, and

that after the second warrant issued there was practically
nothing more of evidence offered, only testimony as to the
meaning and signification of concubinage as practiced in
China.   I fail, however, to find in the transcript of the
record any suggestion that the first warrant was discharged,
much less that the alien was discharged or that she was
found not to have been within any of the grounds charged
in the first warrant.   The second warrant has the statement, "This warrant supersedes and cancels warrant of
arrest issued in this case on March 30, 1915," but that statement is not of necessity to be taken to imply anything in aid
of the alien's claim, but inasmuch as an express finding of
discharge of the immigrant would be the natural thing in
due course of procedure, the inference is much more probable that the second warrant was virtually an amendment
of the first to include, as it does, other and more explicit
grounds than the first warrant,—in order, it may be, to
make the pleadings as it were "conform to the proof."   The
language above quoted from the second warrant seems
merely to express a conclusion of law,—of course the second warrant "superseded" and therefore operated to "cancel" the first.

Let the petition for a writ of habeas corpus be dismissed.

IN THE MATTER OF HATSUJI IWANAGA, A BANK-
RUPT.

January 26, 1916.

Bankruptcy—Clerk's fees—Notice to creditors: Special or extra
compensation is not allowable to the clerk of court, under General
Order in Bankruptcy No. XXXV, sec. 1, for mailing notices to
creditors; his clerical services in such matters,—so far at least as
no extraordinary expenses are involved,—being covered by the filing
fee of ten dollars provided by the Bankruptcy Act, sec. 52, subdiv. a.

In Bankruptcy: On motion of clerk for allowance of
extra compensation for mailing notices to creditors.

Foster L. Davis, clerk, *pro se.*

CLEMONS, J. The question arises whether the clerk of
court may not in bankruptcy cases make a charge for mailing notices to creditors. For several years from and after
the institution of this court it was the practice here for the
clerk to make such a charge. Somehow—for what reason
I have been unable to ascertain,—the practice ceased and
has not been followed for at least seven years. The practice, I am informed by an examiner of the Department of
Justice, is followed in all the Federal courts on the Pacific
coast.

The authority now relied on for such charge, is General
Order XXXV, section 1, adopted by the Supreme Court of
the United States, which reads:

"The fees allowed by the act to clerks shall be in full
compensation for all services performed by them in regard
to filing petitions or other papers required by the act to be
filed with them, or in certifying or delivering papers or
copies of records to referees or other officers, or in receiving
or paying out moneys; but shall not include copies furnished to other persons, or expenses necessarily incurred in
publishing or mailing notices or other papers."

The concluding clause of this provision of the general orders may seem somewhat broader than the statutory provision for compensation of clerks, Bankruptcy Act, section 52, subdivision a, which follows:

"Clerks shall respectively receive as full compensation for their services to each estate, a filing fee of ten dollars, except when a fee is not required from a voluntary bankrupt."

And to a view of this general order as too broad, Mr. Collier gives support in the following language:

"It is thought that General Order XXXV (1) is not in accord with section 52, a; if not, the latter must control." Collier on Bankruptcy, 10th ed., 687, q. v. in extenso.

In my view of the statute, which makes the filing fee of ten dollars the clerks' "full compensation for their services to each estate", it seems that a clerk's services rendered in mailing notices are covered by and included within his "services to each estate." *In re Durham*, 2 N. B. N. Rep. 1104, cited by Brandenburg on Bankruptcy, 3d ed., section 801, to the effect that "the clerk is entitled to charge an additional fee for each notice of bankrupt's application for discharge sent to creditors," is no authority as against my view; for it is controlled by the broader provision of the bankruptcy statute of 1867, section 47, which reads:

"In each case there shall be allowed and paid, in addition to the fees of the clerk of the court as now established by law, *or as may be established by general order for fees in bankruptcy*, the following fees," etc.

I do not go so far, however, as to express disapproval of the rule approved by the Supreme Court in section 1 of General Order XXXV, but rather express my disagreement with the application of this rule by the judges and clerks in other districts. When we regard the phrase of the rule "expenses necessarily incurred in publishing notices", there is no difficulty in so dissenting, for it would be unreasonable, absurd, to burden the clerk, who receives but ten dollars for all his "services", with what is strictly and purely an "expense" incurred by the work of another, an independent, party, the printer of the publication; and so with regard to the "mailing (of) notices or other papers",—only "expenses," are contemplated as the proper subjects of extra allowance, something outside of the clerk's own acts, something done by another, an independent party. See *In re Dunn Hardware and Furniture Co.*, 134 Fed. 997, 14 Am. B. R. 186, 187. And so far as his own clerical acts are involved in mailing notices, his compensation is already provided for in the blanket ten-dollar fee. To repeat the idea in other words, "services" are to be distinguished from "expenses". For the latter the clerk would, under the Supreme Court's general order, and probably as a matter of course quite apart from any such rule, be entitled to reimbursement. But what "expense" is there in mailing notices to creditors? Only that of the paper and envelopes used; the typewriting and other manual labor being "services" and not "expenses". To make a charge for the stationery used would be impracticable and contrary to practice in all other cases, and in any event the amount chargeable for an envelope and a small sheet of paper would be trivial.

Accordingly, the items of mailing notices to creditors, submitted by the clerk as proper subjects of charge under General Order XXXV, are disallowed as such.

Reported, 36 Am. B. R. 285.

IN THE MATTER OF THE APPLICATION OF
EITARO YAMADA FOR A WRIT OF HABEAS
CORPUS.
IN THE MATTER OF THE APPLICATION OF ASANO
MIYAZAKI FOR A WRIT OF HABEAS CORPUS.

February 16, 1916.

1. *Aliens—Immigration—Deportation proceedings—Finality of find-ings of fact:* Findings of fact made by immigration officers in deportation proceedings are final, if a fair hearing has been accorded, even though such findings may have been erroneous. *Chin Yow v. United States*, 208 U. S. 8.

2. *Same—Same—Entry into the United States:* Aliens who came to Hawaii after the treaty of annexation but before the enactment of the Organic Act providing a government for the Territory, are to be regarded as having "entered the United States" within the meaning of the Immigration Act, 24 Stat. 898 as amended.

Habeas Corpus: On return to writ.

J. W. Cathcart for petitioners.
H. W. Vaughan, U. S. District Attorney, for respondents.

CLEMONS, J. For convenience, these cases will be considered together, as they are closely related.   They arise out of an investigation before the immigration officers at the port of Honolulu, resulting in an order of deportation grounded on the fact, to quote from the warrant of the Secretary of Labor,

"That the said Eitaro Yammoto, alias Eitaro Yamada, is unlawfully within the United States in that he has been found assisting a prostitute; and that the said Asano Tsuda, or Asano Yamada, is a prostitute and has been found practicing prostitution subsequent to her entry into the United States."

At the immigration office the cases were heard together, and the transcript of proceedings in case No. 97 is made by reference a part of the record in case No. 99.

[1] The case of the woman, (No. 99), is clearly one in which the finding of the Secretary of Labor cannot be set aside by this court. No unfairness is shown, and there is enough in the record to justify the Secretary's conclusion that this alien had been practicing prostitution subsequent to her entry into the country. See Transcript of Case No. 97, pages (bottom paging) 1-3, 6, 7 (Eitaro), 4 (Asano herself), 9 (Shutaro).

As to the man, the case (No. 97), is not so clear: the evidence is, it seems, wholly circumstantial, much, perhaps, depending on the demeanor of the witnesses. See *Fong Gum Tong v. United States*, 192 Fed. 320, 321. And though I cannot say that I would have come to the same conclusion on the facts, and even though the finding on the facts may have been erroneous (See *Chin Yow v. United States*, 208 U. S. 8, 11-13, Holmes, J.), the case is one in which the court cannot set up its own judgment of the facts to override the conclusion of an independent authority, the executive, having jurisdiction to make a finding in the matter, especially as no unfairness is apparent in the conduct of the proceedings. It is unnecessary to cite the numerous decisions, including those of the Federal appellate courts, so holding. Though the evidence against the man is characterized above as circumstantial, it is by no means weak. We have here a woman, whom this man himself called "a poor old woman"—indicating her dependent condition (Transcript, 7), who lived with the man for some time perhaps as his mistress (Id., 1) but who very soon was practicing prostitution at Iwilei, the "red light" district of Honolulu (see Id., where first cited above) and came to his house whenever physically disabled for her trade. (Id., 3). The conclusion would not be unjustified then, from these, and from all, the circumstances in evidence, that the relation of the woman to the man was not exclusively, if at all, at the later stage, that of a mistress, but that they were on a business basis in which their own relations were not at all sexual. The fact that the man was able to start his pig ranch after the woman began prostitution, is worthy of some attention. (Id., 4). The circumstances tend to support the finding of the Secretary. As to assisting in the sense of protecting from arrest, see Id., 7; as to assisting in the sense of harboring, see Id., 3.

Apart from the case on the facts, however, these petitioners make the point of law that inasmuch as they both came to Hawaii in the year 1899, after annexation of these islands to the United States but before Congress in the Organic Act provided a government for this Territory and extended the Constitution and laws of the United States thereto, they are within the ruling of Judge Dole of this court in the recent case of *Sui Joy* (Habeas Corpus, No. 75), ante, p. 374, and so the immigration law does not apply to them. In that behalf the argument is that neither of these parties ever "entered the United States," because "Hawaii was not an integral part of the United States,— not incorporated in the United States",—until the passage of the Organic Act the next year after their arrival.

But to apply the statute in this way is to construe the statute contrary to its reason and spirit (see Rev. L. Haw. 1915, sec. 12), if not in a manner leading to an absurdity (see Id., sec. 13). As the District Attorney points out, in spite of the language of section 3 of the immigration act (34 Stat. 898 as amended), that

"Any alien who shall be found an inmate of or connected with the management of a house of prostitution or practicing prostitution *after such alien shall have entered the United States,* or who shall receive, share in, or derive benefit from any part of the earnings of any prostitute; or who is employed by, in, or in connection with any house of prostitution or music or dance hall or other place of amusement or resort habitually frequented by prostitutes, or where prostitutes gather, or who in any way assists, protects, or promises to protect from arrest any prostitute, shall be deemed to be unlawfully within the United States and shall be deported";

nevertheless, section 33 having defined the term "United States" to mean for the purposes of the act, "the United States and any waters, territory, or other place subject to the jurisdiction thereof, except the Isthmian Canal Zone." it follows that any person who entered Hawaii after it became "subject to the jurisdiction" of the United States, (as Hawaii was at all times after the treaty of annexation,) is within the letter as well as within the spirit of the statute.

Let the writs of habeas corpus be discharged in both these cases, and the petitioners be remanded to the custody of the respondent, the immigration inspector at the port of Honolulu.

IN THE MATTER OF SUEJIRO TARADA.

February 24, 1916.

Contempt of court—Disobedience of court order—Escape: An immigrant remanded in habeas corpus proceedings to the custody of immigration officers there to "remain as heretofore," but who makes escape from such custody, is guilty of contempt of court, under Judicial Code, sec. 268.

Contempt of Court: On plea to jurisdiction.

S. B. Kemp, Assistant U. S. Attorney, for the United States.

J. Lightfoot for respondent.

CLEMONS, J.   Under decree of this court in the matter
of the application of Suejiro Tarada for a writ of habeas
corpus (Case No. 117), dated January 6, 1916, this respondent Tarada was ordered to "remain as heretofore in the
custody of   .   .   .   Richard L. Halsey, Immigration Inspector in charge at the Port of Honolulu".   He thereafter
filed herein a formal "appeal and notice of appeal" but has
taken no further steps toward the appeal's perfection.   On
January 19th he made what may be called a partial escape,
in breaking away from the narrow place where he was confined in the Immigration Station premises.   On February
22d he made a complete escape, and upon his apprehension, which was soon effected, the United States Attorney
petitioned for an order to show cause why he should not
be punished for contempt.   This was granted, and at the
hearing thereon a plea to the jurisdiction was interposed in
behalf this respondent, the contention being that the
court lost jurisdiction when it ordered the writ discharged
and this respondent remanded to the custody of the immigration officers, that he has offended them and not this
court, and, if not, that in any event his punishment should
be by a criminal proceeding as for an escape or something
of the kind.   Though the respondent made no return to
the order to show cause, and though his counsel then stated
that he was in no position to deny the facts alleged and
above recited in support of the petition for such order, the
court has taken testimony, including that of the respondent
himself who made no objection to testifying, and the facts
above stated have been established beyond any doubt.

A few words are called for on the jurisdictional question
raised in the plea.   Of course, the fact that the respondent
possibly might be punished criminally, is immaterial.   9
Cyc. 32.   On the broad aspect of the question neither counsel nor court has been able to find any cases in point.   The
general rule, however, seems to bring this respondent within the court's power to punish for contempt.   The power

of Federal courts is limited, but it contemplates punishment of "disobedience by any party . . . or other person to any lawful . . . order, rule, decree, or command of the said courts." Judicial Code, sec. 268. The Federal statutory provision is very nearly in the language of Mr. McQuillin's statement of the general rule, 9 Cyc. 8. In my own judgment, this respondent's escape is virtually in disobedience of the court's order: his obligation toward the court would seem to extend to the doing of all things to make its order effective. His escape was in the face of that order. A recent view of the Supreme Court is suggestive, as reflected in the syllabus of the report of *United States v. Shipp*, 214 U. S. 386-387, paragraph 2; see also Id., 425.

The plea to the jurisdiction is overruled, the respondent is found guilty of contempt and sentenced to fourteen days' imprisonment. On completion of the sentence, he will, of course, be returned to the custody of the Immigration Inspector in Charge.

IN THE MATTER OF THE APPLICATION OF TOKU SAKAI FOR A WRIT OF HABEAS CORPUS.

March 4, 1916.

Aliens—Immigration—Deportation proceedings: Under testimony taken before immigration officers in deportation proceedings, finding of such officers not disturbed. Misnomer of alien as "Toku Taki" instead of "Toku Sakai," in preliminary order for arrest in deportation investigation, held immaterial.

Habeas Corpus: Hearing on return to writ.

G. A. Davis and *W. T. Rawlins* for petitioner.
H. W. Vaughan, U. S. District Attorney, for respondent.

CLEMONS, J. This case, in which the writ of habeas
corpus issued, has been submitted on the record, including
not only the record of proceedings before the immigration
officers and before the Secretary of Labor, but also the verified petition of the alien, and the verified return of the
respondent the immigration inspector in charge at the port
of Honolulu and his verified amended return, having
thereto annexed the transcript of record of proceedings in
the whole matter of the alien's arrest as a deportable alien
and of the hearing and consideration pursuant to the warrant authorizing arrest.

The petitioner's counsel claim that she did not, as alleged
by the government, admit having practiced prostitution in
the United States, but that in her examination there was
nothing showing where she had so practiced. But her testimony was that she had "been practicing prostitution"
. . . "about one year and . . . before that time."
(Transcript, 2), and her petition (page 1, par. I) shows
she had been a resident of this Territory for eleven years
before her arrest. The consequent inference is that she was
in the Territory at the time of her unlawful act, and that
inference is an additional reason why the finding of the
Secretary of Labor should not be disturbed. See *In the
matter of Chiye Kajikami* (No. 92) decided Feb. 21, 1916,
unreported; *In the matter of Eitaro Yamada,* (No. 97) decided Feb. 16, 1916, ante, p. 664.

The fact that the alien is named "Toku Taki" in the
preliminary telegraphic order for her arrest, is immaterial.
In subsequent proceedings and orders her name was given,
as here given, "Toku Sakai." And,—to meet an argued
contention,—it does not matter that the prejudicial admis-

sion which the alien made was made in an investigation had pursuant to that order in which she was differently named. This alien was the person who made the admission and it stands against her, and the immigration department rightly took advantage of it, whatever her name might be: her identity, and not her name, is the important thing.

The ground of want of counsel and the other grounds of objection to the deportation proceedings, are insufficient to justify the petitioner's release from custody.

Let the writ be discharged and the petitioner remanded to the custody of the respondent.

————

Affirmed, Toku Sakai v. United States, 239 Fed. 492.

————

IN THE MATTER OF TAKAO OZAWA, A PETITIONER FOR NATURALIZATION.

March 25, 1916.

Aliens—Naturalization—Japanese: A person of the Japanese race born in Japan, is not eligible to citizenship under the naturalization laws. Rev. Stat., sec. 2169.

Petition for Naturalization.

Takao Ozawa, petitioner, *pro se.*
H. W. Vaughan, U. S. District Attorney, and *J. W. Thompson,* Assistant U. S. Attorney, opposed.

CLEMONS, J. This petition for naturalization is opposed by the United States district attorney on the ground that the petitioner, being, as the facts are, a person of the Japanese race and born in Japan, is not eligible to citizenship under Revised Statutes, section 2169, which limits naturalization to "free white persons" and those of African nativity and descent.   The other qualifications are found by the court to be fully established, and are conceded by the government.   Twenty years' continuous residence in the United States, including over nine years' residence in Hawaii, graduation from the Berkeley (Cal.) High School, nearly three years' attendance at the University of California, the education of his children in American schools and churches, the maintenance of the English language in his home, are some of the facts in his behalf.   And he has presented two briefs of his own authorship, in themselves ample proof of his qualifications of education and character.   He makes the main points that in the statute the word "white" is "not used to exclude any race at all" or in other words is used "simply to distinguish black people from others," and that even in a narrow sense of the word "white" the Japanese are eligible to citizenship.   Also, as to the word "free" in the expression "free white persons," the contention is made, that this word designates the quality of person and implies goodness, worthiness, excluding only improper persons.

The first contention is regarded by the petitioner as supported by the learned opinion of Judge Lowell in the case of *In re Halladjian*, 174 Fed. 834.   A brief discussion of this opinion is therefore called for, and may serve to enforce our own conclusions.   In the head-notes the court is reported as holding:

"That the word 'white' was used to classify the inhabitants and to include all persons not otherwise classified, not as synonymous with 'European,' there being in fact no 'European' or 'white' race as a distinctive class, or 'Asiatic' or 'yellow' race, including substantially all the people of Asia; and hence the term 'free white persons' included Armenians born in Asiatic Turkey."

This is a broad ruling, and although a ruling was required only as to the eligiility of Armenians, it may appear even broad enough to divide the eligible classes into Africans and *all others*, subject of course to the exception, created by a statute of later date, in the case of Chinese. Without questioning Judge Lowell's conclusion that Armenians are eligible to citizenship, it seems that he goes too far in saying, Id., 843, that:

"From all these illustrations, which have been taken almost at random, it appears that the word 'white' has been used in colonial practice, in the Federal statutes, and in the publications of the government to designate persons not otherwise classified."

His citation, for example, of the classification of the Massachusetts census of 1764, which included only whites, negroes, mulattoes, Indians, and "French neutrals," and that of the Rhode Island census of 1748, which included only whites, blacks, and Indians, would be far from proof that Oriental races, particularly the Japanese, or even the indefinite yellow race or races, were included or thought of at all. The most that would naturally be inferred from the use of the word "white" as a "catch-all," as Judge Lowell characterizes it, Id. 843, is the inclusion therein of all unclassified inhabitants *then in the country* and not as a rigid classification to endure for all time and to include particularly persons of the Oriental races or of the so-called "yellow" races, who, as will be seen, have always under accepted classifications been regarded as ethnologically distinct from the white race. And the fact that as occasion arose, from the presence of a noticeable number of Chinese or Japanese, those new-comers received in the census reports a special classification, weakens very much the extreme view which may be implied from Judge Lowell's opinion. If the word "white" was a catch-all, why was its use not generally continued, to include those later immigrants? Judge Lowell's opinion itself shows that when the

Oriental population, as represented first by the Chinese, came to be appreciable, beginning with the census of 1860, (i.e., at the first opportunity after the census of 1850), the word "white" ceased to be used as a catch-all to designate those people, but they were specially classified by race. Id. 844; also 842, quoting from the Eleventh Census, part 1, p. xciv.   The adoption of such classification was due more reasonably to the fact that the population of Oriental peoples had become appreciable, than to any idea, such as Judge Lowell's, 174 Fed. 843-844, that it was "after the majority of Americans had come to believe that great differences separated the Chinese, and later the Japanese from other immigrants, [that] these persons were no longer classified as white."   Too much is not to be inferred from the use of the words "white" and "black," or "white" and "Negro", in early times when these were undoubtedly the only, or practically the only, classes here other than the Indians. Nor is undue credit to be given to even much later, and recent, census classifications which were "not uniform in all parts of the country," Id. 842-843, or where much was left to the discretion of the director of the census.   Id., 843. Far more reliance may fairly be placed upon the considered judgments of courts, rendered at least as early as 1878, or perhaps 1854, in contested cases,—upon the judgments of those whose peculiar duty it was to determine the meaning of this word "white."

Such a comprehensive meaning of the word "white" as that contended for, would include Indians, yet the Supreme Court in 1884 did not regard the statute, Revised Statutes, section 2169, as so broad. See *Elk v. Wilkins*, 112 U. S. 94, 104, also the considerably earlier case of *Scott v. Sanford*, 19 How. 393, 420, which says, "Congress might . . . have authorized the naturalization of Indians, because they were aliens and foreigners." If Indians were excepted, then why not also the races of the Orient, who though since found to be more adaptable to our manners and customs,

were in the earlier days regarded as strange peoples, of
manners and customs incompatible with ours. The fact
that more lately we have come to better appreciate, that,
in the language of William Elliot Griffis ("The Japanese
Nation in Evolution," 24):

"There is no necessary distinction between the Oriental
and Occidental, the brown man and the white man. That
the 'yellow brain,' and the Japanese heart are ultimately
different from those of the Yankee or the Briton, is the
notion of tradition, not the fact of science,"

does not justify the setting aside of an interpretation well-
established prior to the date of any of the cases, an incomplete list of fourteen of which is submitted by the petitioner,—there being, it is understood, about fifty in all,—
of Japanese who have been naturalized by State and Federal courts.   The earliest of these fourteen cases, that of
Seizo Matsumoto, naturalized by a court of Pierce County,
Washington, is as recent as January, 1896, two years later
than the case of *In re Saito,* 62 Fed. 126, and sixteen or
more years subsequent to two cases which took a view
broad enough to exclude Japanese: *In re Camille,* 6 Fed.
256, and *In re Ah Yup,* 1 Fed. Cas. 223, No. 104.   Indeed,
as early as 1827* Chancellor Kent, inclined to the same
opinion as the two cases just cited, for he said in his Commentaries, volume 2, page 72:

"The act of Congress confines the description of aliens
capable of naturalization to 'free white persons.'   I presume this excludes the inhabitants of Africa and their de-

---

*Note the following very important additional evidence of what
the word "white," as applied to the human race, meant to those
learned in the law at the time when that word was first used in the
statute; said Francis Lieber, in a treatise on the science of interpretation, published very shortly after Kent's work: "The word
'white' [in the Girard will, under which the beneficiaries were "white
male orphans"] everyone knows is used to indicate the descendants
of the Caucasian race, whose blood has remained unmixed with that
of the Negroes, Indians, or that of any other '*colored*' race.   The provision cannot be invalidated by the objection that no really white
people exist."   Lieber's Hermeneutics, 3d ed., 94-95.—C. F. C.

scendants; and it may become a question, to what extent persons of mixed blood are excluded, and what shades and degrees of mixture of color disqualify an alien from application for the benefits of the act of naturalization. Perhaps there might be difficulties also as to the copper-colored natives of America, or the yellow or tawny races of the Asiatics, and it may well be doubted whether any of them are 'white persons' within the purview of the law."

And in 1854, the dictum of Chief Justice Murray of California in *People v. Hall*, 4 Cal. 399, 403, 404, is that "the word 'white' has a distinct signification, which *ex vi termini* excludes black, yellow and all other colors."

In the case of *Ah Yup*, supra, in holding that Chinese are not white persons, Circuit Judge Sawyer in 1878 said:

"The words 'white person,' as well argued by petitioner's counsel, taken in a strictly literal sense, constitute a very indefinite description of a class of persons, where none can be said to be literally white, and those called white may be found of every shade from the lightest blonde to the most swarthy brunette.   But these words in this country at least, have undoubtedly acquired a well settled meaning in common popular speech, and they are constantly used in the sense so acquired in the literature of the country, as well as in common parlance.   As ordinarily used everywhere in the United States one would scarcely fail to understand that the party employing the words 'white person' would intend a person of the Caucasian race.

"In speaking of the various classifications of races, Webster in his dictionary says, 'The common classification is that of Blumenbach, who makes five. 1. The Caucasian, or white race, to which belong the greater part of the European nations and those of Western Asia; 2. The Mongolian, or yellow race, occupying   Tartary, China, Japan, etc.; 3. The Ethiopian or Negro (black) race, occupying all Africa, except the North; 4. The American, or red race, containing the Indians of North and South America; and. 5. The Malay, or brown race, occupying the islands of the Indian Archipelago,' etc.   This division was adopted from Buffon, with some changes in names, and is founded on the combined characteristics of complexion, hair and skull.

Linnaeus makes four divisions, founded on the color of the skin: '1· European, whitish; 2. American, coppery; 3. Asiatic, tawny; and, 4. African, black.' Cuvier makes three: Caucasian, Mongol, and Negro. Others make many more, but no one includes the white, or Caucasian, with the Mongolian or yellow race; and no one of these classifications recognizing color as one of the distinguishing characteristics includes the Mongolian in the white or whitish race.' See New American Encyclopedia, tit. 'Ethnology.'

"Neither in popular language, in literature, nor in scientific nomenclature, do we ordinarily, if ever, find the words 'white person' used in a sense so comprehensive. Yet, in all, color, notwithstanding its indefiniteness as a word of description, is made an important factor in the basis adopted for the distinction and classification of races. I am not aware that the term 'white person' as used in the statutes as they have stood from 1802 till the late revision, was ever supposed to include a Mongolian. While I find nothing in the history of the country, in common or scientific usage, or in legislative proceedings, to indicate that Congress intended to include in the term 'white person' any other than an individual of the Caucasian race, I do find much in the proceedings of Congress to show that it was universally understood in that body, in its recent legislation, that it excluded Mongolians. . . . Whatever latitudinarian construction might otherwise have been given to the term 'white person', it is entirely clear that Congress intended by this legislation to exclude Mongolians from the right of naturalization."

This case was determined four years before the enactment of a special statute prohibiting the naturalization of Chinese. 22 Stat. 58, 61. It is quoted at length to include its review of the then prevailing race classifications.

In 1880 in *In re Camille*, supra, 6 Fed. 257, Judge Deady approved of Judge Sawyer's view above quoted, though the case involved not a person of an Oriental race but one of Indian blood. See also the specific reference to the Chinese, Id., 258.

In 1894, Circuit Judge Colt, in the case of *In re Saito*, 62 Fed. 127, ruled directly on the eligibility of Japanese. He says:

"The history of legislation on this subject shows that Congress refused to eliminate 'white' from the statute for the reason that it would extend the privilege of naturalization to the Mongolian race, and that when, through inadvertence, this word was left out of the statute, it was again restored for the very purpose of such exclusion.

"The words of a statute are to be taken in their ordinary sense, unless it can be shown that they are used in a technical sense.

"From a common, popular standpoint, both in ancient and modern times, the races of mankind have deen distinguished by difference in color, and they have been classified as the white, black, yellow, and brown races.

"And this is true from a scientific point of view. Writers on ethnology and anthropology base their division of mankind upon differences in physical rather than in intellectual or moral character, so that difference in color, conformation of skull, structure and arrangement of hair, and the general contour of the face are the marks which distinguish the various types. But, of all these marks, the color of the skin is considered the most important criterion for the distinction of race, and it lies in the foundation of the classification which scientists have adopted."

Judge Hanford in the case of *In re Buntaro Kumagai*, 163 Fed. 922, 923, is of opinion that:

"The use of the words 'white persons' clearly indicates the intention of Congress to maintain a line of demarkation between races, and to extend the privilege of naturalization only to those of that race which is predominant in this country."

He cites in support of his opinion the cases of *Ah Yup* and *Saito*, supra, and also the case of *In re Yamashita*, 30 Wash. 234, 70 Pac. 482 (1902). His opinion is followed in the case of *In re Knight*, 171 Fed. 299, in which the applicant was one-quarter Japanese and one-quarter Chinese and in which Judge Chatfield holds. Id., 300, that neither Chinese nor Japanese can be naturalized,—though, it is true, it was only necessary for him to hold for the purposes of the case, that the substantial element of Chinese blood was sufficient to exclude the petitioner, regardless of the eligibility of Japanese. And the Circuit Court of Appeals of the Fourth Circuit in *Bessho v. United States*, 178 Fed. 245, and Judge Cushman in *In re Young*, 198 Fed. 715, hold expressly that Japanese aliens are ineligible to citizenship.

To meet any argument that the enactment of a special statute prohibiting naturalization only of Chinese, implies the eligibility of the Japanese, who are not included in any special prohibition, reference is made to *In re Kanaka Nian*, 21 Pac. 993-994, 6 Utah, 259 (1889), and *Bessho v. United States*, 178 Fed. 245. 248, also *In re Ah Yup*, 1 Fed. Cas., 224, decided as above noted, before the enactment of the special prohibition against Chinese, *In re Saito*, 62 Fed. 127. and *Fong Yue Ting v. United States*, 149 U. S. 698, 716.

As against these authorities, no reported case is known in which a person of the Japanese race has been naturalized, in which the court has rendered a written opinion to justify its ruling or in which there has been a contest to evoke the most thorough consideration. There are recent judicial opinions, that the statute in its present form is not to be "construed in the light of the knowledge and conception of the legislators who passed the original statute in 1790, without regard to the more definite and special knowledge and conception which must be attributed to the legislators who upon reconsideration of the whole subject, enacted subsequent statutes including that now in force." *Dow v. United States*, 226 Fed. 145. 147. See also *In re Muddari*, 176 Fed. 465. 467, and a learned opinion of Judge Morrison of the Superior Court of California, rendered May 7. 1914, in the case of *In re Sakharan Ganesh Pandit*. But the *Dow* case, for example, in using the language just quoted and in referring to more recent legislation, had in mind the legislation of 1875 in which the words "free white persons", omitted by error from the revision of 1873 (62 Fed. 127) were restored. 226 Fed. 147. And, aside from the circumstance that the decisions just referred to were dealing with border-line cases of races closely related to what may be loosely called the "Europeans," who were perhaps in 1790 here considered as the only white people (226 Fed. 145, 147, 148), it is of most practical importance to bear in mind that the ethnological divisions which classed the Japanese as of the Mongolian or yellow race, were what the legislators of 1875 and the courts thereafter down even to the present have had to rely upon as their guides. See quotation in *In re Ah Yup*, supra (1878) from Webster's Dictionary, probably the most widely circulated work in America except the Bible, and even the very recent edition of the Encyclopaedia Britannica, 11th ed., vol. 9, page 851. This classification was undoubtedly well known in this country early in the last century, as it was in Germany before 1790, the date of the original enactment of the statute. Even if, as the petitioner contends, Blumenbach's classification is unscientific (see *In re Dow*, 213 Fed. 355, 358, 359, 365; *In re Mudarri*, 176 Fed. 466-467), nevertheless it has not yet been superseded so far as to assimilate the Japanese with what for many years, at least as early as 1854, and especially before 1875, has been generally regarded as the "white" race.[*]

. Tylor, one of the highest authorities, in his book of 1881, "Anthropology" (Appleton's ed. 63, 96-98), points out that the Japanese have characteristics of the "Mongoloid type of man" in which one prominent feature is that "their skin is brownish yellow." The most recent encyclopaedic authority, 9 Enc. Brit. 11th ed. (1910), 851, classes the Japanese as Mongolic or yellow, though placing the Ainos, a small element of the people of Japan, as Caucasic or white. See

---

[*]See also references to Kent and Lieber of the early 1800's, ante, p. 675.—C. F. C

also 15 Id., 165. In addition to this unobstructed current of authority reference may be had to a very late work, "A History of the Japanese People," by Captain F. Brinkley, included by Dr. William Elliot Griffis ("The Japanese Nation in Evolution," 20) in a list of the English scholars who "have made obsolete most of the old European learning about Japan."

"The Japanese are of distinctly small stature . . . Their neighbors, the Chinese and the Koreans, are taller. . . . Nevertheless, Professor Dr. Baelz, the most eminent authority on this subject, avers that 'the three great nations of Eastern Asia are essentially of the same race,' and that observers who consider them to be distinct 'have been misled by external appearances.' " Brinkley, History, etc. supra, 57-58, see also 59, 60. That the Japanese have, however, an element of white, Caucasian or Iranian, blood is noted. Id. 58, see also 45, 54, 55.

Another recent book may be quoted as giving the opinion of a Japanese educator, "The Life and Thought of Japan," by Okakura Yoshisaburo (published by E. P. Dutton & Co., 1913):

"And as to those swarms of immigration from China and Korea, who crossed the sea at various periods in the early days of Japanese history, it did not take many generations before they came to adopt the views of the people with whom it was their interest in every way to get mixed, and thus they lost their own identity. In this manner, notwithstanding an extensive admixture of foreign elements to our original stock, we find ourselves as closely unified a nation as if we had been perfectly homogeneous from the very beginning. One and the same blood is felt to run through our veins, characterized by one and the same set of religious and moral ideas. This may perhaps be due to the fact that the three elements—the conquering, the conquered, and the immigrating—belonged originally to the same Mongolian race, with every little trace of any mingling of Ainu and Malayan blood." Id. 48, 49.

"You will come, at least to some extent, to acknowledge the truth of the statement so often made in books on Japan, that there are two distinct racial face-types among the present Japanese. . . . Be it remembered that both these types are Mongol. Both have the yellowish skin, the straight hair, the scanty beard, the broadish skull, the more or less oblique eyes, and the somewhat high cheekbones, which characterize all well-established branches of the Mongol race." Id., 41.

"The relation here displayed between the living and the departed may be considered as a characteristic of the Mongolian race to which both the Japanese and the Chinese belong." Id., 54:

Whether these views just quoted are wholly accurate or not, I do not undertake to say. They are at all events, in line with the statements of scientific works which have been, as already intimated, the guides of our courts in all cases known to have been contested or in which the court rendered a written opinion,—even though recognizing that there is in the Japanese an element of white blood. See reference to Brinkley, supra.

Dr. Griffis' interesting book, in a broad spirit of tolerance, notable because of his having been for forty years in closest touch with Japan and for some years a resident there, goes far to demonstrate the conclusion that "the Japanese are not Mongolian." "The Japanese Nation in Evolution." 400. Rev. Dr. Doremus Scudder, of Honolulu, who is himself intimately acquainted with the Japanese people, and who may be termed a friend of the court, has submitted in behalf of the petitioner, this authority as tending at least to support the view that the Japanese are "white persons" even in a narrow sense of those words. But Dr. Griffis, after all, does not seem to be at variance with the common authorities on ethnology. It is plain that he is speaking of the later development of the Japanese away from all that is narrow in the sense of "Mongolic" or "Oriental,"—of their "both deserving and winning success," Id., 400, in competition, or rather comparison, with the most progressive and enlightened peoples of the world. He recognizes the Mongolic element constantly. "White men, belonging to the great

Aryan family and speaking a language akin to the Indo-Germanic tongues, were the first 'Japanese,' who are a composite and not a pure 'Mongolian' race. Their inheritance of blood and temperament partakes of the potencies of both Europe and Asia." Id., 1, also 21, 25, 349. He also recognizes the Malay element, which,—at least "the Malay peoples of the Eastern archipelago,"—the last edition of the Encyclopaedia Brittanica includes in the Mongolic or yellow division of the races, though "less typical" but with the "Mongolic elements so predominant as to warrant inclusion." Says Dr. Griffis, Id., 30, "Those most familiar with the races, the Mongol, Aryan and the Malay, now so differentiated, consider that in the Nippon composite the Malay strain predominates." Also Id., 30-31 et seq. Though Dr. Griffis believes that "the basic stock of the Japanese people is Aino" (a white people) . . . "by 'basic stock' . . . mean(ing) the oldest race in the islands" (Id., 5, also 1), yet he speaks of the Ainos as having been "crowded out" (Id., 9)—elsewhere characterizing the process as absorption not elimination (Id., 26); and Brinkley, History, etc., supra 56, (see also 44), notes the "steady extermination for twenty-five centuries" of the Ainu element, characterized by him as having "left so little trace in the Japanese nation." Id., 58.

Intelligent men, of course, agree with Dr. Griffis that the words "Mongolian" and "Oriental", as mere epithets, can bear no sense of unworthiness or inferiority in the case of the Japanese people.

A few words are called for by the cited examples of the Magyars of Hungary and of the very dark Portuguese, who are both freely admitted to citizenship, in spite of the fact that the former are Mongolic in origin and that the latter are in a strict sense of the word not "white." Many of the decisions admit the difficulties inherent in the statutory classification, and even Judge Lowell has declared that he "greatly hopes that an amendment of the statutes will make

quite clear the meaning of the word 'white' in section 2169."
In re Mudarri, 176 Fed. 465, 467. Indeed in this latter
case his language seems to cast doubt upon the practicability of the rule applied in the *Halladjian* case. He says,
176 Fed. 467:

"No modern theory has gained general acceptance.
Hardly anyone classifies any human race as white, and none
can be applied under section 2169 without making distinctions which Congress certainly did not intend to draw; e. g.,
a distinction between the inhabitants of different parts of
France. Thus classification by ethnological race is almost
or quite impossible. On the other hand, to give the phrase
'white person' the meaning which it bore when the first naturalization act was passed, viz., any person not otherwise
designated or classified, is to make naturalization depend
upon the varying and conflicting classification of persons
in the usage of successive generations and of different parts
of a large country."

But the examples just cited may be regarded as exceptional. Centuries before our first legislation on naturalization, the Magyars had "become physically assimilated
to the western peoples." 17 Enc. Brit., 11th ed., 393-394.
"In their new environment their Mongolic physical type
has gradually conformed to the normal European standard." Webster's New International Dictionary (1913), tit.
"Magyar", quoting A. H. Keane. They have long been "one
of the dominant people of Hungary—which they conquered
at the close of the ninth century", Id.; and they with the
Portuguese of varying degrees of color, are within the meaning of "white", as commonly understood, and as explained
by Judge Cushman, in the case of *In re Young*, 198 Fed.,
716-717:

"The term 'white person' must be given its common or
popular meaning. As commonly understood, the expression includes all European races and those Caucasians belonging to the races around the Mediterranean Sea, whether
they are considered as 'fair whites' or 'dark whites', as classified by Huxley, and notwithstanding that certain of the

southern and eastern European races are technically classified as of Mongolian or Tartar origin.

"It is just as certain that, whether we consider the Japanese as of Mongolian race, or the Malay race, they are not included in what are commonly understood as 'white persons.'"

See also *Dow v. United States*, 226 Fed. 145, 147.

Though the intent of the word "white" is determinative of the case, we may well dispose of the petitioner's argument that the use of the word "free" in the expression "free white persons" emphasizes the element of worthiness, good quality, as against the element of color.   The use of the word "free" in the debates in the Constitutional Convention in 1787 affords most reliable evidence of what the word meant at about and shortly before, its first use in the naturalization laws.   It is recorded that Gouverneur Morris in moving to insert "free" before the word "inhabitants," with reference to the apportionment of members of the House of Representatives, used the word as the opposite of "slave."   Madison's Journal of the Constitutional Convention (Albert Scott & Co., Chicago, 1893), 478.   And such has always been its intent, not only when this statute had its origin but shortly after the Civil War when this statute was revived after a brief suspension—though the retention of the word "free" had then become unnecessary.

As lately as 1906 Congress went over the whole law of naturalization, and yet in the face of the well known rulings of the published decisions which had interpreted the particular section here in question, the section was left just as it was.   This is a very persuasive reason for the conclusion that Congress acquiesced in, and adopted, the interpretation which the courts had put upon its own work. 226 Fed. 145, 148.   The remedy for uncertainty in the statute, or for its unfairness or inconsistency with the theory and spirit of our institutions, lies, of course, with the legislative body.

In view of the foregoing authorities and considerations, the court finds that the petitioner is not qualified under Revised Statutes, section 2169, and must therefore deny his petition; and it is so ordered, in spite of the finding hereby made that he has fully established the allegations of his petition, and, except as to the requirements of section 2169, is in every way eminently qualified under the statutes to become an American citizen.

Pending on appeal in the Supreme Court of the United States, to which certified by the Circuit Court of Appeals.

IN THE MATTER OF MARCOS SOLIS, A PETITIONER FOR NATURALIZATION.

March 25, 1916.

Aliens—Naturalization—Persons eligible; Filipinos: **Under section 30 of the Act of June 29, 1906, 34 Stat. 596, a Filipino, native and citizen of the Philippine Islands, is eligible to citizenship in spite of the provision of Rev. Stat. sec. 2169, limiting naturalization to aliens who are free white persons or of African nativity or descent.**

Petition for naturalization.

Marcus Solis, petitioner, *pro se.*
H. W. Vaughan, U. S. District Attorney, opposed.

CLEMONS, J.   The petitioner Marcos Solis, born in the Philippine Islands October 1, 1892, and a citizen thereof. owing permanent allegiance to the United States, seeks to be made an American citizen.   On the hearing of his petition, he appeared to be in all ways qualified as a person honorably discharged from service in the Navy, under the act of June 30, 1914, 38 Stat. 395; and no question was made as to his qualifications except for the district attorney's contention, in reliance upon the decision in the case of *In re Alverto*, 198 Fed. 689, that Filipinos owing allegiance to the United States are not eligible to citizenship, because, under Rev. Stat. sec. 2169, that privilege is open only to free white persons and persons of African nativity or descent.

But the error of the *Alverto* decision is apparent, though the court's opinion is persuasive and well reasoned from its own premises. Section 2169, above, which was not repealed by the naturalization act of June 29, 1906, 34 Stat. 596, except so far as "inconsistent with or repugnant to the provisions of this act" (Id., sec. 26), limits the naturalization of *aliens* to free white persons and persons of African nativity or descent, and it has no application to any persons except aliens, but on the other hand, section 30 of the naturalization act of June 29, 1906, hereinafter quoted, applies to a class who are *not aliens* at all, but are a class in peculiar and close relationship with the United States. In other words, under section 2169 no alien can be naturalized who is not a white person or an African, and the petitioner here is not an alien to whom this section could apply. Or again, at the risk of repetition, section 2169 applies the provisions of the naturalization laws to aliens who are white persons or Africans, and that is all that it does; while section 30 applies the naturalization laws to an additional and entirely distinct and definite class of persons whom Congress has found it politic and no doubt just to favor.

As against the opinion in the *Alverto* case, there is first, the opinion given July 10th, 1908, 27 Ops. Atty. Gen. 12, by Attorney General Bonaparte, who assumed office almost contemporaneously with the taking effect of the statute in question; for he was appoined December 17, 1906, and the act became effective August 28, of that year.   Contemporary executive construction, and particularly by those in high office and having peculiar duties in relation to the administration of the Act, is of very persuasive authority. The Attorney General says, 27 Ops. Atty. Gen. 12, with regard to the application of the statute to a native Filipino:

"This section seems to have been formed expressly for the people of our insular possessions, who are there accurately described and to whom alone the section can refer."

It was this clear opinion that guided me on June 29th, 1912, in admitting to citizenship Paulino Netto, a person of half Filipino and half Spanish parentage.

And a still more recent authority, the decision of Justice Gould of the Supreme Court of the District of Columbia rendered December 13th, 1915, in the case of *In re Monico Lopez*, sustains the view of the Attorney General so succinctly and convincingly, that I am content to quote from it quite largely:

"The contention of the United States is that petitioner is debarred by Section 2169 R. S. U. S., which provides:

" 'The provisions of this title shall apply to aliens being free white persons, and to aliens of African nativity and to persons of African descent.'

"It is argued that Section 30, of the act of June 29, 1906, and Section 2169 R. S. U. S. must be read together, and that the former Section applies only to persons who are designated in the latter, viz.: 'aliens being free white persons and to aliens of African nativity,' etc.

"The court is unable to agree with the contention of the Government. The language of Section 30, above quoted, is that:

" 'All the *applicable* provisions of the naturalization laws . . . shall apply to and be held to authorize the admission to citizenship of all persons not citizens who owe permanent allegiance to the United States, and who may become residents of any State or organized Territory of the United States.'

"But Section 2169 is not *applicable* to petitioner. He is not an alien nor is he of African nativity or descent.

"By the treaty with Spain, the Philippines were ceded to the United States on April 11, 1899. By the Act of July 1, 1902 (32 Stat. at Large, 691) inhabitants of the Philippines who were Spanish subjects on April 11, 1899, other than those who had elected to preserve their allegiance to Spain, were declared 'to be citizens of the Philippine Islands and as such entitled to the protection of the United States.' Four years later Congress, with the Act of 1902 before it, making Filipinos local citizens and with the knowledge that the Islands were being governed by the United States and that thereby its citizens owed allegiance to the United States, enacted Section 30, with the evident intention of providing means whereby such citizens could become citizens of the United States.

"In the case of *Fourteen Diamond Rings v. U. S.*, 182 U. S., 176, the Supreme Court, speaking of the Philippines, used this language:

" 'The Philippines thereby ceased, in the language of the treaty, 'to be Spanish'. Ceasing to be Spanish, they ceased to be foreign country. They came under the complete and absolute sovereignty and dominion of the United States, over which civil government could be established.

" 'The result was the same although there was no stipulation that the native inhabitants should be incorporated into the body politic and none securing to them the right to choose their nationality. *Their allegiance became due to the United States*, and they became entitled to its protection.'

"This decision was handed down December 2, 1901. Five years later, Congress provided a means whereby those persons described by the quoted language of the Supreme Court, owing allegiance to the United States, might become citizens thereof. To contend that this provision must be read in *pari materia* with a section relating to aliens and persons of African descent is to ignore the evident intent of Congress in extending citizenship to a definite and ascertained class of persons who were neither aliens nor of African descent.

"I am aware that in other jurisdictions, an opposite conclusion has been reached, but to my mind the above considerations are compelling and I will admit the petitioner to citizenship."

The present view of the government may perhaps be indicated by the following from the letter of the Commissioner of Naturalization dated February 15th transmitting in compliance with my request a copy of Justice Gould's decision:

"Request was made by this Department that steps be taken with a view to the review of the decision by the Court of Appeals of the District of Columbia, but the Department of Justice declined to take such action, and stated, in part, as follows:

" 'It is to be noted that in the case of *Lopez* the applicant had resided in this country since 1904, while in the *Alverto* case, . . . there appears to have been no showing that the applicant had ever resided in any state or organized territory of the United States, which, of course, is a prerequisite.' "

As regards any prejudice against the naturalization of any but white persons or Africans, Congress has done no extraordinary thing in here extending citizenship to those who may be other than of the classes just named; for, e. g., by the Organic Act providing a government for the Territory of Hawaii all who were citizens of the Republic of Hawaii at annexation but who by mere annexation were not made citizens of the United States, were collectively naturalized, even though the majority of them were neither white persons nor Africans, and even though some were Chinese. who under 22 Stat. 61. sec. 14, act of May 6, 1882, were not eligible. See 23 Ops. Atty Gen. 509, also Van Dyne on Naturalization, 45, 318.

Let the petition be granted.

See *In re Ocampo*, post. decision of December 30, 1916.

IN THE MATTER OF THE APPLICATION OF SHO-
TARO HOKAMURA FOR A WRIT OF HABEAS
CORPUS.

March 31, 1916.

Aliens—Immigration—Domiciled aliens: The Immigration Act, 34
Stat. 898, as amended, applies to domiciled aliens returning to Hawaii
after temporary absence abroad, regardless of whether they established
their domicile here before or after annexation.

Habeas Corpus: Hearing on return to writ.

John W. Cathcart for petitioner.
H. W. Vaughan, U. S. District Attorney, for respondent.

CLEMONS, J.   There is no need of any extended discussion of the evidence in this case, it being ample to sustain
the deportation order of the Secretary of Labor.

As to the contention, that the alien having come to
Hawaii before Annexation, and established a domicil here,
and being now here on return from a temporary absence,
he is not within the contemplation of the law,—following
the ruling of this court in *In re Ching Lum,* ante, p. 376:
This contention is in my opinion, disposed of by *Lapina v.
Williams,* 232 U. S., 78, in view of the fact that after Annexation the alien went out of the country on a year's visit
to Japan.   Under the authority just cited, the Immigration
Act applies to domiciled aliens returning to the country as
well as to aliens coming here for the first time.

Let the writ be dismissed and the petitioner be remanded
to the custody of the respondent.

IN THE MATTER OF THE APPLICATION OF FU-SANO SASAKI FOR A WRIT OF HABEAS CORPUS.

April 6, 1916.

Aliens—Immigration—Deportation—Effect of marriage to citizen:
A Japanese alien woman, whose acts render her liable to deportation, cannot avoid deportation by marriage to a citizen.

Habeas Corpus: Hearing on return to writ.

J. *Lightfoot* for petitioner.
H. *W. Vaughan*, U. S. District Attorney, for respondent.

CLEMONS, J.· Nothing appears in the record,—on which the case was submitted for the court's determination,—to justify the issuance of the writ of habeas corpus. The petitioner, a Japanese woman, born in Japan, admitted repeatedly that she had practiced prostitution for at least seven or eight months of the year 1913, and subsequent to her entry into the United States. Transcript of Record of Immigration Office, 4, 6. This is corroborated by the statement of Inspector H. B. Brown of Honolulu. Id., 2. Some of these admissions were made in reply to questions of her own attorney. Id., 6.

After filing her petition for the writ, the alien filed a supplementary petition in which she alleges that on January 16, 1915, eight months subsequent to her petition, she was married to a citizen of the United States, and that they have since lived together as husband and wife. On this ground it is strenuously contended, that she is now a citizen of the United States and that the immigration laws do not apply to her. The answer to this is, that not being one "who might herself be lawfully naturalized", her marriage to a citizen does not give her the status of a citizen. Rev. Stat., sec. 1994. *In re Takao Ozawa*, ante, p. 671.

The writ is discharged and the petitioner remanded to the custody of the respondent.

UNITED STATES OF AMERICA *v.* FOUR DIAMOND RINGS.

April 8, 1916.

1. *Criminal law—Pleas—Former acquittal—Variance—Estoppel:* Defendant cannot plead former acquittal as res adjudicata, when such acquittal was had on his own motion for a directed verdict based on the ground of a variance between indictment and proof.

2. *Same—Material variance:* A variance in the proof as to the means used in committing a crime is a material variance. Thus, it is a variance to allege an attempt to smuggle by means of concealing jewelry upon the person and beneath the clothing, and to prove such attempt by false and fraudulent practices and statements that the smuggler had nothing in his pocket except money.

Indictment: Motion in arrest of judgment.

R. W. Breckons and *H. L. Grace* for the motion.
H. W. Vaughan, U. S. District Attorney, and *S. B. Kemp,* Assistant U. S. Attorney, contra.

CLEMONS, J. This is a motion in arrest of the judgment ordered by this court in its decision rendered orally on November 26, 1915, and holding that the property herein sought to be condemned as contraband under the laws against smuggling, should be condemned as prayed in the government's information.

The motion is based on the contention of "former jeopardy." And it appears that in a criminal proceeding for violation of the Tariff Act of October 3, 1913, against Lee Tai, movant here and intervenor as claimant and owner of the property condemned (No. 1100 of our criminal docket), the court ordered a directed verdict on the ground of a variance between the indictment and the proof. The proceedings were as follows:

"Mr. Breckons (attorney for defendant): Now, if the court please, there is only one thing for the defendant to do at this stage and that is to move your Honor for a directed verdict. (Mr. Breckons argues.)

The Court (Dole, J.). I feel that the indictment is not borne out by the testimony and that the law means something different from putting the things into a regular pocket. It is unsound to regard it as a concealment beneath his clothing. If he had slipped these jewels underneath his undershirt or into his shoe, why, it would have been within the statute, but I think the point raised is sound. The law did not mean as a false practice the use of a regular pocket which one uses for his papers or his money and other things. The placing of dutiable goods in such a place would not be a false practice even. The denial of its being there, that would have been a false statement, but it is not alleged. I am impatient of technicalities and do not like to recognize them, but I believe that a man who is indicted is entitled to a strict construction of the indictment as regards testimony, so, gentlemen of the jury, I instruct you to return a verdict of acquittal."

This variance counsel now claims to be *immaterial*. If it is, the motion for directed verdict should not have been granted. But though I do not agree that the variance is immaterial, an admission that it is so does not, and should not, help the movant. He cannot "eat his cake and have it, too." And Judge Dole's "impatience of technicalities", supra, which appears in his decision in the criminal prosecution, may very reasonably and fairly be invoked against the same defendant now claimant here. See *People v. Meakim*, 61 Hun, 327, 15 N. Y. Supp. 917, affirmed 131 N. Y. 667, all judges concurring and regarding the point as so clear as not to require a written opinion. Though that case cites a statute, enacting that "if the defendant were formerly acquitted on the ground of a variance between the indictment and the proof, . . . it is not deemed an acquittal of the same offense," still the decision appears to rest on the broad ground of estoppel. See Id., 917-918, in extenso. It may be noted that the decision there was made in spite of the "insist(ance) that there was no material variance;" and that the court said, *"whether the variance was or was not material,* we think the defendants cannot now be permitted to question the position which they took upon that head on the former trial." Of course, in face of the New York constitutional provision against double jeopardy (see *King v. People,* 5 Hun, 297, 299; N. Y. const., art. 1, sec. 6), the decision cited, 15 N. Y. Supp. 917, could not—as a general proposition—hold that an immaterial variance does not prevent a second trial; for it is only to state the obvious to say that an immaterial variance is no variance. But even in spite of an immaterial variance being no variance, the court held that the party relying upon a variance at trial could not thereafter be heard to say that it was such a variance (immaterial) as was no variance. Id. See, also, *State v. Drakeford,* 78 S. E. 308 (No. Car.), holding that where the fact "that accused was discharged on a former trial at his own instance on the ground of variance between the name of prosecutrix as alleged and proved, was not former jeopardy so as to bar a subsequent prosecution." Syllabus, par. 2.

[2] But, in any event, the variance here was material The indictment alleged an attempt to smuggle "by means of concealing the said jewelry upon his person and beneath his clothing," while the testimony offered as to the "means" used, was (to use the language of the information now before the court) of "certain false and fraudulent practices and statements . . . that he, the said Lee Tai, had nothing in his pocket except money." That an allegation as to the means used in committing the crime, is a material allegation, a matter of substance, see *Stone v. State,* 115 Ala., 121; 22 So. 275; 22 Enc. Pl. & Pr., 579, also 584. And see 12 Cyc. 266-267. Other suggestive cases are: *United States v. Aurandt,* 107 Pac. 1064, 1067, citing Cooley's Constitutional Limitations, 328; *Reynolds v. State,* 124 S. W. 931, and as favoring the movant, *Burch v. State,* 61 S. E. 503.

"The application of the plea of former jeopardy has suffered continual modification since it first arose as a plea at common law." Chatfield, J., in *United States v. Rogoff*, 163 Fed 311, 312. And though one may at first realize no little difficulty in determining what is "double jeopardy" (see *United States v. Ah Poi*, ante, p. 607), yet the court cannot resist the justified tendency to regard questions of jeopardy with the same freedom from over-technicality now fast becoming the general rule in criminal cases. See language of Day, J., in *Garland v. Washington*, 232 U. S., 642, 646-647.

As disposing of any possible argument, that the mere false statement was not an offense, see *United States v. A Lot of Silk Goods*, ante, p. 113, 213 Treasury Decisions, 31 (T. D. 33019).

The motion in arrest of judgment is denied.

UNITED STATES OF AMERICA v. LELOHA KUKILANI AND MAGGIE PERREIRA.

May 2, 1916.

1. *Evidence—Husband and wife—Competency as witnesses against co-defendants of each other in criminal cases:* The Act of March 3, 1887, 24 Stat. 635, sec. 1 (Edmunds-Tucker Act) removing the incompetency of husband and wife as witnesses as against each other in certain cases, does not apply to indictment for adultery, even as against a paramour of the witness' spouse on the trial of both offenders under a joint indictment.

2. *Same—Same—Same—Testimony as to marriage:* The husband of a female defendant in a case of adultery is not a competent witness to prove her marriage.

Indictment: On objection to testimony.

C. S. Davis for defendants.

H. W. Vaughan, U. S. District Attorney, and *S. B. Kemp,* Assistant U. S. Attorney, for the United States.

CLEMONS, J. In this prosecution, under one indictment, of the alleged participants in adultery, the government offers as a witness the husband of the female defendant, to prove marriage,—not as against the wife, however, but only as against the other defendant, her alleged paramour.

The attorney for the defense objects on the ground that the incompetency of one spouse to testify against the other under the common law and under the Revised Laws of Hawaii, 1915, sec. 2613, renders such testimony as is here offered inadmissible, so long as the other spouse remains one of the defendants in the case.

The district attorney makes four points in reply:

[1] The first is, that the United States is not bound by the rules of evidence laid down by the Revised Laws of Hawaii, particularly by section 2613, above cited.

This may be true (without now undertaking to decide), but in any event it will be noted that the provision of the Revised Laws does not change the common-law. To say, as the local statute does, that husband and wife shall be incompetent, "except in such cases where such evidence may now be given," is to make no change at all. And what the common-law is, as viewed by the Supreme Court of the United States, will presently be seen.

The government's next point is, that there is an exception to the common-law incompetency of husband and wife to testify against the other spouse where as here, the act complained of is an injury to, or an act "against" the witness,—that, for example, assault and battery is one of the exceptions and so also is the assault upon the injured spouse's feelings involved in the offense of adultery.

The sufficient answer to this is, that the Supreme Court, by which right or wrong we are bound, holds otherwise in the case of *Bassett v. United States*, 137 U. S. 496, 505, 506 The cases, cited by the district attorney, of *Cohen v. United States*, 214 Fed. 23; *United States v. Gwynne*, 209 Fed. 993; and *United States v. Rissoli*, 189 Fed. 271, may, therefore, be disregarded. As supporting the *Bassett* case, see 5 Chamb. Ev., sec. 3659 and notes 2-5; 30 A. & E. Enc. L., 2d ed., 954; *State v. Gardner*, 1 Root (Conn.) 485; *State v. Welch*, 26 Me. 30; *Groves v. Harris*, 117 Ga. 817, 45 S. E. 239; *Com. v. Sparks*, 7 Allen 534; *People v. Fowler*, 104 Mich. 449, 62 N. W. 572; *State v. Wilson*, 31 N. J. Law, 77, 81.

The next contention is, that, in any event, the Federal Statute, 24 Stats. 635, sec. 1, 1 Fed. Stat. Ann., 708, removes the common-law incompetency of one spouse to testify against the other. But it does not, except in the expressed cases of bigamy, polygamy, and unlawful cohabitation, which are specific, narrow offenses, not broad enough to include adultery or fornication, the latter being merely unlawful sexual intercourse, while the former are something more than that, if indeed they may be held to necessarily imply sexual intercourse at all.

Light is thrown on the matter by the history of the Edmunds-Tucker Act, of which this provision of March 3, 1887, is a part (by amendment of the original Edmunds Act, of March 22, 1882, 22 Stats. 30). See *United States v. Baum*, 74 Fed. 43, 44; also 8 Enc. Britannica, 11 ed., 949, tit. "Edmunds". The evident intent of the provision was to facilitate proof against polygamy, the whole act being mainly directed against flagrant conditions in the Territory of Utah in the eighties. Mere unlawful sexual intercourse was not aimed at, or the words adultery and fornication would have been added to the list. *Expressio unius exclusio alterius.* It is significant that although this amending act in subsequent sections provides penalties for the offenses of adultery and fornication as well as those of bigamy, polygamy, and unlawful cohabitation which were provided for in the amended act, the former are omitted from section 1.

But, says the district attorney, unlawful cohabitation is as a matter of fact broad enough to include adultery. Not so; the accepted definitions, the etymology of the word "cohabitation," are against his contention. Though unlawful cohabitation does in most cases involve either fornication or adultery, it is itself neither one, its gist is the living together of a man and woman as husband and wife when they are not so, a violation of the strict laws relating to marriage,—an offense against public policy, which sets certain formalities and requirements as conditions precedent to lawful marriage. *United States v. Myers,* 99 Pac. 336 (New Mex.), and see dissent, 337.

Now, the only unlawful cohabitation to which section 2 could apply would be unlawful cohabitation in which one of the parties was already married, for the words of the section "husband" and "wife" apply expressly to the parties to a valid marriage; and besides there was never any privilege or testimonial incompetency in favor of any but those who were lawfully married. See 4 Wig. Ev., secs. 2230, 2231; Wig. Code Ev., sec. 1711. So that this section in addition to applying to those who have two spouses (bigamy) or three or more (polygamy), is intended to apply also, and, as the other and only other class, to those who having one spouse attempt to hold out to the world another as his or her own lawful spouse (embraced within unlawful cohabitation, an offense already defined by law before the amending act of 1887: 22 Stat. 31, sec. 3, 1 Fed. Stat. Ann., 706). Section 1 thus covered all possible cases of polygamy or attempted polygamy, and covered only polygamy as distinguished from mere unlawful sexual intercourse.

The fact, in the case now on trial, that there is testimony tending, if true, to show a living together, a holding out to the world of these defendants as husband and wife, is only a circumstance of the alleged adultery, circumstantial evidence tending to show adultery; but such cohabitation is not the offense charged, nor the gist of the offense charged,—the offense on which the government has elected to try these defendants.

The district attorney's interpretation of the words "the lawful husband or wife of the person accused shall be a competent witness and may be called but shall not be compelled to testify . . . without the consent of the husand or wife, as the case may be," to-wit, that the spouse is competent, except that the spouse if reluctant to testify may be compelled to do so on the consent of the other spouse on trial, is clear and seems to be sound in cases to which section 1 applies,—but the section does not apply to adultery.

Finally, and to my mind the government's strongest point, the court is urged to consider that the testimony of the husband of the female defendant is offered not at all as against her but only as against her paramour, the male defendant, and that the court's proper instruction to the jury to that effect, will remove any difficulty.

Though evidence may be received as admissible as against only one of two joint defendants, and the jury instructed to disregard it as against the other: see *Com. v. Miller*, 150 Mass. 69, 70; *Com. v. Bingham*, 150 Mass. 69, 70; *Com. v. Bingham*, 158 Mass. 169, 171; yet "where it can be anticipated at the outset that there will be such evidence, the court will, sometimes, in exceptional cases, and in the exercise of its discretion, grant separate trials", *Com. v. Miller*, supra; and so here it seems that in such an exceptional case as this in which the defendant spouse is entitled to the protection afforded to "the marital relation" under the ruling in the *Bassett* case,—i. e., so long as there is any rule at all of incompetency in adultery cases,—the rule should be so enforced as to afford the complete immunity contemplated by the reason of the rule in that dominant case. Thus, in

McLean v. Barnett, 32 Tex. Cr. App., 521, 24 S. W. 898, in which the fact appears that, although the "proof was offered only against the defendant Kate McLean" under a joint indictment for adultery, and although "the court instructed the jury that they would not consider the same as to the defendant Elias Barnett," Id., 523, yet the appellate court said: "The testimony was as to the acts of adultery as between the parties. It would have been impossible for a reasonable mind to have obeyed the instruction of the court. The error could not be cured by such an instruction." Id., 524. *Morrill v. State*, 5 Tex. App. 447, an earlier case, is cited in our case at bar as tending to the contrary. As supporting the view of the later Texas case of *McLean v. Barnett*, supra, are, however: *Com. v. Gordon*, 2 Brewst. (Pa. Com. Pleas), 569-570; *Com. v. Easland*, 1 Mass. 15 (and see *Com. v. Robinson*, 1 Gray, 555, 560; *Com. v. Sparks*, 7 Allen, 534); *State v. Jolly*, 3 Dev. & B. (No. Car.), 110, 32 Am. Dec. 656, 659-660; *Republic v. Kahakauila and Kilikina Hake*, 10 Haw. 28; *Cotton v. State*, 62 Ala. 12; *Reg. v. Brittleton*, 12 Q. B. D. 266, Coleridge, C. J., Hawkins, Lopes, and Mathew, JJ., Stephen, J., concurring but doubting, but the separate opinions being barren of discussion, the court not having had "the assistance of the argument of counsel," and the Chief Justice not being able to say that the matter is "free from doubt"; *State v. Burlingham*, 15 Me. 104, 106-107; 4 Wig. Ev., sec. 2236, and n. 1; 30 A. & E. Enc. L., 2d ed., 953-954; 40 Cyc., 2216, par. (7).

The practical difficulty emphasized in the *McLean* case, supra, of making the jury maintain the distinction between testimony to be used against one party and testimony to be used only against the other, tends to support the reasonableness of the defendant's position, though, in ordinary cases, we may recognize the principle of the two Massachusetts decisions first above cited.

See also 1 Enc. Pl. & Pr. 308, and Iowa cases cited, to the effect that though in adultery cases "the parties may

be jointly indicted, . . . the better practice is to indict
the parties separately;" also 2 McClain, Cr. Law, sec. 1095.
Such policy may lend some support to the defendant's contention.   And see 4 Wig. Ev., sec. 2236, and notes 1-6.

There is in the books no very satisfactory discussion of
the questions here involved; and there is a very apparent
dissatisfaction with the rule that made a wife competent
to testify where her husband had injured her by physical
violence, yet regarded her as incompetent where her husband had broken her heart by marital infidelity: 4 Wig. Ev.,
sec. 2228, 2234, 2239, (at p. 3060), 2245; 5 Chamb. Ev.,
sec. 3660; but a district judge cannot overrule the Supreme
Court' and its decision in the *Bassett* case, though our own
Circuit Court of Appeals in the case of *Cohen*, supra, 214
Fed. 29, par. 7, may seem to have been for the time unconscious of its superior court's ruling.

The court sustains the objection to the proffered testimony.

Since giving this decision the court has recalled two un-
published rulings of Judge Dole which are of such special
interest in this connection as to justify reference to them
here: The ruling of Judge Dole, made December 17, 1907,
in *United States v. T. S. Choy and No Sang Bong* (No. 344),
allowing the husband to testify to marriage in a case in
which the wife was jointly indicted with her paramour, was
reversed by that judge, November 17, 1908, in *United States
v. Teno and Diki Nomura* (No. 470.)

UNITED STATES *v.* F. L. DAVIS.

May 29, 1916.

1. *Clerks of courts—Clerks of Federal Courts—Deposit of moneys—Duty:* Rev. Stat., secs. 995, 996, respectively provide that all moneys paid into any court of the United States or received by the officers thereof in any cause pending or adjudicated in such court shall be forthwith deposited with the Treasurer, Assistant Treasurer, or a designated depositary, to the credit of the court, but that nothing shall be construed to prevent the delivery of any such money upon security according to the agreement of the parties under the direction of the court, and that no money shall be withdrawn, except by order of the court or judges of the courts. There is no statutory provision authorizing clerks of courts to require deposits to secure their fees specified by Rev. Stat. sec. 828, though such practice is authorized by the rules of court. Bankruptcy Act July 1, 1898, c. 541, secs. 51, 52, 30 Stat. 558, providing for prepayment to the clerk of the fees of clerk, referee, and trustee, do not require such moneys to be forthwith deposited with the Treasurer, Assistant Treasurer, or a designated depositary. Act March 3, 1841, c. 35, 5 Stat. 421, first reduced the emoluments of clerks of courts to sums less than the fees collected, and the United States, though a party to suits, is not required to pay clerks' fees, unless the other sums received shall be insufficient to satisfy the expenses of his office and defray the clerk's salary, while Rev. Stat. sec. 844 requires every District Court clerk, at the time of making his half-yearly return to the Attorney General, to pay into the Treasury or deposit to the credit of the Treasury any surplus of the fees and emoluments of his office, which the return shows there is existing over and above the compensation and office allowance authorized by law to be retained by him. *Held,* that a clerk of a District Court is not required to forthwith deposit with the Treasurer, Assistant Treasurer, or a designated depositary, moneys deposited with him by parties to secure costs; there being no duty to make such deposit until the time of settlement, when the clerk is required to account for all sums in excess of those which he is allowed to retain.

2. *Courts—Clerks of courts—Duties of—Territory of Hawaii:* Though Act April 30, 1900, c. 339, 31 Stat. 141, providing a government for the Territory of Hawaii, declares in section 86 that the District Judge shall appoint a clerk for the court at a salary of $3,000 per annum, the clerk is not relieved from the duty of making

returns of his earnings, and, being entitled to retain out of his fees those sums necessary for the expenses of his office, is not bound to forthwith deposit with the Treasurer, Assistant Treasurer, or designated depositary, the sums deposited with him as security for costs.

3. *Embezzlement—Offense—What constitutes:* Under Penal Code (Act March 4, 1909, c. 321) sec. 99, 35 Stat. 1106, declaring that whoever, being a clerk or other officer of a court of the United States, shall fail forthwith to deposit any money belonging to the registry of the court, or hereafter paid into court or received by the officer's thereof, with the Treasurer, Assistant Treasurer, or a designated depositary, in the name and to the credit of the court, or shall retain or convert to his own use or to the use of another any such money, is guilty of embezzlement, a clerk of the Federal court in Hawaii, who did not forwith deposit sums received by him as security for costs to be incurred, is not guilty of embezzlement, where none of such moneys belonged to the United States, and he had not refused to make the regular settlements for the surplus of fees and emoluments collected above the amounts he was entitled to retain for his services and expenses of his office.

4. *Embezzlement—Offense—What constitutes:* In such case, as the clerk was not required to forthwith deposit moneys received as security for costs, the failure of the deputy clerk to make such deposits did not render him guilty of embezzlement, within Penal Code, section 99.

5. *Indictment and information—Validity—Statutes:* Where an indictment charging an offense follows the language of one particular statute and not that of a second it cannot be sustained as charging a violation of the second statute.

6. *Indictment and information—Offenses—Statutes:* Penal Code, section 97, declares that any officer connected with or employed in the Internal Revenue Service of the United States, and any assistant of such officer, who shall embezzle or wrongfully convert to his own use any money or property of the United States, or any money or property which may have come into his possession or under his control in the exercise of such office or employment, or under color or claim of authority as such officer or assistant, whether the same be the money or property of the United States or of some other person or party, shall, where the offense is not otherwise punishable, be fined not more than the value of the money and property thus embezzled or converted, or imprisoned not more than 10 years, or both. An indictment charged that a deputy clerk of the Federal court of Hawaii, who received moneys deposited with him as clerk of the court by

parties to suits, actions, and proceedings to pay and secure the payment of costs in such proceedings, failed to forthwith deposit them with the Treasurer, Assistant Treasurer, or with a designated depositary, and that he retained, embezzled, and converted to his own use such moneys. *Held*, that as the clerk was not required to make such deposits, and as it did not appear that he had failed to account for such moneys at the regular periods for accounting, and that none belonged to the United States, the indictment did not charge an offense under the section.

Indictment (for violation of Penal Code, sec. 99.): On demurrer to the indictment.

S. C. Huber, U. S. District Attorney, for the United States.

E. C. Peters, R. W. Breckons, C. S. Davis, A. D. Larnach and *L. M. Straus*, for defendant.

Morrow, Circuit Judge (sitting in place of Clemons, J., disqualified). The indictment in this case contains nine counts. In counts numbered 1, 2, 3, 4, 5, 7, 8, and 9 it is charged in substance that during certain specified periods the defendant was a deputy clerk of the United States District Court for the Territory of Hawaii, and as such deputy clerk he had in his possession and under his control certain moneys which he was required by law forthwith to deposit with the Treasurer, or Assistant Treasurer, or a designated depositary of the United States; that he failed forthwith to deposit said moneys as required by law, and did not deposit said moneys with the Treasurer, nor with the Assistant Treasurer, nor with a designated depositary of the United States; that he retained, embezzled, and converted to his own use the moneys mentioned; that the moneys so retained, embezzled, and converted to his own use were moneys deposited with him as deputy clerk of said court by parties to suits, actions, and proceedings in said court to pay and to secure the payment of costs in such proceedings. In count numbered 6 it is alleged that during a certain other period mentioned the defendant was the clerk of the United States District Court for the Territory of Hawaii, and as such clerk he had in his possession and under his control certain moneys which he was required by law forthwith to deposit with the Treasurer, or Assistant Treasurer, or a designated depositary of the United States; that he failed forthwith to deposit said moneys as required by law and did not deposit said moneys with the Treasurer, nor with the Assistant Treasurer, nor with a designated depositary of the United States; that he retained, embezzled, and converted to his own use the moneys mentioned; that the moneys so retained, embezzled, and converted to his own use were moneys deposited with him as clerk of said court by parties to suits, actions, and proceedings in said court, to pay and to secure the payment of costs in such proceedings.

[1] It is nowhere charged that any moneys so deposited with the defendant as clerk or deputy clerk were moneys of the United States. On the contrary, it is specifically alleged in all the counts of the indictment that the moneys so deposited with the defendant as clerk and deputy clerk were moneys of persons other than the United States.

In counts numbered 1, 3, 4, 7, and 8 it is alleged that the moneys so deposited with the defendant as deputy clerk were deposited with him by persons others than the United States, who were parties to suits, actions, and proceedings in said court, other than proceedings in bankruptcy, and the moneys were to pay and to secure the payment of costs in such proceedings. In counts numbered 2, 5, and 9 it is alleged the moneys so deposited with said defendant as deputy clerk were deposited by persons other than the United States, who were parties to proceedings in bankruptcy in said court, and the moneys were to pay and to secure the payment of costs in such proceedings. In count numbered 6 it is alleged that the moneys deposited with defendant as clerk were deposited by persons other than the United States, who were parties to suits, actions, and proceedings in said court, and the deposits were made to pay and to secure the payment .of costs in such proceedings, without distinguishing whether the proceedings were in bankruptcy or in suits and actions between individuals.

To this indictment, the defendant has interposed a demurrer, in which the objection is made that it does not charge any offense against the laws of the United States, and is not sufficient in law to be answered.

Section 99 of the Penal Code of the United States (section 5504 of the Revised Statutes) provides as follows:

"Whoever, being a clerk or other officer of a court of the United States, shall fail forthwith to deposit any money belonging in the registry of the court, or hereafter paid into court or received by the officers thereof, with the Treasurer, Assistant Treasurer, or a designated depositary of the United States, in the name and to the credit of such court, or shall retain or convert to his own use or to the use of another any such money, is guilty of embezzlement, and shall be fined not more than the amount embezzled, or imprisoned not more than ten years, or both; but nothing herein shall be held to prevent the delivery of any such money upon security, according to agreement of parties, under the direction of the court."

The language of the several counts of the indictment indicates that they are all based upon this section of the Penal Code. and the indictment is so .indorsed. Do the facts alleged bring the charges within the terms of the statute?

There are moneys required by law to be paid to and received by the clerk or deputy clerk of the District Court in his official capacity as clerk or deputy clerk, which moneys, when received, the clerk or deputy clerk is required forthwith to deposit with the Treasurer, or Assistant Treasurer, or a designated depositary of the United States. These are moneys which he may receive by virtue of his office, and are required by law to be paid into court and forthwith deposited with the Treasurer, Assistant Treasurer, or a designated depositary of the United States; and the moneys so deposited can only be withdrawn by order of the judge or judges of said court. See sections 995, 996, 4543, and 4545 of the Revised Statutes. The last sentence of the statute providing for the delivery of the deposited money upon security clearly identifies the deposit there referred to as money deposited in court, as distinguished from money paid to the clerk as costs or as security for costs. Are the moneys paid to and received by the clerk or deputy clerk, as deposits made by individuals to pay and to secure the payment of costs, also required by law to be forthwith deposited with the Treasurer, Assistant Treasurer, or a designated depositary of the United States?

It should be stated preliminarily that there is no law requiring individuals to make any deposit of moneys to secure in advance the payment of costs in any action, suit or proceeding in court, except in bankruptcy.

Section 828 of the Revised Statutes prescribes in detail the fees which a clerk of the court may earn for his official services in all cases. Those fees range in amount from 10 cents to $3, and a specific sum is fixed for each individual service rendered, however small. Take, for example, the following items in the long schedule of fees:

"For filing and entering every declaration, plea, or other paper, ten cents.

"For issuing a writ of summons or subpoena, twenty-five cents.

"For issuing and entering every process, commission, summons, capias, execution, warrant, attachment, or other writ, except writ of venire, or a summons or subpoena for a witness, one dollar.

"For making dockets and indexes, issuing venire, taxing costs, and all other services, on the trial or argument of a cause where issue is joined and testimony given, three dollars."

It was found in practice inconvenient and impracticable

to collect these fees from litigants at the time each service was rendered. Thereupon the courts provided by rule for a deposit by them with the clerk of the court of a sum of money to pay and secure the payment of costs of court as they accrued. This method of securing the payment of costs, although not provided for by law, has had the sanction of general adoption by the courts, long usage, and recognition by the Department of Justice in regulations.

In bankruptcy proceedings, the deposit to secure costs is recognized by law. Section 51 of the Act of July 1, 1898, providing a uniform system of bankruptcy throughout the United States (30 Stat. 559), provides that:

"Clerks shall respectively . . . collect the fees of the clerk, referee, and trustee in each case instituted before filing the petition, except the petition of a proposed voluntary bankrupt which is accompanied by an affidavit stating that the petitioner is without, and can not obtain, the money with which to pay such fees; . . . and within ten days after each case has been closed [the clerk shall] pay to the referee, if the case was referred, the fee collected for him, and to the trustee the fee collected for him at the time of filing the petition."

Section 52 of the act provides that:

"Clerks shall respectively receive as full compensation for their service to each estate, a filing fee of ten dollars, except when a fee is not required from a voluntary bankrupt."

There is no law requiring these prepaid fees in bankruptcy or in other cases to be forthwith deposited with the Treasurer, Assistant Treasurer, or a designated depositary of the United States; but the clerk may, as a matter of convenience and for his own safety and security, deposit the moneys so received in bankruptcy and other cases to his individual account or to his account as clerk of the court in any bank, although he is not required by law to make such a deposit anywhere in the name or to the credit of the court. In other words, it is plainly and distinctly not a court fund, nor a fund belonging to the United States.

Prior to the Act of March 3, 1841 (5 Stat. 421, 428, c. 35), the fees and emoluments received by the clerks of the Supreme and District Courts of the United States were their own property; but since the passage of that act the amounts retained by such clerks have been specified sums as compensation, together with office and other expenses allowed by the accounting officers of the Treasury, the overplus to be paid into the Treasury. The purpose of this statute was manifestly to enable the accounting officers of the Treasury to limit the office expenses of the clerks of the courts. It follows that a system of accounting has been required and provided in dealing with the fees, compensation, allowances and accountability of the clerks of courts.

This necessity for a proper system of accounting is further emphasized by the fact that the United States, although a party to many suits, actions, and proceedings in the courts of the United States, makes no deposits to pay or to secure the payment of fees earned by the clerks in United States cases, nor does the United States, since the act of 1841, pay the clerks any fees for services rendered the United States in such cases, unless the fees collected by the clerks in all cases shall be less than the sum allowed them by law for annual compensation and office expenses. In other words, a clerk is entitled to retain out of his earned fees the compensation allowed him by law, together with the amount allowed him for his office expenses; but should his earnings, after the deduction of his compensation and necessary office expenses, exceed the said sum upon any half-yearly emolument return, the surplus must be paid into the Treasury of the United States upon a warrant from the Attorney General. Section 844 of the Revised Statutes.

Pursuant to this feature of the law, the clerk is required to make a quarterly return to the Department of Justice of all fees of every kind earned by him from the United States during the quarter covered by the return; and if at the end of the half year, upon an adjustment of his accounts, it is found that he has earned in fees from individuals a sum more than sufficient to pay his semi-annual compensation and expenses of his office, then he must pay the excess into the Treasury of the United States and he receives nothing from the United States for his services in United States cases; but if the sum earned in fees from individuals is not sufficient to pay his semi-annual compensation and expenses of office, the United States will allow him the difference between the sum earned and the amount of his semi-annual compensation including expenses of office.

[2] The act of Congress entitled "An act to provide a government for the territory of Hawaii," approved April 30, 1900 (31 Stat. 141, 158, c. 339), provides in section 86 that:

"The said District Judges shall appoint a clerk of said court at a salary of three thousand dollars per annum."

But this act does not relieve the clerk from the duty of making a quarterly return of his earnings in United States cases, nor from the duty of making the half-yearly emolument return of all fees and emoluments of his office; nor does it relieve the accounting officers of the Treasury from the duty of auditing and allowing the clerk, over and above his personal compensation provided in the act, his necessary office expenses including clerk hire; and the act does not require that deposits for costs shall be paid into the Treasury prior to such return and audit. The relation of the clerk to such deposits is, therefore, precisely the same in Hawaii as in other districts under the general statute in that behalf.

This method of compensation and allowances for expenses requires a system of accounting, carried on by the accounting officers of the Treasury, to ascertain and determine what portion of the fees earned by the clerk may be retained by him as compensation and for expenses of his office, and what portion he will be required to pay into the Treasury as surplus earnings of his office.

[3] It is not alleged in the indictment that any of the amounts charged to have been embezzled by the defendant was shown by any return of his to be a surplus of fees and emoluments of his office as clerk and deputy clerk, over and above the compensation and allowances authorized by law to be retained by him, or that the accounting officers of the Treasury had so found, or that he had been directed by the Attorney General, after such audit, to pay into the Treasury or to the credit of the Treasurer any of said amounts as surplus fees and emoluments of his office; and such an allegation, if it had been made, would have been wholly inconsistent with the charge that, upon receiving the deposits, it was his duty forthwith to deposit the same with the Treasurer, Assistant Treasurer, or a designated depositary of the United States.

We find the statutes with respect to the clerks' fees fully and clearly discussed and explained in *United States v. Mason*, 218 U. S. 517, 531, where the Supreme Court had under consideration charges of embezzlement preferred against a clerk of the District Court for failure to faithfully keep the public moneys which had come into his possession and control by virtue of his office, said public moneys being a portion of the surplus fees and emoluments of his office. The court held that even the duty to pay the surplus fees, as shown by the return or audit, was not governed by the statutes relating to embezzlement. The court said further:

"The amount with which the clerk is chargeable upon his accounting is not the 'public money' or 'the money or property of the United States' within the meaning of their provisions. The fees and emoluments are not received by the clerk as moneys or property belonging to the United States, but as the amount allowed to him for his compensation and office expenses under the statutes defining his rights and duties, and with respect to the amount payable when the return is made the clerk is not trustee, but debtor.

Any other view must ignore, not only the practical construction which the statutes governing the office have received, but their clear intent."

[4] The United States Attorney contends, however, that the counts in the indictment charging the defendant as deputy clerk with the offense of embezzling the moneys deposited with him in the cases mentioned distinguish the charges in such counts from the charges in the *Mason* case, wherein the defendant was clerk of the court. The contention is that the deputy clerk, having a specific allowance for his services as deputy clerk, has no interest in the deposits to be determined by an accounting, and he is therefore required forthwith to deposit such moneys with the Treasurer, Assistant Treasurer, or a designated depositary of the United States.

The objection to this view of the case is that we are dealing with deposits with the clerk, and not with the compensation of the clerk or deputy clerk. The question is: What was the duty of the clerk or deputy clerk with respect to these deposits? Was it their duty, when the money was received, to forthwith deposit the same to the credit of the court in the depositaries mentioned? If they were not so required, and such is our conclusion, it makes no difference whether the moneys were received by the clerk or a deputy clerk. With respect to a duty of this character, the law does not distinguish between a clerk and a deputy clerk; their duty to the fund is precisely the same.

[5], [6] The United States Attorney further contends that the indictment may be supported under section 97 of the Penal Code (Act Feb. 3, 1879, c. 42, 20 Stat. 280). That section provides:

"Any officer connected with, or employed in, the Internal Revenue Service of the United States, and any assistant of such officer, who shall embezzle or wrongfully convert to his own use any money or other property of the United States, and any officer of the United States, or any assistant of such officer, who shall embezzle or wrongfully convert

to his own use any money or property which may have
come into his possession or under his control in the execution of such office or employment, or under color or claim
of authority as such officer or assistant, whether the same
shall be the money or property of the United States or of
some other person or party, shall, where the offense is not
otherwise punishable by some statute of the United States,
be fined not more than the value of the money and property thus embezzled or converted, or imprisoned not more
than ten years, or both."

The first objection we find to the application of this statute to the charges contained in the indictment is that the
charges in the indictment do not follow the language of
the statute; and the second is that the facts constituting
the charge of embezzlement are set forth with particularity
in the various counts of the indictment, and we have
already found that they do not constitute embezzlement,
nor do they, in our opinion, show that the defendant wrongfully converted to his own use any money or property which
came into his possession or under his control in the execution of his office or employment.   On the contrary, we
have found that he rightfully came into the possession of
the moneys charged to have been received by him and that
he did not convert such moneys to his own use, except in
so far as authorized by statute to take and hold possession
of such moneys until a return and audit had determined
his further duty with respect to these deposits.   As said by
the Supreme Court in the *Mason* case, 218 U. S. at page
529:

"There has thus been established a distinct system with
respect to the fees and emoluments of the clerks.   Its features are to be explained by the history of the clerk's office
and the requirements of its convenient administration.   It
is urged that the fees and emoluments are attached to the
office, and are received in an official capacity. This consideration, however, does not aid the prosecution, for they
were attached to the office before the statute of 1841, when
they belonged to the clerk without any duty on his part to

account for any portion of them. The fees and emoluments stand in a different category from other moneys which he may receive by virtue of his office, as, for example, moneys paid into court. Revised Statutes, sections 995, 996."

Again, on page 530 of 218 U. S., the court says:

"None of the statutes relating to embezzlement of moneys or property of the United States, which we have quoted, affords a basis for the counts in question."

The act of February 3, 1879 (20 Stat. 280), the original of section 97 of the Penal Code, is one of the statutes quoted by the Supreme Court on page 521. The court proceeds:

"There may be an honest difference of opinion with regard to the amount, the payment of which from the fees collected may properly be allowed. Provision has been made for the examination of the matter and for the ascertainment of the amount due. Pending such audit there would be no justification for indicting the clerk as an embezzler, upon the allegation that he had in his hands a surplus which he had converted to his own use. It is not a question of public moneys, which are to be deposited as such, and are to be disbursed in accordance with the Treasury system. A fixed compensation is to be retained, the expenses of the office are to be defrayed, and the question of the necessity of the expenses is to be passed upon, and the clerk is not in default until he refuses or fails to make his return or to pay over the surplus shown by his return to exist, or the amount found upon the audit of his accounts to be payable. We have not before us a case where a clerk has refused or failed to make the return required by statute, or to pay over the surplus shown by his return to exist, or established by the audit."

The case of *United States v. MacMillan*, 209 Fed. 266, 271, is the title to nine actions at law in a District Court of Illinois to recover upon alleged breaches of official bonds. Six of these actions were against clerks of the District Court, and three against the clerk of the Circuit Court of Appeals. The breaches alleged consisted in the failure of the clerks to account and pay over to the United States certain specified sums of money received by the clerks as interest on moneys which had been paid to the clerks as deposits to secure the payment of fees in bankruptcy and other cases. The deposits were identical with the deposits in the present case. To the several declarations pleas were interposed setting forth the proceedings under which the deposits were made with the clerk. The United States demurred to their pleas on the ground that they constituted no defense to the actions. The court overruled the demurrers, following the *Mason* case and holding that the United States had no right or title to any interest the clerk might receive on the fund pending his semi-annual return, either as increment of the fund or as an emolument of the office, and as such to be accounted for. The case appears to us to be an extreme one in favor of the right of the clerk to the exclusive and unqualified possession and use of all deposits made with him to secure the payment of costs until such time as he makes his emolument return and an accounting is had as required by the statute, but we are of the opinion that the decision is justified under the law as declared by the Supreme Court in the *Mason* case.

It follows that, in our opinion, the indictment in the present case does not state an offense against the United States. The demurrer must therefore be sustained, and the indictment quashed; and it is so ordered.

Reversed, United States v. Davis, 243 U. S. 570.

KIM HONG *v.* THE AMERICAN STEAMSHIP "CLAUDINE."

May 24, 1916.

1. *Admiralty—Jurisdiction as affected by local enactment abolishing common-law remedy (Workmen's Compensation Act)*:   The admiralty jurisdiction of the United States District Court for the Territory of Hawaii in cases arising out of injuries to seamen, due to the failure of shipowners to provide safe appliances or safe places of work, is not taken away by the enactment by the legislature of the Territory of Hawaii of a Workmen's Compensation Act, S. L. Haw. 1915, 323, abolishing the right to pursue certain common-law remedies.

2. *Same—Same:* Though an injured seaman may by his acts be held to have elected to take the remedy provided by the Workmen's Compensation Act, yet the mere receipt from the ship or shipowners, of hospital and medical treatment and money for maintenance, is not in itself alone such an election as to deprive the seaman of a remedy in admiralty,—subject, however, to allowance therein by way of set-off for such benefits received.

3. *Same—Pleading—Joinder of causes:*   It is proper, subject to the court's discretion, and to avoid multiplicity of suits, to join in one libel *in rem* causes of action for personal injuries received by a seaman while in the service of a vessel, due to alleged negligence in breach of contract, or of implied duty, to provide proper appliances, places of work reasonably safe under the conditions, and sufficient help. Joinder of suits *in rem* and *in personam* and of suits arising out of contract and tort, considered.

4. *Same—Seamen—Personal injuries from negligence of ship—Assumption of risk:*   In a libel for damages arising out of injuries to a seaman, assumption of risk is not to be presumed in the face of the clear allegation that the risk resulted from the ship's own negligence.

In Admiralty: Exceptions to libel *in rem.*

G. A. Davis for libelant.

E. W. Sutton (*Smith, Warren & Sutton* with him) for claimant.

Clemons, J. This libel *in rem* for recovery of damages
"for breach of marine contract . . . · and for maintenance and support, care, medical attention and for money
expended during illness and for compensation for expenses,"
is based (1) upon the libellee's failure to provide a safe place
of work and proper apparatus,—in respect to a ship's ladder,—resulting in injury (fracture) of the arm of the libelant, a seaman in the libellee's service under a contract
whereby it was "the bounden duty" of the ship and her
owners to furnish such a safe place and reasonably safe
apparatus, and (2) upon the libellee's failure some time
later under a distinct contract of hiring to provide a safe
place of work and proper apparatus,—in respect to the place
and the means of stowing a large, heavy, anchor-chain,—
and, it seems, a proper method of doing this work, and failure to furnish sufficient help for this hazardous work, all
of which negligence resulted in further injury to the injured
arm; also, the wrong of the libellee's officers, under whom
the libelant was working, in ordering him to do this hazardous work of stowage when his arm had not, as was
known to the officers, yet recovered from the earlier injury.
Under this second cause of action, the failure to provide
a safe place of work and proper appliances, is not alleged
as clearly and directly as accords with good pleading, but
in view of the fact that such failure was testified to by the
libelant in his deposition *de bene esse* heretofore taken
herein, the libel will for the purposes of this decision be
regarded as cured by an amendment which the libelant now
offers to supply. It is also alleged that the owner of the
libellee allowed the libelant five dollars a week for fourteen
weeks after the second injury, but refused to pay anything
more to compensate him for his injuries.

The claimant, owner of the libelled steamship, excepts
to the libel on the following grounds, some being here combined for brevity's sake:

(1) The superseding of this court's admiralty jurisdic-

tion by the enactment by the legislature of the Territory of Hawaii, of a Workmen's Compensation Act, S. L. Haw. 1915, page 323, Act 221, approved April 28, 1915.

(2) The libelant's waiver of all right to libel the ship in admiralty "by accepting hospital and medical attendance and care and payments for cost of maintenance made by the claimant under the provisions of said Act."

(3) Duplicity.

(4) Failure to state a cause of action *in rem* against the ship by reason of the second injury alleged, it appearing affirmatively that the second injury was caused not by unseaworthiness or want of proper appliances, but by the libelant's negligence in attempting to work as a seaman and the negligence of his fellow-servants in permitting him to work upon the ship while his arm was in a weakened and dangerous condition from the former injury.

(5) The receipt from the owners by the libelant of all necessary "hospital and medical attendance" in connection with the injuries alleged and all necessary payments on account of maintenance.

(6) The affirmative appearance that the proximate cause of the former injury was the libelant's losing his balance and falling from the ladder, and not any unseaworthiness or failure to supply and keep in order proper appliances.

(7) The affirmative appearance that for the latter injury the libelant is solely responsible in having offered himself as a seaman and held himself out to the master and officers as in fit physical condition for and able to do all work required of seamen, and that the work required is not other than that usually required in such employment.

(8) Assumption of risk in both cases of injury.

[1] Ground (1) is disposed of by the fact that this court cannot be deprived of its jurisdiction as a court of admiralty (Organic Act, sec. 86, 31 Stat. 141, 158, as amended 33 Stat. 1035, c. 1465, sec. 3, 35 Stat. 838, c. 269, sec. 1), by any act of the Territorial legislature,—particularly by this Workmen's Compensation Act purporting to abolish common-law remedies in personal injury cases; assuming, of course, that admiralty has jurisdiction of the case at bar. This very point is so ably covered by Judge Neterer's opin-

ion in *The Fred E. Sander*, 208 Fed. 724 (see also s. c., 212
Fed. 545, 548), that the court is content to refer thereto
without further discussion.   The decision of *Waring v.
Clarke*, 5 How. 441, 459-464, not therein cited, also throws
some light on the point.   And see 1 Cyc. 811; 1 Enc. L. &
P. 1229.

The constitutionality of the Act has not been raised, and
in any event need not be considered, for any such question
would be quite immaterial under the view above expressed.

Ground (2) is not justified by anything appearing in the
libel.   It does not appear that the libelant accepted anything, or that anything was given, as satisfaction under the
Compensation Act, or as anything more than *pro tanto*
compensation under whatever remedies he might have.   See
discussion of Ground (5), post.

Ground (3) is somewhat difficult to dispose of, not only
by reason of the condition of the authorities, but more especially by reason of the prolixity and want of clearness
and directness of the pleader.

This ground is that of duplicity in the allegation of two
causes of action "each independent of the other and based
on different grounds," "one *in rem* against the ship and the
other *in personam* against the owners," who are not, however, made parties.

Considering the above suggested amendment as made
(whether it was necessary or not), and regarding these two
causes of action as arising from breaches of contract to
furnish safe places of work and proper appliances (and perhaps proper methods of work), joinder may be justified by
the rule of Judge Morrow in *The Queen of the Pacific*, 61
Fed. 213-214, approving joinder of a number of claims for
damages growing out of distinct contracts, for the purpose
of avoiding a multiplicity of suits.   See *The Prinz George*,
19 Fed. 653.   It is understood, of course, that the application of this rule may not be a matter of right but of the
court's discretion.   1 C. J. 1295.

And even assuming that, as claimant's proctor contends, the second cause of action is (as it stands without amendment) insufficiently alleged as a breach of contract, and that all that is shown is an injury received in obeying orders of the ship's officers, nevertheless such an injury may be the basis of a suit *in rem. Lafourche Packet Co. v. Henderson,* 94 Fed. 871, 872-873; *The A. Heaton,* 43 Fed. 592, 594; *The Edith Godden,* 23 Fed. 43, 46; 1 Labatt, Master and Servant, 697, sec. 289, par. b and note. And see *Gabrielson v. Waydell,* 67 Fed. 342, 344, and *Johnson v. Johansen,* 86 Fed. 886, 889, though suits *in personam.*

Independently of any contract, the ship owed a duty to the seaman to furnish proper appliances and reasonably safe places of work (*Johnson v. Johansen,* supra, 888), and a breach of this duty would be a tort. The fact that the tort may be coincident with the contract, is immaterial (see 38 Cyc. 428), especially here, as the general nature of admiralty practice is equitable, and in admiralty "the grand object of doing justice between the parties is superior to technical rules and forms." Benedict, Admiralty, 4th ed., secs. 291, 413.

"The strict rules of the common-law in respect to the unity of the cause of action, or the community of interest or of responsibility of parties to actions, are not observed in the maritime courts." *The Merchant,* 17 Fed. Cas. 31, 32, No. 9,434. Betts, J.

And see language of Judge Betts in *Borden v. Hiern,* 3 Fed. Cas. 897, 898, No. 1,655, which though written before the Admiralty Rules narrowed the cases of permissible joinder, is still suggestive where, as here, the causes of action are not within the classes whose joinder is forbidden (Benedict, Admiralty, 4th ed., sec. 294):

"With regard to the joinder of causes of action, the division and nomenclature of actions at common law afford no rule of decision for admiralty courts; because, as a general rule, the remedy under the civil law is commensurate with the right established by the pleadings and proofs in a cause, and is not made dependent upon the specialties of form which embarrass a suit at common law. Wood, Civ. Law, b. 4, c. 3, sec. 3 et seq. . . . There is an obscurity in respect to the right of a libelant to unite distinct causes of action in an admiralty suit, which is essentially owing, I apprehend, to the propensity of the bar and courts, in modern times, to identify the pleadings of this court with those of common law tribunals. . . . The course of procedure in this country must be essentially at the discretion of each individual court, until a permanent direction shall be given to it by the paramount authority of the supreme court. No formula of pleading, in this respect, has as yet been prescribed by that high authority; but it has pointedly implied, in its adjudications, that a libel may embrace causes of action arising *ex contractu,* and those arising *ex delicto.* See *The Amiable Nancy,* 3 Wheat. 16 U. S. 546; s. c., Case No. 331. And I think there is ground to question the propriety of restraining admiralty suits to single causes of action. The reason which sustains that practice at law, very slightly, if at all, applies to the pleadings in admiralty, where no regard is paid to the names or forms of actions, or to modes of complaint or defence, and where it is never made a point of pleading whether the case rests upon contract or tort."

And, inasmuch as the court could, and should, compel a consolidation in a case like this, the objection of duplicity is not practical. Rule 40 of this court; Benedict, Admiralty, 4th ed., sec. 412; *The Prinz George,* supra.

The joining of the two phases of the second injury, tort and contract, is proper under *Welch v. Fallon,* 181 Fed. 875, 877; 1 C. J. 1295; 1 Enc. L. & P. 1287.

Ground (4) if otherwise justified, would at all events be cured by the above amendment. Were it not for such amendment, this ground would be of considerable force.—that is, if we look only at the pleader's explanation of the second injury as not any specific act or circumstance or neglect, or anything outside of the weak condition of his arm,—which for all that appears he knew as well as anybody, and if we regard the fact that the stowing of an anchor chain was manifestly incident to his employment.

Ground (5) is untenable: the libel is wholly inconsistent with the idea of the libelant's receipt of "hospital and medical attendance" as in full settlement of any claim for damages. Though an injured seaman may by his acts be held to have elected to take the remedy provided by the Workmen's Compensation Act, yet the mere alleged receipt from the ship or its owners, of benefits such as these and of money for maintenance, cannot in itself alone be fairly regarded as an election to take the remedies provided by the Compensation Act. See *The Fred E. Sander*, supra, 212 Fed. at 548. But such benefits would be entitled to be credited by way of set-off. And this Court of Admiralty cannot sympathize with the claimant's oral argument, that the libelant because presumed to know the law (including the provisions of the Territorial Act) must designate in some way that any money received from the ship owner is not an acceptance *pro tanto* of compensation under that Act. And, to follow the reasoning of Judge Neterer in the *Sander* case, it would seem that the local legislature could not affect the jurisdiction of admiralty by providing the rule of presumption, Act, sec. 4, that "all contracts of hiring in the Territory shall be presumed to include such an agreement" to accept the remedies under the Act as exclusive of other remedies. See *In re Su Yen Hoon*, 3 U. S. Dist. Ct. Haw. 606, 610. And, as regards the rule of presumption as a rule of procedure, the admiralty court would not be required to follow the local rule. Rev. Stat. sec. 914.

Ground (6) is untenable. Though the libelant's losing of his balance and falling from the ladder immediately preceded the injury, these circumstances are not alleged directly or inferentially as the proximate cause of the injury, but the allegation is that the unsafe condition of the ladder was the cause, and as a matter of pleading that allegation must stand, for all that yet appears—the absence of negligence being negatived by allegation of exercise of due and proper care.

Ground (7) is disposed of by the consideration of Ground (4) above.

So far as the first injury is concerned, assumption of risk, Ground (8), is nowhere apparent in this pleading, and is not to be presumed in the face of the clear allegation that the risk resulted from the ship's own negligence. See 1 Labatt, Master and Servant, sec. 2. And as to the second injury, the risk can not be held to have been assumed. See Id., sec. 289, par. b and cases cited in connection therewith under Ground (3), above.

In accordance with the foregoing views, the exceptions are overruled.

IN THE MATTER OF THE HAWAIIAN JAPANESE DAILY CHRONICLE, LIMITED, BANKRUPT.

June 30, 1916.

Bankruptcy—Privilege of witness: Officer of corporation testifying before referee cannot be compelled, over his claim that his answers would incriminate him, to answer questions if his answers might constitute evidence against him of a violation of law amounting to a criminal offense.

In Bankruptcy: On petition of referee to require witness to answer.

J. Lightfoot for the referee.
E. C. Peters for the witness.

VAUGHAN, J.   The referee has filed a petition praying that H. Tsurushima be required to appear before the court and that the court require him to answer certain questions proponded to him at a hearing before the referee, which the said witness refused to answer, claiming that his answering might criminate him.

The witness, through his counsel, has made certain objections to the form of the proceeding which it is not necessary to notice.

The question before the court is whether or not the witness should be required to answer the questions. If his answers to the questions might constitute evidence against him in a criminal proceeding, he is entitled to claim the benefit of the constitutional provision which prohibits requiring him to give evidence against himself that would criminate him. If the court can say that the witness is mistaken or is acting in bad faith in claiming the privilege and that his answer could not be material evidence against him in any criminal prosecution he should be required to answer.

It is true that the referee should use all legal means to ascertain and seek out the assets of the bankrupt for the purpose of applying them to the payment of its debts. However desirable this may be the witness cannot be compelled to give evidence of the existence of assets if his answers would criminate himself. Other witnesses must be obtained as to such matters. The questions propounded to the witness which he refused to answer relate to two different subjects, the first relates to the matter of certain shares of stock in the bankrupt corporation issued to the witness while he was president thereof; and is as follows:

"I ask you, Mr. Tsurushima, how much you paid for the ten shares of stock which were issued to you on May 23, 1904?"

The witness claimed that his answer to this question might criminate him. The court is unable to say that the wit-

ness is mistaken about this matter for the witness may
have violated sec. 3303 of the Revised Laws of Hawaii by
the issuance of the certificate if he certified in the certificate that the shares of stock had been paid for when in
truth and in fact they had not.

There are also other sections of the statutes which may
have been violated by him rendering him liable to criminal
prosecution and his admission if he were forced to testify
and should admit that he had paid nothing for the stock
might be very important evidence against him in a prosecution for the violation of one or the other of these different
provisions relating to larceny and embezzlement.

In *In re Fieldstein*, 103 Fed. 269 it was held that a witness testifying before a referee in bankruptcy could not be
compelled to answer a question as to what was the consideration of certain checks given him by the bankrupt
where he claims his answer might criminate him. It appears that the purpose of the examination was to show that
the checks were given for gambling debts, the receipt thereof
being a criminal offense under the laws of the State of New
York. Numerous other authorities might be cited to support the view the court takes in the matter.

The other question which the witness refused to answer
relates to the alleged payment of $9,000 to the bankrupt
corporation and is as follows:

"Mr. Tsurushima, I ask you whether or not during the
year 1909 a large sum of money, about $9,000, was paid to
the Hawaiian Japanese Daily Chronicle, Ltd., for their aid
and support in the matter of a so-called Japanese strike?"

The witness refused to answer this question upon the
ground that his answer thereto might criminate him. The
referee seeks to have the witness compelled to answer the
question or stand committed for contempt.

Of course, the mere receipt of the money by the corporation, of which the witness was president, was not a
criminal offense. It could not be said that the witness was

25

guilty of any criminal offense on account of the receipt of the money by the corporation of which he was president, but the answer of the witness, if he should be forced to answer and should admit that the money was paid to the corporation of which he was president, might constitute a very important link in a chain of testimony to establish that the witness appropriated the money to his own use in violation of law, under such circumstances as to make him guilty of a criminal offense.

The constitutional provision protects the witness against being compelled to give evidence against himself under such circumstances. However criminal it may be for an officer of the corporation to appropriate the funds thereof to his own use he cannot himself be compelled to give evidence which might subject him to a prosecution for the offense. The court can very well see how the answers of the witness might constitute important evidence against him in criminal prosecution and is therefore unable to say that the witness is mistaken or that his claim of privilege is not made in good faith.

It is therefore the opinion of the court that the petition to compel the witness to answer these questions should be denied.

UNITED STATES OF AMERICA *v.* THOMAS WHITE.
UNITED STATES OF AMERICA *v.* JOHN McCANN.

July 7, 1916.

Internal Revenue—Possession as evidence of violation of revenue law: In a prosecution under the Harrison Narcotic Act, 38 Stat. 785, the presumption of guilt arising under sec. 8 from possession of narcotic drugs, is applicable only to cases of possession indicating a violation of sec. 1,—i. e., possession by persons required to register but not registered under the latter section.

Indictment: Motion in arrest of judgment.

G. A. Davis for the motion.
S. B. Kemp, Assistant U. S. Attorney, contra.

CLEMONS, J.   The defendants' motion in arrest of judgment has been lately enforced by the decision of the Supreme Court, of June 5, in the case of *U. S. v. Jin Fuey Moy,* 241 U. S. 394, holding not only that it is not every possession of narcotic drugs (with certain exceptions) that is a penal offense under the Harrison act, 38 Stat. 785, but also apparently weakening the presumption created by section 8 of that act as arising from possession.   Thus Mr. Justice Holmes says:

"Only words from which there is no escape could warrant the conclusion that Congress meant to strain its powers almost if not quite to the breaking point in order to make the probably very large proportion of citizens who have some preparation of opium in their possession criminal *or at least prima facie criminal* and subject to the serious punishment made possible by sec. 9.   It may be assumed that the statute has a moral end as well as revenue in view, but we are of opinion that the District Court, in treating those ends as to be reached only through a revenue measure and within the limits of a revenue measure, was right.

"Approaching the issue from this point of view we conclude that 'any person not registered' in sec. 8 cannot be taken to mean any person in the United States but must be taken to refer to the class with which the statute undertakes to deal—the persons who are required to register by sec 1."

And as my charge to the jury following the view of Judge Lacombe and the Circuit Court of Appeals of the second circuit in T. D. of Jan. 27, 1916, No. 4 [*Tom Wilson v. United States,* 229 Fed. 344] was broadly in the words of the statute, section 8, that "if a defendant is shown to have been in possession of this drug then he is presumed to have violated the law," I cannot say that the instructions were not prejudicial to the defendants, even though I did give the defendants the benefit of the following additional instructions:

"But, there is the qualification that no unfavorable presumption against either defendant can be raised by such circumstances of possession or control as carry a reasonable explanation on their own face."

"The mere possession or control of cocaine is no crime or offense under the laws of the United States. It is merely evidence of an offense and the strength of that evidence varies with each set of circumstances under which we find a defendant in possession of the drug."

The *Jin Fuey Moy* decision seems clearly to require something more than these instructions, and that the jury should be told that it is only from a possession indicating a violation of the acts inhibited by section 1, that the presumption of guilt arises.

And the defendants are entitled to some consideration from the fact that the evidence against them was somewhat based on confessions—which are to be received with caution—and that inasmuch as there was evidence only of an attempt to sell, or negotiations for a sale which was never consummated, it might perhaps under what seems to be the weight of authority be held that there was no "dealing in" (on which offense alone the case was submitted to the jury). As to the scope of the words "dealing in," however, I am not satisfied with those definitions which require a plurality of sales as a business, (see, e. g., *Overall v. Bezean,* 37 Mich. 506, 507; *State v. Martin,* 5 Mo. 361, 363; *Goodwin v. Clark,* 65 Me. 280, 284) but without deciding as to that, think that the motion should be granted and a new trial ordered on the Supreme Court's view of the statute above suggested.

. The evidence, if believed, was ample enough for conviction, but we do not know how far the verdict may have been based on mere evidence of possession, apart from any confession or other evidence of an attempted but not completed sale. And the jury might under my instructions have found a verdict from mere possession.

The motion in arrest and for a new trial are granted.

IN THE MATTER OF THE APPLICATION OF JAMES P. CURRAN FOR A WRIT OF HABEAS CORPUS.

August 12, 1916.

1. *Habeas corpus—Writ, when not granted:* The writ of habeas corpus cannot be employed as a substitute for writ of error.

2. *Same—Same:* And should not be granted unless the judgment or writ by authority of which petitioner is held, is void.

3. *Same—Error in procedure not basis for writ; exception:* Error in procedure does not render judgment void unless it consists in the exercise of jurisdiction when none exists or in excess of that conferred by law.

4. *Same—Error in admitting evidence not basis for writ:* Error in admitting evidence is error in procedure and does not render judgment void so as to warrant habeas corpus.

5. *Federal courts—Non-interference with other courts; exceptions:* Federal courts should not interfere with proceedings in State or Territorial courts, except in cases of peculiar urgency.

Habeas corpus: On petition for writ.

C. H. McBride, Andrews & Pittman, and *L. L. Burr* for petitioner.

W. T. Carden, Assistant County Attorney, for respondent.

VAUGHAN, J., The petitioner seeks by the writ of habeas corpus to be released from the custody of the sheriff of the City and County of Honolulu.

While it is true the writ of habeas corpus issues as a matter of right upon an ex parte hearing when the petitioner therefor shows himself to be entitled thereto, it does not issue as a matter of course upon application, but only when petitioner shows that he is illegally restrained of his liberty and that he is entitled to be enlarged. Let us examine the petition in this case and see if it makes any such showing.

It is unnecessary to set out the petition. It shows that the petitioner was convicted in the Circuit Court of the First Judicial Circuit of the Territory of Hawaii of a criminal offense, charged by indictment returned against him by a grand jury of said Court, to have been committed by him within the jurisdiction of said Court in violation of the laws of said Territory; the said Court having jurisdiction of the person of petitioner and of the offense charged against him.

The petitioner claims that his conviction was in violation of the Constitution and laws of the United States because the trial court permitted the prosecution over his objection to read as evidence before the jury the testimony of one Victor Derda, given on a former trial of said cause; that this action of the court denied petitioner his right to be confronted with the witness against him, guaranteed to him by the Sixth Amendment of the Constitution of the United States, and that said trial having resulted in the judgment by virtue of which he is now held in custody by the sheriff, he is illegally restrained of his liberty in violation of his rights guaranteed by the Constitution of the United States.

The petition shows that petitioner duly excepted to the action of the court in admitting said evidence, and in due time filed his motion for a new trial in said court, urging as one of the grounds thereof the action of the court

in admitting said evidence, which motion being overruled the petitioner duly excepted, and thereafter filed his
bill of exceptions duly presenting his objections and exceptions to the rulings of the trial court complained of and
to the verdict and judgment as being erroneous on account
thereof; which exceptions were submitted to the Supreme
Court of the Territory of Hawaii in accordance with the
practice in said Territory; and thereafter the Supreme
Court of said Territory rendered its decision in said cause
overruling petitioner's exceptions.

The petition shows that after the rendition of the aforesaid judgment by the Supreme Court of the Territory a
regular mandate was issued, remanding the cause to the
First Circuit Court aforesaid, in which said cause was tried,
and that thereafter the said First Circuit Court issued a
mittimus directing Charles H. Rose, Sheriff of the City and
County of Honolulu, to take petitioner into custody and to
execute the sentence of said court against petitioner, requiring him to serve a term of four months in the county jail of
the City and County of Honolulu; and that said Rose holds
petitioner in custody by virtue of said mittimus.

The petition shows that the petitioner sought to take his
case to the Supreme Court of the United States by writ of
error and presented his petition therefor in due form to the
Chief Justice of the Supreme Court of the Territory of
Hawaii, and that said court finally denied said petition on
the ground that no final judgment had been entered in said
Supreme Court.

The petition alleges that "under the laws and decisions
of the Territory of Hawaii, a defendant convicted in a
criminal case has two methods of review, to-wit, by way of
writ of error or by exceptions; that a defendant electing to
pursue one of said methods of review, is precluded and
estopped of pursuing the other; that in said case of Territory of Hawaii against your petitioner, counsel for your
petitioner elected to appeal by way of exceptions, which
said exceptions were overruled, as aforesaid, and by reason

of such fact, your petitioner is now unable to have any further or other review of the verdict and judgment in said First Circuit Court; and your petitioner further alleges that, except by the issuance of a writ of habeas corpus herein prayed for, he is without any and all means of relief or remedy in the premises."

In short, the petition shows that the petitioner has been convicted of a violation of the laws of the Territory of Hawaii in a court having jurisdiction of his person and of the subject matter of said controversy between him and said Territory, and that he has appealed from the judgment of conviction "by way of exceptions" and that his exceptions have been overruled by the Supreme Court of the Territory and that he cannot now appeal by writ of error.

Grant for the purpose of discussion that the clause of the Sixth Amendment of the Constitution of the United States which provides that "in all criminal prosecution, the accused shall enjoy the right . . . to be confronted with the witnesses against him," applies to and governs in trials and proceedings in the courts of the Territory of Hawaii; grant also for the purpose of discussion that the action of the trial court in permitting the prosecution, over the objections of the accused, petitioner, to introduce the evidence of the witness without confronting the accused with the witness on said trial was a denial to the accussed of a right guaranteed to him by said clause of said Amendment to the Constitution; to what relief is petitioner entitled under the law? What remedy does the law afford petitioner to obtain such relief? Is he entitled to have the judgment against him set aside and a new trial ordered, or is he entitled to have the judgment against him treated as a nullity? Is he entitled to the writ of habeas corpus?

It must be remembered that this court has no jurisdiction to review the proceedings of the Circuit Courts of the Territory for the correction of error. Such jurisdiction is conferred by the Organic Act upon the Supreme Court of the Territory. That court in the exercise of that jurisdiction has reviewed this matter, and has decided that there was no error in the ruling of the Circuit Court, complained of by the petitioner. Nor has this Court jurisdiction to review the proceedings of the Supreme Court of the Territory for the correction of error. Such jurisdiction is conferred by the Organic Act upon the Supreme Court of the United States, not upon this court. That for the reasons he alleges, or for any reason, petitioner is cut off from the exercise of the jurisdiction of the Supreme Court of the United States and cannot have the proceedings of the Supreme Court of the Territory reviewed by the Supreme Court of the United States for the purpose of correcting the error, if it be error, of the Supreme Court of the Territory, in refusing to sustain his exceptions to the action of the trial court, cannot operate to confer such jurisdiction upon this Court, nor authorize this Court in the exercise of its jurisdiction to review for the purpose of correcting error the proceedings of the Territorial Courts.

[1] The writ of habeas corpus is not for the correction of error; it is not available for the correction of error. It is the writ for the enlargment of those unlawfully deprived of liberty; it results from the very nature of the writ that one held in custody by authority of an order or judgment of a court, to be entitled to be released from such custody by habeas corpus must show that the said court had no authority to make such order or render such judgment. It is not sufficient to show that the court committed error in conducting the proceedings or the trial which resulted in the judgment by authority of which he is held in custody; for all such errors the law gives a remedy to obtain relief; but not the writ of habeas corpus. Such errors may be corrected by the granting of a new trial either by the trial court or the court having jurisdiction on appeal or writ of error to do so; and the trial court will retain jurisdiction and try the case again. The writ of habeas corpus takes the prisoner

from custody and sets him free. It is only when he shows that he is entitled to be set free from custody that the writ of habeas corpus issues. As was said by the Supreme Court of the United States in *Frank v. Nagum*, 237 U. S. 309, 336, "Mere error in point of law, however serious, committed by a criminal court in the exercise of its jurisdiction over a case properly subject to its cognizance, cannot be reviewed by habeas corpus. That writ cannot be employed as a substitute for the writ of error."

It is insisted by counsel for petitioner that the right denied to petitioner is guaranteed by the Constitution of the United States, and that it is the duty of this Court to release petitioner from imprisonment resulting from such denial of his constitutional right. It is also insisted that the denial of the constitutional right rendered the judgment void.

[2] [3] [4] In *Ex Parte Harding*, 120 U. S. 782, the petitioner for the writ of habeas corpus claimed that rights guaranteed him by the Fifth and Sixth Amendments of the Federal Constitution had been denied him by a Territorial Court of the Territory of Montana, and that as a result thereof he had been convicted in said court and was unlawfully "deprived of his liberty and about to be deprived of his life without due process of law," etc. The third ground of his application contained the following averment: "That, at the pretended trial of the petitioner, he, the said petitioner, was denied by said court his rights under Article Six of the Amendments to the Constitution of the United States, in this: He was by said court deprived of his right to have compulsory process for obtaining witnesses in his favor." Chief Justice Waite delivering the opinion of the court said: "This court has no jurisdiction for the discharge on habeas corpus of a person imprisoned under the sentence of a Territorial Court in a criminal case, unless the sentence exceeds the jurisdiction of that court, or there is no authority to hold him under the sentence. *Ex parte Wilson*, 114 U. S. 417, 420, and the cases there cited. The fact that

the law of the Territory allowed an alien who had declared his intention to become a citizen of the United States to sit on a grand jury, and that an alien did in fact sit on the jury that found the indictment against this petiioner, did not deprive the court of its jurisdiction for his trial under the indictment. The objection, if it be one, goes only to the regularity of the proceedings, not to the jurisdiction of the court. The same is true of the allegation in the petition that the petitioner was denied his right to have compulsory process for obtaining witnesses in his favor. For such errors or irregularities, if they exist, a judgment is not void, and a writ of habeas corpus gives this court no authority for their correction."

It is unquestionably true that the Sixth Amendment to the Constitution of the United States does guarantee the accused the right to compulsory process to obtain witnesses in his favor as well as the right to be confronted by the witness against him. If a denial of the right to compulsory process for witnesses is a mere error in procedure and does not render the judgment void, upon what reason or authority can it be held that a denial of the right to be confronted by the witness during the trial operates to deprive the court of its jurisdiction and makes any judgment it may thereafter render in the proceedings void? One is as much an error in procedure as the other; one is procedure before trial, the other during trial. Both are proceedings in exercise of jurisdiction, not in excess of it, if the court has jurisdiction of the subject matter of the controversy and of the person of the accused. "Jurisdiction of a question," as was said by Judge Sanborn, in *Ex parte Moran*, 144 Fed. 604, "is the lawful power to enter upon the consideration of it, and to decide it. It is not limited to making corrected decisions. It necessarily involves the power to decide an issue wrong as well as right." If a court has jurisdiction of a case or a prosecution, certainly it does not lose jurisdiction by rendering an erroneous decision even on the merits.

Can it be seriously contended that it loses jurisdiction of a prosecution by admitting evidence, even if the Constitution forbids the admission of such evidence? .

Counsel for petitioner have presented his application with such ability and zeal that I have considered it with more than usual care; and have carefully read the numerous cases they have cited.   No good purpose could be served, however, by discussing all these cases in this opinion.   Most of them are reviewed in the opinion of Judge Sanborn in *Stevens v. McClaughry,* 207 Fed. 18.

Suffice it to say that no authority has been cited. that an error of procedure, committed in a trial court having jurisdiction of the subject matter of the prosecution and of the person of the accused and authority to render the judgment and to issue the writ by which he is held in custody, authorizes the release of the accused by habeas corpus, even though such error may consist of a denial of a right guaranteed by the Constitution of the United States. Of course, if the error be the assumption and exercise of jurisdiction when the law does not confer it, or beyond or in excess of that conferred by the law, the order or judgment rendered or writ issued without lawful jurisdiction or in excess of it is void; and imprisonment by such order, judgment or writ is unlawful and may and should be terminated by the release of the prisoner by habeas corpus. Such was the case in *Ex parte Wilson,* 114 U. S. 417; the court had no jurisdiction because no indictment had been found by a grand jury; the Supreme Court of the United States held that, the crime being infamous an indictment by a grand jury was necessary to give jurisdiction. Such was the condition in the several cases referred to by counsel, where the petitioner was imprisoned by virtue of a judgment which punished him the second time for the same offense, or after the power of the court to punish had been exhausted, or when the court had no power to punish, as in the case where the court imprisoned the party for the purpose of forcing

him to give criminating evidence against himself. In all
such cases, it was not because the error of the court consisted of a denial of a Constitutional right, but because it
was an exercise of power and jurisdiction not given by law
or in excess of that given by law, in the making of the order
or in the rendition of the judgment of imprisonment that
the petitioner was entitled to the writ of habeas corpus to
be released from unlawful imprisonment.

[5] There is another view which will be noticed. If petitioner shows his imprisonment to be unlawful under the
principles discussed in the foregoing paragraphs, does he
present a case of "peculiar urgency" and take himself out
of the rule announced in those decisions of the Supreme
Court of the United States which forbid the granting of the
writ of habeas corpus to take prisoners from the custody of
State courts, even where imprisonment is shown to be unlawful and the Federal courts have jurisdiction to grant
the writ, except in cases of "peculiar urgency"?   In all such
cases, except those of "peculiar urgency," the remedy to obtain release from unlawful imprisonment by State or Territorial courts is appeal or writ of error to the Supreme
Court of the United States after resort to the court of last
resort in the State or Territory. The Supreme Court of the
United States has often admonished judges of inferior Federal courts not to grant the writ of habeas corpus in such
cases, has reversed judgments of such inferior courts granting the writ in such cases and refused to consider the question of the unlawfulness of the imprisonment except on
appeal or writ of error from the State courts. *Ex parte
Royall*, 117 U. S. 241, *Minn. v. Brundage*, 180 U. S. 499,
Urquhart v. Brown, 205 U. S. 179. The admonition is
equally applicable against interferance of this Court with
procedings in the courts of this Territory This Court has
so held in *Soga, et al. v. Jarrett*, 3 U. S. Dist. Ct. Haw. 502,
decided by Judge Robertson, now Chief Justice of the Supreme Court of the Territory, and *In the Matter of Atch-*

erly, 3 U. S. Dist Ct. Haw. 404, decided by Judge Woodruff. The petitioner shows nothing that takes him out of this rule which forbids the granting of the writ.

It is insisted by petitioner, however, that as he cannot reach the Supreme Court of the United States by writ of error, he is entitled to his remedy in this court. Petitioner chose to appeal to the Supreme Court of the Territory of Hawaii by way of exceptions, and if it be true that on account of his having chosen that method of appeal to the Supreme Court of the Territory he is cut off from reaching the Supreme Court of the United States by writ of error, that would not change his status in this court. If so, every party charged with crime in the Territorial courts of Hawaii, in every case involving a Federal question could choose whether he would pursue writ of error to the Supreme Court of 'the United States or have the judgment of the Supreme Court of the Territory reviewed by habeas corpus proceedings in this court. He would only need to decide which court he would go to. If to this court, he would appeal to the Supreme Court of the Territory by way of exceptions. It seems that the statement of these propositions should be sufficient answer. The writ is denied.

THE UNITED STATES OF AMERICA *v.* YEE MUN WAI.

November 4, 1916.

1. *Courts—Number of Judges constituting:* Under the provision of the Organic Act, sec. 86 as amended, 35 Stat. 838, creating a United

States District Court for the Territory of Hawaii, to "consist of two judges" to have and exercise in that court all the powers conferred by the laws of the United States upon the judges of District and Circuit Courts of the United States, one such judge may carry on the work of the court even though there be a vacancy in the office of the other judge. Wherefore an indictment reported by the grand jury to such single judge presiding during a vacancy in the office of the other judge, is not subject to quashal on the ground that there is then no court.

2. *Indictment—Negativing matters of defense:* The fact that under the Act of January 17, 1914, 38 Stat. 275, amending the Act of February 9, 1909, 35 Stat. 614, prohibiting traffic in opium, opium other than smoking opium may be imported under certain regulations for medicinal purposes only, does not make it necessary for an indictment charging the unlawful importation of opium, to allege that the opium dealt with was smoking opium, or to negative the possible defense that the opium was within the excepted class of opium imported for medicinal purposes.

3. *Constitutional law—Due process of law—Statutory rules of evidence creating presumptions in criminal cases:* Section 2 of the Act of January 17, 1914, 38 Stat. 275, prohibiting traffic in opium, which in certain cases places the burden upon a person indicted under the Act of "explaining" his possession to the "satisfaction" of the jury, is not unconstitutional as requiring the accused to establish his innocence: the rule of presumption thus created is to be interpreted as subject to the rule of "reasonable doubt" under the general burden of proof in criminal cases, and the defendant's "explanation" in order to be "satisfactory" need only go as far as to raise such a doubt,—indeed, any doubt arising from the circumstances of the possession would itself satisfy the statute as regards the defendant's burden without any special explanation by him.

Indictment: Motion to quash.

C. S. Davis (Thompson, Milverton & Cathcart with him) for the motion.

S C. Huber, U. S. District Attorney, and *S. B. Kemp,* Assistant U. S. Attorney, opposed.

CLEMONS, J.   This is a motion to quash an indictment charging violation of section 2 of the Act of January 17,

1914, 38 Stat. 275, amending the Act of February 9, 1909, 35 Stat. 614, prohibiting traffic in opium.

[1] The ground of the motion, that when the indictment was found, there was no District Court for this District, because there was then a vacancy in the office of one of the Judges, must be overruled. Though as counsel states, the provision of the Organic Act, sec. 86, as amended, 35 Stat. 838, is that this court shall "consist of two judges," these judges do not act together,—at least, in most of the court business, and its most important business, the concurring judgment of the two judges has never been required: when there are two judges they divide the work between them and each judge acts independently in the matters assigned specially to him. To read the statute according to counsel's contention would thus be to disregard the urgent reason for appointing a second judge, i. e., to facilitate the disposition of the growing business of the court,—which a court of two judges acting together would hardly accomplish any more than a court of one judge acting alone. And that two judges should be required to preside at trials or, as here, at the return of an indictment by a grand jury or while a grand jury is in session, would be so contrary to the established procedure in Federal courts as not to be presumed as contemplated by Congress; it being noted that the statute provides that these judges "shall have and exercise in the Territory of Hawaii all the powers conferred by the law of the United States upon the judges . . . of District and Circuit Courts of the United States." It would be most unreasonable to read the statute so strictly as to put the court out of business pending a vacancy in the office of one judge, when the other judge is present and qualified to act.

[2] The ground of the motion based on failure of the indictment to allege that the substance dealt with by the defendant was smoking opium or to negative possible exceptions to the operation of the statute, is overruled. The

fact that in certain excepted cases opium other than smoking opium may be imported lawfully, is a matter of defense, which it is not necessary to negative in the indictment, especially as the allegation is that the opium was "imported and brought into the United States in violation of law." The indictment clearly alleges the doing of acts prohibited by the statute, and by that fact this case is distinguished from those cited, of *United States v. Woods*, 224 Fed. 278, and *United States v. Carney*, 228 Fed. 163.

The ground of vagueness, indefiniteness, etc., based upon drag-net allegations of the various acts of receiving, concealing, buying, etc., have been disposed of by repeated rulings of this court. See e. g. *United States v. Leau Hung*, 3 U. S. Dist. Ct. Haw. 552.

[3] The main ground of the motion is the unconstitutionality of the presumptions created by the statute from the fact of possession of opium (section 2 of the Act) or from the finding of smoking opium in the country after a certain date (section 3 of the Act). The statute reads:

"Whenever, on trial for violation of this section, the defendant is shown to have, or to have had, possession of such opium or preparation or derivative thereof, such possession shall be deemed sufficient evidence to authorize conviction unless the defendant shall explain the possession to the satisfaction of the jury" (Sec. 2).

"On and after July first, nineteen hundred and thirteen, all smoking opium or opium prepared for smoking found within the United States shall be presumed to have been imported after the first day of April, nineteen hundred and nine, and the burden of proof shall be on the claimant or the accused to rebut such presumption" (Sec. 3).

The contention of unconstitutionality is based especially on section 2, in that the requirement of that section that a defendant shown to have been in possession of opium, shall "explain the possession to the satisfaction of the jury," is equivalent to compelling him to prove his innocence and is, therefore, not due process of law.

, This point ably presented by counsel, raises a question of apparent difficulty. See *City of Auburn v. Merchant*, 8 N. E., 484, 485 (N. Y.), also 8 R. C. L. 171-172; 10 Id. 863, sec. 6; 4 Wig. Ev. secs. 2494, 2513.

The difficulty is with the word "satisfaction" in the phrase "explain the possession to the satisfaction of the jury." Does this mean, as contended, that the defendant is required to explain beyond a reasonable doubt?—i. e., establish his innocence? If so, the validity of the statutory presumption might be questionable, as repugnant to principles of reason and justice. See *In re Wong Hane*, 108 Cal. 680. But, after all, the statute is to be upheld if possible (see *United States v. Jin Fuey Moy*, 241 U. S. 394, June 5, 1916), and it seems to this court reasonable to regard this presumption as at all times subject to and qualified by the never-shifting burden of proof upon the prosecution, of establishing guilt beyond a reasonable doubt: wherefore, the jury is to be "satisfied" with any explanation which raises a reasonable doubt of guilt,—for the prosecution fails to sustain its ever-continuing burden when the defendant's explanation causes such a doubt. See *People v. Cannon*, 34 N. E. 759, 762, col. 2 (N. Y.); 2 Chamberlayne, Ev. sec. 960.

Such appears to be the view of the court in *United States v. Yee Fing*, 222 Fed. 154, a case involving this very statute, though attention to the use of the words "satisfaction" and "explain" may not have been at all or so urgently directed as by counsel here, and the court's opinion does not explicitly, though it does impliedly, dispose of the question here raised on the strict implication of these words. Especial reference is hereby made to the opinion of Judge Bourquin at pages 155-157, especially to his opinion that quite apart from any "explanation" of the defendant himself, any doubt arising from or suggested by the circumstances of possession would itself be enough to satisfy the statute so far as regards the defendant's burden. And in

People v. Cannon, 34 N. E. 759 (N. Y.), Judge Peckham clearly indicates that in case of a statutory presumption in a criminal prosecution, the necessity of the defendant's "explaining" to the jury, does not avoid the rule of "reasonable doubt". Thus he says:

"A provision of this kind does not take away or impair the right of trial by jury. It does not in reality change the burden of proof. The people must at all times sustain the burden of proving the guilt of the accused beyond a reasonable doubt. It, in substance, enacts that, certain facts being proved, the jury may regard them, if believed, as sufficient to convict, in the absence of explanation or contradiction. Even in that case the court could not legally direct a conviction. It can not do so in any criminal case. That is solely for the jury, and it could have the right, after a survey of the whole case, to refuse to convict unless satisfied beyond a reasonable doubt of the guilt of the accused, even though the statutory prima facie evidence were uncontradicted. The case of *Com. v. Williams*, 6 Gray, 1 supports this view. Without the aid of the statute, the presumption provided for therein might not arise from the facts proved, although the statute says they shall be sufficient to authorize such presumption. The legislature has the power to make these facts sufficient to authorize the presumption, (*State v. Mellor*, 13 R. I., at page 669), and the jury has the power, in the absence of all other evidence, to base its verdict thereon, if satisfied that the defendant is guilty. But the jury must in all cases be satisfied of guilt beyond a reasonable doubt, and the enactment in regard to the presumption merely permits, but cannot, in effect, direct, the jury to convict under any circumstances." (Page 762, col. 2.)

"Of course, the fact from which the presumption is to be drawn may exist without the existence of the main fact. That is true in all cases. In other words, the two facts are not necessarily inseparable. But in this case the fact of the possession of this kind of bottles by a dealer in second hand articles, without the written consent of the owner, while it may be innocent, yet the presumption of an unlawful use or traffic in them is not so forced or so extraordinary as to be regarded by sensible and unprejudiced men as unreasonable or unnatural. It is some evidence of the main fact, and the strength of it is properly a matter for legislative enactment in the first instance, subject to its submission to the jury for its deliberation and determination. So the presumption, from the possession of certain birds out of season, that they were unlawfully killed or taken in the state, is not a certain presumption, in any sense. A person might, of course, have the birds, and have procured them in another state, and therefore not be guilty of a violation of the game law. Yet the presumption of a violation of the statute is not such a forced and unnatural one that the legislature may not enact that it shall be made, and thus leave the defendant to explain it." (Page 763, col. 1.)

And see Id., 763-764, discussing *Com. v. Kelly,* 10 Cush. 69, 70, and other Massachusetts cases, also see this case of *Kelly* at pages 69, 70, wherein it is held that the words of the statute "presumption that the defendant has not been licensed" to sell intoxicating liquors require the defendant to *prove* that he was licensed. Judge Peckham's opinion in the *Cannon* case may be summarized as holding that strict statutory rules of presumption of this kind are not to be taken unqualifiedly or without regard to the dominant rule of reasonable doubt.

State v. Kyle, 45 Pac. 147 (Wash.), involved a statute providing that proof of possession in certain cases should have the effect of throwing on the possessor the burden of explaining such possession. In reply to the contention of unconstitutionality in the casting of the burden of proof upon the accused, the court said, at page 148, col. 2:

"We are unable to agree with the contention that the other section referred to is unconstitutional. It is but an extension of the rule, which has long prevailed, that possession of property recently stolen is sufficient proof that the possessor is guilty of the crime to call upon him to explain his possession; and, so far as we are aware it has never been claimed that the holding of the courts, that such prima facie presumption flowed from the fact of possession, infringed any constitutional right of the defendant."

State v. Potello, 119 Pac. 1023 (Utah), involved a statute very similar to section 2 of this act and provided that "possession of property recently stolen, when the party in possession fails to make a *satisfactory explanation*, shall be deemed prima facie evidence of guilt." Id., 1026, col. 1-2, 1029, col. 1. That provision was held to be valid, yet the court said:

"Not that the jury, on such proven facts [raising a prima facie case], though unrebutted or not discredited by circumstances, are required to convict if upon such proven facts they are not convinced beyond a reasonable doubt of the accused's guilt"—and, we would add, even the less, if upon the facts proven by defendant in explanation the jury are still not convinced beyond a reasonable doubt, i. e., in other words, if the explanation itself raises such a doubt. See Id., 1027-1028, par (3).

This decision may be referred to for its comprehensive statement of the limits of legislative power to prescribe rules of evidence. Within these limits, of reasonableness and fair relation between the ultimate substantive fact and the fact that is declared to be prima facie evidence thereof, the present statutory presumptions fall, as pointed out in the above case of *Yee Fing*, 222 Fed. 156.

And the Supreme Court of the United States also has the view, that where a presumption is raised, or a prima facie case made out against a person accused of crime, the duty upon him as to the burden of proof may be properly expressed by the words "explain" or "rebut" or even by the words "satisfactory explain." *Wilson v. United States*, 162 U. S. 613, 619, 620. The persistence of the rule of reasonable doubt may, it seems to us, be always implied in such cases. The court just cited goes a good way towards suggesting this when it says, at page 620: "The trial judge did not charge the jury that they should be *controlled* by the presumption arising from the fact of the possession of property of one recently murdered, but that they might consider that there was a presumption and act upon it, unless it were rebutted by the evidence or the explanation of the accused." See, also, *Chaffee v. United States*, 18 Wall. 516, 545.

The cases of *Brooke v. People*, 48 Pac. 502 (Colo.), *Campbell v. State*, 49 N. E. 905 (Ind.), *State v. Briscoe*, 50 Atl. 271, 273 (Del.) and *State v. Carr*, 57 Atl. 370-371 (Del.) are referred to as suggestive of support to this statute, and the first of these cases as tending to sustain our view as above indicated. They offset suggestions of argument for the present motion which may be founded on such cases as *Van Straaten v. People*, 26 Colo. 184, 56 Pac. 905, and *Hoge v. People*, 117 Ill. 35, 6 N. E. 796, cited in 2 Chamberlayne, Ev., sec. 1130 b.

No attempt has been made herein, and none was necessary, to show that Congress could, even, go so far as to impose an absolute burden of explanation in disregard of the rule of reasonable doubt. In any event, cases under statute, as here, may possibly be distinguished from other cases as being on a stronger basis. See *Chaffee v. United States*, 18 Wall. 545-546.

What has been said above disposes of the objections to the rule of presumption created by section 3 of the Act.

In accordance with the foregoing opinion the motion to quash is denied.

S. M. KAŇAKANUI, WILLIAM R. CASTLE, and WILLIAM R. CASTLE AS TRUSTEE FOR SAID S. M. KAŇAKANUI v. UNITED STATES OF AMERICA.

December 9, 1916

Eminent domain—Abandonment of proceedings—Suit against government for resultant damages to property-owner: The United States prosecuted proceedings for condemnation of lands to a judgment of condemnation and valuation, which provided in accordance with the laws of Hawaii that upon payment of the damages title should vest in the government. Over two years passed without such payment, and the property owners, respondents in the condemnation suit, sued the United States under the Tucker Act (24 Stat. 505) providing for suit on claims founded upon the Constitution and laws of the United States or upon contracts express or implied, or for damages in certain cases wherein the United States is suable, and under Revised Laws of Hawaii, 1905, sec. 505, providing that upon failure to pay the fixed price within two years all rights under the judgment of condemnation shall be lost to the government and it shall be liable for respondents' costs, reasonable expenses and damages sustained by reason of the bringing of the action; the property owners claiming inter alia that the judgment amounted to a taking of property for which compensation was due under the Constitution, Fifth Amendment. *Held,* that the suit against the United States was not well founded, for the reason, so far as concerns the local law, that the provision of section 505 as to liability is a matter of substantive law and not of procedure and is therefore not controlling under "conformity" statutes adopting local procedure, and, so far as concerns the Tucker Act, that there was no taking of property for which compensation is due or for which there is any contract express or implied for reimbursement, and that, so far as concerns any claim for damages, such claim as sounding in tort is expressly disallowed by that Act.

Action under the Tucker Act, 24 Stat. 505, for damages resulting from abandonment of eminent domain proceedings: On demurrer to complaint.

D. L. Withington (*Castle & Withington* with him) for plaintiffs.

S. C. Huber, U. S. District Attorney, for the United States.

CLEMONS, J. This is an action against the United States to recover damages arising from proceedings to condemn certain land of the plaintiffs. The complaint alleges that on September 7th, 1911, a decree was entered in those proceedings condemning the right, title and interest of the plaintiffs for the public use of the United States and ordering that their right, title and interest should vest in the United States upon the payment of an award of $5,000 damages; that no part of this award has been paid, and that the two years' period fixed by the Revised Laws of Hawaii, 1905, section 505 (Revised Laws of Hawaii, 1915, section 675) within which such award should be paid, has elapsed and under that statute all rights obtained by the United States in the above decree have been lost; and that "by reason of the law and particularly by reason of section 505 of the Revised Laws of Hawaii, 1905," the plaintiffs "are entitled to recover their costs of court, reasonable expenses and such damages as they have sustained by reason of the bringing of said action for condemnation," the specific amounts claimed being $1,100 for attorney's fees in the preparation and trial of the condemnation suit, $64.85 for witness fees and other expenses, $5,000 damages for the loss of the use of the condemned property, and interest on the award of $5,000 at seven per cent. per annum, from October 11th, 1911. The latter date is thirty days (and a little more) after final judgment, evidently following the provision of section 505, aforesaid, which reads:

"The plaintiff must within two years after final judgment pay the amount assessed as compensation or damages; and upon failure to do so all rights which may have been obtained by such judgment shall be lost to the plaintiff; and if such judgment shall be delayed more than thirty days after final judgment, then interest shall be added at the rate of seven per cent. per annum. Such payment shall be made to the clerk of the court rendering the judgment, who shall distribute the same in accordance with the order of

the court.   If the plaintiff shall fail to make such payment
as aforesaid, the defendant shall be entitled to recover his
costs of court, reasonable expenses and such damages as
may have been sustained by him by reason of the bringing
of the action."

The present action is based, as plaintiffs claim, not only
directly upon the local statute just quoted, but especially
upon the Tucker Act, of March 3, 1887, 24 Stat. 505, sections 1 and 2, this court having under the latter section
jurisdiction up to ten thousand dollars (see *United States
v. Foreman,* 5 Okla. 237; *Johnson v. United States,* 6 Utah
403; *United States v. Johnson,* 140 U. S. 703), in case of:

"All claims founded upon the Constitution of the United
States or any law of Congress, except for pensions, or upon
any regulation of an executive department, or upon any
contract, expressed or implied, with the government of the
United States, or for damages, liquidated or unliquidated,
in cases not sounding in tort, in respect of which claims
the party would be entitled to redress against the United
States either in a court of law, equity, or admiralty if the
United States were suable." (Section 1).

The contention is that this action is within the Tucker
Act, as being:

(a) A claim founded upon the Constitution of the United
States;

(b) Under a law of Congress;

(c) On a contract express or implied.

Though, strictly, the complaint appears to have been
drawn in theory on the basis of a right of action under section 505 of the Revised Laws of Hawaii, 1905, nevertheless
the case will be considered as if the plaintiff's allegations
were broad enough to unquestionably permit the claims
under the Tucker Act, as above stated.   And the plaintiffs
might rely upon the comprehensive phrase "by reason of
the law" in the allegation:

"That by reason of the law, and particularly by reason
of section 505 of the Revised Laws of Hawaii, 1905," plaintiffs "are entitled to recover their costs of court, reason-

able expenses, and such damages as they have sustained
by reason of a bringing of said action for condemnation."
But this allegation is deemed appropriate for recovery
under section 505 of the local law, and is not deemed an
allegation of a claim based on a "taking of property" under
the Constitution, or a claim based on a contract express or
implied. The plaintiffs may amend their complaint, if
they wish, so as to remove any question, especially as the
evident desire of the United States Attorney is to have
the case determined on broad and not technical grounds.

As to this action's being "under a law of Congress," the
plaintiffs contend that section 505 of the Revised Laws of
Hawaii, 1905, above quoted, is applicable because made
so by a law of Congress, 26 Stat. 316, Act of August 18,
1890, as follows:

"And hereafter the Secretary of War may cause proceedings to be instituted, in the name of the United States, in
any court having jurisdiction of such proceedings, for the
acquirement, by condemnation, of any land, or right pertaining thereto, needed for the site, location, construction,
or prosecution of work for fortifications and coast defenses,
such proceedings to be prosecuted in accordance with the
laws relating to suits for the condemnation of property of
the States wherein the proceedings may be instituted."

The provision that "such proceedings" are "to be prosecuted" in accordance with the local eminent domain laws.
is merely a provision adopting local procedure —a provision
not needed in view of the "conformity" statute, Rev. Stat.
sec. 914, *Judson v. United States,* 120 Fed. 637, 642-643;
while, on the other hand, the provision of section 505 of
the Revised Laws of Hawaii, 1905, allowing damages, ex‑
penses, and costs against the government is a provision of
substantive law, rather than of procedure.   The former
has to do with remedy, with the means or method of enforcing rights; the latter creates rights in certain cases—
rights which did not exist before, the government being in
the absence of legislation immune from damages or costs.

Carlisle v. Cooper, 64 Fed. 472, 474, 475, (C. C. A., Brown, Circuit Justice, Wallace and Shipman, Circuit Judges); and, as to costs, *Downs v. Reno*, 124 Pac. 582, 583. In the Federal case just cited "a judgment for costs and allowances against the United States upon the dismissal of the condemnation proceedings under the Act of August 1, 1888, c. 728, 25 Stat. 357, was reversed because the court found no authority for awarding costs against the United States in such case in the act or in any other act", even in spite of the existence of the "conformity" statute, Rev. Stat. sec. 914. See *Treat v. Farmers' L. & T. Co.*, 185 Fed. 760, 763.

The contention, which is the main one, that the action is supported by "a claim founded upon the Constitution," a claim for "just compensation" for property taken for public use, has had full attention, and the court is impressed with the moral considerations which call for relief from the heavy expense, not to mention other disadvantages, brought upon the plantiffs by their forced participation in these condemnation proceedings; but, in spite of the able argument in the plaintiffs' behalf, and in spite of the recognized difficulties of the question arising out of the varied provisions of law in different jurisdictions, there is no conviction that there was a "taking" here or that the advantage acquired by the government was "property."

There was certainly no taking of the particular property sought to be condemned. The proceedings were only preliminary to a taking. See *United States v. Dickson*, 127 Fed. 775; *Lamb v. Schottler*, 54 Cal. 319, 327; *Stevens v. Borough of Danbury*, 22 Atl. 1071, 1072 (Conn.); *Carson v. City of Hartford*, 48 Conn. 68, 87, 88, and other cases discussed hereinbelow.

But the strongest argument in behalf of the complaint has been, that by the judgment of condemnation the government virtually acquired an option to purchase the plaintiff's interests for a certain sum of money, that this is a thing of value, property, for which under the Constitution compensation should be paid.   And emphasis is laid on the damage suffered through the fact of the tying up of plaintiffs' property for two years,—the interference with the free use and disposition of it because of the so-called lien or cloud upon it resulting from this judgment by which under section 505 of the local laws, the government by paying the fixed price could at any time within two years acquire title.   It is apparent that the plaintiffs have suffered damage and have been put to expense by reason of the condemnation suit, and the judgment, under which the condemnation was to be consummated on payment of a fixed price, might be said to operate as a cloud on the title, but so, in a measure might the very institution and the carrying on of the proceedings, yet for none of these things is the government liable, unless that cloud results from a "taking" of property.   That, however, there here resulted no such legal cloud or lien, see *Lamb v. Schottler,* 54 Cal. 319, 327.

Was there a taking or acquiring of property by the government in the so-called "lien" or "option" resulting from the judgment of condemnation?   At first sight it might appear so, but on reflection it does not seem that the government has acquired anything new by this judgment: for it had at all times the right or power to acquire for public purposes that particular piece of land and all interests therein,—or in other words, the owners held it subject to that right or power, and the mere definite fixing of the value for condemnation purposes, the mere decree that the plaintiffs' property be condemned to be taken by the government at a certain price does not seem to be, or to amount to, the government's acquiring of a lien or option in any sense of the word.

By using the equivalent expression "right of purchase" instead of "option", the situation will be more clear.   The government had the right of purchase at the beginning and at all times, the main purpose of the proceedings (at least after the determination of the necessity of the taking) being to fix the price; and yet that right of purchase,—in other words, the mere right of eminent domain,—could never in any true sense be called "property," the taking of which necessitates compensation.   Language of the Supreme Court of Connecticut, may be considered as tending to support the above view (*Carson v City of Hartford*, 48 Conn. 87-88):

"But the Council considered only—did not take.   By considering [after the condemnation proceedings had gone so far as to result in the assessment of damages] *no new relation between the city and the land came into being;* for at all times the land of the plaintiff and of every other owner is exposed to the right of the public to take it for public use.   By considering, the taking became more probable than before; but it remained only a possibility; his exclusive possession was not interrupted; the power to sell was not taken from him; his use was made less profitable only by his apprehension lest a possibility might·ripen into a certainty."

And the Supreme Court of California has said, in *Lamb v. Schottler*, 54 Cal. 319, 327:

"When, in the exercise of its sovereign right of eminent domain, the State takes the private property of a person, he has but one right—and that is given him by the Constitution—the right to compensation before he is deprived of his property.   The right to take his property in no sense depends upon any contract between him and the public.   His assent is not required, and his protestations are of no avail.   But, under the Constitution his property cannot be taken until paid for.   Up to that time he holds it as he always held it, subject to the right of the State to take it for public use upon compensating him for it.   When so taken, the right to compensation, which the Constitution gives him, accrues.   That right then, for the first time, would become under the Constitution a vested one.   Up to that time he parts with nothing, and the public receives nothing.   Prior to that, no lien is impressed upon his property, or cloud cast upon his title, in consequence of any preliminary proceedings. 'Nor indeed can it be said in any legal sense that the land has been taken, until the act has transpired which divests the title or subjects the land to the servitude. So long as the title remains in the individual, or the land remains uncharged by the servitude, there can have been no taking, under conditions which, as already stated, preclude the commission of a trespass.— Until the price has been ascertained, the government is not in a position to close the bargain; and when it is ascertained, if the sum is not satisfactory, the government may withdraw. The government is under no obligation to take the land if the terms when ascertained are not satisfactory.' (*Fox. v. W. P. R. R. Co.*, 31 Cal. 538.) We know of no method by which the government could have expressed its dissatisfaction with the price fixed upon the Laguna de la Merced more plainly and positively than by the repeal of the act which provided for its acquisition—and that, too, before any step subsequent to the ascertainment of the price had been taken. It is obvious that *the public had acquired no new right under these proceedings* before the repeal of the act, and quite as clear that the owners of the property had not."

.The plaintiffs in the present case have been prejudiced, it is true, and the more prejudiced as the proceedings advanced to the judgment of condemnation and of valuation, but this is merely *damnum absque injuria.* The so-called taking here seems to be such only as was characterized by Mr. Justice Strong as resulting from "acts done in the proper exercise of governmental powers, and not directly encroaching upon private property, though their consequences may impair its use." He said in the case of *Transportation Co. v. Chicago*, 99 U. S. 635, 641, 642:

"Acts done in the proper exercise of governmental powers, and not directly encroaching upon private property, though their consequences may impair its use, are universally held not to be a taking within the meaning of the constitutional provision. They do not entitle the owner of such property to compensation from the State or its agents,

or give him any right of action.   This is supported by an
immense weight of authority.—The extremest qualification
of the doctrine is to be found, perhaps, in *Pumpelly v.
Green Bay Company*, 13 Wall. 166, and in *Eaton v. Boston,
Concord & Montreal Railroad Co.*, 51 N. H. 504.   In those
cases it was held that permanent flooding of private property may be regarded as a 'taking.'   In those cases there
was a physical invasion of the real estate of the private
owner, and a practical ouster of his possession.   But in
the present case there was no such invasion.   No entry was
made upon the plaintiff's lot.   All that was done was to
render for a time its use more inconvenient."

No authority has been found holding that it is not proper
exercise of governmental powers to abandon a condemnation proceeding even after the fixing of the value of the
property proposed to be taken—see Lewis, Em. Dom. 3rd
ed., sec. 955 (656)—with the exception, of course, of certain decisions controlled by statute, as e. g., in *Plum v. City
of Kansas*, 14 S. W. 657 (Mo.), hereinafter mentioned. And
such exercise of governmental powers is still proper even
though in a few States a remedy is afforded to reimburse
the property-owner for damages, costs, etc., incurred.   10
R. C. L. 239, sec. 200.   In the absence of such a statute,
as section 505 of the local law, under the great weight of
authority, if not all authority, a remedy is afforded only
where there has been unreasonable delay or malice, but
such remedy is expressly excluded by the Tucker Act as
sounding in tort.   See Id., 238, sec. 200, also *In re City of
Pittsburg*, 90 Atl. (Pa.) 329, 331, col. 2, 332, holding that
no such remedy exists apart from the statute.   And see 2
Lewis, Em. Dom., 2d ed., 1693, sec. 957 (658).

The opinion in the case of *Stevens v. Borough of Danbury*, 22 Atl. 1071, 1072, 1073, throws some light on the
question of what is a taking, holding, at page 1072, that the
fixing of the amount to be paid if the land is taken, constitutes "only a proposed taking;" and it has the following,

at pages 1072-1073, on the matter of damages arising from
inconvenience and uncertainty:

"There may be a hardship in compelling a land or mill-
site owner to hold his property in entire uncertainty, after
an assessment, whether it will be taken or not; but the
inconvenience is of the same kind which attends all proceedings for the taking of land for public improvements,
and which is incident to the ownership of property in a
community, and especially in a city. This inconvenience
was shown in a marked degree in the recent case of *Carson
v. City of Hartford,* 48 Conn. 68, where it was held by the
court to give no right."

That there can be no recovery for the mere inconvenience,
trouble and expense resulting from the condemnation proceedings, see also *United States v. Oregon R. & N. Co.,* 16
Fed. 524, 531; *McCready v. Rio Grande Western Ry. Co.,*
83 Pac. 331, 333 (Utah).

In the case of *Plum v. City of Kansas,* 14 S. W. 657
(Mo.), cited in behalf of the plaintiffs, the court says, at
page 658:

"The issue of law here is whether or not interest runs
upon the award of damages assessed as compensation for
land taken for public use by the judgment of the circuit
court, pursuant to the terms of the Kansas City charter
of 1875, (Sess. Acts 1875, p. 244, art. 7.) The situation of
the parties in interest relative to the subject of controversy is this: Neither the plaintiff nor the city was dissat-
isfied with the original award fixing the value of plaintiff's
property, with a view to its appropriation to public use.
The long delay in reaching the end of the condemnation
case arose from the acts of other parties. During it the
plaintiff remained in possession of the land, but his enjoyment and use thereof were not such as belonged to complete ownership. His tenure, then, might be characterized
as a sort of base or qualified fee, liable to be determined
at any moment by the issue of the appellate proceedings.
He could not, with any degree of confidence, improve the
property or make any but the most transient agreements
for its use. He could not dispose of it except subject to the
paramount public easement, which had become impressed

upon it.   So far as concerned his beneficial rights, as
owner, the judgment of condemnation amount to the taking of the property for public use, and the price for such
taking then became justly due him."

But this case is distinguished by the fact that there was no
question, as here, of any compensation on account of abandoned proceedings, but under the Missouri statutes "the
title to the land is thereby (by the judgment of condemnation) vested in the city for public purposes," Id., col. 2,
and such a judgment is differentiated from judgments "under statutes making them merely tentative, or expressly
or impliedly postponing their final effect," Id., page 659,
col. 1.

The cited case of *City of St. Louis v. Hill*, 22 S. W. 861
(Mo.) involved an undoubted taking, an invasion of property rights in the fixing of a building line which prevented
the owner from building on a strip of land forty feet wide.
The following language quoted in plaintiffs' brief has,
therefore, no application here, Id., page 862:

"Property, then, in a determinate object, is composed of
certain constituent elements, to wit, the unrestricted right
to use, enjoyment and disposal of that object.   It follows
from this premise that anything which destroys or subverts
any of the essential elements aforesaid is a taking or destruction pro tanto of property, though the possession and
power of disposal of the land remain undisturbed, and
though there be no actual or physical invasion of the locus
in quo."

If under that language what was done in the case at bar
was a taking, then equally well would the mere institution
of the proceedings be a taking, for in the latter case, though
in a lesser degree, the use and disposal of the plaintiffs'
property was interfered with.   Such interference, as has
been pointed out in the case of *Feiten v. City of Milwaukee*,
2 N. W. 1148, 1151 (Wis.), would result from an ordinary
action of ejectment, and yet in such case there could not
be said to be a taking any more than here.

As to the suggestion of the opinion in the case of *Shoe-maker v. United States*, 147 U. S. 282, 321, upon which the plaintiffs rely, that the assessment of damages in eminent domain presumably includes certain incidental damages such as are here complained of, and that if the proceedings are abandoned there should be compensation to cover such damages, it is enough to say that, under the general expression of the authorities, the right to abandon without liability to pay the damages awarded necessarily means the right to abandon without payment of any of the included elements of damage.

"The weight of authority undoubtedly is that, in the absence of statutory provisions on the question, the effect of proceedings for condemnation is simply to fix the price at which the party condemning can take the property sought, and that even after condemnation or judgment the purpose of taking the property may be abandoned without incurring any liability to pay the damages awarded." Lewis, Em. Dom., 3rd ed., sec. 955 (656).

There is known to us no decision covering the exact question, i. e., no decision in which the acquisition of a so-called "option" or "right of purchase" or "lien" is considered. In *United States v. Dickson*, 127 Fed. 774, 775, Circuit Judge Pardee went so far as to say, that where "appraisers appointed under the practice in the State of Georgia returned a much larger value for the property than the United States had ever expressed a willingness to pay," and "no physical interference had been made with the property," there had not "been any 'taking' of the same in any legal sense." But this is only an opinion of no taking of the property sought to be condemned, and not an opinion of no incidental taking of any property, as, e. g., an option as above. In that case a motion of the government to dismiss the condemnation suit was maintained, it appearing that an intervening Act of Congress had operated as a legislative abatement of the

proceedings *Carson v. City of Hartford,* 48 Conn. 68, is
perhaps more in point.   There an assessment of damages
had been made as to property proposed to be condemned
for a public street.   After proceedings had pended for over
three years, the city council voted to abandon the public
improvement which required the above property,—and under the city ordinance relating to the opening of streets, it
had the right of abandonment, though that fact would not
seem to distinguish the case, for if the power of the city to
purchase at an assessed price is an "option" or "property,"
it is, so long as it lasts, no less so in spite of the final right of
non-exercise of this option.   The court says, pages 87-88, in
the context of what has already been quoted above:

"As we have said that no way was laid out, the court
must stand upon the proposition that if the council considers, for any period however brief, the matter of laying out
a way, and a provisional award of damages is made to an
owner of land if it shall be taken, and he is delayed thereby
in the sale, or omits to make profit by the use of it, the city
is responsible in damages.

"But, the council considered only—did not take.   By
considering no new relation between the city and the land
came into being; for at all times the land of the plaintiff
and of every other owner is exposed to the right of the
public to take it for public use.   By considering, the taking
became more probable than before; but it remained only
a possibility; his exclusive possession was not interrupted;
the power to sell was not taken away from him; his use
was made less profitable only by his apprehension lest a
possibility might ripen into a certainty."

Adverting to cases cited in support of the claim of damages, the court observed, at page 89, "these cases do not
determine the law of an instance of a contemplated but
unaccomplished taking for public use."   Speaking of the
case of *Pumpelly v. Green Bay Co.,* 13 Wall. 166, in which
the defendant flowed the plaintiff's land without compensation, and of other cases, it is said, at page 88, "Practically
each of these acts was a taking of land, was the actual ex-

pulsion and exclusion of the owner from it by force." And
of another line of cases, it is said, at page 91, "These again
are trespasses, and, as we have said, furnish no precedent
for making good to a land-owner profits which he omitted
to make because of his belief that the city would take his
land."

There are numerous State cases, notably in Maryland
courts, holding that where the proceedings are not instituted in good faith, or are kept alive for an unreasonable
length of time, and finally abandoned, the owner is entitled to be compensated for his expenses and loss. 10 R. C.
L. 238, sec. 200. But, as above noted, an action for relief
in such case sounds in tort (Id.) and is expressly excepted
from the operation of the Tucker Act. By way of paren-
thesis, it may be said that, presumably, in the State cases,
the States had by legislation consented to be sued for torts
as well as on contracts. And most of these cases, and probably all of them so far as consequential injuries are concerned, are it seems grounded upon no idea of the taking
of property but rather upon that of the damaging of
property within provisions of law allowing compensation
not only for taking but for damaging. See *Gibson v.
United States*, 166 U. S. 269, 275, also *Bedford v. United
States*, 192 U. S. 217, 225; 15 Cyc. 653-654, and see, e. g.,
Winkelman v. City of Chicago, 72 N. E. 1066 (Ill.), in
which condemnation procedings, delayed for several years,
were abandoned after more than 15 months from entry of
judgment fixing the damages. And see *Black v. Mayor of
Baltimore*, 50 Md. 235, 33 Am. Rep. 320, 323, holding that
damages in such cases of wrong are not dependent upon
whether the assessments of damages for the taking have
been completed or not. See also *Shanfelter v. Mayor of
Baltimore*, 31 Atl. 439 (Md.); also *Ford v. Board of Park
Commissioners*, 126 N. W. 1030, 1032 (Ia.), which says that
"perhaps as many, if not more, of the courts," have held
that there are no damages even in cases unreasonably de-

layed, and which points out that it is by statute in many States that a right of action has been given.

The fact that it has been found necessary, as in Hawaii (section 505 of the local laws aforesaid), Massachusetts (*Downey v. Boston,* 101 Mass. 439), Minnesota (*Minnesota & N. W. Ry. v. Woodworth,* 32 Minn. 452, 21 N. W. 476) and elsewhere (10 R. C. L. 239, sec. 200), to enact legislation giving relief, and the fact that the cases in which relief is given in the absence of such legislation (but doubtless with legislation permitting the government to be sued for torts) are all cases (as the case at bar is not, under the complaint) of unreasonable delay or want of good faith, seem to militate in some degree against the contentions of the plaintiffs.

So far as the latter class of cases is concerned, it is obvious that any question of delay is quite independent of the question of the existence of a taking, and in such cases it is significant that recovery is placed on the ground of unreasonable delay and not on the ground of a taking.

The remedial character of the Tucker Act has been referred to. *United States v. Southern Pacific R. R. Co.,* 38 Fed. 55. That, however, results only in a liberal construction of the Act itself and in no way affects the construction of the word "taking" as used in the Constitution.

If there was not a taking of property, then there could be no basis for a contract express or implied and the claim based on such a contract would fall to the ground. *United States v. Lynah,* 188 U. S. 444, 462, 472; *United States v. Great Falls Mfg. Co.,* 112 U. S. 645, 656, 657; *Peabody v. United States,* 231 U. S. 530, 538, 539; *McCready v. Rio Grande Western Ry. Co.,* 83 Pac. 331, 333; *Lamb v. Schottler,* 56 Cal. 319, 328.

The conclusion from the foregoing considerations, is that the demurrer should be sustained, and it is so ordered.

Pursuant to the suggestion above made, the complaint

may be amended *nunc pro tunc,* and an amended complaint should be filed, so that the case may be regarded as fully determined on its merits—particularly for the purposes of appeal.

———

Affirmed, Circuit Court of Appeals, Ninth Circuit, August 6, 1917.

———

UNITED STATES OF AMERICA *v.* WONG GOON LET.

December 5, 1916.

1. *Adultery—Evidence:* Held sufficient to warrant conviction and therefore to require submission to the jury.

2. *Same—Circumstantial evidence:* Held sufficient to authorize the jury to find the circumstances to be incapable of any reasonable explanation consistent with the innocence of the defendant.

3. *Same—Name of defendant's wife—Necessity of alleging—Variance:* Allegation of name of defendant's wife in indictment may be treated as surplusage, and variance between her name alleged and that proved, held immaterial.

Indictment: On motion of defendant for directed verdict.

S. B. Kemp, Assistant U. S. Attorney, for the United States.

Bitting & Ozawa for the defendant.

VAUGHAN, J. The defendant moves the court to instruct the jury to render a verdict of not guilty upon the ground that the evidence is insufficient to prove that there was carnal intercourse as alleged in the indictment, and upon the further ground that there is a variance between the name of the wife of the defendant as alleged in the indictment and her name as shown by the evidence.

As to the first ground: There is evidence that at about six o'clock P. M. on the 30th day of June, 1916, the defendant, driving an automobile, came down Emma street in Honolulu to a Chinese store on said street just above Beretania street, and stopped at said store; and that the girl, with whom the indictment charges he had intercourse, went up to where he was sitting in the automobile, and he and the girl talked together about ten minutes; and then the defendant left in the automobile; and the girl walked up Emma street a short distance to a lane, and went into the lane. About half an hour afterwards she came out of the lane carrying an overcoat, and walked down Emma and Alakea streets to Hotel street, and turned down Hotel street towards Waikiki; she crossed Richards street and stopped at the corner of Richards and Hotel on the Waikiki side of Richards. About seven o'clock P. M. the defendant came along in an automobile and stopped at the corner where the girl was, and she jumped in the automobile and sat down beside him, and they drove off and turned down Punchbowl street when they got to it. At about eight o'clock P. M. the men who had been watching the movements of the defendant and the girl, accompanied by a companion, arrived at the house in the Kaimuki district, to which the defendant had taken the girl. There is evidence from which it would appear that the house to which the defendant took the girl was about a mile and a half or two miles from the place where she got in the automobile with him. The man who was watching, and his companion, took a street car at the corner of Nuuanu and Hotel streets at 7.30 P. M. and arrived at eight o'clock at the house where the defendant had taken the girl.

There is evidence from which the jury would be warranted in finding that the defendant had been in the house with the girl for half an hour or more before the arrival at eight o'clock of the man who was watching. At eight o'clock the defendant was in the house with the girl, his automobile with lights turned off was near the house and under some banana trees, which prevented it being seen from the street. There was no light in or about the house except a dim light in one of the upper rooms. The defendant remained in the house with the girl from the time the man who was watching arrived with his companion until he was arrested by the marshal at ten minutes after nine o'clock P. M. At nine o'clock the marshal arrived at the house, having been summoned by telephone by the man who was watching. The marshal together with the watcher and his companion, went up the stairway leading to the room in which was the dim light. The door of said room was locked. The marshal kicked it in and entered. The electric light in said room was covered with a newspaper, and there was no other light in the room or in the adjoining room in which the defendant and the girl were. The marshal turned his flash light upon the adjoining room through the door between the two rooms. By means of the flash light the marshal and the two other witnesses saw the defendant and the girl together in the adjoining room. They were both undressed; she was sitting on the side or edge of the bed and was buttoning up her drawers; she had on only her chemise and drawers. The defendant was standing beside the bed near the girl and was buttoning up his drawers. He had on only his undershirt and drawers. There is evidence of the condition of the bed, from which the jury could infer that the defendant and the girl had been lying on it together. The defendant was a full grown man, apparently between 30 and 40 years of age, and was married to another woman; and his wife was then living. The girl he was with was about 21 years old. Immediately after breaking into the room and seeing the defendant and the girl therein, the marshal arrested the defendant and read to him a warrant for his arrest on a charge of adultery with the same girl, which was alleged to have been committed some time prior thereto. There is no evidence that the defendant at any time made or attempted to make any explanation of his presence with the girl in said house at said time to the marshal, or that he said anything about it, or that he demanded or requested an explanation by the marshal of the marshal's conduct in breaking into said room where he and the girl were. There is no evidence showing who owned the house to which defendant took the girl, but evidently he had access to it.

[1] While evidence that the defendant had an opportunity to commit the offence is not sufficient to raise any presumption against him, much less to convict, when the evidence shows not only an opportunity to commit the offense but additional circumstances which the jury could justly find to be incapable of any reasonable explanation other than that the meeting which afforded the opportunity for the intercourse was for that purpose and that the defendant availed himself of the opportunity and had intercourse with the female, the question of his guilt should be submitted to the jury for them to determine under proper instructions.

[2] Could not the jury very justly and very properly find that the defendant's presence with the girl at the house at the time, as shown by the evidence, is incapable of any reasonable explanation other than that they were there for the purpose of having intercourse?

Could not the jury very justly and very properly find that the length of time they were together with each other, both undressed, in the dark room, and their proximity to the bed when the light was flashed on them, and other circumstantial evidence, as before stated, are incapable of any reasonable explanation other than that they had had intercourse at the time the room was entered by the marshal?

In the opinion of the court both these questions should be answered in the affirmative.

There are numerous cases in the reports, cited in the digests, in which the circumstances in evidence were not more convincing, nor less capable of reasonable explanation consistent with the innocence of the accused than the circumstances in evidence in this case, and the evidence was held by the court sufficient to warrant conviction.   It is unnecessary to review them.   It is sufficient to cite some of them: *Ramsey v. State,* 84 S. E. 984 (Ga.) ; *Cummins v. State,* 81 S. E. 366 (Ga.) ; *Commonwealth v. Mosier,* 135 Pa. St. 221, 19 Atl. 943; *State v. Schaedler,* 90 N. W. 91, 116 Iowa, 488.   For numerous other cases, see Dec. Dig., Adultery, Key number 14.

As to the second ground:

[3] The indictment not only alleges that the defendant was a married man and had a wife then living other than the woman with whom it charges he committed adultery, but it alleges that the wife's name was Wuai Kam Let. The witness who testified that he was present at the marriage of defendant to his wife, pronounced her name; but the court is unable to remember just how he pronounced it, and is unable to say whether there is any similarity between her name as pronounced by the witness and her name pronounced according to the way it is spelled in the indictment; but according to the view the court takes of the matter, it was unnecessary for the indictment to allege the name of the wife, and the allegation of it may and should be treated as surplusage; and if the evidence shows her name to be different from that alleged in the indictment, this does not constitute a material variance between the allegations and the proof because the allegation itself is unnecessary and immaterial.   The general rule is that

the proof must correspond with the allegations; and a material variance between the same is fatal; but the variance must be material and upon allegations of which proof is required. Unnecessary particularity in alleging facts which must be alleged sometimes imposes the burden of proving the particulars unnecessarily alleged; but it is unnecessary to prove facts which need not have been alleged even though they have been alleged with particularity. That the defendant was at the time of the alleged intercourse *a married man,* is a fact which it was necessary to allege. The name of his wife is another fact which it was unnecessary to allege; and the unnecessary allegation of it does not impose the burden of proving it; and a variance between the name alleged and that proved is immaterial.

The offense consists when committed by a married man with an unmarried woman, in having unlawful intercourse with her, not in being a married man, even though such intercourse would not be adultery if he were unmarried.

In order to inform the defendant fully of the accusation against him, so as to enable him to prepare his defense and be not taken by surprise, it is necessary to inform him of the name of the woman with whom he is charged with having had the unlawful intercourse, and to inform him of the fact that the prosecution proposes to prove that he was a married man at the time, and that the woman was not his wife. But what reason is there for informing him of the name of his wife? He is neither more nor less guilty or innocent, whatever his wife's name may be; and the allegation of her name in the indictment would not apprise him of anything charged against him, nor render more definite the charge against him. There are a number of cases reported in which the question has been before the court, and the authorities are abundant to sustain the proposition that the name of the defendant's wife need not be alleged or proved. One of the latest of such cases is *Bodkins v. State*, 172 S. W. 216, decided by the Court of Criminal Appeals of Texas, in which the indictment alleged the name of the defendant's wife, but defendant contended that the court's charge was erroneous, in that it only required the jury to find that the defendant was married to another person, and did not require them to find that he was married to Lillian Bodkins, alleged in the indictment to be his wife. The court said that the allegation of the name of the wife was wholly unnecessary and was properly treated as surplusage, and cited as authority *Collum v. State*, 10 Tex. App. 712. An examination of the *Collum* case, referred to, will show that the court held that the allegation of the name of the defendant's wife, was not a descriptive averment as to the subject of the crime, such as must be proved when unnecessarily pleaded. In *Reynolds v. United States*, 103 S. W. 762, decided by the Court of Appeals of the Indian Territory, on writ of error to the United States Court for the Western District of the Indian Territory, evidently the prosecution was for a violation of the very section of the Penal Code involved in this case. I think it is apparent from the report of the case that the indictment did not allege the name of the defendant's wife, though it is nowhere specifically stated that it did not. It was held sufficient.

The digests cite many cases in which the question has been more or less involved, and after examination of them, I am of the opinion that the allegation of the wife's name is unnecessary, and that when it is alleged the allegation should be treated as surplusage.

The motion to instruct the jury to render a verdict for defendant is denied.

Affirmed, Wong Goon Let v. United States, 245 Fed. 745.

IN THE MATTER OF THE APPLICATION OF ALFRED FLORES OCAMPO FOR NATURALIZATION.

December 30, 1916.

1. *Aliens—Naturalization:* Section 2169 of the Revised Statutes was not repealed by the Act of June 29th, 1906, "to establish a uniform rule of naturalization," etc.

2. *Same—Same:* Section 30 of the Act of June 29th, 1906, authorizes the naturalization of the class of persons specified therein by applying to them all the applicable provisions of the laws providing for the naturalization of aliens, and relieving them from the necessity of renouncing foreign allegiance.

3. *Same—Same:* That one does not come within the classes of persons designated in section 2169, does not make it *inapplicable* to him. It applies to and forbids his naturalization unless he does come within one of the classes specified.

4. *Same—Same:* It is no answer to say that the section applies to aliens, and that the applicant is not an alien. It is by virtue of the provisions of the laws for the naturalization of aliens, that he must be admitted, if at all.

5. *Same—Same:* Section 30 itself applies all the provisions of the naturalization law including section 2169 of the Revised Statutes to the persons specified therein.

6. *Same—Same—Filipinos:* A native of the Philippine Islands, of the Filipino race, being neither a white person nor of African nativity or descent, is not eligible to citizenship under our naturalization laws.

Naturalization: Hearing on petition.

Alfred Flores Ocampo, petitioner, *pro se.*

VAUGHAN, J. Alfred Flores Ocampo, a Filipino, born January 27, 1888, in the Philippine Islands, where he had lived prior to coming to Honolulu on November 14, 1907. seeks to be admitted to citizenship under section 30 of the Naturalization Act of June 29, 1906.

Is he eligible? Does the law authorize that he be admitted to citizenship? He may be admitted unless section 2169 of the Revised Statutes of 1878 applies in his case and forbids.

The decision of the question is not free from embarrassment. This court has held in the case of *Marcos Solis*, in an opinion rendered by Judge Clemons, for whose opinions the writer has great respect, "that under section 30 of the Act of June 29th, 1906, a Filipino, a native and citizen of the Philippine Islands, is eligible to citizenship in spite of the provision of Rev. Stat. sec. 2169, limiting naturalization to aliens who are free white persons or of African nativity or descent.

The opinion of Attorney General Bonaparte, given July 10th, 1908, and the opinion of Justice Gould, of the Supreme Court of the District of Columbia, in the *Lopez* case, are cited to support the decision of the court; and they certainly do sustain it as far as the authority of the precedent can. On the other hand directly the contrary has been held by Judge Thompson of the United States District Court for the eastern district of Pennsylvania in the *Alverto* case, 198 Fed. 688, which has been cited with approval and followed in a short opinion by Judge Hand, in the *Lampitoe* case, 232 Fed. 382.

Let us examine the question. The authority of the courts to grant citizenship to those who are not citizens of the United States, whether aliens or inhabitants of possessions subject to the sovereign jurisdiction of the United States, owing allegiance thereto, is derived from and limited by the provisions of the naturalization laws. From the passage of the first naturalization act down to 1870 our laws permitted none to be admitted to citizenship except "free white persons." See *in re Ah Yup*, 1 Fed. Cas. No. 104. In 1870 an Act was passed containing the following provision:

"That the naturalization laws are hereby extended to aliens of African nativity and to persons of African descent."

As was stated by Judge Sawyer in the *Ah Yup* case:

"At the time of the amendment, in 1870, extending the naturalization laws to the African race, Mr. Sumner made repeated and strenuous efforts to strike the word 'white' from the naturalization laws or to accomplish the same object by other language."

All his efforts to do so failed, and the words limiting the aliens admissible to citizenship to white persons remained in the law as from the beginning, and the amendment simply extended the privilege of admission to citizenship to those of African nativity or African descent.

As was said by Judge Ward in *United States v. Balsara*, 180 Fed. 694:

"The revisers of the laws of the United States whose revision was adopted at the first session of the Forty-third Congress, 1873 to 1874, reported (section 2169, title 30), on the subject of naturalization in the following words: 'The provisions of this title shall apply to aliens of African nativity and to persons of African descent.' As the revisers were not authorized to change the law, the omission of the words 'free white persons' was evidently an oversight and it was corrected by Act Feb. 18, 1875, c. 80, 18 Stat. 318, entitled, "An Act to correct errors and to supply omissions in the Revised Statutes of the United States' as follows: 'Sec. 2169 is amended by inserting in the first line after the words 'aliens' the words 'being free white persons and to aliens.' "

It will thus be seen that when from some cause the revisers omitted the words "free white persons," Congress restored them by express enactment, and as a result the Revised Statutes of 1878 contain under the title "Naturalization" the following:

"Section 2169. The provisions of this title shall apply to aliens being free white persons, and to aliens of African nativity and to persons of African descent."

The uniform construction given by the courts to section 2169 has been that it forbids the granting of citizenship to any except free white persons and to those of African descent or nativity. Numerous decisions have been rendered by the courts in which those who were not white persons nor of African descent nor of African nativity were denied citizenship. Those of Chinese, the Malay, the Japanese, the Indian and the Hawaiian races were denied on account of section 2169. Even the half white and half Indian, born in America, in British Columbia, was denied on account of that section.

As to the Chinese, see the following cases: *In re Ah Yup*, 1 Fed. Cas., No. 104 (1878); *In re Gee Hop*, 71 Fed. 274 (1895); *In re Po*, 28 N. Y. S. 383 (1894).

As to the Japanese, see: *In re Saito*, 62 Fed. 126, (1894); *In re Takuji Yamashita*, 30 Wash. 234, 70 Pac. 482, 59 L. R. A. 671 (1902).

As to the Hawaiian, see: *In re Kanaka Nian*, 6 Utah, 259, 21 Pac. 993, 4 L. R. A. 276 (1889).

As to the Indian, see: *In re Camille*, 6 Fed. 256 (1880); *In re Burton*, 1 Alaska, 111, (1900).

[1] On June 29, 1906, H. R. 15442, 34 Stat. 596, "An Act to provide for a uniform rule of Naturalization of Aliens throughout the United States, and to establish the Bureau of Naturalization," having passed both houses of Congress, was approved by the President and became a law, superseding all laws on the subject in conflict with it. Was section 2169 of the Statutes repealed by the Act? At the time it was passed the Congress was familiar, it must be presumed, with the effect of section 2169, and the construction given to it by the courts. All the opinions referred to in the foregoing had been published in the reports at the time. After a careful examination of the Congressional Record during the time the bill was before Congress, I have not found any mention of section 2169 or of the decisions relating thereto. It is not mentioned in the Act. Section 26 of the Act expressly repeals sections 2165, 2167, 2168 and 2173 of the Revised Statutes, and section 39 of

Chapter 1012 of the Statutes at Large for the year 1903, 32
Stat. 1222, "and all Acts and parts of Acts inconsistent with
or repugnant to the provisions of this Act."

As was said by Judge Goff, in *Bessho v. U. S.*, 178 Fed.
245:

"By this legislation, (referring to the Act of June 29,
1906), a new and complete system of naturalization was
adopted, all of the details of which together with the
method of procedure, and the courts having jurisdiction of
it, were set forth and designated and all Acts or parts of
Acts inconsistent with or repugnant to its provisions were
repealed. In section 26 of that Act is found an express
repeal of sections 2165, 2167, 2168 and 2173 of the Revised
Statutes. These repealed sections are all included in title
50 of said Revised Statutes, and demonstrate beyond doubt
that Congress carefully considered all the provisions of that
title and that it intended that the unrepealed sections
thereof should still remain in force. Among those unrepealed is section 2169, which we thus find to be virtually
re-enacted, and declared to be one of the rules under which
future naturalizations are to be conducted."

Evidently Congress did not consider section 2169 inconsistent with or repugnant to any of the provisions of the Act.
It repealed the sections immediately preceding it and one
a few numbers succeeding it, but left 2169; and was so
careful to be certain to repeal all Acts and parts of Acts inconsistent with or repugnant to the Act, that it used express words though it was unnecessary to do so.

In some cases the courts have expressly held that section
2169 was not repealed by the Act of June 29th, 1906, United
States v. Balsara, 180 Fed. 649, 103 C. C. A. 660; *Bessho
v. United States*, 178 Fed. 246, 101 C. C. A. 605. In others,
the question is not noticed, but the decisions assume that
it was not repealed. *In re Buntaro Kumagai*, 163 Fed.
922; *In re Knight*, 171 Fed. 299.

The effect of leaving section 2169 unrepealed was virtually to re-enact it, as is stated by the court in the *Bessho*

case, supra. So that the case stands as if the Act of June 29th, 1906, contained section 2169 as one of its provisions, declaring,

"The provisions of this Act shall apply to aliens being free white persons and to aliens of African nativity and to persons of African descent."

It is claimed, however, that section 2169 limits the naturalization of *aliens* to free white persons and to persons of African nativity or descent, and that it has no application to any persons except *aliens*; and that section 30 of the Act of June 29th, applies to a class of persons who are *not aliens,* and provides for their naturalization   That is true, but how does section 30 provide for the naturalization of this class of persons, which it authorizes?   By applying to such persons all the applicable provisions of the laws providing for the naturalization of aliens.

[2], [3], [4], [5] Is not section 2169 of the Revised Statutes an applicable provision of Naturalization laws? The very language of it makes it read itself into every provision of the naturalization laws.   None of the provisions of the naturalization laws apply to any except free white persons and those of African descent or nativity.

In the *Lopez* case Justice Gould said:

"But section 2169 is not applicable to petitioner.   He is not an alien nor is he of African nativity or descent."

He should have added, nor a white person.   But Justice Gould erred in holding that these facts made section 2169 inapplicable to the petitioner.   That one does not come within the classes of persons designated in section 2169, does not make it *inapplicable* to him.   It applies, and forbids his naturalization unless he does come within one of the classes therein specified.   It is no answer to say that the section applies *to aliens,* and that the petitioner is not an alien.   It is by virtue of the provisions of the laws made for the naturalization of aliens, into every one of which

by its very terms section 2169 reads itself, that the petitioner for naturalization, claiming to come within the class
of persons designated in section 30 of the Act of June 29th,
1906, must be admitted if at all. Section 30 itself applies
all the applicable provisions of the laws governing the naturalization of aliens to the class of persons whose naturalization it authorizes in the same manner as aliens except
that they are not required to renounce allegiance to any
foreign sovereignty, shall make their declarations of intention to become citizens of the United States at least two
years prior to admission, and their residence within the
jurisdiction owing allegiance to the United States is regarded as residence within the United States within the
meaning of the clause requiring five years' residence.

If section 2169 of the Revised Statutes does not limit the
class of persons authorized by section 30 of the Act of
June 29th, 1906, to be naturalized, then there is no limitation.   Those of the Chinese, the Japanese and the Malay,
as well as the Filipino races, "all persons not citizens who
owe permanent allegiance to the United States, and who
may become residents of any State or organized Territory
of the United States," may all come in and be naturalized
under section 30.

If section 30 takes the Filipino out of the operation of
section 2169, it takes out all other races.

Did Congress have any such purpose in the incorporation of that section in the Naturalization Act? I do not
think so.

Let us examine a little further into the matter.   The
Act of June 29th, 1906, was passed for the purpose of restricting rather than increasing naturalization.

The language of section 30 was not in the bill when it
was introduced nor when it passed the House.   It was put
in by an amendment offered by Senator Foraker, who said
at the time:

"I offer this amendment which simply provides that when a Porto Rican comes to the United States he may stand equally as favorable before the naturalization laws of the United States as the Spaniard or any other alien, and may become a citizen of the United States.   The thing that stands in his way now is that he has no allegiance to any foreign potentate or power to renounce, and this simply opens to him a way to become a citizen if he comes here."   See Congressional Record 59th Congress, 1st Session, vol. 40, part 10, page 9360.

It is evident that such was the sole purpose of the amendment which became section 30 in the Act.   It reads as follows:

"Sec. 30.   That all the applicable provisions of the naturalization laws of the United States shall apply to and be held to authorize the admission to citizenship of *all persons not citizens* who owe permanent allegiance to the United States, and who may become residents of any State or organized Territory of the United States, with the following modifications: The applicant shall not be required to renounce allegiance to any foreign sovereignty; he shall make his declaration of intention to become a citizen of the United States at least two years prior to his admission; and residence within the jurisdiction of the United States, owning such permanent allegiance, shall be regarded as residence within the United States within the meaning of the five years' residence clause of the existing law."

There was but little discussion upon the amendment, which was agreed to without objection.   And the bill was further amended by inserting the words, "and Porto Rico" after Alaska in the section conferring jurisdiction on courts, so as to confer jurisdiction on the United States District Courts in Porto Rico as well as those of the other Territories, to grant naturalization, the author of this last amendment, Senator Mallory, of Florida, saying at the time, that he would not go so far as to exclude the courts of the Philippine Islands.   Can it be doubted that if there had been any effort to repeal section 2169 or to make it inapplicable to the class of persons authorized by section 30 to be naturalized, there would have been opposition and discussion?

[6] Does the section provide for the naturalization of persons who owe permanent allegiance to the United States or persons who do not owe such permanent allegiance? It reads, "all persons not citizens who owe permanent allegiance to the United States." The language has been construed to mean persons *who owe permanent allegiance to the United States, who are not citizens;* and the clause, "owing such permanent allegiance," in the last sentence of the section, and other circumstances support such construction. Do the citizens of the Philippine Islands owe *permanent* allegiance to the United States? It is unnecessary to go into the discussion of the question   I do not question in the least the correctness of the decisions of the Supreme Court of the United States thereon. But, if the citizens of the Philippine Islands come within the meaning of the words "persons not citizens who owe permanent allegiance to the United States," in my opinion section 30 does not authorize the naturalization of any of them except those who are free white persons or of African nativity or descent, because section 2169 of the Statutes forbids.

Congress has passed various Acts providing for the naturalization of various classes of persons, those who have served in the Navy and Army, and the Marine Corps; and in every instance where the question has been before the courts, it has been held that section 2169 was a limitation upon the class of persons provided for. *Bessho v. U. S.*, 178 Fed. 245; *In re Knight*, 171 Fed. 299; *In re Buntaro Kumagai*, 163 Fed. 922. With this fact in mind it is all the more evident, as was said by Judge Thompson, in the *Alverto* case, supra, "If Congress had not intended its provisions (section 2169) to apply to section 30 of the Act of 1906, such intention would naturally appear in the Act."

There is nothing in section 2169 of the Statutes incon
sistent with or repugnant to section 30 of the Act; and th
latter section can be construed in harmony with the for
mer, and it should therefore be so construed.   I am there
fore of the opinion that section 30 does not authorize th
naturalization of any of the class of persons specified ther
in unless they are free white persons or of African nativit
or descent.

The petitioner does not come within the classes of per
sons designated and his application is denied.

Contra: In re Solis, ante, p. 686; *In re Bautista,* 245 Fed
765 (Morrow, J.).   As to reversal of earlier decisions o
same court, see *United States v. Hoshi,* 3 U. S. Dist. Ct
Haw. 439 (Woodruff, J.), *United States v. Ishibashyi, Id.*
517 (Robertson, J.).

APPENDIX

IN THE MATTER OF THE REPORT OF THE GRAND JURY FOR THE APRIL, 1911, TERM.

July 31, 1911.

1. *Grand Jury—Reports by, proper limits of—Secrecy:* It is improper, and a breach of the oath of secrecy, for a grand jury in a report of its doings, to comment on the failure of a person under its investigation to take the stand and testify in explanation of his alleged misconduct

2. *Same—Same—Comment on matters beyond jurisdiction:* It is, also, not within the just powers of a grand jury of this Federal court to make adverse comments on anybody's qualifications, moral or otherwise, for an office held by him under a distinct department, the department of education of the Hawaiian Territorial government, in no way within the court's jurisdiction,—even though that person be under investigation by the grand jury.

Grand Jury Report: Motion to expunge.

Lorrin Andrews and *LeBlonde & Smith* for movant.

CLEMONS, J. (Memorandum). The grand jury for the April, 1911, term of this court, in a partial report of their actions filed herein on May 15, 1911, said among other things:

"By means of the public press, and through general discussion, our attention was called to certain matters connected with the Hilo High School. The information was so public and general in its nature that we concluded it merited notice from us, if any law of the United States—as was intimated—had been violated by certain persons. The matter was of further interest, inasmuch as it involved the administration of the schools of the Territory. We therefore determined to make as complete investigation as possible concerning the charge of a violation of the laws of the United States alleged to have taken place, and for this purpose had before us numerous witnesses whose testimony might throw any light on the question.

"We beg leave at this time, to make a report thereon. In

making this report we have taken into consideration the
charge of your Honor, that in performing our duties, we
should find no indictments unless reasonably satisfied that
a trial jury, on the evidence heard by us, would probably
convict. With that charge in view we have returned no indictments. Nevertheless, the matter has been of so great
public interest, that we feel constrained to make this report
thereon. We are not unmindful of the charge of your Honor
to the effect that no mention should be made of cases investigated by us wherein no prior legal charge has been entered unless indictments are returned, and that proceedings
before the Grand Jury and actions taken by the Grand
Jury, where no indictments are returned, should be kept
secret. That the investigation in question has been going
on, however, has been well known, and by making a report
of the same we feel that we do not, at least in spirit, go
contrary to your Honor's instructions relative to secrecy.

"The conduct and actions of . . [a certain teacher]
of the Hilo High School [naming him] were investigated by
us. When considerable testimony had been received relative thereto, we felt that in fairness to [him] . . he should,
if he wished, be given ample opportunity to explain what
might, without explanation, appear to us to have been incriminating evidence. He was brought before us, with his
attorney, and it was stated to him that his conduct was being investigated; that certain witnesses had testified concerning that conduct; and that if he desired, we would be
glad to hear anything he might have to say, which would
tend to explain what witnesses had testified to. After consulting with his attorney . . [he] stated that he did not
desire to testify or make any statement whatsoever. We
were therefore left, as to his conduct, with the uncontradicted statements of several witnesses relative to his actions. While we are loath to say it, and while we do not
think the evidence would justify a verdict of guilty of a
violation of the United States statutes, yet we are of the
opinion, from the evidence elicited by us, that [he] . .
has conducted himself in a very questionable and immoral
manner, which renders him, in our opinion, unfit to act as a
teacher of children.

"The conduct of . . [a certain woman teacher, naming
her] was also investigated by us, in connection with the

matter, and we are of the opinion that the testimony given by this witness was in no way shaken or shown in the slightest degree to be untruthful."

Thereupon this gentleman, by his attorneys, moved to expunge from the partial report the above-quoted paragraphs relating to him, on the following grounds:

"1· That the said portion of the said report violated the charge of the presiding Judge of this Court to the said Grand Jury, whereby the said Grand Jury was directed that no mention should be made of cases investigated wherein no prior legal charge had been entered unless indictment should be returned, and that proceedings before the Grand Jury and action taken by the Grand Jury where no indictments are returned, should be kept secret.

"2· That the Grand Jury was without authority to comment upon the character or morality of any person investigated by it in cases wherein no indictment was found, and was therefore without authority to comment upon the character or morality of this movant in the said report.

"3· That the said Grand Jury was without authority to report upon the fitness or unfitness of any Territorial employee to occupy his position or to take any action relative to such employee, except to determine whether or not said employee had violated a Federal statute.

"4· That the said Grand Jury was without authority to disclose whether or not this movant appeared before that body or submitted himself to an examination thereby, or to disclose what effects, if any, such failures to appear had upon the deliberation and decision of that body.

"5· That the statement made in the above mentioned passage, that 'while we do not think the evidence would justify a verdict of guilty of a violation of the United States statutes, from the evidence elicited by us, that . . the person in question has conducted himself in a very questionable and immoral manner, which renders him, in our opinion, unfit to act as a teacher of children,' is an ambiguous and unwarranted reflection upon the character of this movant by a body holding its investigation in secret, and whose grounds for such reflection neither this movant nor the public have any means of learning.

"6. That the said portion of the said report is scandalous, impertinent, unprivileged, and libelous *per se.*"

And he moved also to expunge the last paragraph of the report above quoted relating to the woman under investigation, on the grounds following:

"1. That the said portion of the said report constitutes a violation of the charge of this Court as to comment and secrecy.

"2· That it is an unauthorized comment upon the evidence of a witness who gave testimony before said Grand Jury against this movant.

"3· That it is unfair and prejudicial to this movant as comment upon the statements of a witness, whose evidence neither this movant nor the public have any means of knowing."

Inasmuch as the motion was heard *ex parte,* the 'district attorney not deeming his office called upon to make any appearance, and with no opportunity for the grand jury to defend or even state its position, it seemed fair to call the grand jurors in, as the court did, on their return from the intervening adjournment and, before ruling on the motion, discuss with them the whole matter, instruct them as to the law of the case, meet their objections, if any, and leave the matter in their hands with the expectation that they would take such action as accorded with the court's instructions. To them, therefore, the court stated the fact of the filing of this motion and the grounds thereof, and read the following from Edwards on the Grand Jury, 157-160, as applying to the questions raised by the motion:

[1] "When the grand jurors have completed all the duties which will devolve upon them, it is now customary for them to prepare a written report of their work, which is signed by their foreman and handed to the court crier with the indictments. In this report they frequently take occasion to discuss various matters affecting the public welfare, criticise public officials, act as censors of the morals of the com-

munity, and make recommendations which it is impracticable and impossible to carry into effect. That they are acting outside of their duties as grand jurors in making such presentments will hardly be doubted. As the official accuser for the government, their duty is to present persons not things.   That this practice should be continued upon the ground that it calls to the public eye abuses in the administration of government or the existence of vice in the community, is a proposition which rests upon no logical basis. If they have any evidence of the things which they thus set forth, it is their duty to the public and to themselves under their oath, to present the individuals guilty of such offenses. See Judge Stowe's *Charge to Grand Jury*, 3 Pitts. Rep. (Pa.) 179. If they have no personal knowledge of the facts, they are then proceeding in a manner contrary to law. *Case of Lloyd and Carpenter*, 3 Clark (Pa.) 188. If they know the things which they present, they should present individuals; if they do not know, they are committing a wrong in making broad accusations, which, while they cannot be sustained, grievously injure those to whom they indirectly apply.

"This practice received severe condemnation over seventy years ago at the hands of Honorable Daniel Davis then Attorney-General for the State of Massachusetts, who says: 'The practice, not uncommon in some parts of the United States, of bringing forward, in the form of presentments, what are denominated public grievances, relative to the political or moral state of the country, is altogether extra-official, and may be and has been adopted and pursued for purposes foreign to, and inconsistent with, the nature of the institution; and perhaps it is not too much to assert, that the opportunity has been used and perverted to party purposes, and with an intent to produce an effect upon public measures and the public mind. Whenever this shall be the case it is to be considered in the same light as any other usurpation or abuse of the judicial authority. It may, with the same propriety, be exercised by any other branch of the judicial power, by the court, or the traverse jury, as well as the grand jury.'   Precedents of Indictments, 11.

"In the case of *Rector v. Smith*, 11 Iowa 302, the grand jury made a written report to the court wherein libellous statements were made relating to the conduct of a person then in public office. An action for libel was begun against the clerk of the grand jury who had brought the report into court and there read it. An answer was filed by the defendant, who claimed the report was a privileged communication, to which answer the plaintiff demurred but the demurrer was overruled by the lower court. On appeal, the Supreme Court affirmed the judgment and expressly ruled that the report was not a privileged communication. In delivering the opinion of the court, Baldwin J., says:

" 'The grand jury have no power, nor is it their privilege or duty to present any person for a criminal offense except by indictment. If the misconduct of an officer does not amount to a crime, and is not of such magnitude as will justify the jury in finding an indictment, their powers over the offense complained of, are at an end . . . A report by a grand jury presents nothing upon which the court can act, unless it is in reference to the condition of the prison. The court can take no jurisdiction over the complaint charged by such report. Nor can a person thus presented have an opportunity to show himself innocent of the matters complained of. With this view of the question we conclude that the report presented by the defendant as a juror, was not a privileged communication and that he cannot plead this in bar of plaintiff's right to recover.'

"When the grand jury in their presentment thus go beyond their lawful authority, whether they refer to persons by name, title, or innuendo, or to any particular matter or thing, it becomes a serious question whether or not their presentment should be permitted to stand. Clearly in such instance they have exceeded their authority, and in such event their presentment rests upon no legal foundation. There would consequently seem to be no valid reason why a motion to quash or dismiss the presentment, or strike it, or the objectionable part thereof, from the files should not be made. If the grand jurors have exceeded their authority in making such presentment, it is clearly invalid and illegal and may be subjected to attack either by the attorney for the state or by the person or persons to whom the presentment may relate, in the same manner as any presentment or indictment may be attacked. This course has been pursued in George (*Presentment of Grand Jury*, 1 R. M., Charlt. 149) where the grand jury made a presentment reflecting upon the judges of the Superior Court. The attorney-general moved to expunge the presentment from the minutes which was accordingly done."

Quotations were also then read from *Rector v. Smith*, 11 Iowa, 302, 307, and *In re Jones*, 92 N. Y. Supp. 275, 278, 279, dissent (An appeal in this case was dismissed as unauthorized, 74 N. E. 226). See *In re Gardiner*, 64 N. Y. Supp. 760, 762, holding a report may be improper but still beyond the court's control, a proposition with which this court does not agree. See Edwards, Grand Jury, 163-165, and notes; *State v. Cowan*, 38 Tenn. (1 Head) 280, 281. A valuable opinion of Justice Goff, which came to hand later, follows the dissent in the *Jones* case, supra: *In re Osborne*, 125 N. Y. Supp. 313, 315-319; though it is recognized as arguable that the New York cases might, though they do not seem to, have been influenced by statute. Id. 318-319; *In re Heffernan*, Id. 737, 738.

It was clear that under these authorities the court regarded the motion as well taken, and the jury was dismissed with the assurance that there would be no ruling on the motion until they had had an opportunity to consider the court's suggestion. It soon became apparent that the jury, if not reluctant to act in the matter, were at least uncertain as to how they should or could act. They felt, as several of the jurymen said, that the report was nothing more than what the public was expecting, almost demanding from them, that they had acted in good faith, and most of all that the report was true, and the facts the common knowledge of the community,—that, while the court was right as to the law, they were right as to the facts and that to amend the report by striking that part to which exception had been taken would be to take back what they had said and admit their error of fact. How could they so stultify themselves?

The question of one juror, even, asked in open court at the time of the court's informal charge or discussion, was whether such a retraction would not place the members of the jury in a position of liability to the person whose acts had been under investigation,—in reply to which, it may be said, he was referred to the Iowa decision, supra, at page 308.

The court quite appreciated the jury's position; and the difficulty presented by their attitude then appeared insurmountable. But it seemed best not to be in haste to take the next logical step of expunging the objectionable matter from the report, or the extreme measure of giving the grand jury a dishonorable discharge; and they were excused until the following morning, without final action on the motion. The court then met the jury again, feeling that possibly they had not understood, or fully appreciated the law as before given, according to which their action was, as had been intimated, without authority and a breach of their duty, and the strongest case supposable was put to them, in an endeavor to make clear by a simple illustration the error of their action, and, also, by way of meeting the objections, to show them that even any demand of the public for a report, or even any good that the report may have done, was quite immaterial, except, perhaps, as bearing on their fair, if not well advised, motives and to assure them that the court was not asking them to say "Our report is untrue,—we take it back because it is untrue," but was instructing them that it was right and proper to take it back because it was unauthorized,—because it was no part of their duty, but an abuse of their powers, to make such a report.

It may be said that the court also in the instructions of the day previous had, in passing, told the jury that their report might be taken as a breach of their obligation of secrecy. They had, it is true, as introductory to their report on this matter, stated that the facts were of such notoriety as to make any reference to them no abuse of confidence, but it must be repeated, as was merely suggested to the grand jury, that they should be on their guard against the slightest disclosure of what has taken place before them as a body, and that the only safe course is to preserve absolute secrecy, irrespective of whether the matter is one of notoriety, or not. In one regard, however, the jury did violate their oath of secrecy; the fact of the movant's having refused to take the stand was not notorious and in any event should not have been divulged. It was his constitutional right not to testify and, most certainly his assertion of such constitutional right should not be made the basis of unfavorable comment or inference by a body which is an impartial instrument in the working out of justice under the Constitution. It is no more becoming for a grand jury, than for a petit jury, or counsel in arguing to a jury, or a judge in instructing a jury, to so comment on a defendant's assertion of his constitutional rights.

[2]   The extreme suppositious case which was put to the grand jury at this second meeting, in order to make clear their breach of duty, was, in substance, this:

"Suppose you were a trial jury and, in trying the person now concerned for the same alleged offense as was under investigation here, returned a verdict as follows: 'We, the jury find the defendant not guilty. However, for the good of the public school service (the alleged offender being a school teacher), and also because the people are demanding it, we here state our opinion that there was evidence against the accused which showed him to be an improper person to have charge of school children. He had an opportunity to answer the complaints against him, but he availed hmself of his constitutional right to refuse to testify.' We may suppose that the effect of this extraordinary verdict was good, that it stirred some tardy executives to do their duty (This is only an illustration, not an implication of dereliction of any executive), that there was a clamor for somebody to take some action and that as you were sitting at the time, the appeal was directed particularly to you; even granted your perfect good faith and a worthy end, still, what only could the court do? The matter would call clearly for the removal somehow of this irrelevant, unauthorized statement from the record. . . As the opinion cited yesterday, of the New York judge, well said, we test a law not by what has been done under it but by what may be done under it. *In re Jones*, 92 N. Y. Supp. 278. It is dangerous for public bodies or officers to go outside of their powers, even to do good. Who is to be the judge? This is not a question of worthy motives or good faith, or of the good your report actually did, or of any public demand to which the report may have been a response. It is a question of law and of rights under it. We must regard the constitutional rights of every person under investigation or accused of crime,—accused rightfully, it may be, but entitled to the benefit of the constitutional guaranty of a trial by a properly constituted body, and of the constitutional guaranty that he shall not be compelled to testify against himself, or at the behest of his accusers, or even to take the stand at all against his free, voluntary consent."

The grand jury, immediately upon their then ensuing session, withdrew the report in question and presented a substitute report as follows (omitting the introductory paragraph, which is the same as that of the original report):

"While the investigation disclosed to our satisfaction that affairs in the Hilo High School were not in a satisfactory condition, yet there was not evidence before us sufficient to return any indictments against any persons whose actions were investigated by us."

In addition to what was said to the grand jury in the court's special charges set forth above, it may be pointed out that the matter on which the body reported, to-wit, the fitness or unfitness of this school teacher as an educator of children, was one over which the court had no jurisdiction, but a matter wholly within the cognizance of the Hawaiian Territorial government. Suppose the grand jury were investigating the Mayor of Honolulu on an unfounded charge of opium smuggling, but incidentally discovered him to be without the essential mental or moral qualifications for the office, would they not be exhibiting officiousness, and going out of bounds, to report that, though the particular charge be not sustained, they take occasion to say the accused is not a fit person to be Mayor?" Where would the precedent of such criticism, though prefaced as was the report in this case by a gentle apology for its publication, lead the grand jury,—a body of great powers but still of powers exercisable within narrow limits? See *Hale v. Henkel*, 201 U. S. 43, 64, quoted post.

The particular case, because of its alleged flagrancy, may seem to be one which we should be slow to say did not call for a report, but the principle controlling it is clear enough, against such exercise of power. That the foregoing examples of possible abuse are not extreme may be seen in the history of the grand jury in New York county. "Mayor Gaynor, a high legal authority, is one of those who hold it is not any part of the business of a grand jury, ... [though] instructed to do so by a judge on the bench, to bring in [even] presentments, so-called, criticising or dealing with the conduct of the city government, or indeed, relative to any other subjects than indictments founded on ascertained violations of the law." Brooklyn Standard-Union, 1911. See at length *In re Osborne*, *supra* and *In re Heffernan*, supra.

"That the powers of the body are inquisitorial to a certain extent is undeniable; yet they have to be exercised within well defined limits." *Hale v. Henkel*, 201 U. S. 43, 64, quoting *In re Lester*, 77 Ga. 143.

In view of the action of the grand jury in following the law as laid down by the court, no necessity remains for any order on the motion to expunge. The court appreciates this attitude of the grand jurors, and would have regretted exceedingly any possible necessity of discharging with dishonor a body which rendered such valuable services as this particular jury.   Its report, so far as it relates to the matter of conditions on the immigrant ship "Orteric" in alleged violation of the Passenger Act, 22 Stat. 186 [see the case of *United States v. Findley*, ante, p. 166] was distinctly within its domain, and, in contrast with its observations in the matter of the Hilo High School, stands as an example of the exercise of its just powers.

———

For a similar view, not officially reported, of the United States District Court for the Northern District of California, Van Fleet, J., see San Francisco Chronicle, August 9, 1913; see also opinion of Heen, J., First Circuit Court, Territory of Hawaii, reported in Honolulu Star-Bulletin, January 3, 1918, Pacific Commercial Advertiser, January 4, 1918.

RULES

OF THE

United States District Court

FOR THE

TERRITORY OF HAWAII

Adopted as compiled January 31, 1918, based on Compiled
Rules of May 5, 1902, as amended.

1.

The title of this court shall be: "UNITED STATES DIS-
TRICT COURT FOR THE TERRITORY OF HAWAII."

2.

A. All officers and persons in the court room shall rise
and remain standing while the marshal or bailiff is making
proclamation at the opening and closing sessions of the
court. It is the duty of the officer making the proclamation
to strictly enforce the observance of this rule.

B. When the oath of citizenship is being administered
to any applicant for naturalization, all persons in the court
room, including the officers of the court, shall rise and remain standing until the applicant has been sworn in as a
citizen of the United States.

CALENDAR RULES.

3.

A.　Before the first day of every stated term, the clerk shall prepare two calendars, one for the use of the court, and the other for the use of the bar.　Such calendars shall contain the titles of the causes, the names of proctors or attorneys, and the dates of issue.

B.　Causes called on the day calendar during the first ten days of the term may for cause shown be at once set down for a later day in the term, or marked off the term by the court.　Such causes shall be put on the day calendar for the next term in order, after the causes on the last day's calendar not disposed of.

C.　The following causes shall be preferred:

1.　Where the property shall be in the actual custody of the marshal;

2.　For seaman's wages;

3.　Where all the testimony has been taken out of court.

D.　Monday shall be the law and motion day of this court, when all such matters will be heard at the hour of 10 o'clock a. m. subject to the order of the court.

E.　In all possessory actions, the process shall be made returnable on Friday of the week after the filing of the libel, unless otherwise ordered by the judge.　In such actions, the answer will be required to be filed upon return of the process duly served, and a day of hearing will then be fixed unless otherwise ordered for cause shown.　Notice by publication will not be required in possessory actions unless specially ordered.

F. When an answer is filed to the libel in open court on the return of process, either party may have the cause placed upon the calendar *instanter* for hearing in its order, without further notice.

G. In summary cases under rule 98 on the return of process in open court, duly served, the cause may be put *instanter* upon the calendar, and either party, without other notice, may proceed therein to proofs and hearing; and the party obtaining a continuance of the cause, if *in rem*, shall bear all expenses taxed for keeping the thing attached until the final hearing. In such a cause a fee shall not be taxed for more than one witness to prove the same facts, unless it appears that the witness was impeached or his testimony contradicted.

H. When an answer is required, in a suit *in rem*, of a party having no interest in the subject matter, he may file an exceptive allegation or disclaimer, and notice the same *instanter* for hearing. If the decree of the court is in affirmance of his plea, he shall be discharged the action.

I. In case of seizure of property in behalf of the United States, an appraisement for the purpose of bonding the same may be had by any party in interest, on giving one day's previous notice of motion before the court, or the judge in vacation, for the appointment of appraisers. If the parties or their proctors and the district attorney are present in court, such motion may be made *instanter*, after seizure, and without previous notice.

J. All questions certified by the referee in bankruptcy to a judge of this court for his opinion, shall be placed on the calendar for argument, and heard and submitted to the court for decision at the opening of the court on the first Monday after the filing of the certificate with the clerk, unless otherwise ordered by the court.

K. The defendant may before filing his answer except to the jurisdiction or to the sufficiency of the libel, and if the exception is sustained and the libel is not amended within such time as the court shall allow, it shall be dismissed.

Exception to the libel or answer may be heard at any time upon one day's notice.

L. Exceptions to the answer shall be taken within two days after notice of the filing of same, which exceptions shall briefly specify the parts excepted to or the grounds of exception, whereupon the party answering or claiming shall in two days either give notice of his submitting to the exceptions, or set down the exceptions for hearing and give one day's notice thereof. In default whereof the like order may be entered as if the exceptions had been allowed by the court.

M. Cases which have been pending in this court for more than one year without any proceeding having been taken therein may be dismissed as of course, for want of prosecution, by the court on its own motion at a call of the calendar. Such cases may also be dismissed for want of prosecution at any time on motion by any party upon notice to parties adversely interested or their attorneys. This rule is not to be construed as a limitation upon the exercise of the power of dismissal for want of prosecution in cases in which it is now permissible according to the practice and other rules. (Adopted Jan. 24, 1918.)

GENERAL AND MISCELLANEOUS RULES.

4

In common law causes all original and final process issued in conformity with section 911 of the United States Revised Statutes, shall be served by the marshal, or by his deputy, except when he is a party.

5.

In common law causes the parties shall be entitled to the same rights and remedies as respects attachments against the property of the defendant, and as respects proceedings supplementary to execution as are now provided by the laws of the Territory of Hawaii in common law causes, which laws in respect to attachments and supplementary proceedings are hereby adopted by this court.

6.

On an indictment found by the grand jury, the district attorney may forthwith sue out a bench warrant, capias, or attachment, under the seal of the court, for the arrest and commitment of the party indicted; such writ may also issue, if the defendant fails to appear pursuant to his recognizance given after indictment found; and also upon information duly filed by the district attorney.

7.

When a fine is imposed by the court on any person for any cause other than upon a judgment or sentence in a penal cause, and the party is not thereupon committed, and such fine is not discharged previous to the close of the term, the clerk on application of the United States attorney shall issue to the marshal a warrant of execution, commanding him to levy and make such fine of the goods and chattels, or in default thereof of the lands and tenements of the party. Such fine may, on application by the party, and sufficient cause shown, before payment of the same out of the court, into the treasury or otherwise, be mitigated or remitted, at any term succeeding that in which it was imposed.

8.

The amount of all the fines imposed and collected shall be paid into court, to be accounted for by the clerk with the United States treasury.

9.

In cases where the collector of customs is entitled to receive the moneys in court, the same, after deducting the costs, shall be paid him by the clerk; upon an order to be entered of course for that purpose.

10.

Special bail may be put in and filed, for the purpose of surrendering the principal, before the return day of the writ. Bail to the arrest may surrender the principal, or he may surrender himself in their exoneration, upon the bail bond given on his arrest. Copies of the bail bond, certified by the marshal or his deputy, may be used for that purpose, in the same manner as certified copies of the bail piece.

11

In no case shall the marshal or his deputies or any attorney or proctor of this court be surety in any suit depending therein; except that a proctor or attorney may in the first instance be surety on the stipulation for costs; but if objected to, other security shall be furnished.

12.

Upon the commencement of any action the moving party shall advance twenty dollars at least for costs of the clerk and marshal. The adverse party or parties shall each advance ten dollars at least, on entering their first appearance or filing for the first time any answer or other paper.

13.

Parties shall promptly furnish to the adverse parties or their attorneys or proctors of record copies of all papers and briefs filed by them in court or with the judge.

13 a.

In cases tried without a jury, briefs shall be filed on both sides at or before the argument, unless otherwise ordered by the court.

14.

Court files shall not be withdrawn from the office of the clerk by parties or their attorneys or proctors save for use in court or in chambers, unless written authority therefor be given by the judge.

15.

Process in actions or causes not otherwise provided for shall be made returnable twenty days after service unless otherwise ordered by the court or judge. Answer will be required to be filed upon the return of the process duly served, and a day of hearing will then be fixed unless otherwise ordered for cause shown.

16.

All motions shall be in writing and filed with the clerk, and, when grounded on facts, shall be verified by affidavit.

17.

The Christian names of all persons shall be written in full in all pleadings and papers filed in court.

18.

All papers, not otherwise provided for by law, shall be filed, and shall be plainly and fairly engrossed without erasures or interlineations materially defacing them. If papers not conforming to this rule are offered, the clerk before receiving them shall require the *allocatur* of the judge to be endorsed thereon.

19.

In all actions, suits and proceedings in this court which are commenced by the filing of a verified complaint, whether a verified complaint be required by the rules of this court or not, it shall be the duty of the opposing party to verify his answer or other pleading in bar.

20.

In all civil actions tried by a jury, where the United States is not a party, each party shall deposit with the clerk of the court $36, being the amount of the fees of the jury for each day; upon the finding of the verdict, the party in whose favor said verdict shall be found, shall, through the clerk, pay the fees of the jury, and shall tax said fees in his cost bill as costs against the losing party. The funds deposited by the losing party shall upon the coming in of the verdict be returned to him by the clerk. (As amended Oct. 13, 1902).

21.

The transcript of the testimony and exceptions on appeal or writ of error in any cause, shall be submitted to opposing counsel for correction and approval; and if the counsel on both sides fail to agree upon and settle the testimony and exceptions within a reasonable time, the same shall be settled by the court. As soon as the record, evidence and exceptions are agreed upon or settled, they shall be filed forthwith in the office of the clerk of this court from which office they shall not be removed for any purpose except on the order of the court.

22.

No papers or motions of any character shall be filed in this court in any matter or proceeding on appeal or error, nor will any matter or thing with reference thereto be heard or passed upon by the court, until the transcript of the evidence in the case is duly filed in the office of the clerk.

23.

' The clerk is authorized to enter satisfaction of record of any judgment on behalf of the United States on filing acknowledgment of satisfaction thereof by the United States attorney; in other cases, upon filing due acknowledgment of satisfaction made by the judgment creditor or his proctor or proctors, within two years from the entry of the judgment, and thereafter upon acknowledgment made by the judgment creditor or by his legal representatives or assigns with evidence of their representative authority.

24.

The clerk is authorized to tax or certify bills of costs, and to sign judgments, and also take acknowledgments of the satisfaction of judgments, and all affidavits and oaths out of court, as in open court, in all cases where the same are required by law to be taken in open court.

25.

The deputies (or chief clerks) of the clerk, not exceeding two in number, named and designated by an appointment filed in the office of said clerk, are each authorized to perform all duties appertaining to the clerk which are not required by law to be performed by the clerk in person.

26.

The clerk shall provide a book in which he shall keep a full and particular account, in each cause depending in the court, of all moneys brought into court, and of the payment of the same, with the dates thereof; and any particular account therein shall be open to the inspection of any person interested in the same.

27.

All bills of costs and of charges to be paid under any order or decree of this court shall be taxed and filed with the clerk before payment thereof; and. if the same shall include charges for disbursements other than to the officers of the court, the proper and genuine vouchers, or an affidavit thereof (in case of loss of vouchers), shall be exhibited and filed; and, if such bill shall be taxed without two days' notice to all parties concerned, it shall be subject to a retaxation, of course, on application by any such party not having had notice, and at the charge of the party obtaining such taxation. The clerk's costs of entering satisfaction of judgment and issuing execution may be taxed as a disbursement. The costs shall in all cases be taxed as aforesaid within ten days after the rendition of the judgment, decree or decision; otherwise the clerk shall tax the same and enter the amount in the order, judgment or decree.

Any party aggrieved by taxation of costs or the exaction of fees by an officer whose office is in the same building with the court, may apply to the court for relief *instanter,* upon notice to the adverse party and to the officer taxing the costs or exacting the fees.

DRAWING AND EMPANELLING JURIES.

28.

A. The clerk of said court shall, at such time or times as may be designated by order of the court, draw, in the presence of a judge of said court, from the box containing the names of the persons originally selected for jury duty, the names of such a number of persons as the court may by order designate to serve as grand jurors, and also the names of such a number of persons as the court may by order designate to serve as petit jurors. The regularity of such drawing shall be certified to by the judge and clerk. Nothing in these rules or in this paragraph shall be construed to prevent the drawing either of the names of grand jurors, or of the names of the petit jurors; nor shall anything in these rules or in this paragraph be construed to prevent the drawing of such jurors, whether grand or petit, either for the existing or the next succeeding term.

As to drawing from part of district, see United States v. Standard Oil Co., 170 Fed. 988.

B. If the name of any person is drawn from said original box who is deceased or insane, or who may have permanently removed from the Territory of Hawaii, or who may have become exempt or incapable for any reason to serve as juror, and the fact shall be made to appear to the satisfaction of the judge, the name of such person shall be omitted from the list of jurors, and the slip of paper having such name on it shall be destroyed, and another juror drawn in his place, and the fact shall be set forth in the said certificate. If the person whose name is drawn resides at a point so remote from the place of holding court as to render it impracticable, in the opinion of the judge, to summon him to attend the forthcoming term of court, the slip containing his name shall be put into a separate place to be kept during such term of court, and at the end of the term it shall be replaced in the said original box. The fact of finding it impracticable to summon such person shall be set forth in the said certificate. The said certificate shall be copied in full in the minutes of the court as of the first day of the regular or special term for which said jurors are drawn.

C. The clerk shall, within twenty-four hours after such drawing, deliver to the marshal of the district a venire containing the names of the jurors so drawn, in order that they may be duly summoned to attend the court.

D. Every grand jury impaneled before this court shall consist of not less than sixteen nor more than twenty-three persons. If of the persons summoned less than sixteen attend, they shall be placed on the grand jury, and the marshal shall, under the court's order, summon, either immediately or for a day fixed, from the body of the district,

and not from the bystanders, a sufficient number of persons
to complete the grand jury. And whenever a challenge to a
grand juror is allowed, and there are not in attendance other
jurors sufficient to complete the grand jury, the marshal
shall, under a like order, summon a sufficient number of
persons for that purpose.—Judicial Code, sec. 282.

United States v. Eagan, 30 Fed. 608, 609 (Brewer, J.), 611 (Thayer,
J.); United States v. Lewis, 192 Fed. 633, 640; United States v.
Mitchell, 136 Fed. 896; Wolfson v. United States, 101 Fed. 430, 432;
United States v. Nevin, 199 Fed. 831, 834, 834-836; United States v.
Breeding, 207 Fed. 645-653; Id. 650; Stockslager v. United States,
116 Fed. 590-596, special terms of court; Id., 596, drawing in vacation
instead of in open court. People v. Sehorn, 48 Pac. 495, 497 (Cal.);
State v. Rockwell, 48 N. W. 721, 722 (Iowa); Germolgez v. State, 13
So. 517 (Ala.); Peters v. State, 13 So. 334. 335 (Ala.). Objections
merely to irregularity of organization of grand jury, not viewed with
favor, Wolfson v. United States, 101 Fed. 430, 433.

E.   At the trial of any case requiring a jury in this court,
the clerk shall draw such jury to the number of twelve,
from the box containing the names of such persons as have
been duly summoned to attend as jurors; and if any of
the said twelve be challenged or set aside for cause, he shall
continue to draw from said box until twelve impartial jurors
are obtained, when they shall be sworn as the jurors for
the trial of such case.

 F.   No person shall serve as a petit juror more than one
term in a year; and it shall be sufficient cause of challenge
to any juror called to be sworn in any cause that he has been
summoned and attended this court as a juror at any term of
court held wthin one year prior to the time of such challenge.—Judicial Code, sec. 286.

United States v. Reeves, 27 Fed. Cas. 750, No. 16,139; Brooke v.
People, 48 Pac. 502 (Colo.); McFarlin v. State, 49 S. E. 267 (Ga.);
State v. Ward, 14 Atl. 187, 193 (Vt.); State v. Cox, 52 Vt. 471; Wise
v. Otter Creek Lumber Co., 48 N. W. 695-696 (Mich.)

G.   When the marshal or his deputy is not an indifferent
person, or is interested in the event of the case, the court
may appoint some fit person to serve writs of venire facias,
or to return jurymen to fill any incomplete panel, and he

shall be sworn to truly and impartially serve and return the writ or perform the service required.—Judicial Code, sec. 279.

H. When, from challenges or otherwise there is not a petit jury to determine any civil or criminal case, sufficient jurymen to complete the panel shall be returned from the bystanders by the marshal, or his deputy, or in case they are not indifferent, by a person appointed by the court.— Judicial Code, sec. 280.

St. Clair v. United States, 154 U. S. 131, 146-147; Andersen v. United States, 170 U. S. 481, 501. As to who are "bystanders," see United States v. Loughery, 26 Fed. Cas. 998, No. 15,631; Patterson v. State, 4 Atl. 449, 452 (N. J. Law).

I. (Amendment of April 1, 1912.) Any person summoned to appear as a juror, who is exempt from service, and who desires to claim such exemption, shall transmit to the clerk of this court, at least two weeks before the day upon which he is summoned to appear, a statement in writing giving the facts upon which he bases his claim.

Any person summoned to appear as a juror and not exempt as aforesaid, who desires to be excused from such service, shall transmit to the clerk at least two weeks before the day upon which he is summoned to appear, a statement in writing signed by him or his agent, of the reasons upon which the request is based.

Upon the drawing of a panel of jurors, the clerk shall forthwith mail a copy of this rule, together with a copy of sections 2407 and 2408 of the Revised Laws of Hawaii of 1915, relating to exemptions and excuse from service, to all jurors drawn.

It is provided, however, that this rule shall not apply to any special drawing of jurors made after the opening of the term to fill out a panel partially or wholly depleted.

CHALLENGES OF JURORS FOR CAUSE.

29.

IN CIVIL CASES.

Challenges of jurors for cause in civil cases may be taken on one or more of the following grounds:

1.   That the juror is not a citizen of the United States and of the Territory of Hawaii.

2.   That he cannot speak and read and write the English language.

3.   That he has been convicted of a felony and not pardoned.

4.   That he has served as a juror in this court within one year.

5.   Consanguinity or affinity within the third degree to either party; or if the juror has, directly or through such relative, any pecuniary interest in the issue to be tried.

7.   Bias for or prejudice against either party.

8.   That he has served as a juror or been a witness in a previous trial between the same parties for the same cause of action, or is a witness in the instant cause.

9.   That he has formed or expressed an unqualified opinion or belief as to the merits of the action.

Opinions which do not disqualify, see 1 Thompson on Trials, 2d ed., sec. 79; opinions which require evidence to remove them, see Id., sec. 80.

30.

IN CRIMINAL CASES.

The following shall be good cause for challenge to any person called as a juror on any criminal trial:

1.   That he is not a citizen of the United States and of the Territory of Hawaii.

2.   That he cannot speak and read and write the English language.

3. That he stands in the relation of debtor or creditor, guardian or ward, master or servant, employer or clerk, principal or agent to the defendant.

4. That he is related within the third degree to the person alleged to be injured by the offense charged, or to the prosecuting witness, or to the defendant.

5. That he was a member of the grand jury which found the indictment.

6. That he has served as juror in this court within one year.

7. That in an indictment for an offense the punishment whereof is capital, his opinions are such as to preclude him from finding the accused guilty of an offense punishable by death.

8. That he has been convicted of a felony and not pardoned.

9. That hc is biased for or prejudiced against the de-
Code, sec. 287.
fendant.

10. That he has formed or expressed an opinion on the guilt or innocence of the defendant. Provided, that if such opinion be based upon newspaper reports alone, the juror shall not be disqualified for that reason if he answer that notwithstanding such opinion he could render a fair and impartial verdict.

See note to rule 29, subdiv. 9. As to duty of prosecution to furnish list of jurors in capital cases, see Rev. Stats., sec. 1033; also Stewart v. United States, 211 Fed. 41, 46, par. 5.   ....

31.

PEREMPTORY CHALLENGES.

In civil cases each party has 3 peremptory challenges. The right shall be exercised by the plaintiff first, and alternately thereafter. Where there are several plaintiffs or several defendants the parties on each side shall be deemed a single party for the purpose of challenges.—Judicial

In treason or capital cases the defendant is entitled to 20 and the United States to 6 peremptory challenges. The United States shall have the first challenge, and the defense shall then have five challenges; and thereafter the United States and the defense may alternate with one and three challenges, respectively.—Id.

In other felonies the defendant is entitled to 10, and the United States to 6 peremptory challenges. The United States shall have the first challenge, the defense shall then have five challenges, and thereafter the United States and the defense may alternate with one challenge each.—Id.

In all other criminal cases the United States and the defense each have 3 peremptory challenges. The United States shall have the first challenge, and alternate with the defense thereafter.—Id.

In all criminal cases where there are several defendants, they shall be deemed a single party for the purpose of challenges.—Id.

All challenges, whether to the panel or to the array, or to individual jurors for cause or favor, shall be tried by the court without the aid of triers.—Id.

32.

Attorneys of this court shall not administer oaths or affirmations in any case or matter in this court wherein they appear as attorneys of record, under penalty of having the paper or pleading so verified stricken from the files of the court.

33.

Except in cases arising under the internal revenue laws, and in cases where an offender is endeavoring to escape, the commissioners of this district shall not entertain a complaint or issue a warrant of arrest in any criminal case unless first authorized to do so by the United States attorney or his assistant.

34

Applications for admission to the bar of this court shall be by petition, signed by the applicant and setting forth his age, birthplace, nationality, last place of residence, and the character and term of his study. Certificates of the applicant's good moral character shall accompany the application. Upon the filing of the application and certificates the court shall appoint a committee of three members of the bar to examine into the qualifications of the applicant, and to report thereon to the court, and thereupon such order shall be made as may be just.

Proctors, attorneys, counsellors and advocates of any district court of the United States or of the supreme court of any State or Territory may be admitted to this court on motion of an attorney or proctor of this court, upon signing the roll and taking the oaths prescribed by the constitution and laws of the United States. The admission fee shall be $1. Members of the bar of the supreme court of the United States shall be admitted free of charge.

35.

In all cases not provided for by the rules of this court, the practice therein shall be regulated by the rules and practice of the supreme court, or of the circuit court of appeals of the United States for this district, for the time being (whether adopted before or after these rules), so far as the same may be applicable.

36.

The hours of meeting of this court shall be at ten o'clock in the morning and two o'clock in the afternoon unless otherwise ordered by the court.

37.

The office hours of the clerk of this court shall be from nine o'clock a. m. to four o'clock p. m.; Saturday nine a. m. to twelve m.

37a.

It shall be considered highly improper for any party, or attorney, solicitor, counselor or proctor for any party, or any other person, in the presence or hearing of either of the judges of this court, or of any juror in attendance at the court, to discuss or talk about any question of law or fact in any cause, action or proceeding in law, equity or admiralty, pending in this court, except in open court when such cause, action or proceeding is before the court for hearing, and except at the hearing of applications for orders, and at hearings in chambers.

Any breach of this rule will be punished as for contempt. (Adopted March 26, 1917.)

RULES IN ADMIRALTY.

38.

Libels, petitions, and answers thereto, unless otherwise ordered by the court for cause, and except on behalf of the United States, shall be verified; the verification shall be made by the party, or by one of the parties, or in his or their absence by the agent, attorney in fact, or proctor, acquainted with the facts. When the verification is not made by a party, the affiant's means of knowledge or information in such case, and the reason why the verification is not made by a party, shall be stated. If the personal oath of the party be demanded, proceedings may be stayed a reasonable time to enable such verification to be taken by commission or *dedimus protestatem*.

This court, as a court of admiralty, and as a court of equity, shall be deemed always open, for the purpose of filing any pleading, of issuing and returning mesne and final process, and of making and directing all interlocutory motions, orders, rules and other proceedings preparatory to the hearing, upon their merits, of all causes pending therein. And the judge may, upon reasonable notice to the parties, make, and direct and award, at chambers, or in the clerk's office, and in vacation as well as in term, all such process, commissions, orders, rules and other proceedings, whenever the same are not grantable of course, according to the rules and practice of this court.—Rev. Stat., sec. 574.

39.

Amendments, or supplementary matters, must be connected with the libel or other pleading by appropriate references, without a recapitulation or restatement of the pleading amended or added to.

40.

Persons entitled to participate in the recovery, and in suits for wages any other seamen claiming wages for the same voyage, not made parties in the original libel, may, upon petition, be admitted to prosecute as co-libelants upon such terms as the court may deem reasonable. Suits may also be joined or consolidated as provided by law.

41.

When various actions are pending, all resting upon the same matter of right or defence, although there be no common interest between the parties, the court, by order, at its discretion may compel said actions to be tried together, and will enter a decree in each cause conformably to the evidence applicable thereto.

42.

Whenever, from the death of any of the parties, or changes of interest in the suit, defect in the pleadings or proceedings, or otherwise, new parties to the suit are necessary, the persons required to be made parties may be made such either by a petition on their part or that of the adverse party. In either mode, it shall be sufficient to allege briefly the prayer of the original libel, the interest which the party sought to be added or substituted has in the action, the several proceedings in the cause and the date thereof, and to pray that such persons required to be made parties in the suit may be made such parties. On service of a copy of such petition and of notice of the presenting thereof, such order will be made for the further proceeding in the cause as shall be proper for its speedy and convenient prosecution as to such new parties; and the same stipulations and security shall, in all such cases, be required and given, as in cases of persons becoming originally parties to suit.

43.

No libel, petition, appearance or answer shall be received, or third party permitted to intervene or claim, except on the part of the United States, or on the special order of the court, or when otherwise provided by law, unless a stipulation for costs shall be first entered into by the party, conditioned that the principal shall pay all costs awarded against him by this court, and in case of appeal, by the appellate court; such stipulations to be with at least one surety resident in the Territory of Hawaii, and to be in the sum of $500 in cases *in rem*, and $200 in cases *in personam*.

But seamen suing for wages in their own right and for their own benefit for services on board American vessels, salvors coming into port in possession of the property libelled, petitioners for money in the registry of the court, and the Territory of Hawaii, shall not be required to give such security in the first instance. The court, however, on motion with notice to the parties, will, for adequate cause shown, order the usual stipulations to be given.

44.

When not otherwise provided for by law, suits can be prosecuted or defended *in forma pauperis* by express allowance of the court only, and in such cases no stipulation for costs will be required; but process *in rem* in such cases, unless specially allowed by the court, shall not issue except upon proof of twenty-four hours' notice of the filing of the libel, for opportunity to appear. In the absence of the judge the allowance may be made by the clerk.

45.

Process to be used in commencing suits may be *in personam* or *in rem*, or both, when not otherwise provided; and shall be issued by the clerk.

Process *in personam* may be:

(1) A simple motion *in personam*.

(2) Such monition united with a clause of attachment of defendant's goods and chattels if the defendant is not found.

(3) Such monition and attachment united with a foreign attachment of the defendant's goods, moneys, choses in action, credits, or effects in the hands of third persons; the names of such third persons and the specific property in their hands to be attached as stated in the libel, shall be expressed in the process, with a citation to the garnishee to appear and answer on oath concerning the same. But except on a libel for liquidated damages not exceeding $500, no process of attachment or foreign attachment shall issue under this, or the preceding subdivision (2), unless allowed by special order of the court, upon due proof of the demand and of the propriety of the attachment being first made.

(4) A warrant of arrest of the person, upon the special order of the court, in cases allowed by law, either alone or united with an attachment.

Process *in rem* may be:

(1) A warrant to arrest the property libelled, with a general monition to all persons interested therein.

(2) Such warrant and monition united with any process *in personam* above specified, when such joinder is allowable.

46.

Final process, in this court, in all cases for the sale of property, shall be by writ of execution, in the nature of a *fieri facias*, or *venditioni exponas*.

47.

In all actions the process shall be made returnable on Friday of the week after the filing of the libel, unless otherwise ordered by the judge. The answer or other pleading will be required to be filed upon return of the process duly served, and a day of hearing will then be fixed unless otherwise ordered for cause shown. Notice by publication will not be required in possessory actions unless specially ordered. (As amended June 30, 1905).

48.

On service of foreign attachment the party holding the property, funds, credits, or effects attached, shall, on the return day of the process, file an affidavit containing a full and true statement of the property, funds, credits or effects in his hands belonging to the defendant at the time the attachment was served and at the time the affidavit was made; and declare whether he had any, and, if any, what claim to any, and what part thereof; and unless he shall then on motion of the libelant, pay into court such amount as he shall not claim, or such amount as may be ordered by the court, he shall give stipulation with sufficient surety to hold the same with interest thereon to answer the exigency of the suit, and to abide the further order or decree of the court in relation thereto; and on his default in this behalf or in default of his appearance to answer interrogatories on oath, an order may be entered that an attachment

issue against him unless he shall show cause in four days, or on the first day the court shall be in session thereafter.

49.

When the property, effects, or credits named in any process of foreign attachment, are not delivered up to the marshal by the garnishee or trustee, or are denied by him to be the property of the party defendant, it shall be a sufficient service of such foreign attachment to leave a copy thereof with such garnishee or trustee, or at his usual residence or place of business, with notice of the property attached; and on due return thereof by the marshal the libelant, on proof satisfactory to the court that the property belongs to the defendant, may proceed to a hearing and final decree in the cause. If the defendant appears, further proceedings may be had as is usual in suits *in personam.*

In proceedings *in rem*, process against freight or proceeds of property in possession of any person, and all orders granted by the court under rule 38 of the admiralty rules of the supreme court, may be served in like manner.

50.

In proceedings *in rem* in behalf of the United States, when the goods are under seizure by the collector and in his possession, the clerk, at the instance of the district attorney, may omit the attachment clause in the monition.

In such suits, and also in other suits *in rem* when the things libelled are in the custody of the collector of customs under authority of any revenue law of the United States, it shall be a sufficient service of the motion and warrant, in the first instance, to leave a copy thereof with the said collector, with notice of the attachment of the property therein described, and requiring such collector to detain such property in custody until the further order of the court; and in case the collector is not found within the district, then to leave also such copy and notice with the custodian of the property within the district; with notice, also, except in customs seizure cases, to the owner or his agent, if found within the district; subject, however, to such further special order as the court may make thereon.

51.

No process shall be received on file unless duly returned by the proper officer.

All process to the marshall shall be returned on the return day thereof; if not so returned by him, nor within four days after written notice so to do, an order may be entered of course that he show cause why an attachment should not issue against him.

Upon process *in rem* the return shall state the day of seizure or of sale, as the case may be.

52.

Processes, orders to show cause and notices of motion shall, upon the return day thereof, be called by the clerk, and thereupon, when there is no opposition, the orders prayed for in accordance with the practice of the court, may be entered by the clerk, whether the judge be personally present or not; and in like manner orders, which, according to the practice of the court, are granted as of course, may be entered, reserving to any party affected thereby the right to apply to the judge at the earliest opportunity to vacate or modify the same. In the event of opposition, the papers may, in the absence of the judge, be left with the clerk, to be by him submitted to the judge for decision thereon, or the clerk may adjourn the matter until the judge shall be in attendance.

53.

Property seized by the marshal may be released as follows:

First. By giving bond as provided in section 941 of the Revised Statutes.

Second. In all suits for sums certain, by paying into court the amount sworn to be due in the libel, with interest computed thereon from the time it was due to the stated term next succeeding the return day of the attachment, and the costs of the officers of the court already accrued, together with the sum of $250, to cover further costs; or by filing an approved stipulation for such sworn amount, with interest, costs and damages, conditioned as in the next subdivision stated; and by payment into court of the costs of officers of the court as provided by Rule 56; and in either case the claimant may thereupon have an order entered *instanter* for delivery of the property arrested without appraisement.

Third. In all suits other than possessory or petitory actions by filing an approved stipulation for the amount of the appraised or agreed value of the property seized with interest (unless the same is modified by order of the court), conditioned to abide by all orders of the court, interlocutory or final, and to pay the amount awarded by the final decree rendered by this court, or by any appellate court, if any appeal intervene, with interest.

Fourth. In possessory and in petitory actions, upon the order of the court only, and on such security and terms as ordered.

Fifth. By an order duly entered upon the written consent of the proctor for the party or parties on whose behalf the property is detained.

54.

If, in a possessory suit, after decree for either party, the other shall make application to the court for a proceeding in a petitory suit, and file the proper stipulation, the property shall not be delivered over to the prevailing party

until after an appraisement is made, nor until he shall give
a stipulation with sureties to restore the same property
without waste, in case his adversary shall prevail in the
petitory suit, and also to abide as well all interlocutory
orders and decrees as the final sentence and decree of the
District Court, and, on appeal of the appellate court.

55.

In case of the attachment of property, or the arrest of
person, in causes of civil and admiralty jurisdiction (except
in suits for seamen's wages when the attachment is issued
upon certificate pursuant to sections 4546 and 4547 of the
Revised Statutes), the party arrested, or any person having
a right to intervene in respect to the thing attached, may
upon evidence showing any improper practices or a manifest want of equity on the part of the libelant, have a mandate from the judge for the libelant to show cause *instanter*
why the arrest or attachment should not be vacated.

56.

No property in the custody of the marshal or other officer of the court shall be delivered up without the order of
the court, but, except in possessory actions, such order may
be entered, of course, by the clerk, on filing a written consent thereto by the proctor in whose behalf it is detained;
or after filing an approved stipulation or an approved bond
to the marshal, as provided by law. But except in proceedings under section 941 of the Revised Statutes, the
marshal shall not deliver property released on stipulation
or on deposit of moneys, until the accrued costs and charges
of the officers of court shall first be paid into court by the
party receiving the property, to abide the decision of the
court in respect to the amount of costs due to them.

57.

All stipulations in causes civil and maritime, shall be

executed and acknowledged by the principal party, if
within the island where the libel is filed, and at least one
surety resident in the Territory, and shall state the street
and number, if there be any, of the surety's residence, and
his occupation, and be accompanied by the surety's acknowledgment and his justification by affidavit that he is
worth double the amount thereof over all his debts and
liabilities; and such stipulation shall contain the consent
of the stipulators, that in case of default or contumacy on
the part of the principal or sureties, execution to the
amount named in such stipulation may issue against the
goods, chattels and land of the stipulators. Parties not residing in the district must supply at least two sureties.

58.

Stipulations to release property from attachment or
arrest may be taken out of court on short notice before the
clerk, or a commissioner, or a notary public, or under a
dedimus protestatem. The officer taking the stipulation
shall, if required by the opposite party, examine the sureties under oath as to their sufficiency, and annex their
depositions.

To obtain the judge's approval thereof, if not consented
to, reasonable notice of application therefor shall be given.
In the absence of the judge, the approval of the clerk, or
deputy clerk, on like notice, shall be sufficient.

Sureties in stipulations for costs may be examined in
like manner on demand thereof served upon the proctors
of the party giving the stipulation, who shall thereupon
give reasonable notice of the time and place of the justification of surties.

59.

In all cases of stipulations in civil and admiralty causes,
any party having an interest in the subject matter may,

at any time on two days' notice, move the court on special cause shown for greater or better security; and any order made thereon may be enforced by attachment, or otherwise.

60.

In suits *in personam*, stipulators on the arrest of the defendant may be discharged from their stipulation before or after the return of the warrant, on the surrender of the principal by them or by himself, except in respect to costs in this court or in any other court to which the case may be appealed.

61.

The clerk shall provide a book in which shall be entered all stipulations filed in causes civil and admiralty, which shall be open to the examination of all parties interested.

62.

In case of seizure of property in behalf of the United States, an appraisement for the purpose of bonding the same may be had by any party in interest, on giving one day's previous notice of motion before the court, or the judge in vacation, for the appointment of appraisers. If the parties or their proctors and the district attorney are present in court, such motion may be made *instanter*, after seizure, and without previous notice.

63.

Orders for the appraisement of property under arrest at the suit of an individual, may be entered, of course, by the clerk at the instance of any party interested therein, or upon filing the consent of the proctors for the respective parties.

64.

Only one appraiser is to be appointed in suits by individuals, unless otherwise ordered by the judge, and, if the respective parties do not agree in writing upon the appraiser to be appointed, the clerk shall forthwith name him, either party having a right to appeal *instanter* to the judge from such nomination, for adequate cause.

65

Appraisers, before executing their trust, shall be sworn or affirmed to its faithful discharge before the clerk, or his deputy, a United States commissioner or notary public, and shall give one day's notice of the time and place of making the appraisement, by notifying the proctors in the cause and by affixing the notice in a conspicuous place adjacent to the United States court rooms, and where the marshal usually affixes his notices, to the end that all persons concerned may be informed thereof; and the appraisement, when made, shall be returned to the clerk's office.

66.

Appraisers acting under an order of the court shall be severally entitled to at least five dollars for each day necessarily employed in making the appraisement, to be paid by the party at whose instance the same shall be ordered.

67.

Upon any seizure in suits *in rem*, or upon any information *in rem* or *in personam* wherein publication is required by law, such publication by the marshal shall, except as otherwise ordered, be made in the newspaper designated for that purpose by the court by general order.

68.

Notice of the arrest of property in suits *in rem* other than in behalf of the United States, shall be published and affixed as required in case of seizures on the part of the United States, unless the judge by special order directs a shorter notice than 14 days; the publication need contain only the title of the suit, the cause or nature of the action, the amount demanded, the time and place of the return of the monition, with notice to all persons interested to appear, or that default and condemnation will be ordered, with the names of the marshal and proctor.

69.

Where the *res* remains in the custody of the marshal, the cause will not be heard until after publication of process shall have been made in that cause, or in some other pending cause in which also the property is held in custody; but no final decree shall be entered after hearing or by default, or on consent of parties, ordering the condemnation and sale of property not perishable, arrested on process *in rem*, unless publication of process in that cause shall have been duly made; nor except on default or by consent of the parties appearing, will any sale of the *res* be ordered by interlocutory decree before the sum chargeable thereon is fixed by the court, unless by the express order of the court because of the perishing or perishable condition of the *res*.

70.

In any admiralty proceeding *in rem* where no proctor has appeared for any claimant, a *venditioni exponas* will not be issued, nor a decree entered, unless proof be furnished of actual notice of the action to an owner or agent of the vessel proceeded against, or to the master in command thereof, in addition to the proof of publication of the notice

of arrest of the vessel or unless it be made to appear on
special application to the court that such actual notice is
unnecessary.

71.

Notice of sale of property after condemnation in suits
in rem (except under the revenue laws and on seizure by
the United States) shall be daily for at least six days before sale unless otherwise directed in the decree; and shall
be published in manner directed by Act of Congress on
condemnation under the revenue laws.—Rev. Stat., sec.
939.

72.

A tender *inter partes* before the suit shall be of no avail
in defence or in discharge of costs unless on suit brought
and before answer, plea or claim filed, the same tender is
deposited in the court to abide the order or decree to be
made in the matter.

At any time not less than 13 days before trial the respondent or claimant may serve upon the libelant's proctor
a written offer to allow a decree to be taken against him
for the sum of money therein specified, with costs to the
date of the offer to be taxed, which the libelant may within
one day thereafter accept and enter judgment accordingly;
if not so accepted, and the libelant fail to obtain a more
favorable decree, he cannot recover costs from the time of
the offer; but if the respondent or claimant deposits the
amount of his offer, or tender, and the clerk's fees for paying out the same, with the clerk, the respondent shall recover costs from the time of the deposit, if the libelant does
not recover a more favorable decree.

73.

At any time after an interlocutory decree in favor of the libelant, the claimant or respondent without admitting liability and without prejudice as to the right to appeal, may serve upon libelant's proctor a written offer to allow libelant's damages to be assessed at a sum of money therein specified, and unless the libelant shall finally obtain a decree for a larger sum, besides interest, he shall not recover any subsequent costs and expenses upon any reference after the offer.

74.

The libelant may at any time on notice take order for the withdrawal of so much of the tender or amount deposited as the court may allow, without prejudice to his subsequent litigation for a larger amount, leaving in the registry a sum sufficient to cover the defendant's costs, in case the amount deposited should be held in this court, or in any appellate court, to be sufficient to meet the libelant's demand.

If the respondent serves on the proctor of the libelant written notice of consent that the whole, or any specific part of the tender deposited be paid over to the libelant, the respondent shall not in any event be liable thereafter for interest on so much of the libelant's claim.

75.

No claim can be made without proof of a subsisting interest of the claimant in the subject matter of the claim. This proof may, in the first instance, be the oath of the claimant; but subject to denial and disproof on the part of the libelant or any other party to the suit, on issue thereto if allowed by the court, or on summary petition.

76.

When an answer is required, in a suit *in rem*, of a party having no interest in the subject matter, he may file an exceptive allegation or disclaimer, and notice the same *instanter* for hearing. If the decree of the court is in affirmance of his plea, he shall be discharged the action.

77.

If separate answers or claims are put in by the same proctor, or by different proctors connected in business, all costs thereby unnecessarily incurred shall be disallowed on taxation.

78.

The defendant may before filing his answer except to the jurisdiction or to the sufficiency of the libel, and if the exception is sustained and the libel is not amended within such time as the court shall allow, it shall be dismissed.

Exception to the libel or answer may be heard at any time upon one day's notice.

79.

Exceptions to the answer shall be taken within two days after notice of the filing of the same, which exceptions shall briefly specify the parts excepted to or the grounds of exception, whereupon the party answering or claiming shall in two days either give notice of his submitting to the exceptions, or set down the exceptions for hearing and give one day's notice thereof. In default whereof the like order may be entered as if the exceptions had been allowed by the court.

80.

If a party submit to exceptions he shall amend his pleadings within four days after notice of his submitting, unless the time be extended by written stipulation filed with the clerk. If the exceptions are allowed on hearing, he shall amend his pleadings within such time as the court shall direct; and if the hearing of the exceptions shall not be duly brought on, or the amendment duly put in, the libel, claim or answer excepted to shall, if the exception was for insufficiency, be treated as a nullity and the default of the party be entered; if the exceptions were for irrelevancy the matter excepted to may be stricken out by the clerk.

81.

Answers to interrogatories may be excepted to in the same manner as answers or claims put in by a defendant, and shall, in all respects, be subject to the provisions of the rules in relation to exceptions; and, if the libelant making answers shall not perfect the same after exception allowed, the libel shall be dismissed for want of prosecution. But this rule shall not in any case be deemed to require answers to interrogatories on the part of the United States, in suits brought in their behalf.

82.

In suits *in rem* in collision cases, if one of the colliding vessels be wholly lost so that no cross libel against her could be maintained, the defendant, if he shall desire to recoup or offset any damage to his own vessel in case it shall be determined on the trial that the collision occurred through the fault of both vessels, must in his answer state the facts and his own damages, in like manner as upon filing a cross libel; and such statement of damage shall be without prejudice to any defence he may make that the collision was wholly the fault of the other vessel.

83.

Commissions for taking testimony shall be moved for in ten days after the claim or answer is filed and perfected (if the same shall have been excepted to); but, if interrogatories shall be propounded for the other party, by the party who moves for a commission, he shall have ten days for moving after the answers to the interrogatories shall be perfected; otherwise such commission shall not operate to stay proceedings; but, on a proper case shown, application for a commission and for a stay of proceedings may be made at any time before final decree.

Affidavits on which a motion for a commission is made shall specify the facts expected to be proved, together with the names of the witnesses, and the shortest time within which the party believes the testimony may be taken and the commission returned. On special cause shown, an order for the examination of parties not named may be applied for on notice to the adverse party.

84.

A commission will not be allowed to stay proceedings, except by order of court, if the opposite party admits in writing that the witnesses will depose to the facts stated in such affidavits; such affidavit, with the admission, may be read on the trial or hearing, and will have the same effect as a deposition to those facts by the witness or witnesses named.

85.

Interrogatories for the direct and cross-examination in case the parties disagree respecting them, shall be presented to the judge for his allowance at one time, and one day's notice of settlement shall be given the party objecting to the opposite interrogatories; such interrogatories or cross interrogatories may be allowed provisionally, subject to objection at the trial.

Cross interrogatories shall be served within two days after the direct have been received, unless further time shall be ordered. If no notice of settlement before the judge is given within three days after both direct and cross interrogatories have been served, each party shall be deemed to have assented to the interrogatories served. The interrogatories, direct and cross, as agreed to by the parties, or settled by the judge, shall be annexed to the commission. Directions as to the execution and return of the commission signed by the clerk shall accompany the commission.

86.

Depositions taken under commission, or otherwise, shall be forwarded to the clerk immediately after they are taken, and be filed on their return to the clerk's office, in term or vacation, and notice thereof shall be forthwith given by the party for whom they were taken to the proctor of the opposite party, and they shall be opened by order, of course, on notice by either party to the other. And all objections to the form or manner in which they were taken or returned shall be deemed waived, unless such objection shall be specified in writing and filed within two days after the same are opened, unless further time shall be granted by the judge.

87.

All reports of commissioners, assessors, adjusters, etc., in all matters referred by the court shall be filed in the office of the clerk of the court, and prompt notice thereof given by them to the proctors of the parties appearing. But such commissioners, etc., are not required to file such reports until their proper fees and charges thereon are paid. The same may be taxed by the clerk if required by either party;

and the proctors of the party procuring the reference shall
be personally liable to the commissioner, etc., for payment
of fees as taxed.

88.

After the filing of a commissioner's report, either party
may except thereto, and either party may set down such
exceptions for hearing on two days' notice.

89.

Upon the filing of the report an order of confirmation *nisi*
may be entered of course without notice, unless otherwise
ordered by the court, or the report shall be excepted to;
and if no exceptions be filed within two days after service
of notice of such confirmation *nisi* on the proctors of the
other parties, decree final may be entered.

90.

If the libelant takes no proceedings upon the report
within two days after notice of the filing thereof given by
the respondent, the respondent may move the court on two
days' notice to dismiss the libel for want of due prosecution.

91.

For service rendered by commissioners acting under rule
44 of the admiralty rules of the supreme court, compensation for which is not otherwise provided by law, a reasonable compensaton shall be allowed and taxed.

92.

Where proceedings on a decree shall not be stayed by
an appeal, and the decree shall not be fulfilled or satisfied
in ten days after notice to the proctor, if there be any, of
the party against whom it shall be rendered, it shall be of

course to enter an order that the sureties of such party
cause the engagement of their stipulation to be performed,
or show cause in four days, or on the first day of jurisdiction afterwards, why execution should not issue against
them, their lands, goods and chattels, according to their
stipulation; and, if no cause be then shown, due service
having been made on the proctor of the party, if there be
any, a summary decree shall be rendered against them on
their stipulations, and execution issue; but the same may
be discharged on the performance of the decree and payment of all costs and clerk's charges. This rule does not
apply to sureties on bonds given under section 941 of the
Revised Statutes.

93.

Whenever after judgment or decree for a sum certain and
before execution issued thereon, any party shall pay into
court the amount thereof, with interest, costs, and the
clerk's statutory charges for receiving and paying out the
money; or whenever the marshal (or the proper officer)
shall return process of execution fully executed, and shall
pay the said amounts into court, including the said charges
of the clerk, which shall also be collected on execution, the
clerk shall forthwith and without other authorization, enter
satisfaction of record on such judgment or decree, at the
charge of the party in whose favor such judgment or decree
may be rendered.

94.

When any moneys shall come to the hands of the marshal
under or by virtue of any order or process of the court, he
shall forthwith pay over the gross amount thereof to the
clerk, with a bill of his charges thereon and a statement of
the time of the receipt of the moneys by him; and, upon
the filing of such statements, and the taxation of such

charges, the same shall be paid to the marshal out of such moneys; and an account of all property sold under the order or decree of this court, shall be returned by the marshal and filed in the clerk's office, with the execution or other process under which the sale was made.

95.

In proceedings *in rem*, after a sale of the property under a final decree, claims upon the proceeds of sale, except for seamen's wages, will not be admitted in behalf of lienors filing libels or petitions after the sale, to the prejudice of lienors under libels filed before the sale, but shall be limited to the remnants and surplus.

96.

A party shall not be held to enter his appeal from any decree or order of the court as final, unless the same is in a condition to be executed against him without further proceedings therein in court. In his notice of appeal the appellant shall state whether he intends to make new pleadings or take new proofs on appeal; and the apostles, or record on appeal must contain a summary statement of the proceedings in the cause.

97.

In appealable cases, ten days from the time of service of a copy of the decree on the opposite proctor, with notice of its entry, shall be allowed to enter an appeal, within which time the decree shall not be executed.

98.

In admiralty and maritime causes, wherein the matter in demand does not exceed fifty dollars, the proceedings for recovery thereof may be summary.

The monition, or citation, or attachment, in such suit, may be made returnable in three days after the service of process *in rem* in suits by individuals.

99.

In suits *in personam* for wages, where the amount sworn to be due, in the libel, is less than fifty dollars, the clerk shall not issue process without the usual stipulation for costs, unless the libel be accompanied by satisfactory proof that the respondent is about to leave the district; or by an *allocatur* of the judge, or by a certificate of a commissioner of the court, that, upon due service of a summons to the respondent to appear before him, sufficient cause of complaint whereon to found process appeared. Such summons shall be served at least one day previous to the day of hearing therein mentioned, and if it shall appear, on the hearing, to the satisfaction of the commissioner, that the wages claimed have been paid or forfeited, he shall refuse the certificate. And if a reasonable offer of compromise be made on such hearing, by either party, and be rejected by the other, the commissioner shall add a certificate of such fact. In case of final recovery by the party rejecting such offer, he shall recover no costs. No costs shall be taxed for the proceeding, unless the commissioner shall certify that a demand of wages was made by the seamen a reasonable time previous to taking out the summons. No costs shall be taxed for fees of marshal, clerk or witness on such proceedings, unless by special mandate of the judge a subpoena or attachment is issued to compel the attendance of witnesses. The commissioner's fees for his services thereon shall not exceed two dollars for a single sitting, and every adjournment granted shall be at the expense of the party obtaining it; if, however, it is required by the parties that the commissioner take down in writing the testimony heard on the summons, he shall be allowed therefor the customary fees for like services. Proof so taken in writing may be used by either party, on the hearing in court, in case the suit is further prosecuted.

100.

A guardian *ad litem* will be appointed on petition verified by oath, stating a proper case for such appointment. Infants may be sued by *prochein ami*, to be first approved by the court; the guardian or *prochein ami* shall give stipulation for the costs in the same manner as if personally the party in interest.

101.

A guardian *ad litem* will be appointed on petition verified by oath, stating a proper case for such appointment. Infants may sue by *prochein ami*, to be first approved by the court; the guardian or *prochein ami* shall give stipulation for the costs in the same manner as if personally the party in interest.

102.

The commission allowed to the marshal shall be computed upon the gross proceeds, in case of sale; or upon the appraised or agreed value, if bonded; but the marshal, in case of an agreed valuation between the parties, not assented to by him, may have an appraisement in the usual mode.

103.

In other than admiralty causes the marshal shall be entitled upon a settlement by the parties of the debt or claim without a sale of the property, to the like commissions as are provided for in admiralty cases by section 829 of the Revised Statutes.

RULES IN PROCEEDINGS TO LIMIT LIABILITY.

104.

Petitions or libels to limit liability must state:

1. The facts showing that the application is properly made in this district.

2. The voyage on which the demands sought to be limited arose, with the date and place of its termination; the amount of all demands including all unsatisfied liens or claims of liens, on contract or on tort, arising on that voyage, so far as known to the petitioners, and what suits, if any, are pending thereon; whether the vessel was damaged, lost or abandoned, and if so, when and where; the value of the vessel at the close of the voyage, or in case of wreck, the value of her wreckage, strippings or proceeds, if any, as nearly as the petitioners can ascertain, and where and in whose possession they are, also the amount of any pending freight, recovered or recoverable. If any of the above particulars are not fully known to the petitioner, a statement of such particulars according to the best knowledge, information and belief of the petitioner, shall be sufficient.

105.

If a *surrender* of the vessel is offered to be made to a trustee, the libel or petition must further show whether there is any prior paramount lien on the vessel, and whether she has made any, and if so, what voyage or trip since the voyage or trip on which the claims sought to be limited arose, and any existing lien or liens, maritime or domestic, arising upon any such subsequent voyage or trip, with the amounts and causes thereof, and the names and addresses of the lienors, so far as known; also the special facts on which the right to surrender the vessel is claimed, notwithstanding such subsequent trip or voyage, and whether the vessel sustained any injury upon or by reason of, such subsequent voyage or trip.

Upon surrender of the vessel no final decree exempting from liability will be made until all such liens as may be admitted or proved, prior to such final decree, to be superior to the liens of the claims limited shall be paid or secured independently of the property surrendered, as may be ordered by the court; and the monition in cases of surrender, shall cite all persons having any claim upon the vessel to appear on the return day or be defaulted, as in ordinary process *in rem*.

106.

If, instead of a surrender of the vessel, an appraisement thereof be sought for the purpose of giving a *stipulation for value*, the libel or petition must state the names and addresses of the principal creditors and lienors, whether on contract or in tort, upon the voyage on which the claims are sought to be limited, and the amounts of their claims, so far as they are known to the petitioner, and the attorneys or proctors in any suits thereon; or if such creditors or lienors be very numerous, then a sufficient number of them properly to represent all in the appraisement; and notice of the proceedings to appraise the property shall be given to such creditors as the court shall direct, and to all the attorneys and proctors in such pending suits.

107.

The stipulation for value upon such appraisement shall be given with sufficient sureties and upon justification as required under these rules in actions *in rem*, and shall provide for the payment of the appraised amount with interest from the close of the voyage, unless otherwise ordered by the court.

108.

If issue is taken by the pleadings upon the right of the petitioners to any limitation of liability, or upon the liability of the petitioners for the claims alleged against them, such issue will not be heard and determined until the publication of the monition, unless otherwise ordered on application to the court.

109.

Proof of claims presented to the commissioner shall be made by or before the return day of the monition by affidavit specifying the nature, grounds and amount thereof, the particular dates on which the same accrued, and what, if any, credits were given thereon, and what payments, if any, have been made on account; with a bill of particulars giving the respective dates and amounts; if the same consists of several different items. Such proof shall be deemed sufficient, unless within five days after the return day of the monition, or after interlocutory decree in case of issue joined by answer to the petition or within such further time as may be granted by the court, the allowance of the claim shall be objected to by the petitioner or by some other creditor filing a claim, who shall give notice in writing of such objection to the commissioner and to the proctors of the claim objected to, if any. Any claim so objected to must be established by further legal *prima facie* proof on notice to the objecting party, as in ordinary cases; but any creditor desiring to contest the same upon any specific defence, must, with his notice of objection, or subsequently, if allowed by the commissioner or the court, state such defence, or be precluded from giving evidence thereof; and the unsuccessful party to such contest may be charged with the costs thereof. The commissioner shall on the return day of the monition, file in open court a list of all claims presented to him.

110.

RULES AS TO INFORMATIONS.

Proceedings *in rem* for a forfeiture, and *in personam* for an offence, fine, penalty or debt, may be joined in one information when having relation to the same transaction.

111.

On filing an information *in personam* or *in rem*, the clerk shall issue process thereon, corresponding as nearly as may be with that employed in the instance court of admiralty in similar cases. But process *in personam* may be, in the first instance, a capias when allowed, or an attachment against goods to compel an appearance, or a simple monition, at the election of the complainant.

112.

No person shall be arrested and held to bail on an information *in personam* without the mandate of the judge, except where such bail is required or authorized by the statute.

113.

All rules applicable to the service of, or proceedings in relation to, process in plenary causes in admiralty, shall equally apply to process on informations.

114.

If the information filed is multifarious or ambiguous, or does not supply plain allegations upon which issue can be taken, or a distinct reference to the statute upon which it is founded, the defendant or claimant may move the court to have it reformed, giving two days' previous notice, together with a specification of his objections, to the district attorney or proctor in whose name it is filed. It may be amended, of course, in conformity with such notice; if not reformed within two days after being pronounced defective by the court, the defendant may take an order of discharge from the action.

115.

In informations *in rem* a delivery, on stipulation, of property seized, or a sale of perishable articles, may be had, as in case of proceedings in the instance court of admiralty.

116.

The claimant shall appear and interpose his claim or plea on information *in rem,* within the same time and in the same manner as in causes on the instance side of the court of admiralty; and shall appear and plead to informations *in personam* within the same time and in the same manner as in causes at common law.

117.

Instead of a traverse of each separate cause of forfeiture alleged in the information, the defendant may plead, as a general issue to an information *in rem,* "that the several goods in the information mentioned did not, nor did any part thereof, become forfeited in manner and form as in the information in that behalf alleged."

118.

Putting in and justifying bail on behalf of the defendants on arrest, and the proceedings to and on trial and execution, where a trial by jury must be had, shall be the same as in cases of common law jurisdiction.

119.

In all cases where a marshal takes possession of a distillery, by virtue of a process issued for violation of the internal revenue laws, he shall immediately cause the head of the still to be taken off, or the machinery to be disconnected in such manner as to render it impossible for distillation to be carried on. The expense thereof shall be returned by the marshal as a part of his disbursements in the cause; and whenever any premises are held in custody by the marshal, under process issued for violation of the internal revenue laws, admission to such premises shall at all times be permitted for any internal revenue officers who would be entitled to admission were the same not in custody of the marshal.

120.

RULES IN HABEAS CORPUS.

The petition for writ of habeas corpus shall in all cases be signed by the applicant, or good and sufficient reason for such omission shall be given therein. When the verification is made by another person for the petitioner, he shall state his relationship to, or character of acquaintance with, the petitioner, and the means of acquiring such acquaintance; that he knows of his own knowledge that the petitioner is the identical person he represents himself to be; that he makes the verification in good faith and not for the purpose of aiding in the evasion of any of the laws of the land.

121.

The petition in behalf of any Chinese person claimed to have the right to land in the United States, shall set forth the city, village, parish, or vicinage, and the county, state and country where, and the day and year when, he was born; the names of his parents and their present place of residence in complete detail; the place and date of his departure for the United States; the name of the vessel on which he sailed; if he claims a residence in the United States he shall also describe such place of residence or abode, giving city, town, village or locality, and the name of the street and number, if any, of the residence or its exact location; the full name of the firm, store or business, if any, with which petitioner claims connection; and the names of the individuals owning and managing the same. There shall be attached to said petition for purposes of identification a photograph of the applicant which shall be made a part thereof by special reference.

122.

In all cases where it is the duty of the United States attorney to appear for the respondent in a writ of habeas corpus, a copy of the petition therefor shall be furnished personally to such attorney at least one hour before the same is presented to the court or judge.

123.

Copies of all papers and briefs filed with the clerk or judge shall be furnished the clerk for use of opposing counsel.

123a.

Excepting in cases of emergency, or where in the judgment of the court or judge before whom the application shall be made the circumstances shall otherwise require, the writ of habeas corpus shall not issue until after an order to show cause shall have been made and a hearing had upon the petition and the return to the order to show cause. (Adopted August 29, 1913.)

124.

Appeals from the final decisions of the court or judge upon an application of a writ of habeas corpus in the cases provided by statute, may be taken to the circuit court of appeals for the ninth judicial circuit, notice of which appeals shall be given before the judge in open court at the time decisions are made.

125.

Pending notice and perfection of appeal the petitioner may be admitted to bail by the court where the same is permitted by law; otherwise the custody of the prisoner shall not be disturbed.

126.

The transcript of the petition, writ of habeas corpus, return thereto, pleadings, motions, evidence, and proceedings and orders therein shall be presented for allowance and the appeal perfected within ten days after the final decision is rendered.—Rev. Stat., sec. 765.

127.

RULES IN BANKRUPTCY.

1. In every case where a person, corporation, or firm is by the court adjudicated a bankrupt, the cause in which such adjudication is made, shall immediately, without any special order of the court, stand referred to the referee in bankruptcy living nearest the residence of such bankrupt; the said referee thereafter to exercise in such cause jurisdiction as conferred upon referees in bankruptcy by the "Act to establish a uniform system of bankruptcy throughout the United States," approved July 1, 1898. And in addition to such general authority, the said referee is authorized to cause notice to be given of the time and place of the first meeting of creditors and all other notices required by law.

2. No petition by or against a person, corporation or firm shall be filed in bankruptcy, unless at the time when the same is presented for filing, there is deposited with the clerk in addition to the $30 prescribed by the statute, the sum of $10 for the purpose of paying the cost

of publication of notices in the proceeding, and of giving notice to creditors and for the record book of the referee in such proceeding. The cost of publication of notices and of giving notice to creditors and the cost of the record book of the referee shall be deemed costs in the proceeding, and the petitioner shall have a claim against the estate for the amount of such deposit to be paid out of the assets of said estate as other costs.

3.   The petition by or against a person in bankruptcy shall be heard only in open court.

4.   The money deposit required by Bankruptcy Rule 2 shall be immediately paid by the clerk to the referee to whom the cause in which such deposit has been made shall have been referred, and the referee shall disburse the same in accordance with said rule and render an account thereof to the court.

5.   All motions or applications for orders in any bankruptcy proceeding, except such as are addressed to the referee in bankruptcy, will be heard only at the opening of the morning session of the court.

6.   The First National Bank of Hawaii (the same being the United States Depository) at Honolulu, Island of Oahu, the Bank of Maui, Limited, at Wailuku, Island of Maui, and The First Bank of Hilo, at Hilo, Island of Hawaii, are hereby designated as depositories for moneys of bankrupt estates in conformity with section 61 of the Bankruptcy Act of 1898, upon their giving bonds to the United States to be specified by the judge of this court presiding in bankruptcy, and said bonds to be approved by said judge. (As amended January 31, 1918.)

7.   Checks or warrants drawn pursuant to general order No. XXIX of the general orders in bankruptcy adopted November 28th, 1898, shall be countersigned by the referee having jurisdiction of the case to which the moneys so drawn against belong. Copies of this rule and of

said general order shall be furnished by the clerk to each depository within this district.

8. When there are no assets, and no trustee has been appointed, and no application for a trustee is pending, after a meeting of creditors duly called, the case shall be deemed closed for the purpose of the payment by the clerk to the referee of the deposit for his services, when a discharge has been granted or refused to the bankrupt, or when three months have elapsed after the first meeting of creditors, without an application by the bankrupt for his discharge.

9. Where a trustee has been appointed, the case shall be deemed closed and the deposit for his services paid to him on the confirmation of a composition, or an approval of the trustee's final account and payment of the final dividend, or upon the trustee's verified report that no assets have come into his hands or were discoverable. When the case is closed if no trustee has been appointed, the deposit for trustee's services shall be paid by the clerk to the petitioner's attorney.

10. All questions certified by the referee to a judge of this court for his opinion, shall be placed on the calendar for argument, and heard and submitted to the court for decision at the opening of the court on the first Monday after the filing of the certificate with the clerk, unless otherwise ordered by the court.

11. *Discharge and Composition.* Application for the discharge of a bankrupt shall be filed with the clerk of the court. Thereupon the clerk shall forthwith file in the case an order made in the name of the judge then presiding in bankruptcy directing all creditors and other persons to attend before the judge upon a day certain to show cause why the petition should not be granted, the day of hearing to be fixed at such time as to permit thirty days' notice to be given as provided by Bankruptcy Act of 1898, section 58,

as amended by act of June 25, 1910. And the clerk shall thereupon transmit a copy of the order so made to the bankrupt, the creditors and all other parties or persons in interest, and shall publish once in some newspaper of general circulation a notice in substantially the following form, to-wit:

(Title of court and cause.)

Notice: Hearing on Discharge.

Notice is hereby given that said bankrupt has filed petition for discharge from his debts in bankruptcy, and that creditors and other persons are ordered to attend the hearing on said petition before the judge presiding in bankruptcy, at the court room, Model Block, Fort Street, Honolulu, on _____ day, the _____ day of _____ , 19_____, at 10 o'clock a.m., then and there to show cause, if any, why said petition should not be granted, and also to attend the examination of the bankrupt thereon.

Dated _____ , 19_____.

_____
Clerk.

If, for any reason, it is found impossible or impracticable to give notice for the day fixed in the order, the clerk may amend the order without further direction of the court.

Before the discharge is granted there must appear in the court files proof of publication and the clerk's certificate of the mailing of notices.

Applications for confirmation of a composition duly verified, shall be filed in the first instance with the referee in charge of the case, who will thereupon fix a day for the hearing before the judge, which may be upon any Monday at 10 o'clock a. m., and give the requisite notices thereof to all creditors or other persons interested, and thereafter transmit to the clerk of the court two days prior to the return day, due proof of the service of such notices, together with the composition.

On the return day, the default of all creditors not appearing in opposition to the discharge or composition shall be entered by the clerk. Upon due filing of written specifications of the grounds of opposition, to the discharge of the composition, the same shall, unless otherwise ordered by the court, be referred to the referee in charge of the case, to take the proof and testimony offered by the parties and to ascertain and report the facts. The hearing thereon before the referee may be brought on by either party on four days' notice to the other. (As amended April 12, 1916, and January 31, 1918.)

12. When the court refers any matter specially to a referee to take evidence, or to report upon any specified issue or issues of law or fact, the referee shall be entitled to a per diem composition at the rate of $10 per day for each day he is necessarily engaged under said order of reference. The fees of the referee and the costs for taking and transcribing the testimony under each order of reference shall be stated in his report, and may be excepted to by the bankrupt or any party in interest. Said fees shall be chargeable in the first instance to the party opposing the adjudication, or application for discharge or composition, and may be demanded by the referee before proceeding with the hearing, but the sum so paid may in the event that such opposition is successful, be allowed by the court as a charge against the estate.

13. A petition for a review by the judge of an order made by the referee, as provided in general order No. XXVII of the general orders in bankruptcy, must be filed with the referee within ten days from the date of notice of such order, unless for good cause shown, such time is extended.

14. A person entitled to file a petition for review or a petition for the re-examination of any claim filed against the bankrupt's estate, shall at the time of filing, deposit with the referee such sum as the referee may designate as required to cover the cost of such proceeding.

15. All applications for attorneys' fees in the matter of all bankruptcy proceedings shall be made by filing with the clerk of the court a written petition setting forth the appraised value of the estate of the bankrupt and the amount of its liabilities; and also including in said petition an itemized statement of services rendered duly verified; all of said applications to be heard in open court.

NOTE: Rule 15 of the Rules of May 2, 1902, reading as follows, is omitted, having been repealed on the adoption of these new Rules:

15. The referee shall be entitled to receive for use of office in each case $2, and in addition thereto for use of office, the sum of one dollar for each day the same is used in the taking of testimony in any proceeding before him, provided that the charge for office rent shall in no case exceed the sum of $5.00.

SURETIES.

128.

Sureties in bonds and undertakings of any character shall be resident owners of interests in real estate, or in goods, wares and merchandise in store or warehouse, worth in the aggregate the amount specified in the bond or undertaking over and above their just debts and liabilities exclusive of property exempt from execution; *provided*, that in criminal cases, each surety shall qualify in the full amount specified in the bond or undertaking. They shall justify by affidavit and may be further required to answer under oath respecting such property owned by them and their liabilities. Bonds, and the sureties thereon, in civil proceedings shall be subject to the approval of the United States commissioner in commitment cases and by the clerk of the court in indictments.

The affidavit which shall be attached to the instrument shall be substantially as follows:

United States of America, Territory of Hawaii, ss. ...., parties to the above ...., being duly sworn, do depose and say, each for himself, that he is worth the sum of .... dollars, over and above his just debts, liabilities and exemptions, and that his property is situate in said Territory and subject to execution.

This rule shall not apply to corporations referred to in the Act of August 13 1894, 28 Stats. 279, amended by Act of March 23, 1910, 36 Stat. 241. (As amended Aug. 3, 1909).

129.

OFFICIAL STENOGRAPHER.

The official court reporter shall report and keep a record of all actions and proceedings tried and held before this court. The compensation of the official court reporter shall, in addition to his salary provided by law, be $10 per day and $5 per half day for reporting in civil cases, and twenty cents per folio for transcribing his notes, to be paid by the party requiring the transcript. The per diem expenses in such cases shall be paid by the parties, in advance, excepting the United States, and shall be taxable as costs in the case. When the court shall require a transcript of the reporter's notes in civil cases, the charge therefor shall be paid by the parties, excepting the United States, and shall be taxable as costs in the case.

The stenographer shall take down and keep a record of all actions and proceedings tried before this court. Each of the respective parties in civil cases, excepting the United States, shall pay one-half of the per diem of the expenses thereof, the same to be taxable as costs in the case. (As amended January 31, 1918.)

NATURALIZATION.

130.

A.   Petitions for naturalization may be made and filed during term or vacation of this court, and shall be docketed the same day as filed. In no case shall final action be had upon such a petition until at least 90 days shall have elapsed after filing the same and posting the notice of such petition. The last Saturday of each calendar month shall be the stated day for hearings upon applications for naturalization, subject to continuances granted by the court. (As amended Feb. 18, 1910).

B.   In every petition for naturalization in which no final order has been made within six months after the date of the filing thereof, the clerk of the court shall cause a notice to be mailed to the last known address of the petitioner to the effect that unless such petitioner shall appear in court with his witnesses for the final hearing of his petition on the next regular day set for hearing naturalization matters, provided, that it be thirty days after the date of said notice (and if said next regular day set for hearing naturalization matters be not thirty days after the date of sending such notices, the following next regular day set for hearing naturalization matters shall be the day designated), or shall within such time show to the court good reason for his failure so to appear, the said petition shall be dismissed; and in all cases in which, after such notice, the petitioners fail so to appear or show the court good reason for such neglect or failure to appear, the petition shall therein be dismissed, provided, that the thirty days preceding any general election shall not be included in computing the time within which a petitioner shall appear for final hearing. (As amended March 23, 1908).

CERTAIN FEDERAL STATUTES APPLICABLE.

Sealing and testing of writs: All writs and processes issuing from the courts of the United States shall be under the seal of the court from which they issue, and shall be signed by the clerk thereof. (Rev. Stat. sec. 911.)

Teste of process, day of: All process issued from the courts of the United States shall bear teste from the day of such issue. (Rev. Stat. sec. 912.)

Mesne process and proceedings in equity and admiralty: The forms of mesne process and the forms and modes of proceeding in suits of equity and of admiralty and maritime jurisdiction in the [circuit and] district courts shall be according to the principles, rules and usages which belong to courts of equity and admiralty, respectively, except when it is otherwise provided by statute *or by rules of court* made in pursuance thereof; but the same shall be subject to alteration and addition by the said courts respectively, and to regulation by the supreme court, by rules prescribed from time to time, to any [circuit or] district court, not inconsistent with the laws of the United States (Rev. Stat. sec. 913.)

Practice and proceedings in other than equity and admiralty: The practice, pleadings, and forms and modes of proceeding in civil causes, other than equity and admiralty causes, in the [circuit and] district courts, shall conform, as near as may be, to the practice, pleadings, and forms and modes of proceeding existing at the time in like causes in the court of record of the state within which such [circuit or] district courts are held, any rule of court to

Court practice to be regulated by own rules: The several [circuit and] district courts may from time to time, and in any manner not inconsistent with any law of the United States, or with any rule prescribed by the supreme court under the preceding section [Rev. Stat., sec. 917, giving power to the supreme court to regulate the practise of district courts] *make rules and orders* directing the return of writs and processes, the filing of pleadings, the taking of rules, the entering and making up of judgments by default, and other matters in vacation, and otherwise regulate their own practice as may be necessary or convenient for the advancement of justice and the prevention of delays in proceedings. (Rev. Stat. sec. 918.)

Suits and writs of error or appeals, etc., by poor persons without prepayment of or security for fees or costs; affidavit of poverty: Any citizen of the United States entitled to commence or defend any suit or action, civil or criminal, in any court of the United States, may, upon the order of the court, commence and prosecute or defend to conclusion any suit or action, or a writ of error, or an appeal to the circuit court of appeals, or to the supreme court in suit or action, including all appellate proceedings, unless the trial court shall certify in writing that in the opinion of the court such appeal or writ of error is not taken in good faith, without being required to prepay fees or costs or for the printing of the record in the appellate court or give security therefor, before or after bringing suit or action, or upon suing out a writ of error or appealing, upon filing in said court a statement under oath in writing that because of his poverty he is unable to pay the costs of said suit or action or of such writ of error or appeal, or to give security for the same, and that he believes that he is entitled to the redress he seeks by such suit or action or writ of error or appeal, and setting forth briefly the nature of his alleged cause of action, or appeal. (27 Stat. 252; 36 Stat. 866.)

Suing as poor person after demand for fees or security for costs; false swearing in affidavit of poverty, perjury: After any such suit or action shall have been brought, or that is now pending, the plaintiff may answer and avoid a demand for fees or security for costs by filing a like affidavit, and wilful false swearing in any affiavit provided for in this or the previous section, shall be punishable as perjury is in other cases. (27 Stat. 252.)

Suits, etc. by poor persons; issue and service of process, etc., by officers; attendance of witnesses: The officers of court shall issue, serve all process, and perform all duties in such cases, and witnesses shall attend as in other cases, and the plaintiff shall have the same remedies as are provided by law in other cases. (27 Stat. 252.)

Suits, etc. by poor persons; assignment of attorney; dismissal of cause: The court may request any attorney of the court to represent such poor person, if it deems the cause worthy of a trial, and may dismiss any such cause so brought under this act, if it be made to appear that the allegation of poverty is untrue, or if said court be satisfied that the alleged cause of action is frivolous or malicious. (27 Stat. 252.)

Suits, etc. by poor persons; judgment for costs; United States not liable therefor: Judgment may be rendered for costs at the conclusion of the suit as in other cases; Provided, That the United States shall not be liable for any of the costs thus incurred. (27 Stat. 252.)

Suits by seamen without prepayment of or bond for costs: Courts of the United States shall be open to seamen, without furnishing bonds or prepayment of or making deposit to secure fees or costs, for the purpose of entering and prosecuting suit or suits in their own name and for their own benefit for wages or salvage and to enforce laws made for their health and safety. (39 Stat. 313.)

Handwriting of person competent as basis for comparison to prove or disprove genuineness of handwriting: In any proceeding before a court or judicial officer of the United States where the genuineness of the handwriting of any person may be involved, any admitted or proved hand-writing of such person shall be competent evidence as a basis for comparison by witnesses, or by the jury, court, or officer conducting such proceedings, to prove or disprove such genuineness. (39 Stat. 683.)

United States District Court, Hawaii; two judges; appointment of judges, district attorney and marshal; jurisdiction; powers of judges, district attorney and marshal; writs of error and appeals; jury trial; terms; clerk; reporter: There shall be established in the said Territory a district court to consist of two judges, who shall reside therein and be called district judges, and who shall each receive an annual salary of six thousand dollars. The said court while in session shall be presided over by only one of said judges. The two judges shall from time to time, either by order or rules of court, prescribe at what times and in what class of cases each of them shall preside. The said two judges shall have the same powers in all matters coming before said court.

The President of the United States, by and with the advice and consent of the Senate of the United States, shall appoiont two district judges, a district attorney, and a marshal of the United States for the said district, and said judges, attorney, and marshal shall hold office for six years unless sooner removed by the President.

The said court shall have, in addition to the ordinary jurisdiction of district courts of the United States, jurisdiction of all cases cognizable in a circuit court of the United States, and shall proceed therein in the same manner as a circuit court; and the said judges, district attorney, and marshal shall have and exercise in the Territory of Hawaii all the powers conferred by the laws of the United States upon the judges, district attorneys, and marshals of district and circuit courts of the United State.

. . And the laws of the United States relating to juries and jury trials shall be applicable to said district court. The laws of the United States relating to appeals, writs of error, removal of causes, and other matters and proceedings as between the courts of the United States and the courts of the several States shall govern in such matters and proceedings as between the courts of the United States and the courts of the Territory of Hawaii. Regular terms of said court shall be held in Honolulu on the second Monday in April and October, and special terms may be held at such times and places in said district as said judges may deem expedient. The said district judges shall appoint a clerk of said court at a salary of three thousand dollars per annum and shall appoint a reporter of said court at a salary of one thousand two hundred dollars per annum. (Organic Act, sec. 86, 31 Stat. 141, 158; 35 Stat. 838.)

NOTE.—For valuable notes on the history of the foregoing legislation, Organic Act, sec. 86, as also that hereinafter quoted, see 2 U. S. Comp. Stat. 1916, pages 1389, 1465, 1704, and 1705; 4 U. S. Comp. Stat. 1916, pages 4688-4689.

Appeals and writs of error from United States District Courts: Appeals and writs of error may be taken from the district courts, including the United States district court for Hawaii and the United States district court for Porto Rico, direct to the Supreme Court in the following cases: In any case in which the jurisdiction of the court is in issue, in which case the question of jurisdiction alone shall be certified to the Supreme Court from the court below for decision; from the final sentences and decrees in prize causes; in any case that involves the construction or application of the Constitution of the United States; in any case in which the constitutionality of any law of the United States or the validity or construction of any treaty made under its authority is drawn in question; and in any case in which the constitution or law of a State is claimed to be in contravention of the Constitution of the United States. (Judicial Code, sec. 238, as amended Jan. 28, 1915, 38 Stat. 804.).

Jurisdiction, Circuit Courts of Appeals; when judgment final: The circuit court of appeals shall exercise appellate jurisdiction to review by appeal or writ or error final decisions in the district courts, including the United States district court for Hawaii and the United States district court for Porto Rico, in all cases other than those in which appeals and writs of error may be taken direct to the Supreme Court, as provided in section two hundred and thirty-eight, unless otherwise provided by law; and, except as provided in sections two hundred and thirty-nine and two hundred and forty, the judgments and decrees of the circuit court of appeals shall be final in all cases in which the jurisdiction is dependent entirely upon the opposite parties to the suit or controversy being aliens and citizens of the United States or citizens of different States; also in all cases arising under the patent laws, under the trade-mark laws, under the copyright laws, under the revenue laws, and under the criminal laws, and in admiralty cases. (Judicial Code, sec. 128, as amended Jan. 28, 1915, 38 Stat. 803.).

Index to Court Rules

[References are to rule numbers, unless otherwise indicated.]

INDEX

ADMIRALTY—Continued.

13. *Discharge of seaman in foreign port:* Discharge of a member of a crew in an out-of-the-way foreign port unjustifiable, except for offenses of a very serious and aggravated character.—*Id.*

14. *Disobedience of seamen—Discharge:* Admiralty precedents do not favor the discharge of seamen for a single offense, unless it is of aggravated character.—*Muishneck v. The St. Helens,* 457.

15. *Same—Same—Reinstatement:* A seaman discharged for such offense should generally be given an opportunity to return to the employment of the ship, with such penalty as is reasonable under the circumstances.—*Id.*

16. *Evidence of position of a ship under way—Position in relation to line to landmark—Distance:* The testimony of a witness as to the position of a ship under way, in relation to a line from the witness to a conspicuous landmark, is more reliable than his estimate of the distance of such object from himself.—*Puget Sound Commercial Co. v. Inter-Island Steam Navigation Co.,* 488.

17. *Two witnesses observing vessel from different points—Landmarks —Intersection of lines of direction to landmarks:* Where two witnesses, observing a vessel under way from different standpoints, testify that her position at a particular time is on lines from their respecttive standpoints to conspicuous landmarks, which lines cross each other, such point of crossing fixes the position of the vessel, and, coming from credible witnesses, may be regarded as conclusive.—*Id.*

18. *Towing sailing vessel—Safe offing—Res ipsa loquitur:* A sailing vessel without cargo or ballast was towed out to sea and let go by the tug before her crew had completed setting her sails. They had the heavy hawser to take in, the wind being baffling and changeable, and the sea against her; she attempted to gain the open sea, tacking several times to port and starboard but losing for the most part, and finally going ashore and becoming a total loss. *Held* that the doctrine of *res ipsa loquitur* applied, the result showing that she was left in an unsafe place,—unless it should appear that the loss was due either to the fault of those on board or to inevitable accident.—*Id.*

19. *Responsibility of master after being let go:* Under such circumstances the master was justified in persisting in the attempt to make the open sea up to the point where such persistence would expose his ship to obvious danger. At such point he had a good opportunity of giving up such attempt and running in to a safe

ADMIRALTY—Continued.

anchorage. *Held* that he should have made the most of such opportunity, and failing to do so made the owner liable, partially at least, for her subsequent loss.—*Id.*

20. *Liability of tug for failure to give tow safe offing and subsequent assistance, and of tow for failure of good judgment and seamanship:* Held, in view of the negligence of the tug in letting go of such vessel in an unsafe place, and her neglect to render assistance, when it became evident that she was losing ground and approaching danger in her attempt to gain the open sea, and of the failure of the master of such vessel to exercise good judgment and seamanship at such juncture, that both the owner of the tug and the owner of the sailing vessel were jointly liable for her subsequen loss.—*Id.*

21. *Jurisdiction as affected by local enactment abolishing common-law remedy (Workmen's Compensation Act):* The admiralty jurisdiction of the United States District Court for the Territory of Hawaii in cases arising out of injuries to seamen, due to the failure of shipowners to provide safe appliances or safe places of work, is not taken away by the enactment by the legislature of the Territory of a workmen's compensation act, S. L. Haw. 1915, 323, abolishing the right to pursue certain common-law remedies.—*Kim Hong v. The Claudine*, 717.

22. *Same* Though an injured seaman may by his acts be held to have elected to take the remedy provided by the workmen's compensation act, yet the mere receipt from the ship or shipowners, of hospital and medical treatment and money for maintenance, is not in itself alone such an election as to deprive the seaman of a remedy in admiralty,—subject, however, to allowance therein by way of set-off for such benefits received.—*Id.*

Costs: See Costs, UNITED STATES MARSHAL, 3-5.

Deposits to cover awards, unclaimed: See Courts, 4.

Immigration rules: See IMMIGRATION, 24.

Negligence: See NEGLIGENCE, 1-11.

Pleading: See PLEADING, 2-3.

Stowage of lumber: See NEGLIGENCE, 1-5.

ADULTERY.

1. *Immigration—Exclusion of alien for commission of:* The commission of adultery is a ground of deportation under section 2 of the

ADULTERY—Continued.

immigration act, this being an offense "involving moral turpitude."—*Matter of Tome Tanno,* 266.

2. *Definition:* The statute, Penal Code, secs. 316, 318, sufficiently defines fornication and adultery in merely providing that those offenses, naming them without further description, shall be punished in a certain manner.—*U. S. v. Ah Sing,* 582.

3. *Evidence: Held* sufficient to warrant conviction and therefore to require submission to the jury.—*U. S. v. Wong Goon Let,* 763.

As involving moral turpitude: See IMMIGRATION, 9, 42, 47.

Indictment; name of wife of co-defendant: See INDICTMENT, 27.

Polygamous marriages: See CONFLICT OF LAWS, 2.

AFFIDAVIT.

Sufficiency of, in support of motion to dismiss indictment: See INDICTMENT, 3.

AGENCY.

Principal and agent—Pleading—Joinder of principal and agent as defendants: One who contracts with a disclosed principal through the latter's agent, has no right of action against the agent for breach of the agreement, and it is improper to join the agent as a party defendant in an action against the principal on such agreement.—*Mayne v. The Makura,* 43.

ALIENS. See also CHINESE EXCLUSION, CITIZENSHIP, DOMICIL, HABEAS CORPUS, IMMIGRATION, NATURALIZATION.

1. *Immigration laws—Right of domiciled alien to re-enter:* Domiciled aliens returning from a temporary absence abroad, are not excluded from admission to the United States by the immigration act, even though of the criminal class, or afflicted with a dangerous contagious disease.—*Matter of Suekichi Tsuji,* 52.

2. *Right to land claimed on ground of domicil—Denial on question of law—Habeas corpus:* Where the right of an alien to enter the United States is claimed on the ground of domicil, a denial thereof by the immigration officers on a question of law, may be reviewed on an application for a writ of habeas corpus.—*Matter of Tsuru Tomimatsu,* 97.

3. *Resident alien returning to United States after temporary absence:* An alien who has acquired a domicil in the United States cannot be treated as an immigrant on his return to the United States

ALIENS—Continued.

after a temporary absence not involving a change of domicil.—*Id.*

4. *Domicil—Presumption of law:* An alien coming to Hawaii as a farm laborer continued that occupation for years and then returned to his own country and, after a visit of eight months, returned to Hawaii bringing his wife with him with the purpose of resuming his former occupation in the same locality as before. *Held,* that the facts relating to his first coming created a presumption that he thereby acquired a domicil in Hawaii, and that presumption is fortified by his temporary trip to Japan and return with his wife to resume his occupation and residence in Hawaii.— *Matter of Ryuzo Higa,* 233.

5. *Change of domicil—Presumption of law:* Any expectation by the alien to return to Japan after a further stay in Hawaii of about ten years, standing alone, would not affect such domicil, which once established is presumed to continue until acually changed. —*Id.*

6. *Domiciled alien—Immigrant—Jurisdiction of board of special inquiry:* The facts showed the petitioner to be a resident alien, and as the statute of 1907, under which the proceedings occurred, provides only for the deportation of alien immigrants, the board of special inquiry was without jurisdiction to deport him.—*Id.*

7. *Alien immigrant, fiancee of domiciled alien:* A woman, resident of a foreign country, with whom a domiciled alien has entered into an agreement to marry upon her arrival, is not a "non-immigrant" alien, but is subject to the provisions of the immigration act.— *Matter of Tome Tanno,* 266.

8. *Domicil—Dangerous contagious disease—Admission:* An alien immigrant owning land in his own country, who comes to the United States for work leaving his wife at home, and after a couple of years returns home, remaining there four years or more during which time a child is born to him, and then returns, without his family to the United States and is found on applying for admission to be afflicted wih a "dangerous contagious" disease, is properly denied the right to land, as under the circumstances he has acquired no domicil in the United States.—*Matter of Maekawa,* 230.

9. *Same—Admission to the United States:* On a hearing as to the right to land of an alien afflicted with a dangerous contagious disease, who had formerly resided in the United States and had been absent on a prolonged visit to his own country, the first question to be considered by the immigration officers is whether or

ARREST. See WARRANTS.

1. *Probable cause:* Arrest of persons without probable cause, unauthorized.—*Matter of Ching Lum (Chung Lum),* 374.
2. *Grounds:* Upon arrest of a person, he or his counsel should be informed of the grounds thereof.—*Id.*
   Deportation of aliens, preliminary arrest, requisites: See IMMIGRATION, 13, 14, 20, 21, 30, 46.
   Detention under immigration laws: See *Id.,* 14.

ATTORNEYS.

Fees in bankruptcy: See BANKRUPTCY, 2, 3, 4, 15, 16, 20.

BANKRUPTCY. See BURDEN OF PROOF, 2; also TRUSTS.

1. *Process, subpoena—Return day:* In determining the return day of the writ of subpoena, it is erroneous to exclude intervening Sundays in counting the fifteen days prescribed by the bankruptcy act, sec. 18, subdiv. a.—*Matter of Levy Outfitting Co.,* 84.
2. *Attorney's fees of creditors' counsel:* The fees of attorneys for petitioning creditors in proceedings in involuntary bankruptcy are to be determined by the condition of the estate, as one of the main considerations,—i. e., by the results effected, the assets saved.—*Id.,* 86.
3. *Same—No fees for services necessitated by own negligence:* Attorneys for the creditors are not entitled to a fee for arguing in opposition to a motion to quash growing out of an error of the clerk of court in fixing the return day, which error might by due diligence have been mitigated by the attorneys' early efforts. Nor are they to be allowed a fee for effecting amendments to the petition necessitated by their own oversight. Nor for arguing a motion due to their neglect to file a replication.—*Id.*
4. *Attorney's fees of bankrupt's counsel—For contesting proceedings —For attending creditors' meetings:* The attorney for an involuntary bankrupt is not allowed a fee for contesting a petition for adjudication; nor is he allowed a fee for merely attending a first meeting of creditors where it does not affirmatively appear that his presence was of any aid to the bankrupt in performing the duties prescribed by law.—*Id.*
5. *Partnership petition—Non-joining partner—Notice:* In a proceeding in which one of the members of a copartnership petitions for the adjudication of the firm as a voluntary bankrupt, the adjudication is vacated upon it appearing that one of the partners did

BANKRUPTCY—Continued.

not actually authorize, or consent to, the petition made for and in his behalf, and was not given notice either of the filing of the petition or of the hearing thereon.—*Matter of City Contracting & Building Co.*, 142.

6. *Same—Nonbankrupt partners—Schedules:* In a partnership bankruptcy, a firm member who is not himself adjudged bankrupt is not required to file schedules of his individual assets and liabilities; for the reason, in the main, that his individual estate may not without his consent be administered in the firm proceeding.—*Id.*, 145.

7. *Same—Adjudication of firm and members in one proceeding:* On petition of a partner for adjudication of his firm as a bankrupt, any of the respondent partners who appear at the hearing and ask to be adjudged bankrupt as individuals in the same proceeding, may be so adjudged, and without payment of separate filing fees,— but with payment, however, of expenses of advertising notices to individual creditors.—*Id.*

8. *Schedules, requirements:* A statement of assets and liabilities which does not furnish a direct and full answer as to each item of the official form of schedules adopted by the Supreme Court, is insufficient.—*Id.*

9. *General orders construction:* The general orders in bankruptcy prescribed by the Supreme Court are not to be taken as enlarging the statute, but must if possible be construed consistently with it; and so far as they cannot be so construed, they must be disregarded.—*Id.*

10. *Subpoena to respondent—Service by publication:* Requisites of order and notice under bankruptcy act, sec. 18, discussed.—*Matter of McDonald*, 221.

11. *Same—Publications, number and time of:* The provision of section 18 of the bankruptcy act, for publication of subpoena "not more than once a week for two consecutive weeks" is satisfied by two publications, one on a certain day of the week, and another on the same day of the week following.—*Id.*

12. *Same—Return day:* The words "return day," as used in said section 18, refer to the day fixed as the latest limit for the marshal's, or other serving officer's, return of the writ of subpoena into court.—*Id.*

13. *Insolvency—Burden of proof:* The burden of proving solvency, under section 3, clause d, of the bankruptcy act, is not shifted from the alleged bankrupt to the petitioning creditors merely by

BANKRUPTCY—Continued.

cation in bankruptcy of an allegation charging him with a conveyance of property with intent to hinder, delay, and defraud his creditors, is sufficient, without explanation for the cancellation of such conveyance.—*Id.*

29. *Clerk's fees—Notice to creditors:* Special or extra compensation is not allowable to the clerk of court, under General Order in Bankruptcy No. XXXV, sec. 1, for mailing notices to creditors; his clerical services in such matters,—so far at least as no extraordinary expense is involved,—being covered by the filing fee of ten dollars provided by the bankruptcy act, sec. 52, subdiv. a.—Matter *of Iwanaga*, 661.

30. *Privilege of witness:* Officer of corporation testifying before referee cannot be compelled, over his claim that his answers would criminate him, to answer questions if his answers might constitute evidence against him of a violation of law amounting to a criminal offense.—*Matter of Hawaiian Japanese Daily Chronicle, Ltd.*, 724.

BIRTH CERTIFICATES. See Immigration 22, 29.

BOND.

Extrinsic evidence to show bond's legal object: See EVIDENCE 5.

Remission proceedings—requirement of bond from applicant: See
. ESTOPPEL, PUBLIC OFFICERS 2.

Surety's liability: See SURETYSHIP.

BUILDING CONTRACTS.

1. *Building material—Cost of transportation—Reasonable value at place of delivery:* The cost of the transportation of building materials furnished by sub-contractors for the construction of public works, is an element of their value at the place of delivery.— *U. S. v. Burrell Construction Co.*, 400.

2. *Materials and labor—Tools and machines:* Tools and machines used in the construction of buildings under an engagement to furnish materials and labor are not within such contract.—*Id.*

BURDEN OF PROOF.

1. *Customs duties—Forfeiture—Measure of proof:* In case of probable cause for an information in rem for forfeiture under subsec. 9, sec. 28, c. 6, of the tariff act of 1909, the burden is placed on the claimant by Rev. Stat. sec. 909; and the government is not in any event, required to prove its case by anything more than a preponderance of the evidence.—*U. S. v. A Lot of Silk Goods*, 113.

BURDEN OF PROOF—Continued.

2. *Insolvency:* The burden of proving solvency, under sec. 3, clause "d" of the bankrupt act, is not shifted from the alleged bankrupt to the petitioning creditors merely by reason of the fact that the respondent's books, papers, and accounts are in the custody of the marshal under an order to seize and hold.—*Matter of Desha & Willfong,* 247.

3. *Stowage of lumber—Safe place to work—Responsibility:* The stowage of lumber being under the control of the owners makes them responsible, and it is incumbent upon them to have it so stowed that those whose duty it is to unload shall have a safe place to work. The evidence throws upon the owners the burden of showing that they used due care in loading.—*Monroe v. The Salvator,* 285.

Explaining possession of opium, etc.: See CONSTITUTIONAL LAW, 5; INTERNAL REVENUE.

Showing right to remain in country after arrest for deportation: See IMMIGRATION, 46.

CARRIERS. See ADMIRALTY, 4; IMMIGRATION, 24.

CENSUS.

1. *Schedule—Refusal to answer unauthorized question—Penalty:* A refusal to answer a question set forth in a census schedule, which question is not authorized by the statute, does not subject the person so refusing to the statutory penalty provided for such of the designated persons as "shall refuse or willfully neglect to answer" the questions in the schedules. *U. S. v. Carter,* 198.

2. *Tenure—Construction:* The word "tenure" in the phrase "tenure of home," required by the statute to be placed in the census schedules relating to population, refers to the manner and upon what terms and conditions the same is held, and not to the strictly technical meaning of the word relating to feudal rights in land. —*Id.*

CERTIFICATE.

Of Chinese resident of Philippines applying for admission to United States: See CHINESE EXCLUSION, 1, 2.

Of Hawaiian birth: See IMMIGRATION, 22, 29.

CHINESE EXCLUSION. See also ALIENS; HABEAS CORPUS; IMMIGRATION.

1. *Habeas corpus—Chinese resident of Philippines applying for admission into the United States—Certificate:* A Chinese subject, previously a resident in the Philippine Islands, applying for admission into the United States who shall exhibit his certificate of identification and permission issued by the Chinese Consul General in and for the Philippine Islands, viseed by the collector of customs at Manila, thereby establishes his right of entry into the United States unless such certificate is contraverted and the statements thereof disproved by the United States authorities.—*Matter of Li Chiong*, 337.

2. *Life of certificate of identification and permission:* There is no ruling limiting the life of such certficate except the words in the act of 1884, i.e., "who shall be about to come to the United States," and these permit reasonable delays for business and social purposes, and stoppages on the journey for the same objects.—*Id.*

3. *Habeas corpus—Bail:* Under the provision of section 5 of the Chinese exclusion act of May 5, 1892, 27 Stat. 25, that on an application to any court or judge of the United States in the first instance for a writ of habeas corpus by a Chinese person refused admission into this country, no bail shall be allowed, bail is not allowable upon the issuance of the writ, or before a final hearing on the merits after return to the writ.—*Matter of Wong Kum Wo*, 534.

4. *Admission of minor son of resident merchant, born of a polygamous marriage:* The minor son of a resident Chinese merchant, the issue of a marriage contracted by the father in China when the father had a lawful wife living in Hawaii, is not entitled to admission to this country, unless on other grounds than that of being the son of such resident; even though the prior marriage was dissolved subsequent to the son's birth.—*Matter of Look Wong*, 568.

5. *Deportation—Arrest—Burden of proof:* An alien Chinese may not be arrested as deportable within the Act of September 13, 1888, c. 1015, sec. 13, 25 Stat. 479, without a warrant based on circumstances showing him to be unlawfully within the United States; but upon such lawful arrest the burden is on him of showing his right to remain.—*Matter of Ho Tim*, 653.

CIRCUMSTANTIAL EVIDENCE. See EVIDENCE, 4.

CONFLICT OF LAWS—Continued.

marriage was entered into during the existence of a prior lawful marriage contracted in Hawaii between the father and a woman other than the mother of the immigrant, except on another ground than the mere relation of father and son.—*Matter of Look Wong*, 568.

Conflict of Revised Statutes with preexisting laws: See STATUTES, 4.

CONSTITUTIONAL LAW.

1. *Eminent domain—Rule for just compensation; opposing statutes:* Even if the silence of federal and local statutes as to interest upon awards can be construed as prohibiting it, they must give way to the constitutional provision for "just compensation," whenever the owners would be deprived of it without the payment of interest.—*U. S. v. Thurston*, 33.

2. *Police power—Opium:* The statute entitled "An act to prohibit the importation and use of opium," 35 Stat. 614, is a valid exercise of the police power of Congress.—*Matter of Hausman*, 202.

3. *Due process of law—Possession of opium as prima facie evidence of crime:* The constitutional guaranty of due process of law is not infringed by the provision of the opium act, that possession of contraband opium "shall be deemed sufficient evidence to authorize conviction unless the defendant shall explain the possession to the satisfaction of the jury."—*U. S. v. Hausman*, 210.

4. *Search and seizure—Self-incrimination:* The incidental seizure of an incriminating account book in the execution of a search warrant for contraband opium, is not an unreasonable search or seizure or an infringement of the guaranty against self-incrimination.—*U. S. v. Fong Hing*, 73.

5. *Due process of law—Statutory rules of evidence creating presumptions in criminal cases:* Sec. 2 of the Act of January 17, 1914, 38 Stat. 275, placing the burden upon a person indicted for traffic in opium, of "explaining" his possession, is not unconstitutional. This rule of presumption is satisfied if the defendant's explanation or the circumstances of the possession raise a reasonable doubt of the defendant's guilt.—*U. S. v. Yee Mun Wai*, 739.

Evidence, self-incrimination: See BANKRUPTCY, 30; IMMIGRATION, 32, 45.

Fair hearing and due process in immigration cases. See IMMIGRATION, 5, 9, 12, 21, 25, 31, 32, 34, 36, 38, 39, 41, 43, 44, 45, 48, 49.

Fair trial: See TRIAL.

CONSTITUTIONAL LAW—Continued.

   Jeopardy: See CRIMINAL LAW, 6-9.

   Self-incrimination: See IMMIGRATION, 32, 45.

CONSTRUCTION. See STATUTES.

1. *Bankruptcy—General orders:* The general orders in bankruptcy prescribed by the Supreme Court are not to be taken as enlarging the statute, but must if possible be construed consistently with it; and so far as they cannot be so construed they must be disregarded. —*Matter of City Contracting and Building Co.*, 145.

2. *Bond—Surety's liability:* Though the liability of a surety be a matter *strictissimi juris*, yet his undertaking is to be construed by the same rules as other contracts and gauged by the fair scope of its terms, and, if possible, so as to be upheld.—*U. S. v. Findlay*, 191.

3. *Census schedule—Tenure:* The word "tenure" in the phrase "tenure of home," required by the statute to be placed in the census schedules relating to population, refers to the manner and upon what terms and conditions the same is held, and not to the strictly technical meaning of the word relating to feudal rights in land.—*U. S. v. Carter*, 198.

CONTEMPT OF COURT.

   Disobedience of court order—Escape: An immigrant remanded in habeas corpus proceedings to the custody of immigration officers there to "remain as heretofore," but who makes escape from such custody, is guilty of contempt of court, under Judicial Code, sec. 268.—*Matter of Terada*, 667.

   See EVIDENCE, 11.

CONTRACTS.

   Breach of contract of carriage: See ADMIRALTY, 4.

CORPORATIONS. See FOREIGN CORPORATIONS.

   Admiralty—Process—Service upon foreign corporation: Service of process upon a foreign corporation in the manner prescribed by the laws of the Territory of Hawaii, is valid, in the absence of any special governing provision of federal statute or practice. *Mayne v. The Makura*, 39.

COSTS. See Fees; Salvage, 11.

> *Expenses—Transcript of testimony:* Cost of a transcript of testimony furnished to counsel as the trial proceeded and to enable them to handle the case to best advantage, approved as a necessary expense of litigation.—*The Loch Garve,* 107.

COURTS. See also Clerks of Courts.

1. *Rules of decision—Decision of appellate court:* The United States district court for Hawaii is bound, as a rule, to follow the decision of its superior court, the circuit court of appeals for the ninth circuit, in a similar case.—*Matter of Suikichi Tsuji,* 52.

2. *Decision of associate judge:* The ruling of one member of the court should be followed by his associate unless extraordinary reasons for its reconsideration.—*Id.*

3. *Federal court—Jurisdiction—Military reservation:* The United States district court for Hawaii has jurisdiction of an assault committed upon a military reservation in the Territory of Hawaii. The words "exclusive jurisdiction of the United States" construed. —*U. S. v. Motohara,* 62.

4. *Unclaimed moneys in registry of—Deposit in federal treasury after five years:* Balances of assets in bankruptcy cases deposited with clerks of courts by trustees or referees on closing estates instead of having been distributed with the final dividends, and deposits to cover awards in admiralty cases, should after remaining unclaimed for five years, be transferred from the registry of the court to the account of the United States Treasury.—*Matter of Unclaimed Moneys on Deposit,* 355.

5. *Number of judges constituting:* Though there be a vacancy in the office of one of the judges of the United States district court for the Territory of Hawaii, an indictment reported to the remaining judge is not subject to quashal on the ground that there is then no court.—*U. S. v. Yee Mun Wai,* 739.

6. *Federal court—Non-interference with other courts; exception:* Federal courts should not interfere with proceedings in state or territorial courts, except in cases of peculiar urgency.—*Matter of Curran,* 730.

CRIMINAL LAW. See also Indictments, and for particular crimes, see Adultery, etc.

1. *Evidence—Confession—Inducement:* The defendant having consented to open a trunk to examination of what its contents might

CRIMINAL LAW—Continued.

disclose, a subsequent suggestion of favor or leniency by the district attorney, though precedent to such examination, is not such an inducement of hope of favor as to render involuntary and incompetent as evidence a confession made at, or before and near, the time of such examination.—*U. S. v. Hausman*, 210.

2. *Accessory before the fact:* Penal Code, sec. 332, authorizes the charging of an accessory before the fact as a principal.—*U. S. v. Popov*, 386.

3. *Post offices—Deposit of obscene matter in mail:* One who prepares for another person an obscene communication with knowledge that the other is to deposit it in the post office for mailing and delivery to a third person, may by virtue of Penal Code, sec. 332, be indicted and convicted as a principal under the Penal Code, sec. 211.—*Id.*

4. *Practice—Application of Territorial statutes to United States District Court:* A statute in force in the Hawaiian Islands at the time of their annexation to the United States and continued in force in the territorial courts, providing that two successive trials in a criminal case shall operate as an acquittal, does not govern the United States district court for the Territory of Hawaii.—*U. S. v. Bower*, 466.

5. *Penal statutes—Definition of crime—Construction by aid of common-law:* When the name of an offense is used in a statute instead of a full description of it the common law may be looked to in determining the legislative intent, provided, of course, the common law affords a certain definition.—*U. S. v. Ah Sing*, 582.

6. *Former conviction—Similarity of offenses:* A conviction in the District Court of Honolulu for the unlawful possession of opium under the territorial statute, R. L. Hawaii, 1915, sec. 2075, is no bar to an indictment in this court for the receipt, purchase, sale, concealment, etc., of opium under the federal statute, 35 Stat. 614, am. 38 Stat. 275.—*U. S. v. Ah Poi*, 607.

7. *Former conviction—Evidence—Burden of proof—Possession of opium:* This is true even though the federal statute makes possession prima facie evidence of receipt, purchase, sale, concealment, etc., of opium.—*Id.*

8. *Jeopardy—Mistrial on one count of indictment, acquittal on another:* Where under an indictment of two counts charging violation of the white slave traffic act, 36 Stat. 825, and one count charging adultery, there is an acquittal on the two former counts

CUSTOMS DUTIES—Continued.

fairly equivalent to a direct disclosure.—*Id.*

6. *Declaration and entry—Customs regulations and procedure:* The fact that an anomalous, or an extraordinary procedure is being pursued by the customs officers, of getting merchandise through the customs line, affords no excuse to a passenger who attemps by devices of concealment to introduce merchandise into this country in violation of subsection 9 aforesaid.—*Id.*

7. *Same—Same—Locus poenitentiae:* In such case, there is no locus poenitentiae, extending until the customs officer shall pursue the regular, or usual, course; but the goods intended to be unlawfully entered or introduced may be seized as forfeited at any time after the concealment is discovered when once the passenger has started the goods through the customs line with intent to use the devices of concealment to evade duties.—*Id.*

8. *Entry of imported merchandise—Time for completing entry:* The fifteen-day limit within which to complete entry of imported merchandise, under R. S. sec. 2785, does not apply to the case of a passenger's taking his goods with him immediately through the customs line, so as to afford a locus poenitentiae to an importer who has concealed articles in his baggage with intent to evade duties; nor do Customs Regulations, 1908, article 1092, providing that certain goods shall be sold if not entered within one year, give a locus poenitentiae or a privilege of making complete entry at any time within that period.—*Id.*

9. *Smuggling—Forfeiture—Circumstantial evidence*: In a forfeiture proceeding under subsection 9, sec. 28, c. 6, of the tariff act of 1909, letters found in a passenger's baggage, indicating a plan to smuggle goods for purpose of sale, may be sufficient circumstantial evidence to sustain a finding, against the passenger, of a fraudulent attempt to enter or introduce, so as to satisfy that part of the statute requiring the entry or introduction to be an entry or introduction into the commerce of the country; even though the passenger is not himself the addressor or the addressee or referred to in the correspondence.—*Id.*

10. *Forfeiture—Burden of proof—Measure of proof:* In case of probable cause for an information in rem for forfeiture under subsection 9 aforesaid, the burden is placed on the claimant by R. S. sec. 909; and the government is not in any event, required to prove its case by anything more than a preponderance of the evidence.—*Id.*

Construction of forfeiture provisions of statute: See STATUTES 2.

CUSTOMS DUTIES—Continued.

Forfeiture sales under customs laws: See UNITED STATES MARSHAL, 1, 2.

DAMAGES.

See also ADMIRALTY, 9, 10; EMINENT DOMAIN; SALVAGE, 7-9.

Breach of contract—Expected profits: An objection to an alleged claim of damages as "largely composed of loss of expected profits," overruled.—*Mayne v. The Makura*, 43.

DEPORTATION PROCEEDINGS.

See CHINESE EXCLUSION, 5; HABEAS CORPUS, 1; IMMIGRATION, 10, 13, 18-21, 30, 33-35, 46, 47, 49, 52.

DEPOSITIONS.

1. *Disinterestedness:* Rev. Stat. sec. 863, requires a deposition de bene esse to be taken before one not interested in the case. The reason for disinterestedness in an examiner under the admiralty and equity rules of the Supreme Court is equally imperative.—*Martin v. The Fort George*, 92.

2. *Reasonable notice:* What is reasonable notice to the opposite party of the time of taking a deposition, when there is no statutory time, depends on the circumstances, the main things to be considered being distance, number of witnesses, facility of communication and proper representation.—*Id.*

3. *Irregularity—Waiver:* The presence of counsel for the opposite party and his participation in the examination, is a waiver of any existing irregularity in the taking of a deposition.—*Id.*

4. *Reference to take and report testimony:* Admiralty rule 44, providing for reference of "any matters arising in the progress of the suit to one or more commissioners, to be appointed by the court to hear the parties and make report therein," includes authority to appoint commissioners or examiners to take and report testimony.—*Id.*

5. *Certain requirements—Admissibility—Waiver:* A deposition not reduced to writing under the direction of the examiner, and not read to the deponent or signed by him, is inadmissible as evidence unless such requirements are waived,.—*Id.*

DISCONTINUANCE.

Agreement of settlement and dismissal: Agreement out of court between parties to litigation, viewed with suspicion by courts, but this suspicion may be overcome by preponderance of evidence.—*Sullivan v. The Edward Sewall,* 637.

DISQUALIFICATION.

Of judge: See JUDGES 1.

DIVORCE. See CONFLICT OF LAWS 1.

DOMICIL. See ALIENS.

1. *Residence—Intention:* Residence in a certain locality for a period of years with one's family and the conduct of regular employment there, will prevail on the question of domicil, over any floating purpose such person may entertain to return at some indefinite future time to a former place of residence to reside.—*Matter of Tsuru Tomimatsu,* 97.

2 *Married woman—Temporary residence away from home:* Temporary residence of a married woman away from home cannot, in ordinary circumstances, be set up against the presumption of law that the domicil of the husband is the domcil of the wife.—*Id.*

3. *Domiciled alien returning to U. S. after temporary absence:* An alien who has acquired a domicil in the United States cannot be treated as an immigrant on his return thereto after a temporary absence not involving a change of domicil.—*Id.*

4. *Proof—Intent—Acts:* Mere evidence of intent is insufficient to prove domicil. Acts indicative of purpose are essential.—*Matter of Maekawa,* 226.

5. *Same—Dangerous contagious disease—Admission:* An alien immigrant owning land in his own country, who comes to the United States for work leaving his wife at home, and after a couple of years returns home, remaining there about four years during which time a child is born to him, and then returns, without his family, to the United States and is found on applying for admission to be afflicted with a "dangerous contagious" disease, has not acquired a domicil in the United States and is properly denied the right to land.—*Id.,* 230.

6. *Alien—Presumption of law:* An alien coming to Hawaii as a farm laborer continued that occupation for four years and then returned to his own country, and, after a visit of eight months, returned to Hawaii, bringing his wife with him with the purpose of resuming his former occupation in the same locality as before. *Held,*

DOMICIL—Continued.

that the facts relating to his first coming created a presumption that he thereby acquired a domicil in Hawaii, and that presumption is fortified by his temporary trip to Japan and return with his wife to resume his occupation and residence in Hawaii.— *Matter of Ryuzo Higa*, 233.

7. *Same—Change of domicil—Presumption of law:* Any expectation of an alien to return to Japan after a further stay in Hawaii of about ten years, standing alone, would not affect such domicil, which once established is presumed to continue until actually changed.—*Id.*

Habeas corpus in aid of domiciled alien: See HABEAS CORPUS, 2.

Married woman temporarily away from home. See MARRIED WOMEN.

Questions to be considered by immigration officers on admission of alien to United States: See IMMIGRATION, 12.

Right of domiciled alien to reenter: See IMMIGRATION, 1, 4, 17-19, 50, 51.

Right of wife, etc., of domiciled alien to enter: See *Id.*, 8, 15; also CHINESE EXCLUSION, 4.

DUE PROCESS OF LAW. See CONSTITUTIONAL LAW, 3, 5; also HABEAS CORPUS; IMMIGRATION; TRIAL.

EMBEZZLEMENT.

1. *Offense—What constitutes:* Under Penal Code (Act March 4, 1909, c. 321, sec. 99, 35 Stat. 1106), declaring that whoever, being a clerk or other officer of a court of the United States, shall fail forthwith to deposit any money belonging to the registry of the court, or hereafter paid into court or received by the officers thereof, with the treasurer, assistant treasurer, or a designated depositary, in the name and to the credit of the court, or shall retain or convert to his own use or to the use of another any such money, is guilty of embezzlement a clerk of the federal court in Hawaii, who did not forthwith deposit sums received by him as security for costs to be incurred, is not guilty of embezzlement, where none of such moneys belonging to the United States, and he had not refused to make the regular settlements for the surplus of fees and emoluments collected above the amounts he was entitled to retain for his services and expenses of his office.—*U. S. v. Davis*, 703.

EMBEZZLEMENT—Continued.

2. *Offense—What constitutes:* In such case, as the clerk was not required to forthwith deposit moneys received as security for costs, the failure of the deputy clerk to make such deposits did not render him guilty of embezzlement, within Penal Code, sec. 99.—*Id.* See INDICTMENTS, 24, 25.

EMINENT DOMAIN. See EVIDENCE.

1. *Just compensation for property taken for public use:* Just compensation for property taken for public use includes not only "a full and perfect equivalent for the property taken," but also for the necessary and direct loss produced by the taking.—*U. S. v. Thurston,* 10.

2 *"Just compnsation":* The rule established by the precedents of the Supreme Court of the United States in regard to compensation to be made for the taking of private property for public uses under the law of eminent domain, is, that the "just compensation" required by the Constitution is limited to an equivalent for the property taken.—*U. S. v. Thurston,* 12.

3. *Same—Movable fixtures:* Such rule taken to include damages resulting from the necessary removal of movable fixtures from the property taken but not the expense of such removal.—*Id.*

4. *Movable fixtures:* There is a distinction between "movable fixtures" and loose furniture like chairs and tables; they are not "fixtures" strictly. Although fixed, they may be moved without injury to the building, making a distinction between them and fixtures that cannot be moved without such injury.—*S. S. Thurston,* 10.

5. *Damages for their removal:* Movable fixures made to fit certain rooms or vaults sometimes cannot be moved without injury, and usually without expense in fitting them to a different building. Lessee entitled to damage for such injury and expense or compensation for their value, if he elects to leave them.—*Id.*

6. *Just compensation:* Private property may not be taken for public use without "just compensation."—*U. S. v. Thurston.* 16.

7. *Same:* Just compensation includes a full equivalent for the property taken and for any injury to other property of the owner, caused by the taking. It is the fair market value of the property at the time of the taking, which is what it would bring at a sale without pressure, together with the damage caused by the taking to other property of the owner.—*Id.*

8. *Appraisement of value:* Ordinarily the lessors' interests, together

EVIDENCE—Continued.

petency of husband and wife as witnesses as against each other in certain cases, does not apply to indictment for adultery, even as against a paramour of the witness's spouse on the trial of both offenders under a joint indictment.—*U. S. v. Kukilani*, 696.

14. *Same—Same—Testimony as to marriage*: The husband of a female defendant in a case of adultery is not a competent witness to prove her marriage.—*Id.*

15. *Circumstantial evidence: Held* sufficient to authorize the jury to find the circumstances incapable of any reasonable explanation consistent with the innocence of the defendant.—*U. S. v. Wong Goon Let*, 763.

Admissions: See BANKRUPTCY, 28.

Birth certificates. See IMMIGRATION 22, 29.

Chinese identification certificates: See CHINESE EXCLUSION, 1, 2.

Confessions: See IMMIGRATION, 45.

Fees of witnesses: See WITNESSES.

Foreign law: See STATUTES 5.

Impeachment of witnesses by statements not referred to in trial: See IMMIGRATION, 5.

Interpreters: See IMMIGRATION, 44.

Log-book as evidence: See ADMIRALTY, 11, 12.

Newly-discovered evidence: See HABEAS CORPUS, 23.

Possession as evidence of violation of law: See CONSTITUTIONAL LAW, 3; INTERNAL REVENUE.

Proof of domicil: See DOMICIL,. 4.

Proof of marriage: See MARRIAGE, 1.

Self-incrimination: See BANKRUPTCY, 30; IMMIGRATION, 32, 45.

EXCLUSION OF ALIENS.

See CHINESE EXCLUSION, HABEAS CORPUS, IMMIGRATION.

EXECUTIONS.

See UNITED STATES MARSHAL.

FACTS.

See EVIDENCE, 9, 15; also ADULTERY, 3; TRIAL, 2.

1. *Habeas corpus—Consideration of grounds of detention—Law—Jurisdiction*: While avoiding any retrial of the case on the facts, the court must consider the facts as questions of law may be raised by them, and also as to the genuineness and bona fides

FACTS—Continued.

of the hearing, in order to ascertain whether the court has jurisdiction.—*Matter of Maekawa*, 226.

2. *Same—Return—Conclusions*: The return to the writ of habeas
corpus must be explicit as to the grounds of detention. A statement
of the conclusions of a board of special inquiry without giving facts
upon which such conclusions were based is insufficient.—*Id.*

3. *Testimony of collateral facts as affecting testimony of facts
germane to the issue*: Slight inaccuracies of testimony as to
collateral facts cannot be used to evade conclusions necessarily
arising from testimony of facts germane to the issue.—*Matter of
Wong She*, 426.

Special findings of fact: See TRIAL, 2.

FAIR TRIAL.

See TRIAL; also CONSTITUTIONAL LAW, 3, 5; HABEAS CORPUS; IMMI-
GRATION 5, 11, 12, 21, 25, 32, 34, 36, 38, 39, 41, 43, 44, 45, 46, 48.
4, 6, 9.

FEES. See BANKRUPTCY 2, 3, 4, 7, 15, 16, 20, 29; COSTS; UNITED STATES
MARSHAL; WITNESSES, 2-4.

FELLOW SERVANTS. See NEGLIGENCE, 4, 9, 10.

FINES. See FORFEITURES.

FOREIGN CORPORATIONS. See CORPORATIONS.

Failure to comply with local laws—Jurisdiction of federal court:
Failure of a foreign corporation, respondent in an admiralty suit,
to comply with the local laws requiring such corporations to provide persons upon whom service of process may be made, does
not deprive the United States district court of jurisdiction of
that respondent when duly served through its agent.—*Mayne v.
The Makura*, 39.

FORFEITURES. See CUSTOMS DUTIES 3, 4, 9, 10; PENALTIES, 1, 2.

Construction of forfeiture provisions of customs law: See
STATUTES, 2.
Evidence in forfeiture remission proceedings: See EVIDENCE, 5.
Marshal's fees and expenses on sale: See UNITED STATES MARSHAL.

FORMER ACQUITTAL AND CONVICTION. See CRIMINAL LAW,
4, 6, 8, 9.

FORNICATION.

> *Definition*: The statute, Penal Code, secs. 316, 318, sufficiently defines fornication and adultery in merely providing that those offenses, naming them without further description, shall be punished in a certain manner.—*U. S. v. Ah Sing*, 582.
>
> Indictment, joinder of participants: See INDICTMENTS, 18.

FRAUD. See BANKRUPTCY, 24; CUSTOMS DUTIES, 2, 3, 4, 9, 10.

GRAND JURY. See JURY, 4.

> 1. *Reports by, proper limits of, Secrecy*: It is improper, and a breach of the oath of secrecy, for a grand jury in a report of its doings, to comment on the failure of a person under its investigation to take the stand and testify in explanation of his alleged misconduct.— *Matter of Report of the Grand Jury*, 780.
>
> 2. *Same—Comment on matters beyond jurisdiction*: It is, also, not within the just powers of a grand jury of this federal court, to make adverse comments on anybody's qualifications, moral or otherwise, for an office held by him under a distinct department, the department of education of the Hawaiian territorial government, in no way within the court's jurisdiction, even though that person be under investigation by the grand jury.—*Id.*

HABEAS CORPUS. See CHINESE EXCLUSION, 1, 3; IMMIGRATION, 3, 5, 6, 28, 30.

> 1. *Chinese exclusion law—Practice—Order to show cause*: Where a petition for a writ of habeas corpus for relief of one ordered deported under the Chinese exclusion law, discloses the same facts as those of a case previously determined, the court, instead of granting the writ in the first instance, orders the respondent to show cause why the writ should not issue.—*Matter of Wong On*, 59.
>
> 2. *Alien's right to land claimed on ground of domicil—Denial on a question of law*: Where the right of an alien to enter the United States is claimed on the ground of domicil, a denial thereof by the immigration officers on a question of law, may be reviewed on an application for a writ of habeas corpus.—*Matter of Tsuru Tomimatsu*, 97.
>
> 3. *Jurisdiction of immigration officers*: When proceedings before immigration authorities show that they have acted without jurisdicton, relief may be had by writ of habeas corpus.—*Id.*

HABEAS CORPUS—Continued.

11. *Chinese resident of Philippines applying for admission to United States—Certificate*: A Chinese subject, previously a resident of the Philippine Islands, applying for admission to the United States, who shall exhibit his certificate of identification and permission issued by H. I. C. M. consul general in and for the Philippine Islands, viseed by the collector of customs at Manila, thereby establishes his right of entry into the United States unless such certificate is contraverted and the statements thereof disproved by the United States authorities.—*Matter of Li Chiong*, 337.

12. *Jurisdiction—Issues of fact*: The court, upon petition for a writ of habeas corpus, is without jurisdiction to modify or reverse the decision of the board of special inquiry denying admission to the applicant, where the case involves solely issues of fact and appears to have been fairly tried.—*Matter of Mitobe*, 340; *Matter of Matsuye*, 351.

13. *Same—Dangerous contagious disease*: The court in habeas corpus proceedings is without jurisdiction to review a finding of the board of special inquiry that an alien applying for admission to the United States is afflicted with a "dangerous contagious" disease.—*Matter of Maekawa*, 230.

14. *Delay of writ until remedies below exhausted*: On a petition for habeas corpus the court will not usually grant the writ, except under peculiar and urgent circumstances, until the petitioner has exhausted his remedies before the authority detaining him and on appeal therefrom.—*Matter of Ching Lum*, 374.

15. *Return to writ, or order to show cause*: Upon the issuance of a writ of habeas corpus, or an order to show cause why such writ should not issue, the return should be explicit, giving facts which justify the detention.—*Matter of Lucy Tomson*, 434.

16. *Same—Allegations of admissions*: A return is not made sufficient by allegations of admissions by the petitioner of conduct which, if true, would show him to be unlawfully in the United States, when it contains no charges of such conduct.—*Id.*

17. *Return—Practice*: Attack on the sufficiency of a petition for a writ of habeas corpus should under the settled practice be made by motion to quash or vacate, and not in the return to the writ.—*Matter of Lee Leong*, 258.

18. *Accident and mistake as grounds for—Pleading*: A petition for writ of habeas corpus which alleges as one of its grounds the failure through accident or mistake to perfect an appeal in a former similar proceeding before the same court, must state fully and explicitly the manner in which the accident or mistake oc-

IMMIGRATION—Continued.

44. *Same—Interpretation of testimony*: Qualifications of interpreters and elements of fair interpretation considered.—*Id.*

45. *Examination of alien immigrant before immigration officers— Self-incrimination—Confessions*: The immigration officers may place an alien immigrant on the witness stand and any answer which he gives voluntarily may be used against him.—*Id.*

46. *Deportation—Arrest—Burden of proof*: An alien Chinese may not be arrested as deportable within the act of Sept. 13, 1888, c. 1015, sec. 13, 25 Stat. 479, without a warrant based on circumstances showing him to be unlawfully within the United States; but upon such lawful arrest the burden is on him of showing his right to remain.—*Matter of Ho Tim*, 653.

47. *Deportation—Moral turpitude:* In considering an alleged offense of moral turpitude as a basis of deportation under the immigration laws, moral turpitude is held to mean moral turpitude according to our own standards and not according to those of alien races.—*Id.*

48. *Same—Hearing—Aid of counsel*: Claim of an unfair hearing by reason of want of assistance of counsel, overruled.—*Id.*

49. *Deportation proceedings—Finality of findings of fact*: Findings of fact made by immigration officers in deportation proceedings are final, if a fair hearing has been accorded, even though such findings may have been erroneous.—*Matter of Yamada*, 664.

50. *Entry into the United States*: Aliens who came to Hawaii after the Treaty of Annexation but before the enactment of the organic act providing a government for the Territory, are to be regarded as having "entered the United States" within the meaning of the immigration act, 24 Stat. 898 as amended.—*Id.*

51. *Domiciled aliens:* The immigration act, 34 Stat. 898, as amended, applies to domiciled aliens returning to Hawaii after temporary absence abroad, regardless of whether they established their domicile here before or after annexation.—*Matter of Hokamura*, 691.

52. *Deportation—Effect of marriage to citizen*: A Japanese alien woman whose acts render her liable to deportation, cannot avoid deportation by marriage to a citizen.—*Matter of Sasaki*, 692.

53. *Deportation proceedings—Misnomer of alien:* Under testimony taken before immigration officers in deportation proceedings, finding of such officers not disturbed. Misnomer of alien as "Toku Taki" instead of "Toku Sakai" in preliminary order for arrest in deportation investigation, *held* immaterial, there being not doubt of her identity.—*Matter of Sakai*, 669.

INDICTMENTS—Continued.

it appears that the defendant would be prejudiced or embarrassed without such election.—*Id.*

8. *Description of defendant as within class of offenders contemplated by statute*: When a statute denominates as an offender any one of a certain class of persons who shall do or omit a certain act, an indictment for an offense within the statute must describe the defendant as one of that class.—*U. S. v. Smith*, 422.

9. *Variance—Conviction for lesser offense embraced within greater*: Where an indictment, endorsed as covering an offense under Penal Code, sec. 291, assault by master of a vessel upon a seaman, nevertheless fails to describe the defendant as such master, but aptly describes an offense under Penal Code, sec. 276, assault upon the high seas, the case may be proceeded with as a prosecution under the latter section. Rev. Stat., sec. 1035 applied.—*Id.*

10. *Endorsement varying from body in describing offense*: Where the endorsement of an indictment indicates a different offense from that described in the body of the indictment, it may be disregarded.—*Id.*

11. *Duplicity*: An indictment charging in one count the commission of adultery "on or about the 15th day of January, 1911, and between the 15th day of January, 1911, and the last day of August, 1912, at various times, the exact date of which is to the grand jurors unknown," is bad for duplicity. Also, an indictment charging in one count the commission of adultery "on or about the 10th day of December, 1913, and between the 20th day of November, 1913, and the 23rd day of December, 1913."—*U. S. v. Doyle.* 452.

12. *Demurrer—Practice on sustaining*: On sustaining demurrer to indictment upon such ground of duplicity, the court rules that if the government will elect to proceed upon a single offense first charged, the case may proceed upon such election; otherwise the indictment to be dismissed and the defendants discharged.—*Id.*

13. *Adultery—Naming spouse*: In an indictment for adultery the designation of the defendant's spouse as "one —— Scholl whose full and true name is to the grand jurors unknown," is not a fatal defect.—*Id.*

14. *Sufficiency of allegations—Breaking into postoffice*: An indictment does not charge an offense under Penal Code, sec. 192, in alleging "the breaking and entering a certain building used in whole or in part as a postoffice," without describing the portion entered as being used for postoffice purposes.—*U. S. v. Ensena*, 479.

INDICTMENTS—Continued.

second it cannot be sustained as charging a violation of the second statute.—*U. S. v. Davis*, 703.

25. *Offenses—Statutes*: An indicment of a clerk of court for embezzlement under Penal Code, sec. 97, does not charge an offense under that section when it does not show that he failed to account for moneys at the regular periods for accounting and that none of them belonged to the United States.—*Id.*

26. *Negativing matters of defense*: An indictment under act of January 17, 1914, 38 Stat. 275, amending act of February 9, 1909, 35 Stat. 614, need not negative the possible defense that opium in possession was within the excepted class of opium imported for medicinal purposes.—*U. S. v. Yee Mun Wai*, 739.

27. *Name of defendant's wife—Necessity of alleging it—Variance*: Allegation of defendant's wife's name in indictment may be treated as surplusage; and variance between her name alleged and that proved, *held* immaterial.—*U. S. v. Wong Goon Let*, 763.

INTEREST. See EMINENT DOMAIN, 16, 18, 30-34.

INTERNAL REVENUE.

Possession as evidence of violation of revenue law: In a prosecution under the Harrison narcotic act, 38 Stat. 785, the presumption of guilt arising under sec. 8 from possession of narcotic drugs, is applicable only to cases of possession indicating a violation of sec. 1,—i. e., possession by persons required to register but not registered under sec. 1.—*U. S. v. White*, 727.

INTERPRETERS. See IMMIGRATION, 44.

JUDGES.

1. *Disqualification—Acting as counsel, or other participation, in cause*: Under the statutes, the fact of having been counsel of record as member of a firm of attorneys which had been retained in a suit, disqualifies a judge from sitting in that suit even though he had never taken any part in the cause and has no further pecuniary, or other, interest in it.—*U. S. v. Thurston*, 1.

2. *Same; exception in case of necessity*: *Quaere*, Whether a judge though disqualified by having been of counsel, may not sit in case of absolute necessity in order to prevent failure of justice.—*Id.*

3. *Same; exception in merely formal matters*: A judge, though disqualified, may act in merely formal matters.—*Id.*

One judge following ruling of his associate: See COURTS, 2.

JUDGMENTS.

1. *Draft of judgment, order or decree*: The winning party should without unnecessary delay present draft of judgment, order or decree for signing and filing.—*Matter of Young Chow* Yee, 245.

2. *Modification by lower court after remand by appellate court:* After remand by the appellate court fixing a salvage award at a certain sum, the lower court is without authority to make any deductions from such award, even in order to do equity between the parties. The award being in court, counsel fees may, however, be charged against it for services in the interest of all the awardees in an attempt, subsequent to the remand, to have the award bear interest from the date of the decree appealed from.—*The Celtic Chief*, 332.

JUDICIAL NOTICE.

Of executive orders of the President: See EVIDENCE, 3.

JUDICIAL SALES. See UNITED STATES MARSHAL.

JURISDICTION.

In habeas corpus, consideration of grounds of detention or exclusion of aliens: See HABEAS CORPUS, 6, 7, 12, 13; IMMIGRATION, 28.

Of foreign corporations: See FOREIGN CORPORATIONS.

Of United States court of assault on military reservation: See COURTS, 3.

JURORS. See JURY.

JURY. See GRAND JURY.

1. *Jurors—Summoning—Service of wrong party*: Where a person not drawn as a juror, but having the same name as a person on the jury list, has by error been served with summons to appear, the court may set the service aside and direct the marshal to summon the proper party.—*Matter of Petit Jury*, 105.

2. *Waiver of Jury—Special findings*: The court having tried an action at law jury waived and having entered judgment including a general finding in favor of plaintiff, it declines to entertain a motion for special findings at a subsequent term.—*U. S. v. Findlay, et. al.*, 193.

3. *Waiver*: Jury may be waived by proceeding to trial in the

MORTGAGES.

Tenure: A modern mortgage of real estate is a charge upon the mortgaged property in the nature of a lien,—a mere security for debt, and as such, does not affect the tenure.—*U. S. v. Carter*, 198.

MOTIONS.

To dismiss, affidavit in support of: See INDICTMENTS, 3.
To quash, grounds supporting: See INDICTMENTS, 4.

NATURALIZATION.

1. *Residence—Member of marine corps, honorably discharged*: Under 28 Stat. 124, an alien who has been honorably discharged from service in the marine corps, after having served for the term of one enlistment, may be admitted to citizenship without other proof of residence, such service being taken in lieu thereof.— *Matter of Bischof*, 60.

2. *Qualifications—Conflict between applicant's religious beliefs and possible civic duties*: An applicant for naturalization is not disqualified for citizenship by reason of religious scruples against war or against the taking of life in defense of country, in view of the exemption extended by Congress, 32 Stat. 775, to adherents of religions teaching such scruples.—*Matter of da Silva*, 347.

3. *Witnesses—Posting*: The requirement of section 5 of the naturalization act of June 29, 1906, 34 Stat. 596, that the names of the witnesses whom the applicant for citizenship expects to summon in his behalf, shall be posted with the notice of his petition for ninety days, applies equally to such substitute witnesses who cannot be produced at the final hearing.—*Matter of Kahn*, 578.

4. *Japanese*: A person of the Japanese race born in Japan is not eligible to citizenship under the naturalization laws. Rev. Stat. sec. 2169.—*Matter of Ozawa*, 671.

5. *Filipinos*: Under section 30 of the act of June 29, 1906, 34 Stat. 596, a Filipino, native and citizen of the Philippine Islands, is eligible to citizenship in spite of the provision of Rev. Stat. sec. 2169, limiting naturalization to aliens who are free white persons or of African nativity or descent.—*Matter of Solis*, 686.

6. *Naturalization*: Section 2169 of the Revised Statutes was not repealed by the act of June 29th, 1906, "to establish a uniform rule of naturalization" etc.—*Matter of Ocampo*, 770.

7. Same: Section 30 of the act of June 29th, 1906, authorizes the naturalization of the class of persons specified therein by applying

NEGLIGENCE—Continued.

than for loading it, and that less experienced men answer for unloading than for loading, in view of the fact that the careening of
a vessel toward the wharf to facilitate its unloading tends to diminish the stability of the tiers in the side of the hold opposite the
wharf, *held* that absence of supervision of the unloading by the
master or an expert agent was negligence.—*Id.*

6. *Negligent act—Custom and usage*: A negligent act cannot be justified by custom or usage.—*Id.*

7. *Res ipsa loquitur*: Under the evidence in the case, the rule of *res
ipsa loquitur* applies.—*Id.*; see also, *Puget Sound Commercial
Co. v. Inter-Island Steam Navigation Co.*, 488.

8. *Cause of injury to libellant*: Injuries received by libellant *held*
due to a want of due care in the loading of the libellee, and to the
absence of expert supervision of unloading the same at her destination on the part of the owners and their agent.—*Monroe v. The
Salvator*, 285.

9. *Fellow servants*: As a rule the master is not liable for injury to a
servant caused by the negligence of a fellow servant in the course
of the master's business.—*Kaulana v. Oahu Railway and Land
Co.*, 447.

10. *Incompetent fellow servant—Burden of proof*: Where exception
to this rule is claimed by a servant by reason of injury resulting
from the master's employment of an unskilled or incompetent
fellow servant, the burden is on the injured servant to show the
master's negligence in employing or retaining the unskilled or
incompetent servant.—*Id.*

11. *Assumption of risk*: In a libel for damages arising out of injuries
to a seaman, assumption of risk is not to be presumed in the face
of the clear allegation that the risk resulted from the ship's own
negligence.—*Kim Hong v. The Claudine*, 717.

Pleading, joinder of causes: See PLEADING, 8.

Stowage and protection of cargo: See ADMIRALTY, 7-10, 18-22.

Towing: See ADMIRALTY, 18-20.

Workmen's Compensation Act: See ADMIRALTY, 21-22.

OBSCENE PUBLICATIONS.

See POSTOFFICES.

1. *The tests*: Question of obscenity of published words or pictures,
dependent on their suggestion. If that tends to make the procreative functions of men and women subjects of levity, the law is
violated.—*U. S. v. Kam Moon*, 595.

OBSCENE PUBLICATIONS—Continued.

2. *Same*: The impressions such publications make upon a community of average men and women as to their decency, and as to their probable effect upon the young.—*Id.*

3. *Knowledge as to nature of publication*: One exhibiting words and pictures is chargeable with knowledge of their character if he understands the words. In the case of nude figures accompanied with words, it is the duty of the exhibitor to acquaint himself with the meaning of the words in relation to the pictures before exposing them.—*Id.*

4. *Combination of words and pictures*: Where words and pictures are combined it is the impression of men as a whole that is to be considered. It is no defense if the words or the pictures taken separately are unobjectionable, if their combination suggests indecency of conduct or calls forth impurity of thought.—*Id.*

OFFICERS. See PUBLIC OFFICERS.

OPIUM.

See CONSTITUTIONAL LAW, 5; CRIMINAL LAW, 7; INDICTMENTS, 5-6, 26; INTERNAL REVENUE.

1. *Constitutional law—Police power*: The statute entitled "An act to prohibit the importation and use of opium," 35 Stat. 614, is a valid exercise of the police power of Congress.—*Matter of Hausman*, 202;.

2. *Due process of law—Possession as prima facie evidence of crime*: The constitutional guaranty of due process of law is not infringed by the provision of the opium act, that possession of contraband opium "shall be deemed sufficient evidence to authorize conviction unless the defendant shall explain the possession to the satisfaction of the jury."—*U. S. v. Hausman*, 210. also *U. S. v. Yee Mun Wai*, 739.

PENALTIES.

1. *Public officers—Remission proceedings—Requirement of bond from applicant*: The secretary of commerce and labor has authority, under Rev. Stat. sec. 5294, as amended, to exact or accept from an applicant for remission of statutory penalties, a bond to secure payment thereof in case of the application's disallowance.—*U. S. v. Findlay*, 166.

2. *Estoppel—To deny public officer's authority—Penalty—Remission proceedings*: A ship's master violating the passenger act of 1882,

PENALTIES—Continued.

22 Stat. 186, as amended, who on his own request and for his own advantage obtains clearance of his vessel under bond for payment of such penalties as may be determined by the department of commerce and labor to have been incurred," on submission of the facts, and whose pursuant submission admits the violation but sets up alleged extenuating circumstances, is estopped to deny the submission to be an application for remission of penalties within the secretary's power under Rev. Stat. sec. 5294, as amended, when, otherwise, the master and his ship would escape satisfaction of such penalties.—*Id.*

3. *Census—Refusal to answer unauthorized question*: A refusal to answer a question set forth in a census schedule, which question is not authorized by the statute, does not subject the person so refusing to the statutory penalty provided for such of the designated persons who "shall refuse or willfully neglect to answer" the questions in the schedules.—*U. S. v. Carter*, 198.

PHILIPPINE ISLANDS.

Chinese resident of, applying for admission into the U. S.: See CHINESE EXCLUSION ACT, 1, 2.

Filipinos, naturalization of: See NATURALIZATION, 5, 11.

PLEADING.

1. *Principal and agent—Joinder of, as defendants*: One who contracts with a disclosed principal through the latter's agent, has no right of action against the agent for breach of the agreement, and it is improper to join the agent as a party defendant in an action against the principal on such agreement.—*Mayne v. The Makura*, 43.

2. *Argumentative or inferential allegations*: Allegations of the ownership of the *res* in a libel in rem should be direct and not by way of inference.—*Id.*

3. *Amendment—Joinder of actions in rem and in personam*: The libelant having brought his action substantially in rem and in personam, the action in rem having been held to be unfounded, and the respondents having withdrawn an exception to such joinder, the court allows the libelant by amendment to proceed in personam.—*Id.*

4., *Damages—Breach of contract—Expected profits*: An objection to

PLEADING—Continued.

an alleged claim of damages as "largely composed of loss of expected profits," overruled.—*Id.*

5. *Sham or frivolous allegations*: Sham or frivolous allegations are to be discountenanced and especially in an extraordinary proceeding such as habeas corpus.—*Matter of Tome Tanno*, 274.

6. *Verification*: It should appear distinctly either from the verification or from the verification taken in connection with the petition for the writ, what allegations are made on personal knowledge and what on information and belief.—*Id.*

7. *Allegations on beliefs*: Allegations on belief merely, without some showing of knowledge or information to support such belief, are insufficient.—*Matter of Nobu Mitobe*, 342.

8. *Pleading—Joinder of causes*: It is proper, subject to the court's discretion, and to avoid multiplicity of suits, to join in one libel in rem causes of action for personal injuries received by a seaman while in the service of a vessel due to alleged negligence in breach of contract, or of implied duty, to provide proper appliances, places of work reasonably safe under the conditions, and sufficient help. Joinder of suits in rem and in personam and of suits arising out of contract and tort, considered.—*Kim Hong v. The Claudine*, 717.

POLICE POWER.

Constitutional law—Opium: The statute entitled "An act to prohibit the importation and use of opium," 35 Stat. 614, is a valid exercise of the police power of Congress.—*Matter of Hausman*, 202.

POLYGAMY. See Conflict of Laws, 2.

POST OFFICES. See Obscene Publications.

Deposit of obscene matter in the mails: One who prepares for another person an obscene communication with the knowledge that the other is to deposit it in the post office for mailing and delivery to a third person, may by virtue of Penal Code, sec. 332, be indicted and convicted as a principal under Penal Code, sec. 211.—*U. S. v. Popov*, 386.

PRACTICE. See Habeas Corpus, Judgments, Jury, Trial, and other titles of practice.

PRINCIPAL, ACCESSORY. See Criminal Law, 2.

REMOVAL OF CAUSES—Continued.

of others, by the surveyor of the port of San Francisco, an officer
of the customs of the United States, while investigating in Honolulu alleged unlawful importation of opium by persons other than
and unknown to the plaintiff, is removable from the circuit court
of the Territory of Hawaii to the United States district court for
the Territory of Hawaii, on the ground within 36 Stat. 1097, sec. 32,
act of March 3, 1911, of being a suit against an "officer appointed
under or acting by authority of (a) revenue law of the United
States. . . . on account of (an) act done under color of his office or
of any such law, or on account of any right, title or authority
claimed by such officer . . . under any such law."—*Farm Cornn v.
Wardell*, 601.

2. *Jurisdiction of parties—Residence*: A non-resident defendant who
secures removal to this court of a suit brought against him in an
Hawaiian Territorial court, cannot then have the suit dismissed
for a United States court's want of jurisdiction of non-residents,
under Judicial Code, section 51.—*Id.*, 605.

3. *Courts—Jurisdiction—General appearance on removal of cause*:
In a cause so removed the defendant waives any right of objection
to this court's jurisdiction of the person by entering into stipulation here extending time to answer.—*Id.*

RES IPSA LOQUITUR. See Negligence, 7.

RESIDENCE. See Domicil; Married Women; Naturalization, 1.

REVISED STATUTES. See Statutes, 4.

SALES.

See United States Marshal, 1, 2.

SALVAGE. See also Costs; Courts, 4.

1. *Distribution of salvage fund*: The old rule of allowance of 1-3 of
the salvage fund to the owners and 2-3 to the crew "in ordinary
cases" of salvage performed from sailing vessels, radically
changed with the advent of steam vessels. Prevailing allowance
being from 1-4 to 1-3 to the officers and crews: preponderance of
ordinary cases favoring the 1-4 allowance, and 1-5 and 1-6 being
sometimes given.—*Spreckels & Bros. Co. v. The Loch Garve*, 107.

2. *Same—Consideration of special services*: Special consideration is
given to special services, like carrying a line attached to a hawser
to a stranded vessel a hundred fathoms away, by boat in a dark

SALVAGE—Continued.

and squally night.—*Id.*

3. *Same—Person specially engaged for the salvage enterprise*: A person engaged specially for the salvage enterprise, included in the distribution of salvage money, the chance of making something by way of salvage in addition to his pay, having been held out to him by the master in engaging him.—*Id.*

4. *Same—Disposition of amount not claimed*: The master not claiming salvage money the amount he would otherwise have received inures to the owners.—*Id.*

5. *Same—Deck hands*: Favorable consideration of claims of deck hands discussed.—*Id.*

6. *Improper rivalry of salvors as affecting award*: The award of a salvor may be reduced or denied by reason of an improper spirit of rivalry, prejudicial to the salvage operations and particularly to the interests of the other salving agencies.—*The Celtic Chief*, 299.

7. *Basis of compensation*: Salvage compensation may be based, inter alia, on the conditions of danger from which a stranded vessel is rescued, the perishability of her cargo on exposure to sea water, the value of the property saved, the undamaged condition in which it is recovered, the time consumed in the operations, the value of the salving agencies, the number of men employed, the risk to which the men and the salving agencies are subjected,, and the expenses incurred and losses suffered by the salvors.—*Id.*

8. *Right to compensation—Forfeiture*: A tug went to the assistance of a steamship stranded on a reef outside the harbor of Honolulu, and for more than 50 hours, most of the time with other vessels, pulled constantly, rendering valuable service in preventing the swell from driving the stranded ship further on the reef. At the end of that time she refused the request of the master of the ship to give her place to a larger vessel, and her hawser was cut and she was discharged from further service, but continued to stand by. *Held*, that while she was properly discharged for refusing in give up her place, she did not, because of such refusal, forfeit her right to compensation for the service rendered; and she was awarded $4,000.—*Id.*

9. *Compensation—Release of stranded steamship*: Another salvor employing four vessels in assisting the stranded ship, the lowest aggregate value of the vessels employed at any one time being $240,000, and the minimum number of men employed at any one time being 97, all being used in pulling on the ship and in lightering over 360 tons of cargo, *held* entitled to a salvage award of

SALVAGE—Continued.

of $17,500 and allowance for certain extra expenses; the value of the ship and cargo salved being about $135,000, of which the cargo represented about $111,000, and the service extending over three days and nights in ordinary but threatening weather, with great danger to the ship through her pounding on the reef, and great danger to the cargo because of its perishability on exposure to sea water. And another salvor, employing five smaller vessels, and a large anchor and other equipment aggregating not over $22,000 in value and employing from 45 to 60 men at all times during three days and nights in pulling on a laid-out anchor and in lightering about 240 tons of cargo, *held* entitled to $8,000 and allowance for certain extra expenses; the awards aggregating $29,500, in addition to expense allowances aggregating $3,446.71.—*Id.*

10. *Special awards to officers and crews*: In the above award to owners of salving ships, it is ordered that one-fourth be divided among officers and crews pro rata according to salaries or wages, except that in case of certain officers extra sums are first given for especially meritorious services.—*Id.*

11. *Costs—Penalizing prevailing libellants for excessive claims*: By reason of excessive claims of libellants, the court orders the taxable costs to be divided between them pro rata according to the amount of their claims.—*Id.*

12. *Salvage*: A salving vessel having towed a vessel in a dangerous position to a supposedly safe place, would lose all claims to remuneration, should it neglect to attempt to save it a second time, when the salved vessel is carried by the same tempestuous weather into a new danger.—*The Halcyon*, 640.

13. *Danger to salving vessel*: Remuneration to a salving vessel is enhanced through its being exposed to loss in the salvage operations.—*Id.*

14. *Lesser danger to cargo of libellee than to libellee itself in case of non-salvage affecting decree*: In case the libellee has not been salved but had become a total wreck upon a sand beach on the occasion of her second peril, the fair possibility that a good proportion of her cargo of lumber might be saved at some expense justifies a lesser proportionate decree against the cargo than against the vessel.—*Id.*

SEAMEN. See ADMIRALTY, SALVAGE.

SELF-INCRIMINATION. See BANKRUPTCY, 30; IMMIGRATION, 32, 45.

SEARCH WARRANTS.

Statutory authority for search warrants in case of contraband opium: See *U. S. v. Fong Hing*, 73.

SHIPPING: See ADMIRALTY; MARITIME LIENS; SALVAGE.

SMUGGLING.

Customs duties—Forfeiture—Circumstantial evidence: In a forfeiture proceeding under subsec. 9, sec. 28, c. 6, of the tariff act of 1909, letters found in a passenger's baggage, indicating a plan to smuggle goods for purpose of sale, may be sufficient circumstantial evidence to sustain a finding against the passenger, of a fraudulent attempt to enter or introduce, so as to satisfy that part of the statute requiring the entry or introduction into the commerce of the U. S.; even though the passenger is not himself the addressor or the addressee or referred to in the correspondence. —*U. S. v. A Lot of Silk Goods*, 113.

STATUTES.

1. *Construction*: As a rule, the intent of a statute is to be ascertained solely from the language used.—*Matter of Suekichi Tsuji*, 52.

2. *Construction of forfeiture provisions of customs law*: Though the statutes authorizing forfeiture for violations of the law of customs administration, are subject to strict construction, they are also to be construed reasonably and so as to give effect, if possible, to every word thereof.—*U. S. v. A Lot of Silk Goods*, 113.

3. *Construction of amendment or revision*: Authoritative construction of a statute holds good as to a revision or amendment thereof when the features which have been so construed remain substantially unchanged and do not suggest, in the revision or amendment, any intention of the legislature to change them.—*Matter of Tsuru Tomimatsu*, 97.

4. *Revised statutes—Conflict with preexisting laws*: In interpreting the Revised Statutes, resort may be had to original antecedent acts of Congress except in case of ambiguity of the revision.— *U. S. v. Findlay*, 166.

5. *Foreign law—Presumption of continuity*: When under the law of a foreign state adultery is shown by a decision of its highest court to have been a crime in 1903, it will be presumed that it continued to be a crime there in 1905.—*Matter of Tome Tanno*, 266.

STATUTES—Continued.

6. *Construction—Exceptions to letter of law*: An exception to the letter of a statute may not be raised on the ground that a matter is not within its spirit, unless the reason for the exception be imperative or at least reasonably clear.—*Id.*, 271.

STOWAGE.

Of cargo: See ADMIRALTY, 7-10; NEGLIGENCE, 9, 10, also 1-8.
Of lumber: See NEGLIGENCE, 1-8.

SUBPOENA.

1. *Bankruptcy—Service by publication*: Requisites of order and notice, under sec. 18 of the bankruptcy act, discussed.—*Matter of McDonald*, 221.

2. *Same—Number and time of publications*: The provision of sec. 18 of the bankruptcy act for publication of subpoena "not more than once a week for two consecutive weeks" is satisfied by two publications, on a certain day of the week and another on the same day of the week following.—*Id.*

3. *Same—Return day*: The words "return day," as used in sec. 18 of the bankruptcy act, refer to the day fixed as the latest limit for the marshal's, or other serving officer's, return of the writ of subpoena into court.—*Id.*

SURETYSHIP.

Construction of bond—Surety's liability: Though the liability of a surety be a matter strictissimi juris, yet his undertaking is to be construed by the same rules as other contracts, and gauged by the fair scope of its terms—and, if possible, so as to be upheld.—*U. S. Findlay*, 191.

TECHNICALITIES. See *U. S. v. Doyle*, 452, 456; *U. S. v. Four Diamond Rings*, 694, 696.

TENDER.

Unclaimed—Deposit in federal treasury: A tender paid into court in behalf of a libellee, but not withdrawn although the tender had not been accepted, the suit had gone to judgment and the judgment had been fully satisfied, should after remaining unclaimed for five years, be transferred from the registry of the court to the account of the United States treasury.—*Matter of Unclaimed Moneys on Deposit*, 355.

UNITED STATES MARSHAL.

1. *Fees and expenses—Forfeiture sales under customs laws*: In the the marshal's bill of fees and expenses in a judicial sale (under decree of forfeiture of goods for violation of customs laws), the statute (Rev. Stat. sec. 829), providing for a fee for service of writs, does not allow a charge for delivering a copy of the notice of sale to the advertising medium designated in the decree, nor for delivering to the auctioneer a certified copy of the decree.—*U. S. v. A Lot of Silk Goods*, 137.

2. *Same—Auctioneer's charges as expense of sale*:—In the marshal's bill of fees and expenses in a judicial sale, he is allowed (by Rev. L., Hawaii, sec. 1889, adopted under Rev. Stat. sec. 829, subdiv. 6) certain commissions, from which he must pay any auctioneer engaged; but with consent of the parties in interest the marshal may be allowed something extra required to compensate an auctioneer whose just charges amount to more than these statutory commissions.—*Id.*

3. *Fees and expenses—Service of petition*: In the marshal's bill for fees items of $2 each for serving copy of petition and copy of order for process are disallowed, and $1 allowed instead,.—*Karlson v. The J. M. Weatherwax*, 646.

4. *Same—Service of notice of monition upon publisher*: There is no authority for the marshal's charging for "service" of the publication notice of monition, upon the publisher. And the marshal's act in such case does not constitute a "service."—*Id.*

5. *Same—Service of release and venditioni exponas*: Item for "serving release and venditioni exponas" disallowed as covered by the sale commission.—*Id.*

UNITED STATES TREASURY.

Moneys in hands of clerks of courts: See CLERKS OF COURTS.
Transfer of unclaimed moneys from registry of court to: See COURTS 4; TENDER.

VARIANCE. See INDICTMENTS, 9, 23, 27.

WARRANTS. See ARREST.

Warrant of arrest, mittimus—Sufficiency, requirements not technical: Warrants of arrest, and of commitment, are not to be tested by the same technical standards as those by which an indictment is tested, but are sufficient if they disclose even by general language or statement of conclusions, a prior lawful basis therefor.—*Matter of Hausman*, 202.

WITNESSES.

1. *Mileage fees for attending voluntarily*: In the case of witnesses living out of the jurisdiction of the court and more than 100 miles distant therefrom, whose testimony is necessary to the settlement of the issue, and who voluntarily attend the trial and give their evidence, their mileage fees may be taxed as costs of court against the other side when it is the losing party.—*U. S. v. Burrell Construction Co.*, 404.

2. *Fees of witnesses for indigent defendants in criminal cases*: Where in a criminal case an indigent defendant, by affidavit under Rev. Stat. sec. 878, as to materiality of proposed testimony, obtains subpoena for a witness who at trial proves to know nothing of matters as to which he is expected to testify, the defendant's motion for costs of process and witness fees in such case is disallowed.—*U. S. v. Dagoman*, 635.

3. *Government officers—Expenses*: Under Rev. Stat. sec. 850, a government officer attending as a witness for the government at a place away from his office, may be allowed in a reasonable amount for expenses of steamer chair; but not for gratuities or tips to stewards and waiters, the latter not being a "necessary" expense within the statute.—*Matter of Wardell*, 648.

WORDS AND PHRASES.

"Abet," "aid": *U. S. v. Popov*, 387-388.

"Exclusive jurisdiction of the United States": *U. S. v. Motohara*, 62.

"Involving moral turpitude": *Matter of Tome Tanno*, 269; *Matter of Matsumoto*, 629; *Matter of Ho Tim*, 653.

"Just compensation": *United States v. Thurston*, 10, 13, 20, 22.

"Picture bride": *Matter of Tome Tanno*, 267.

"Reasonable notice" as to taking depositions: *Martin v. The Fort George*, 94-95.

"Return day": *Matter of McDonald*, 223, 225.

"Tenure of home": *U. S. v. Carter*, 200.

WORKMEN'S COMPENSATION ACT. See ADMIRALTY, 21, 22.

WRIT OF ERROR.

Time when may be taken: The time when writs of error for review in the circuit court of appeals may be taken or sued out, begins to run when the judgment, order or decree is filed.—*Matter of Young Chow Yee*, 245.

STATUTES—Continued.

6. *Construction—Exceptions to letter of law*: An exception to the letter of a statute may not be raised on the ground that a matter is not within its spirit, unless the reason for the exception be imperative or at least reasonably clear.—*Id.*, 271.

STOWAGE.

Of cargo: See ADMIRALTY, 7-10; NEGLIGENCE, 9, 10, also 1-8.
Of lumber: See NEGLIGENCE, 1-8.

SUBPOENA.

1. *Bankruptcy—Service by publication*: Requisites of order and notice, under sec. 18 of the bankruptcy act, discussed.—*Matter of McDonald*, 221.

2. *Same—Number and time of publications*: The provision of sec. 18 of the bankruptcy act for publication of subpoena "not more than once a week for two consecutive weeks" is satisfied by two publications, on a certain day of the week and another on the same day of the week following.—*Id.*

3. *Same—Return day*: The words "return day," as used in sec. 18 of the bankruptcy act, refer to the day fixed as the latest limit for the marshal's, or other serving officer's, return of the writ of subpoena into court.—*Id.*

SURETYSHIP.

Construction of bond—Surety's liability: Though the liability of a surety be a matter strictissimi juris, yet his undertaking is to be construed by the same rules as other contracts, and gauged by the fair scope of its terms—and, if possible, so as to be upheld.—*U. S. Findlay*, 191.

TECHNICALITIES. See *U. S. v. Doyle*, 452, 456; *U. S. v. Four Diamond Rings*, 694, 696.

TENDER.

Unclaimed—Deposit in federal treasury: A tender paid into court in behalf of a libellee, but not withdrawn although the tender had not been accepted, the suit had gone to judgment and the judgment had been fully satisfied, should after remaining unclaimed for five years, be transferred from the registry of the court to the account of the United States treasury.—*Matter of Unclaimed Moneys on Deposit*, 355.

UNITED STATES MARSHAL.

1. *Fees and expenses—Forfeiture sales under customs laws*: In the the marshal's bill of fees and expenses in a judicial sale (under decree of forfeiture of goods for violation of customs laws), the statute (Rev. Stat. sec. 829), providing for a fee for service of writs, does not allow a charge for delivering a copy of the notice of sale to the advertising medium designated in the decree, nor for delivering to the auctioneer a certified copy of the decree.—*U. S. v. A Lot of Silk Goods*, 187.

2. *Same—Auctioneer's charges as expense of sale*:—In the marshal's bill of fees and expenses in a judicial sale, he is allowed (by Rev. L., Hawaii, sec. 1889, adopted under Rev. Stat. sec. 829, subdiv. 6) certain commissions, from which he must pay any auctioneer engaged; but with consent of the parties in interest the marshal may be allowed something extra required to compensate an auctioneer whose just charges amount to more than these statutory commissions.—*Id.*

3. *Fees and expenses—Service of petition*: In the marshal's bill for fees items of $2 each for serving copy of petition and copy of order for process are disallowed, and $1 allowed instead,.—*Karlson v. The J. M. Weatherwax*, 646.

4. *Same—Service of notice of monition upon publisher*: There is no authority for the marshal's charging for "service" of the publication notice of monition, upon the publisher. And the marshal's act in such case does not constitute a "service."—*Id.*

5. *Same—Service of release and venditioni exponas*: Item for "serving release and venditioni exponas" disallowed as covered by the sale commission.—*Id.*

UNITED STATES TREASURY.

Moneys in hands of clerks of courts: See CLERKS OF COURTS.
Transfer of unclaimed moneys from registry of court to: See COURTS 4; TENDER.

VARIANCE. See INDICTMENTS, 9, 23, 27.

WARRANTS. See ARREST.

Warrant of arrest, mittimus—Sufficiency, requirements not technical: Warrants of arrest, and of commitment, are not to be tested by the same technical standards as those by which an indictment is tested, but are sufficient if they disclose even by general language or statement of conclusions, a prior lawful basis therefor.—*Matter of Hausman*, 202.

Lightning Source UK Ltd.
Milton Keynes UK
UKHW020050231118
332756UK00005B/106/P